THE COMPREHENSIVE
COUNTRYMUSIC
ENCYCLOPEDIA

FROM THE EDITORS OF
COUNTRY MUSIC MAGAZINE

THE COMPREHENSIVE

ENCYCLOPEDIA

FROM THE EDITORS OF
COUNTRY MUSIC MAGAZINE

A COUNTRY MUSIC MAGAZINE PRESS BOOK

RANDOM HOUSE

Introduction

In 1974, two years after starting *Country Music Magazine*, we published the *Country Music Encyclopedia*. There was nothing else like it at the time. It served a useful function and a lot of copies were sold. In fact, up through the 1980's, if you had asked the Library of Congress for recommended reading on the subject of country music, the two books always mentioned first were our *Country Music Encyclopedia* and another book we published, *The Illustrated History of Country Music*.

But 20 years have passed. Not only has a lot happened in country music since 1974 (Garth Brooks was 12), but new facts have come to light, old "facts" have been discovered to be incorrect and, more importantly, the young and relatively inexperienced *Country Music* staff of 1974 has become mature, experienced, professional and absolutely reeking with authority.

So, recognizing the need for an up-to-date book of this kind, rather than simply revising the original, we decided to start from scratch and produce a completely new book, the *Comprehensive Country Music Encyclopedia*. A revision would have been simpler, quicker and less expensive, but it would not have been as good—for three main reasons. First, the earlier book was written as short biographical notes without much historical connection. Second, while the writing and scholarship involved was satisfactory, it was not at the level we are capable of now. Third, the photographs were uninspiring compared to what we have gathered since. The ways in which we and our resources have changed over the years combine to make the *Comprehensive Country Music Encyclopedia* a very different kind of book. In addition, we include 680 entries, more than half again as many as in 1974, and over 600 photographs, many rare and not previously published in any book.

Inevitably, due to time and practicality, we had to make choices about what to emphasize and what to exclude. We could certainly fill up twice as many pages on the subject of country music. But these are the choices we made.

THE EDITORS
COUNTRY MUSIC MAGAZINE
WESTPORT, CONNECTICUT
AUGUST 1994

Editor-in-Chief
Russell D. Barnard

Art Director
Katheryn Gray

Managing Editor
George Fletcher

Research Editor
Rich Kienzle

Copy Editors
Bob Allen
Helen Barnard
Dan Woog

Research Associates
Dave Samuelson
Charles Wolfe

Graphic Production
Nick de la Mare
Skip Ploss

Electronic Pre-press
American Color Graphics

Typesetting and design were done on Power Macintosh computers using *Aldus PageMaker*™ software. Headings are set in Egyptienne bold condensed. Text is Garamond.

Contributors

The initials of the contributor appear at the end of each entry in the book.

BOB ALLEN (B.A.) is an editor-at-large for *Country Music Magazine*, and has written for the magazine since 1977. His articles on country music have also appeared in *Esquire, Playboy, Saturday Evening Post, The Washington Post, The Baltimore Sun, The Atlanta Journal-Constitution, Rolling Stone* and *The Journal of the American Academy for the Preservation of Old-Time Country Music*. Allen is also the author of *George Jones: The Life and Times of a Honky Tonk Legend*, and edited the *Blackwell Guide to Recorded Country Music*. He has worked as a writer and consultant for Time-Life Records, and is a part-time faculty member at Towson State University in Maryland. He lives in rural Maryland with several dozen chickens, two dogs, two cats and two pigs.

MICHAEL BANE (M.B.) is a former editor of *Country Music Magazine* and is a 15-year veteran in the editor-at-large position for the magazine. Bane is the author of 15 books, including the recent biography with Travis Tritt, *Ten Feet Tall and Bulletproof*. He co-authored the autobiography of Hank Williams Jr., *Living Proof*, which was made into a successful television movie. (It can still be seen occasionally in the wee hours of the morning.) In addition to country music, Bane has written extensively on personal computers, food, guns and high-risk sports. He is presently the executive editor of *Over the Edge*, the journal of adventure sports.

GEORGE FLETCHER (G.F.) is senior editor of *Country Music Magazine*, managing editor of *The Journal of the American Academy for the Preservation of Old-Time Country Music* and editor of the Country Music Society of America *Newsletter*. He's been employed by Silver Eagle Publishers since his 1990 graduation from Northeastern University in Boston. In college he worked at the *Boston Globe* and edited a local Massachusetts country music publication. In addition to a wide-ranging interest in music, he is also a rail enthusiast who has written for *Passenger Train Journal*, and whose photography has been featured in *Passenger Train Journal, Railpace Newsmagazine* and the Conrail Technical Society Calendar.

DOUGLAS B. GREEN (D.G.) is a Western music authority who formerly served as oral historian and editor of *The Journal of Country Music* at the Country Music Foundation. He authored the book *Country Roots* and is a former *Country Music Magazine* contributing editor. He's also written for *The Journal of the American Academy for the Preservation of Old-Time Country Music*. Green is best known to the public as "Ranger Doug" of Riders in the Sky.

DAVID HOLT (D.H.) is a musician, storyteller and historian. He has also hosted *Fire on the Mountain, American Music Shop* and *Celebration Express* for The Nashville Network and the PBS series *Folkways*. His writings have appeared in *The Journal of the American Academy for the Preservation of Old-Time Country Music*.

RICH KIENZLE (R.K.) is a *Country Music Magazine* contributing editor and has written for the magazine since 1973. He began his Buried Treasures reissue review column in 1978, the CMSA *Newsletter's* Legends of Country Music feature in 1984 and the Essential Collector video and book column in 1990. He is also the senior editor of *The Journal of the American Academy for the Preservation of Old-Time Country Music* and the country columnist for *Request Magazine*. His articles and interviews have appeared in *Music City News, Guitar Player, Pulse!, Guitar World, The Journal of Country Music, Country Guitar, Rock and Roll Disc, Country Sounds* and *Goldmine*. He's written over 100 sets of liner notes for historical reissues by Time-Life Music, Rhino Records, Bear Family, Liberty and Columbia Country Classics. In 1994, he co-produced Bear Family's Merle Travis boxed set, *Guitar Rags and a Too Fast Past*.

RICK PETREYCIK (R.P.), a guitarist and writer/editor, was born in Aberdeen, Maryland and raised in Black Rock, Connecticut. He attended nearby Fairfield University, where he received a master's degree in corporate communications. He has contributed to *Guitar Player, Musician, Acoustic Guitar, Country Guitar, Fender Frontline, Profit* and *The Hartford Courant*, among other publications. He is senior editor for Pitney Bowes Inc. and lives with his wife and daughter in Black Rock, Connecticut.

Acknowledgments

RONNIE PUGH (R.F.P.) is the Head of Reference at the Country Music Foundation in Nashville. He is a leading authority on Ernest Tubb whose biography he is currently writing. He has written on Tubb and others for *The Journal of the American Academy for the Preservation of Old-Time Country Music* where his entry on Porter Wagoner first appeared. He has a Master's Degree from Stephen F. Austin State University in Nacogdoches, Texas, for his thesis on Tubb.

DAVE SAMUELSON (D.S.) is a free-lance writer, occasional musician and producer more than 30 folk, country, bluegrass and jazz recordings. As a child in Chicago, Samuelson became hooked on the music he heard on the WLS *National Barn Dance* and Randy Blake's *Suppertime Frolic* on WJJD. In college, he and collector Norman Carlson reissued classic stringband recordings on LP. In 1972 he started the Puritan label for both reissues and new recordings. In 1974 he helped organize the Indiana Fiddlers' gathering. He lives in Battle Ground, Indiana, with his wife and three children. He writes frequently for *The Journal of the American Academy for the Preservation of Old-Time Country Music* .

CHARLES WOLFE (C.W.) is the author of some 14 books and numerous articles on folk and country music, including biographies of Grandpa Jones, Lefty Frizzell, Bill Monroe, Mahalia Jackson and others. He has annotated over 150 albums, and has been nominated for Grammy awards three times for his liner note writings. His book, *The Life and Legend of Leadbelly* (co-authored with Kip Lornell), won the ASCAP-Deems Taylor award for music writing in 1993. He writes and teaches from his base of Middle Tennessee State University near Nashville. A widely-known country music historian and archivist, his writings and photographs have appeared in *The Journal of the American Academy for the Preservation of Old-Time Country Music* among many other places.

STACEY WOLFE (S.W.) lives and works near Nashville, with interests that range from contemporary country to heavy metal. A graduate student at Middle Tennessee State University, she has for five years been associated with The Center for Popular Music, one of the South's leading music archives.

In addition to the contributors' research and writing, lots of interest, care and attention and of lots of hard work, weekends and late nights went into this book. I am grateful for that and want to express my thanks in print to those who made the effort.

THE STAFF: senior editor George Fletcher and art director Katheryn Gray made a prodigious contribution shepherding all the material from writer to production while still doing their regular jobs. Of course, they had assistance from our computer graphics whiz, Nick de la Mare. Bob Allen was uprooted from his Maryland farm and separated from his house pig for two weeks, adding to editorial muscle. Coach Dan Woog made lots of good stops from his copy editing position. The rest of the staff put up with our raving and crankiness, keeping the routine business going while pitching in on anything from typing and proofreading to getting pizza and rushing to Federal Express: Moira Allaby, Joyce Brown, Warren Beardow, Tony Bunting, Michele Jones and Leonard Mendelson. Special thanks to managing editor Rochelle Friedman and senior editor Helen Barnard who saw to it that *Country Music Magazine* got out while we were doing this.

THE PUBLISHERS: no use putting together a book unless someone wants to package, print, promote, advertise and sell it. We have the best: Random House/Times Books, who have been very enthusiastic about this book from the beginning. Thanks and go-get-'em to our editor, Steve Wasserman, and his colleagues Peter Osnos, Robbin Schiff, Della Mancuso and to the intractable Martha Trachtenberg, whose eagle eye spotted many defects in the text.

The editors also wish to thank the following people and institutions for their contributions: Harold Bradley, president, Nashville Chapter, American Federation of Musicians; Ronnie Pugh, Country Music Foundation; Dane Bryant; Mrs. Ralph Mooney; John Morthland; Charlie Seemann; Cindy Wolfe; Hazel Smith; Mae Axton; Jeff Richardson; Hugh Cherry; New England Country Music Historical Society; Gene Bear; Les Leverett; Donna Jackson; Frank Driggs; and the Southern Folklife Collection at the University of North Carolina.   —R.D.B.

THE COMPREHENSIVE

Country Music

ENCYCLOPEDIA

FROM THE EDITORS OF
COUNTRY MUSIC MAGAZINE

Roy Acuff

BORN: September 15, 1903
BIRTHPLACE: Maynardsville, Tennessee
DIED: November 23, 1992

Just how popular was Roy Acuff during his heyday? In the latter days of World War II, Japanese soldiers in the Pacific would try to psych out American Marines by yelling taunts like, "To hell with Franklin Roosevelt! To hell with Babe Ruth! To hell with Roy Acuff!" Back in San Diego, soldiers and sailors from all over the country would hold "Roy Acuff contests," in which the object was to see who could do the best imitation of the singer. Acuff records were so popular that the government had to issue them on V-discs so overseas troops could hear hits like "Low and Lonely." It was not unusual for 15,000 fans to show up at Acuff concerts, and not unusual to see the Acuff name ranking with Frank Sinatra and Benny Goodman in popularity polls among servicemen. Nobody in the music business was really surprised to see Roy Acuff run for governor of Tennessee in 1948.

Contemporary fans who were used to seeing Roy Acuff as the stately, white-haired elder statesman of the Grand Ole Opry may have wondered what all the fuss was about and whether Acuff's role was partially the result of Opry hype. It wasn't. Acuff was actually the music's first great stylist after the death of Jimmie Rodgers and was a major influence on younger singers like Hank Williams, Lefty Frizzell and George Jones. Though he had only three modest hits from 1950 on, his longtime presence on the Grand Ole Opry gave him a platform from which he continued to influence country music: as a publisher, a media pioneer, a spokesman and, in later years, a defender of older traditions and performers. His nickname, "The King of Country Music," may sound a bit mawkish and old-fashioned, but in many ways it is remarkably accurate.

Acuff actually came from the Smoky Mountains. He was born "in a little three-room house," he re-

called, modest enough circumstances even though his father attended a local college and served as a lawyer and the preacher of the local Baptist church. His father taught him to play the fiddle and sent him to an occasional church singing school, but as a teenager Roy was more interested in baseball and fighting. "There was nothing I loved as much as a physical fight," he said, and though he was small for his age, he soon developed a reputation as a scrapper around Knoxville, where he'd moved. Old-timers still talk about a brawl in which Roy took on seven local policemen at a ballpark melee and wound up in jail.

Though he was a good enough ballplayer to be invited to a major league training camp for a tryout, he suffered severe sunstroke on a fishing trip to Florida in 1929. Recovering, he honed his skill as a fiddler and apprenticed himself to a local medicine show man, Doc Hauer. Here he learned show business: the comedy, the hucksterism, the way to work an audience. He did imitations—he had learned to do a neat train whistle while working as a railroad "call boy" as a teenager—and tricks that called for balancing things on his nose. These skills led to a job on Knoxville's WROL with a local band called The Tennessee Crackerjacks. An announcer later dubbed the band "The Crazy Tennesseans," and soon they were playing $25 schoolhouse gigs all over East Tennessee. "Mostly, we fiddled and starved," Roy remembered.

All this changed one day in early 1936. Acuff and fellow band member Red Jones met up with a young Bible college student named Charley Swain, who had been working part-time as a radio singer. Swain had been featuring an unusual gospel song called "The Great Speckled Bird," which both Red and Roy liked. When Roy learned that Swain was moving and would not be singing the song in Knoxville any more, he offered him 50 cents to write down the words. Swain agreed—though Jones recalled, "We had to borrow an extra quarter to pay him." Soon Acuff was singing the song over WROL; that October it landed them a recording deal with the American Recording Company. In 1938, when Acuff and his band were offered a chance to audition for the Grand Ole Opry, "Great Speckled Bird" was one of the songs he sang. Thousands of letters poured in, and the surprised Opry management realized they had a new star on their hands.

At first, the Acuff band—now dubbed The Smoky Mountain Boys, a name the Opry management thought more dignified than The Crazy Tennesseans—tried to follow the Western swing formula, mixing old-time country with pop material like "Coney Island Baby." Roy didn't like this, though, and in 1939 three members left. Among the replacements Roy recruited was Pete "Oswald" Kirby, whose soulful tenor singing and breathtaking dobro work were soon permanent elements in the Acuff sound. Roy's preference for the "mountain sound" over the Western sound was underscored when he starred on the NBC network portion of the Opry in 1939. It was also an issue in the seven Hollywood films he made in the 1940's, when he refused demands of Hollywood directors to turn his outfit into a cowboy band.

Fans rewarded him with hit records. The lonesome, sentimental songs were the biggest: "Beneath That Lonely Mound of Clay" (1940), "The Precious Jewel" (1940), "Wreck on the Highway" (1942), "Fire Ball Mail" (1942), "Wait for the Light to Shine" (1944) and "Two Different Worlds" (1945). "Wabash Cannonball," an old song which had been recorded in the 1920's by The Carter Family, had been a favorite with Acuff fans since The Crazy Tennesseans first recorded it back in 1936. Ironically, Roy did not sing the song on that record; Dynamite Hatcher did. It wasn't until 1947 that Roy re-cut the song for Columbia, able to sing his own theme song on wax at last.

In 1942, primarily to preserve his own publishing interests, Acuff joined forces with veteran songwriter Fred Rose to open the first modern publishing company in Nashville, Acuff-Rose. It was immediately successful, and later became a major country publisher, signing everyone from Don Gibson to The Louvin Brothers to Hank Williams. This business interest helped Acuff survive the hard times of the 1950's and enabled him to take advantage of the folk revival of the 1960's. In 1962, he was elected to the Country Music Hall of Fame.

By the 1970's he had decided to return to his roots, to the older, acoustic sounds that first brought him fame. Following his participation in the 1971 Nitty Gritty Dirt Band collection, *Will the Circle Be Unbroken* (a project he was initially dubious about), Acuff saw his audience expand noticeably. In the years following, he continued to follow his instincts, hone his fiddle playing, resurrect old songs and defend the faith to a Nashville scene that all too often has a short memory of its music's past. Despite failing health he continued as an Opry member right up until the time of his death, November 23, 1992.   —C.W.

Acuff-Rose Publishing Company

On October 13, 1942, on a handshake and $25,000 in seed money, Opry star Roy Acuff and Chicago-born ex-pop/Tin Pan Alley/Hollywood songwriter Fred Rose founded a music publishing concern which, in the coming decades, would grow to be one of the mightiest multi-million-dollar conglomerates in the national music publishing business and one of the true cornerstones of the Nashville music industry. Acuff's motivation for this venture was modest: he was simply tired of having New York and Hollywood publishers coming into town and buying up the copyrights of his original songs for a song and a dance.

The sterling song catalogue of Acuff and later Hank Williams (which included a number of titles co-written by Fred Rose, a particularly gifted and prolific songwriter) became the foundation of Acuff-Rose's steadily growing catalogue. The Bailes Brothers and Pee Wee King and his Golden West Cowboys were other early signees. (King gave the company a big boost with "Tennessee Waltz," a song he co-wrote with Red Stewart that has since become a country and pop standard.)

In the ensuing decades the company numbered among its staff writers some of the most prolific and oft-recorded songwriters in the business—Don Gibson ("Oh Lonesome Me," "I Can't Stop Loving You"), Leon Payne ("I Love You Because," "Lost Highway"), Marty Robbins, Bob Luman, J.D. Loudermilk, Felice and Boudleaux Bryant ("Wake Up, Little Susie," "Dream, Dream, Dream" and other early Everly Brothers hits), Jimmy Work ("Making Believe," "Tennessee Border"), Melvin Endsley ("Singing The Blues"), Mickey Newbury ("American Trilogy") and Doug Kershaw being just a few of them. In 1954, Acuff-Rose launched its own successful record label, Hickory, and thus enhanced its immense stature in the industry even further. After Wesley Rose's death in 1990, Acuff-Rose and Hickory were purchased by the Opryland Music Group.   —B.A.

Alabama

In the pre-Garth Brooks world of country music, no individual or group stood higher than Alabama. The four "good ole boys" from Fort Payne, Alabama, a geographical spit in the shadow of Lookout Mountain, were the first country music supergroup, virtually defining country music in the early 1980's. They sold heaven knows how many records (over 11 million at last count); swept away all the big country music awards, including multiple Entertainer of the Year awards from both the Country Music Association and the Academy of Country Music, and scored 21 Number One hit records in a row.

The music that came to define the country of that period was, not surprisingly, a remix of the old ingredients—the hardshell Southern bar music filtered through a distinct 1960's pop group sensibility—sort of The Allman Brothers Meet The Beatles. When the music worked—"Tennessee River" or "She and I"—it did, in fact, transcend its genre. When it didn't—"Roll On Eighteen Wheeler," for example—it was the country music equivalent of fingernails on a chalkboard.

Randy Owen, Teddy Gentry, Jeff Cook and Mark Herndon followed the tried-and-true path to Hillbilly Heaven—a decade on the grueling Southern bar circuit before an executive with RCA Records thought

the group deserved a shot on a "new talent" showcase. The core of the group was and is the two cousins, Owen and Gentry (Cook is also a distant cousin), who, like so many others before them, got their start in th,eir church—in their case, the Lookout Mountain Holiness Church. In 1969, the three cousins did their first paying gig, at the American Legion hall, earning each the princely sum of $5.37. In 1973, against the strenuous advice of family and friends, the three cousins left their day jobs (hanging drywall and laying carpet) and turned pro, heading to the clubs and honky tonks along South Carolina's Myrtle Beach. They eventually landed a regular gig at a place called The Bowery, a hardcore, sawdust-on-the-floor place, six nights a week for tips. "We'd play some nights until we got blisters," Gentry remembers. "Then we'd play 'til the blisters popped. But it sure beat working the swing shift in a sock factory."

Though they'd managed to put together a series of independent deals (as well as pick up Herndon, a rock drummer), they didn't get The Break until 1980, when they earned a shot on the "New Faces" show at Nashville's annual Country Radio Seminar. Suffice to say they blew the assembled DJs away. RCA signed the group, and their first single, "Tennessee River," went immediately to the top of the charts—the first of their long string of chart toppers.

Part of the group's early problems (they weren't allowed to play their instruments or have drummer Herndon on stage, for example, at their showcase) was that Music City was uncomfortable with the idea of a band, as opposed to a group. The ubiquitous Statler Brothers were a group—four guys who sang harmony. But Alabama was a band: four guys who played their own instruments and sang harmony. Bands tended to be volatile, fragmenting under the pressure of success, was the idea; plus the whole thing smacked of rock 'n' roll. Nashville took one look and thought, "Uh, oh! Lock up the women and children!" The emerging country audience, though, having grown up with rock bands, was perfectly comfortable with Alabama—as was Nashville when the sales figures started coming in. Alabama was the breakthrough country music had been looking for—a conduit to younger markets.

As is pretty typical, Alabama stayed a little too long at the party—the Southern Rock Lite formula began fraying around the edges about the time the "hat" acts began appearing in the late 1980's. The young audience was already committed to country, and they were looking for something different. While the band still has hits and campaigns for the admirable cause of environmental responsibility, it is no longer the dominant force it once was. Ironically, their recent albums have fared somewhat better with critics, despite diminishing sales.　　—M.B.

Deborah Allen

BORN: September 30, 1953
BIRTHPLACE: Memphis, Tennessee

A well-known Nashville songwriter and performer, Deborah Allen was born Deborah Lynn Thurmond in Memphis, Tennessee, on September 30, 1953. Ever since she was a little girl, Deborah had her sights set on stardom. When she was 19, she moved to Nashville, working as a backup singer and playing the club circuit. She eventually landed a chorus job at Opryland USA, which in turn provided her the opportunity to tour the Soviet Union with Tennessee Ernie Ford in 1974.

When Deborah returned, Jim Stafford invited her to work on his TV variety show in Los Angeles. She jumped at the opportunity.

In 1977, she moved back to Nashville and signed a songwriting deal with MCA. She hit the big time when Janie Fricke went to Number One with Deborah's "Don't Worry 'Bout Me Baby."

Record buyers became more familiar with Deborah's powerful voice when she recorded a trio of duets with the late Jim Reeves. Deborah's vocal tracks were melded onto Reeves' tapes, and two of the re-releases, "Don't Let Me Cross Over" and "Oh, How I Miss You Tonight," became smash successes.

In 1982, Deborah married Nashville songwriter Rafe Van Hoy (whom she divorced in the early 1990's). The following year, she signed with RCA and topped both the country and pop charts with the crossover hit, "Baby I Lied," which was co-written by her husband.

Rafe also produced Deborah's first RCA album,

Cheat the Night, which contained additional Top Ten hits such as "I've Been Wrong Before" and "I Hurt for You."

Her follow-up album, *Let Me Be the First*, received critical acclaim and further showcased Deborah's excellent songwriting skills as well as her clever combination of country, R&B, pop and gospel elements.

She continued writing and recording into the 1990's, including a lengthy foray into the pop and rock fields that resulted in several unreleased albums, including some tracks produced by rock star Prince. Her return to the country fold yielded a well-received album, *Delta Dreamland* (1993), for Giant Records. Among the many artists Deborah has written for are T.G. Sheppard, Tammy Wynette, John Conlee, Tanya Tucker, Patty Loveless and ex-Fleetwood Mac guitarist Billy Burnette.　　—R.P.

Rex Allen

BORN: December 31, 1921
BIRTHPLACE: Willcox, Arizona

Born December 31, 1921, in Willcox, Arizona, singer/actor Rex Allen came to represent the voice of the American cowboy to an entire generation. As a teenager, Rex made a name for himself as a rodeo performer before tackling a musical career in earnest in 1944, when he  landed his own show on WTTM in Trenton, New Jersey. Other radio jobs followed, and he joined the WLS *Barn Dance* in 1945. In 1948 he left Chicago for the West Coast. He signed with the increasingly influential Mercury Records in the late 1940's. Rex's rise in the music business coincided with the fledgling television industry's fascination with cowboys, and even before his recording career took off, Rex found himself starring in a popular CBS-TV show, *Frontier Doctor,* in 1949-50.

In 1951, perhaps as a result of his growing TV following, Allen scored his first Mercury hit, "Don't Go Near the Indians." The song made the country

Top Ten around the same time Allen was making it big as a movie star. With his horse Koko, he starred in a number of cowboy pictures throughout the 1950's while appearing as a regular cast member of Los Angeles' *Town Hall Party*. He also cut another Top Ten single, the 1953 tune "Crying in the Chapel," on Decca Records.

In the early 1960's he became a regular host of the short-lived NBC country music series, *Five Star Jubilee*. He cut several Mercury albums in the 1960's, including *Faith of a Man* and *Rex Allen Sings and Tells Tales*. Around the same time he also began narrating TV shows and nature films for Walt Disney Productions. Allen's career slowed down somewhat in the 1970's, though he continued to appear in an occasional Disney film (by the end of the 1970's his Disney projects totaled over 80). He also served as a trustee of the Cowboy Hall of Fame, to which he had been elected in 1968.

Rex used the time off from performing to pursue another love: songwriting. Throughout his long career Allen relied so heavily on traditional Western ballads like "Old Faithful" and "On Top of Old Smoky" that few of his fans realized he was also a prolific songwriter. By the late 1970's he had over 300 original songs to his credit. His son, Rex Allen Jr., rose to fame as a country singer in the 1970's.   —M.B.

Rex Allen Jr.

BORN: August 23, 1947
BIRTHPLACE: Chicago, Illinois

Born in Chicago, Illinois, on August 23, 1947, Rex Allen Jr., the son of singing cowboy legend Rex Allen Sr., enjoyed brief popularity in Nashville in the 1970's and early 1980's as a Western revivalist-turned mainstream country singer. The winner of *Country Music Magazine*'s annual "Bullet Award" for "Entertainer of the Year" in 1979, Allen's breakthrough was "Can You Hear Those Pioneers," a brilliant radio hit that briefly did a lot to "put Western back in the country sound."

Rex Jr. began his recording career in Los Angeles in 1966, but his association with Liberty/U.A. Records there was cut short when he was drafted into the Army, trained for advanced infantry, and instead wound up singing in the Special Services.

In 1971, after spending several more years going

nowhere in the L.A. club scene, he and his wife Judy spent their $600 in shared savings moving to Nashville. His famous surname notwithstanding, Allen found the sledding in Nashville pretty tough at first. "It was six or seven months before I played my first date. My income that first year was less than $3,000," he told journalist Bob Allen in a 1981 interview with *Country Music Magazine*.

Eventually, though, Allen had a pretty good run on Warner Bros. Records—nearly a dozen albums and a slew of chart records in the 70's and early 80's, including a half dozen or so Top Tens in the 70's: "Two Less Lonely People," "No, No, No (I'd Rather Be Free)," "With Love" and "Me and My Broken Heart," among them. But as the 80's wore on, Nashville turned out to be a lot less interested in the Western sound than Allen had first imagined. When last heard from, he was back where his heart had been all along: working the vital cowboy music scene, as well as appearing regularly on The Statler Brothers' Nashville Network variety show   —B.A.

Rosalie Allen

BORN: June 27, 1924
BIRTHPLACE: Old Forge, Pennsylvania

Rosalie Allen grew up in the northeastern Pennsylvania coal country as June Marlene Bedra, a chiropractor's daughter, and fell in love with the Western image. As Rosalie Allen, "The Prairie Star," she became one of the early female country stars on the East Coast. By the late 1930's, when still a teenager, she caught on with singer-songwriter Denver Darling's radio program. Her popularity continued through the 1940's and 50's. She worked with other New York-based country acts, including Zeke Manners, and began working with Elton Britt. Along the way she became a skilled yodeler. In the mid-40's she signed with RCA where she had two hits in 1946, a cover version of Patsy Montana's "I Wanna Be a

Cowboy's Sweetheart" and "Guitar Polka." She and Britt also recorded duets, and in 1950 the duo had Top Ten records with "Beyond the Sunset" (with The Three Suns) and "Quicksilver" (with The Skytoppers). Never fond of touring, she worked in the 1950's as a disc jockey over WOV Radio, and did TV as well. Gradually she ended her singing career, owned a record store and moved to the South.   —R.K.

Amazing Rhythm Aces

Formed in 1972 by vocalist/guitarist Russell Smith and drummer/percussionist Butch McDade, The Amazing Rhythm Aces, which also consisted of Billy "Byrd" Burton (guitar, dobro), Billy Earhart III (keyboards) and Jeff Davis (bass), were essentially a country band that also incorporated elements of rhythm and blues, rock and gospel into their repertoire.

In 1974 the group hit the national pop as well as country charts with "Third Rate Romance," a tune written by Smith that was later successfully covered by Jesse Winchester and Rosanne Cash. The single was featured on the band's ABC Records debut, *Stacked Deck*—a recording that garnered favorable reviews in both the rock and country press. "Amazing Grace (Used to Be Her Favorite Song)," the follow-up single from the album, also scored big on the country charts, and in 1975 The Aces released their second album, *Too Stuffed to Jump*. A third album, *Toucan Do It Too*, was released in 1976, but it failed

to receive the critical acclaim of the first two. However, that same year The Aces did win a Grammy award for Best Country Vocal Performance by a Group for Smith's "The End Is Not in Sight," which was featured on the album.

During the mid-1970's the group had a hefty touring schedule, often opening for Outlaw artists such as Waylon Jennings and Willie Nelson. However, the heavy road schedule eventually took its toll on Burton, who left the band amicably in the late 1970's. He was replaced by Duncan Cameron, a guitarist with Dan Fogelberg, (who later joined Sawyer Brown).

In 1978, the band released its fourth album, *Burning the Ballroom Down*. In 1979 came *Amazing Rhythm Aces*, which was basically R&B-tinged, but also featured the country-rocking "Lipstick Traces (On a Cigarette)," which was a pop hit for the Philadelphia soul group, The O'Jays, in 1965. Both albums failed to capture the public's attention. In 1980 the group recorded a single for Warner Bros. titled "I Musta Died and Gone to Texas." The song peaked at Number 77 on the country charts before Smith and McDade formally disbanded the group. In 1986, Earhart joined The Bama Band. Smith embarked on a solo career in the early 1980's, and then joined Run C&W in 1992. He is also a very successful Nashville songwriter.   —R.P.

Bill Anderson

Born: November 1, 1937
Birthplace: Columbia, South Carolina

James William Anderson III grew up interested in both music and journalism, earning a degree in the latter from the University of Georgia while singing and playing country music in his spare time. He worked in Commerce, Georgia, after graduating, and combined working as a DJ, a part-time newspaper correspondent and a singer to make a living. One night in Commerce, he was inspired by the lights of the small town to write the ballad, "City Lights." He recorded it for the tiny TNT label, and after Ray Price covered the song in 1958, making it one of the biggest hits of the year, Anderson's career took off. Decca signed him that year, largely on the strength of "City Lights." Still writing songs, he had his first Top 20 records in 1959, his first Top Ten records in 1960 with "The Tip of My Fingers," "Walk Out Backwards"

(covered by Rick Trevino in 1994) and "Po' Folks," the latter inspiring the name of his band.

He joined the Grand Ole Opry in 1961. Recording in the Nashville Sound style favored by his producer, Owen Bradley, Anderson had back-to-back Number Ones with "Still" in 1962 and "Mama Sang a Song" in 1963, each spending seven weeks at the top. His low-keyed, sentimental vocal style earned him the nickname "Whispering Bill," and he also used recitations in certain numbers for effect. "Me" in 1964 and "Three A.M." in 1965 were his biggest hits those years.

Anderson and The Po' Boys began to build a topflight touring show, adding Jimmy Gately and, in the late 60's, singer (and Anderson duet partner) Jan Howard. Anderson's songs were still hits for others. He wrote Connie Smith's first big hit, "Once a Day," as well as hosting his own syndicated half-hour TV show. Also in the late 60's, Anderson hit a streak of Top Ten and Number One recordings, among them "I Love You Drops" and "I Get the Fever" in 1966 (the latter a Number One record). His duets with Jan Howard included "I Know You're Married (But I Love You Still)," a number that has become a minor classic of cheating songs. "For Loving You" remained Number One four weeks in 1967. From the late 60's into the early 70's, he was barely out of the upper end of the charts with songs like "Wild Week-End," "Happy State of Mind" (1968) "My Life (Throw It Away

If I Want To)," "But You Know I Love You" (1969), "Love Is a Sometimes Thing" (1970), "Quits," (1971), "Don't She Look Good" (1972), "The Corner of My Life" and the Number One "World of Make Believe" (1975). After Jan Howard left, Anderson hired singer Mary Lou Turner for his act. He had one final Number One in 1976 with "Sometimes," a duet with Turner.

Anderson had lesser hits through the late 70's and remained with Decca after the label became MCA. In the early 80's he moved on, recording for the small Southern Tracks and Swanee labels. He never quit writing prose, contributing a column to *Country Song Roundup*, and hosted the TNN game show, *Fandango*. He later penned his autobiography, *Whispering Bill*, which dealt in part with his efforts to rehabilitate his wife Becky after a near fatal car crash. During the Persian Gulf War, he recorded an updated version of "Deck of Cards" for Curb Records. Anderson, still a member of the Opry (he sang with Roy Acuff on Acuff's final night at the Opry), later hosted TNN's *Grand Ole Opry Backstage*. He was also the subject of a video biography (which he hosted), and wrote another book, this one filled with amusing country music road stories taken from himself and fellow artists, *I Hope You're Living as High on the Hog as the Pig You Turned Out to Be*, in 1994.

—R.K.

John Anderson

BORN: December 13, 1954
BIRTHPLACE: Orlando, Florida

John Anderson and Ricky Skaggs were the first artists to symbolize the shift in the early 1980's to a sound that subsequently became known as New Traditionalism, and were the stylistic ancestors of Randy Travis. Yet Anderson did not establish the sound; he was merely the first sign of a shift. Born in Orlando, he was raised in Apopka, Florida, and played in rock bands early in his career, later singing with his sister. He was deeply influenced by the singing of both Merle Haggard and Lefty Frizzell. In 1972 he moved to Nashville and landed a position as a staff writer with Gallico Music. Two years later he made his first recording for the tiny Ace of Hearts label.

It was not until he signed with Warner Bros. in 1977 that he found success. Through the late 70's he had some modest hits, including two Top 20's, "Your Lying Blue Eyes" and "She Just Started Liking Cheatin'

Songs." In 1981 he had his first Top Ten with "1959," followed by his now-classic version of Billy Joe Shaver's "I'm Just an Old Chunk of Coal (But I'm Gonna Be a Diamond Someday)." The flip-side, "Chicken Truck," was also a Top Ten record. His album had the distinction of being the final one recorded in Columbia Records' Studio B, the old "Quonset Hut," before it was dismantled. Anderson's momentum built even more with "I Just Came Home to Count the Memories" and "Would You Catch a Falling Star." He had two Number Ones in a row in late 1981 and early 1982: "Wild and Blue" and "Swingin'" (co-written with Alton Delmore's son, Lionel), which won the Country Music Association's Single of the Year award. In 1983 "Black Sheep" became his third Number One record. That year he won the CMA's Horizon Award. "Let Somebody Else Drive" and "She Sure Got Away with My Heart" were his big hits in 1984. Anderson gradually moved to-

ward a more rocking sound, which he also tackled well. He even covered the 1964 Rolling Stones hit, "It's All Over Now."

Ironically, as New Traditionalism began to fill the charts in the mid-80's with the success of Travis and Dwight Yoakam, Anderson's career stalled. His 1987 move to MCA, with Jimmy Bowen producing, yielded few hits. He regained his initiative after signing with BNA Records in 1991. Early in 1992, "Straight Tequila Night" became his first Number One record in nine years, followed by the Top Tens "When It Comes to You," "Seminole Wind," "Let Go of the Stone," and his 1993 Number One, "Money in the Bank." —R.K.

Lynn Anderson

BORN: September 26, 1947
BIRTHPLACE: Grand Forks, North Dakota

The daughter of country singer/songwriter Liz Anderson (who wrote "The Fugitive" and "My Friends Are Gonna Be Strangers" for Merle Haggard and had several chart hits of her own, including the 1960's Top Fives, "Mama Spank" and "The Game of Triangles"), Lynn Anderson was born in Grand Forks, North Dakota, on September 26, 1947, years before her mother ever placed a song with a country performer. When she was a child, the family moved to California where, as a teenager, she entered a talent competition sponsored by a local country TV program called *Country Corners*. This exposure helped her land a spot in the regular cast of *The Lawrence Welk Show* in 1967.

Around the same time, Anderson signed her first recording contract with Chart Records and cut a hit single, "Too Much of You," as well as a debut album, *Ride, Ride, Ride*. After marrying producer R. Glenn Sutton in 1968, she moved to Nashville and recorded successful albums for Chart, including *Promises, Promises, Uptown Country Girl, Songs My Mother Wrote* and *Songs That Made Country Girls Famous*.

Anderson signed with Columbia in 1970 and cut two albums that year, *Stay There 'Til I Love You* and *No Love at All*. While both albums did well, it was Lynn's cover of the Joe South standard, "Rose Garden," released later that year, that made her an international star. It was an instant hit with pop and country audiences; its American sales alone earned the song platinum record status, while foreign sales earned her 13 other Gold records from around the world. The album of the same name, the first of many produced by her then-husband Glenn Sutton, was also a smash hit, and when Grammy time came around, Anderson was named Best Female Country Vocalist of 1971. She also received the Country Music Association's award for Female Vocalist of the Year.

On the heels of "Rose Garden," she struck Gold once again with the Number One "You're My Man," which spent 15 weeks on the country charts in 1971. Her other Number One singles included "How Can I Unlove You" later that year, "Keep Me in Mind" in 1973, and "What a Man, My Man Is" in 1974. Also rising high on the charts were a passel of love songs including "Sing About Love," "I've Never Loved Anyone More," "I Love What Love Is Doing to Me" and "Last Love of My Life."

Anderson remained a top country-pop act for much of the decade, touring throughout the U.S. and Europe. For years she was a constant fixture on TV talk shows, appeared frequently on *Hee Haw*, and even ate breakfast at the Nixon White House. By the latter part of the 70's, though, her hits slowed. The 80's produced some modest chart records, including a cover of the pop hit, "Under the Boardwalk" and a Top Ten 1983 duet with Gary Morris, "You're Welcome to Tonight," for Mercury Records. Most recently, Anderson recorded a Western album for the indie label, Delta Music. —M.B.

Eddy Arnold

BORN: May 15, 1918
BIRTHPLACE: Henderson, Tennessee

Legendary singer Eddy Arnold was born Richard Edward Arnold near Henderson, Tennessee, on May 15, 1918. The son of a sharecropper, the "Tennessee Plowboy" learned to play guitar from his mother. He made his radio debut in 1936 on a station in Jackson, Tennessee; six years later he was hired full time, and

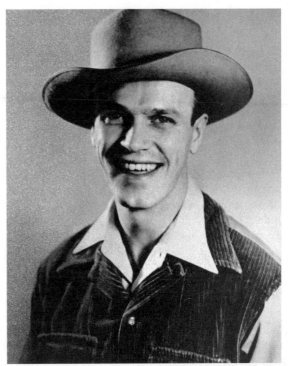

soon became one of the station's most popular performers.

His radio following brought Arnold to the attention of Pee Wee King, who invited him to join his Golden West Cowboys, a popular Grand Ole Opry act of the 1940's. The experience helped Arnold land a recording contract with RCA Records in 1944. Managed by Colonel Tom Parker (who would later go down in history as the manager of Elvis Presley), the Plowboy quickly churned out a series of hits that lasted well into the 1950's. In 1948 alone he placed a total of nine hits in the country Top Ten, some of which he wrote or co-wrote. Among them were four Number One singles, including "A Heart Full of Love," "Any Time" and "Texarkana Baby." The fourth, the smash hit "Bouquet of Roses," spent an unbelievable 54 weeks in the country Top 40, setting a record no country artist has since been able to match. His intimate sound on record was enhanced by the Hawaiian steel guitar of Little Roy Wiggins. Interestingly, one of Arnold's signature songs, "Cattle Call," went nowhere when first recorded in 1944. Re-recorded in 1955, it became a Number One hit.

The rise of rock 'n' roll changed the music marketplace, and traditional country found less favor with audiences. As a result, Arnold's chart hits began to taper off as the 50's wore on. He responded with drastic changes in his sound. Under the direction of Chet Atkins, Arnold's "Tennessee Plowboy" persona disappeared, replaced with an urbane crooner who led the "countrypolitan" movement. Recording now with orchestras and lush string sections, Arnold played at supper clubs, with symphony orchestras and at other non-country venues. It was a pattern that would be repeated by many top stars of the day, notably Ray Price and Jim Reeves. The shift worked, and while it angered some of his earlier fans, Arnold's hit-making continued through the 60's. Among his Top Tens in this era were "A Little Heartache," "After Loving You," "Tears Broke Out on Me," "Here Comes the Rain Baby," "It's Over," "The Last Word in Lonesome Is Me," "Here Comes Heaven," "I Thank My Lucky Stars" and "Molly." He also scored his share of Number One hits, including "What's He Doing in My World" and "Make the World Go Away" in 1965; "Tips of My Fingers" and "Somebody Like Me" in 1966; "Lonely Again" and "Turn the World Around" in 1967; and "Then You Can Tell Me Goodbye" in 1968. Arnold was named to the Country Music Hall of Fame in 1966, and when the Country Music Association gave out its first Entertainer of the Year award in 1967, he was the obvious choice.

While his record sales slowed in the 1970's, Arnold put out albums on RCA, including *Love and Guitars* (1970), *Portrait of My Woman* and *Chained to a Memory,* both in 1972. His personal magnetism and infectious laugh made the transition from country star to television personality seem inevitable. He hosted more than 20 TV specials, many of them part of the *Kraft Music Hall* series, served as co-host of the *Mike Douglas Show* and occasionally stood in for Johnny Carson as guest host of *The Tonight Show.*

In the mid-1970's, Arnold's nearly 30-year association with RCA came to an end, and he began recording on the MGM label. While his MGM sales were modest compared with what he'd accomplished at RCA, he still managed to put songs on the charts, including "Just for Old Time's Sake" and "She's Got All I Need" in 1974, and "Butterfly," "Red Roses" and "Middle of a Memory" in 1975. Arnold returned to RCA in 1976 and resumed a successful collaboration with the label without missing a beat. Among his charted singles were three Top Ten hits: "Rocky Mountain Music/Do You Right Tonight" in 1976, and "If Everyone Had Someone Like You" and "What in Her World Did I Do," both in 1979.

In 1980 Arnold placed three more singles on the country charts: "That's What I Get for Loving You," "If I Ever Had to Say Goodbye to You" and "Let's Get It While the Getting's Good," earning him the distinction of making country hits over five decades. After more than 50 years in the business, Arnold has become a true country music legend. The best-selling solo country act of all time, Eddy has sold over 70 million records and developed a following of fans the world over. He continues to record for RCA into the 90's.   —M.B.

Clarence "Tom" Ashley

BORN: September 29, 1895
BIRTHPLACE: Bristol, Tennessee
DIED: June 2, 1967

Clarence "Tom" Ashley's career spans from Appalachian medicine shows before World War I to the urban folk revival. His re-emergence in the early 60's also launched the career of his neighbor, Doc Watson.

Ashley was born Clarence Earl McCurry, but he later adopted the last name of the maternal grandfather who raised him. As a youngster, Ashley was fascinated by transient musicians who boarded at his family's. After absorbing many of their jokes, songs and banjo and guitar specialties, he joined his first medicine show in 1913. During his early years, he split his time between sawmilling, farming and entertaining.

He began recording as a string band musician around 1927, initially with The Blue Ridge Entertainers. Ashley's best known ensemble recordings were with Byrd Moore and His Hot Shots on Columbia, and The Carolina Tar Heels on Victor. A 1929 solo session for Columbia preserved Ashley's versions of "The Cuckoo Bird" and "The House Carpenter." In 1943 Ashley quit the medicine show circuit, although he later worked as a comedian with Charlie Monroe's Kentucky Partners and The Stanley Brothers.

In 1960 a chance encounter with folklorist Ralph Rinzler convinced Ashley that many listeners still cared about his music. When Rinzler and collector Eugene Earle set up a recording session at Ashley's home later that year, Ashley invited Doc Watson to join him. In 1961 Ashley, Watson, Clint Howard and Fred Price began appearing at Northern folk festivals and clubs. Folkways issued two albums of their music; a third album featured Ashley and Tex Isley.   —D.S.

Ernest Ashworth

BORN: December 15, 1928
BIRTHPLACE: Huntsville, Alabama

Ernie Ashworth began his career in Alabama radio before joining WSIX in Nashville. He made his first mark as a songwriter, impressing Wesley Rose of Acuff-Rose who helped him obtain an MGM recording contract in 1955. After unsuccessfully recording under the name "Billy Worth," he found his first success with Decca with the single, "Each Moment (Spent With You)," which went Top Five in 1960.

Other successes followed until Rose signed Ashworth to Acuff-Rose's Hickory label in 1962. After Top Tens with "Everybody But Me" and "I Take the Chance," "Talk Back Trembling Lips" reached Number One in 1963. Ashworth joined the Grand Ole Opry in 1964, but after his 1965 hit, "The DJ Cried," he never had another Top Ten. He continued as an active Opry member and also moonlighted as the "Opry artist in residence" at a large recreational vehicle park in Alabama.   —R.K.

Asleep at the Wheel

Two young Philadelphia musicians, guitarist Ray Benson and steel guitarist Reuben "Lucky Oceans" Gosfield, formed Asleep at the Wheel around 1970 in Paw Paw, West Virginia. Captivated by both country music and the Western swing of Bob Wills, they played bars and lodge halls in the area and added other musicians, including vocalist Chris O'Connell. In 1972 they moved to Berkeley, California, where they played bars (often billed with the similarly focused Commander Cody and His Lost Planet Airmen). Other talented musicians joined, including Leroy Preston, who had a rhythm and blues and country focus, and pianist Jim Haber, known as "Floyd Domino." Signed to United Artists Records that year, their debut was not successful. In 1974 the group relocated to Austin, Texas, just in time for that city's musical renaissance. An Epic album that year went nowhere, but their career took off when they signed with Capitol in 1975. The acclaimed album, *Texas Gold*, produced a hit single, "The Letter that Johnny

Walker Read," and their success helped fuel the Western swing revival. In the freewheeling Bob Wills tradition they eventually grew, added a full horn section, and expanded their musical scope to include R&B and big band swing. They often used ex-Texas Playboys like Johnny Gimble and Eldon Shamblin on their records. Most of their other Capitol albums were as well-received, and in 1978 they won a Grammy for their version of Count Basie's 1930's big band classic, "One O'Clock Jump." After Capitol dropped them, they briefly signed with MCA for one album, then recorded for the independent Stony Plain label before returning to Epic and, later, Arista. Dozens of musicians have circulated through the band, and only Benson remains of the original group. Founding member Gosfield (Lucky Oceans) is now in Australia, heading a much respected band called Dude Ranch. Early member Haber (Floyd Domino) has become a leading session man and has played on numerous George Strait records. The band has appeared in several movies, and in 1993 Benson produced a Grammy-winning all-star tribute to Bob Wills for Liberty Records titled *Tribute to the Music of Bob Wills and His Texas Playboys,* featuring AATW, ex-Texas Playboys, and former AATW members and guests including Dolly Parton, Garth Brooks, Vince Gill, Huey Lewis, George Strait, Marty Stuart, Lyle Lovett and Willie Nelson.   —R.K

but by 1922, they returned east to Ohio. He did his first radio show in 1928, and continued performing on Louisville radio while a student at the University of Kentucky. A Chicago radio station owner heard him and encouraged him to move there. In 1932 he began broadcasting over three stations there, which attracted the attention of ARC's Art Satherley, who encouraged Atcher to move to a larger station. In 1935 he went to WSB in Atlanta, but within three years was back in Chicago, where he made records with Satherley (including duets with female singer Bonnie Blue Eyes). Atcher was the first to record the Western classic, "Cool Water." Following World War II service he returned to Chicago-area radio work and recording for Columbia. By 1948 he'd joined the WLS *National Barn Dance.* Since he was not exclusively tied to WLS, he did other local TV and radio shows as well. After moving to the Chicago suburb of Schaumburg in the mid-1950's, he became active in the community, serving as mayor from 1959 to 1975, and played a major role in Schaumburg's incorporation as a town and its dramatic residential and industrial expansion. He still performed over the *Barn Dance* after it moved to Chicago's WGN in the 1960's, remaining with the show until it ended in 1971. He kept performing around the area after leaving office, until moving to Kentucky in 1989. He died of cancer on October 30, 1993.   —R.K.

Bob Atcher

BORN: May 11, 1914
BIRTHPLACE: Hardin County, Kentucky
DIED: October 30, 1993

Robert Owen Atcher, born in Hardin County, Kentucky, on May 11, 1914, began his career as a country singer, but later took his career far beyond music. The son of a tobacco farmer, he grew up with music all around, and played with his brothers. The Atchers moved to a ranch in North Dakota when Bob was five,

Chet Atkins

BORN: June 20, 1924
BIRTHPLACE: Luttrell, Tennessee

Chet Atkins' contributions to country music are broad-based. As a guitarist, he combined pop and jazz elements with the Merle Travis-based finger picking style he developed. His dozens of solo albums legitimized the country guitar soloist and established the fact that Nashville musicians were capable of more than three-chord hillbilly songs. And as a record producer, he helped redefine country music for a generation.

At RCA for many years, Atkins launched many new stars and helped veteran stars like Hank Snow and Eddy Arnold thrive amid changing times. His production influenced the success of Jim Reeves, Floyd Cramer, Hank Locklin, Don Gibson, Skeeter Davis, Connie Smith, Dottie West, Jerry Reed, Waylon, Willie, Porter Wagoner, Dolly Parton, Charley

Pride and George Hamilton IV, among others.

Despite the sophistication and polish that became his trademark musically, Chester Burton Atkins' roots were stone country. He was born June 20, 1924, to James and Ida Atkins on a farm near Luttrell, Tennessee, a whistle stop in the Clinch Mountain foothills not far from Knoxville. His father taught music; the first guitarist in the family was Chester's older half-brother, Jimmy, James' son by a previous marriage.

Chester fought asthma throughout his youth. His parents separated and eventually divorced. Jimmy left to stake out a musical career; Chester and another brother, Lowell, helped work their small farm to avoid poverty. Chet traded his stepfather two rifles for a spare guitar he owned and began trying to play. He also learned to fiddle reasonably well, and by age ten was playing informally.

When Chester's asthma worsened in 1935, James Atkins took his son back to Georgia, where he was living. One night in the late 30's while listening to his crystal radio, Chester heard Merle Travis finger picking over 50,000-watt Cincinnati station WLW. Chet figured out his own version of the style. Meanwhile Jimmy Atkins, now part of electric guitarist Les Paul's trio on bandleader Fred Waring's NBC radio show, was another inspiration.

World War II brought changes. In an era when many musicians were being drafted, Chester—exempt because of his asthma—had little trouble working. He became a fiddler at WNOX in Knoxville, Tennessee. Station manager Lowell Blanchard decided to feature him as a guitar soloist on the station's *Mid-Day Merry-Go-Round*. To learn more material, Atkins listened to all types of music in the WNOX library, a self-education greatly influencing his future.

He first recorded as a sideman in 1944 in Atlanta with three WNOX acts who signed with Capitol. After brief stints in Cincinnati and Raleigh, he was hired by Red Foley and moved to Nashville, where he made his first solo record for Bullet Records in 1946: the funky "Guitar Blues." After leaving Foley he worked briefly in Richmond, Virginia, then in 1947 moved to KWTO in Springfield, Missouri. There his friend, station booking agent Si Simon, nicknamed him "Chet." But his smooth, polished playing earned him a pink slip from other KWTO officials, who wanted a more "hillbilly" guitarist.

Chet's idol, Merle Travis, was a major recording star for Capitol by then, and other labels sought a similar artist. Chet was working in Denver when he got an unexpected phone call from RCA Victor producer Steve Sholes. Si Simon had sent Sholes some transcription discs of Chet's playing, and Sholes offered the guitarist an RCA contract. His first RCA session was in Chicago in August 1947, playing and singing in the Travis style. Late that year he returned to WNOX, working with guitarist Homer Haynes and mandolinist Jethro Burns, whom he'd met at WLW. Then Chet signed on as featured guitarist with Mother Maybelle and The Carter Sisters, working in Knoxville and Springfield. They moved to the Opry in 1950.

Increased recording activity in Nashville helped Chet supplement his income. When not working with The Carters, he played guitar on scores of recording sessions with both major and minor artists. Among the hits he played on were Hank Williams' "I'll Never Get Out of This World Alive" and The Carlisles' "No Help Wanted" in 1953. He no longer sang on records but concentrated on pungent instrumentals like "I've Been Workin' on the Guitar" and "Galloping on the Guitar." He was often backed by Homer & Jethro, who could be heard on tunes like 1949's "Galloping on the Guitar," 1952's "Downhill Drag" and his 1953 classic, "Country Gentleman." All sold extremely well, as did his albums. In 1954, in conjunction with the Gretsch guitar company, he designed their candy-apple red CA 6120, the original "Chet Atkins" electric guitar, a measure of his growing stature.

Chet's friendship with RCA's Steve Sholes led to his appointment as Sholes' Nashville assistant in 1952, setting up RCA recording sessions and occasionally producing if Sholes couldn't make it. Sholes saw Chet's clear-cut skills as a session leader, and when RCA opened its own Nashville studio, Sholes placed him in charge of it. By 1957 Chet was managing all Nashville recording operations for RCA.

He faced an immediate challenge. Country record sales were nose-diving in Elvis' wake. People were clearly tired of the fiddle and steel sound. Chet was one of a trio of producers (Decca's Owen Bradley and Columbia's Don Law were the others) who saw that the sound of country records had to change to survive. Both he and Bradley, a former danceband leader who knew pop music, began making records without fiddles and steel. Instead they tried guitars, piano, vocal choruses and new, unusual instrumental sounds as backing for the artists. Chet also helped non-RCA artists, and played a major role in the creation of The Everly Brothers' classic rock hits.

Chet's early successes with the new sound include Jim Reeves' 1957 hit "Four Walls," and Don Gibson's 1958 double-sided smash, "Oh Lonesome Me" and "I Can't Stop Lovin' You." His ear for the unusual was uncanny. In 1960 Chet received a demo of songwriter Don Robertson singing his tune "Please Help Me, I'm Falling," accompanying himself on piano and bending the piano notes like a steel guitar. Chet knew the song was perfect for Hank Locklin, but also had Nashville session pianist Floyd Cramer teach himself Robertson's piano style for Locklin's session. Two smash records emerged: Locklin's hit and Floyd Cramer's classic, "Last Date." "Pedal piano" became Cramer's trademark.

In 1968 Chet became an RCA vice president, supervising other producers, signing artists, producing and doing his own recordings (many of them made in his home studio), mixing flamenco, country, pop and rock. As a solo artist he performed and recorded with the Boston Pops. His influence on rock guitar players was immense, since he was using many of the electronic effects now common, such as "wah-wah," on his albums in the 50's. "Yakety Axe," a guitar version of Atkins discovery Boots Randolph's "Yakety Sax," was a Top Ten record in 1965.

Among those he signed were Dolly Parton, Jerry Reed, Waylon Jennings and Willie Nelson. He bravely signed country music's first black singer, Charley Pride, after many other Nashville executives, respecting Pride's talent but fearing controversy, had declined. He also helped produce various RCA pop sessions done in Nashville by Perry Como and others. Onstage he usually performed with Floyd Cramer and Boots Randolph. In 1973 he underwent successful surgery for colon cancer. Inducted into the Country Music Hall of Fame that same year, he was at the time the youngest individual to be so honored. A year later he and his mentor, Merle Travis, cut an album that won a Grammy. In 1976 he recorded *Chester and Lester* with his old friend and idol, Les Paul, winning another Grammy.

Through the 70's he gravitated back to his first love: the guitar. He began ceding his executive responsibilities to others. Disheartened at the increasingly corporate direction of making records, he resigned from RCA in 1981. In 1982 he signed with Columbia as a recording artist—after 35 years with RCA. The Gretsch guitar company then defunct, he began working with Gibson on the Chet Atkins line of guitars they now sell.

In recent years Chet has recorded all types of music, from fusion jazz to a recent effort with old friend and protégé Jerry Reed. He was a regular performer on Public Radio's *Prairie Home Companion*, and still remains active as a musician. In May 1991, a small street near Music Row was renamed Chet Atkins Place.

Chet Atkins came far from the hollows of Luttrell. Though proud of his other achievements, in many ways he remains a guitar picker at heart. As true as that may be, at age 70, through his producing skills, his vision and most of all his guitar-playing, he is one of a handful of men who truly changed the face of country music. —R.K.

Austin City Limits

Through the ups and downs of country music on television, one show has remained constant since its January 2, 1976, premiere: Public Broadcasting's *Austin City Limits*. The concert program, generally featuring one or two performers each episode, is taped at PBS affiliate KLRU in Austin and distributed to some 300 PBS affiliates across the country. The pilot episode featured Willie Nelson, who has been a frequent guest over the show's 19 seasons. The line-ups are known for their diversity—everyone from Asleep at the Wheel to B.B King to The Indigo Girls, Leonard Cohen, Delbert McClinton, Waylon Jennings, Nanci Griffith and Lyle Lovett have appeared right alongside more mainstream Nashville fare. —G.F.

Gene Autry

BORN: September 29, 1907
BIRTHPLACE: Tioga, Texas

One of the most famous and successful cowboy singers ever, Orvon Gene Autry initially modeled his singing and yodeling style on Jimmie Rodgers. Autry grew up on ranches in Texas and Oklahoma. As a teenager he worked with a medicine show, learned to play guitar and became enamored of the music of Rodgers. He was encouraged by legendary Oklahoma humorist Will Rogers, who met young Autry, then a telegraph operator, in his telegraph shack by the side of the railroad. Art Satherley of the American Recording Company signed Autry in 1929. He achieved success with Rodgers-style material, performing over KVOO in Tulsa (the future home of Bob Wills), but found even greater popularity in Chicago. On the WLS *National Barn Dance*, he became known as "America's Singing Cowboy." One of his first six recordings, "That Silver Haired Daddy of Mine," which he wrote, sold five million copies.

Autry's career in cowboy movies began in 1934 when he sang "Silver Haired Daddy" in the Ken Maynard western, *In Old Santa Fe*. That part led to his own movie contracts. Autry did more singing in his movies than most earlier singing western heroes. His records continued to do well, particularly his "Mexicali Rose," his theme song "Back in the Saddle Again," and a song that became a pop music standard, "South of the Border." His films became a Saturday afternoon pastime with young Americans, and in early 1940, with radio increasingly popular, he began his CBS *Melody Ranch Show*. He also became part of Columbia Records after CBS bought the American Recording Company.

He built a strong performing organization on the West Coast in the 1940's. His group included comics like Smiley Burnette, and musical acts like The Jimmy Wakely Trio with Johnny Bond (Wakely would become a singing cowboy star in his own right). Throughout the World War II years he had hits like "I'm Thinking Tonight of My Blue Eyes" and "Don't Fence Me In," even while he served in the Army Air Corps. His biggest hit of these years was the wartime number, "At Mail Call Today," which remained Number One for eight weeks. After returning in 1945 he picked up his film, radio and recording career. His postwar hits included "I Wish I Had Never Met Sunshine" and "Someday You'll Want Me to Want You."

In 1948 his recording of "Here Comes Santa Claus" became a Christmas standard, followed in 1949 by his definitive "Rudolph the Red-Nosed Reindeer." His final hits came in 1950 with his version of "Peter Cottontail," and "Old Soldiers Never Die" in 1951. He never had another hit on the charts. Roy Rogers' popularity increased, but Autry had little to complain about even after *Melody Ranch* ended as a network TV show in 1956. After returning from the war, he had become more focused on business interests. These included real estate, oil, broadcasting, song publishing and ownership of Republic Pictures, which owned many of his classic films. His final western appeared in 1953, the 93rd of his career.

For years he owned Los Angeles' television station KTLA, and to this day owns the California Angels baseball team. He was inducted into the Country Music Hall of Fame in 1969. However, Autry has remained close to his roots, continuing to perform on television until the early 1970's. When *Melody Ranch* TV show finally went off the air in the mid-80's, Autry and his longtime sidekick, Pat Buttram, hosted old Autry westerns on The Nashville Network's *Melody Ranch Theater*. Though largely out of the public eye at his advanced age, Autry continues to be revered throughout the Western film and music community as an elder statesman. His Gene Autry Western Heritage Museum stands in North Hollywood. —R.K.

Hoyt Axton

BORN: March 25, 1938
BIRTHPLACE: Duncan, Oklahoma

Hoyt Axton is the son of songwriter Mae Boren Axton. He began his career as a West Coast folkie, playing the coffeehouses of California and getting involved in the acoustic/country/folk scene there. He had several chart hits on A&M, MCA and his own Jeremiah label, including the Top Ten "Boney Fingers" in 1974, but covers of his songs by rock group Three Dog Night were even more prominent. They brought his "Joy to the World" to Number One on the pop charts in 1971, and had a Top Ten with his "Never Been to Spain." Hoyt focused mostly on acting through the 80's, including roles in the films *Gremlins* and *The Black Stallion*, and numerous TV appearances. He returned to recording in 1991 with the album *Spin of the Wheel*, on independent label DPI. —G.F.

Mae Boren Axton

BORN: September 14, 1914
BIRTHPLACE: Bardwell, Texas

Mae Boren Axton (mother of country-pop singer/songwriter/film actor Hoyt Axton and sister of retiring Oklahoma senator David Boren) has been for years a colorful fixture on Music Row: a perennial behind-the-scenes career broker and perpetual friend to the stars whose engaging personality and non-stop creativity brought her success in a variety of different fields.

As a songwriter, Axton's most enduring credit is as co-writer of Elvis Presley's "Heartbreak Hotel." (That song has brought her a healthy five-figure royalty check every year since it was first released in 1956.) Over the years, her original tunes were also covered by Faron Young, Conway Twitty, Hank Snow, Patsy Cline and Floyd Tillman.

Axton, who earned a degree in journalism from Oklahoma University, also made a mark as a journalist (*Life Magazine*, for example); a Nashville radio and TV personality; and a public relations trouble shooter who played a role in the early careers of Dolly Parton, Willie Nelson and Mel Tillis, among others. —B.A.

Backup Bands

Country music's early string bands of the 1920's and 1930's were mainly groups of talented instrumentalists (even if the leader sometimes sang). Some had designated leaders, such as Gid Tanner and The Skillet Lickers or Charlie Poole and The North Carolina Ramblers; nevertheless, the focus was on the group. In Western swing bands, the same was largely true, though the leaders were a bit more prominent: for example, Milton Brown, the solo vocalist who led The Musical Brownies, and Bob Wills, the fiddling leader of The Texas Playboys. When solo singers began to dominate, things changed for bands. The singer was now the star.

The real shift came with Roy Acuff. Though Acuff played fiddle, his Smoky Mountain Boys existed primarily to provide instrumental backup to his vocals, as did Gene Autry's group and Ernest Tubb's Texas Troubadours.

By the 1950's, however, certain backup bands, like The Troubadours, Hank Williams' Drifting Cowboys and Carl Smith's Tunesmiths, established strong identities in their own right. Some groups even made their own records.

Touring in such groups was, and still is, a valuable apprenticeship for learning the music business. A selected listing of stars who began this way supports that view: Willie Nelson (bassist with Ray Price), Cal Smith and Jack Greene (ex-Texas Troubadours), Ricky Skaggs, Rodney Crowell and Tony Brown (Emmylou Harris' Hot Band). —R.K.

DeFord Bailey

BORN: December 14, 1899
BIRTHPLACE: Bellwood, Tennessee
DIED: July 2, 1982

One of the earliest and biggest stars of Nashville's Grand Ole Opry, and the first of only a handful of successful black country artists, DeFord Bailey was born in Bellwood, Tennessee, in 1899. By the time the Grand Ole Opry came into existence in 1926, Bailey (often referred to as "The Harmonica Playing Wizard") was already a popular entertainer on the WSM *Barn Dance*, the radio show that preceded the Opry. From 1926 to 1941, Bailey was one of the Opry's most popular headliners. In 1928 alone, he made 49 appearances on the Opry in 52 weeks—twice as many as any other single Opry act.

The diminutive singer (he stood only 4'11" and was slightly crippled due to a childhood bout with polio) learned his musical licks from family members who played old-time fiddle and banjo music—what Bailey himself later referred to as "black hillbilly music." Starting in 1928, he also became one of the first artists to record regularly in Nashville. "Ain't Gonna Rain No More," "Shoe Shine Boy Blues," "Lost John," "John Henry," "Ice Water Blues," "Pan-American Blues," "Muscle Shoals Blues," "Fox Chase," "Old Hen Cackle" and "Alcoholic Blues" were some of the better known numbers from his repertoire.

During his Opry years, Bailey often toured with the Opry troupe and appeared frequently with both Roy Acuff and Bill Monroe. He often outdrew everybody. "I carried him with me because they wanted to see him," Roy Acuff recalled in *DeFord Bailey*, an excellent biography of the singer, written by David C. Morton and Charles K. Wolfe. "There was quite a demand to see him....He always had very nice crowds." There were strong suggestions of racial discrimination surrounding the Opry management's rather abrupt dismissal of Bailey at age 42, when he was at the height of his popularity. As the singer himself, who died in 1982, recalled in his posthumously published biography, "They turned me loose to root hog or die. They didn't give a hoot where I went."

—B.A.

Razzy Bailey

BORN: February 14, 1939
BIRTHPLACE: Five Points, Alabama

Razzy Bailey was born on February 14, 1939, in Five Points, Alabama. After initially achieving some success—and financial stability—working the nightclubs of the South, and making a couple of stabs at recording on MGM and Capricorn, Bailey captured Nashville's attention when Dickey Lee  recorded his song, "9,999,999 Tears." The single was a hit, and eventually led to Bailey's signing with RCA. A string of Top Tens followed from 1978 to '82, including five Number One hits: "Loving Up a Storm," "I Keep Coming Back," "Friends," "Midnight Hauler" and "She Left Love All Over Me." Bailey failed to establish a strong identity with record buyers, and by the time he signed with MCA in 1984, his hitmaking days were largely over.

—G.F.

Baillie & The Boys

BORN: Michael Bonagura, March 26, 1953, Newark, New Jersey; Kathie Baillie, February 20, 1951, Morristown, New Jersey

Native New Jerseyans and husband and wife Michael Bonagura (born March 26, 1953 in Newark, New Jersey) and Kathie Baillie (born on February 20, 1951 in Morristown, New Jersey) had been making music for almost 15 years before landing an RCA Records contract in Nashville. But when that break came, things still didn't get any easier: in 1988, just as their momentum was picking up, founding member and bassist Alan LeBoeuf quit. He was replaced with Lance Hoppen, and the group went on. The group's folk/pop/country stylings, Baillie's vocals, and the songwriting skills of she and Bonagura have earned much critical praise. Top Tens included "Oh Heart," "Long Shot," "Heart of Stone" and "Can't Turn the Tide." The hits continued through 1991, with "Treat Me Like a Stranger," their most recent chart entry.   —G.F.

Moe Bandy

BORN: February 12, 1944
BIRTHPLACE: Meridian, Mississippi

There was a period of time in the mid and late 1970's when the slick country-pop of Kenny Rogers and John Denver, and the counter-culturally tinged Outlaw sound of Waylon & Willie was all the rage. Credit journeyman Texas singer Moe Bandy with keeping the twin fiddle/steel guitar, Texas-style honky tonk music alive during these years.

Before younger and more telegenic hard country singers like George Strait began taking the wind out of his sails, Bandy had a pretty good run in the charts. Between 1974 and 1989 (when he made his last trip into the Top 20), he scored repeatedly with "cheatin' and drinkin'" hits like "Hank Williams You Wrote My Life," "I Just Started Hatin' Cheatin' Songs," "Bandy the Rodeo Clown," "Honky Tonk Amnesia," "It Was Always So Easy to Find an Unhappy Woman (Till I Started Looking for Mine)" and "Just Good Ol' Boys" (with Joe Stampley). He and Joe Stampley had a series of successful duets, mostly novelties.

Born in Meridian, Mississippi, on February 12, 1944, Bandy grew up in San Antonio, Texas, where his father headed a popular local band called The Mission City Playboys. Bandy soon followed in his father's footsteps, and by his teens had formed his own band. Coming of age, Bandy spent a dozen years working sheet metal for a plumbing company and playing Texas honky tonks by night. Determined to somehow crash into the recording business, Bandy got his first break when he heard that Nashville producer Ray Baker was in Texas on a hunting trip. Though he'd never met Baker, Bandy summoned his courage, knocked on Baker's motel room door, and gave him a tape.

Baker soon took Bandy into the studio at his own expense, but their first joint efforts were turned down by every label in Nashville. They finally struck pay dirt the hard way when the two of them paid out of their own pockets to record and press copies of the song that would eventually become Bandy's first hit, "I Just Started Hatin' Cheatin' Songs Today." They released the record on their own tiny basement label, and sent copies out to radio stations. It was eventually re-released on GRC, an independent Atlanta label, and did well enough (Top 20) to attract the attention of Columbia, for whom Bandy subsequently recorded most of his big hits.

Over time, Bandy abandoned his honky tonk

sound for a more pop-oriented style that resulted in less success. After leaving Columbia in 1986 he briefly signed with MCA,where he had one hit ,"Till I'm Too Old to Die Young," in 1987; in the late 80's he signed with Curb. Today, Bandy often performs at his Americana Theater in Branson.   —B.A.

Banjo

The exact origin of the banjo is unknown, although evidence suggests it developed from a four-string, fretless instrument that slaves brought to America in the 18th century. A fifth string was added during the mid-19th century; minstrel performer Joel Walker Sweeney claimed credit for this innovation. Around 1880 banjo makers began adding frets to the fingerboard, allowing for greater volume and truer pitches.

The instrument inspired two distinct modes of playing: an intricate classical style popular with turn-of-the-century Northern urban musicians, and folk styles evolved from minstrel strums and independent experimentation with mail-order and homemade banjos.

Early Southern banjo players frequently used clawhammer and various finger-picking styles. The clawhammer style, also known as "frailing," uses the middle fingernail to strike downward on the strings, with the thumb hooking upward on the fifth string. Among the best-known clawhammer banjoists are Uncle Dave Macon, Wade Ward, Clarence Ashley, Grandpa Jones, Cousin Emmy and Stringbean. Some early country finger-style banjoists used a thumb and index finger, such as Wade Mainer and Bascom Lamar Lunsford. Others fashioned different three-finger approaches, including Macon, Charlie Poole, Sam McGee, Dock Boggs and Doc Walsh.

In the early 40's Johnnie Whisnant, Don Reno and Earl Scruggs independently learned a fundamental three-finger roll based on the playing of Snuffy Jenkins, a member of Byron Parker and His Mountaineers. However, Scruggs was the first to perfect the broken, syncopated pattern that made the sound of Bill Monroe's 1945-48 Blue Grass Boys so distinctive. By the end of the decade other pioneering bluegrass banjo players refined their own approaches to Scruggs' basic style, most notably Reno, Ralph Stanley, Rudy Lyle, Joe Medford, Don Stover and Larry Richardson. By the mid-50's Sonny Osborne, Allen

Shelton, Johnny Clark, Bill Emerson, Eddie Adcock, Curtis McPeake and J.D. Crowe emerged as highly individual bluegrass players.

In the 50's some players began breaking away from established picking patterns to play chromatic melodies within bluegrass tempos. Jim Smoak and Bobby Thompson were among the first bluegrass banjo players to explore the banjo's chromatic potential; New York folk musician Billy Faier was doing similarly in folk music circles. The style gained widespread attention in 1963 when Monroe hired Boston musician Bill Keith. Keith's clean, fluid playing on Monroe's Decca recordings of "Salt Creek," "Devil's Dream," "Shenandoah Breakdown" and other instrumentals had enormous impact on a young generation of bluegrass banjo players.

Other important chromatic players emerged during the 60's, including Doug Dillard, Billy Ray Lathum, Eric Weissberg, Herb Petersen, Larry McNeely, Courtney Johnson and John Hartford. By the 70's the style had became an integral component of contemporary bluegrass and newgrass. Pat Cloud, Tony Trischka and Bela Fleck successfully applied it to jazz and funk. Even clawhammer-style players adapted chromatic ideas, most notably Bob Carlin.

While the short-necked, four-stringed tenor banjo is usually associated with traditional or Dixieland jazz, it also provided the rhythmic foundation for most early Western swing bands. Notable players include Ocie Stockard, Sleepy Johnson and Johnnie Lee Wills. Postwar guitar soloists Arthur Smith and Joe Maphis also doubled on tenor banjo. In 1955 Smith and Don Reno recorded "Feuding Banjos," a "tenor versus five-string" novelty, for MGM; Eric Weissberg and Steve Mandell revived the number as "Dueling Banjos" for the 1972 movie, *Deliverance*.   —D.S.

Bobby Bare

BORN: April 7, 1935
BIRTHPLACE: Ironton, Ohio

Bobby Bare is an important vocalist for several reasons. His material, though it began as straightforward country, evolved over time into a durable, folk-flavored style that caught on and helped to broaden the music's appeal. Bare was among the younger singers whose music anticipated the more complex songs of the Outlaw era. Inspired by the singing cowboys, he left home at age 16 and did day work, playing music in Ohio and West Virginia before moving to California in 1953. Playing clubs, he met steel guitarist Speedy West, who convinced Capitol producer Ken Nelson to sign Bare in 1956. Nothing happened there, same goes for his brief period with Challenge Records. By 1958 Elvis was about to be drafted, and so was Bare. He wrote a novelty about Presley's imminent induction titled "All American Boy," and for various reasons allowed his friend Bill Parsons to have both label and songwriter credit. Parsons actually toured to promote the record. During his Army period, Bare recorded for Fraternity. Though the records didn't click, they convinced Chet Atkins of Bare's potential, and Atkins signed him to RCA in 1962. There he began recording songs by popular folk artists such as Bob Dylan. But his first big hit came in 1963 with Mel Tillis' song, "Detroit City." Though a straightforward country song, his next hit, "500 Miles Away From Home," had a strong folk flavor, as did later hits like "Miller's Cave" in 1964, "Streets of Baltimore" (a song that dared to mention prostitution in 1966) and "Margie's at the Lincoln Park Inn," a 1969 hit that was a Tom T. Hall number about cheating. He had another hit with Hall's "How I Got to Memphis" in 1970. Bare also recorded duets with Skeeter Davis, but one of his biggest hits came in 1973 with "Daddy What If?," a duet with his eight-year-old son, Bobby Jr. In 1974 "Marie Laveau" became his biggest hit ever, and his only Number One record. Bare also recorded the album *Singing in the Kitchen* with his entire family, including daughter

Cari, who died in 1976 of a heart ailment. In 1978 he moved from RCA to Columbia, where he had more modest success, including *Down & Dirty* (1980), and what many critics thought was his career masterpiece, *As Is* (1981), produced by Rodney Crowell...a testament to the combined talents of the veteran Bare and the up-and-coming Crowell. Bare remained with Columbia until 1985, when he joined EMI-America. In the mid-80's he hosted a TV show on The Nashville Network. He continues to tour today.   —R.K.

Bass

Early country string bands didn't use bass fiddles often. Grand Ole Opry pioneer Dr. Humphrey Bate began using a full-sized stand-up string bass played by Oscar Albright when he started working around Nashville in the early 1920's.

Bass became more prevalent in the Southwest in the early 1930's, used by Milton Brown and His Musical Brownies (played by Wanna Coffman). By the 1930's, string bands such as Roy Acuff's Crazy Tennesseeans and similar groups all began using bass players.

Virtually all Western swing bands, with their emphasis on dance music, began using bassists, though Bob Wills' Texas Playboys' problems finding adequate bassists led rhythm guitarist Eldon Shamblin (who joined in 1938) to compensate by playing bass runs. Wills solved the problem by making bass players of his brothers Luke and Billy Jack. Though there were no real innovators at the time, and most bass players doubled as baggy-pants country comics, the instrument was common by the late 1930's and early 40's. The first great bassists in country included Ernie Newton, formerly with The Les Paul Trio, who did extensive Nashville studio work in the 40's and 50's.

The bass fiddle's bulkiness ultimately caused transportation problems. The solution came from Leo Fender in California, who began designing a solidbody electric bass in 1950 and introduced the "Precision Bass" in 1951. Little Jimmy Dickens' Country Boys were one of the first country bands to adopt it. The electric bass made transporting basses easier, and the solidbody design reduced the damage that moisture or rough handling caused a string bass. Still, many bluegrass and traditional country acts continued using string bass, as did Elvis Presley, whose bassist, Bill Black, made bass-slapping (used infrequently in country) an essential part of rockabilly. Several outstanding studio bassists appeared in Nashville, most notably Bob Moore, who played on well over 18,000 sessions.

Today, the electric bass is dominant on both stage and records, though Nashville's Roy Huskey Jr. continues using string bass, as did his late father, studio bassist Junior Huskey. Many Nashville bass players today come from the rock field, including Joe Osborn and Willie Weeks.   —R.K.

Dr. Humphrey Bate

BORN: 1875
BIRTHPLACE: Castalian Springs, Tennessee
DIED: 1936

One of the earliest pioneers of country music, Dr. Humphrey Bate (born in 1875 in Castalian Springs, Tennessee) was an authentic country doctor who happened to be an excellent harmonica player, and who also happened to lead the first band to appear over WSM's Grand Ole Opry. From the very earliest broadcasts of WSM in 1925 until Dr. Bate's death in 1936, his band, The Possum Hunters, opened the show with "There'll Be a Hot Time in the Old Town Tonight." When Judge Hay, the Opry founder, referred to Bate as "the Dean of the Opry," he was not far wrong.

Bate's band existed from at least 1903, and featured an odd line-up: harmonica, fiddle, two banjos, sometimes a cello, a guitar and a "doghouse bass." Their repertoire included very old folk tunes like "Old Joe," "Ham Beats All Meat," "Goin' Uptown" (which became the first Opry song to be published in sheet music) and "Take Your Foot Out of the Mud and Stick it in the Sand." Another favorite, "How Many Biscuits Can You Eat?," was later revived by Grandpa Jones, and then by bluegrass legends Flatt and Scruggs. In 1928 they recorded 12 of their best pieces for Brunswick, preserving at least some of their remarkable music. A number of these cuts have been reissued on various albums, including several by the Library of Congress.

Bate taught songs to many younger Opry stars, including The Crook Brothers, Fiddlin' Arthur Smith, Uncle Dave Macon and The McGee Brothers. He was also instrumental in getting DeFord Bailey, the Opry's

first black star and a fellow harmonica player, his job on the Opry. After Bate died in 1936, The Possum Hunters continued to flourish as one of the show's "hoedown bands," usually led by Staley Walton or by Bate's daughter, Alcyone Bate Beasley.   —C.W.

Bear Family Records

Bear Family, founded in 1975 by German record collector Richard Weize, grew out of his love for American folk and country music. Though the company releases some new recordings by contemporary country, folk and rockabilly artists, its specialty is licensing vintage (and often long-neglected) American country, rhythm and blues and rock material from record companies and reissuing it in elaborate packages. The goal of founder Richard Weize is to provide definitive chronicles of the music he chooses to release, preserving it for posterity and increasing the knowledge of the artist and his performances. The company's releases, both boxed sets and individual compact discs, all feature remastered sound, almost always from the original tapes, booklets laden with rare photos, specially commissioned liner notes (in English, often done with the artists' cooperation), and exhaustive recording data. Bear's country boxed sets have covered virtually the entire careers of Lefty Frizzell, Jerry Lee Lewis, Hank Snow, Johnnie and Jack, Jimmie Rodgers and Tommy Collins, and large portions of the careers of Carl Perkins, Merle Travis and Webb Pierce, and many others. Aside from contributing much from a historical point of view, Bear Family's excellent releases have, in many cases, spurred major American labels to raise the often shoddy standards of their own in-house historic reissues. —R.K.

The Bellamy Brothers

BORN: Howard, February 2, 1946, Darby, Florida;
David, September 16, 1950, Darby, Florida

The worldwide success of the Bellamy Brothers' second single (in 1976), "Let Your Love Flow," set the pace for the brothers, who have scored more charted singles than any other duo in country music history. The song was a Number One pop hit in the United States and elsewhere, and reached the country Top 20. Their brotherly harmonies and 60's-inspired sound—a blend of country, pop, folk, rock and island music—have given them Gold and platinum sales success in the United States and in Europe (where they remain a widely popular touring act). Their songwriting, sometimes mildly raunchy (as in the Number One hit, "If I Said You Had a Beautiful Body Would You Hold It Against Me"), sometimes slight, but often humorous and always listenable, has covered everything from rednecks to hippies to baby boomers, and of course the old stand-by, love. Over the years the brothers have recorded for Warner, Curb, MCA and Atlantic, racking up 26 Top Ten singles,

including 10 Number Ones. They're now on their own label, Bellamy Brothers Records, and continue to live on, and run, their family's ranch in Florida—now up to 2,500 acres from the original 150. Every October the brothers host a benefit concert, "The Snake Rattle & Roll Jam." —G.F.

Byron Berline

BORN: 1944
BIRTHPLACE: Caldwell, Kansas

This Kansas-born, Oklahoma-raised former championship fiddle player cut his teeth listening to great fiddlers of yesteryear like Benny Thomasson and Eck Robertson. Serving the requisite apprenticeship in Bill Monroe's Blue Grass Boys, Berline launched a solo career of his own, which was augmented by his warm reception when he appeared at the Newport Folk Festival. Over the years, he has established himself as one of the leading innovators of the progressive bluegrass (newgrass) fiddle. He co-founded Country Gazette, and he has recorded extensively both as a solo artist and in collaboration with everyone from Vince Gill and The Rolling Stones to Sam Bush and The Dillards. —B.A.

John Berry

BORN: September 14, 1959
BIRTHPLACE: Aiken, South Carolina

Born in 1959 in South Carolina and raised in Atlanta, Georgia, singer/songwriter/ guitar player John Berry first hit the charts in 1993, when his self-titled debut album was released on Liberty Records. His sound has been described as neo-honky tonk, with a good bit of Southern rock/boogie thrown in. He had a Top 20

single with "Kiss Me in the Car" (a country dance club favorite), and a Number One hit in 1994 with "Your Love Amazes Me." In May 1994, he underwent stereotactic endoscopic surgery to drain a cyst located deep within his brain. The surgery was deemed successful, and Berry was singing again by summer 1994.   —G.F.

Big D Jamboree

This popular live radio "barn dance" show (in the spirit of the Grand Ole Opry and *Louisiana Hayride*) was broadcast over KRLD Radio in Dallas, Texas, in the 1940's and early 50's. It proved a haven for local country stars of the day like The Shelton Brothers and The Callahan Brothers, and served as a stepping stone to fame for newcomers like Lefty Frizzell, Sonny James and Billy Walker.   —B.A.

Bigsby

Paul A. Bigsby, a machinist, pattern maker and amateur inventor based in Downey, California, built a steel guitar for Spade Cooley's steel guitarist, Joaquin Murphey, around 1947. That same year he met Merle Travis, who was just on the verge of stardom. Travis, unhappy with the string-bending vibrato tailpiece on his guitar, asked Bigsby to design a new unit. Bigsby did, then built a new neck with the tuners on one side for Travis' Martin acoustic guitar.

Travis also conceived an idea for a solidbody electric guitar that would anchor the strings in the body like a steel guitar (though this was not the first solidbody electric). In 1948, Bigsby built this guitar from a drawing Travis made, again with the tuners on one side. It is now in the Country Music Hall of Fame. It impressed Leo Fender, another inventor, inspiring his legendary Telecaster guitar design (though he later denied it). Bigsby designed Speedy West's pedal steel, as well as solidbody guitars for Hank Garland and Grady Martin and an electric mandolin for Texas Playboy Tiny Moore. Bigsby also invented a vibrato for Travis that became used on Gibson, Gretsch and other brands. In the 1960's he sold the company to retired Gibson president Ted McCarty. Bigsby died in 1972.   —R.K.

Clint Black

BORN: February 4, 1962
BIRTHPLACE: Long Branch, New Jersey

Clint Black is one of the most talented and popular stars rising from the trendy "Hat Pack" phenomenon of the late 1980's: a veritable wave of young, studly, photogenic and (for the most part) reasonably talented male singers foisted on the world by the Nashville record labels, each in search of a George Strait clone it could call its own.

At first these "Hat Packers" seemed virtually indistinguishable from each other with their amiable smiles, deft stage moves, tight blue jeans, big belt buckles and George Strait-style headgear. But within weeks of the release of *Killin' Time*, Clint Black's critically acclaimed 1989 debut album (which resulted in a record-breaking five consecutive Number One singles), Black swiftly pulled away from the pack. It's a yardstick of Black's immense popularity (which has eroded only a little in more recent years) that his first three albums sold more than six million copies, combined.

Black was born in Long Branch, New Jersey, on February 4, 1962, and grew up in Houston, Texas. As a boy he played in his older brother's country band, and sang, and received a good deal of encouragement from his father, who—in Black's words— "lives and breathes country music." Yet as Black came of age as a Houston club singer (often making ends meet by working days as a fishing guide or construction hand), his repertoire gradually expanded to reflect both his family's country background and his own more urbane tastes. His stylistic versatility and the range of his relaxed baritone enabled him to put together a song list that included not only Merle Haggard and George Strait favorites, but country-rock classics by Jimmy Buffett, The Eagles, Jackson Browne and Loggins & Messina, as well.

"I'm probably more ignorant about the origins of

a lot of music than people might presume," Black readily conceded to veteran music journalist John Morthland in a 1990 *Country Music Magazine* interview. "I didn't grow up with Bob Wills and Hank Thompson and all that; I grew up with the people that grew up with them, like Merle Haggard and Gene Watson and George Strait."

In the late 1980's, Black had the foresight and good fortune to hook up with two people without whom his career might never have happened. One was Houston super-manager Bill Ham, who has masterminded Texas rock band ZZ Top's platinum studded career for years and who was actively looking for a country artist to break. The other was Houston guitarist Hayden Nicholas, whom Black met in the local clubs and got to know while recording demos at the guitarist's eight-track studio. Nicholas not only joined Black's band, but has since helped the singer write many of his most memorable hits.

It's arguable that with Ham's immense deal-making clout behind him, Black would have achieved some measure of success even if he hadn't matured into such a fine singer and songwriter.

Shortly after its release, *Killin' Time* hit Number One in the *Billboard* album charts, went platinum, and resulted in the Number One hits "A Better Man," "Killin' Time," "Nobody's Home," "Walking Away" and "Nothing's News." Black also won the CMA's coveted Horizon award in 1989. However, *Put Yourself in My Shoes*, Black's 1990 sophomore album, was marred by unevenness. Though it contained some fine songs and some spirited vocal performances, it fell short of the standards set by *Killin' Time*.

The Hard Way (1992), Black's third album, got things back on track, for the most part. *No Time to Kill* (1993) also had its moments, yet was over-laden with Black-Nicholas originals which were too often marred by wordiness and thematic paucity.

No Time to Kill's lack of focus may be related to a lack—or at least shift—in direction in Black's own life. After having sung his share about the Lone Star State being the true center of the universe, Black has ended up in a Hollywood mansion, married to TV star Lisa Hartman (they wed in October 1991). His once-fruitful management deal with Bill Ham disintegrated into acrimony and multi-million-dollar counter-suits. Though Black—like most newlyweds—professed to be happier than ever, he gave the impression of being strangely adrift from his own roots and unable to recapture the inspiration of his bril-

liant debut album. In the end, a talent has irrepressible as Black's seems destined to prevail over such vicissitudes. "We try to push the line and still remain traditional," Black noted recently of his music. He's been an Opry member since 1991.   —B.A.

The Blackwood Brothers

Though country fans may know The Blackwood Brothers mainly through their influence on Elvis Presley, or their albums with Porter Wagoner, the group was the most influential and popular Southern gospel act in the country in the 1950's and 1960's. Coming from a family of Mississippi sharecroppers, the basic group consisted of three brothers—Roy (born December 24, 1900), Doyle (born August 22, 1911) and James (born August 4, 1919)—and Roy's son R.W. (born October 23, 1921). They began singing in the early 1930's, working at times for the Stamps-Baxter publishing company, and singing over stations as diverse as KWKH in Shreveport and KMA in Shenandoah, Iowa. In 1950 they relocated to Memphis, where their shrewd promotion (they were one of the first acts to have their own record company) and ability to adopt black gospel quartet music to their own style won them a nationwide reputation. Many of their records became models for arrangements later used by Elvis Presley, and at one point Presley actually auditioned for a Blackwood "farm club" group, The Songfellows. Signed to RCA Victor in 1952, they produced hits like "Have You Talked to the Man Upstairs," "Rock My Soul" and "Swing Down Chariot." After a series of personnel changes (partially as a result of a tragic plane crash in June 1954 that killed two of the group), the act continued to record a long of series of albums for RCA before turning to the Skylite label.   —C.W.

Blue Sky Boys

BORN: Bill, October 28, 1917
          Earl, November 16, 1919
BIRTHPLACE: Hickory, North Carolina

Today, The Blue Sky Boys (Bill Bolick, born October 28 1917, and Earl Bolick, born November 16, 1919, both in Hickory, North Carolina), are viewed as hav-

ing helped set the standard for close-harmony "brother" duets, as well as a having been a fountainhead of material that found its way into the repertoires of many bluegrass acts. The Bolicks began playing music early in life, with Bill on five-string banjo, then mandolin and guitar. The two joined together after Bill taught Earl guitar. Steeped in the hymns that were popular in their home, Bill began playing in a group called The Crazy Hickory Nuts. When that group disbanded, Bill started a new band called The Good Coffee Boys (in honor of their sponsor), including Earl and fiddler Homer Sherrill. By 1936 the group was working over WGST in Atlanta. They first recorded for Victor in 1936. Bill Bolick and their Victor producer, Eli Oberstein, decided on the name "Blue Sky Boys." They recorded extensively for Victor through the 1930's. After World War II military service, they reunited in 1946 at WGST, adding fiddler Curly Parker to the lineup and doing comedy as well. They made additional recordings for RCA Victor. Early in 1951, while working at a Raleigh, North Carolina, station, they decided to seek other careers. Called out of retirement in the early 60's, they recorded two albums for Starday in 1963, began doing some limited appearances at folk mu-

sic festivals, and recorded a Capitol album. They later performed at bluegrass festivals and recorded one more time for Rounder in 1975, before calling it quits for good. Their influence on the close harmony sound of The Louvin Brothers and The Everly Brothers has made them a revered act of the past. —R.K.

Bluegrass

In many ways, bluegrass could be considered country music's equivalent of jazz; yet at the same time it continues its older stringband traditions. And like Western swing, bluegrass relies on a tight ensemble with room for improvised solos. Its primary lead instruments are the fiddle, mandolin, a five-string banjo and occasionally a dobro; rhythm instruments are usually an acoustic guitar and a bass. The mandolin also plays rhythm on a quick backbeat, producing a percussive effect. Vocals tend to be pitched high, contributing to the music's intense sound.

The first group to fully implement all the elements associated with bluegrass was Bill Monroe's 1945-48 Blue Grass Boys. Monroe contributed a strong sense of timing and rhythm, as well as his taut Kentucky tenor. Lester Flatt sang in a relaxed low tenor and played a full, open-chorded rhythm guitar. Chubby Wise fiddled with a slow, fluid bow stroke that borrowed elements from Texas and other contemporary Southwestern styles. Earl Scruggs served up a fresh, syncopated banjo roll modified to fit Monroe's rhythmic sense. With such a tight ensemble, bassist Howard Watts broke away from conventional "root/fifth" patterns to explore the fingerboard of his instrument.

After hearing Monroe's groundbreaking band on WSM and his Columbia releases, other young musicians tried to duplicate his sound. One of the earliest bands to emulate Monroe's style was The Stanley Brothers, based at WCYB in Bristol, Virginia. When Columbia signed them to a recording contract in late 1948, an angry Monroe jumped to Decca Records, claiming that the brothers had stolen his sound.

By 1952 virtually every major label had contracted at least one artist or band built on Monroe's basic sound: RCA Victor had The Lonesome Pine Fiddlers; Dot had Mac Wiseman; Columbia had Lester Flatt and Earl Scruggs; Capitol had Carl Sauceman and Jim and Jesse; King had Don Reno and Red Smiley;

Mercury's roster included Carl Story. Small Southeastern independents like Rich-R-Tone and Blue Ridge were recording bluegrass groups that had regional followings.

Bluegrass went into a decline in 1956 as rock 'n' roll polarized traditional country music audiences and radio playlists became more standardized. The music continued to thrive where it received considerable radio airplay, notably southwestern Ohio and the Baltimore/Washington area. By the end of the decade bluegrass attracted a new following: young Northern musicians active in the folk music revival. The Stanley Brothers, Hylo Brown and Earl Scruggs appeared at the 1959 Newport Folk Festival. By 1963 virtually every major city and college town sported its own bluegrass band. Innovative Northern musicians began working in established Southern bands, most notably Boston-based banjoist Bill Keith, who brought his chromatic banjo style to Monroe's Blue Grass Boys.

Interest in bluegrass hit a peak in the mid-60's. Flatt and Scruggs performed the theme music to CBS-TV's *The Beverly Hillbillies;* their 1962 Columbia recording of "The Ballad of Jed Clampett" was the first bluegrass record to reach Number One on *Billboard's* country chart. The 1968 hit film, *Bonnie and Clyde,* used a 19-year-old Mercury record of Flatt and Scruggs' "Foggy Mountain Breakdown" during its chase scenes. Five years later Eric Weissberg and Steve Mandell's duet version of "Dueling Banjos" was included in the movie, *Deliverance*, and became a Number Two pop hit.

In 1965, promoter Carlton Haney organized the first multi-day festival exclusively devoted to bluegrass. Held in Roanoke, Virginia, over Labor Day weekend, it attracted enthusiasts from the North and South. In addition to a stage show, the festival gave musicians a chance to swap licks and other information. Although initial attendance was only fair, Haney continued to sponsor this annual Labor Day festival; it became bluegrass' major event until it was surpassed in the early 70's by Bill Monroe's June festival in Bean Blossom, Indiana. The bluegrass community was further unified by the establishment of *Bluegrass Unlimited* in 1966. Originally a mimeographed newsletter, it expanded into a full-sized magazine by 1970.

The audience for bluegrass changed in the 70's, and the music changed with it. The Washington, D.C.-based Seldom Scene mixed bluegrass instrumentation with contemporary folk vocals. The New Grass Revival from Louisville, Kentucky, took as much inspiration from The Grateful Dead as it did from Bill Monroe. A short-lived New York band, Breakfast Special, fused bluegrass with bop concepts and eastern European harmonies. In California, David Grisman headed an instrumental quintet featuring two mandolins, a guitar and an acoustic bass. While firmly rooted in bluegrass, Grisman's group essentially played acoustic string jazz.

During the 80's the music's predominant style was "contemporary bluegrass," as formulated by The Seldom Scene, the later Country Gentlemen, and J.D. Crowe and The New South. It generally sounds less countrified and less syncopated than the traditional bluegrass of Monroe and other pioneers. Another enduring style is "newgrass," named after The New Grass Revival. It frequently includes extended, free-form solos, a prominent electric bass and a repertoire borrowed from and inspired by modern rock music.

Despite being shunned by the country music industry, radio programmers and many retail record chains, bluegrass has thrived into the 90's. Independent labels like Rebel, Rounder, Copper Creek, Flying Fish, Old Homestead, CMH and Sugar Hill produce hundreds of new releases every year. Bluegrass festivals attract thousands of loyal fans each summer. Traditional and contemporary bands have sprung up in western Europe, Japan, Australia and New Zealand; Kukuruza, a Russian band, made two American tours in the early 90's.

A trade organization, the International Bluegrass Music Association, was founded in 1985 to unify businesses, artists and agencies serving and promoting bluegrass music. The association sponsors a convention, trade show and awards ceremony in Owensboro, Kentucky, each September. Additionally, *Bluegrass Unlimited*, now a monthly magazine, remains on the scene.   —D.S.

Dock Boggs

BORN: February 7, 1898
BIRTHPLACE: West Norton, Virginia
DIED: February 7, 1971

Few of the old-time singers who recorded during the 1920's had as much intensity and emotion as Dock Boggs, a banjo player from Norton, Virginia. The eight sides he recorded for Brunswick in 1927 capture a performer who fused black blues and white musical traditions into a deeply personal musical style.

He was the youngest of ten children. By age 12 he was working in the local mines; eight years later he began playing banjo for his enjoyment. In late 1926 or early 1927 he successfully auditioned for Brunswick executives at the Norton Hotel; he was invited to New York for his first session. Among the songs he recorded was "Down South Blues," which he learned from a Rosa Henderson blues record, and such traditional pieces as "Country Blues," "Danville Girl," "Pretty Polly" and "Sugar Baby." The records sold well in Boggs' home territory, but demand was not strong enough to enable him to quit mining. He recorded four additional sides in 1929 for an independent label. The Depression ended any possibilities of making future recordings. Discouraged, he pawned his banjo and left music entirely until 1963, when he was contacted by Mike Seeger. Encouraged by the younger musician, Boggs was surprised to hear that a new audience was interested in his early recordings. He successfully performed at the University of Chicago, the Newport Folk Festival and other events. Three new albums for Folkways revealed that Boggs' powers remained undiminished after 30 years of inactivity.   —D.S.

Noel Boggs

BORN: November 14, 1917
BIRTHPLACE: Oklahoma City, Oklahoma
DIED: October 1974

Noel Edwin Boggs became one of the major innovators of pre-pedal Western swing steel guitar. His influence touched countless steel players from the 1940's to the present. Born in Oklahoma, Boggs initially worked in that region before moving to New Orleans in the 1930's. There aspiring Western swing bandleader Hank Penny heard him, and by 1939 Boggs was a member of Penny's band, The Radio Cowboys. His sharp tone and skillful chord work stood him in good stead. By the early 1940's he was working in California, and in 1945 he joined Bob Wills' Texas Playboys, where he recorded the memorable instrumental, "Texas Playboy Rag," and others. After leaving Wills, Boggs worked again with Hank Penny, who featured him on his 1946 Top Ten re-

cording of "Steel Guitar Stomp." Through the rest of the 1940's, and into the 50's, much of Boggs' career involved recording session work and performing with Spade Cooley's band. He recorded on his own in the 1950's without success, and faded into obscurity, in part because he refused to embrace pedal steel guitar. He died in 1974, and was inducted into the Steel Guitar Hall of Fame in 1981.   —R.K.

Suzy Bogguss

BORN: December 30, 1956
BIRTHPLACE: Aledo, Illinois

After near a half-dozen albums, Suzy Bogguss finally seems poised for stardom in the mid-1990's, as she continues to bring her diverse stylistic influences into tighter focus.

Bogguss hails from the Mississippi River farming community of Aledo, Illinois. After an idyllic small town All-American youth of Girl Scouts and acting in high school plays, she began singing in folk clubs while attending Illinois State University. She eventually earned her degree in metalsmithing and jewelry-making—skills that have come in handy in recent years as she's begun designing and marketing her own line of jewelry and leather apparel.

After college Bogguss spent several years on the club circuit, not only booking her own shows and hanging her own posters, but sometimes even advertising her appearances with impromptu performances at the local mall or town square. She often made the rounds in those days traveling with her pet dog in her camper truck. But in 1984 she finally decided to make the plunge into country music and moved to Nashville, where she happened to have a couple of acquaintances in the music business. She soon found work singing on demos and performing at venues as diverse as the local Tony Roma's rib joint and Dolly Parton's Dollywood in the Smoky Mountains.

Despite her early folk and country-rock proclivities (she names Linda Ronstadt, Emmylou Harris and Patsy Montana as her biggest influences) Bogguss' major label debut on Capitol Records, *Somewhere Between* (1989), was a lovely, confident exercise in country revivalism. *Somewhere Between* not only featured a splendid rendition of the Merle Haggard-penned title tune, but also lovingly inspired covers of Hank Williams and Patsy Montana oldies, as well.

Bogguss' recent albums—*Moment of Truth* (1990), *Aces* (1991), *Voices in the Wind* (1992) and *Something Up My Sleeve* (1993)—have been co-produced by Bogguss herself, along with Jimmy Bowen, and have tended to steer her in a more contemporary direction. (Her hit rendition of Nanci Griffith's and Tom Russell's folk-flavored "Outbound Plane" is an indication of her more recent musical directions.)

Though less satisfying to more tradition-oriented country fans, these newer records have enabled Bogguss to drive a wedge into the often stubbornly closed door of country radio, and have earned her the sort of following she's long deserved. As of the mid-1990's, she's also earned her first Gold record (for *Aces*) and was the recipient of the Country Music Association's 1992 Horizon award.   —B.A.

Johnny Bond

BORN: June 1, 1915
BIRTHPLACE: Enville, Oklahoma
DIED: June 12, 1978

Inspired by Jimmie Rodgers and Vernon Dalhart recordings, Cyrus Whitfield Bond began working in groups in 1934, attending the University of Oklahoma while performing in Oklahoma City with a group called The Bell Boys that included singer Jimmy Wakely. Gene Autry met The Bell Boys (then The Jimmy Wakely Trio) when Autry toured Oklahoma, and offered the trio work in California. They moved there in 1940 and joined his organization. In 1941 Bond began recording for Columbia. His first hits came in 1947 with cover versions of the Merle Travis hits, "Divorce Me C.O.D." and "So Round! So Firm! So Fully Packed!," as well as his own "The Daughter of Jole Blon" and "Oklahoma Waltz" (1948). In 1950 his "Love Song in 32 Bars" made it into the Top Ten. Bond, who also worked in films throughout the 1940's, also wrote the classic Western number,

"Cimarron," and the ballads, "I Wonder Where You Are Tonight" and "I'll Step Aside." In 1953 he joined the cast of L.A's *Town Hall Party* TV program, remaining until the show ended in 1960. After leaving Columbia in 1957 he recorded for various labels before signing with Starday in 1962. There he recorded mainstream country, trucker tunes and drinking songs. In 1965 his re-recording of "Ten Little Bottles" (he originally recorded it in 1954), remained Number Two for four weeks. Bond wrote biographies of Gene Autry and Tex Ritter, as well as his autobiography *Reflections*, published in 1976. While he was recovering from a stroke, a second one ended his life, on June 12, 1978.   —R.K.

Bonnie Lou

BORN: October 27, 1924
BIRTHPLACE: Bloomington, Illinois

Bonnie Lou Kath, born in Bloomington, Illinois, was typical of the many regional performers of the 1940's and 50's who managed—if only for a brief moment—to hit big on the national scene. Originally known for her yodeling, she worked on the radio in Kansas City in the early 40's before joining WLW in Cincinnati in 1945. She remained a regular on the station's

Midwestern Hayride, and signed with Cincinnati-based King Records in the early 1950's. A WLW executive named her Bonnie Lou. Her brief stab at success came in 1953 when "Seven Lonely Days" (a pop hit around that same time for singer Georgia Gibbs) and "Tennessee Wig Walk" both went Top Ten. Later she recorded for another Cincinnati label, Fraternity, without much success. She remained a part of the *Hayride* cast well into the 1960's, happy to remain a regional star. —R.K.

Jimmy Bowen

BORN: November 30, 1937
BIRTHPLACE: Santa Rita, New Mexico

 Throughout the 1980's and well into the 90's, Jimmy Bowen has been a powerful and ubiquitous force in country music, as a producer and record executive. Working with dozens of recording artists—superstars like Reba McEntire, George Strait, Hank Williams Jr., Waylon Jennings, Conway Twitty and John Anderson, to name but a few—he has cranked out dozens of million-selling albums and Number One records.

A relentless, aggressive power broker and self-promoter since landing in Nashville in the mid-70's, Bowen has been chief executive of the country divisions of six different labels: MCA, Elektra/Asylum, Warner Bros., MCA (twice!), Universal and, most recently, Liberty (formerly Capitol). Along the way Bowen has—for better or worse—shoved the country record business headlong into the future, encouraging utilization of the latest studio technology and corporate marketing techniques. Often, he's also seemed to rewrite the rules of "insider ethics" in the process. (He is one of the first Nashville producers—maybe the first—to produce hit artists for one label while serving as chief executive for another. Once, when asked why he'd signed a veteran artist with a less than mediocre track record to his label,

he explained with a grin that it was all part of a bet he'd lost over a round of golf.)

Bowen was born in Santa Rita, New Mexico, on November 30, 1937, and grew up in the Panhandle region of Texas. Before facing the realization that he could barely carry a tune in a bucket, he had a brief stint as a rockabilly singer and teen idol in the late 1950's. His bass playing in Buddy Knox's Rhythm Orchids was featured on Knox's 1957 hit, "Party Doll," and Bowen also sang the song on the B-side. When it hit Number One, it earned Bowen a minor niche in rock 'n' roll history. Gravitating toward the business side of the music, Bowen worked as a DJ, then ended up on the West Coast heading a publishing company. Eventually he became A&R man and producer for Frank Sinatra's Reprise Records. ("That's Life" and "Strangers in the Night" are two all-time Sinatra favorites that bear the Bowen production stamp.) As a producer, he also revived the recording career of singer/comedian Dean Martin with a string of hits.

By 1968 Bowen was heading Amos Records, his own label (which later went belly-up), where he worked with Kenny Rogers and The First Edition, J.D. Souther and Glenn Frey and Don Henley (who would later form The Eagles). He also briefly held the reins at MGM Records.

After a several-year hiatus, Bowen landed in Nashville full-time after having made numerous professional forays there in search of songs. Bowen's first Nashville headquarters was a small room behind Mel Tillis' gift shop, and his first independent projects as a producer were with hit artists of the day like Tillis, Roy Head and Red Steagall. Working in Tompall Glaser's now legendary "Hillbilly Central" (a studio a few blocks off Music Row that became the unofficial headquarters of Waylon & Willie and the Outlaws—see Outlaw entry), Bowen recalls that he took a three-year crash course in country music: "I basically spent about 20 hours a day for three years in that studio. Tompall and some of his friends were the ones who taught me what country music was and what it had become."

Calling repeatedly on his West Coast corporate connections, Bowen began his surging upward career spiral in 1978 as vice president and general manager of MCA/Nashville. He produced both George Strait and, independently, Hank Williams Jr. As of the mid-1990's, he is still going strong, heading Liberty Records and helping guide the career of that label's flagship artist, Garth Brooks. —B.A.

Boxcar Willie

BORN: September 1, 1931
BIRTHPLACE: Sterratt, Texas

Lecil Travis Martin (born September 1, 1931 in Sterratt, Texas) created the Boxcar Willie character after spotting a hobo on a passing freight train who reminded him of Willie Nelson. An aspiring country singer at the time, Martin wrote a song about it, then filed it away when he became a radio DJ. In 1975, he dusted off his country music career, and the Boxcar character was born. He joined the Grand Ole Opry in 1981, and though he's never had a hit single, he's sold millions of records—first through television offers, and now at his theater in Branson, Missouri. He's also a popular entertainer in Europe.   —G.F.

Harold Bradley

BORN: January 2, 1926
BIRTHPLACE: Nashville, Tennessee

 While his older brother Owen Bradley has become legendary for his pioneering efforts to establish the Nashville recording industry and his production of Ernest Tubb, Patsy Cline and others, Owen's younger brother Harold Ray Bradley was also present throughout those days. Known as the dean of Nashville's session guitarists, he grew up as a jazz fan until Owen got him a job with Ernest Tubb in 1943.

A skeptical Harold found playing Tubb's simple music a challenge, and, after Navy service from 1944 to 1946, he returned to Nashville and began working on recording sessions. Harold spent increasing time doing sessions and, with Owen, opened the Bradleys' first Nashville studio in 1953. They later opened the legendary Bradley Film and Recording on 16th Avenue South (which included the equally legendary "Quonset Hut" facility) and, in the 60's, the Bradley's

Barn studio east of Nashville. Harold played on countless hits and, for a time in the early 1960's, recorded his own pop guitar albums for Columbia. He became the first president of Nashville's chapter of the National Academy of Recording Arts and Sciences. As a new generation of session musicians took over, Harold gravitated to production himself. He produced much of Eddy Arnold's later output, and in 1991 became President of Nashville's chapter of the American Federation of Musicians.   —R.K.

Owen Bradley

BORN: October 21, 1915
BIRTHPLACE: Westmoreland, Tennessee

Owen Bradley is the only country record producer portrayed in two major movies: *Coal Miner's Daughter* (the Loretta Lynn story) and *Sweet Dreams* (the Patsy Cline story). He produced both artists, and few individuals played a larger role in the development of Nashville as a worldwide recording center. Bradley began his career as a pianist in pop dance orchestras in the 1930's, and, in 1940 became musical director at WSM in Nashville. He also led his own dance band. But unlike many trained musicians, Bradley did not look down on the Opry, developing friendships with many of its artists. Many of Nashville's early country studio pickers, like guitarist Jack Shook and drummer Farris Coursey, were actually members of Bradley's orchestra.

He became an assistant to Decca Records country producer Paul Cohen in 1947, working on recordings by Red Foley, Ernest Tubb and many others. When Cohen left Decca in 1958, Bradley took his place producing Decca country artists, eventually giving up his WSM position. He built two recording studios in town before, in 1955, building his legendary Bradley Film and Recording studio, which included the equally legendary "Quonset Hut" studio. That studio, built at a time when Decca was considering moving their recording activities to Dallas, is often credited with saving Nashville's status as a recording center.

Bradley's instinctive production sense, which helped define the Nashville Sound, was best epitomized by his work with Patsy Cline, whom he had produced since she signed with Four Star. His pop background allowed him to use sophisticated orchestrations with some artists, yet he was just as comfortable with earthier Decca performers like Ernest Tubb, The Wilburn Brothers and Kitty Wells. Typical of his varied approach, he kept Loretta Lynn's records hardcore country. His track record led to a 1968 vice presidency at Decca. In the late 50's, he and his brother Harold produced a half-hour TV series, *Country Style U.S.A.* The Bradleys sold their Nashville studio to Columbia Records in 1961 and shortly after that, built Bradley's Barn in a converted barn near Mt. Juliet, Tennessee. Inducted into the Country Music Hall of Fame in 1974, he kept on producing for MCA until retiring in the early 1980's. Despite occasional health problems, he continues to be active today. He produced k.d. lang's 1988 *Shadowland* album and takes on other freelance studio projects.   —R.K.

Branson, Missouri

Although tourism has always been one of Tennessee's leading industries, visitors to Music City have, for years, had a persistent complaint: Nashville's lack of live country music. Though most of country's leading stars live and record in Nashville, few (for a variety of reasons) perform there on a regular basis.

Over the past decade or so Branson, a small, once-insignificant little Ozark Mountain town in Missouri, has since filled the breach, turning itself into a live country music mecca, and easily challenging Nashville as the nation's leading country music tourist center. On any given day, a visitor has the choice of seeing as many as 50 or more different live music shows by stars of yesterday (and in some cases, of today) in nearly as many different theaters. Ray Stevens, Roy Clark, Mel Tillis, Glen Campbell, Danny Davis, Jim Stafford, David Allan Coe, Moe Bandy, Johnny Cash, Boxcar Willie and Andy Williams are just a few of the dozens of veterans who have either permanently or temporarily set up shop in Branson.

The theory behind Branson is simple enough: to give all those vacationing Americans who annually flock to Las Vegas to see the shows rather than gamble a place where they can just see shows—and for a whole lot cheaper, at that. And instead of sending all those veteran and often aging country entertainers out on the endless tour grind to seek their out their audiences, someone realized it might be simpler to just plop them all down in one place with a beautiful natural setting and cheap motel rates and let the public come to them. It was an idea that worked brilliantly.

Branson first became a tourist attraction as long ago as the 1890's, when visitors started coming to see nearby Marvel Cave. In the 1940's, some enterprising souls hit on the idea of renting out the cave's gigantic Cathedral Room for square dances. The Ozark Jubilee, a popular local group, was the first act to set up in Branson on a regular basis. (For years, *The Ozark Jubilee*, a country radio and ABC-TV musical variety show whose popularity rivaled The Opry's in the late 1950's, was broadcast from Springfield, Missouri, just down the road.) Roy Clark, one of modern-day Branson's entertainment pioneers, first opened his theater there in 1983 and helped start the present-day gold rush. These days, more than seven million show tickets are sold in an average summer, and the place is still growing by leaps and bounds. It's hard to find any veteran country recording artist who's still above ground who hasn't opened a theater in Branson.   —B.A.

Rod Brasfield

BORN: August 22, 1910
BIRTHPLACE: Centerview, Tennessee
DIED: September 12, 1958

After joining the Grand Ole Opry shortly after World War II, this Centerville, Tennessee, native soon became its most popular comedian, beloved for his trademark baggy suits, staccato speech and familiar cry of "By Ned!" From the 1940's until shortly before his death in 1958, Brasfield and Minnie Pearl (Sarah Collie) did many routines together. (Collie, in fact, always felt in awe of Brasfield's talents and has always cited him as an immense influence on her own comic style.) The naive hillbilly persona that Brasfield fashioned for himself enabled him to get away with the sort of racy (at least for the era), double-entendre humor that would have gotten a less affable character booted off the air. He also branched out into acting, with a featured role in the 1957 film, *A Face in the Crowd*, starring Andy Griffith. Brasfield was elected to the Country Music Hall of Fame in 1987.   —B.A.

Elton Britt

BORN: June 27, 1917
BIRTHPLACE: Marshall, Arkansas
DIED: June 23, 1972

A country superstar of the 1940's who recorded prolifically for RCA, Elton Britt (born James Britt Baker), was an early member of the California Western group The Beverly Hillbillies in the mid-30's before embarking on his solo recording career for RCA in 1937. In 1944, when World War II patriotic songs were rampant, Britt earned the first Gold record ever awarded a country performer for his 1942 recording of "There's a Star Spangled Banner Waving Somewhere." Britt, who made most of his records in New York in the years before Nashville was a serious recording center, often was backed by jazz and pop sidemen. Other hits included "Wave to Me, My Lady" and "Chime Bells." He also did some successful duets with Rosalie Allen, such as "Beyond the Sunset" and "Quicksilver." He had little success in the late 1950's and early 60's, but his RCA recording of "The Jimmie Rodgers Blues" broke the Top 30 in 1968 and his final chart appearance was "The Bitter Taste" in 1969.   —R.K.

Brooks & Dunn

BORN: Brooks, May 12, 1955, Shreveport, Louisiana
          Dunn, June 1, 1953, Coleman, Texas

Before reaching platinum heights as Brooks & Dunn, Leon Eric "Kix" Brooks and Ronnie Gene Dunn had each been making inroads into the music business on their own. Brooks was a successful Nashville songwriter, on staff at Tree Publishing for six years, with songs cut by Sawyer Brown, Highway 101, Ricky Van Shelton and others. He'd also released a solo album on Capitol in 1989. Dunn was plugging away in the clubs of Texas and Oklahoma; he won the Marlboro Talent Search in 1989 before also linking up with Tree. After hearing a demo of a song the two co-wrote, Arista Records head Tim DuBois signed them up. The result was a triple-platinum 1991 debut album, *Brand New Man*, and five Top Ten singles, including four Number Ones ("Brand New Man," "My Next Broken Heart," "Neon Moon" and "Boot Scootin' Boogie"). They helped spawn the country line dance craze with their high-energy, beat-heavy, rock-inspired tunes. The two are also known for their wild, party-atmosphere stage shows. Their next album, 1993's *Hard Workin' Man*, reached similar heights, in sales and chart position, giving the duo another batch of four Number One singles.   —G.F.

Garth Brooks

BORN: February 7, 1962
BIRTHPLACE: Tulsa, Oklahoma

As the decade of the 90's dawned, an Oklahoman named Garth Brooks took the entertainment world by storm with one of the most commercially viable sounds in contemporary music. Born in Tulsa, Oklahoma, on February 7, 1962, but raised in nearby Yukon, Troyal Garth Brooks came from a musically-inclined family. His father was a guitar-playing ex-Marine, and his mother, Colleen Carol Brooks, was a country singer who had recorded for Capitol Records in the mid-1950's and performed with Red Foley on his *Ozark Jubilee* TV show.

Among the records Garth heard the most while growing up were those by country greats such as Johnny Horton, Merle Haggard and George Jones, as well as 60's and 70's singer/songwriters such as Peter, Paul and Mary, Tom Rush, Townes Van Zandt, Arlo Guthrie, Janis Ian, Janis Joplin, Rita Coolidge, James Taylor and Dan Fogelberg.

While in grammar school Garth sang in talent shows, but his real interest was in sports. During his high school years he played baseball, basketball, football and track. At 17 Garth began taking more interest in music, started playing guitar and formed a band called The Nyle. He entered Oklahoma State University in Stillwater on a track scholarship, but became discouraged when he failed to make the Big Eight finals during his senior year. At that point he decided to focus on advertising and a career in music. He graduated with a degree in marketing, began performing at various clubs in the Stillwater area and met his future wife Sandy before departing for Nashville and a crack at the big time in 1985.

But fame and fortune didn't come easy. There were dues to pay, and he knew he wasn't quite ready. He left Nashville after one day, disillusioned. During the next two years he married Sandy, formed a pop-country band called Santa Fe, and began playing the club circuit throughout Texas, Oklahoma and New Mexico. By 1987 he knew he was ready, and decided to make another assault on Music City. He sang jingles and performed on demos while holding down a job as a clerk in a Nashville boot shop. This time Garth broke through. Within seven months of his arrival, he had a record deal with Capitol Records.

His first album, *Garth Brooks* (1989), was straight-ahead country, complete with fiddles and steel guitars. It garnered good reviews in the country press. The first three singles from the album—"Much Too Young (To Feel This Damn Old)," "If Tomorrow Never Comes" and "Not Counting You"—made the country Top Ten. But the fourth, "The Dance," and its provocative video, established him as the country music superstar of the 1990's.

During the next few years, Garth literally dominated the country and pop charts. His follow-up album, *No Fences*, produced four more Number Ones, and his third release, *Ropin' the Wind*, yielded two. The latter release made music history when advance orders stood at four million and it debuted on both country and pop charts at Number One.

From 1989 to 1991, his three albums sold a staggering 30 million copies, accounting for more than 68 percent of Capitol's sales. Those numbers were unprecedented in country music history and placed Garth squarely in the company of pop and rock greats such as Elvis Presley, The Beatles and Michael Jackson. More importantly, the sales phenomenon turned a broader, younger audience on to country music and paved the way for future Music City hopefuls. In 1990, the Grand Ole Opry made him a member.

Aside from the record sales, Garth's other attention grabber was his electrifying stage performance. A disciple of the arena-rock acts of the 70's and 80's such as Kiss, Queen, Boston and Styx, Garth's raucous rock-outs included rope-swinging antics and dramatic smoke and lighting effects. In 1991 and 1992, he outsold every major rock and pop act in stadium performances throughout the United States.

Garthmania exploded in 1992 when *The Chase*, Garth's fourth release, entered the pop and country charts at Number One in its first week—a feat never before accomplished by a country music performer. *The Chase* produced three chart-topping singles: "We Shall Be Free," "Somewhere Other Than the Night" and "Learning to Live Again." *In Pieces* followed in 1993, yielding two more Number Ones with "Ain't Goin' Down (Til the Sun Comes Up)" and "American Honky Tonk Bar Association."

By 1993 Brooks had won more than 50 major industry awards, including the Entertainer of the Year Award from both the CMA and the ACM and the CMA Video of the Year award for "The Thunder Rolls" which, with its vivid portrayal of a battered woman shooting and killing her cheating husband, was banned by TNN and CMT.   —R.P.

Hylo Brown

BORN: April 20, 1922
BIRTHPLACE: River, Kentucky

Frank Brown Jr. was nicknamed "Hylo" in the late 1940's for his ease in singing high and low vocal parts. Born April 20, 1922, in River, Kentucky, he made his recording debut singing harmony with Bradley Kincaid on a 1950 Capitol session. He had no intentions of pursuing music as a career until Capitol producer Ken Nelson signed him in 1954 after auditioning his song demo of "Lost to a Stranger."

Between 1955 and 1959 Brown was usually a featured performer with other bands, first with Jim & Jesse, and later with Lester Flatt and Earl Scruggs.

In 1958 Martha White Mills, who sponsored Flatt and Scruggs, offered Brown a chance to head his own traveling unit. Although together for only a year, Hylo Brown and The Timberliners—mandolinist Red Rector, fiddler Clarence "Tater" Tate, banjo player Jim Smoak and bassist Joe Phillips—is considered one of bluegrass music's all-time great bands.

The group appeared at the 1959 Newport Folk Festival and made a classic album, *Hylo Brown*, for Capitol. Brown's career continued through the 1960's and early 70's with recordings for Starday, Rural Rhythm and Jessup. Health problems curtailed most of his musical activities after 1973. —D.S.

Jim Ed Brown

BORN: April 1, 1934
BIRTHPLACE: Sparkman, Arkansas

Jim Ed Brown always seems to be attached to some other phrase—"a member of the famous group, The Browns, in the 1960's," or "singing partner for Helen Cornelius in the late 1970's." Both are true, but overlook the fact that Jim Ed Brown was a major star in his own right during country music's countrypolitan phase.

Born in Sparkman, Arkansas, on April 1, 1934, Brown began singing early on with his sisters Maxine and Bonnie as The Browns. In 1955 they cut one of the sappiest songs ever, "The Three Bells," which, in keeping with the times, became a huge crossover pop hit. By 1967, the sisters had opted for home and family. Jim Ed's first solo hit was the classic Top Five,

"Pop-a-Top," in 1967, which, by all rights, should be recut sometime soon.

In the mid-1970's, Jim Ed was looking for a new backup singer when he came across newcomer Helen Cornelius. She refused to do backup, but the duo clicked for a string of hits, most notably their first, "I Don't Want to Have to Marry You," a Number One in 1976, and their second, "Saying Hello, Saying I Love You, Saying Goodbye," which hit the Number Two spot. As a duo, they had a run of hits through the mid- to late 70's.

Brown has been a member of the Grand Ole Opry since 1963. (See also, The Browns.) —M.B.

Marty Brown

BORN: July 25, 1965
BIRTHPLACE: Maceo, Kentucky

Few performers get their start with a profile on a network news program, yet that's precisely what happened to Marty Brown in 1991. Kentucky-born Brown grew up listening to his father's Merle Haggard and Jimmie Rodgers records. That background shaped his hard-core, traditional approach to country music.

After enduring a failed marriage and the frustration of rejection in Nashville, Brown landed an MCA recording contract in 1991, his struggle chronicled on the CBS documentary program, *48 Hours*. Though his first two MCA albums, *Marty Brown* (1991) and *Wild Kentucky Skies* (1993), received critical acclaim, radio felt his music, with its unpolished overtones of Hank Williams Sr., was too raw and largely ignored him.

Brown countered with his "Cadillac Tour," during which, in addition to concert appearances, he promoted his albums at Wal-Mart stores. This was a highly original move that without question took him to his rural audience. —R.K.

Milton Brown

BORN: September 8, 1903
BIRTHPLACE: Stephenville, Texas
DIED: April 18, 1936

Milton Brown was second only to his friend Bob Wills as a Western swing innovator. He always enjoyed singing, but never found the chance to turn professional until the Depression had cost him his job as a cigar salesman. After sitting in with Wills and his guitarist, Herman Arnspiger, at a 1930 house party, Milton and his younger brother, guitarist Durwood Brown, joined Wills' group. They began working on radio, becoming The Light Crust Doughboys in 1931, after the Burrus Mill and Elevator Company of Dallas, makers of Light Crust Flour, began sponsoring them. In 1932 Burrus general manager W. Lee O'Daniel barred the group playing dances for extra money. The Brown brothers quit, and Milton formed The Musical Brownies, adding bassist Wanna Coffman, fiddlers Jesse Ashlock and Cecil Brower, and Fred "Papa" Calhoun, the first Western swing pianist. Like The Doughboys, The Brownies' repertoire mixed country, blues, pop and jazz. In 1934 they recorded for Bluebird, then for Decca Records. In 1935 Bob Dunn, country music's first electric steel guitarist, joined; fiddler Cliff Bruner replaced Ashlock. Based at the Crystal Springs dancehall near Fort Worth, the group had an enormous influence on Texas musicians. On April 13, 1936, Milton's vehicle struck a utility pole along Dallas' Jacksboro Highway, killing a female passenger. Though his injuries were minor, he died after pneumonia set in. Some 3500 fans at-tended his funeral in Stephenville. Durwood Brown attempted to continue the group, but it quickly dis-integrated as Cliff Bruner and Bob Dunn formed their own bands.   —R.K.

T. Graham Brown

BORN: October 30, 1954
BIRTHPLACE: Atlanta, Georgia

A soul man who grew up on the likes of Otis Redding, Percy Sledge and Aretha Franklin in Arabi, Georgia, Anthony Graham Brown first tuned in to country music through David Allan Coe. He honed his country/soul/R&B/rock sound while a songwriter for CBS Songs, then hooked up with Capitol Records in 1985. His gritty, hard-hitting voice and Muscle Shoals-inspired production led to a string of Top Tens, including three Number Ones: "Hell and High Water," "Don't Go to Strangers" and "Darlene." His most recent Top Ten was 1990's "Don't Go Out," a sultry duet with Tanya Tucker. Brown has also acted in films and served as pitchman for Taco Bell, McDonald's and Budweiser.   —G.F.

Tony Brown

BORN: December 11, 1946
BIRTHPLACE: Greensboro, North Carolina

It tells us something about his immense impact that Nashville producer Tony Brown made *Newsweek's* 1992 list of America's Top Ten "Cultural Elite"—right alongside Bill Cosby, Bill Moyers, Madonna and Spike Lee. Indeed, in the early 1990's, Brown has emerged as one of Nashville's most influential, prolific and commercially successful country producers.

If producer Billy Sherrill had the Midas Touch for

the 70's, then Tony Brown has the platinum thumb of the 90's. Yet unlike Sherrill (who was often known for his domineering, and sometimes condescending, attitude toward the very music he made) Brown is almost universally revered by his peers. First and foremost this is due to the fact that he himself spent years as a musician, and thus has a special affinity and fondness for the many artists with whom he's made hit records. A few of them, like Rodney Crowell and Vince Gill, are even former bandmates.

Some of the artists who, through Brown, got their first shot on a major label include: Patty Loveless, Trisha Yearwood, Lyle Lovett, Steve Earle, Mark Chesnutt, Nanci Griffith, Kelly Willis, Marty Stuart, Marty Brown, McBride & The Ride, and The Maver-

icks. Then there are the numerous veteran superstars whose careers he has either revived or sustained, with his studio savvy and hit-making prowess—artists such as Vince Gill, Reba McEntire, George Strait, Wynonna, Rodney Crowell and Steve Wariner.

Brown was born in Greensboro, North Carolina, on December 11, 1946. His father was a dairy farmer who became an itinerant evangelical preacher and gospel musician after being diagnosed with terminal cancer. (Ironically, the elder Brown ended up living another 20 years.) By age 13, Tony was already playing piano in the family's gospel road show. A few years later, he landed a similar spot with the then all-gospel group, The Oak Ridge Boys.

In 1975, Brown's career took a major step forward when he ended up playing piano in Elvis Presley's road band. He stuck with Presley until The King's death two years later. Not long afterward, he ended up playing keyboard in Emmylou Harris' now legendary Hot Band, and in Rodney Crowell's similarly revered ensemble, The Cherry Bombs.

By the late 70's Brown had segued into the Nashville music industry. Working at first as an A&R man with RCA Records, he was instrumental in bringing future superstars like Alabama and Vince Gill on board

that label. In 1984, he jumped ship and went across the street to MCA for an opportunity to produce.

Today, Brown is president of MCA/Nashville, and was named "Number One Country Producer" by *Billboard Magazine* in 1990, '91 and '92. The argument can easily be made that by the mid-1990's he had become one of the most influential producer/executive in country music.   —B.A.

Brown's Ferry Four

If there is such a genre as "country gospel," it was an all-star quartet named The Brown's Ferry Four that defined it. Formed at station WLW Cincinnati in June 1943, the quartet originally consisted of Grandpa Jones, The Delmore Brothers and Merle Travis, all of whom were then working at the station. Alton Delmore organized the group (taking the name from his old hit, "Browns' Ferry Blues").

Alton taught the singers how to read the old shape notes, commonly used in old-time gospel material, and remained one of the few constant members of the quartet. In 1946 The Four recorded its first record, a double-sided hit for King, "Will the Circle Be Unbroken" and "Just a Little Talk with Jesus." This led to a long series of King sides from 1945 to 1952, with shifting personnel that included Red Foley, Clyde Moody, Zeke Turner and Red Turner, as well as Grandpa and The Delmores. The records featured just the four voices and a guitar, and often spotlighted the songs of Albert E. Brumley. The name itself was owned by WLW, and that station kept a parallel quartet on the air for years. (See also, entries on individual members.)   —C.W.

Jann Browne

BORN: March 14, 1954
BIRTHPLACE: Anderson, Indiana

It's one of life's minor mysteries why the lovely, vastly talented Jann Browne has not yet found a comfortable niche in contemporary country music. This eminently gifted singer/songwriter emerged in the late 1980's as part of the same Southern California country scene that had, just a year or two earlier, given us Dwight Yoakam. Yet despite a stint or two with ma-

jor Nashville labels (which resulted in chart records like "You Ain't Down Home" and "Tell Me Why"), Browne is, as of this writing, label-less.

Browne was born in Anderson, Indiana, in 1954. Her grandparents were accomplished professional square dancers who occasionally danced on the Grand Ole Opry. Browne ended up in Southern California in 1977, where she quickly earned a reputation as a club singer. In 1981 she joined Ray Benson's premier Western swing revival band, Asleep at the Wheel. After touring with The Wheel for two years, she left the road to concentrate on her songwriting. She spent several ensuing years as a gospel singer.

An uncompromising champion of hard-hitting, tradition-conscious country music, Browne's presence would certainly be welcome in Nashville's current stylistic wilderness. As *The Los Angeles Times* wrote of her a few years ago: "Browne is country. She can discuss Wynn Stewart, Rose Maddox, and just about any other old-line country singer at length—keeping country's classics alive is as important to Browne as getting her own songs to the public. It's no surprise that Emmylou Harris is a big Jann Browne fan. Harris said in the early 1990's, when Browne opened for her in San Juan Capistrano, 'There is something about the way she sings that is so pure and honest, and her writing is wonderful.'" —B.A.

The Browns

BORN: Jim Ed, April 1, 1934, Sparkman, Arkansas
       Maxine, April 27, 1932, Samti, Louisiana
       Bonnie, July 1, 1937, Sparkman, Arkansas

Jim Ed Brown's early exposure came as part of this brother-sister duo-turned-trio. Initially, Jim Ed and Maxine sang together, and first attracted notice when they won a talent contest in Little Rock. That led to a spot on the *Louisiana Hayride* in the early 1950's. Like other *Hayride* artists they wound up recording for Fabor Records, their first hit being the upbeat "Looking Back to See" in 1954. Their sister Bonnie joined them for their next hit, "Here Today and Gone Tomorrow," in 1955. Another sister, Norma, briefly filled in when Jim Ed went into the military. In 1956 they signed with RCA, where success came with "I Take the Chance" (a Louvin Brothers song) that year and "I Heard the Bluebirds Sing" (1957). Yet their biggest hit was anything but country. "The Three Bells" was a French number, originally recorded by French chanteuse singer Edith Piaf. Translated into English, the version done by The Browns topped both country and pop charts in 1959.

After a second Top Ten with the folk tune, "Scarlet Ribbons," in 1960, the group's stature grew. They joined the Opry in 1963, finally disbanding in 1967. By then Jim Ed's solo career had already begun. Maxine also made a stab at a solo career; she had one minor hit in 1968 with "Sugar Cane Country." (See also, Jim Ed Brown.) —R.K.

Ed Bruce

BORN: December 29, 1940
BIRTHPLACE: Keiser, Arkansas

William Edwin Bruce Jr. began his career as a teenager, recording for Sun Records. After moving to Nashville in 1964, he had a lucrative career in jingles and commercials, working as "The Tennessean." Throughout his recording career he worked with six different labels, but his biggest hits came during the early 1980's on MCA Records. Among them were such Top Tens as "You're the Best Break This Old Heart Ever Had," "Ever, Never Lovin' You" and "My First Taste of Texas." His recording career, however, was overshadowed by his songwriting skill: He is responsible for such classics as "Mamas Don't Let Your Babies Grow Up to Be Cowboys," "The Last Cowboy Song," "The Man That Turned My Mama On" and "Texas When I Die." And that's all right with Ed. In a *Country Music Magazine* interview in 1979, he said, "If I had to maintain any one facet of what I do, I guess it would be songwriting. I get more thrill out of hearing one of my songs on the radio than I do hearing one of my own records."   —G.F.

Cliff Bruner

BORN: April 25, 1915
BIRTHPLACE: Houston, Texas

Fiddler Cliff Bruner made his initial mark as a member of the groundbreaking Western swing band, Milton Brown and His Musical Brownies. Following Brown's death in 1936, Bruner organized his own band, The Texas Wanderers, and began recording for Decca in 1937. Some later recordings came out under the name Cliff Bruner and His Boys, which included Moon Mullican on piano and vocals, and steel guitar innovator Bob Dunn. In 1939 Bruner's band recorded the first truck driving song ever recorded: Ted Daffan's composition, "Truck Driver's Blues." After World War II Bruner recorded for the Houston-based Ayo label, and eventually left the music business for a career in insurance in the Houston area.

Following the Western swing revival of the 1970's, he performed and recorded again, including a guest appearance on Johnny Gimble's 1980 *Texas Swing Pioneers* album on the CMH label.   —R.K.

Boudleaux and Felice Bryant

BORN: Boudleaux, February, 13, 1920, Sheldon, Georgia; Felice, August 7, 1925, Milwaukee, Wisconsin
DIED: Boudleaux, June 26, 1987

Of all the songwriting teams of the 1950's and 60's, few were as unique as the husband-wife team of Boudleaux and Felice Bryant. Boudleaux, a classically-trained violinist, worked with the Atlanta Symphony in 1938. In 1939 he joined Hank Penny and His Radio Cowboys, then working at WSB in Atlanta, to earn extra money.

He originally scorned country music, though his recordings with Penny show him to be an excellent swing fiddler (he wrote the instrumental, "Mississippi Muddle," during his time with Penny). After leaving Penny he went into jazz. He met Felice, then an elevator operator, in Milwaukee, during a tour there. The pair casually started writing country songs together, and in 1948 sent one, "Country Boy," to Nashville's Acuff-Rose song publishers. Owner Fred Rose not only bought the song, he gave it to Little Jimmy Dickens, who had a hit with it (his second Top Ten) in 1949. Rose saw enough talent in the Bryants, particularly their unabashedly rural attitudes, that he urged them to move to Nashville. There, they became Acuff-Rose songwriters and set off on a streak of success that included Carl Smith's "Hey, Joe!" and "Back Up Buddy" and Dickens' "A-Sleeping at the Foot of the Bed" and "Out Behind the Barn." Boudleaux and Chet Atkins co-wrote "Midnight" and "How's the World Treating You," 1953 hits for Red Foley and Eddy Arnold, respectively.

The Bryants' writing transcended the country field after Wesley Rose, Fred's son (who took over Acuff-Rose after Fred's death in 1954), teamed the Bryants' writing with Don and Phil Everly. Boudleaux and Felice created such Everly Brothers classics as "Bye Bye Love," "Bird Dog," "All I Have to Do Is Dream,"

"Take a Message to Mary," "Love Hurts," "Problems" and "Poor Jenny," all pop classics. When The Everlys left Nashville, Boudleaux and Felice kept writing for pop artists. Bob Luman's "Let's Think About Living" was a Bryant tune, as was Bob Moore's "Mexico" and Buddy Holly's "Raining in My Heart." They continued writing for country acts, too, including standards like "Rocky Top" for The Osborne Brothers and "Come Live with Me" for Roy Clark in 1973. In 1986 the Bryants joined the Nashville Songwriters' Hall of Fame. Boudleaux died of cancer in 1987. In 1991, the team was deservedly elected to the Country Music Hall of Fame. —R.K.

Jimmy Bryant

BORN: March 5, 1925
BIRTHPLACE: Moultrie, Georgia
DIED: September 22, 1980

For a brief period in the early 1950's, the dazzling country-jazz guitarist and fiddler Jimmy Bryant was one of the most recorded guitarists in the world. John Ivy Bryant Jr. , the oldest of 12 children, learned fiddle from his father, a sharecropper. He joined the Army in 1943. After being wounded in Europe in 1945, he recuperated at a Washington, D.C., military hospital, teaching himself guitar. He eventually became an excellent jazz guitarist. After his discharge he moved to Los Angeles, working as an extra in Western films and playing bars, where he first met steel guitarist Speedy West. His first major exposure came when he played a hot solo on Tex Williams' 1950 recording of "Wild Card." That year, Bryant joined Speedy on Cliffie Stone's *Hometown Jamboree*, where they not only backed singers but, dubbed "The Flaming Guitars," created complex, dynamic instrumentals. Bryant was among the first country musicians to play a Fender Broadcaster (later Telecaster). Signed to Capitol, he and West recorded original instrumentals such as Bryant's "Stratosphere Boogie" and "Whistle Stop." They did hundreds of sessions with country and pop artists in L.A. through the early 1950's. Bryant's outspokenness led him to quit *Hometown* in 1955 and, subsequently, Capitol.

In the 60's he played sessions and by mid-decade did five albums for Imperial, four solo and one with L.A. steel guitarist Red Rhodes (under the pseudonym "Norval and Ivy"). Bryant penned the 1968 Waylon Jennings hit, "The Only Daddy That'll Walk the Line." He lived in Nashville in the 1970's, where he and Speedy recorded a reunion album. His doctors discovered lung cancer in 1978; he eventually returned to Georgia where he spent his last days. Contemporary country guitarists like Albert Lee and bluegrasser Eddie Adcock are among the pickers who cite Bryant as an influence. —R.K.

Jimmy Buffett

BORN: December 25, 1946
BIRTHPLACE: Mobile, Alabama

Jimmy Buffett was born in Mobile, Alabama, on December 25, 1946. He got his first taste of performing in local clubs in New Orleans in the mid-1960's. After earning a degree in journalism, he moved to Nashville and landed a job as a record reviewer for *Billboard Magazine*. It wasn't long before he signed a recording contract with Barnaby Records and released two albums in the early 1970's. When his records

sold poorly, Buffett decamped for Los Angeles before discovering Key West, Florida, which has been his home base ever since.

From Key West he spent a year pitching demo tapes in the hopes of landing another contract, and finally signed with ABC/Dunhill in 1973. While his ABC debut, *A White Sport Coat and a Pink Crustacean*, didn't exactly take audiences by storm, it sold well enough to convince ABC execs to produce another one, *Livin' and Dyin' in 3/4 Time*. Around the same time Buffett wrote songs for and acted in the Frank Perry film, *Rancho Deluxe*. He went on to cut two more albums, *A1A* and the more successful *Havana Daydreamin'*, before 1977's *Changes in Latitudes, Changes in Attitudes* made Jimmy Buffett a household word. The album climbed to the top levels of both country and pop charts and yielded a Gold single, "Margaritaville." The following year his sixth album on ABC was an immediate hit; in less than a month Buffett had his second Gold album. Later in the year came a live album, *You Had to Be There*. While his blend of pop, folk and country had clearly struck a chord with fans, Buffett went on to explore new musical territory with the Caribbean-styled album, *Volcano*, in 1979. It was a risk, but fans clearly approved: the album also went Gold.

While Buffett had fewer hits in the early 1980's, there was still a vast audience for his music: His 1985 greatest hits album, *Songs You Know by Heart*, went platinum, and Buffett remained a popular headliner, as he is today. In the mid-80's, he moved over to MCA Records. During the same period he became increasingly involved in political and environmental causes, notably the campaign to save the endangered Florida manatee.

Buffett began the 1990's with a bang: his 1990 album, *Feeding Frenzy*, was a hit with old and new fans alike, and quickly achieved Gold status. Two years later his *Boats, Beaches, Bars & Ballads* boxed set went platinum. Also keeping him occupied in the 90's is his custom record label, Margaritaville Records, which is distributed by MCA.   —M.B.

Bullet Records

Bullet Records, one of Nashville's first substantial record companies, was founded in 1945 by WSM announcer Jim Bulleit. The label did most of its re-

cordings in the country and rhythm and blues field.

One of their first modest country hits was "Zeb's Mountain Boogie" by "Brad Brady and his Tennesseeans," featuring Zeb Turner on lead guitar. This boogie instrumental was arranged by WSM Music Director and dance band leader, Owen Bradley, and featured horns, a progressive move for the time.

Other Bullet artists included Zeb Turner, Autry Inman, Bradley Kincaid, country boogie pianist Roy Hall, Hardrock Gunter, Chet Atkins and Pee Wee King and The Golden West Cowboys (before both Atkins and King signed with RCA Victor), The York Brothers and Charline Arthur. Bullet's biggest hit record by far was the pop song, "Near You," by veteran Nashville orchestra leader, Francis Craig. It was one of the biggest pop hits of 1947.

Other country hits on Bullet included "Rag Mop" and "Peter Cottontail" by Johnnie Lee Wills.

Leon Payne did his original recording of "Lost Highway' for the label. Ray Price made his first recording ever for Bullet in 1949.

Bullet also had a number of gifted R&B artists, some of whom made their first recordings for the label, including B.B. King, Wynonie "Mr. Blues" Harris and Cecil Gant.

Despite the success of "Near You," Bullet never had enough truly big hits to become a major concern and finally shut down in 1954.   —R.K.

Wilma Burgess

BORN: June 11, 1939
BIRTHPLACE: Orlando, Florida

Wilma Burgess was born in Orlando, Florida, on June 11, 1939. She listened to pop music until an Eddy Arnold concert introduced her to country music. At first, she had no plans for a music career, and entered Stetson University in Florida as a physical education major. After finishing college she recorded a demo for a songwriter friend. This demo attracted attention and resulted in her signing with Decca Records. "Baby" (1966) was her first Top Ten country single. "Misty Blue" appeared on her second album, and was her second Top Ten hit.

Wilma Burgess' other important songs include "Don't Touch Me" (1966), "Fifteen Days" (1967), "Tear Time" (1967) and "Wake Me Into Love" (1973) with Bud Logan.   —S.W.

Smiley Burnette

BORN: March 18, 1911
BIRTHPLACE: Summum, Illinois
DIED: February 16, 1967

A renowned comedian and songwriter, Lester Alvin "Smiley" Burnette worked as a comedian on the WLS *National Barn Dance* in the early 40's, then briefly at WLW in Cincinnati before moving to the West Coast during World War II. There he became part of Gene Autry's organization, as both an accordionist and comedian. He made a total of 81 films with Autry, not counting other appearances with other Western stars. In 1945 Burnette wrote and recorded the bluesy novelty tune, "Hominy Grits." He also wrote "I Might Have Gone Fishing" and recorded for a number of labels including ARA, Bullet, Abbott, Columbia, Decca and Capitol. He recorded transcribed shows with The Whippoorwills for RadiOzark Transcriptions in Springfield, Missouri, and also did children's albums. Burnette died at age 55—on February 16, 1967—of leukemia.   —R.K.

Johnny Bush

BORN: February 17, 1935
BIRTHPLACE: Houston, Texas

Born in Houston, Texas, in 1935, John Bush Shin is a long-time Willie Nelson associate, best known as the composer of "Whiskey River," the song that has since become Nelson's theme song. (Nelson, who is Bush's former bandmate from at least one Texas bar band,

certainly helped Bush's pension fund by including versions of "Whiskey River" on five different million-selling albums.)

Bush began playing professionally in the clubs of San Antonio, Texas; he and Nelson first met when they both served as sidemen behind some long-forgotten local club singer.

Later, after serving stints as a drummer in Ray Price's band and in a backup band Nelson put together during his early recording career in the 60's, Bush went on to modest solo success. Nelson, who never forgets an old friend, financed Bush's first recording sessions. Bush's own version of "Whiskey River" was a Top 20 single on RCA in 1972. Other Bush hits include "Undo the Right" (a Top Ten in 1968) and "You Gave Me a Mountain" (Top Ten in 1969) on Stop Records.   —B.A.

Carl and Pearl Butler

BORN: Carl, June 2, 1927, Knoxville, Tennessee
             Pearl, September 20, 1927, Nashville, Tennessee
DIED: Carl, September 4, 1992; Pearl, March 1, 1988

Though Carl and Pearl Butler made their reputations during the heyday of the smooth Nashville Sound, their music was anything but smooth. Clad in flashy Western outfits, they sang hard-edged traditional music with decidedly unpolished harmonies.

Carl Roberts Butler began singing as a boy, and after working on radio in Knoxville and Raleigh, North Carolina, went on to join the Opry in 1948. He recorded for Capitol Records, where he had little success but wrote two country favorites: "Crying My Heart Out Over You" (a hit for both Flatt and Scruggs and Ricky Skaggs), and "If Teardrops Were Pennies" (a hit for Carl Smith).

He signed with Columbia and had his first solo hit, "Honky-Tonkitis," in 1961. His wife Pearl sang harmony with him on the ballad, "Don't Let Me Cross Over." Its success, remaining Number One eleven weeks on the *Billboard* charts in 1962, made it clear they'd found a niche as a duo. That same year they joined the Opry and had other hits for Columbia, the biggest being "Too Late to Try Again" and "I'm Hanging Up the Phone" (1964). They continued recording for Columbia through the late 60's, appearing in the B-movie, *Second Fiddle to a Steel Guitar*. They recorded for Chart Records, for their own Pedaca label and for CMH. Butler did some performing after Pearl's death in 1988, but basically retired from music, his own death coming in 1992. —R.K.

Billy Byrd

BORN: February 17, 1920
BIRTHPLACE: Williamson County, Tennessee

Billy Byrd, born and raised in the Nashville area, aspired to a career as a jazz guitarist. As a teenager, he and his friend Harold Bradley regularly got together to study the innovative electric jazz guitar of Benny Goodman's pioneer guitarist, Charlie Christian. But like Bradley, Byrd didn't make his mark in the jazz field. In the 1940's he began playing with Ernest Tubb's Texas Troubadours. Playing the simple melodic style that Tubb's first guitarists, Smitty Smith and Jimmy Short pioneered, Byrd found that his formidable jazz talents often went unrecognized.

In 1955 he and his friend, Nashville studio guitarist Hank Garland, designed a hollowbody electric guitar for Gibson. The "Byrdland" became popular with country and, later, with rock guitarists. Byrd recorded for Starday and recorded four albums for Warner Bros. on his own. —R.K.

Jerry Byrd

BORN: March 9, 1920
BIRTHPLACE: Lima, Ohio

Before pedal steel guitar dominated the country music scene, Jerry Byrd was the dominant influence on most country steel players. His buttery, warm tone and exquisite sense of touch made him instantly identifiable and much imitated. He grew up in Ohio, not encouraged in his music by his family. Deeply influenced by the great Hawaiian steel guitarists, he eventually moved into country music, working at WLW in Cincinnati and catching on first with Ernest Tubb's Texas Troubadours and then with Red Foley's band, The Pleasant Valley Boys. The Foley band became the first touring band to double as a studio recording

band, and backed various singers on records. Byrd, for example, played on Hank Williams' "I'm So Lonesome I Could Cry" and made his own instrumental records for Mercury, including "Steelin' the Blues" (with Rex Allen Sr. on vocals) in 1949.

Eventually Byrd became a top session player in Nashville, until the pedal steel's rise in the early 50's left him less in demand. He still recorded for Decca and later for Monument, but his refusal to switch to pedals hurt him as musical tastes changed. He even played bass on some Nashville sessions. During the 1970's he left Nashville for Hawaii to pursue his love of Hawaiian steel guitar music. Hawaiians considered him a master of their music, and he remains there today, still recording and playing occasional steel guitar conventions on the mainland.

He was inducted into the Steel Guitar Hall of Fame in 1978. —R.K.

Tracy Byrd

BORN: December 18, 1966
BIRTHPLACE: Vidor, Texas

Raised in the Beaumont area—like Clay Walker, Mark Chesnutt and others—Byrd mines territory similar to yet another Texan, MCA labelmate George Strait, though with a bit less depth and maturity (so far, anyway, but he is young yet). Byrd's self-titled 1993 MCA debut contained the Number One single, "Holdin' Heaven." He co-wrote one track on his debut, and two on his second album, 1994's *No Ordinary Man*. Interestingly, Byrd and Mark Chesnutt both got their start in the same Beaumont nightclub, Cutter's. —G.F.

The Byrds

Though best-known for their mid-1960's folk-rock, The Byrds' country roots made them influential far beyond that era. Bassist Chris Hillman was originally a bluegrass mandolinist, and Byrds numbers like "Mr. Spaceman" had obvious country overtones.

Eventually leader Roger McGuinn was ready to move the band more resolutely in that direction. When Gram Parsons joined the group in 1968, with a strong love of hard country and a gift for songwriting, the

group began to change, a shift that culminated in the classic *Sweetheart of the Rodeo* album that year. *Sweetheart of the Rodeo* inspired the country-rock movement and included Parsons' classic "Hickory Wind" along with country favorite "I Am a Pilgrim."

The group played the Grand Ole Opry in 1968, but faced a conservative and hostile audience. Their biting, satirical "Drug Store Truck Drivin' Man" was directed at Ralph Emery's musical conservatism.

When Los Angeles bluegrass guitarist Clarence White joined the band, the country sound continued, even though Parsons and Chris Hillman left to form The Flying Burrito Brothers. White's flatpicking and pedal steel type licks (played on a converted Fender Telecaster) retained the group's country orientation to some extent.

The group disbanded around 1972.   —R.K.

Cain's Dancing Academy

Cain's Dancing Academy, originally a Tulsa, Oklahoma, dancehall and dancing school, became famous in 1934 as the home of Bob Wills and His Texas Playboys, who had moved to Tulsa from Waco, Texas. Cain's became the site of Wills' legendary noontime broadcasts from 1934 until The Playboys disbanded in 1942. When The Playboys weren't on the road playing dances around Texas, Oklahoma and neighboring states, they were broadcasting or performing at Cain's. Bob's manager, O.W. Mayo, ran much of Bob's business affairs from Cain's. When Bob disbanded The Playboys during his seven months in

the Army, his brother Johnnie Lee Wills took over the broadcasts, and after Bob moved to California, Johnnie Lee used Cain's as his home base. Cain's, looking much as it always has, has continued ever since to host various musical acts in Tulsa, its connection with the Wills brothers making it immortal.   —R.K.

Cajun Music

Cajuns are French-speaking people with roots in Acadia, which is now the Canadian province of Nova Scotia. In the 18th century, genocidal practices by the British forced a mass exodus of Acadians (memorialized by Henry Wadsworth Longfellow in the poem "Evangeline") into Louisiana, a land that was just as rich in French culture and resources as Acadia had been.

Upon their arrival in Louisiana, the Acadians, or Cajuns, brought with them a unique musical tradition that was dominated by the fiddle. Supplemented by hand claps and kitchen utensils, the music conveyed a sense of joyous celebration.

During the railroad and rice boom years of the 1880's, German immigrants from the Midwest began remigrating south to Texas and Louisiana. They also had a rich musical heritage, and they, in turn, introduced the Cajuns to the accordion, which gradually replaced the fiddle as the undisputed champ of Cajun music.

However, in the 1930's and 1940's, the fiddle made a dramatic comeback in Cajun music. During that period, Governor Huey Long was building roads and establishing English-language schools throughout the French Triangle. Consequently, English-language radio stations began to crop up, and Cajuns began hearing the fiddle incorporated in a host of other musical genres such as Western swing and hillbilly.

Between 1946 and 1949, a Cajun fiddler named Harry Choates formed a band that fused Cajun with swing, and, in the process, played a significant role in bringing Cajun music into the mainstream. Among the Cajun tunes Choates helped popularize are "Jole Blon" ("Pretty Blond"), "Allons a Lafayette" ("Going to Lafayette") and "Poor Hobo."

In the 1960's, Cajun music went through a major revolution when artists such as Jimmy Newman and Doug Kershaw went electric and headed for Nashville. Kershaw, who was born in Lake Arthur, Louisiana, spoke no English as a child and learned to play fiddle as well as 28 other musical instruments. At the age of 20 he joined the *Louisiana Hayride*, went on to play the Grand Ole Opry and gave Cajun music some national exposure when he performed "Louisiana Man" and "Diggy Diggy Lo" on TV's *Johnny Cash Show*.

With his lightning speed and rhythmic nuances, Kershaw paved the way for younger Cajun musicians to explore a variety of instrumental and melodic combinations that were still rooted in the traditional Acadian form.

One example of this new breed was the short-lived group Coteau, founded by Jimmy Newman's son Gary. The group's "progressive" Cajun sound combined elements of Austin and Nashville country and western with some doses of rock and bluegrass. After the group split, Mike Doucet, Coteau's fiddler, founded the popular Beausoleil, which became a Cajun mainstay throughout the 1980's and 1990's, and even accompanied country superstar Mary-Chapin Carpenter on her hit, "Down at the Twist and Shout."

Another strain of Cajun-influenced music is called Zydeco, which is a Cajun idiomatic expression meaning "beans aren't salty." A hybrid of West Texas country, boogie-woogie and Cajun, the genre's leading practitioners include the late Clifton Chenier, Rockin' Dopsie and Buckwheat Zydeco.   —R.P.

the same station that started Chet Atkins, Homer and Jethro and Don Gibson—where his rendition of the elderly character "Grandpappy" made him a local star. He worked with Bill Carlisle's group by the early 1940's (Atkins became the group's fiddler). After Navy service in Florida during World War II, Campbell returned to WNOX, and by 1952 hosted his own TV show over WATE in Knoxville. That show ended in 1958 when he joined the Opry's Prince Albert Show and signed with RCA (he also briefly recorded for Starday). His word-twisting routines like "Rindercella" (the Cinderella story) made him a favorite. He and singer Lorene Mann made some vocal recordings as well, including, oddly enough, late 60's rhythm and blues hits like "Dark End of the Street" and "Tell It Like It Is."

A charter member of the *Hee Haw* cast, he was head writer and performed as various characters. After The Nashville Network began, he hosted a historical series, *Yesteryear in Nashville*, in addition to his *Hee Haw* duties. He had various business interests, but continued on the show until his 1987 death from a heart attack.   —R.K.

Archie Campbell

BORN: November 7, 1914
BIRTHPLACE: Bull's Gap, Tennessee
DIED: August 29, 1987

Archie Campbell was a popular country comedian before joining TV's *Hee Haw* when it debuted on CBS in 1968, but that show made him a household name far beyond Nashville. He'd worked in comedy from the late 1930's on WNOX Radio in Knoxville—

Glen Campbell

BORN: April 22, 1936
BIRTHPLACE: Delight, Arkansas

Glen Campbell is best known for the immensely popular string of pop and country hits with which he scored big in the 1960's and early 70's: "Wichita Lineman," "By the Time I Get to Phoenix," "Rhinestone Cowboy," "Gentle on My Mind," "Where's the Playground, Susie," "Dreams of the Everyday Housewife" and "Southern Nights," among others.

Yet Campbell's roots have always run deep in country music, to whose folds he has returned in more recent years. The son of a sharecropper, Campbell was born in the throes of the Great Depression. The seventh son in a family of 12 kids, he grew up knowing what hard times were all about. But he found his own ticket out of hardscrabble Arkansas at age four when his father bought him a five-dollar guitar. Within a couple of years, he was already an accomplished picker.

Campbell was still in his teens when he began working as a guitarist in various bands on the dancehall circuit in and around New Mexico, including a Western swing outfit headed by his uncle, Dick Bills. He soon organized his own first band, The Western Wranglers.

An impeccable guitarist and accomplished vocalist, Campbell, by age 24, was on the West Coast working as a session guitarist/harmony singer on the road and in the studio for everyone from Elvis Presley, Ray Charles and Merle Haggard to Frank Sinatra, Dean Martin and The Mamas and Papas. After a few minor early successes as a recording artist—most notably with a modest hit called "Universal Soldier"—he did a brief stint in the hit harmony rock group, The Beach Boys. In 1969, with his solo career well under way, Campbell launched his own nationally broadcast television show, *The Glen Campbell Goodtime Hour*, which became a showcase not only for Campbell, but for many other country artists as well. Campbell also appeared in a few feature films, including a supporting role in *True Grit*, with John Wayne.

But as the 1970's wore on and his fame grew, Campbell began to flame out on the double pyre of alcohol and cocaine addiction. During the late 1970's and early 1980's he garnered more tabloid headlines for his tumultuous, mutually abusive engagement to singer Tanya Tucker than for his music.

But like so many 70's and 80's country bad boys, Campbell has, in middle age, traded in debauchery for religion and righteousness. Recently, he confessed all the sins of his youth in his steamy autobiography, *Rhinestone Cowboy*, and has found refuge in predictable places: born-again Christianity and conservative politics.

Along the way, he's proven once again that show business is one of the few professions where a reckless, somewhat misspent youth can actually end up bearing big dividends. "I'm frequently asked these days whether I plan to go into the ministry," Campbell, who these days serenely devotes most of his time to God, golf and Branson (where he performs at his Goodtime Theater) notes in *Rhinestone Cowboy*. "My answer is that I'm already in it....I have a ministry in my music, much of which is focused on God and all of which is performed for God."   —B.A.

Capitol Records

Founded in 1942 by songwriter Johnny Mercer, Los Angeles record store owner Glenn Wallichs and film producer Buddy DeSylva, the Los Angeles-based Capitol became a formidable force in country music early on. Its first country artist was Tex Ritter, followed by

Jack Guthrie (cousin to Woody) and Wesley Tuttle. Following World War II, the label's roster took off as Jack Guthrie, Jimmy Wakely, Merle Travis and Tex Williams began to have major hit records.

Williams gave the label its first million-seller with "Smoke! Smoke! Smoke! (That Cigarette)" in 1947. Capitol's original country producer was former big band musician Lee Gillette, who worked closely with Cliffie Stone, founder of *Hometown Jamboree* and a Capitol talent scout and producer. Cliffie brought Tennessee Ernie Ford to the label in 1949. By 1951, Gillette moved elsewhere within Capitol. His friend, former Chicago radio station guitarist Ken Nelson, replaced him as country producer. He produced classic records by Hank Thompson, Wanda Jackson, Jean Shepard, Sonny James, Ferlin Husky and Faron Young in the 50's. He also helped create the Bakersfield Sound of Buck Owens and Merle Haggard in the 60's. After Nelson retired in the 70's, Capitol used various producers, but continued to remain vital, mainly through the hits of Glen Campbell. Capitol's original owners sold the company to the British EMI organization in 1955, which still owns the label today. Though Garth Brooks began as a Capitol artist, a 1991 reorganization moved the label's country roster over to the newly re-activated Liberty label, also owned by EMI.   —R.K.

Captain Midnight

BORN: March 6, 1931
BIRTHPLACE: Durand, Michigan

This Michigan-born DJ (he had a program on KDA in Nashville for a while) and some-time journalist (he wrote liner notes to at least one classic Waylon Jennings album from the early 70's), whose real name was Roger Schutt, was a minor but colorful figure in the early 70's Outlaw movement.

For quite a while, the closest thing he had to a home was the sofa at Glaser Sound Studios at 916 19th Avenue South, the unofficial "Hillbilly Central" headquarters of the so-called Outlaws, which was owned by Outlaw producer/recording artist Tompall Glaser and his brothers. Though Schutt himself was neither an artist nor a songwriter, he became, in the words of one survivor from that scene, "a guru...He played pinball with Waylon and Tompall, and he knew everybody—he knew the good guys and the bad guys, who to trust and who not to."

When last heard from, Schutt was still around Nashville, still friends with Waylon & Willie and the boys, had gotten married, settled into relative normalcy, and was producing a radio show from his home for a Chicago station.   —B.A.

Henson Cargill

BORN: April 5, 1941
BIRTHPLACE: Oklahoma City, Oklahoma

Like many country artists, Henson Cargill was an "overnight" sensation that was over a decade in the making. Born in Oklahoma City in 1941, Cargill spent years playing small clubs in Oklahoma before cutting a successful debut album, *Skip a Rope*, in 1968. The title single reached the top of the charts in a period of time when people were anxious about youth, the subject of the song. In 1969, Henson became the host of Avco Broadcasting's *Country Hayride*, a retitled, syndicated version of the old *Midwestern Hayride*. He continued with the popular television show into the 1970's. After signing with Atlantic Records in the early 70's, he cut the hit single, "Some Old California Memory," in 1973, then found himself temporarily without a label when Atlantic closed down its country division. He later signed with Copper Mountain Records, placing two singles, "Silence on the Line" and "Have a Good Day," on the charts in 1980. Later, he turned to full-time cattle ranching in Oklahoma. —M.B.

The Carlisle Brothers

BORN: Cliff, May 6, 1904, Taylorsville, Kentucky
Bill, December 19, 1908, Wakefield, Kentucky
DIED: Cliff, April 2, 1983

Half of the legendary Carlisle Brothers (the other half was his brother Bill), Cliff Carlisle was a gifted and influential musician who pioneered the use of Hawaiian or slide guitar in country music. Though his earliest recordings were made with guitarist Wilbert Ball, his greatest fame came when he recorded with Bill, with whom he worked until 1947.

In the late 1930's, the brothers ran their own barn dance stage show over WLAP Radio in Louisville. Their biggest hit record was "Rainbow at Midnight" in 1946. Cliff retired in 1947; shortly thereafter, in 1948, Bill had a solo hit record with "Tramp on the Street." Cliff briefly returned to performing with Bill in Knoxville in the early 50's, then returned to retirement and remained inactive until his death. Every dobroist, from Oswald to Josh Graves to Jerry Douglas, owes an enormous debt to Cliff. (See also, The Carlisles.) —R.K.

The Carlisles

The Carlisles, not to be confused with their earlier incarnation as The Carlisle Brothers, began when Cliff Carlisle left retirement to reunite with his brother Bill at WNOX in Knoxville in 1951. After gospel singer Martha Carson joined them, they signed with Mercury that summer, specializing in up-tempo novel-

ties like Bill's original number, "Too Old to Cut the Mustard," their first hit. After Carson left and Cliff retired again, singers Roy Sneed and Betty Amos replaced them. Their 1952 hit, "No Help Wanted," remained Number One for four weeks. That April, they joined the Opry. Three Top Tens followed in 1953: "Knot Hole," "Is Zat You Myrtle" and, late that year, "T'ain't Nice (To Talk Like That)."

After their Mercury contract ended in 1959, they recorded for smaller labels. Bill had a solo hit record in 1966 with "What Kinda Deal Is This," and The Carlisles remained Opry members into the early 1990's (they became members in 1953). Despite various personnel changes, Carlisle, whose vigorous onstage antics earned him the nickname "Jumping" Bill Carlisle, still led the group in the early 1990's, with Opry staff musician Joe Edwards often playing lead guitar. Bill underwent successful heart surgery in 1993. (See also, The Carlisle Brothers.) —R.K.

Mary-Chapin Carpenter

BORN: February 21, 1958
BIRTHPLACE: Princeton, New Jersey

New Jersey-born, Brown University educated, Mary-Chapin Carpenter would appear an unlikely prospect for country stardom, but her intelligent, introspective, witty songwriting and folk/rock-leaning style have found a solid place in the Nashville music scene.

After early years in Princeton, New Jersey, Carpenter spent part of her childhood in Japan, where her father served as a publishing executive for *Life Magazine*. The family then settled in the Washing-

ton, D.C., area, where Chapin still makes her home today. She began writing songs as a teenager, making her debut at a D.C. bar called Gallagher's in 1977. She played the bars during her college years at Brown University, continuing to do so after her return to Washington. In the early 80's, she met up with John Jennings, who became her guitar player and co-producer. After achieving a high degree of local fame—winning a number of Washington Area Music Awards (Wammies)—and, whenever she had the money, recording demo tapes of her songs in Jennings' basement, she attracted the attention of Columbia Records. So impressed were they by the demo tape—which Chapin intended to sell locally— that they released it as her first album, *Hometown Girl*, in 1987. It wasn't a commercial hit, but critics applauded it, and it started the ball rolling.

Her next album, 1989's *State of the Heart*, received even more attention, yielding four Top 20 hits ("How Do," "Never Had It So Good," "Quittin' Time" and "Something of a Dreamer"), and achieving Gold status. Industry accolades included the Academy of Country Music's Top New Female Vocalist award. Further sealing Carpenter's status as an artist to be reckoned with was her performance on the 1990 Country Music Association Awards show. She knocked the audience dead with her song, "Opening Act," a hilarious look at opening for a less-than-kind headliner. She received a standing ovation from a roomful of her peers, and anyone who hadn't been paying attention before most certainly was afterward.

Four more Top 20's came from her next album, the platinum-selling *Shooting Straight in the Dark*, including the Grammy-winning "Down at the Twist and Shout." It would be the first of three (so far) consecutive Best Female Country Vocal Performance Grammys Carpenter has earned. In 1992, she released her fourth album, *Come On Come On*, which contained seven Top 20 singles, including the Number One, "He Thinks He'll Keep Her." The album went

double-platinum and Chapin picked up Country Music Association Female Vocalist of the Year awards in both 1992 and 1993.

Despite all of these tangible signs of "success" in the business, Carpenter herself is more philosophical. "I never even thought about record sales or awards and those things until they were kind of in my lap...I started playing music because it meant something to me, because it fulfills me. The awards, all that, have never been the motivation," she said in a *Country Music Magazine* interview in 1993.—G.F.

Fiddlin' John Carson

BORN: March 23, 1868
BIRTHPLACE: Fannin County, Georgia
DIED: December 11, 1949

Though preceded by various vaudevillians and fiddlers who performed music that could be called country, Fiddlin' John Carson was in many ways the first real country entertainer to make records. His 1923 sides for the Okeh label were the first to combine genuine Southern singing and fiddling, and were the ones that alerted the record companies that a new type of music was on the scene. Carson spent his youth riding race horses and working in cotton mills. By 1913 he was playing the fiddle well enough to enter local contests, and by 1918 he was playing for carnivals, dances and medicine shows. His success at these, and over WSB Radio in Atlanta in 1922, led to his 1923 recordings, done at a temporary studio in Atlanta. This famous "first country record" featured Carson alone singing and fiddling on "The Little Old Log Cabin in the Lane," backed with "The Old Hen Cackled and the Rooster's Going to Crow." Released without even a catalog number, it soon became a best-seller, and embarrassed Okeh officials scrambled to bring him to New York to record more. He eventually did over 150 sides between 1923 and 1934; other hits were "You Will Never Miss Your Mother Until She Is Gone," "Be Kind to a Man When He Is Down" and "It's a Long Way to Tipperary." Carson toured widely during his glory days, often with his daughter "Moonshine Kate," and later recorded with a string band, The Virginia Reelers. He spent his later years working as an elevator operator at the Georgia State Capitol.   —C.W.

Martha Carson

BORN: March 19, 1921
BIRTHPLACE: Neon, Kentucky

A member of the musically gifted Ambergay family that also produced songwriter Jenny Lou Carson, Irene Ambergay (Martha Carson) began working as a teenager over WHIS in Bluefield, West Virginia, with other members of her family. She married James Carson and worked with him on WSB in Atlanta and as a member of The Coon Creek Girls. After she divorced James in 1951, she concentrated on songwriting (Jenny Lou had written the standard, "Jealous Heart"). She also briefly joined The Carlisles at WNOX in Knoxville. Her early 50's recordings for Capitol featured minimal backing in the style of The Carlisles.

Her song, "Satisfied," a gospel original, became a standard (and a favorite of Elvis Presley). In the 50's she sang a big-band style of pop-flavored gospel music and recorded extensively in this style (as well as some semi-rock 'n' roll material) for RCA. She eventually retired after marrying booking agent and manager Xavier Cosse.   —R.K.

Carlene Carter

BORN: September 26, 1955
BIRTHPLACE: Madison, Tennessee

Carlene Carter, the granddaughter of Mother Maybelle Carter and the daughter of June Carter (now June Carter Cash) and Carl Smith, worked with The Carter Family during the late 1960's and early 1970's. She took a stab at modeling, moved to England and then embarked on a solo career that combined a country sensibility with a rock 'n' roll heart.

Carlene was swayed by London's thriving club scene, which was dominated by pub-rock groups such as The Rumour and the legendary Rockpile. She married Nick Lowe, Rockpile's bassist and producer of punk godfather Elvis Costello, and in 1978, she recorded a self-titled debut album for Warner Bros. The record, which was produced by Rumour guitarist Brinsley Schwarz and keyboard player Bob Andrews, won immediate critical acclaim and helped establish Carlene as a major proponent of the progressive country-rock movement of the late 1970's and early 1980's.

Two Sides to Every Woman, which was recorded in New York City, followed in 1979 and featured more of a hard-rock edge than its predecessor. However, with the release of the good-timey, rockabilly-flavored *Musical Shapes* in 1980, Carlene returned to the crossover territory she helped stake out. The record was produced by Lowe.

During the early 1980's, Carlene's career was stalled at the starting gate. She and Lowe divorced, and she also parted ways with Warner Bros. She recorded a commercially dismal album for Epic Records in 1982, and then appeared in the London production of *Pump Boys and Dinettes*. In 1986, she toured England with her mother June and aunts Helen and Anita as part of The Carter Family Road Show, and in the process, rediscovered her country roots.

In 1990, Carlene returned with a bang. She resigned with Warner Bros., and then released *I Fell in*

Love, a musical powerhouse that blended her grandmother's roots with some vigorous country-rock. The record, which was produced by Howie Epstein, bassist for Tom Petty and The Heartbreakers, garnered Carlene a Grammy award nomination in 1991 for Country Female Performance, and also an Academy of Country Music nomination for Best New Female Vocalist the same year. In 1993, Carlene struck Gold again with *Little Love Letters*, which yielded the hit single, "Every Little Thing."   —R.P.

The Carter Family

To the big-time recording scout from Victor Records in New York, they were not very impressive. "He is dressed in overalls and the women are country women from way back there—calico clothes on—the children are very poorly dressed. They look like hillbillies." He was A. P. Carter, and the woman holding the autoharp was his wife Sara; the other woman with the big guitar was Sara's cousin, Maybelle. They had driven a Model A Ford 25 miles down mountain roads and across rocky streams to get to the tryouts, and now they were face to face with a fast-talking, moon-faced young man named Ralph Peer. It was the summer of 1927, in a temporary recording studio set up on State Street in Bristol, Tennessee. Country music history was about to go into high gear.

After their first audition Peer realized that these hillbillies could sing. "As soon as I heard Sara's voice," he recalled, "that was it. I knew it was going to be wonderful." And it was. The first song he recorded that hot August day, "Bury Me Under the Weeping Willow," was the start of the most incredible dynasty in the annals of American music. For 50 years now, some part of this original Carter Family has been a fixture on the country scene, from the pure folk sound of the original trio to the rock-flavored sound of Maybelle's granddaughter, Carlene. "Carter Family songs" is a term that has become synonymous with old-time country standards, and includes a wide range of pieces either written by or introduced by The Carters: "Will the Circle Be Unbroken," "Keep On the Sunny Side," "I'm Thinking Tonight of My Blue Eyes," "Hello, Stranger" and "Worried Man Blues" are just a few. "They didn't have Gold records in those days," says a modern Nashville record executive. "But if they had, The Carters would have had a wall full."

Most of this foundation work was laid, of course, by the group people today have taken to calling "The Original Carter Family" to distinguish them from the various later Carter Families or Carter offshoots. It's that original group that got voted into the Hall of Fame in 1970, and whose scratchy, primitive 1920's and 1930's records still stay in print in an age of CD's and digital tape. They made six records for Peer that day in 1927 and went back to their mountain farm. A. P. returned to his regular job of selling fruit trees. It wasn't until three months later, when the local Victor dealer hunted A.P. up to give him his first royalty check, that the trio began to sense that there might be something to the record business.

Not long after that they were brought up to New York, where they recorded again—and did a song called "Wildwood Flower." In it Maybelle figured out a way to pick the melody on the lower strings of her guitar while she strummed chords on the higher strings, thereby creating the most influential guitar style in country music. The song itself was an old one A.P. had learned in the mountains; though he didn't know it, it was actually an old 1859 composition that had been a hit in sheet music form before the Civil War. If there had ever been any doubt about The Carters' popularity on records, "Wildwood Flower" ended it. Not only was it sold by record stores around the country, it was also peddled by Sears, Roebuck in their catalog, by Montgomery Ward and by dime-store chains like Woolworth.

In the years from 1927 until 1941, The Carters went on to record some 270 records for every major American label. There were old folk songs, gospel songs, blues, comedy songs, sentimental tearjerkers and even a few social protest songs like "Coal Miner's Blues" and "No Depression in Heaven." And though A.P. was supposedly the leader of the group, and the emcee at their stage shows, most of the music was really done by Sara and Maybelle. Maybelle later recalled of A.P.: "If he felt like singing, he would sing, and if he didn't, he would walk around and look at the window. So we never depended on him for anything." In one sense, then, The Carter Family could be thought of as country music's first successful female singing group, since most of the records focused on Sara and Maybelle's duet work. A. P.'s great talent was finding songs; he would travel far into the mountains to seek out old ones, some of them hundreds of years old, and then rearrange them and rework them for modern tastes.

Unlike modern stars, The Carters never really figured out how to capitalize on their record hits. As late as 1929 they were not even performing regularly on tours or on radio, and A.P. was even working in Detroit for a time. Their idea of promoting a tour was having a bunch of handbills printed up ("This program is morally good," read one), tacking them up to trees and storefronts and renting a country schoolhouse to play for 200 people.

As early as 1933 Sara and A.P. had separated, but got back together again when the group finally got a chance at big-time radio broadcasting over XERA, the notorious "border radio" station that beamed its powerful signal all over the United States. This was in 1938, and by now the Carter show included Maybelle's youngest daughter, Anita, and A.P. and Sara's 15-year-old daughter, Janette; Maybelle's older girls, Helen and June, later joined the show. Thousands of fan letters were pouring in, and for a time it looked as if the group would finally reap some just rewards.

In 1939 A.P. and Sara split for good, and Sara moved to California; XERA went off the air in 1941. There was one last get-together—a six-month contract at WBT in Charlotte. A photographer from *Life Magazine* came down to do a major photo spread. It looked like the big break might come after all. The photographer filled up a waste basket with flash bulbs, but the story never came out: war news pushed it out of the issue. When the contract ended, finally, Sara decided to really call it quits. A.P. went back to his home in the mountains of Virginia, and Maybelle started up a new act with her daughters. All the Carters would stay active in music for another 20 years, but the original trio was history. In 1970, that original group was elected to the Country Music Hall of Fame. Their legacy was a hundred great songs and a definition of duet singing—enough to be an inspiration for generations who followed.   —C.W.

June Carter

BORN: June 23, 1929
BIRTHPLACE: Maces Springs, Virginia

Valerie June Carter was born on June 23, 1929, in Maces Springs, Virginia, and learned to sing as soon as she could talk. Her mother was Maybelle Carter, who along with uncle A.P. and aunt Sara, formed the legendary Carter Family. June and sisters Anita and

Helen eventually began touring with the group.

The road experience proved to be a boon for June. She discovered that in addition to possessing a soaring voice, she also had a knack for comedy routines—a trait that earned her a stint with Elvis Presley's road show. She married country singer Carl Smith, and together they had two daughters—Carlene and Rosie. The marriage, however, ended in divorce.

In 1961, June joined Johnny Cash's road show, and along with Merle Kilgore, penned Cash's classic tune, "Ring of Fire." In 1967, June and Cash picked up a Grammy for Best Country Performance Duet for the song "Jackson." On March 1, 1968, the pair married in Franklin, Tennessee, and in 1969, the CMA named them Vocal Group of the Year.

Throughout the late 1960's and early 1970's, the couple continued to roll out Top 20 singles such as "If I Were a Carpenter" (1970) and "No Need to Worry" (1971).

In 1974, June was cited as Wife and Mother of the Year. Although her recording career was relatively quiet during the 1970's and 80's, June wrote two books and a screenplay and did some acting. She also toured with her sisters, their children and Carlene as part of The Carter Family Road Show.

In 1990, she, along with Anita and Helen, appeared on The Nitty Gritty Dirt Band's award-winning album, *Will the Circle Be Unbroken, Volume 2*, and in 1992, she appeared with husband Johnny at an all-star tribute to rock legend Bob Dylan at New York City's Madison Square Garden. Together, the couple performed Dylan's "It Ain't Me, Babe," which had been a Top Ten country hit for them in 1964. She and members of the Carter family currently tour as part of The Johnny Cash Show. (See also, The Original Carter Family.)   —R.P.

Wilf Carter

BORN: December 18, 1904
BIRTHPLACE: Guysboro, Nova Scotia, Canada

Singer-songwriter Wilf Carter, better known as Montana Slim, was born in Guysboro, Nova Scotia, in 1904. He started out as a Canadian cowboy and subsequently wound up with his own radio show on CFCN in Calgary, Alberta, in the early 1930's. At the same time, Wilf began recording for RCA Victor in the States. While performing on a CBS radio program in New York City, he adopted the name Montana Slim. Wilf was largely influenced by the yodeling and singing cowboys of the period, including Jimmie Rodgers and Gene Autry.

He also wrote more than 500 tunes, including "The Hindenburg Disaster" and "I'm Only a Dude in Cowboy Clothes." One of the longest-running acts in country and western music, Wilf celebrated 60 years in show business in 1993.   —R.P.

Lionel Cartwright

BORN: February 10, 1960
BIRTHPLACE: Gallipolis, Ohio

Lionel Cartwright was born in Gallipolis, Ohio, on February 10, 1960, and was raised in nearby Glendale, West Virginia. He took piano lessons as a child and, by the time he was ten, he could play ten instruments.

In high school, Cartwright was influenced by the singer-songwriters of the early 1970's, especially James Taylor, Paul Simon and Billy Joel, as well as country artists such as Merle Haggard and Buck Owens. In

his early teens, he landed a spot as a regular on a country music radio show in Milton, West Virginia, and eventually became a featured singer/musician on WMNI's *Country Cavalcade* in Columbus, Ohio. While attending Wheeling College in Wheeling, West Virginia, Cartwright worked his way through by serving as a backup pianist and later as a featured performer and musical director at the *WWVA Jamboree* in Wheeling.

Upon graduation in 1982, he moved to Nashville, where he received a part as a cast member of The Nashville Network's sitcom, *I-40 Paradise*. While in Music City, Cartwright also struck up a friendship with Felice and Boudleaux Bryant, from whom he learned additional songwriting techniques, which eventually led to a recording contract with MCA Records in 1988.

His debut album that year, *Lionel Cartwright*, yielded four country hits, "You're Gonna Make Her Mine," "Like Father, Like Son," "Give Me His Last Chance" and "In My Eyes." The album also showcased Cartwright's adept musicianship on a number of instruments, including guitar, mandolin, fiddle and piano.

In 1990, "I Watched It All (On My Radio)," the title track to Cartwright's second MCA release, shot all the way to the top of the charts. The following year, Cartwright topped the charts again with "Leap of Faith" from his third album, *Chasin' the Sun* (1991).   —R.P.

Johnny Carver

BORN: November 24, 1940
BIRTHPLACE: Jackson, Mississippi

Born in Jackson, Mississippi, in 1940, Johnny Carver began singing at age five as part of his family's gospel group. By high school, he'd formed his own band and entered the world of secular music. Before coming to Nashville he sang with the house band at the famed Palomino Club in Los Angeles.

As a country artist, Carver never quite achieved stardom, but nonetheless had numerous chart records between 1967 and the early 1980's.

His biggest success came as a purveyor of warmed-over country versions of pop hits of the day, like "Tie a Yellow Ribbon ('Round the Old Oak Tree)," "Afternoon Delight," "Sweet City Woman" and "Living Next Door to Alice."   —B.A.

Johnny Cash

BORN: February 26, 1932
BIRTHPLACE: Kingsland, Arkansas

In 1954 when Johnny Cash, Luther Perkins and Marshall Grant auditioned at the Sun studios in Memphis, Garth Brooks was still eight long years away from appearing on earth. And in 1969 when Cash, riding a phenomenal wave of popularity, became a household word, Billy Ray Cyrus was only eight years old. In the course of his long career, Cash raised America's consciousness about country, enlightening millions who thought of Nashville only as Tennessee's state capitol, or associated the Grand Ole Opry with some kind of "hoedown" music. The road to fame meant conquering poverty, working to succeed in a highly competitive profession and dealing with the demands of stardom. Through it all, he defied those who urged him to remain silent on social issues. And regardless of cost, his complex personality and its darker sides were as open as the rest of his life. Small wonder that as a cultural icon, his appeal crossed age and class boundaries. Regardless of detours and downsides, Cash always held to the basics that defined both his music and himself.

Certainly the future was not that promising at first. J.R. Cash, born February 26, 1932, in Kingsland, Arkansas, was a child of the Great Depression. It wreaked havoc across America, hitting the rural South particularly hard. His parents, Ray and Carrie Cash, took the work ethic seriously and imparted it to all their children. As President Franklin Roosevelt was desperately trying to solve the problems of the Depression, Ray Cash elected to participate in one of Roosevelt's innovations: Dyess Colony. This experiment involved creating a farming community (with cotton the specialty) in the Delta country of Arkansas near the Mississippi River. The Cashes got 20 acres of land and a house when they moved there in 1935.

Ray Cash liked to sing; Carrie Cash played piano and guitar; the entire family knew the hymns from the Church of God. Roy Cash, J.R.'s older brother, even played in a band called The Rhythm Ramblers. The death of another older brother, the deeply religious Jack, in a 1944 sawmill accident, affected J.R. deeply. In school he acted and sang, listening to country singers on the radio whenever he could. By age 16 he became so serious about singing that Carrie Cash took in laundry to pay for his formal singing lessons. In 1950 he graduated from high school. After a brief, miserable period working in a Fisher Body plant in Detroit, he joined the U.S. Air Force. He got the name "John" there.

Having spent much of his hitch in Germany, Cash emerged a civilian in 1954. He'd learned to play guitar in the service, and began writing songs, including "Hey Porter," published as a poem in the military newspaper, *Stars and Stripes*. After his 1954 discharge, he married Vivian Liberto, whom he'd met in San Antonio, Texas, during his basic training. They moved to Memphis to begin a family. Cash sold appliances while training to become a radio announcer.

A musical career was his true goal. Roy Cash worked in the garage of a local Chevrolet dealer and introduced John to two guitar-playing co-workers, Luther Perkins and Marshall Grant. Soon Cash, Perkins, Grant and a steel player (who later dropped out) were working out songs, many of them gospel. It was inevitable that they would gravitate to Sun Records, the local label that discovered Elvis. Scotty Moore, Elvis' guitarist, suggested Cash contact Sam Phillips. It took many tries to get through. When John came in alone, Phillips was impressed enough to invite him back with his band. When they auditioned in the spring of 1955, Sam Phillips discouraged the gospel music but recorded Cash's song, "Hey Porter," asking John to come up with a second song for the single. Cash returned with "Cry! Cry! Cry!"

The now-classic Cash "boom-chicka-boom" sound wasn't a calculated creation but a product of the considerable musical limitations of the three men. But they were innovative. To compensate for the lack of a drummer, Cash put tissue paper under his acoustic guitar strings to imitate a snare drum. Grant obtained a $25 bass fiddle and had to learn it from scratch. Perkins, a primitive lead guitarist, could do little more than play simple licks and alternating notes on the lower strings. This was the Cash "boom-chicka-boom" sound, and with the addition of the legendary Sun "slapback" echo, it became a sparse but powerful vehicle for Cash's voice. Issued in June 1955, by late that year "Hey Porter," by "Johnny" Cash (an attempt to emphasize his youth) and The Tennessee Two, came in at Number 14 on the *Billboard* charts. Still, nobody quit their day jobs—yet.

Both sides of the next Sun single, "So Doggone Lonesome" and "Folsom Prison Blues," reached Number Four nationally. The third single, "I Walk the Line," stayed six weeks at Number One on the country charts and broke into the pop Top 20. Cash began making decent money, and in mid-1956, he joined the Grand Ole Opry. He began doing national TV appearances and worked with Sun producer Jack Clement, who added vocal choruses to later hits like "Home of the Blues" and "Guess Things Happen that Way," another crossover hit. Cash eventually moved the family to California.

In 1957, Columbia country producer Don Law persuaded him to sign with them when his Sun contract ended the following year. Cash's momentum continued on Columbia. His first Number One on the label came as he began exploring American history in his songs, with the Western gunfighter song, "Don't Take Your Guns to Town," in 1959. It landed him an appearance on the *Ed Sullivan Show* on CBS-TV. In 1960 he added a drummer, former Carl Perkins drummer W.S. Holland (who remains with him today), and the renamed Tennessee Three continued touring.

The early 60's saw Cash beginning to abuse pills (and becoming legendary for "redecorating" his hotels on tour). Nonetheless he grew as an artist. He recorded historical albums; mariachi horns appeared on his 1963 crossover hit, "Ring of Fire." His growing maturity allowed him to perform at the Newport Folk Festival and strike up a friendship with a young Bob Dylan. Unlike many of his peers, Cash stared controversy in the face, recording the hard-hitting Peter LaFarge song, "The Ballad of Ira Hayes," and other songs protesting the mistreatment of American Indians.

His touring show improved, first with the addition of The Carter Family (Mother Maybelle, Helen, Anita and June), then with old Sun Records friend, Carl Perkins, and finally with The Statler Brothers. His personal life was less successful. In 1965, the same year he made a vocal hit out of the old fiddle tune, "Orange Blossom Special," he was busted for drugs in El Paso, Texas (and got off with a suspended sentence and fine). Following his divorce from Vivian in 1966, his relationship with June Carter grew, but his pill problems worsened. It took several near-fatal episodes and encouragement from friends for Cash to kick his addiction. In 1967, healthier than he'd been in years, he recorded a live album at Folsom Prison, the classic *Johnny Cash at Folsom Prison.* Things weren't totally triumphant—Luther Perkins died in a fire. But the *Folsom Prison* album had phenomenal sales, reaching out far beyond the standard country audience. His new, live version of "Folsom Prison Blues" went to Number One and crossed over to pop success. By the time he married June in 1968, he was the subject of growing media attention.

His version of Carl Perkins' composition, "Daddy Sang Bass," spent six weeks at Number One late in 1968, and by 1969, Cash landed his own ABC-TV variety show. Bob Dylan did a rare guest appearance on the premiere show, and the series did so well that ABC added it to the fall schedule. His 1969 version of Shel Silverstein's novelty, "A Boy Named Sue," recorded live at San Quentin Prison (part of another best-selling album), topped the country charts and came in at Number Two on the pop charts.

Cash's eagle eye saw new talent in Nashville songwriters like Kris Kristofferson and Larry Gatlin. In recording their songs and promoting them, he helped pave the way for the entire Outlaw movement, though no one realized that at the time (Waylon Jennings had been a former Nashville roommate for a time in the mid-60's). In 1968, 1969 and 1970, Cash won the CMA Entertainer of the Year Award, and Male Vocalist of the Year the latter two years. He won Grammys in 1969 and 1970 as well. Through the 70's, the TV show and tours continued. He produced a religious film, *Gospel Road*, and appeared with Kirk Douglas in the film, *The Gunfighter.*

After losing his musical direction in the mid-70's by allowing his records to be slickly produced, he returned to the "boom-chicka-boom" sound with the 1976 novelty, "One Piece at a Time." That sound remained in place when he celebrated his 25th anniversary in the business in 1980. That same year, at 48, Cash became the youngest inductee to the Country Music Hall of Fame. The Carters remained with his show; Perkins and The Statlers left.

Cash's personal problems weren't over. Pills resurfaced in the early 80's, and he nearly died battling abdominal problems. After 28 years, he and Columbia parted ways. Though always a strong draw in concert, his record sales inevitably trailed off, though his visibility remained high. He was part of the all-star quartet, The Highwaymen, with Willie Nelson, Kris Kristofferson and Waylon Jennings. A 1987 recording contract with Mercury yielded little success, but he starred in a number of TV movies. The pill problems persisted, and he wound up at the Betty Ford Center in 1985. In early 1989 he underwent open heart surgery. In the early 90's he left Mercury/Polygram, signing with the non-Nashville label, American Records.

Today, Johnny Cash is 62 years old, still touring with The Carter Family and a band built around Fluke Holland on drums, Bob Wootton on guitar (Luther Perkins' replacement), and pianist Earl Poole Ball. Cash was elected to the Rock 'n' Roll Hall of Fame in 1992.

He became a hot media item once again with the 1994 release of *American Recordings*, his debut for the American label. Featuring just Cash and his guitar, it landed him anew on the pages of magazines like *Time, People, Vanity Fair, Rolling Stone* and his twelfth cover of *Country Music Magazine*. Cash will joke about his more restrained style, minus the tight pants and "exploding stages" of other performers. But without Johnny Cash, many of today's hot country artists might not have a stage to explode. (See also, June Carter, Rosanne Cash, Tommy Cash.)   —R.K.

Rosanne Cash

BORN: May 24, 1955
BIRTHPLACE: Memphis, Tennessee

Rosanne Cash records only sporadically (eight major label albums in 15 years) and seldom tours. Yet on account of her smoldering vocal style, compelling rock 'n' roll attitude, and subjective and confessional songwriting, she has nonetheless earned a reputation as one of the most influential and outspoken women in modern country music.

The daughter of Johnny Cash, Rosanne was born in Memphis, Tennessee, on May 24, 1955. Her parents divorced when she was 11, and she was raised by her mother, Vivian Liberto, in Ventura, California. Before launching her recording career with an album for the obscure Ariola label in Germany, Cash studied acting at the famed Lee Strasberg Institute and creative writing at Nashville's Vanderbilt University. She also worked at a desk job for Columbia

Records' London office for a while and toured as a singer with her father's road band for several years.

Cash was married to singer/songwriter/producer Rodney Crowell from 1979 until 1992. (They have three daughters.) And through the years Crowell became an instrumental part of her success, producing nearly all of her critically acclaimed albums and hit records, and co-writing many of them with her. Cash's first Number One single, "Seven Year Ache" (1981), established her sultry, smoky, quietly anguished style, much as did subsequent Crowell-produced chart-toppers like "My Baby Thinks He's a Train" (1981), "Blue Moon with Heartache" (1981), "I Don't Know Why You Don't Want Me" (1985), "Never Be You" (1985), "Tennessee Flat Top Box" (a 1987 remake of her father's 1961 hit) and "It's Such a Small World" (a 1988 duet with Crowell).

By the early 1990's, as her marriage to Crowell was unraveling, Cash poured her anguish, bitterness, and eventual emotional rejuvenation into a pair of stark, revealing albums—*Interiors* (1990) and *The Wheel* (1993)—which she produced herself and which, with their minimalist arrangements and subjective lyrics, tended to fly in the face of country conventions. Yet at the same time, these latter albums charted the continued growth of one of popular music's most intense, musically adventurous and idiosyncratic figures. (See also, Johnny Cash.) —B.A.

Tommy Cash

BORN: April 5, 1940
BIRTHPLACE: Dyess, Arkansas

Brother of the legendary Johnny Cash, Tommy spent the early 1960's working at Johnny's publishing company before pursuing his own recording career on the Epic label late in the decade. He had his first Number One single, "Six White Horses," in 1970, followed by a string of Top 20 hits including "So This Is Love." He recorded a number of albums with his band, The Tomcats, including *Tommy Cash Country* (1971) and *American Way of Life* (1972). Another country case of, as Hank Williams Jr. once put it, "living in the shadow of a very famous man." While his chart hits have stopped, he's still making records, releasing an early 90's album on Playback Records. (See also, Johnny Cash.)   —M.B.

Curly Chalker

BORN: October 22, 1931
BIRTHPLACE: Enterprise, Alabama

Harold Lee Chalker was one of those Nashville session legends largely unknown except to other steel players captivated by his jazzy, sophisticated playing. An accomplished steel guitarist by his teens, he started working with his bass player brother, Jim. By the early 1950's Curly caught on with a group hired by Lefty Frizzell to be his touring band. Chalker appeared on Lefty's recordings of "Mom and Dad's Waltz" and "Always Late." He then joined Hank Thompson's Brazos Valley Boys, remaining with them until he was drafted in 1952. In that band he became friendly with Merle Travis, who often toured with Thompson. In 1961 Travis used him on his 1962 *Travis!* album, which impressed many. Chalker also worked in Las Vegas with both Wade Ray's and Hank Penny's bands before moving to Nashville in 1965.

In 1966 he recorded an album for Columbia, and his jazzy approach could be heard on hits like Carl Smith's "I Love You Because." His greatest exposure came with the *Hee Haw* staff band in the early 80's. Eventually Chalker returned to Las Vegas, where health problems ended his steel playing. He was inducted into the Steel Guitar Hall of Fame in 1985.   —R.K.

Ray Charles

BORN: September 23, 1930
BIRTHPLACE: Albany, Georgia

With the release of *Modern Sounds in Country and Western Music* in 1962, singer/pianist Ray Charles introduced an important new audience to both country music and his remarkable vocal talents.

Born September 23, 1930, in Albany, Georgia, Ray Charles Robinson began losing his sight at age five, probably from glaucoma. From 1937 to 1945 he attended the Florida State School for the Blind in St. Augustine. During those years he was exposed to many types of music: big bands, boogie woogie, jazz, blues and country. The King Cole Trio and Charles Brown were among his favorite performers. The youth soon became skilled on piano and reeds; after leaving school he landed jobs throughout eastern and central Florida. His early performing years included a 1947 stint with a Tampa country band.

After moving to Seattle in 1948, he changed his name to avoid confusion with boxer Sugar Ray Robinson. As Ray Charles he made his first recordings with his McSon Trio, a group modeled on Nat "King" Cole's.

Relocating to Los Angeles in 1949, Charles continued recording for Swingtime and later toured with Lowell Fulsom. In 1952, New York-based Atlantic Records bought his contract. After several releases in a jump blues style, Charles developed the powerful, gospel-tinged vocals that set him apart from his rhythm and blues contemporaries. In the mid-50's, songs like "I Got a Woman" and "Hallelujah, I Love Her So" established Charles as a major recording artist; Atlantic also promoted him as a jazz instrumentalist. Charles flirted with country music during his tenure at Atlantic; Hank Snow's "I'm Moving On" was the follow-up single to his 1959 pop smash, "What'd I Say."

After moving to ABC Paramount in late 1959, Charles began broadening his audience by recording albums that appealed to a middle-of-the-road pop

audience. A single release of Hoagy Carmichael's "Georgia on My Mind" topped the *Billboard* pop charts in the fall of 1960. In 1962 Charles recorded an album of country songs using similar arrangements. *Modern Sounds in Country and Western Music* topped the album charts and spawned three Top Ten pop singles: "I Can't Stop Loving You," "You Don't Know Me" and "You Are My Sunshine." A second *Modern Sounds* volume was issued in 1963; virtually every ABC/Paramount album he made through the early 70's included one or two country standards. His 1966 cover of Buck Owens' "Cryin' Time" netted two Grammy awards.

In 1982 Charles signed with Columbia's Nashville division. He recorded four country albums during the next five years; *Friendship*—a 1985 collection of ten duets with different country performers—was a major success. A duet with Willie Nelson, "Seven Spanish Angels" topped the *Billboard* country chart in March 1985. A few more country recordings followed in the late 80's, along with additional rhythm and blues, jazz and pop recordings. In the 90's, he did a series of television commercials for Pepsi.   —D.S.

Hugh Cherry

BORN: October 7, 1922
BIRTHPLACE: Louisville, Kentucky

One of the nation's top country disc jockeys in the 50's and 60's, Hugh Cherry began as a staff announcer at WKAY, a 250-watt station in Glasgow, Kentucky. Stints in Chattanooga and Louisville followed. There,

at WKLO, he did his first country music program. Pee Wee King, based in Louisville, heard the show. Impressed by Cherry's style, free of the exaggerated rural dialect many country disc jockeys used at the time, King familiarized Cherry with the country music scene in Nashville and suggested Cherry go there. King's father-in-law/manager, J. L. Frank, helped Cherry sign on with WKDA in Nashville. From there, Cherry became a Nashville insider, with greater access to the stars than any other disc jockey at the time. He became close to many artists, attended their recording sessions and did the first major radio interviews with Lefty Frizzell, Bill Monroe and Hank Williams. Cherry briefly hosted WLW's *Midwestern Hayride* in 1956, then returned to Nashville's WSIX-TV as a newscaster.

After relocating to Los Angeles in 1960, he joined legendary KFOX radio, becoming one of four KFOX personalities inducted into the Country Music Disc Jockey Hall of Fame. He was a country music DJ for Armed Forces Radio and has written and lectured extensively.   —R.K.

Mark Chesnutt

BORN: September 6, 1963
BIRTHPLACE: Beaumont, Texas

This gifted neo-honky-tonk singer not only hails from the same region of southeast Texas (he was born in Beaumont, in 1963) as the great George Jones; he's also earned effusive praise from Jones. "I think this boy from Beaumont, Texas, is the real thing," Jones wrote in the liner notes for *Too Cold at Home*, Chesnutt's debut 1990  album. "Mark Chesnutt sings country music from his heart."

Chesnutt is himself the son of a Texas country musician: His father, Bob, put out several records on small labels in the 1960's and 70's. Chesnutt followed his old man's footsteps into the local honky tonks at age 15. By 17, he was appearing at such celebrated Texas clubs as Gilley's, in suburban Houston. And he released several records on regional Texas labels, Cherry and AXBAR Records.

Chesnutt had been playing the clubs for a decade or so and had made many empty-handed trips to Nashville before finally catching the ear of ace MCA producer/executive Tony Brown.

Chesnutt has proven a popular performer. He released two more albums since his debut (*Longnecks and Short Stories*, 1992, and *Almost Goodbye*, 1993) and by 1994 hit the Number One spot in the singles charts four times, with every one of his first 12 singles reaching the Top Ten. —B.A.

Lew Childre

BORN: November 1, 1901
BIRTHPLACE: Opp, Alabama
DIED: December 3, 1961

Few early country music entertainers were as versatile as "Doctor Lew'" Childre. While traveling with medicine shows and on vaudeville circuits during the 1920's, he polished his talents as a comedian, buck dancer, singer and instrumentalist.

Childre began his show business career in the early 20's as a singer and drummer with local bands. After completing pre-med studies at the University of Alabama, he joined the Milt Holbert tent show as a pop singer. Childre became interested in country music in 1925. Teaching himself to play Hawaiian guitar, he began performing cowboy songs and folk ballads for the Harley Sadler tent shows.

He began his radio career in 1929, performing as a solo or with Wiley Walker as "The Alabama Boys." By 1933 he was a popular entertainer and commercial pitchman over WWL in New Orleans. Between 1938 and 1944 he broadcast over XERA in Del Rio, Texas, WWVA in Wheeling, and WAGA in Atlanta. In 1945 he joined the Grand Old Opry. Between 1946 and 1948 he performed a comedy act with Dave "Stringbean" Akeman. Long-time WSM listeners fondly remember his long-running *Warren Paint Time* series. Childre left the Opry in 1959 to join the cast of *Jubilee U.S.A.*, ABC-TV's Saturday night country music show.

Childre made relatively few records during his 40-year career. In 1961 Starday recorded him in a relax-ing, informal setting with Cowboy Copas, Josh Graves and Junior Husky. The resulting album, *Old-Time Get-Together*, is a country music classic. Childre died December 3, 1961, soon after its release. —D.S.

Harry Choates

BORN: December 26, 1922
BIRTHPLACE: Rayne, Louisiana
DIED: July 17, 1951

Harry Choates has the distinction of being the first Cajun performer to truly break through to the country mainstream with his 1946 hit, "Jole Blon." He grew up, unschooled, in Port Arthur, Texas, where he learned fiddle, guitar and accordion, playing on the streets of the city. He did his first recording with Happy Fats and his Rayne-Bo Ramblers in 1940. He served briefly during World War II, then began pursuing a musical style that combined Cajun with the immensely popular Western swing and honky tonk that developed in Texas. "Jole Blon," recorded for Gold Star, was the result; sadly, Choates sold the rights to the song for some money and a fifth of whiskey.

It's been recorded dozens, perhaps hundreds of times, in the years since. A heavy drinker since his youth, he worked clubs around Louisiana and Texas, recording for labels including Macy's and Hummingbird. His drinking interfered severely with his performing and his personal life.

By 1950 he had divorced his wife and wound up being arrested for failing to provide support for her and their children. Arrested and jailed in Austin, the sudden withdrawal from alcohol proved too much, and he died in the jail (under circumstances that remain clouded to this day) before help could be summoned. A memorial heralding his music was finally erected at his grave in 1981. —R.K.

Guy Clark

BORN: November 6, 1941
BIRTHPLACE: Rockport, Texas

A poet/songwriter oftentimes associated with the Austin, Texas, music scene, Guy Clark was born in Rockport, Texas, on November 6, 1941. During his early years, he lived with his grandmother in a run-down hotel in West Texas. In fact, many of his songs, which are rich in dramatic flourish and keen detail, stem from the memories of people he encountered during those years.

Guy taught himself guitar as a youngster, played the Houston and Austin coffeehouse circuit, and in the 1960's moved to Los Angeles, where he earned a living by making dobros in the Dopyera brothers' guitar factory. He also began to concentrate heavily on songwriting.

In 1971 Guy and his wife, Susanna, a talented artist and songwriter herself, moved to Nashville, where Guy kept busy writing and pitching songs to publishing houses and recording studios. Slowly but surely, his reputation as an accomplished writer began to spread. Jerry Jeff Walker was the first to tap Guy's catalog, featuring "L.A. Freeway" and "That Old Time Feeling" on his first album. He also included Guy's "Desperadoes Waiting for a Train" on his critically-acclaimed *Viva! Terlingua*.

Other artists subsequently began mining Guy's songwriting talents, including The Earl Scruggs Revue, The Everly Brothers, Tom Rush, Rita Coolidge, The Highwaymen (Willie Nelson, Waylon Jennings, Kris Kristofferson and Johnny Cash), David Allen Coe, Ricky Skaggs, George Strait and Rodney Crowell.

Guy also released a number of solo albums for RCA, Warner Bros. and Elektra. Almost all of them, particularly *Old No. 1* (RCA, 1975) and *Boats to Build* (Elektra, 1992) received rave reviews, but failed to crack the charts. —R.P.

Roy Clark

BORN: April 15, 1933
BIRTHPLACE: Meherrin, Virginia

Roy Clark's reputation was growing long before he hosted *Hee Haw* and, ironically, the man who helped launch him had fired him years earlier. Clark, the son of a tobacco farmer, grew up in a highly musical family and learned guitar and banjo. He became such an outstanding banjoist that he won two national competitions in the late 1940's. By the early 50's he was working in Washington, D.C., as the guitarist for Jimmy Dean's Texas Wildcats, who did local TV. Dean, a demanding boss, admired his talent, but Roy's repeated lateness got him fired. For a time he worked with singer Marvin Rainwater and later with George Hamilton IV; he was also guitarist with Wanda Jackson's band in Las Vegas and did a stint with Hank Penny's Vegas unit, where he further developed his comedy skills. In 1963 he signed with Capitol Records, where he had a Top Ten record with "The Tips of My Fingers." Clark excelled in flashy guitar instrumentals, and in the 60's, Jimmy Dean, by then a mainstream star due to his successful ABC-TV show, guest-hosted TV's *The Tonight Show* and, letting bygones be bygones, invited Clark to appear. Playing on such shows boosted his visibility. In 1968 he signed

with Dot Records. A year later he became a charter member of the *Hee Haw* cast. He had a second Top Ten record with "Yesterday, When I Was Young," an American adaptation of a French pop hit. Clark's records generally incorporated heavy amounts of pop music, and as a result he never had sustained popularity as a country recording artist even during his peak years. In 1970 "I Never Picked Cotton" and "Thank God and Greyhound" were Top Ten. In 1972 "The Lawrence Welk-Hee Haw Counter-Revolution Polka" celebrated the success of both Welk's TV show and *Hee Haw*, by then in syndication after having been dropped by the major networks. His sole Number One was "Come Live With Me" in 1973. He won the CMA's Entertainer of the Year award that same year. His final Top Ten record was "If I Had to Do It All Over Again." On *Hee Haw* he moved between comedy, musical interludes with his old family band, including his father, and Western swing with Curly Chalker. He did albums with black blues and country musician Gatemouth Brown and joined the Opry in 1987. Clark recorded for Dot after it was absorbed by ABC and MCA. After leaving them, he recorded for Songbird, then Churchill, before moving on to Silver Dollar and Hallmark. Clark, based in Oklahoma, now performs actively in Branson. In 1994, Clark and jazz guitarist Joe Pass recorded an album of Hank Williams songs just before Pass' death.   —R.K.

Lee Clayton

BORN: October 29, 1942
BIRTHPLACE: Russellville, Alabama

This Alabama-born, east Tennessee-raised former jet fighter pilot—a minor figure in the 1970's Outlaw movement—was one of Nashville's most well-liked "Cosmic Cowboys" from that era. Clayton is the composer of one of the songs generally recognized as the inspiration for the entire 70's Outlaw/progressive country phase: His "Ladies Love Outlaws" was recorded by Waylon Jennings as the title cut to a 1972 album. Willie Nelson also had a Top Five hit with Clayton's "If You Can Touch Her at All" in 1978.

Clayton himself recorded several noteworthy but largely forgotten albums in the late 70's and early 80's—most notably *Border Affair*, in 1978. Featuring cryptic lyrics, surrealistic Dylanesque vocal performances, and startling imagery, his efforts were too far ahead of their time and out of the mainstream to penetrate the country charts, but nonetheless drew rave reviews from sources as far afield as *Rolling Stone Magazine*. "Silver Stallion," a particularly outstanding cut from *Border Affair*, was reprised by The Highwaymen (Nelson, Jennings, Johnny Cash and Kris Kristofferson) and became a minor hit in 1990.

Clayton, though unknown to U.S. audiences, became a minor star in parts of Europe in the early 80's and toured there sporadically. After a long hiatus from the music scene, he was recently spotted back on Music Row, still writing songs.   —B.A.

Jack Clement

BORN: April 5, 1931
BIRTHPLACE: Memphis, Tennessee

"Cowboy" Jack Clement (who has opened a couple of studios and founded at least one record label during his years in Nashville) is one of the most influential, eccentric and hard-to-read producers in country music history. He is a man who has had any number of great commercial successes over the years, even though he has often given commercial considerations a back seat to his strong-headed artistic and creative whims. Clement's amazing professional resume—as a producer, songwriter, music publisher, label head and occasional recording artist—hardly begins to reflect the true impact

his presence has had on modern country music.

Clement has, at one time or another, produced many of the biggest names in the music: Elvis Presley, Johnny Cash, Jerry Lee Lewis, Carl Perkins, Charley Pride (for whom he produced 19 consecutive Number One records), Charlie Rich, Waylon Jennings, The Glaser Brothers, Don Williams, John Prine and Stoney Edwards, among many others. He also wrote many of the signature songs from these same artists' early careers, including the Johnny Cash hits, "Ballad of a Teenage Queen" and "Guess Things Happen That Way"; Jerry Lee Lewis chart-toppers like "Fools Like Me" and "It'll Be Me"; and a long string of chart records for The Glaser Brothers, including "The Moods of Mary" and "Gone Girl." Clement was even present at the creation, so to speak, when Memphis rockabilly took the nation by storm in the mid-1950's. Working as Sam Phillips' sound engineer and some-time producer at Sun Records, he manned the control booth on many of the now immortal Cash, Lewis and Perkins recording sessions.

Nearly two decades later, Clement was a similar behind-the-scenes force and spiritual guiding light in the early 1970's Outlaw movement. He produced *Dreamin' My Dreams*, a vivid song collection that is not only one of Waylon Jennings' all-time best albums, but which also helped lay the groundwork for the free-wheeling musical philosophy which eventually coalesced into the Outlaw movement.

Clement hails from White Haven, Tennessee, a suburb of Memphis, where he was born in 1931. While stationed in Washington, D.C., as a member of the Marine Corps drill team, he formed his first group, a bluegrass band. Later, he was in a band called Buzz and Jack and The Bayou Boys that appeared on the Wheeling *WWVA Jamboree*, and at other notable country venues. Back in Memphis, in 1954, Clement attended Memphis State University on the G.I. Bill and made his production debut (using a home tape recorder he'd bought for a few bucks) with a record he cut on rockabilly singer Billy Lee Riley. He took the tape to Sun Records to have it mastered, and Sam Phillips liked what he heard so much that he not only released the record, but also hired Clement as a $90-a-week producer/engineer/go-fer. That proved to be the first chapter of Clement's long, wayward epic of a career, which has wound like a crazy yet important thread through the greater tapestry of post-1950's country music.

Clement's notable foray as a recording artist in his own right came in 1978, with *When I Dream*, an album which was hailed as a masterpiece by some critics and dismissed as faintly amusing by others.

The always verbose, eminently quotable, yet maddeningly elliptical Clement has emerged over the years as one of Nashville's most lovable arch-eccentrics— a figure who, because of his sheer devotion to the somewhat antiquarian notion of making music for the music's sake, has always had a way of inspiring even artists he didn't directly work with.

The Cowboy is still in residence today at his Nashville headquarters, The Cowboy Arms Hotel and Recording Spa, a mecca for many, and always a safe haven for beleaguered *Country Music Magazine* writers and editors. —B.A.

Vassar Clements

BORN: April 25, 1928
BIRTHPLACE: Kinard, South Carolina

Fiddler extraordinaire Vassar Clements was born in Kinard, South Carolina, on April 25, 1928. He started out as a session player, and soon developed a reputation not only for dazzling speed but for an uncanny ability to convey emotions ranging from jubilation to forlornness at the stroke of a bow. He has played in the bands of Bill Monroe, Jim and Jesse, Faron Young and The Earl Scruggs Revue, and, in the early 1970's, he turned a newer and younger audience on to bluegrass music when he was featured in Old and In the Way, a bluegrass outfit formed by the Grateful Dead's Jerry Garcia.

Some of Vassar's best studio work can be heard on John Hartford's album, *Aereo Plain*, and The Nitty Gritty Dirt Band's *Will the Circle Be Unbroken*. Clements continued performing and recording, and in 1993 produced an all-star tribute album to Merle Travis, on which Clements played and sang. —R.P.

Zeke Clements

BORN: September 6, 1911
BIRTHPLACE: Empire, Alabama
DIED: June 4, 1994

Zeke Clements' stardom came less from hit records than from songwriting and live appearances. His career began at age 17 on the WLS *National Barn Dance* in 1928. A stint with the Western stage act Otto Gray and His Oklahoma Cowboys followed before he came to the Grand Ole Opry as part of a group known as The Bronco Busters around 1933. He left the Opry some time later to work in Hollywood, where he made his most notable non-musical contribution by performing in films and doing the voice of "Bashful" in Walt Disney's *Snow White and the Seven Dwarfs*. By 1939 he'd returned to Nashville and began concentrating on a solo performing and songwriting career. He remained there through World War II, and though he himself had no hit records, his songs did considerably better. Bob Wills and Red Foley each had hit versions of Clements' anti-Axis anthem, "Smoke on the Water." His "Why Should I Cry," "Just a Little Lovin'" and "Somebody's Been Beating My Time" were all hits for Eddy Arnold in the late 40's and early 50's. Though Clements eventually left the Opry again, he remained an elder statesman of the music. He died after a long illness in 1994.   —R.K.

Patsy Cline

BORN: September 8, 1932
BIRTHPLACE: Winchester, Virginia
DIED: March 5, 1963

History books seem intent on determining whether the "Queen of Country Music" title should be bestowed on Kitty Wells or Patsy Cline, but it really shouldn't be a case of either/or—enough categories exist in country music that crowns can be bestowed without invading someone else's territory. And Patsy definitely charted new territories when she entered the country music scene.

Patsy danced into the entertainment world at age four, winning a tap dance contest in her hometown. As a youngster, she started singing on street corners, at churches and benefits—and a gift of a piano when she was eight sealed her destiny as an entertainer.

When her father left her mother, she quit school to clerk in a drugstore to help support the family but continued to sing wherever she could, including with name acts who performed in Winchester. It was Wally Fowler, who along with his Oak Ridge Quartet performed regularly with Roy Acuff's Nashville radio show, who convinced Patsy, then 15, to go to Nashville to audition for the Grand Ole Opry. Despite a job offer from Acuff, Patsy's money ran out, forcing her to return to Virginia where she resumed clerking and singing locally. During this period, in 1953, Patsy married Gerald Cline; the marriage lasted three years.

Patsy's style—pure country influenced greatly by pop artists Kay Starr and Patti Page—was too good to remain local talent forever. She began touring with Opry stars Faron Young and Ferlin Husky, appeared on the Grand Ole Opry, and—upon signing a recording contract with Four Star Records—released her first record, "A Church, a Courtroom and Then Good-Bye" in 1955.

But it wasn't until January 21, 1957, when Patsy appeared on the nationally televised *Arthur Godfrey's Talent Scouts*, singing a song she didn't want to sing, that she became the proverbial overnight success. The song, of course, was "Walkin' After Midnight," and after Patsy's rendition literally froze the applause meter, bringing the audience to its feet, Decca Records, Four Star's distributor, signed her and heavily promoted her.

"Walkin' After Midnight" was her first song to hit the charts (country Number Three, pop Number 12). Despite a couple of follow-ups, she retired shortly afterwards when she married her second husband, Charlie Dick, on September 15, 1957. Charlie and Patsy had two children, Julia and Randy, and for a couple of years, she was the happy housewife. In 1959, however, the bug bit her again, and she and the family moved to Nashville where, on January 9, 1960, Patsy became a member of the Grand Ole Opry.

After signing a new contract with Decca, Patsy released her first Number One record, "I Fall to Pieces." Seven more hits followed—"Sweet Dreams," "Crazy," "She's Got You," "Faded Love," "Leavin' on

Your Mind," "South of the Border" and "You Made Me Love You." The sessions that produced these hits were directed by Owen Bradley, whose name has become inextricably linked with hers, and who was responsible for helping her develop her instinctive talent for the Nashville Sound, more commercially viable in those years than twangy country.

"Crazy," written by Willie Nelson and considered one of Patsy's most famous songs, was recorded in 1961 while she was recuperating from a serious car accident that hospitalized her for over a month. It was two years later, on March 5, 1963, that Patsy was killed in another accident, when the plane in which she was returning to Nashville following a benefit concert in Kansas City crashed near Camden, Tennessee. Killed with her were Hawkshaw Hawkins, Cowboy Copas and Cline's manager, Randy Hughes.

In 1973, 20 years after her death, Patsy was the first woman elected to the Country Music Hall of Fame as a solo act. And more than 30 years after that fateful crash, Patsy's versions of "Crazy" and "I Fall to Pieces" still stand as benchmarks for a heartfelt country-pop song.

As of 1993, no fewer than 27 different reissues of compilations of her music were in print on CD; her records still outsell many contemporary hit-makers. More than 30 years after her death, her influence on country music remains immense, and her vocal talents stand as a benchmark against which those have come since are sooner or later measured.   —M.B.

Jerry Clower

BORN: July 28, 1926
BIRTHPLACE: Liberty, Mississippi

Country humorist Jerry Clower has been making records for MCA since 1970, when *Jerry Clower from Yazoo, Mississippi Talkin'* was released. To date, 23 of his story-telling albums have appeared on the label.

A Grand Ole Opry member since 1973 and former fertilizer salesman (he quips that some may say he's still in that business), Clower's humor focuses on the everyday doings of small-town life, all told in his trademark Mississippi dialect.

Favorite characters inhabiting his stories of Yazoo City include Marcel Ledbetter and the whole Ledbetter clan, along with his own family.   —G.F.

Hank Cochran

BORN: August 2, 1935
BIRTHPLACE: Isola, Mississippi

Garland Perry Cochran became one of the "new breed" of country songwriters of the 1960's, along with Mel Tillis and Willie Nelson.

Both parents died when he was young, and he grew up in Tennessee before taking off on his own. An uncle in New Mexico taught him guitar, and Cochran started writing his own material.

After moving to California around 1955, he played music in his spare time, eventually turning professional when he joined young country singer and (unrelated) guitarist Eddie Cochran.

Dubbed The Cochran Brothers, they were popular in suburban Los Angeles before Eddie left to become a rock 'n' roll legend. After a brief military stint, Hank Cochran landed a writer's contract with Pamper Music.

Within a year of his 1959 move to Nashville, he met another newcomer: Willie Nelson, just in from Texas. The two became close friends, and Cochran brought Willie to Pamper as a writer. Cochran also recorded without success for Liberty.

His songs were another matter. Among his achievements were Patsy Cline's "She's Got You," "Make the World Go Away" (a hit for both Ray Price and Eddy Arnold), Price's "Don't You Ever Get Tired of Hurting Me," Arnold's "I Want to Go With You" and George Jones' "You Comb Her Hair."

He also penned Jeannie Seely's 1966 hit "Don't Touch Me." Seely and Cochran later married.

Though Cochran never made it as a singer (despite stints on five different labels between 1962 and 1980), his association with Willie Nelson continued. The two of them dueted on "Ain't Life Hell," a minor chart record Cochran released on Capitol in 1978. He also wrote Willie's 1981 hit, "Angel Flying Too Close to the Ground."   —R.K.

David Allan Coe

BORN: September 6, 1939
BIRTHPLACE: Akron, Ohio

At first his wild clothing and prison-dominated past (most of it exaggerated) were part of his image. Coe was, however, a songwriter of depth. His first album, in the early 70's, was one trading on his wilder days, for Shelby Singleton's SSS label, known as *Penitentiary Blues*. It and its follow-up, *Requiem for a Harlequin*, did little for Coe's singing career. His writing, however, made him a substantial reputation. He wrote such hits as Tanya Tucker's early hit "Would You Lay With Me (In a Field of Stone)." The rise of the Outlaw era made his style of singing and songwriting more acceptable, and in 1972 he began recording for Columbia. His first album for that label, *The Mysterious Rhinestone Cowboy*, gained him some attention. His biggest hit, the Top Ten "You Never Even Called Me by My Name," came in 1975, followed by the 1976 Top 20 number, "Longhaired Redneck." Other singles didn't do as well, though he released a steady stream of albums. Johnny Paycheck had a Number

One single in 1977 with Coe's "Take This Job and Shove It." Coe made a substantial surge again in 1983 with the Hank Williams fantasy number, "The Ride," which peaked at Number Three, while in 1984 "Mona Lisa Lost Her Smile" remained at Number Two for two weeks. Early in 1985 "She Used to Love Me a Lot" made it to the Top 20. Coe's connection with Columbia lasted until 1987. Though not affiliated with a major label, Coe still performs and runs a museum in Branson, Missouri. —R.K.

Paul Cohen

BORN: November 10, 1908
DIED: April 1, 1971

This long-time Decca Records executive was instrumental in the rise of country music in the 40's and 50's and was also one of the first to realize Nashville's potential as a recording center. During his years producing for Decca (1945-58), Cohen recorded giants like Patsy Cline, Red Foley, Webb Pierce, Ernest Tubb, Kitty Wells, Red Sovine and many others. He was also a mentor to Owen Bradley, who would become one of the most influential producers in Nashville during 50's, 60's and 70's. Both Cohen and Bradley played a large part in shaping Decca (now part of MCA Records) into the powerhouse country label that it became. In 1958, he took over Coral Records. Cohen also served as the President of the Country Music Association and was elected to the Country Music Hall of Fame in 1976. —B.A.

Mark Collie

BORN: January 18, 1956
BIRTHPLACE: Waynesboro, Tennessee

Mark Collie's arrival on the country scene in the early 90's was somewhat obscured in the dust clouds of hype surrounding the rise of more celebrated newcomers like Travis Tritt, Hal Ketchum and Aaron Tippin. But if Collie, after three albums and a handful of chart records, has not yet achieved the sort of make-it-or-break-it hit success that the above-mentioned neophytes have enjoyed, it is certainly not for lack of talent, stage presence or consistently excellent songwriting. Collie possesses a growling, drawl-

ing, thoroughly magnetic vocal style and musical persona that is reminiscent of greats of yesteryear like Waylon Jennings and Johnny Cash.

One of six children, George Mark Collie hails from the little southwestern Tennessee town of Waynesboro which, significantly, is somewhere around midway between Memphis and Nashville—the twin Tennessee cities which have both influenced Collie's rockabilly—and honky tonk—informed style.

Before launching his own recording career with his fine 1989 MCA debut *Hardin County Line* (a startlingly impressive album, full of fine original material), Collie had already found success in Music City turning out hits for other artists like Aaron Tippin, Randy Travis and Marty Stuart. (He and Tippin cowrote "Something with a Ring to It," which, in 1990, became Collie's first chart single.)

Hardin County Line—as well as *Born and Raised in Black and White* and *Mark Collie*, his two subsequent albums—have proven Collie to be not only a favorite of the critics, but also a songwriter of unusual insight and vision, and a performer with uncommon fire and originality. Two of his biggest chart successes to date are "Even the Man in the Moon Is Crying" (Number Five in 1992) and "Born to Love You" (Number Six in 1993). *Unleashed*, his 1994 album, seemed to hold the momentum well.   —B.A.

Tommy Collins

Born: September 28, 1930
Birthplace: Oklahoma City, Oklahoma

Collins, the Bakersfield singer-songwriter immortalized in Merle Haggard's 1981 hit, "Leonard," was born Leonard Raymond Sipes, in Oklahoma City, Oklahoma, and grew up in a modest household. His father farmed and worked for the county. His mother wrote poetry, and that love of words was passed on to her son. He was playing guitar as a teenager, and by the time he began attending college in 1948, was also working on an Oklahoma City radio station. By age 21 he made his first records with his band, The Rhythm Okies. After a brief stay in the Marines, he wound up in Bakersfield, California, in 1952. Local singer Ferlin Husky helped him get his start, and by 1953 he had a Capitol recording contract (Ferlin played lead guitar on Collins' first session). He received his stage name at a Husky session when he brought someone the mixed drink known as a Tom Collins. His first big hit came in 1954 with the original novelty number, "You Better Not Do That" (with

Buck Owens on lead guitar). He followed it up with several other novelties including "Whatcha Gonna Do Now" (1954), "Untied" and "It Tickles" (1955), and wrote the Faron Young hit, "If You Ain't Lovin' (You Ain't Livin')." In the late 50's, he began studying for the ministry and served as a pastor until 1963. He still recorded for Capitol, with little success. After Johnny Cash helped him sign with Columbia in 1965, one single, "If You Can't Bite, Don't Growl," made the Top Ten in 1966. Problems with alcohol and drugs surfaced; meanwhile, in the late 60's, Collins, who'd been touring with his former sideman turned superstar Buck Owens, worked with Merle Haggard. In 1976 he moved to Nashville. That same year Merle Haggard had a Number One record with Collins' "The Roots of My Raising." The Collins-Haggard connection then yielded "Leonard," Haggard's Top Ten tribute to him in 1981. In the early 80's, Collins finally beat his drinking and today lives outside of Nashville. —R.K.

Jessi Colter

BORN: May 25, 1947
BIRTHPLACE: Phoenix, Arizona

Born Miriam Johnson, Jessi Colter took her stage name from her great-great uncle, Jesse Colter, who was a member of the notorious James Gang. The daughter of an auto mechanic and a Pentecostal minister, Jessi began her musical career as a pianist in her mother's church at the age of 11. When she was 16, she auditioned as a backup singer for rock 'n' roll guitarist Duane Eddy, and was subsequently chosen for the part. Jessi accompanied Eddy on a whirlwind tour of England, Germany, South Africa and other countries, and then married him in 1962.

In the mid-1960's, Jessi recorded an album produced by Eddy and Lee Hazelwood, but it didn't fare well commercially. It was at this time that she met country superstar Waylon Jennings during some recording sessions in Phoenix. In 1965, she divorced Eddy and moved to Nashville, where she landed a recording contract with RCA and cut the critically acclaimed album, *A Country Star Is Born* in 1966. Jessi's reputation as a first-class songwriter also began to spread, and artists such as Eddy Arnold, Dottie West, Anita Carter and Don Gibson were asking for her material. In 1968 she hooked up with Jennings again, and in 1969 the pair married.

In 1974, Jessi signed a solo contract with Capitol Records and scored big with "I'm Not Lisa"—a tune which was Number One on the country charts in addition to being a giant pop-crossover hit. In 1976, she recorded an album for RCA with Waylon, Willie Nelson and Tompall Glaser called *Wanted—The Outlaws*, which went platinum. The record also earned her a CMA Album of the Year award in 1976. Throughout the rest of the 1970's and into the 1990's, Jessi has continued recording and touring with Waylon. Their famous duet, "Storms Never Last," wa a Top 20 hit in 1981. (See also, Waylon Jennings.) —R.P.

Columbia Records/Epic Records

Founded in 1889, Columbia was one of the earliest companies to focus on the phonograph as an entertainment device rather than a dictation machine. The Columbia Graphophone Company recorded light operatic pieces, military bands and instrumental novelties. By 1900 it was the world's largest record company, with offices in New York and Europe.

In March 1924, not long after Fiddlin' John Carson's initial Okeh releases opened the market for authentic country music, Columbia recorded its first Southern rural artists: Gid Tanner and Riley Puckett. The following year the label launched a separate 15000-D series of "Old Familiar Tunes." Its primary artists included Gid Tanner and The Skillet Lickers, Riley Puckett, Charlie Poole and The North Carolina Ramblers, Tom Darby and Jimmie Tarlton, The Smith Sacred Singers, Al Craver a/k/a Vernon Dalhart, and The Leake County Revelers. The label issued 781 records in this series through November 1932. In October 1926, Columbia acquired the General Phonograph Corporation, owners of the Okeh label. Columbia and Okeh were operated independently through 1934.

After Columbia's British parent company filed for bankruptcy in November 1933, Columbia and Okeh were acquired by the American Record Company. ARC's country and western recordings then appeared on the budget-priced Vocalion, Sears Roebuck's Conqueror or one of five "chain-store" labels. Popular ARC artists during the 30's included Roy Acuff, Gene Autry, The Carter Family, The Chuck Wagon Gang, The Light Crust Doughboys, Lulu Belle and Scotty, The Hoosier Hot Shots, The Prairie Ramblers and Bob Wills and The Texas Playboys. The Columbia Broadcasting System purchased ARC in 1939. To resolve name ownership conflicts, CBS replaced Vocalion with a new Okeh label in June 1940.

Country and western music returned to the full-priced Columbia label in mid-1945. Between May 1948 and November 1956, Columbia issued its "folk" product under a 20000 numerical. This series symbolizes country music's "Golden Age." Mainly supervised by Art Satherley and Don Law, the series covered everything from the hard country of Wilma Lee and Stoney Cooper, Carl Butler, Jimmy Dickens, Carl Smith and Molly O'Day; to Texas honky tonk legend Floyd Tillman; country pop singers George Morgan and Billy Walker; the Western styles of Johnny Bond, Spade Cooley and Gene Autry; sacred singers The Chuck Wagon Gang, Stuart Hamblen and The Masters Family; bluegrass pioneers Bill Monroe, The Stanley Brothers and Flatt and Scruggs; Cajun singers Link Davis and Vin Bruce; and early rockabilly artists like The Collins Kids, Onie Wheeler, Jimmy Murphy, Johnny Horton and Sid King. Particularly noteworthy artists during this series were three influential singers whom Don Law produced at Jim Beck's Dallas studio between 1950 and 1956: Lefty Frizzell, Ray Price and Marty Robbins.

Many Columbia country artists enjoyed considerable popular crossover sales during the late 50's and early 60's, often through story or saga songs, which reflected the public's growing interest in folk music and topical songs. Horton's "When It's Springtime in Alaska" and "The Battle of New Orleans" established the format; other Columbia artists who followed Horton's lead were Marty Robbins, Stonewall Jackson, Jimmy Dean, Johnny Cash, Flatt and Scruggs and Claude King. Many of these artists successfully migrated into album sales.

In 1963 CBS hired songwriter/producer Billy Sherrill to supervise Nashville recordings for its Epic subsidiary. Sherrill's lush countrypolitan productions became an industry benchmark and helped develop Northern audiences for country music. Among the artists he nurtured were David Houston, Tammy Wynette and Tanya Tucker. In the early 70's he revitalized the careers of Charlie Rich, Bob Luman, Johnny Paycheck and, most notably, George Jones. By the end of the decade Sherrill was vice president and executive producer of CBS/Nashville.

Sherrill objected to Columbia's release of Willie Nelson's minimally produced concept album, *The Red-Haired Stranger*, in 1975. The album became an enormous critical and popular success and spawned two crossover hit singles. Sherrill's ambitious productions now seemed unfashionable; he left CBS in 1980 to become a free-lance producer. In 1981 CBS signed former bluegrass picker Ricky Skaggs. His first Epic album generated two Number One country hits and helped launch the New Traditionalist movement of the 80's. Another key Columbia artist of the era was Rosanne Cash; her breakthrough album, *Seven Year Ache*, was released in 1981. Other important Columbia/Epic artists of the 80's included John Conlee and veteran singers George Jones, Merle Haggard and Mickey Gilley.

Columbia marked the late 80's with hit recordings by other highly distinctive new artists, notably Ricky Van Shelton, The O'Kanes, Mary-Chapin Carpenter and Rodney Crowell. The label also garnered attention with The Highwaymen, a supergroup consisting of Johnny Cash, Waylon Jennings, Kris Kristofferson and Willie Nelson. Columbia and Epic, like the rest of the CBS Records empire, are now part of Sony Music.

—D.S.

Commander Cody & The Lost Planet Airmen

This important 1970's country rock act was the brainchild of Michigan art student George "Commander Cody" Frayne and other college kids in the Ann Arbor area. They became captivated by older country music, particularly honky tonk, rockabilly, Western swing and trucker songs. In part, they genuinely liked the music; in part, they loathed the psychedelic rock that then dominated the pop concert stages and airwaves. With key members including singers John Tichy and later Billy C. Farlow, guitarist Bill Kirchen and others, they moved to Berkeley, and garnered a following in the bars there. Farlow became the rockabilly singer; Kirchen handled ballads and Western swing; Frayne played boogie woogie piano and sang "Talking Blues" numbers like Tex Williams' "Smoke! Smoke! Smoke! (That Cigarette)." In 1971, after some good notices in the rock press, Paramount Records signed them. Musically, the addition of California Western swing steel player Bobby Black improved the band. They had a respectable pop hit in 1972 with a remake of Charlie Ryan's "Hot Rod Lincoln." They never had another hit but found great popularity in Austin, Texas, around the time the Outlaw movement began. In 1974 Warner Bros. signed them and tried in vain to give them more formal production. Success failed to materialize. The band broke up in the summer of 1976. Cody later revived the group, and various members continue to perform under various names.   —R.K.

Confederate Railroad

The rough and rowdy Southern rock/country hybrid of Confederate Railroad is a sound they established in more than ten years as a working band. Led by Danny Shirley on lead vocals, the boys paid their dues touring as the road band for both David Allan

Coe and Johnny Paycheck, as well as opening for Lynyrd Skynyrd. They eventually signed with Atlantic Records and released their self-titled album in 1992. It spawned six singles, including three Top Tens, "Jesus and Mama," "Trashy Women" and "Queen of Memphis." Their second album, *Notorious*, was released in 1994. In addition to Shirley, the line-up includes Mark Dufresne on drums, Michael Lamb on guitar, Chris McDaniel on keyboards, Wayne Secrest on bass and Gates Nichols on steel.   —G.F.

John Conlee

BORN: August 11, 1946
BIRTHPLACE: Versailles, Kentucky

Born in Versailles, Kentucky, in 1946, John Conlee was raised on a 400-acre Kentucky farm. He worked as a farmer, rock DJ and mortician before finally breaking into country music in the late 1970's. Blessed with a wry, mellow baritone (which stylistically weighs in somewhere  in the surprisingly narrow band between the raw, honky-tonk edge of a John Anderson and the humorous, irony-tinged growl of a Jimmy Buffett), Conlee broke into the charts in 1978 with "Rose Colored Glasses" (co-written with George Baber)—one of several immensely impressive original songs with which he made his mark. Other noteworthy Conlee hits include: "Lady, Lay Down" (his first Number One single, in 1978), "Backside of Thirty" (also an original), "Friday Night Blues," "I Don't Remember Loving You" and "Common Man."

Though Conlee's music sounded timely and sometimes even quasi-traditional in Nashville's pop-laden late 70's, by the mid-1980's his producer Bud Logan's fondness for lush strings and background singers had fallen out of sync with the times. Around the same time, Conlee ran out of steam as a songwriter. He suffered the added burden of simply being the wrong size and shape (short and round) to become a part of the long and lean "New Country" chic of the late 80's and early 90's.

Though Conlee no longer records for a major label, he does divide his time these days between farming his impressive spread in Tennessee and performing—occasionally on the Grand Ole Opry, where he's been a member since 1981, or at benefits for American farmers. —B.A.

Earl Thomas Conley

BORN: October 17, 1941
BIRTHPLACE: Portsmouth, Ohio

Earl Thomas Conley was one of the most prolific and consistent singer/songwriters of the 1980's, scoring nearly 20 Number One hits and selling more than two million albums.

Born in Portsmouth, Ohio, on October 17, 1941, Earl was exposed to music at an early age through his father—a hard-working railroad man who played traditional country music on guitar and banjo. Earl also took a liking to the silky-smooth croonings of Nat King Cole as well as the raucous rock 'n' roll of Jerry Lee Lewis and Elvis Presley and the country stylings of Jim Reeves.

When he was 18, Earl enlisted in the Army and was stationed in Germany. Upon his release, he decided that music was the career he wanted. Earl managed to earn a living by painting, sculpting and working in a steel mill in Ohio, but in his spare time, he'd write songs and then commute back and forth to Nashville to try to sell them. In 1974, he moved to Huntsville, Alabama, where he began to get some steady club dates, then moved on to Nashville. His big break came in 1975 when Mel Street recorded his "Smokey Mountain Memories," which became a Top Ten hit. The following year, Conway Twitty hit the top of the charts with another of Earl's tunes, "This Time I've Hurt Her More Than She Loves Me."

Earl continued to work hard at the music business, churning out a series of singles for a small independent label. The persistence paid off. In 1978, he was signed by Warner Bros., and in 1979, he scored his biggest hit so far with "Dreamin's All I Do." To avoid confusion with country artists John Conlee and Con Hunley, Earl took the name Thomas as his middle name. In 1980, Earl Thomas moved to the smaller Sunbird label and scored his first Number One hit with "Fire and Smoke." In 1981, he signed with RCA and began a fruitful association with the label that lasted nearly 12 years. During this period, he topped the charts with almost every release, most notably "Somewhere Between Right and Wrong" (1982), "Your Love's on the Line" (1983), "Holding Her and Loving You" (1983), "Angel in Disguise" (1984) and "Right from the Start" (1987).

In 1990, Earl Thomas underwent throat surgery, which forced him to put his singing career on hold for nearly two years. Conley is no longer on a major label. —R.P.

Spade Cooley

BORN: February 22, 1910
BIRTHPLACE: Grand, Oklahoma
DIED: November 23, 1969

Donnell Clyde Cooley grew up in rural Oklahoma. One-quarter Cherokee Indian, he learned classical fiddle and cello in an Indian school. His card-playing prowess earned him the nickname of "Spade," and he worked with various musical units on the West Coast in the 1930's before moving to Holly-

wood. There, he played music and did movie stunt work. By 1942 he had formed his own band with an unconventional, sophisticated, Hollywood Western swing sound that featured classical harp, tightly arranged fiddles (a product of his classical training), smooth vocalist Tex Williams and gifted teenage steel guitarist Earl "Joaquin" Murphey. Signed to Columbia, Cooley had hits in 1945 with "Shame on You" (his biggest), "A Pair of Broken Hearts," "I've Taken All I'm Gonna Take From You," "Detour" and "You Can't Break My Heart" (1946) and "Crazy Cause I Love You" (1947). A difficult employer, Cooley fired Tex Williams in June 1946, and most of the band went with Tex. Though Cooley's reorganized band boasted full horn sections, their RCA recordings went nowhere. Though Cooley did some national tours, he remained primarily a West Coast act. His KTLA-TV variety show, *The Hoffman Hayride*, which premiered in 1948, was one of L.A.'s top TV attractions until the early 50's. Cooley, who suffered his first heart attack in 1950, was semi-retired by the mid-50's though he recorded for Decca and did a final album for Raynote in 1959. Living north of Los Angeles, he focused on real estate development. His wife was Ella May Evans, a former singer in his band. On April 3, 1961, as the marriage collapsed, a drunken Cooley beat Ella May to death. After his arrest and conviction, he served his time at California's Vacaville medical facility, where he became a model prisoner. He often performed for the inmates, and was about to be paroled when he performed at a Sheriff's benefit. After his performance, he dropped dead of a heart attack. —R.K.

Coon Creek Girls

This female quartet was founded by Lily May Ledford, a Kentucky native who began playing music as a child. WLS *National Barn Dance* promoter John Lair picked her out of a group including her sister Rosie and a brother in 1936. At WLS Ledford worked solo and with other acts for a time before Rosie came north again in 1937. By then, Lair had decided to form his own barn dance program, the *Renfro County Barn Dance*, over WLW Radio in Cincinnati. He built a female band around Lily May and Rosie by adding teenaged fiddler Evelyn ("Daisy") Lange and mandolinist-guitarist Esther ("Violet") Koehler. Lair himself

named the group. They debuted over WLW on October 9, 1937, and by 1939 were popular enough to be invited to the White House. The group began to disintegrate by late 1939 when Koehler and Lange left. Lily and Rosie Ledford remained, adding their younger sister Minnie. At one point the two fragments of the act each used the name Coon Creek Girls with new members. The Ledfords continued at *Renfro Valley* through World War II and afterward, though family responsibilities sometimes warranted temporary replacements for the band. Martha Carson and her sister Mattie O'Neil worked for a time as Coon Creek Girls. The Ledfords still performed occasionally after they retired in 1957. Of the original group, only Evelyn Lange Perry remains alive. —R.K.

Wilma Lee & Stoney Cooper

BORN: Stoney, October 16, 1918, Harman, West Virginia
   Wilma Lee, February 7, 1921, Valley Head, West Virginia
DIED: Stoney, March 22, 1977

Wilma Lee Cooper (born Wilma Leigh Leary, in Valley Head, West Virginia, in 1921) rose to country fame with her husband Stoney (born Dale Troy Cooper, in Harman, West Virginia, in 1918) on various country radio stations, including WWVA, and later as members of The Grand Ole Opry, which they joined in 1957.

 Both the Coopers were heavily steeped in rural

In the coming years, in Nashville, the Coopers found continued success as recording artists—both jointly and separately. The two of them continued recording and performing, almost up until the time of Stoney's death, in 1977. Wilma Lee, as of the mid-1990's, was still making appearances on the Grand Ole Opry.   —B.A.

Cowboy Copas

BORN: July 15, 1913
BIRTHPLACE: Adams County, Ohio
DIED: March 5, 1963

Nearly every biography on Lloyd "Cowboy" Copas mentions his death in the plane crash that claimed Patsy Cline, Hawkshaw Hawkins and Patsy's manager Randy Hughes (Copas' son-in-law). Most biographies note that Copas was an authentic Oklahoma-born cowboy. Actually, he was born and raised on an Ohio farm and started in music as a 14-year-old guitarist with The Hen Cacklers, a string band. In

1929 he began working with Midwest promoter Larry Sunbrock's stage show. Copas later worked in West Virginia before moving to WLW's *Boone County Jamboree* in the late 30's. Pee Wee King discovered him in 1940. At that point, Copas concocted the Oklahoma cowboy story. In 1944 he briefly replaced Eddy Arnold as vocalist in King's Golden West Cowboys. He signed with King records in 1945, and his first hits were "Filipino Baby" and "Tragic Romance," the latter reaching Number Four on the *Billboard* charts in 1946. Copas soon joined the Grand Ole Opry cast and in early 1948 had hits with "Signed, Sealed and Delivered" and Pee Wee King's "Tennessee Waltz." His 1949 hits included "Tennessee Moon," "Breeze" and "I'm Waltzing with Tears in My Eyes," George Morgan's "Candy Kisses" and "Hangman's Boogie." His 1951 duet with daughter Cathy, "The Strange Little

musical traditions as children. Stoney learned mountain music and traditional Elizabethan ballads from his family and was adept on both fiddle and guitar by his early teens. Wilma Lee (who earned a degree in banking from Davis-Elkins College) began singing gospel music with her parents and two sisters at a very early age. After the Leary Family won a local talent contest, Stoney was hired as their $10-a-week fiddle player. The Learys' local popularity spread, and they eventually signed on with the prestigious *WWVA Wheeling Jamboree* in the early 1940's.

Wilma Lee and Stoney married in 1941 and first began singing as a duet team called The Musical Pals, while still members of The Leary Family. By the mid-1940's, they were out on their own, performing on radio stations as far flung as Chicago and Great Plains, Nebraska. By the late 1940's, they resurfaced on the *WWVA Jamboree*, and were signed to Columbia Records in 1949. A handful of the rustic songs they recorded in the next decade—"Come Walk With Me" (a top five single in 1958), "Big Midnight Special" (which hit Number Four in 1959), "There's a Big Wheel" (a Number Three in 1959), "This Old House" (1960), "Wreck on the Highway" (a Top Ten in '61), "Sunny Side of the Mountain," "West Virginia Polka," "Thirty Pieces of Silver" and "Legend of the Dogwood Tree" among them—have since become country and gospel standards.

Girl," also did well. He even had a pop hit with "Don't Leave My Poor Heart Breaking," a duet with pop singer Rosalind Patton. backed by Elliot Lawrence's orchestra (the label referred to him as "Lloyd Copas"). In 1952 he had one hit with "Tis Sweet to Be Remembered." After leaving King he briefly joined Dot in 1956. After signing with Starday in 1960, "Alabam'," a reworking of an old Frank Hutchison number titled "Coney Isle," remained Number One on the country charts for 12 weeks. He repeated the success in 1961 with the singles, "Flat Top" and "Sunny Tennessee." At Christmas of 1962 he returned to the Evergreen Baptist Church near his birthplace and sang the song "Goodbye Kisses," which Starday planned to issue that spring. After his death in 1963, the song broke into the Top 20. —R.K.

Helen Cornelius

BORN: December 6, 1941
BIRTHPLACE: Hannibal, Missouri

Helen Cornelius was born near Hannibal, Missouri, on December 6, 1941, and grew up listening to the Grand Ole Opry. In high school, she formed a vocal trio with her sisters, and later, as a soloist, appeared on the *Ted Mack Amateur Hour*. In the late 1960's, she established herself as a songwriter. She is best known for her work on Jim Ed Brown's television show, *Nashville on the Road* (1976-1980). Their Top Ten country singles include "I Don't Want To Have to Marry You" (1976), "Saying Hello, Saying I Love You, Saying Goodbye" (1976), "If the World Ran Out of Love Tonight" (1978), "Lying in Love With You" (1979), "Fools" (1979) and "Morning Comes too Early" (1980). Shortly after the last hit, Brown unceremoniously fired her from his show; later solo efforts for Elektra and Dot led nowhere. In 1988 the team reunited for a comeback tour, and in later years occasionally did guest shots on the Grand Ole Opry. —S.W.

Country All Stars

When Chet Atkins moved to Nashville in 1950, he became part of a select group of Nashville session musicians. These individuals played on many of the growing number of recording sessions held in various Nashville studios.

Trading on his close relationship with RCA, Atkins occasionally recorded both vocals and instrumentals with various groupings of these players—including himself, Homer (Haynes) & Jethro (Burns), Jerry Byrd and others—which were often produced by Steve Sholes, from 1952 to 1955.

Much of the All Stars' repertoire included vintage pop and jazz tunes with Homer or Jethro occasionally adding a vocal.

Two of their most memorable numbers were "Fiddle Sticks" and "Fiddle Patch," featuring session fiddler Dale Potter.

None of the records were hits, but all revealed the versatility of these musicians. Bear Family records later reissued the complete All Stars recordings, which had been sought after by fans of country instrumentals for years. —R.K.

Country America

Founded in October 1989, *Country America Magazine* is owned by Country America Corporation, a joint venture between the Meredith Corporation (*Ladies' Home Journal, Better Homes and Gardens, Successful Farming, Golf for Women* and other magazines) based in Des Moines, Iowa, The Nashville Network and Group W Marketing.

At the same time Meredith Corporation was entertaining the idea of starting a new magazine devoted to country life, The Nashville Network (TNN) was interested in publishing a program guide to publicize its cable television channel.

TNN's advertising agency, Decker, Decker & Freas, knew of Meredith's intentions, and suggested that TNN pitch Meredith the idea of incorporating a program guide within the new publication. The pitch worked, and so *Country America* was born. The lifestyle magazine features a mix of articles dealing with country entertainment, country living, travel, cooking, heritage, decorating and fashion . —R.P.

Country Gentlemen

One of bluegrass' most distinguished groups with a long history that began in 1957, The Country Gentlemen have achieved much over the years. They were the catalyst for the growing bluegrass scene around Washington, D.C., which remains strong today. The original members were Charlie Waller, John Duffy, Bill Emerson and Eddie Adcock. The lineup eventually changed as new members joined. The group also played an enormously important role in expanding the bluegrass repertoire by adding folk songs, material by Bob Dylan and songs from mainstream honky tonk artists like Lefty Frizzell, a trend that continues in bluegrass today. Over the years, their alumni have also included J.D. Crowe, John Starling and Ricky Skaggs, and they've recorded extensively for various labels.—R.K.

Country Music Association (CMA)

Founded in 1958 by an influential group of recording artists and country music executives (publishers Wesley Rose, Jim Denny and Jack Stapp, promoters Hubert Long and Connie B. Gay, and BMI executive Frances Preston, producers Steve Sholes, W.D. Kilpatrick, Ken Nelson and Don Pierce, artists Mac Wiseman and Cindy Walker and veteran WSM director Harry Stone, among others), the Country Music Association has always had a single goal: the worldwide promotion of country music as a viable commercial and popular art form. The membership of this suit-and-tie trade organization has, since its founding, grown from less than 250 to more than 10,000.

The CMA (as it is commonly called), which was, for years, under the leadership of executive director Jo Walker-Meador (who started out as the CMA's first full-time employee—a glorified secretary) has endeavored by many different means to raise the cultural profile of country music and enhance its overall market share. During the 60's this mainly meant expanding country's radio market, something which the CMA did brilliantly. In 1961, there were just 81 fulltime country radio stations in the U.S. But through lavish and extensive promotions of all kinds, the CMA managed to expand the number to 606 stations as of 1969.

One of the CMA's most ambitious brainchilds was the Country Music Hall of Fame and Museum (see separate entry), which is now an independent organization. However, the real centerpiece of the CMA's various programs is its annual country music awards ceremony—the CMA awards are unquestionably the most prestigious awards given in the field of country music (the West-Coast based annual Academy of Country Music Awards being second, in terms of both credibility and prestige). The annual CMA Awards program was initiated in 1967, and was televised nationally a year later, under the sponsorship of Kraft. Today, the CMA Awards ceremonies, broadcast from the Opryland Theater complex, are the most important—and glitzy—event in country music. The CMA's role in the growth of country music's popularity in recent decades has been significant. That said, if the organization has one glaring fault, it has been its tendency to embrace sheer growth in terms of market share, even at the expense of the soul and integrity of the music itself. At times, the CMA has seemed too eager to put commercial considerations ahead of artistic ones: to downplay traditional country's innate twang in favor of the more urbane crooning of a John Denver or an Olivia Newton-John, and to replace the old-time hay bale and blue jeans imagery with something more sleek and stylish.

Jo Walker-Meador retired in 1991, with Ed Benson taking the reins of the organization. That same year, the CMA moved into a new building on Music Row.
—B.A.

Country Music Foundation/ Hall of Fame

Since it first opened its doors to the public in 1967, The Country Music Hall of Fame and Museum has been one of the most popular tourist attractions in Nashville. Before Branson, Missouri, stole Nashville's thunder as the nation's leading country music mecca, the Hall of Fame played host to more than half a million tourists a year.

Besides its extensive films, displays and exhibits devoted to country music—most notably the Hall of Fame and the Walkway of the Stars—the museum also houses the world's most extensive library and research facility devoted exclusively to country music. The entire complex is operated by the Country Music Foundation, a non-profit, educational umbrella organization that was chartered in 1964 to preserve the history of country music and to further research its rich history.

The Hall of Fame itself, originally established in 1961 by the Country Music Association, is a shrine and memorial to many of the most influential figures in country music history; and as such, this pantheon of greats is fundamental to country music's abiding sense of its own history and identity.

Fittingly, Jimmie Rodgers, songwriter/publisher Fred Rose and Hank Williams were the first inductees into the Hall of Fame, in 1961. As of 1994, 53 more members have been inducted—most recently

George Jones and Willie Nelson. Selections to the Hall of Fame are arrived at through a rather involved nominating and voting process overseen by the CMA. Each year a field of 10 to 20 candidates is presented by a Hall of Fame nominating committee (composed of 12 knowledgeable CMA members and industry leaders) to an anonymous panel of 300 CMA members known as the Hall of Fame electors, who are selected by the CMA's board of directors. The electors then winnow the list down to five finalists. In a second balloting, the 300 electors then vote on the list of five to come up with the winner for that year. Special measures are taken to ensure that Hall of Fame inductees include not only musicians, but also executives and other figures who have had a massive impact in shaping the modern country record industry.   —B.A.

Country Music Magazine

Country Music Magazine was founded by the partnership of Russell D. Barnard, Jack Killion and Spencer Oettinger. The magazine was conceived by Russ Barnard, who had grown up a fan in Texas and had been an executive at CBS Records in New York from 1963 to 1970. The first issue was published in New York City in September 1972.

The editorial goal was to produce a magazine of comprehensive coverage of the people who write, record and perform country music, aimed at the most serious, knowledgeable fan. Through interviews, profiles, essays and critical reviews, *Country Music* covers current country music while always helping keep the rich historical connections alive.

In publishing terms it was an instant success, reaching 200,000 circulation in its first year—more than its main predecessors *Country Song Roundup* and *Music City News* combined. Most notably it was critically acclaimed by Nashville's professional community. First

among those to praise *Country Music* was Johnny Cash—an icon then and an icon 22 years later—who said in March 1973, "It's the best the country music business ever had." On the 10th Anniversary, with circulation over 400,000, Cash said, "*Country Music* has set a new standard for music publications." On the 20th Anniversary, with circulation over 600,000, Cash added, "The best report I've ever seen...."

Cash, Tom T. Hall, Tammy Wynette, Willie Nelson, Marty Stuart and other Nashville insiders have shown their connection by writing articles for *Country Music*. Meanwhile *Country Music*'s regular writers and editors were quickly recognized for their knowledge and talent. The core group which has maintained the magazine's high editorial quality over 20 years includes Bob Allen, Michael Bane, Patrick Carr, Rich Kienzle and John Morthland.

In 1984, the organization launched a membership organization, the Country Music Society of America (CMSA), to provide members with a vehicle for sharing news, views and reviews with each other relative to their common interest in country music and its history through the *CMSA Newsletter*. By 1994 membership had passed 200,000. In 1991, the organization established another association, The American Academy for the Preservation of Old-Time Country Music. More than 80,000 have joined. The Academy publishes *The Journal of the American Academy for the Preservation of Old-Time Country Music*, devoted strictly to covering country music roots and history.
—R.D.B.

Country Music Television

Taking to the airwaves on March 6, 1983 (one day before The Nashville Network), Country Music Television (CMT) focused only on showing music videos, a difficult task in those days as few country artists were making videos and industry involvement was at a minimum. Upon realizing the potential of the medium (MTV's success was quite convincing), record companies were soon cooperating. The network, purchased by Gaylord Entertainment (owners of The Nashville Network) in 1991, now reaches about 25 million households. In October 1992, CMT Europe was launched. CMT attracts a younger audience than TNN and is credited with helping launch new artists.
—G.F.

Country Song Roundup

The oldest country music fan magazine still in publication, *Country Song Roundup* was established in 1949 by Charlton Publications of New York (and later, Derby, Connecticut), which had also founded *Hit Parade* seven years earlier.

Over the years, *Country Song Roundup*'s mainstay has not only been its breezy, upbeat feature stories on country artists and songwriters, but also its inclusion of the lyrics of many popular country songs of the day.

Bill Anderson (who has written a question-and-answer column for the magazine for years) is one of several country personalities who have been associated with the publication. *Country Song Roundup* was acquired by the Peretta Media Corporation in the late 1980's.
—B.A.

Billy "Crash" Craddock

BORN: June 16, 1939
BIRTHPLACE: Greensboro, North Carolina

Born June 16, 1939, in Greensboro, North Carolina, Billy "Crash" Craddock acquired his famous nickname as a running back on his high school football team.

He was playing at a local club when he was spotted by a Columbia talent scout in 1959. Craddock went to Nashville and cut a number of heavily pop-influenced singles that fell flat.

Within two years he was back in North Carolina, working construction by day and playing honky tonk bars at night.

It was 1968 before Craddock got his second chance. Dale Morris, a traveling pharmaceuticals salesman, was so impressed with Craddock that he spent two years trying to form a record company to record Billy's songs.

Two years later, the infant Cartwheel Records released Craddock's first hit single, "Knock Three Times." The song made it all the way to Number One and paved the way for two more hits, "Ain't Nothin' Shakin'" and "Dream Lover." Craddock's success attracted the attention of ABC Records, which bought out Cartwheel for no other reason than to get a piece of Billy Craddock.

Craddock went on to score a number of hits in the mid-1970's including "Rub It In," "Ruby, Baby" in 1974, "Easy as Pie" (1975) and "Broken Down in Tiny Pieces" (1976). By 1977 he had placed 17 singles in the country Top Ten for ABC/Cartwheel.

Billy and The Dream Lovers moved to Capitol in 1977. At that point the band consisted of guitarist

Charlie Walker, bassist Robert Yates, mandolinist James Gondreaux and banjoist Richard Smith. They cut an album called *Billy Crash Craddock*, which was produced by Dale Morris. The debut single, "I Cheated on a Good Woman's Love," became Craddock's 18th Top Ten hit. They went on to score a number of lesser hits for Capitol, including "If I Could Write a Song as Beautiful as You," "Robinhood" and "My Mama Never Heard Me Sing," all of which made the Top 30 in 1979.

He remained on Capitol until 1983, resurfacing on Atlantic Records in 1989, with little chart success. —M.B.

Floyd Cramer

BORN: October 27, 1933
BIRTHPLACE: Samti, Louisiana

Born in Samti, Louisiana, on October 27, 1933, songwriter/pianist Floyd Cramer was a principal architect of the now-infamous "Nashville Sound." Along with guitarists Chet Atkins, Grady Martin, Hank Garland and saxophonist Boots Randolph, Cramer shares the credit—or blame—for devising the smooth blend of pop and honky tonk that attracted mainstream audiences to country in the 1950's and 60's.

Cramer learned piano by ear as a child and got his start on Shreveport's *Louisiana Hayride*, playing in the band of future country star Webb Pierce. A highly regarded session player, he soon attracted the attention of Chet Atkins, who asked him if he could produce the slip-note sound heard in the songs of New York songwriter Don Robertson for a Hank Locklin session. The technique, which emulates the twangy guitar sound of Mother Maybelle Carter, was a hit with fans: Locklin's single made it to Number One and slip-note became an almost ubiquitous fixture of country music for over a decade.

Cramer moved to Nashville in 1955 and soon joined the Grand Ole Opry. He had his first moderately successful pop hit in 1958, "Flip, Flop and Bop." He went on to record a long string of crossover hits, beginning with "Last Date" in 1960. He toured extensively throughout the 60's and 70's, both as a soloist and as a featured performer with major symphony orchestras. By the late 1970's, he had over 40 RCA albums to his credit. In 1974 Cramer was awarded the Golden Metronome award for his lifelong contributions to Music City.

—M.B.

The Crook Brothers

One of Judge Hay's original "hoedown bands" that helped start the Grand Ole Opry, The Crook Brothers had a distinctive sound that was built around leader Herman Crook's driving harmonica playing. When the band first played on the Opry, in the summer of 1926, it featured Herman and his brother Matthew playing twin harmonica leads on pieces like "Love Somebody" and "Going Across the Sea." Matthew quit in 1927, and Herman replaced him with banjoist-singer Lewis Crook, who was, by coincidence, no relation whatsoever. The band participated in the very first Nashville recording session—for Victor—in 1928, but spent the rest of its time content to do radio work. Sparked by a series of fine fiddlers that included Floyd Ethridge and Ed Hyde, the band remained intact until June 10, 1988, when Herman passed away. Their only other recordings were part of an album for Starday in 1963.

—C.W.

Crossover

The term "crossover" is used throughout this encyclopedia. It refers to country hits that have "crossed over" to become successes in other fields, most notably pop music. Record buyers were far more segregated in previous decades than today. Pop music fans bought records by pop artists, country records by country singers, rhythm and blues by black performers and so on. That began to change when pop record buyers found appeal in certain specific country records. Some of the first big country crossover hits came in the 1940's and included Al Dexter's "Pistol Packin' Mama," Elton Britt's "There's A Star-Spangled Banner Waving Somewhere" and Tex Williams' "Smoke! Smoke! Smoke! (That Cigarette)," which enjoyed strong sales and chart success in the pop field. Occasionally in the 1940's black jazz numbers even crossed over to become hits among country record buyers, most notably The Nat "King" Cole Trio's "Straighten Up and Fly Right" in 1944 and jazz bandleader Benny Carter's "Hurry! Hurry!" became hits among country record buyers. When the Nashville Sound came into being in the late 50's, one of the goals was to produce country records that would appeal enough to pop fans to "cross over." Over time this caused controversy, fans and some in the industry feeling that records should cross over on their own merit, not because the records were "tailored" by producers to do so. In the 90's Garth Brooks and Billy Ray Cyrus epitomize a new, more rock-oriented form of crossover through their success at attracting pop fans, reflected in more accurate measures of album sales. And the controversy over crossover's merits continues. (See also, Nashville Sound, Urban Cowboy.)

—R.K.

Alvin Crow

BORN: September 29, 1950
BIRTHPLACE: Oklahoma City, Oklahoma

Born in Oklahoma, Alvin Crow briefly rose to prominence as part of the vital live music scene in Austin, Texas, that attracted national attention in the wake of the 1970's Outlaw movement in country music.

Crow is best known for fronting The Pleasant Valley Boys, a noteworthy Austin-based Western swing

band which had a couple of national chart records ("Yes She Do, No She Don't," "Crazy Little Mama at My Front Door," "Nyquil Blues") in 1977. Crow also played a significant role in the late 70's and early 80's Western swing revival; and for a while, he headed other impressive, if short-lived ensembles, including The Broken Spoke Cowboys and The Neon Angels. Crow has had continued success through the years recording for various independent Texas-based labels, briefly worked with Doug Sahm, and has even made a few minor film appearances.   —B.A.

J.D. Crowe

BORN: August 27, 1937
BIRTHPLACE: Lexington, Kentucky

This revered progressive bluegrass banjo player for years led The New South, an influential newgrass (progressive bluegrass) ensemble that not only made some fine music, but was also a training ground for other newgrass notables like Ricky Skaggs, Tony Rice,

Larry Rice, Jerry Douglas and future country star Keith Whitley.

Crowe grew up near Lexington, Kentucky, listening not only to bluegrass, but to blues and rock 'n' roll, as well. When he was 13, Flatt & Scruggs began making regular appearances around Lexington; he became so fascinated with the banjo that a Saturday night seldom passed when he wasn't at one of their shows. By 1956, he was in Detroit, playing banjo with Jimmy Martin. As the years passed, Crowe developed a distinctive style of his own by infusing his banjo picking with aspects of blues guitar technique and fusing his country-rock influences with Earl Scruggs-inspired bluegrass.

After playing around Lexington, Crowe, by now heading his own band, began recording for Starday in 1973 as J.D. Crowe and The New South. Mandolinist Doyle Lawson and guitarist Tony Rice and his brother, mandolinist Larry Rice were just a few notables who passed through Crowe's band during this era. Around this same time, Crowe also followed the lead of the Osborne Brothers and injected his evolving bluegrass style with electric instrumentation.

Crowe's 1975 album, *J.D. Crowe and The New South*, featured the rather stellar line-up that by now comprised his band: Tony Rice on guitar, Ricky Skaggs on vocals/mandolin/guitar and Jerry Douglas on dobro. It was Crowe's first album for Rounder, and it turned out to be one of the most influential bluegrass albums of the decade. It also established Rounder as a leader in the bluegrass field.

It's safe to say that over the years, no two albums by the always experimental, always innovative Crowe have sounded alike. With Keith Whitley as his lead singer during the late 70's and early 80's, Crowe recorded two more remarkable albums. *My Home Ain't in the Hall of Fame* was a wonderful fusion of bluegrass and honky tonk, featuring Whitley singing a few of his favorite Lefty Frizzell songs to a largely acoustic bluegrass accompaniment. *Somewhere Between*, which followed a year or two later, was almost a straight honky tonk album, and really proved the stepping stone for Whitley's segue from bluegrass to mainstream country.

In 1981 Crowe teamed with Tony Rice, Doyle Lawson (of the group Quicksilver), fiddler Bobby Hicks, and bassist Todd Phillips to make another immensely influential bluegrass "supergroup" (or, as one critic dubbed it "supergrass") album, titled simply, *The Bluegrass Album*.   —B.A.

He recorded several critically acclaimed albums for Warner Bros.—*Ain't Livin' Long Like This, What Will the Neighbors Think, Rodney Crowell*, and a fourth one that was never released—in the late 70's and very early 80's. Yet no hits were forthcoming.

It was not until the late 1980's, when he finally took on his former band member-turned-producer, Tony Brown, as his co-producer, that Crowell had his first real chart success, with an album titled *Diamonds & Dirt*.

This, his 1988 breakthrough, resulted in five consecutive Number One singles (all of them written by Crowell) and won a Grammy award. He's since followed with *Keys to the Highway* (1989), *Life Is Messy* (1992) and *Let the Picture Paint Itself* (1994), which are not only some of the most intelligent, but also simply some of the best albums made in the last decade.

The thing that has always set Crowell apart and given him his added creative edge is his brilliant imagination and incessant creative exploration. Hank Williams, Guy Clark, artist Georgia O'Keefe, jazz master Miles Davis, author Raymond Carver, novelist Leo Tolstoy, and the French poet Rimbaud are just a few of the artists from vastly diverse mediums who have influenced him over the years.

Crowell's long musical journey began in Houston, Texas, where he was born in 1950. His father was a Tennessee-born construction worker and part-time local honky tonk musician. (Crowell has always taken considerable pride in the fact that his mother and father met at a Roy Acuff concert in Tennessee.) By the time Crowell was 13, he was already drumming and occasionally singing in his father's band. After a brief stint in college, Crowell headed for Nashville in 1972.

He went through the usual starvation period. "I was 21, didn't know a soul, didn't have a penny. I slept out at the lake in my car," he told *Country Music Magazine*'s Bob Allen in a 1989 interview. "But then I met Guy Clark and he gently shoved me toward influences like Townes Van Zandt, Mickey Newbury and Billy Joe Shaver. I was lucky to meet Guy. He's certainly one of the biggest influences on me. He's like the Picasso of country writers."

Crowell did a stint as vocalist/guitarist in Emmylou Harris' legendary Hot Band. Harris was also one of the first of many artists to record Crowell's original songs. Others include: rocker Bob Seger ("Shame on the Moon"), Waylon Jennings ("Ain't Livin' Long

Rodney Crowell

BORN: August 7, 1950
BIRTHPLACE: Houston, Texas

Rodney Crowell may well be the most talented country artist of his generation—a singer/songwriter/producer/entertainer who has constantly forged ahead into new musical and thematic territory during times when too many of his compatriots have timidly clung to the straight and narrow. Yet, despite—or perhaps because of—his wide-ranging, diverse musical gifts, success as a recording artist was a relatively long time in coming for Crowell.

Like This"), Willie Nelson ("Till I Gain Control Again"), The Oak Ridge Boys ("Leavin' Louisiana in the Broad Daylight") and The Nitty Gritty Dirt Band ("Long Hard Road").

On the strength of his early albums, Crowell also put together his own road band, The Cherry Bombs. Seen in retrospect, The Cherry Bombs' stellar line-up is another testimonial to his sheer good taste in musicians: its personnel included three men who have since become Nashville's hottest producers (Tony Brown, Richard Bennett and Emory Gordy Jr.), along with Vince Gill and famed session guitarist Albert Lee.

When Crowell's early Warner Bros. albums failed to jump-start his recording career, he backed into yet another side occupation: producing records.

He not only produced most of the hit records of Rosanne Cash (to whom he was married from 1979 to 1991), but has also manned the console as producer on projects with actress Sissy Spacek, actor Robert Duvall and on Bobby Bare's magnificent 1980 album, *As Is*.

More recently, he produced Jim Lauderdale's critically acclaimed debut album, *Planet of Love*. In 1993, Crowell left Columbia Records and signed with MCA. His 1994 debut album for that label, *Let The Picture Paint Itself*, was extremely well received. —B.A.

Bobbie Cryner

BORN: September 13, 1961
BIRTHPLACE: Woodland, California

One of the most traditionally-oriented—and critically acclaimed—of 1993's crop of newcomers, Epic's Bobbie Cryner was born in Woodland, California, on September 13, 1961. Later, her family moved to Kansas. She grew up with the sounds of Merle Haggard, Tammy Wynette, Loretta Lynn, George Jones and Buck Owens, all of whom she cites as influences,

both in her singing and in her songwriting. There's also a bit of Bobbie Gentry in her deep, smoky vocals. Her self-titled 1993 debut album included the singles "He Feels Guilty," "You Could Steal Me" and "Daddy Laid the Blues on Me." —G.F.

Dick Curless

BORN: March 17, 1932
BIRTHPLACE: Fort Fairfield, Maine

Dick Curless developed a following as the "Rice Paddy Ranger" broadcasting his music to U.S. troops in Korea via the Armed Forces Korea Network. In 1965 he met songwriter Dan Fulkerson and recorded Fulkerson's song, "A Tombstone Every Mile," which became one of the biggest hits of that year, on Tower Records. By the end of 1965, Curless had three more hits: "Tater Raising Man," "Travelin' Man" and "Six Times a Day." Around the same time, he toured the U.S., Europe and Asia with the Buck Owens American Music Show. In 1968, he recorded the soundtrack for the film *Killers Three*, starring Merle Haggard and Dick Clark. Signing with Capitol in 1969 and cut two more albums: *Doggin' It* and *Comin' on Country*, and a number of Top 40 hits, but no Top Tens. After leaving Capitol in 1973, he recorded for a number of smaller labels. In the mid-90's, he was still living in his home state of Maine and still performing throughout New England. —M.B.

Billy Ray Cyrus

BORN: August 25, 1961
BIRTHPLACE: Flatwoods, Kentucky

"Achy Breaky Heart" earned a reputation as one of the fluffiest pieces of controversy in country music history. Whether you loved it—as the nine million or so people did who bought Billy Ray Cyrus' first album—or hated it, you tapped your toe to its catchy beat. Fueling the controversy was Billy Ray Cyrus himself, heartthrob in a sea of hunks, who tapped into the libidos of thousands of country music fans. The Flatwoods, Kentucky, native draws comparisons to Elvis with his sex-charged, rock 'n' roll-country shows. Head-shaking scandals revolving around the singer included: the "was-he-or-wasn't-he-a-Chippendale-dancer" question; Travis Tritt's inflammatory assertion that "what we're going to have to do to be popular is get into an ass-wiggling contest between one another"; and the revelation of an out-of-wedlock Cyrus-sired son, Christopher Cody.

Not bad press for the grandson of a country fiddle-playing preacher who started his musical career as a pre-schooler with his father's gospel quartet. But before Billy Ray decided music would be his calling, his dream was a career in professional baseball. When his Johnny Bench-vision of catching for the major leagues evaporated, he turned his attention to music, bought a guitar and formed a band, Sly Dog. Sly Dog was a popular local bar band, even cutting a few independent singles, but Billy Ray's efforts to land a major record deal went nowhere for ten years, despite countless trips to Nashville—and then they literally went up in flames, when the band's equipment was destroyed in a fire.

Taking his dreams to Los Angeles, Billy Ray sold Oldsmobiles for a day job, concentrating on his music at night, until he finally decided to return to Ashland, Kentucky, in 1986. Again, he and his band consistently packed the Ragtime Lounge, and he doggedly continued his almost weekly treks to Nashville, where he finally made the right connections: Manager Jack McFadden (Buck Owens, Keith Whitley, Lorrie Morgan) and PolyGram's Harold Shedd (Alabama, Kentucky HeadHunters). Mercury Records signed Billy Ray in 1990 after hearing "Some Gave All," the song he wrote after a touching encounter with a Vietnam veteran. Although his debut album bore that name and consisted of ten songs written or co-written by Billy Ray, it was "Achy Breaky Heart," written by Don Von Tress, that propelled him to stardom.

Appropriately, the single's release in 1992 was carefully orchestrated, and included a choreographed line dance shipped via video to dance clubs with instructions, and a video of Billy Ray that, according to Paul Kingsbury, editor of *The Journal of Country Music,* "made Cyrus look like the second coming of Elvis." The marketing strategy worked, and when the single was finally released, it planted itself at Number One on country radio within a month; sold platinum (extremely rare for a country single), and even made it to Number Four on the pop charts. Then the album was released: it debuted at Number One on both the country and pop charts, selling nine million copies before 1992 was over, making it one of the fastest-selling debuts in the history of pop music. In addition, the song single-footedly launched the line dance craze and, by the end of 1992, had won the Country Music Association Single of the Year.

A hard act to follow and, indeed, Billy Ray's biggest concern seemed to be how to avoid becoming just another one-shot wonder. The other big, but not nearly as big, singles from *Some Gave All* are "Where'm I Gonna Live?," "It Could Have Been Me" and "She's Not Cryin' Anymore." He scored at least a few points with the defiant title of his 1993 follow-up album, *It Won't Be the Last,* which produced the hits "In the Heart of a Woman" and "Somebody New," among others.
—M.B.

Ted Daffan

BORN: September 21, 1912
BIRTHPLACE: Beauregard Parish, Louisiana

One of honky tonk's pioneer songwriters, steel guitarist Ted Daffan enjoyed stardom himself in the 1940's. Raised in Houston, Theron Eugene Daffan gravitated to steel guitar and eventually to electric steel, playing in a Hawaiian music band known as The Blue Islanders. By 1934 he'd signed on with The Blue Ridge Playboys and started writing songs, including the first trucker number, "Truck Driver's Blues." Daffan formed his own band, known as The Texans, and with them enjoyed a brief run of stardom with originals like "No Letter Today" and his "Born to Lose," written under the pseudonym of "Frankie Brown." During World War II, both of Daffan's Columbia recordings of these songs, as well as "Headin' Down the Wrong Highway," became enormously popular—"Born to Lose" is now considered a standard. Daffan's instrumental, "Blue Steel Blues," was a favorite among steel guitarists. The Texans relocated to the West Coast during the war, becoming regulars at Venice Pier. After the war, Daffan returned to Texas and continued performing and recording. He wrote other honky tonk favorites including Faron Young's 1956 hit, "I've Got Five Dollars and It's Saturday Night," and Hank Snow's 1957 hit, "Tangled Mind." For a time he and Snow ran a publishing company in Nashville before Daffan returned to Texas in 1961. One more major standard emerged from his pen: the ballad "I'm a Fool to Care." Daffan ran his own song publishing operation for awhile and remains today an elder statesmen of honky tonk's earliest days.

—R.K.

Vernon Dalhart

Born: April 6, 1883
Birthplace: Jefferson, Texas
Died: September 18, 1948

Vernon Dalhart (Marion Try Slaughter) was one of the most prolific country recording artists ever (several thousand sides) and among its first solo stars. Never a "country" singer as such, Dalhart had no interest in such music in his earliest days. His voice suggested that his true potential might lie in legitimate operatic singing. He set his sights on opera, moving to New York to take vocal training. There he discovered the growing popularity of phonograph records.

He made his first record in 1916 and over the next several years, in addition to singing in vaudeville, he confined his recording activity to popular song and what was then known as "light opera." Trends began changing in the 1920's and he realized he needed something new. The idea of recording rural music came to mind, and in 1924 he recorded "Wreck of the Old 97," which someone else had previously cut. The flip side was a number called "The Prisoner's Song," based on an old poem. Released by Victor Records, it sold in the millions. The singer devised his new performing name much as Conway Twitty later did: by combining the names of two small towns in Texas to create the name Vernon Dalhart. The record launched Dalhart on an entirely new career; he began recording more and more rural ballads even as he grew wealthy from royalties from sales of "The Prisoner's Song." He also recorded for other labels under various pseudonyms. Eventually his career tapered off as country music became more diverse and popular. He eventually left music to take more conventional employment. He was elected to the Country Music Hall of Fame in 1981.   —R.K.

Lacy J. Dalton

Born: October 13, 1946
Birthplace: Bloomsburg, Pennsylvania

It is certainly not for lack of talent or devotion to her craft that this soulful, gravely-voiced singer never lived up to the predictions of superstardom and mountains of hype that Columbia Records buried her under shortly after she was signed to the label by legendary producer Billy Sherrill in 1979. Dalton is, in fact, one of the most singularly gifted vocalists to hit Music Row after Wanda Jackson and before Wynonna Judd. As the Country Music Foundation's *Country on Compact Disc* noted: "Her wounded and smoky voice is a thing of wonder—an instrument that matches George Jones' clenched-teeth moaning for sheer drama."

Dalton was born Jill Byrem, in rural Pennsylvania, and as a child dreamed of someday being a great

painter. She ended up majoring in art for a while at Brigham Young University in Provo, Utah, before moving on to California where she tried her hand both as a folk singer and as the lead for a rock 'n' roll band.

Dalton had kicked around the California music scene for quite a few years, married, had a child, and was well into her early 30's before backing into country music. Her proverbial "big break" came when a record she'd made with her own money landed on the desk of Billy Sherrill, then one of Nashville's most powerful producer/star-makers. Sherrill loved what he heard, and hoped to break Dalton (whose voice is often reminiscent of the late Janis Joplin's) as a sort of female Outlaw: a rough and rowdy feminine counterpart to Willie & Waylon.

Though Dalton (who was the Academy of Country Music's Top Female Vocalist in 1980) never became the sort of honky-tonk/country-rock diva that Sherrill had in mind, she did score a number of Top Tens for the label, including "16th Avenue," "Takin' It Easy," "Everybody Makes Mistakes" and "Hard Times."

Her hits trailed off by the mid-80's, but she found success with the short-lived label Universal, where she had a Top 20 record with "The Heart." Moving over to Capitol after Universal folded, she scored another Top 20 in 1990 with the dramatic single, "Black Coffee." But after several albums with minimal chart success, she was dropped by the label. —B.A.

Charlie Daniels

BORN: October 28, 1936
BIRTHPLACE: Wilmington, North Carolina

Charlie Daniels was one of the principal inventors of the Southern rock sound popularized by The Marshall Tucker Band, Lynyrd Skynyrd and The Allman Broth-

ers. Daniels assembled his first band, The Rockets (later known as The Jaguars), in the late 1950's. Around the same time he got seriously involved in songwriting; his composition, "It Hurts Me," was a hit for Elvis Presley in 1963.

Daniels moved to Nashville in the early 1960's and became a sought-after session player, working with artists as diverse as Bob Dylan (he played guitar on Dylan's classic 1969 *Nashville Skyline* album), Leonard Cohen, Pete Seeger and Flatt & Scruggs. By the late 1960's Daniels was also producing, including the critically acclaimed Youngbloods album, *Elephant Mountain*.

In 1970 Daniels assembled The Charlie Daniels Band, which included guitarist Tom "Bigfoot" Crain, keyboardist Joel "Taz" DiGregorio, bassist Charlie Hayward and drummers Fred Edwards and Don Murray (who was replaced by Charlie Marshall in 1978). Though the band cut one album on Capitol

Records in 1971, it featured mostly Daniels performing solo with studio musicians.

A year later the band began recording on Buddah Records' Kama Sutra label; the album, *Te John, Grease and Wolfman*, wasn't a major commercial success but sold well enough for Buddah to send the band into the studio again. The next two albums, *Honey in the Rock* and *Way Down Yonder*, produced the band's first charted singles, "Uneasy Rider" and "Whiskey," but it wasn't until their 1975 album, *Fire on the Mountain*, that The Charlie Daniels Band struck gold. The album went platinum in 1976 and produced the hit singles, "No Place to Go" and "The South's Gonna Do It Again," which became the band's signature song.

The band switched to Epic Records in 1976 and cut two chartbusting albums in as many years: *Saddle Tramp* and *High Lonesome*. Around the same time Daniels was instrumental in establishing Nashville's Tennessee Volunteer Jam, an annual festival celebrating Southern rock.

While the Jam did much to revive interest in Southern rock, it was Daniels' next Epic album, *Million Mile Reflections*, that really brought the sound to the musical forefront.

With the phenomenally successful fiddle tune, "The Devil Went Down to Georgia," Daniels rose to the top of both pop and country charts and finally gained acceptance as a full-fledged country performer. The album went platinum, and Daniels received two Country Music Association awards, for Single of the Year and Musician of the Year.

Daniels continued his winning streak the following year with another wildly successful album, *Full Moon*. He also performed on the platinum-selling soundtrack of the 1980's film, *Urban Cowboy*, along with other crossover favorites like Kenny Rogers and Linda Ronstadt.

The Charlie Daniels Band appeared on the charts again in the late 80's with the albums *Homesick Heroes* and *Simple Man*, both of which stirred up controversy as Daniels introduced his current social and political philosophies to his music (just as he'd done in a markedly different vein on liberal-sounding 70's and early 80's hits like "Uneasy Rider" and "Long Haired Country Boy"): this time around, he appeared to embrace such concepts as vigilantism, lynching and gay-bashing, a far cry from the earlier anti-Vietnam, drug-friendly spirit evident in those earlier songs. In 1994, Daniels released a gospel album.   —M.B.

Darby & Tarlton

BORN: Darby, 1884, Columbus, Georgia
   Tarlton, May 8, 1892, Chesterfield County, South Carolina
DIED: Darby, August 20, 1971; Tarlton, November 29, 1979

Tom Darby and Jimmie Tarlton were the two most famous white bluesmen of the 1920's, known for their two-sided 1927 hit, "Birmingham Jail" and "Columbus Stockade Blues." Between 1927 and 1933, they recorded some 60 sides, many featuring Tarlton's innovative acoustic steel guitar work and the duo's odd falsetto singing and yodeling. Tarlton was a widely traveled vaudevillian and busker, born in Chesterfield County, South Carolina, on May 8, 1892; Darby was descended from full-blooded Cherokees, born in Columbus, Georgia, in 1884. Their "Birmingham"/ "Columbus" disc sold over 200,000 copies, making it one of Columbia's best selling records, and making the songs country standards. Other hits by the team included "Birmingham Jail No. 2," "Lonesome Railroad," "Traveling Yodel Blues" and "After the Ball," all from the late 1920's. The pair had a brief comeback in the 1960's. —C.W.

Dave & Sugar

Beginning their career as Charley Pride's backup singers and opening act, vocal trio Dave & Sugar found an opportunity for success at one of country music's low points—the saccharine, country-lite era just after the Outlaw movement and just before Urban Cowboy. Singer Dave Rowland (born in Los Angeles, January 26, 1942) and an ever-changing line-up of blonde, and occasionally, brunette female "Sugars" (the originals were Vicki Hackeman and Jackie Frantz) had 11 Top Ten hits from 1975 through '81, most of them on RCA, a few on Elektra. Three songs hit Number One: "The Door Is Always Open," "Tear Time" and "Golden Tears." Now without a recording deal, Dave & Sugar still tour the lounge circuit and appear at Fan Fair. —G.F.

Gail Davies

BORN: April 4, 1948
BIRTHPLACE: Broken Bow, Oklahoma

Gail Davies became one of the first female country artists to sing, play guitar, write her own songs and produce her own records.

As a young girl, she was surrounded by music. Her father was a country singer-guitarist who played on the *Louisiana Hayride*. At home, he used to play the recordings of country legends Patsy Cline, Webb Pierce and Carl Smith on the family jukebox. Gail's mother also had a fine voice and liked to sing. When she was five, her parents split up and her mother moved Gail and her two younger brothers to Seattle, Washington. Her interest in music continued during high school, influenced by The Everly Brothers and The Beatles. After graduating, she joined a rock band as a singer and hit the road for almost nine years.

In 1978, Davies moved to Nashville with her sights set on becoming a songwriter. She scored a major hit in 1978 when Ava Barber reached the country Top 20 with Gail's "Bucket to the South." That same year, Davies signed with Lifesong/Epic Records and recorded a self-titled debut album that received critical acclaim. A single from the album, "Someone Is Looking for Someone Like Me," became a best-seller and stayed on the country charts for four months.

In 1979, Davies left Lifesong/Epic for Warner Bros. Her first single for the label, "Blue Heartache," hit the Top Ten in early 1980. Two more songs reached the Top Ten the same year—"Like Strangers" and "Good Lovin' Man." In 1984, Davies signed with RCA and topped the charts with the pop-crossover hit, "Jagged Edge of a Broken Heart." Two follow-up singles failed to match the caliber of her earlier releases, and in 1986, she joined the group Wild Choir, which had a couple of minor hits.

Her songs have been covered by other artists, including K.T. Oslin. In 1991, Davies signed with Jimmy Bowen's Capitol Records and released *The Best of Gail Davies*. —R.P.

Danny Davis and The Nashville Brass

BORN: April 29, 1925
BIRTHPLACE: Dorchester, Massachusetts

Born George Nowlan, in Dorchester, Massachusetts, April 29, 1925, Danny Davis first played trumpet in high school bands. After attending the New England Conservatory of Music, he played in ensembles with jazz greats Gene Krupa, Sammy Kaye and Bob Crosby. Later, as a producer for the Joy and MGM labels, he had several Number One hits with Connie Francis. On a trip to Nashville, Davis met producer/guitarist Chet Atkins and, in 1965, became Atkins' production assistant. Not long afterward, he conceived the idea of adapting the Herb Alpert-style Tijuana Brass sound to a country-pop rhythm section. The result was The Nashville Brass, which he formed in 1968.

Davis & The Nashville Brass enjoyed a handful of modest chart instrumental records—"Wabash Cannonball," "Please Help Me, I'm Falling," "Night Life" and similar remakes of country standards—between 1970 and the mid-1980's. Davis also won the Country Music Association's Instrumental Band of the Year award for six straight years ('69-'74), as well as a Grammy in 1969. In the years since, he has continued to perform and record sporadically. —B.A.

Jimmie Davis

BORN: September 11, 1902
BIRTHPLACE: Quitman, Louisiana

James Houston Davis, born in Quitman, Louisiana, in 1902, and twice elected governor of the state of Louisiana (in 1944, and again in the mid-1960's), had one of the most colorful careers in country music history. Davis began his recording career in the 1920's as a talented Jimmy Rodgers imitator who flirted

adeptly with both blues and Western swing stylings. Though best known today for sentimental classics like "You Are My Sunshine" and "Nobody's Darling But Mine," Davis also recorded a number of important and (at least for the times) risqué honky tonk numbers. In 1936, he bought the rights to "It Makes No Difference Now," which was written by Floyd Tillman. It wasn't a hit for Davis, but it did introduce the classic. (Tillman later bought the rights back.) In his early years, Davis earned a master's degree, and, for a while, was a professor of history at Dodd College. During his heyday as a musician and politician (he often combined the two pursuits, using his music to put fire in his gubernatorial campaigns), he also starred in a 1944 feature film, *Louisiana*. In his later years, Davis (perhaps in repentance for his racy honky tonk hits) turned to gospel and found great favor with hits like "Supper Time," "Honey in the Rock," "Take My Hand" and "Columbus Stockade Blues." Davis was elected to The Country Music Hall of Fame in 1972. He's now retired from both music and politics. —B.A.

Linda Davis

BORN: November 26, 1962
BIRTHPLACE: Carthage, Texas

A contemporary country singer in the vein of Reba McEntire—though somewhat less dynamic vocally—Davis moved to Nashville from her hometown of Dotson, Texas, in 1982. Supporting herself through commercial jingle and lounge singing, she had three non-hit singles on Epic in 1988. Next came a deal with Liberty (then known as Capitol) Records, with two album releases. Again no real success, though a couple of singles reached the lower rungs of the charts. Meanwhile, the Reba McEntire connection intensified—Reba and her husband, Narvel, signed Davis to their management company, Starstruck. She toured with Reba, singing backup vocals, and duetting with McEntire on 1993's Number One hit, "Does

He Love You." This attracted the attention of Arista Records. In 1994, her Arista debut album, *Shoot for the Moon*, was released.   —G.F.

Mac Davis

BORN: January 21, 1942
BIRTHPLACE: Lubbock, Texas

Born January 21, 1942, singer/songwriter Mac Davis began writing songs as a teenager and went on to become a successful country music songwriter. Mac formed his own rock band in the early 1960's but eventually turned to management, landing a job as Atlanta district manager of Vee-Jay Records. In 1965 he began working with Liberty Records and ended up managing Metric Music, Liberty's music publishing division. With an extensive canon of original songs, Mac quickly drummed up interest in his songs and before long had two hit credits: Lou Rawls' release of "You're Good to Me" and Glen Campbell's single of "Within My Memory." By 1968 Davis had sold Elvis Presley's manager Colonel Tom Parker on

his songwriting abilities; within two years he provided Elvis with three hit songs: "In the Ghetto," "Memories" and "Don't Cry Daddy."

During the same period other artists were putting Mac's songs on the charts: Bobby Goldsboro ("Watching Scotty Grow") and Kenny Rogers and The First Edition ("Something's Burning"). But it wasn't until a few years later that Mac made a name for himself as a soloist. He signed a recording contract with Columbia Records and cut a debut album, *Mac Davis: Song Painter*, in 1971. He promptly placed two singles on the country charts: "Beginning to Feel the Pain" and the crossover hit, "I Believe in Music," both his own compositions. The momentum carried into 1972, with his second album, *I Believe in Music*. Later that year Mac scored his first Gold album, *Baby, Don't Get Hooked on Me*, with its Number One title track.

By the mid-1970's Mac's recording career had begun to slow down as he devoted more and more time to TV appearances. He had a short-lived NBC variety show which later became a series of specials. He made his acting debut in the 1979 film, *North Dallas Forty* with Nick Nolte, and had a leading role in the 1980 comedy, *Cheaper to Keep Her*. In the early 1980's Mac re-focused his energies on recording. He switched to the Casablanca label and scored his first Top Ten hit in years: "It's Hard to Be Humble," which turned up as the title track of a Gold album later that year. He also placed two singles in the Top Ten: "Let's Keep It That Way" and "Texas in My Rear View Mirror." Most recently, he duetted and co-wrote with Dolly Parton on her *White Limozeen* album. —M.B.

Skeeter Davis

BORN: December 30, 1931
BIRTHPLACE: Dry Ridge, Kentucky

Born Mary Frances Penick in Dry Ridge, Kentucky, in 1931, Skeeter Davis was one of country music's most distinctive female voices—and outspoken women—for three decades. Skeeter began her career in 1952 as one-half of the duo, The Davis Sisters, with her friend Betty Jack Davis. The duo racked up a Number One hit for RCA in 1953 with "I Forgot More Than You'll Ever Know" before Betty Jack's death in a car crash in August of that year. After a brief period of performing with Betty Jack's older sister, Georgie, Skeeter struck out on a solo career, remaining with RCA Records. Between 1958 and 1973, the singer/songwriter recorded over 60 singles and 30 albums for the label and was nominated for five Grammys. *Cashbox Magazine* wisely named her its Most Promising Female Country Vocalist in 1958, af-

ter which Skeeter went on to produce hits including "Set Him Free" (1959), "I'm Falling Too" (1960), "Where I Ought To Be" (1962) and "The End of the World," which hit the top of both the country and pop charts in 1963 to become Skeeter's first Gold record. In the 1970's she became known for her renditions of sacred songs and often appeared in the programs of televangelist Oral Roberts. She was married to Ralph Emery from 1960 to '64, and is currently married to Joey Spampinato of the rock group, NRBQ, with whom she sometimes records. She's been a member of the Grand Ole Opry since 1959. In 1993 she chronicled her life in her autobiography, *Bus Fare to Kentucky*, which told a story of the considerable ups (and downs) of her career. It also took many jabs at ex-husband Emery. —M.B.

Jimmy Day

BORN: January 9, 1934
BIRTHPLACE: Tuscaloosa, Alabama

James Clayton Day got his start as a teenaged steel guitar player on the *Louisiana Hayride*, working with a number of *Hayride* artists in the late 40's including Hank Williams and Faron Young. He also made an instrumental recording for Abbott Records in the early 50's. Day, who eventually moved to a pedal steel, later worked extensively with Ray Price's Cherokee Cowboys (in the late 50's) and made two albums for Philips in 1962 and 1963. He met Willie Nelson in the early 60's while Willie worked in The Cherokee Cowboys, and played on the often-reissued series of Nelson demo recordings for Pamper Music. In the

mid-60's, Day worked on and off with Price and then toured with Willie.

In addition, Day did substantial recording session work in Nashville. Day also worked with Willie after Willie moved to Austin in the early 70's, including work on his *Shotgun Willie* album in 1973. Day also did an album for DeWitt Scott's Mid-Land label in the late 70's. He was inducted into the International Steel Guitar Hall of Fame in 1982. —R.K.

Billy Dean

BORN: April 2, 1962
BIRTHPLACE: Quincy, Florida

Born April 2, 1962, in Quincy, Florida, Billy Dean made a living acting in TV commercials before achieving success first as a songwriter, then as a singer. As a finalist in the Wrangler Country competition, Billy got his first taste of Nashville. Though he didn't win the contest, he decided to make the move to Nashville, where he formed a band that opened for major country stars like Mel Tillis and Ronnie Milsap. At the same time, Billy's original songs were being recorded by the likes of Milsap, Randy Travis and The Oak Ridge Boys. Billy signed with Capitol/SBK in 1989 and cut a debut album, *Young Man*; one of the tracks from that album, "Only Here for a Little While," turned out to be a career-making hit. The follow-up single, "Somewhere in My Broken Heart" (co-written with Richard Leigh), went to the top of the country and adult contemporary charts. His second album, *Billy Dean*, went Gold. The Academy of Country Music named Billy its Best New Male Vocalist in 1992. In 1993, his third album, *Fire in the Dark*, yielded a few more of his contemporary-styled hits. His fourth album, *Men'll Be Boys*, was released in 1994. —M.B.

Jimmy Dean

Born: August 10, 1928
Birthplace: Plainview, Texas

Jimmy Ray Dean grew up poor in Texas, working in the cotton fields and doing other farm work. Poverty and brutal labor set a strong work ethic in his mind and a determination to break out of that lifestyle. Having learned to play several instruments, including piano, guitar, accordion and harmonica, Dean at first looked on music as a hobby. While serving in the U.S. Air Force, he found himself stationed in the Washington, D.C., area and began playing music on the side. After his 1948 discharge, he remained in music and eventually connected with radio station owner/promoter Connie B. Gay. By 1952 he had a band titled The Texas Wildcats, built around himself and his accordion, and landed a recording contract with Four Star. "Bummin' Around" became his first hit record in 1953. Dean, who had begun hosting a local TV program, *Town and Country Time*, in 1955, took on Roy Clark as a guitarist. Patsy Cline also became an early regular on this program; the hard-driving Dean eventually fired Clark in a dispute over chronic lateness.

By 1957, though Dean had few hit records, his popularity expanded into a full-blown CBS morning show, done from his Washington home base. Dean next landed a recording contract with Columbia, and while preparing for his first session, wrote the classic coal mine drama, a recitation titled "Big Bad John." It spent five weeks at Number One on *Billboard's* pop chart, two weeks on the magazine's country chart in 1961. Dean had a Top Ten with "Dear Ivan," a Cold War-inspired number, that same year. He did a number of other recitation recordings, the biggest being "P.T. 109," inspired by John F. Kennedy's 1943 P.T. boat collision, then the subject of a feature film.

Dean's continuing popularity led to his own prime-time ABC series in 1963, a show important for a number of reasons. He had considerable control over the content, and presented a variety of country stars with dignity and class, be it George Jones, Buck Owens or Roger Miller. The show also gave early exposure to puppeteer Jim Henson's Muppets. The show lasted from 1963-66. For a time he was popular as a talk show guest host and used a *Tonight Show* guest host shot to give Roy Clark his first major national exposure. After one final Number One with "The First Thing Every Morning (And the Last Thing Every Night)" on Columbia, Dean went to RCA, where he remained until 1972. After a brief return to Columbia, he signed with Casino, where he had his final Top Ten with "I.O.U." in 1976. Along the way, Dean formed his own company producing sausage and other meat products, and he continues to appear in the company's advertisements.   —R.K.

The Delmore Brothers

Born: Alton, December 25, 1908
      Rabon, December 3, 1910
Birthplace: Elkmont, Alabama
Died: Alton, June 8, 1964
      Rabon, December 4, 1952

The Delmore Brothers are not only among the premiere brother vocal duets of all time, they are among the few such groups to succeed in the pre-World War II years and then succeed again after the war when country music had changed considerably. They grew up on their parents' tenant farm in Alabama with gos-

pel music all around them. They began singing to-gether as children. Though their first recording for Columbia in 1931 went nowhere, they joined the Grand Old Opry in 1932. In 1933 they began recording for RCA Victor's Bluebird label; their output included their classic recordings of "Brown's Ferry Blues" and "Gonna Lay Down My Own Guitar." Their popularity on the Opry surged and their records sold well. After leaving the Opry in 1938, they worked on radio stations throughout the South before settling at WLW in Cin-cinnati during World War II. In addition to their own performing, they formed The Brown's Ferry Four gos-pel quartet with fellow WLW performers Grandpa Jones and Merle Travis. They were among the earliest artists to record for Cincinnati's King Records, and, after mov-ing to Memphis, they incorporated blues and boogie woogie into their music. This shift in their music was obvious on post-war King recordings like their 1946 hit, "Freight Train Boogie" (with harmonica player Wayne Raney). Their 1949 recording of "Blues Stay Away from Me," became their only Number One. Af-ter Rabon's death from lung cancer in 1952, Alton tried to continue, but eventually left music. Some years af-ter Alton's death in 1964, the Country Music Founda-tion published his autobiography. Alton's son, Lionel, has written a number of modern country classics, in-cluding John Anderson's "Swingin'." —R.K.

Iris DeMent

BORN: January 5, 1961
BIRTHPLACE: Paragould, Arkansas

Iris DeMent, who made her debut with her 1992 album on Philo/Rounder, *Infamous Angel*, received such critical and popu-lar acclaim (though no country radio airplay) that Warner Bros. signed her and re-re-leased the album in 1993. Growing up, DeMent took in the sounds of Loretta Lynn, Tammy Wynette, Bob Dylan, Johnny Cash and even Aretha Franklin and Joni Mitchell, all of whom inspired her writing. DeMent has, as one *Country Music Magazine* writer put it, "one of those bold, unconstrained country/folk voices that seems to echo back across the de-cades to purer times. She reminds us of a long-gone era when rural music was free of contemporary com-mercial adulterations and spoke directly to the ab-solutes of the soul and the stark imponderables of life." Her second album, *My Life*, was released in 1994 to equal critical praise. —G.F.

James R. Denny

BORN: February 28, 1911
DIED: August 27, 1963

Elected to the Country Music Hall of Fame in 1966, James R. ("Jim") Denny, a long-time manager of the Grand Ole Opry, and a highly successful music pub-lisher and talent agent, played a huge behind-the-scenes role in the growth of the Nashville music es-tablishment in the 1950's. Denny's greatest contribu-tion was—mainly through his acumen as a promoter and developer of talent—helping ensure the growth in popularity of the Opry during the 50's when simi-lar barn dance-style country music shows were bit-ing the dust all around the country in the face of rock 'n' roll.

Denny, along with Jack Stapp, who'd preceded Denny as Opry manager (see entry on Stapp), is given much credit for changing the face of the Opry. As historian Douglas B. Green noted in *The Illustrated History of Country Music*: "Denny and Stapp are the men who wrested control of the Opry away from founding manager George D. Hay in the early 1940's, determined to 'modernize' the show. This was not an easy period for performers, but Stapp and Denny's efforts turned the Opry from a popular barn dance into a star-studded super-show, packed not with high-spirited fiddle bands but with singing stars. The cast grew enormously, and most of the major recording stars of the period became Opry members, turning the show into every performer's ultimate goal. Un-der Stapp, and later Denny, the Grand Ole Opry lost its barn dance flavor and became a showcase of stars, having lost something on one hand and gained some-thing on the other."

However, Denny was eventually fired from WSM (the Opry's parent company) amidst allegations of conflict of interest stemming from his activities as a publisher and manager. He was accused of discriminating against Opry members who did not publish their songs with Cedarwood, the publishing enterprise which he co-founded with singer Webb Pierce (then the Opry's biggest star) in 1954. Cedarwood grew to contain one of the most formidable song catalogues on Music Row. Denny, who also launched an eminently successful booking agency, was a longtime board member of the CMA.   —B.A.

John Denver

BORN: December 31, 1943
BIRTHPLACE: Roswell, New Mexico

Born John Deutschendorf in 1943, in Roswell, New Mexico, John Denver is best known for the string of eminently popular fresh-air-and-sunshine pop hits with which he dominated popular music in the 1970's: "Country Roads," "Thank God I'm a Country Boy," "Rocky Mountain High," Back Home Again" and more.

Without really trying, Denver also made a huge—and arguably somewhat dubious—impact on country music during the rootless, crossover-crazy early 70's when a large segment of the Nashville music industry was intent upon watering down the traditional hard country sound in pursuit of pop sales and airplay. Though Denver's best-selling records were not specifically promoted as country, they nonetheless were embraced by country radio, and by Nashville (which presumably felt that Denver personified what modern country music should sound like). Denver's pop smashes became country hits as well. The end result was that, in 1975—much to the chagrin of many "keep it country" traditionalists and purists, who felt they were being pushed out of the country "Hot 100" by interlopers like Denver—this pop superstar was named the Country Music Association's Entertainer of the Year. His hit single, "Back Home Again," was also voted the CMA's Song of the Year in '75. A similar outcry was heard from some in Nashville when Olivia Newton-John won the award for Female Vocalist of the Year in 1974.

Though Denver's massive chart-crossing popularity began to dwindle by the later 1970's, he revisited the country charts in 1979 with "What's on Your

Mind." He has also recorded a memorable duet with Emmylou Harris ("Wild Mountain Skies"), and, in the early 90's, returned with an independent label album.   —B.A.

The Desert Rose Band

Though The Desert Rose Band was founded by veteran 1960's country-rocker Chris Hillman, it was steeped in country tradition. Hillman, a former bluegrass mandolinist, had been part of the legendary 60's rock band, The Byrds, one of the first American rock bands to venture into country-rock years before The Eagles ever existed. When fellow Byrds member Gram Parsons, who had inspired the band's ventures into country, left to found his Flying Burrito Brothers, Hillman became a co-founder, but soon left the group to work with various rockers. In 1985, Hillman founded The Desert Rose Band with guitarist John Jorgenson and former Burrito Brother Herb Pedersen, along with pedal steel guitarist Jay Dee Maness, bassist Bill Bryson and drummer Steve Duncan. Their first chart entry, in 1987, after they signed with Curb, was a remake of Johnnie and Jack's "Ashes of Love." Following that, they found substantial success in 1987 with "Love Reunited" and "One Step Forward." "He's Back and I'm Blue" and "Summer Wind" were their 1988 hits, followed by their biggest record ever, "I Still Believe In You," which peaked in early 1989 at Number One. That year they also had hits with "She Don't Love Nobody" and a remake of Orville Couch's "Hello Trouble," along with "Start All Over Again." In

1990 "Story of Love" was their sole Top Ten. Through the early 90's, the group's success on records has flagged considerably, and the lineup has changed. Maness, Jorgenson, Gibson and Duncan have all departed, and the group's future is uncertain. Their most recent album, in 1994, didn't have a U.S. release, but came out on a small German label. —R.K.

Al Dexter

Born: April 5, 1902
Birthplace: Troup, Texas
Died: January 28, 1984

Al Dexter was a founding father of honky tonk; one number of his, "Pistol Packin' Mama," became a virtual standard during the World War II years. Born Albert Poindexter, he began as a laborer, painting houses before starting to perform. By the early 30's, in the diverse musical atmosphere of Texas, he'd formed an all-black musical unit to play around Longview, a daring step at the time. Signed to the American Recording Company in 1936, he came out with "Honky Tonk Blues," the first country song to use that term. Dexter also owned a honky tonk bar in Turnertown, Texas. One day a jealous armed woman came in, looking for a woman who'd been romancing her husband. Dexter used the musical structure of Bob Wills' "Take Me Back to Tulsa" and the woman's story to create "Pistol Packin' Mama." Up until then, Dexter's recording career hadn't been successful. Producer Art Satherley knew that Dexter's days at Columbia were numbered if he soon didn't get a hit. When Satherley heard "Pistol Packin' Mama," he knew Dexter had found his brass ring. Released in 1943, the song dominated American jukeboxes, a hit with both pop and country fans. Bing Crosby and The Andrews Sisters recorded a successful "cover" version of the song at the same time. That one smash didn't end his success. "So Long Pal," "Guitar Polka," "Too Late to Worry" (which also became a standard) and "Wine, Women and Song" were all huge hits. Nevertheless, Dexter's singing skills and his sound were always rather limited, and after leaving Columbia, his career quickly faded. Recordings for King, Decca and Capitol failed. Yet his singing and writing left him wealthy enough to live off investments. In 1971 he became a member of the Nashville Songwriters Hall of Fame. He died in 1984. —R.K.

Diamond Rio

Diamond Rio consists of six highly accomplished musicians; together they bring to the band a unique fusion of country, bluegrass and rock. Both lead singer Marty Roe (born December 28, 1960, in Lebanon, Ohio) and lead guitarist Jimmy Olander (born August 26, 1961, in Minneapolis) were professional musicians by the age of 12. The other members are bassist/vocalist Dana Williams (born May 22, 1961, in Dayton, Ohio), drummer Brian Prout (born December 4, 1955, in Troy, New York), fiddler/pianist Dan Truman (born August 29, 1956, in St. George, Utah) and mandolinist Gene Johnson (born August 10, 1949, in Jamestown, New York).

Originally known as The Tennessee River Boys, the band was opening for George Jones when they were "discovered" by Arista Records executive Tim DuBois. By the time they released their self-titled debut album a year later, they'd changed their name to Diamond Rio. The Gold album yielded three solid hits, "Meet in the Middle" (their debut single release, which hit Number One in 1991), "Mirror, Mirror" also in 1991 and "Mama Don't Forget to Pray for Me" in 1992. Diamond Rio was named Best Vocal Group of 1992 by the Academy of Country Music. Subsequent albums have yielded similar success. —M.B.

Little Jimmy Dickens

BORN: December 19, 1920
BIRTHPLACE: Bolt, West Virginia

Though James Cecil Dickens grew up as a disciple of Roy Acuff's anguished, unvarnished ballad singing style, he gradually found his own direction. The son of a West Virginia coal miner, his four-foot, 11-inch height as an adult became part of his image early on. His first musical work came at WJLS in Beckley, West Virginia, in the late 30's, where he signed the station on the air. Deeply influenced by Acuff's vocal style, Dickens performed there with Mel Steele and his band before joining Johnnie Bailes and his Happy Valley Boys, where he was known as "The Singing Midget" or "Jimmy The Kid."

In 1941 he moved to a Fairmont radio station, then in 1942 moved to Indianapolis, then to WLW in Cincinnati and finally to a station in Saginaw, Michigan. There he met Roy Acuff, who liked his voice enough to recommend him to both the Grand Ole Opry and Columbia Records' Art Satherley in 1948. Dickens' first recordings were done with members of Acuff's band. The first hit was "Take an Old Cold

'Tater and Wait," which, according to historian Ivan Tribe, was a 1920's hillbilly song Dickens learned in Fairmont from banjoist Sonny Grubb. The song charted in 1949. Hank Williams, who became friendly with Dickens after he came to the Opry in '49, nicknamed Dickens "'Tater," after the song. Dickens had two more hits in 1949, "Country Boy" and "My Heart's Bouquet," and one in 1950, "A-Sleeping at the Foot of the Bed." Dickens also formed an excellent backup band from the remnants of Paul Howard's Arkansas Cotton Pickers, with twin lead guitars played by Grady Martin and Robert "Jabbo" Arrington. Novelty songs, many of them written for him by Felice and Boudleaux Bryant, became his specialty, including "Hillbilly Fever" and "Out Behind the Barn," yet Dickens' Acuff-inspired ballad singing, though never as successful, was equally moving. Numbers like his 1950 hit, "My Heart's Bouquet," and his version of "Tramp on the Street" reveal just how powerful a vocalist he was without the novelty tunes.

His band was considered one of the best in Nashville, featuring such talent as steel guitarists Walter Haynes and Buddy Emmons. Though he made some attempts to record rock, he never succeeded with it, and his hits dropped off, though he remained with Columbia. In 1965, someone played him a novelty song at a recording session and the band worked up a quick arrangement. "May The Bird of Paradise Fly Up Your Nose" became his biggest  record yet, becoming a country Number One and a pop Top 20, and earning him guest spots on rock 'n' roll "dance party" shows. Dickens tried to capitalize on this with more novelties, but had no success.

Though he remained on the Opry and toured the world, his hitmaking days were ending. In 1968 he signed with Decca, but did no better with them or with United Artists. Inducted into the Country Music Hall of Fame in 1983, Dickens continues performing on the Opry. In the early 90's, Rounder Records reissued some of his ballad singing on the album, *From the Heart*. —R.K.

Joe Diffie

BORN: December 28, 1958
BIRTHPLACE: Tulsa, Oklahoma

Neo-honky-tonker Joe Diffie blasted onto the scene with his masterful 1990 Epic debut album, *A Thousand Winding Roads*, which resulted in four consecutive Number One singles: "New Way to Light Up an Old Flame," "Home," "If You Want Me To" and "If the Devil Danced (In Empty Pockets)." Diffie's debut, along with its follow-ups—*Regular Joe* (1992) and *Honky Tonk Attitude* (1993)—have shown Diffie to be a stalwart George Jones/Merle Haggard hard country disciple who occasionally rises above the heavy hand of these influences to assert a style all his own.

Diffie was born in Oklahoma in 1958, and lived the majority of his years in that region before coming to Nashville. Like so many country singers, he learned his licks listening to his father's record collection. But Diffie took a while to get around to following his musical muse full-time. He attended college in Lawton, Oklahoma, dropped out, married and had kids, worked in the Texas oil fields, and sang in a gospel group. Later, back in Oklahoma, he worked in an iron foundry for quite a few years while operating his own eight-track demo studio on the side. But the iron foundry shut down in 1986, and his marriage folded up around the same time.

Unable to find any other work in his home state, he borrowed some money from his parents and headed for Nashville. He found steady work in the Gibson Guitar factory near Nashville. He also plunged into songwriting in earnest and found side work as a demo singer. With hundreds of Diffie-sung demos floating around Music Row, it was only a matter of time before the powers at Sony Music heard one of them and offered Diffie his first major league recording contract on their Epic label. He was made a member of the Grand Ole Opry in 1993.
—B.A.

The Dillards

Founded by Illinois-born brothers Doug and Rodney Dillard, The Dillards cut their first album, *Backporch Bluegrass*, in 1963 on the Elektra label. With mandolinist Dean Webb and bassist Mitch Jayne, the band cut two more albums in as many years, *The Dillards Live—Almost* and *Pickin' and Fiddlin'* (a now classic collaboration with fiddler Byron Berline). Around the same time the band began a lengthy stint playing the slow-witted Darlin family on *The Andy Griffith Show*, gaining a national audience for their lighthearted brand of bluegrass. Doug Dillard left the group in 1968 and formed a band of brief duration with ex-Byrd Gene Clark; his replacement, guitarist/banjo player Herb Pedersen (presently a member of The Desert Rose Band), stayed with the group for three years before leaving to form his own band, Country Gazette. Pedersen's replacement, Billy Ray "Hot Rod Banjo" Latham, joined the group for their next two albums, *Roots and Branches* (Anthem/UA Records, 1972) and *Tribute to the American Duck* (Poppy Records, 1973). After a period of inactivity, the band met up again in August 1979, to play a reunion concert in Salem, Missouri. All the former band members as well as four generations of the Dillard family were represented. The concert itself was later released as a live album for Flying Fish Records, and was filmed as a segment for the NBC-TV series, *Real People*. The band continues to record occasional albums.
—M.B.

Dean Dillon

BORN: March 26, 1955
BIRTHPLACE: Lake City, Tennessee

Though he has had modest success as a recording artist (his half dozen or so albums include two particularly noteworthy efforts for Atlantic Records: 1991's *Out of Your Ever Lovin' Mind* and 1993's *Hot, Country and Single*), Dean Dillon's real mark has been as a songwriter. George Strait alone has recorded more than 30 Dillon originals, including "Easy Come, Easy Go," "Unwound," "Marina Del Rey," "Ocean Front Property," "The Chair," "Nobody in His Right Mind," "I've Come to Expect It from You," "If I Know Me" and "Holding My Own."

Other classics from Dillon's extensive catalogue include "Set 'Em Up, Joe," "Is It Raining at Your House" (both recorded by Vern Gosdin), "Tennessee Whiskey" (George Jones), and "Miami, My Amy" and "Homecoming '63" (both hit singles for Keith Whitley).

A native of East Tennessee, Dillon survived a wayward childhood (his father abandoned the family when he was born, his mother left a few years later, and he was raised by his grandparents) and began performing music at age 14. He came to Nashville in the 1970's with hopes of becoming a star. Since then, however, songwriting has proven his real ticket. Hardly a fortnight seems to pass without the release of yet another hit country album with at least one Dean Dillon song on it. —B.A.

The Dixon Brothers

BORN: Dorsey, October 14, 1897; Howard, June 19, 1903
BIRTHPLACE: Darlington, South Carolina
DIED: Dorsey, April 17, 1968; Howard, March 24, 1961

During the late 1930's The Dixon Brothers was one of the most popular country acts on RCA Victor's Bluebird label. Accompanying themselves on guitar and Hawaiian guitar, the brothers specialized in traditional ballads and Dorsey Dixon's poignant compositions, including "I Didn't Hear Anybody Pray" (better known as "Wreck on the Highway"), "The Intoxicated Rat" and "Weave Room Blues."

Dorsey Murdock Dixon and Howard Briten Dixon were textile workers by profession. The brothers originally accompanied themselves on fiddle and guitar. When they met Jimmie Tarlton, the tenor singer and Hawaiian guitarist who recorded with Tom Darby, Tarlton taught Howard Dixon how to play with a steel bar.

In 1934 the duo began playing over WBT's *Saturday Night Jamboree;* their popularity caught the attention of Bluebird recording executive Eli Oberstein, who signed them to a contract in 1936. They produced 60 masters during the next three years—some as duets and others with fellow mill workers, Mutt Poston and Frank Gerard. The brothers quit playing music after the Bluebird contract expired.

In 1963 Eugene Earle and Archie Green persuaded Dorsey Dixon to make a new album for Testament and appear at the Newport Folk Festival. Howard died in 1961, Dorsey followed in 1968. —D.S.

Dobro

Eager to produce a louder acoustic Hawaiian guitar for vaudeville performers, the California-based Dopyera brothers developed the dobro in the late 20's. The instrument is basically a six-string wooden guitar with a circular, multi-component metal sound chamber. The bridge sits directly on the sound chamber; a screw permits manual adjustment of the tone and volume. Most models have square necks and raised nuts and are designed to be played with a steel bar; others are fretted and sport conventional necks, standard nuts and fretted fingerboards. Some specially made dobros feature fretted five-string banjo, eight-string mandolin or 12-string guitar necks.

The first major country singer to adopt the dobro was Cliff Carlisle, but its sound is most associated with two members of Roy Acuff's Smoky Mountain Boys: Clell "Cousin Jody" Sumner and Beecher "Brother Oswald" Kirby. Other important early players were Jenks "Tex" Carman, Ray "Duck" Adkins, George "Speedy" Krise and Harold "Shot" Jackson.

The musician who fully unleashed the dobro's

potential was Burkett "Buck" Graves, who was also known as "Uncle Josh." While working with Wilma Lee and Stoney Cooper in the early 50's, Graves developed a driving three-finger roll similar to what Earl Scruggs used on the banjo. He introduced the instrument to bluegrass in 1955 when he joined Flatt and Scruggs' Foggy Mountain Boys. Later in the decade Robert "Tut" Taylor used a flat pick to create a different bluegrass dobro technique.

Two important dobro stylists emerged in the late 60's and early 70's: Mike Auldridge and Jerry Douglas. Auldridge, a member of Emerson and Waldron's New Shades of Grass and later The Seldom Scene, developed a subtle, understated technique that differed from Graves' aggressive, blues-tinged approach. Auldridge's two solo Takoma albums, from 1972 and 1974, are classics. Ohio native Jerry Douglas expanded upon many of Auldridge's ideas in the early 70's. After serving apprenticeships with The Country Gentlemen and Boone Creek in the 70's, Douglas moved to Nashville and became a successful session musician. 　　　　　　　　　　　　　　—D.S.

Pete Drake

BORN: October 8, 1932
BIRTHPLACE: Atlanta, Georgia
DIED: July 29, 1988

Producer Billy Sherrill once compared pedal steel guitarist Pete Drake to a "machine." That was a compliment, meaning that for Sherrill, who supervised every note of his recordings, Drake could play precisely whatever the producer required. Initially he played standard guitar around Atlanta before turning to pedal steel after Webb Pierce's 1953 hit record of "Slowly," featuring Bud Isaacs on pedal steel, popularized pedal guitars. Drake had one of the first in the Atlanta area. His older brother, Jack, played bass with Ernest Tubb's Texas Troubadours.

Drake finally moved to Nashville in 1959 and started getting recording session work, making his mark in 1960 on Roy Drusky's hit, "Anymore," and George Hamilton's "Before This Day Ends." Drake, who, like many studio musicians, liked to experiment, began using an motorized device created by pop steel guitarist Alvino Rey that made the steel guitar "talk" through a tube in the guitarist's mouth. His recording of "Forever," built around the gimmick,

broke the pop Top 30. Drake's "Talking Steel Guitar" became his trademark.

He also owned the small, Nashville-based Stop label. In the late 60's Bob Dylan used him on his *John Wesley Harding* and *Nashville Skyline* albums. Soon other pop musicians sought out Drake, including ex-Beatles George Harrison and Ringo Starr. Drake produced Ringo's 1969 country album, *Beaucoups of Blues*. In the 1970's, Drake owned his own recording studio. His First Generation label gave veteran artists like Ernest Tubb and Stonewall Jackson a recording outlet after the major labels dropped them. In the late 70's, Drake masterminded the all-star Tubb tribute album, *The Legend and the Legacy*.

In 1987, he was inducted into the International Steel Guitar Hall of Fame. Drake died in 1988 of a respiratory ailment. 　　　　　　　　　　　—R.K.

Jimmy Driftwood

BORN: June 20, 1907
BIRTHPLACE: Mountain View, Arkansas

Though he is little-known by contemporary country fans, Jimmy Driftwood's contributions to country music and American folk music are many. He wrote a handful of true country classics (most notably "The Battle of New Orleans," which was a Number One hit for Johnny Horton in 1959, and "Tennessee Stud," a hit for Eddy Arnold that same year).

He also recorded a number of albums of his own over the years, for RCA, Monument and other labels. Driftwood's only entry into the country charts was with his own version of "The Battle of New Orleans," which climbed as high as Number 24 in 1959.

Driftwood's greatest significance in the overview of American music has been as a preservationist of traditional American folk music. He has diligently collected, performed and thus kept alive many of the folk songs he heard growing up in rural Arkansas—some of which date back to Elizabethan England. Driftwood has further kept this musical heritage alive by writing dozens of songs of his own in the traditional American folk music vein.

Born James Corbett Morris, in Mountain View, Arkansas, Driftwood, as a youth, became proficient on banjo, fiddle and a home-made guitar given to him by his uncle. He later earned a bachelor's degree in education from Arkansas State Teachers College and began teaching while also performing at local folk festivals. During the 50's folk revival, Driftwood's popularity grew until he was playing at festivals all over the U.S. and was offered a recording contract by RCA.

During the 60's, Driftwood (who seldom strayed far from his native Arkansas) settled into a career as a high school principal. He also helped found such organizations as the Rackensack Folklore Society and the Arkansas Folk Festival. Through the years he

performed frequently as a guest on the Grand Ole Opry. Well into the 1970's, Driftwood continued to appear occasionally at folk festivals.   —B.A.

Drums

For decades, drums were considered too uptown by many in country music. Ironically, many of those who held the line admired the late Jimmie Rodgers, who'd used a drummer on his 1929 recordings of "Desert Blues" and "Any Old Time." In Texas, Milton Brown and His Musical Brownies used a drummer on specific dance jobs, and in, 1935, Bob Wills hired Smokey Dacus as drummer for his Texas Playboys. Wills played to vast dance crowds, and needed Dacus, who occasionally used a brush on one of his drum cases to push the beat. In later years, Wills used other drummers with strong Dixieland roots, including Gene Tomlins and Monte Mountjoy, who worked with him in the 1940's; talents in later editions of Playboys including Johnny Cuvilello and his own younger brother, Billy Jack Wills. Adolph Hofner's San Antonians also used a drummer by the 1940's. West Coast bands such as Spade Cooley's routinely used drummers on all engagements, many of them ex-big band drummers like Muddy Berry.

At the Grand Ole Opry, drums were expressly forbidden, though Bob Wills defied the ban when he performed there on December 30, 1944, with Monte Mountjoy playing his entire drum set onstage. Pee Wee King's band used a drummer, "Sticks" McDonald, but not on the Opry stage. Likewise, Paul Howard's Arkansas Cotton Pickers, another Western swing act on the Opry, briefly employed Joe Morello, later known for his work with jazz pianist Dave Brubeck. One of the first country drummers in Nashville was Farris Coursey, who played in Owen Bradley's dance band. Still, most Nashville and Southeastern artists avoided drums (though Hank Williams briefly used a drummer in Alabama before he became a star). Coursey, who slapped his thighs on Red Foley's 1950 hit recording of "Chattanoogie Shoe Shine Boy," was used on some sessions, though in other cases, muted rhythm guitar was used to provide percussion. Carl Smith's 1954 hiring of Nashville big band drummer, Buddy Harman, caused further controversy at the Opry. Opry managers still refused to allow a drum set on stage, but eventually relented to the point of allowing Harman to play a snare drum, with brushes, behind a curtain—only to have new Opry boss Dee Kilpatrick briefly ban them again. After rock 'n' roll hit, more performers added drums to their bands and their records. Buddy Harman helped Ray Price develop his famous "shuffle" beat.

Drums have been routinely used in country music ever since, except in traditional bluegrass. The Osborne Brothers, however, used Buddy Harman on records beginning in 1958.

Several country drummers used the instrument to break into the business before becoming stars, including Roger Miller, who drummed with Faron Young, and Jack Greene, who worked with Ernest Tubb.

Even Roy Acuff used a snare drum with brushes on the Opry after the drum was allowed to be seen. In 1973, when the Opry moved to Opryland, full drum sets were permitted on the stage at last. —R.K.

Roy Drusky

Born: June 22, 1930
Birthplace: Atlanta, Georgia

This low-key Georgia-born singer has been a minor but respected member of the Grand Ole Opry since 1958. A vocalist of smooth but relatively modest dimensions, Drusky had several dozen chart singles between 1960 and the very early 1970's. Some of the most successful of these were "Another" (which reached Number Two in 1960), "Three Hearts in a Tangle" (1961), "Second Hand Rose" (1962) and "Yes, Mr. Peters" (a Number One "cheatin'" duet with Priscilla Mitchell, released in 1965). Drusky, who also recorded a few duets with Kitty Wells, dabbled in songwriting (Faron Young covered his "Alone with You") as well as acting, and was also briefly an executive with SESAC, the music performance rights organization. —B.A.

Dave Dudley

Born: May 3, 1928
Birthplace: Spencer, Wisconsin

Singer, guitarist and songwriter Dave Dudley (born David Pedruska) helped create the legend of the truck driver as an American folk hero. While two of his singles for Mercury Records, "Mail" and "Last Day in the Mines," topped the charts in 1964, it wasn't until he cut "Six Days on the Road" the following year that Dudley really found his stride. The single was an instant hit with truckers, and became a sought-after jukebox pick in truck stops from coast to coast. It is still one of the great road songs of all time.

Dudley continued to make records for Mercury until the mid-70's; the split relegated him to state and county fairs for the next several years.

He reappeared briefly on several smaller labels. His Sun Records single—and final chart entry—"Rolaids, Doan's Pills and Preparation H" spent several weeks on the charts in 1980, but, despite the...eclectic...title never had quite the ring of "Six Days." —M.B.

The Duke of Paducah

BORN: May 12, 1901
BIRTHPLACE: DeSoto, Missouri
DIED: June 20, 1986

This Missouri native, born Benjamin F. "Whitey" Ford, was known to millions of Opry fans for years for his unique brand of down-home comedy. Ford broke into show business playing with a Dixieland jazz band and made numerous vaudeville tours with early Western bands. He also starred in the popular NBC radio show, *Plantation Party*. From his debut on the Opry in 1942 until shortly before his death in 1986, "The Duke," with his vast repertoire of jokes and his familiar tag line ("I'm goin' to the wagon, boys—these shoes are killin' me!"), was beloved by several generations of Opry audiences. Always meticulous, he allegedly kept the jokes in a carefully indexed and cross-indexed file that numbered more than a half million. He was elected to the Country Music Hall of Fame in 1986, the year of his death.   —B.A.

Johnny Duncan

BORN: October 5, 1938
BIRTHPLACE: Dublin, Texas

Johnny Duncan was born on October 5, 1938, into a musical Texas family: His cousin Jimmy Seals was half of the 1970's pop duo, Seals & Crofts, while another cousin, Dan Seals, performed as England Dan with pop singer John Ford Coley.

While doing a spot on a local morning TV show in the late 1960's, Duncan was "discovered" by a Columbia Records executive and quickly signed to the label. He had a number of successful singles in the early 1970's including "Fools" (1972) and "Jo and the Cowboy" (1975)—the latter co-written with Larry

Gatlin, with vocals by a then-unknown Janie Fricke. In the mid-1970's Duncan teamed up with veteran producer Billy Sherrill. Almost immediately the collaboration yielded two Number One hits, "It Couldn't Have Been Any Better" and "Thinkin' of a Rendezvous," plus a highly successful recording of Kris Kristofferson's "Strangers." Duncan went on to score a string of other hits in the late 1970's including "Song in the Night" in 1977, "She Can Put Her Shoes Under My Bed (Anytime)," "Hello Mexico" in 1978, "Slow Dancing" and "The Lady in the Blue Mercedes" in 1979. Duncan's name continued to appear on the charts in the early 1980's, with "Play Another Slow Song" (1980) and "All Night Long" (1981). By the early 80's he left Columbia, and later recorded for the small Pharoah label, scoring a few minor hits in the mid-80's.   —M.B.

Tommy Duncan

BORN: January 11, 1911
BIRTHPLACE: Hillsboro, Texas
DIED: July 25, 1967

After Milton Brown left The Light Crust Doughboys in 1933, Bob Wills auditioned 67 singers before finding Thomas Elmer Duncan, who was heavily influenced by Jimmie Rodgers, Bing Crosby and singer-yodeler Emmett Miller. He remained with Wills in The Lightcrust Doughboys until Wills left the band in 1933 to form the original Playboys. Duncan left with him and remained for the next 15 years, his versatility and personality becoming an integral part of The Texas Playboys. He joined the Army after Pearl Harbor but completed his hitch in time to rejoin The Playboys for their 1943 move to California. Various conflicts between Duncan and Wills led to Wills firing him in 1948. Duncan organized his own Western swing band and recorded for Capitol, where one song, a version of Jimmie Rodgers' "Gambling Polka Dot Blues," became a hit. Though he recorded for Intro and Coral, among others, he never found the success he enjoyed with Wills. Wills never found another vocalist with Tommy's charisma, either. In the early 1960's Wills and Duncan briefly reunited for appearances and recordings for Liberty. Duncan continued performing, mostly on the West Coast, until his death in 1967 from a heart attack. —R.K.

Bob Dunn

BORN: February 8, 1908
BIRTHPLACE: Braggs, Oklahoma
DIED: May 27, 1971

Bob Dunn began his musical career like many musicians: playing Hawaiian steel guitar at a time when that instrument was all the rage. But Dunn was not satisfied to play mere Hawaiian tunes. He loved jazz and developed a solo technique on the instrument that took more from horn players than from guitarists. When Milton Brown added him to The Musical Brownies in 1935, Dunn was playing an instrument that started a revolution. It was a small Martin acoustic, the strings raised, amplified with a Volu-Tone pickup and amplifier. He had to magnetize the strings before playing. But with The Brownies, on tunes like "Taking Off" and "Yes Sir!," Dunn created dynamic solos that used the amplifier to enhance the sound. Though some of these solos may have sounded crude, Dunn paved the way for every electric steel guitarist who came after him. After joining The Texas Playboys, Leon McAuliffe, who idolized Dunn, talked Bob Wills into buying him an amplified steel to get a similar sound. After Brown's death in 1936, Dunn worked with various groups, recording with some, and leading his own group, The Vagabonds. As the 1940's approached and new steel guitarists emerged, Dunn's career waned. By the early 60's, he ran a Houston music store. His contributions were never properly acknowledged by historians until Bill C. Malone's book, *Country Music U.S.A.*, appeared with a discussion of The Brownies. Malone did obtain some rudimentary information from Dunn, who unfortunately died before the true revival of interest in Western swing began. In 1992, his accomplishments were recognized when he was posthumously inducted into the International Steel Guitar Hall of Fame. —R.K.

Holly Dunn

BORN: August 22, 1957
BIRTHPLACE: San Antonio, Texas

Though full-fledged stardom has thus far eluded her, Holly Dunn, one of country music's most gifted women songwriters, has been a significant presence in the charts throughout the late 1980's and the early 1990's. "Daddy's Hands" (a song she wrote about her father, a preacher, which was first recorded by The Whites), "Love Someone Like Me" (her first Number One single), "A Face in the Crowd" (a Grammy-nominated duet with Michael Martin Murphey), "Are You Ever Gonna Love Me," "There Goes My Heart Again" and "You Really Had Me Going" are some of her better known chart records.

Dunn was born in San Antonio, Texas, in 1957, and earned a college degree in public relations and advertising before setting her sights on a full-time music career. In Nashville she first struck gold as a

songwriter, turning out tunes for Terri Gibbs, Sylvia, Marie Osmond, Louise Mandrell and The Whites, among others. When MTM, her publishing company, offered her a record contract in 1986, success soon followed. She recorded three albums for MTM—*Holly Dunn, Cornerstone, The Blue Rose of Texas*—before moving to Warner Bros. in 1990. She recorded for them until moving over to the new River North label in '94. Dunn's been an Opry member since 1989. Her brother, Chris Waters, is a frequent songwriting collaborator.   —B.A.

Bob Dylan

BORN: May 24, 1941
BIRTHPLACE: Hibbing, Minnesota

One of the most gifted and influential 20th-century American popular songwriters, Bob Dylan is most often associated with folk music (in the 1960's) and rock 'n' roll. Yet when asked about his musical roots, and specifically about his idol, folk singer Woody Guthrie, in a *Playboy* interview some years ago, Dylan replied: "I could have listened to the Stanley Brothers and gotten to the same place."

Dylan's influence on and contributions to the country field have indeed been substantial. He recorded three albums in Nashville in the late 1960's, including 1969's *Nashville Skyline;* a full-blown country outing. Not only did Johnny Cash write the liner notes and duet with Dylan on *Nashville Skyline;* instrumental accompaniment was served up on this and on Dylan's two previous Music City albums—1966's *Blond on Blonde* and 1968's *John Wesley Harding*—by A-Team Nashville session pickers like Charlie McCoy, Pete Drake, Kenny Buttrey, Hargus "Pig" Robbins, Charlie Daniels, Norman Blake and Wayne Moss. Dylan's trifecta of Music City albums did much to set loose the Southern California-meets Nashville country-rock explosion of the late 60's and early 70's, which was personified by groups like The Flying Burrito Brothers and The Byrds (who had a tremendous amount of chart mileage with Dylan compositions).

Dylan's excursion into country music in the 1960's more or less coincided with a period in Johnny Cash's career when he became intrigued with the music and social concerns of the Manhattan-based folk music scene. The friendship that developed between the

two men, in retrospect, seemed inevitable.

Besides recording a number of duets together (a few of which ended up on both men's solo albums) Cash and his wife, June, had a Top Five hit with Dylan's oft-covered "It Ain't Me, Babe" in 1965. On June 7, 1969, when Dylan made a rare television appearance on the debut broadcast of Cash's ABC-TV musical series (on which the respective kings of folk-rock and country duetted on Dylan's "Girl from the North Country"), it seemed to symbolize a coming together of the two often disparate fields of music and captured the imagination of America's increasingly anti-establishment youth movement, which was then just beginning to turn on to the sounds of slightly left-of-center country artists like Kris Kristofferson. Kristofferson (whose early career was boosted immensely by appearances on Cash's TV show) also forged a friendship with Dylan that has since resulted in several songwriting collaborations and a joint appearance in the 1973 feature film, *Pat Garrett and Billy the Kid.*

Through the years, any number of other country artists—everyone from John Anderson and Doc and Merle Watson, to Claude King and Judy Rodman—have covered Dylan's songs.   —B.A.

Steve Earle

BORN: January 17, 1955
BIRTHPLACE: Fort Monroe, Virginia

Despite the fact that he made only a passing dent in the country charts in the mid and late 1980's, and even though he rather unceremoniously burned his bridges with the country music industry by re-hitching his star to the rock 'n' roll world and living like there was no tomorrow, Steve Earle's impact on the mid-1980's New Traditionalist movement was immense. Looking back, Nashville's mid-80's musical renaissance had as much to do with a renewed openness to diversity as it did with mere revivalism. The times produced not only Randy Travis and Alan Jackson, but also Lyle Lovett, Nanci Griffith, k.d. lang...*and* Steve Earle.

If Earle were only judged by his remarkable 1986 debut album, *Guitar Town*, he would still emerge as one of the most important figures of those times. No surprise that the album (produced by Tony Brown and Emory Gordy Jr. and released in 1986) hit Number One on the country album charts and won Earle first place in the rock magazine *Rolling Stone's* annual critics poll for best country artist. *Guitar Town*, the title tune of which made it to Number Seven in the singles charts, was an inspired, muscular and uncompromising piece of music that reverberated with a bold, exuberant, latter-day Duane Eddy-style, larger-than-life electric guitar sound. The album was also chock full of vintage Earle originals which, like the best work of John Mellencamp or Bruce Springsteen, teemed with all the anger, longing, frustration and abandon of being young, restless and wild in small-town America. Much like Dwight Yoakam's *Guitars, Cadillacs, Etc., Etc.* (which was released around the same time), Earle's debut also bristled with a scowling, sneering, anti-establishment

raunch and rebellion. As such, it was like a stone being hurled into the placid waters of Nashville. Earle—like Yoakam—never more than thinly veiled his personal contempt for Music City's rather incestuous, small-town, behind-the-scenes politics, and refused to jump through the usual hoops. Unlike a clean cut crowd-pleaser like George Strait or Randy Travis, the impolitic Earle wasn't afraid to go on stage wearing a dirty T-shirt and ragged-ass jeans. And he certainly wouldn't smile and grovel and say "Thank you, ma'am" unless he felt like it.

Born in Virginia and raised in Texas, Earle spent quite a few years in Nashville on the periphery of an immense talented, iconoclastic clique of Texas-to-Nashville songwriters that included Guy Clark, Townes Van Zandt and a young Rodney Crowell. Besides teaching Earle the art of their craft (his songs have been recorded by everyone from Waylon Jennings to Kelly Willis), these young renegades also taught him a few lessons about the struggle one faced on Music Row in putting the creative imperative ahead of mere commercial considerations. The brash rebelliousness that Earle brought not only to his record-making, but to his whole style of living (a half dozen or so marriages and still counting, sporadic brushes with the law for everything from petty drug violations to failure to show for jury duty) quickly made him a hero with the critics while more or less crucifying him, career-wise, within the industry itself.

Ultimately Earle's idea of artistic purity proved to be a strange one, indeed—one which evidently only he alone could envision and which ultimately led him down the road to creative ruin and personal disaster. After making a couple more uneven albums in Nashville after *Guitar Town*, he switched his allegiance to the rock 'n' roll field, made several more albums, then quickly vanished into that career black hole that ultimately swallows most Nashville artists who openly court rock stardom. In the end, Earle pursued his musical vision down a dangerous dead-end street which, by the early 90's left him in a shambles of drug addiction, major health problems and not the slightest hint of a career.

Yet if there is anyone with the personal history to launch the sort of dramatic come-back from which modern legends are fashioned, it's got to be Earle. A talent as bull-headed and fiercely original as his, no matter how self-destructive, can never be completely counted out.
—B.A.

Ray Edenton

BORN: November 3, 1926
BIRTHPLACE: Mineral, Virginia

Though Ray Quarles Edenton never became quite as well known as Hank Garland, Grady Martin and other hot Nashville sidemen of the 50's, 60's and 70's, he was a rhythm guitar ace and part of the Nashville A-Team of session pickers during those years. He began playing around his home area, then served in the Army during World War II. In 1946, he returned to Mineral and started working as an electric guitarist with a local band, The Radio Rangers. He worked with them and with other acts around Virginia and, by 1948, was playing bass with Joe Maphis' Corn Crackers band in Richmond on WRVA's *Old Dominion Barn Dance*. In 1949 he and several WRVA musicians moved to WNOX, where he met Chet Atkins. Following a two-year bout with tuberculosis, Edenton moved to Nashville in 1952. He began working with various Opry artists and decided to concentrate on rhythm guitar. He started working sessions about 1953, and, on many, he played acoustic rhythm in a way that imitated a snare drum. He played on the Kitty

Wells-Red Foley hit duet, "One By One," and by the mid-50's was doing extensive session work. One of his few lead guitar solos was on Marty Robbins' "Singin' the Blues." Though rock 'n' roll set his session work back for a time, Edenton rebounded by becoming a crucial part of The Everly Brothers' sound, playing the acoustic rhythm licks with Don Everly. Through the 60's he was on dozens of hit records and did an album on his own for Columbia. He continued to be active into the 70's, and has been honored by the Nashville recording industry, including awards as NARAS' Superpicker of the Year.   —R.K.

Joe Ely

BORN: February 9, 1947
BIRTHPLACE: Amarillo, Texas

Though Joe Ely has never been a hitmaker, his influence on the progressive country of the 1970's and beyond has been immense. Primarily an album artist, Ely grew up in Lubbock, Texas, and lived in Fort Worth for a time in the 60's. He later played music and worked in the dramatic field in England for a time. In the 70's, when he returned home, the so-called Austin Sound that focused attention on Texas singers and songwriters was just taking shape. Ely teamed up with singer-writers Butch Hancock and Jimmie Dale Gilmore to form a group called The Flatlanders, who played their own unique mix of country. They made an album around 1972. After returning to the Lubbock area, Ely struck out on his own and formed a hard-driving electric band. His mix of the music of Texas, blues, honky tonk, Tex-Mex, rhythm and blues, rock and hard country, combined with original material, earned him an MCA contract in 1977, and every album he made earned him critical acclaim. *Joe Ely, Honky Tonk Masquerade, Down on the Drag* and other albums like *Musta Notta Gotta Lotta* and the live album, *Live Shots*, earned him considerable respect and made him a popular live attraction. Unfortunately, he didn't sell albums in sufficient numbers, and MCA dropped him in the mid-80's. Ely continued on, recording for small labels until he returned to MCA in 1990. Ely was seen as such a musical fountainhead, as the careers of former bandmates Butch Hancock and Jimmie Dale Gilmore surged, that MCA reissued his early albums and had him recording new ones. Though never a Garth-like star, Ely has carved out a formidable—and lasting—niche for himself and his music.   —R.K.

Ralph Emery

BORN: March 10, 1933
BIRTHPLACE: McEwen, Tennessee

Walter Ralph Emery is more than just the world's best-known country disc jockey and air personality. Over the years he's become nearly as legendary a figure as many of the stars whose careers he has helped launch: Dolly Parton, Marty Robbins, The Judds, Patsy Cline, Loretta Lynn, Willie Nelson, Conway Twitty, Johnny Horton, Barbara Mandrell and Jimmy Dean among them. (Emery even has his own fan club with over 5,000 members.)

Emery has been a fixture on WSM-Radio—the flagship station of the Grand Ole Opry and, for years, the most powerful clear-channel AM station in the South—for what seems like ages. For quite a few years, his visibility was also expanded by his role as announcer for the Opry. An admitted workaholic, Emery also balanced his radio work with the additional role of TV personality. He hosted the immensely popular early-morning *Ralph Emery Show* on Nashville's WSMV-TV from 1972 until recently, and also chaired The Nashville Network's musical variety/talk show, *Nashville Now*, from 1983 until '93. Though sorely lacking in Carson's quick wit, Emery has nonetheless been referred to by *Cable Guide Magazine* as "the Johnny Carson of cable." Singer Ronnie Milsap once observed that Emery, in his heyday, was "to country music what Dick Clark is to rock 'n' roll."

Born in 1933 in McEwen, Tennessee, Emery came to Nashville at an early age with his mother after she divorced his alcoholic father. He attended Belmont College, worked as a movie usher and emceed local

wrestling matches before breaking into broadcasting—first with WAGG, in Paris, Tennessee, and later with brief stints at WNAH and WSIX (Nashville), and WLLS (Baton Rouge). In 1957, at age 24, Emery, with great trepidation, auditioned for "the graveyard shift" on WSM, which was then already one of the most widely listened-to stations, heard in 38 states and even parts of Canada.

It was the open house policy that Emery soon developed on his radio shows that ultimately gave him such an instrumental role in the careers of the music's biggest names. In the middle of the night, artists—anyone from virtual unknowns to superstars of the day like Waylon Jennings, Johnny Cash and Buck Owens—would drop by to sing some songs, play their latest releases, or bare their souls on the air about their latest divorces. Despite his chumminess with the stars and his droll charm, Emery admits that he could also be brusque, boorish, even downright boring, at times. (In recent years, he's sometimes had the unfortunate tendency to occasionally forget the names of younger artists he invited on the show, and often comes across as your least favorite, humorless, fuddy-duddy uncle.)

In 1991, Emery documented his colorful life and career with an immensely entertaining and revealing autobiography, *Memories*, which became a surprise best-seller. In *Memories*, he candidly recalls his four marriages, occasional financial woes and bouts with pills and alcohol, as well as his own couple of (mainly forgettable) efforts as a recording artist. ("Hello Fool," Emery's "answer song" to Faron Young's "Hello Walls," somehow managed to straggle to Number Four in the country singles charts in the early 60's.) The book's popularity prompted him to write a sequel, *More Memories*, in 1993. Today, he hosts occasional specials for The Nashville Network. —B.A.

Buddy Emmons

BORN: January 27, 1937
BIRTHPLACE: Mishawaka, Indiana

One of the pedal steel guitar's greatest virtuosos, Buddy Gene Emmons was encouraged to take up steel by his country music-loving parents. As a youth in Indiana, he worked with everyone from local acts to jazz guitarist Arvin Garrison. While appearing in Detroit, Little Jimmy Dickens heard Emmons and hired him to replace Walter Haynes in Dickens' Country Boys in 1955. After several years with Dickens, he joined Ernest Tubb's Texas Troubadours. Emmons and steel guitarist Shot Jackson collaborated on a steel guitar design that became the Sho-Bud pedal steel in the mid-1950's. Their Nashville-based operation enjoyed great success with country steel players since Bigsby, the favored brand of pedal guitar, had a long waiting list for deliveries. Emmons went on to work with Ray Price and in 1963 recorded *Steel Guitar Jazz* for Mercury Records, the first pedal steel jazz album ever done. Around that same time, after

splitting from Sho-Bud, he founded the Emmons Steel Guitar company to build steels. Emmons' trademarks were his lightning-fast single string solos, which were deeply influenced by jazz, though he could capably handle standard country licks as well. He left Price in 1967 to play bass with Roger Miller, and lived in California until 1974. Back in Nashville, Emmons kept recording with others and made his own recordings for a number of labels, including instruction videos. Today, in addition to his recording and instructional work, he regularly tours with The Everly Brothers. He's been a member of the International Steel Guitar Hall of Fame since 1981. —R.K.

Melvin Endsley

BORN: January 30, 1934
BIRTHPLACE: Heber Springs, Arkansas

Melvin Endsley never enjoyed the career he deserved as a singer, but his songs assure him a secure place in country music history. "Singing the Blues" and "Knee Deep in the Blues" were among Marty Robbins' and Guy Mitchell's biggest records. In the summer of 1957 Andy Williams made "I Like Your Kind of Love" a Top Ten pop hit, while pop thrush Jill Corey pushed "Love Me to Pieces" into the pop Top 20.

Endsley was born on January 30, 1934, in Heber Springs, Arkansas. A bout with polio at age three left him without the use of his legs. He learned slide guitar around 1947 during a two-year hospital stay in Memphis, and began writing songs soon after returning to his home in Drasco, Arkansas. In July 1955, Endsley and a friend drove to Nashville, hoping to pitch "Singing the Blues" and other songs to Webb Pierce. Marty Robbins was impressed with what he heard, and arranged an Acuff-Rose songwriting contract for him.

In December 1956, Endsley began recording for RCA Victor. During the next two years the label released seven singles featuring his blues-tinged baritone; many included his bottleneck-style rhythm guitar. Despite their quality, his RCA singles failed to catch on, nor did later sides on MGM, Hickory or his own Mel-Ark label. Ironically, various reissues of these recordings have met with critical acclaim, bringing Endsley belated recognition as a recording artist. —D.S.

Epiphone

The Epiphone musical instrument company grew out of the House of Stathopoulo, which was founded in 1873 by Anastasios Stathopoulo in New York City. Anastasios' son, Epaminondas—or "Epi"—followed in his father's musical footsteps, became a luthier and subsequently lent his name to the company's now-famous emblem. During the 1920's, the company became one of the leading banjo manufacturers in the country, creating instruments that were extraordinarily ornate as well as brilliant sounding.

However, by the end of the decade the banjo began to decline in popularity, so the company shifted its focus to guitar building. The move was a windfall. During the 1930's, Epiphone had one of the most esteemed reputations in the archtop guitar arena. Throughout the decade, the company gave its archrival, Gibson, some fierce competition.

After World War II, however, Epiphone fell on some hard times. In 1953, the Stathopoulo family sold the business to the C.G. Conn Company, a well-known maker of musical instruments. In 1957, Gibson bought Epiphone. Today the company, headquartered in Nashville, continues to make quality electric and acoustic guitars. Among the country singers using Epiphone guitars was Ernest Tubb.   —R.P.

Dale Evans

BORN: October 31, 1912
BIRTHPLACE: Uvalde, Texas

Dale Evans began her film and music career even before marrying Roy Rogers in 1947. She was born Frances Octavia Smith on October 31, 1912, in Uvalde, Texas. The Smith family left Texas when Frances was very young and moved to Osceola, Arkansas, where Frances married Thomas Frederick Fox at the

age of 16. After her divorce two years later, she set out to make a name for herself as a singer.

Smith, then known as Dale Evans, performed on radio programs in Memphis, Dallas and Louisville before hooking up with Anson Weeks' band in Chicago in the late 1930's. She made her Hollywood debut in the 1943 film *Swing Your Partner*. It was at around this time that she met Roy Rogers, who would become her frequent co-star and, more importantly, her husband. The pair wed on December 31, 1947. They starred together on television's *The Roy Rogers Show* in the 50's and, in the 60's, on the *Roy Rogers & Dale Evans Show*. In the 80's, Roy and Dale hosted the *Happy Trails Theater* on cable television's Nashville Network. (See also, Roy Rogers.)   —M.B.

Leon Everette

BORN: June 21, 1948
BIRTHPLACE: Aiken, South Carolina

Though born in South Carolina, Everette was raised in Queens, New York (one of the boroughs of New York City).

He began his career in country music recording for the independent labels Doral, True and Orlando (which was started by Everette's manager) in the late 70's.

After some minor chart success, including the Top Ten "Over," RCA signed him in 1980. Over the next four years, Everette placed six songs in the Top Ten— "Hurricane," "Midnight Rodeo" and "I Could'a Had You" among them.

But Everette never really broke through to superstar status, and moved over to Mercury Records in 1985.

Subsequent singles—in a more contemporary vein than his earlier material—fared less successfully on the charts, and in 1986 Everette returned to the Orlando label, charting two more singles.   —G.F.

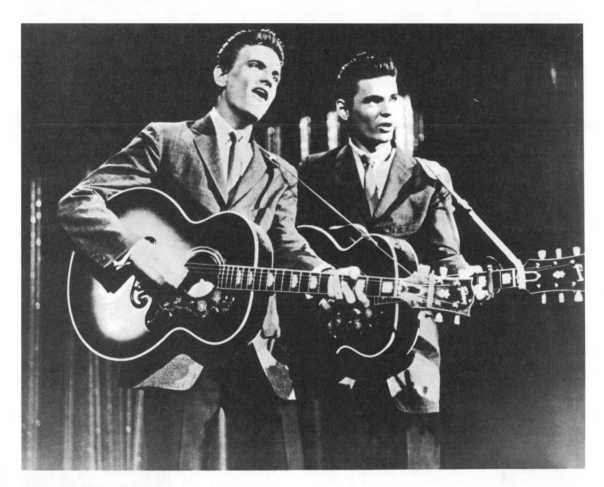

The Everly Brothers

BORN: Don, February 1, 1937, Brownie, Kentucky
Phil, January 19, 1939, Chicago, Illinois

Legendary rock 'n' rollers Don and Phil Everly have deep Kentucky roots. Their late father, guitarist Ike Everly, came from the western Kentucky school of finger pickers that spawned Merle Travis. Ike, in fact, was one of several pickers who actually taught Merle to play. Don and Phil got their start as kids working on shows and on small radio stations with their parents. They began singing in the close harmony duet styles made popular by The Blue Sky Boys and The Louvin Brothers. In the early 50's, Ike Everly took them to a performance where they met Chet Atkins, who had taken his own guitar inspiration from Travis. Atkins, not yet a major power in Nashville, nonetheless got them an audition with Columbia Records, where they recorded four songs in 1955, backed by Carl Smith's Tunesmiths.

Those songs went nowhere. Still, the family moved to Nashville and the brothers started getting some work on the country circuit. Columbia passed on a long-term relationship, but by 1957, with rock 'n' roll gaining strength in Elvis' wake, they signed with Cadence Records, owned by pop bandleader Archie Bleyer.

Acuff-Rose head Wesley Rose introduced them to the husband-wife songwriting team of Felice and Boudleaux Bryant, who would write most of their early hits, including "Bye Bye Love" and "Wake Up Little Susie." The success of these two singles in 1957 propelled Don and Phil into stardom, and they sold to both teenagers and the country audience.

All these hits were recorded in Nashville with Chet Atkins, Hank Garland, Ray Edenton and other country sidemen. They recorded a number of albums for Cadence, and freely paid homage to their country roots on *Songs Our Daddy Taught Us*.

Departing Cadence for Warner Bros. in 1960, The Everlys moved away from country into a stronger pop identity. Hits like "Cathy's Clown" attested to the soundness of this move. Their *Country Hits* and *Roots* albums again saluted their country backgrounds. By the mid-1960's their popularity had receded somewhat, though the occasional single, like "Bowling Green," kept their profile reasonably high, as did their short-lived, early 70's TV show on ABC, a replacement for Johnny Cash's program.

In 1973, long-standing tensions exploded between Don and Phil, culminating in a rancorous onstage breakup during a series of performances at Knott's Berry Farm in California. For the next decade they pursued solo careers that yielded minimal success. Finally in 1983 they reconciled, returning to the stage at London's Royal Albert Hall. Several albums followed. The Everlys continue touring today with an all-star band, including guitarist Albert Lee and steel guitar virtuoso Buddy Emmons.　　　—R.K.

Exile

This country-rock band, formed in Lexington, Kentucky, in 1963, segued into country music after fleeting success in the rock field (with the million-selling single, "Kiss You All Over"). Their heyday came in the 1980's with a string of tepid Number One singles, including "Woke Up in Love," "Give Me One More Chance," "Hang on to Your Heart," "She's Too Good

To Be True" and "I Can't Get Close Enough." With various personnel shifts, Exile continued recording into the early 1990's. Throughout the years their music has been uniformly pleasant and thoroughly competent, yet hindered by a recurring blandness—in other words, expertly performed "chart fodder."

Original members J.P. Pennington (vocals and lead guitar) and Les Taylor (vocals and rhythm guitar) both left the band to pursue solo careers. Pennington's debut album, *Whatever It Takes*, was released in 1991. Taylor's two solo outings, *That Old Desire* and *Blue Kentucky Wind*, were released in 1990 and 1991, respectively.

Other Exile members over the years have included Sonny Lemaire, Steve Goetzmann, Paul Martin, and Lee Carroll.　　　—B.A.

Barbara Fairchild

BORN: November 12, 1950
BIRTHPLACE: Lafe, Arkansas

Born in Lafe, Arkansas, in 1950, Barbara Fairchild signed her first recording contract at age 15; a few years later, after impressing music publisher Jerry Crutchfield with her original songs, she moved to Nashville and signed with Kapp Records. Crutchfield arranged an audition with legendary Colum-  bia record producer Billy Sherrill, and before long Fairchild had a handful of singles on the Columbia label: "Love Is a Gentle Thing" and "A Woman's Hand" in 1969, and her own "A Girl Who'll Satisfy Her Man" and "Loving You Is Special" in 1970.

By 1972, after three albums and a string of singles, Fairchild still hadn't scored a hit when an Atlanta DJ played a cut from her *A Sweeter Love* album called "The Teddy Bear Song." The station was bombarded with requests for the song, and Columbia, encouraged, released it as a single. By early 1973 it had reached Number One on the country charts and crossed over to the pop charts as well. Barbara

Fairchild had arrived.

She had several more Top Ten singles in the early 70's, including "Kid Stuff" and "Baby Doll," but "The Teddy Bear Song" would remain her biggest hit. As a songwriter under contract to MCA she wrote material for artists such as Loretta Lynn, Liz Anderson and David Sloane.

Fairchild left Columbia in the late 1970's. She recorded for some smaller labels, with her final chart entry appearing in 1986. For a time, Fairchild even left music and worked as a waitress. Today, she records sacred material for small, independent labels.   —M.B.

Donna Fargo

BORN: November 10, 1949
BIRTHPLACE: Mount Airy, North Carolina

Donna Fargo was born Yvonne Vaughn on November 10, 1949, in Mount Airy, North Carolina. She burst on the country scene in 1972. A powerful singer and gifted

songwriter, Fargo seemed destined for long term country stardom when the onset of a debilitating illness stifled her career in the late 70's.

After years of paying her dues—teaching English by day and writing and performing at night—Fargo signed with Dot Records and wrote the once-in-a-lifetime song that brought her to the top of country music: "The Happiest Girl in the Whole U.S.A." The song made it to Number One, spent 23 weeks on the charts, in 1972 and won the Country Music Association's Single of the Year award. It also won Fargo a Grammy for Best Performance by a Country Female Vocalist.

It was the beginning of a seven-year streak that would include 15 more Top Ten hits, five of which would make it to Number One: "Funny Face" in 1972, "Superman" and "You Were Always There" a year later, plus "You Can't Be a Beacon (If Your Light Don't Shine)" (1974), and, after moving over to Warner Bros., "That Was Yesterday" (1977).

In 1978, at the age of 29, Fargo was diagnosed with multiple sclerosis. She continued recording though, scoring chart entries for RCA, Columbia, Mercury and, in 1991, the independent label Cleveland International.

Today she lives a relatively quiet life with her husband in Williamson County, Tennessee, and still performs regularly.   —M.B.

The Farr Brothers

BORN: Hugh, December 3, 1903, Llano, Texas
        Karl, April 25, 1909, Rochelle, Texas
DIED: Hugh, March 17, 1980
        Karl, September 20, 1961

Guitarist Karl Farr and his fiddling brother Hugh Farr, best known for their work with The Sons of the Pioneers, also recorded several guitar-fiddle duets in 1934 and 1935 on their own. Their instrumentals differed considerably from The Pioneers' material, often drifting into unadulterated jazz in the style of jazz violinist Joe Venuti and his partner, guitarist Eddie Lang. While The Pioneers recorded for Standard Transcriptions in the 1930's, The Farrs also recorded separately as The Cornhuskers.

Hugh left the Pioneers in 1958; Karl was with them until he died in 1961. Karl Farr's guitar playing also had a major influence on Hank Snow's flatpicking style. Hugh died on March 17, 1980.   —R.K.

Narvel Felts

BORN: November 11, 1938
BIRTHPLACE: Bernie, Missouri

At 14, Narvel Felts picked $15 worth of cotton to buy himself a guitar from the Sears, Roebuck catalogue. Twenty years later, the Missouri-born singer had a Top Five single. In the early 1960's Felts did some session work in Nashville, but not until he signed with Pink Records in the late 1960's did he enjoy some measure of success. After a few mildly successful singles, Felts and a friend set up their own record label, Cinnamon, in 1972. The following year, Felts had the Top Five single, "Drift Away," followed by the Top 20, "All in the Name of Love," and the Top Ten, "When Your Good Love Was Mine." In 1975 Felts signed with ABC Records and became a regular on the country charts, with singles like "Reconsider Me" (Number Two in 1975), "Lonely Teardrops" (Top Five in '76), "I Don't Hurt Anymore" (1977) and "Everlasting Love" and "Moment by Moment," both in 1979. Around this time ABC merged with MCA Records, and Felts fell by the wayside, recording for smaller labels up until 1987. —M.B.

Fender Guitar

Clarence Leo Fender, born in 1909 in Orange County, California, never played an instrument, but his innovations had an enormous impact on country music's artists and its sound. Electricity, engineering and tinkering fascinated him, and, by 1938, he quit his job with the government to open a shop in Fullerton, fixing radios, record players and early musical instrument amplifiers. A lover of Hawaiian guitar and country music, he began studying those instruments and their pickups. In 1943 he and his friend, Doc Kauffmann, designed an instrument pickup and an electric solidbody Spanish guitar based on Rickenbacker's Electro solidbody (it is now in Opryland's Roy Acuff instrument collection). By 1945 Fender and Kauffmann were building "K&F" brand Hawaiian steels and amplifiers. By 1946 Fender was working on his own, founding the Fender Electric Instrument company, building steel guitars and amplifiers. With the burgeoning country music scene in California, and that scene's greater emphasis on electric guitars, his timing was perfect. Only Rickenbacker preceded him there. Fender began building multineck steel guitars (though he was not the first to do this) in 1947, and his first went to Spade Cooley sideman, steel virtuoso Noel Boggs. Soon Bob Wills had become a friend, and

Fender regularly gave amplifiers to The Playboys and steel guitars to Playboy steel guitarist Herb Remington. The musicians would use the amps on the road and bring them back to Fender with recommendations for improvements. Leon McAuliffe also became an early supporter of Fender steel guitars, using an early Fender double-neck, and later, a four-neck "Stringmaster" model. Fender also helped Cliffie Stone on dances that Stone promoted in nearby Placentia. After borrowing Merle Travis' solidbody Bigsby– whose strings went through the body like a steel guitar's—he used that instrument's fundamentals, adding many ideas of his own, to introduce the Fender

Broadcaster solidbody Spanish guitar in 1950. Two of the first country pickers to use it were Jimmy Bryant and Hank Penny, as well as Jimmy Wyble of Spade Cooley's band. After Gretsch protested, since they had a "Broadkaster" drum set on the market, Fender changed the name to "Telecaster" in 1951. That same year, Fender introduced the electric solidbody bass guitar to the market. Other Western acts followed Wills' lead in using Fender guitars and/or amps, including Hank Thompson's band, The Brazos Valley Boys. Wills was so loyal to Fender that when one of his musicians worked out an endorsement deal with Rickenbacker behind Wills' back, Wills fired the musician on the spot. In 1954, California country guitarist Bill Carson began working for Fender and played a major role in designing the Fender Stratocaster. Texas Playboy Eldon Shamblin got one of the prototype models. Fender began to make pedal steels, and Speedy West became an early endorser, later going to work for Fender. Steel guitarist Freddie Tavares, who formerly worked with Foy Willing and The Riders of the Purple Sage, helped Fender design his Jazzmaster guitar in 1958.

The Telecaster became the most popular country guitar, becoming an essential part of the Bakersfield sound. Buck Owens bought his first model in 1952 and later, Don Rich, his lead guitarist, played a "Tele" as well. Studio guitarist James Burton used a Tele with Elvis, Emmylou Harris and other acts. So did Merle Haggard's longtime lead guitarist, Roy Nichols, and Johnny Cash guitarists, Luther Perkins and Bob Wooton. Waylon Jennings' leather-encased Telecaster became one of the symbols of the Outlaw movement, and Fender's acoustic guitars have also proved popular with various singers.

Fender sold his company to CBS in 1965 for $13 million, and though the company grew, cost-cutting hurt its reputation badly. Many old hands left. Leo Fender's sale agreement forbade him from making instruments for five years. In 1971 he helped his Vice President, Forrest White, begin the Music Man company, which began production in 1975. By the early 80's, Leo started G&L to make guitars and basses. Meanwhile, in 1985, former Fender employee Bill Schultz bought the company back from CBS. Under Schultz, Fender's earlier reputation has been restored and Fender instruments, as well as other brands building instruments with obvious Fender-inspired designs, continue to be an important part of country music in the 90's. Leo Fender died in 1991.   —R.K.

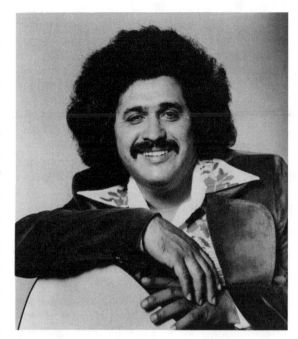

Freddy Fender

BORN: June 4, 1937
BIRTHPLACE: San Benito, Texas

Despite his vast emotional power as a vocal stylist, Freddy Fender had been kicking around for years with only marginal success when Cajun producer Huey Meaux hooked him up with an aching, wistful country ballad called "Before the Next Teardrop Falls" in 1975. When "Before the Next Teardrop Falls" topped the country charts, and got some pop play as well, Fender (real name: Baldemar Huerta), much to his own amazement, found himself a country star. Other hits—like "Wasted Days and Wasted Nights" (which sold two million copies after its 1976 release), "Secret Love," "You'll Lose a Good Thing" and "The Wild Side of Life"—soon followed.

"It was weird, man," Fender told *Country Music Magazine*'s Bob Allen in 1984. "When I first heard 'Teardrop,' I thought it was a bad gringo song...I mean, I used to ridicule country music. I thought anybody who listened to it was a hillbilly or somethin'. And I'd always thought I was this real cool Pachuco dude with my long hair, sideburns, chain hangin' down outa my pocket and all that shit—a real San Benito city slicker. Then, sheeitt! Here I am all of a sudden, Freddy Fender, the country music star!"

Fender was born in San Benito, Texas, in June

121

1937, in a dirt-floor shack. His father, an illiterate laborer, died when Fender was seven, leaving Fender's mother to try and fend for their nine children alone. From then on, Fender's life seemed ill-starred. By his early teens he was roving the country as a migrant farm laborer. At 16 he joined the Marines but was booted out with a bad conduct discharge a couple of years later for brawling, drinking and stealing food from the mess hall.

Back in civilian clothes he plunged into music full-time, since it seemed to be his only possible road out of poverty. Billing himself as "El Bebop Kid," he enjoyed fleeting success in the mid-50's with a Spanish version of "Don't Be Cruel," prompting fans to dub him Elvis Presley Mexicano. In 1959, he hit the regional charts again with an early version of "Wasted Days and Wasted Nights." But in 1960 he was busted on a minor drug charge in a Baton Rouge club, and he spent the next three years at the grim Louisiana State Penitentiary at Angola. After prison, Fender went back to a dreary life of singing in beer joints and working minimum wage jobs, and wound up back in jail at least once on a vagrancy charge. He'd recorded (by his own reckoning) over 200 singles and nine Spanish-language albums and was working a $1.80-an-hour car wash job when he hooked up with Meaux and "Teardrop" in the mid-70's.

By the early 80's, the bloom was already off Fender's recording career, and he found himself beset by the same sort of personal, financial and marital problems that had plagued him in the years before his big break. But in more recent years, he's found new life and creative inspiration in The Texas Tornados, a celebrated quartet which also includes Doug Sahm, Flaco Jimenez and Augie Meyers. Fender also briefly ventured into acting, turning in a particularly impressive supporting role in Robert Redford's 1988 *The Milagro Beanfield Wars*. (See also, Texas Tornados.) —B.A.

Fiddle

One of the most demanding instruments to master, the fiddle predates the banjo and guitar in country music. The first major country artists to record, Eck Robertson and Fiddlin' John Carson, were essentially solo fiddlers.

Most American fiddle styles derive from British, Irish and Scottish traditions. As the country expanded westward, musicians within isolated cultures developed their own approaches to the standard fiddlers' repertoire. The most distinct geographical changes are reflected in bowing techniques, amount of ornamentation and rhythmic approach. A Texan might approach a tune with long, bow strokes and considerable embellishment, while a Georgian might play the same tune with short, rhythmic strokes and minimal adornment.

The rise of radio and records brought outside influences that affected, if not entirely replaced, regional fiddle styles. During the 1930's, talented young country fiddlers freely took ideas from popular violinists like Fritz Kreisler, Dave Rubinoff and Joe Venuti. The hybridization of styles was inevitable; bluegrass fiddling owes as much to French swing violinist Stephane Grappelli as it does to Tex Atchison, Fiddlin' Arthur Smith, Curly Fox, Howdy Forrester and other influential pre-World War II fiddlers.

Two of the most popular bandleaders of the late 1930's and early 40's were fiddlers: Roy Acuff in the Southeast and Bob Wills in the Southwest. Both Acuff and Wills usually gave solo space to more accomplished fiddlers in their bands. Most Western swing fiddlers were influenced by Wills and Cliff Bruner, but their swinging improvisations came from jazz fiddlers like Joe Venuti, Stephane Grappelli and Stuff Smith. The instrument was frequently heard in the honky tonk country sounds that emerged after 1945; fiddlers Tommy Jackson and Dale Potter became important Nashville session men. Since 1957 the fiddle has moved in and out of fashion in mainstream country music, although it remains a key instrument in bluegrass and old-time music. In the early 80's its popularity was bolstered by the New Traditionalist movement and new interest in Western swing.

Today, the predominant American fiddling styles and their most well-known practitioners are: Texas (Johnny Gimble, Dale Potter, Byron Berline); bluegrass (Chubby Wise, Kenny Baker, Benny Martin); Cajun (Doug Kershaw, Michael Doucet), and old-time (Ramona Jones, John Hartford, Mike Seeger). Lines between styles cannot always be neatly drawn. Berline introduced Texas fiddling to bluegrass when he joined Bill Monroe in 1967. Versatile modern fiddlers like Vassar Clements, Buddy Spicher, Bobby Hicks, Mark O'Connor, Sam Bush and Alison Krauss draw inspiration from bluegrass, Texas styles, blues, jazz and rock music. —D.S

Lester Flatt

BORN: June 19, 1914
BIRTHPLACE: Overton County, Tennessee
DIED: May 11, 1979

Half of the greatest bluegrass team of all time, Lester Flatt first worked with Charlie Monroe before joining Bill Monroe in 1944. He and five-string banjo innovator Earl Scruggs propelled Bill Monroe's Blue Grass Boys to greater music than ever before, then left in 1948 to work as a team. Monroe didn't speak to Flatt again until the early 1970's. The "Lester Flatt G-run" is a standard among flatpickers of all styles. After he and Scruggs went their separate ways in 1969, Flatt continued with the hardcore traditional bluegrass sound with his band, The Nashville Grass, which included Flatt and Scruggs alumni Curly Seckler and, for a time, fiddler Paul Warren. Flatt recorded for RCA, including a duet album with Mac Wiseman. In part because of his dedication to traditional bluegrass, Flatt and Bill Monroe reconciled during a Flatt appearance at Monroe's bluegrass festival at Bean Blossom. From then on they remained close, Monroe even making a guest appearance on a live Flatt album in the 1970's. Marty Stuart, a mandolin prodigy from Mississippi, got his professional start working with Flatt in 1971. The Nashville Grass also recorded extensively for CMH Records until Lester became ill. He endured heart surgery and continued performing until a later stroke and added heart trouble ended his life in 1979. (See also, Flatt & Scruggs.) —R.K.

Flatt & Scruggs

BORN: Flatt, June 19, 1914, Overton County, Tennessee
Scruggs, January 6, 1924, Cleveland County, North Carolina
DIED: Flatt, May 11, 1979

Though Lester Flatt and Earl Scruggs first worked together after Scruggs joined Bill Monroe, they came into their own in 1948 when they left Monroe's Blue Grass Boys to start their own act. They first settled in Danville, Virginia, where they set up a band not originally identified as "bluegrass": They felt that term applied only to Monroe's music, and never liked being categorized in that field. Inspired by The Carter Family song "Foggy Mountain Top," they named their group The Foggy Mountain Boys. Working at WDNA radio in Danville, they hired guitarist Jim Eanes, soon replaced by Mac Wiseman, along with ex-Monroe bass player Howard Watts (better known as Cedric Rainwater) and fiddler Jim Shumate. After a short time they relocated to Bristol, Virginia, and signed with Mercury Records. They did their first recording dates in Cincinnati, with some songs featuring Scruggs picking guitar instead of banjo. Other songs recorded then became Flatt and Scruggs classics, including, in 1949, "Foggy Mountain Breakdown." Over the next couple of years they based themselves at radio stations in Tennessee, Kentucky, Virginia, North Carolina and Florida. After Wiseman left, they added mandolinist Curly Seckler, who remained until the end. In 1950, during their time in Florida, they recorded "Roll in My Sweet Baby's Arms" and "Salty Dog Blues," both longtime staples of their repertoire. In 1951 they signed with Columbia, where their fortunes grew greater, and in 1953 began their WSM radio show for Martha White Flour. In part due to the ill feeling between themselves and Monroe, they didn't join the Grand Ole Opry until 1956.

Their first three hit records were "'Tis Sweet to Be

123

124

Remembered" (1952), "Cabin in the Hills" (1959) and "Crying My Heart Out Over You" (1960—revived in 1981 by Ricky Skaggs). In 1961, "Go Home" became a Top Ten record. The band lineup gradually settled around a core group that included dobroist Josh Graves, fiddler Paul Warren and mandolinist Curly Seckler. Through shrewd promotion, much of it initiated by their manager (Scruggs' wife, Louise), Flatt and Scruggs received more media attention than any other bluegrass act (which infuriated Bill Monroe's supporters, who felt his role unfairly downplayed). Major articles in general circulation magazines and the group's increasing popularity on college campuses spoke to their growing popularity. Their appearances on CBS-TV's *The Beverly Hillbillies* comedy series also sent their visibility and popularity skyrocketing. In 1962 they had their biggest hit record with their version of the show's theme, "The Ballad of Jed Clampett," and another hit song related to the show, "Pearl, Pearl, Pearl." The recording of their 1963 Carnegie Hall concert has become a classic. In 1968 their original Mercury recording of "Foggy Mountain Breakdown" wound up in the soundtrack to the smash hit film, *Bonnie and Clyde*.

By the late 1960's, Scruggs' eclectic listening tastes, which embraced folk-rock, blues and jazz, were affecting the Flatt and Scruggs repertoire; on occasion they recorded songs by Bob Dylan and other contemporary folk rock numbers and even appeared at San Francisco's famous Fillmore Auditorium. As added studio musicians began showing up on Flatt and Scruggs albums, older fans and Flatt himself became upset. The strain increased, and the final breakup came in 1969. The two never worked together again, though they personally reconciled before Lester's death in 1979. In 1985, the duo was elected to the Country Music Hall of Fame. (See also, Lester Flatt and Earl Scruggs.)   —R.K.

Rosie Flores

BORN: September 10, 1950
BIRTHPLACE: San Antonio, Texas

One of the key figures of the eclectic Los Angeles and Austin country music scenes, Rosie Flores was born in San Antonio in 1950. Her earliest musical influences included the local Tex-Mex sounds, as well as the raw rock 'n' roll of Elvis Presley and Buddy

Holly and the country of Brenda Lee, Wanda Jackson and Buck Owens. In 1967 the family moved to San Diego, where 12-year-old Rosie soaked up styles like surf, blues and California country-rock. At 16, Flores formed Penelope's Children, an all-female rock band, and in 1978 she fronted Rosie and The Screamers, a group that blended heavy doses of classic rockabilly and hard-driving country in a repertoire that included many Flores originals. In 1984, she formed The Screaming Sirens, an all-female cow-punk quintet. The band released *Fiesta* on Enigma Records in 1984.

In 1986 she recorded a self-titled solo album for Warner Bros./Reprise. the record, which was produced by Pete Anderson, Dwight Yoakam's guitarist/producer, showcased Flores' aggressive guitar playing, as well as her vocal prowess and songwriting talent. More importantly, it garnered immediate critical acclaim from both the rock and country press. Between 1986 and 1988 Flores played the Texas honky tonk circuit before relocating to Los Angeles in 1990. In 1992 she signed with HighTone Records and released *After the Farm* (1992) and *Once More With Feeling* (1993).   —R.P.

The Flying Burrito Brothers

After Gram Parsons and Chris Hillman left The Byrds in 1968, they set out to form The Flying Burrito Brothers to explore Parsons' vision of country music, a vision that proved to be enormously influential. Having already been involved in the recording of The Byrds' classic *Sweetheart of the Rodeo* album, they now merged with Sneaky Pete Kleinow (steel), Jon Corneal (drums) and Chris Ethridge (bass) and went on to create some of the most visionary country-rock of all time. Their 1968 debut album, *The Gilded Palace of Sin*, featuring the group clad in customized Nudie outfits, is considered a classic today, with its visions of 1960's upheaval mixed with Parsons' drug-enhanced view of California, the whole blended with traditional country instrumentation. The band went through various personnel changes, and, following the appearance of the album *Burrito Deluxe*, Parsons left for a solo career. The group continued on with a fairly fluid roster. By the early 70's the band expanded by adding Byron Berline, Kenny Wertz, Roger Bush and Al Perkins on steel. The personnel changes continued throughout the decade, and the group recorded extensively for Columbia. In the 1980's the group continued, but the vision of Parsons had expanded far beyond The Burritos. Though he died in 1974, his influence on Emmylou Harris' music in particular, as well as that of The Eagles and numerous other performers (including Hillman's Desert Rose Band) remained. —R.K.

Red Foley

BORN: June 17, 1910
BIRTHPLACE: Blue Lick, Kentucky
DIED: September 19, 1968

Red Foley began his career with occasional performances as a vocalist with The Cumberland Ridge Runners on the WLS *National Barn Dance* in the 1930's. He hosted WLS *National Barn Dance* road shows in the late 30's and early 40's, and started recording for Decca in 1941. His first big record was the sentimental "Old Shep." He had several other big hits, including the World War II tune, "Smoke on the Water." He left WLS in 1946 to replace Roy Acuff as host of the Grand Ole Opry's Prince Albert Tobacco segment. (Acuff had quit the segment in a contract dispute.) Coming to Nashville with a band that included Chet Atkins, Foley brought the house down at his debut performance. And though some on the Opry had been upset when Prince Albert's ad agency hired an outsider, the cast quickly accepted him.

Foley had a string of hits throughout the 1940's including "New Jole Blon" (1947), "Tennessee Saturday Night" (1948) and "Tennessee Border" (1949). In 1950, "Chattanoogie Shoe Shine Boy" topped both the pop and country charts; the flip side, "Sugarfoot Rag," featuring Hank Garland on guitar, sold strongly, too. He recorded a number of hit novelty duets with Ernest Tubb for Decca in the late 1940's and early 50's. He also cut other boogie numbers like "Birmingham Bounce." His 1951 version of "(There'll Be) Peace in the Valley (For Me)" quickly became a gospel standard. Adverse publicity began to dog Foley in 1952, when his wife committed suicide, allegedly over his constant philandering. Two years later, his daughter, Shirley, married Pat Boone. That same year, Foley remarried.

In 1954 Foley left the Opry to become the star of Springfield, Missouri's *Ozark Jubilee*, but by then his hitmaking career was on the wane. Over time, his alcoholism worsened.

In the late 50's, he found himself in trouble with the Internal Revenue Service. Though he continued performing after the *Jubilee* ended, including a role in the TV series, *Mr. Smith Goes to Washington*, his career never recovered.

Ralph Emery's autobiography, *Memories*, discusses Foley's increasing alcoholic and emotional dissipation. Inducted into the Country Music Hall of Fame in 1967, he died while on tour, at a Fort Wayne, Indiana, motel in 1968. Hank Williams Jr. had been with him on the tour, and later recorded "I Was With Red Foley (The Night He Passed Away)." —R.K.

Tennessee Ernie Ford

BORN: February 13, 1919
BIRTHPLACE: Bristol, Tennessee
DIED: October 17, 1991

Tennessee Ernie Ford found himself in a strange position in late 1955. Busy with a CBS Radio show, a daily NBC-TV show and concert dates galore, he had little time to record for Capitol Records, his record company since 1949, and they had nothing to release on him. Earlier that year his version of the "Ballad of Davy Crockett" had gone Top Ten on both the pop and country charts, but now he was almost in breach of contract.

On the afternoon of September 20, 1955, Ernie went into the Capitol studio with Jack Fascinato's band—the band that backed him on his NBC show— and recorded a song that had worked well with both his TV and his live audiences. That song, written by one of Ford's old friends from *Hometown Jamboree*, the Los Angeles country music radio and TV program that had launched him seven years earlier, was Merle Travis' coal mining ballad, "Sixteen Tons." Travis had recorded his version in 1946. That afternoon, Ford recorded the upbeat, hip, jazzy arrangement he sang on the show and onstage. Released in mid-Oc tober, "Sixteen Tons" became a national event, selling 400,000 copies in just 11 days and remaining at Number One for ten weeks on the country charts and eight weeks on the pop charts. Journalists wrote about the song's social commentary, and Travis' Kentucky hometown erected a monument honoring both Travis and the song. Between the record and the show, Ford became a household word.

Thirty-five years later, Ford's importance may not be obvious to everyone, but his 1990 induction into the Country Music Hall of Fame was altogether fitting. Through a combination of talent, versatility and good timing, he proved that country singers could make respectable television personalities without compromising. In doing so, he opened the door for many others. In addition, his early recordings reveal a buoyant, robust singer who created exciting hillbilly boogie. And, finally, in the late 1950's, when singles were still the major means of selling country records, Ford, ahead of his time, concentrated on recording albums.

He was born in Bristol, Tennessee, in 1919, to parents who were both religious and musical. His first job was as a staff announcer at WOPI in Bristol. He studied singing in Cincinnati in 1939 but returned to announcing to pay the bills, working in both Atlanta and Knoxville. During World War II he was an Army Air Corps officer stationed in California. Following his discharge he and his new wife, Betty, settled in Southern California.

Ford eventually joined KFXM in San Bernardino, where he alternated routine announcing and newscasts with a country DJ program that inspired the "Pea Picker" character he made famous. In a sassy, exaggerated hillbilly voice, he introduced the hits of the day and occasionally sang along with the records. Loyal King, owner of KXLA radio in Pasadena, heard him and hired him. He also gave him a morning DJ show, *Bar Nothing Ranch Time*, for which Ford reprised the down-home "Pea Picker." Meanwhile, KXLA's *Dinner Bell Round-Up* show, emceed by bass player and announcer Cliffie Stone, was just getting started; Stone liked what he heard from the station's new DJ, and invited him to sing on the show. Ford was cautious, not wanting to jeopardize his announcing job. But by 1948, when the show, renamed the *Hometown Jamboree*, became one of the major programs on KXLA's new TV station, Ford was ready to join the cast, singing and doing comedy. Stone, also a Capitol Records sideman and the label's country

producer, took Ford to Capitol's head producer, Lee Gillette, who signed him immediately.

The potential of the boogie-woogie beat in country music first became apparent in various hits by The Delmore Brothers and in Arthur Smith's "Guitar Boogie." Ford himself liked boogie, but his first Capitol release was a simple cover of Red Foley's hit, "Tennessee Border," that made it to Number Eight. His next single, "Country Junction," was his first boogie tune. It went to Number 14. Many of Ford's early records featured dazzling backing by the team of guitarist Jimmy Bryant and steel guitar wizard, Speedy West, both regulars in the *Hometown Jamboree* staff band. His 1949 single, "Smokey Mountain Boogie," a salute to his home area near the Great Smoky Mountains, made it to Number Four, but the next, a version of Frankie Laine's pop hit, "Mule Train," gave Ford his first Number One, holding that spot for four weeks. The B-side, "Anticipation Blues," a novelty number Ford wrote in salute to his wife Betty's pregnancy with their first son, reached Number Three.

The 1950 follow-up was a change of pace: the dramatic "Cry of the Wild Goose," which reached Number Two. Ford's potential was clear to Lee Gillette, who was always willing to experiment, and in 1950 he teamed him with pop singer Kay Starr for the bluesy "I'll Never Be Free." The single's success amazed everyone: Number Two in the country field and Number Three in pop. Ford's original tune, "The Shot Gun Boogie," inspired by his frequent hunting trips—a bigger country hit than "Sixteen Tons"—stayed at Number One on the country charts for 14 weeks early in 1951 and reached the Top 20 on *Billboard*'s pop charts.

Gillette continued to experiment. He teamed Ford with ragtime pianist Lou Busch (known on records as Joe "Fingers" Carr) for the rollicking "Tailor Made Woman," a Number Eight recording. Ford's 1951 interpretation of Patti Page's pop hit, "Mister and Mississippi," gave him a Number Two country song, while "The Strange Little Girl" was a Top Ten ballad that year for three different artists: Ford, Cowboy Copas and the duet team of Ernest Tubb and Red Foley. Ford's 1952 hit was "Blackberry Boogie," with wild accompaniment by Bryant and West. In 1953 "Hey! Mr. Cotton Picker," co-written by actor Robert Mitchum, reached Number Eight. In England, the boogie numbers sold so well that in 1953 Ford performed at the London Palladium. His "River of No Return," from the film of the same name, went to Number Nine in 1954. At this point Cliffie Stone, who still emceed the *Hometown Jamboree*, became Ford's manager.

Mainstream America may have had a stereotyped notion of country singers as ignorant, uneducated rubes, but Ford demolished that image. His announcing experience made him comfortable in the role of host, the "Pea Picker" character gave him instant identity and his *Hometown* experience gave him comedy skills. He was the ideal country artist to make the move to national TV.

Following the success of "Sixteen Tons" in 1956, NBC folded Ford's daytime show, and on October 4th debuted *The Ford Show*, a prime-time showcase sponsored by Ford Motors. It remained a success until the entertainer left it in 1961. His high visibility made him a sought-after guest star on other top shows as well, including the old CBS *Jack Benny Program*, *This Is Your Life* and even *Make Room for Daddy*. As his TV career rose, demand for his singles tapered off. Instead, he focused on albums. *Hymns*, his first sacred album, released in 1957, remained on *Billboard's* Top album chart for 277 weeks—over five years. Two follow-up sacred albums also did well.

When the grind of managing Ford's booming career began to affect Stone's health, he bowed out. In 1959 his assistant, Jim Loakes, took over. Loakes remained Ford's manager for more than 30 years. When the NBC show ended in 1961, Ford began broadcasting a daytime show for ABC from San Francisco. The show included such regulars as ex-*Hometown* singer-guitarist Billy Strange. Strange and bass player, Johnny Mosher, were the only two musicians who backed Ford on his intimate 1964 album of country standards, *Country Hits...Feelin' Blue*. That year "Hicktown," his final Top Ten single, peaked at Number Nine.

In the late 1960's Ford continued recording (mostly bland, pop-flavored country) for Capitol, doing concerts and appearing on various country TV shows. Gradually, however, he scaled down. In 1974 he went to Russia as the star of the *Country Music USA* show sponsored by the U.S. State Department. The cast put on 27 concerts in five Russian cities. In 1976, after nearly 30 years, he and Capitol parted ways. In the late 1970's he hosted three specials for Public Broadcasting, and made occasional appearances on *Hee Haw*.

Ford's wife Betty died on February 27, 1989, not long after Ford's 70th birthday. He married Beverly Wood-Smith on June 11, 1989, the same year he taped his special, *50 Golden Years*, for TNN. His induction into the Country Music Hall of Fame in 1990 called attention to him again, proving that his excellence as a singer wasn't forgotten. He died on October 17, 1991, of liver disease, which had plagued him for several years. Today, Ernie Ford's musical contributions speak for themselves. And every country performer who's successfully made the transition to TV—Jimmy Dean, Johnny Cash, Roy Clark, Glen Campbell, The Mandrells and others—owe a debt to the pioneering work of the ol' Pea Picker himself.　　—R.K.

The Forester Sisters

Hailing from Lookout Mountain, Georgia, Kathy, June, Kim and Christy—collectively known as The Forester Sisters—became one of the more successful female groups in country music in the mid-to-late 80's by topping off traditional and contemporary instrumentation with sweet, soaring harmonies. The sisters started honing their harmony skills as children singing in their local church choir. Eventually, they began performing at clubs and parties in the Chattanooga, Tennessee, area.

After the church and club scene, Kathy and June went to college, got their degrees and then put together a band. Kim and Christy quit their studies and joined their older sisters in 1982. A demo recorded by the sisters in Muscle Shoals, Alabama, found its way into the hands of Jim Ed Norman and the executives at Warner Bros. By the end of 1984,

the sisters were rewarded with a recording contract.

Their very first single, "(That's What You Do) When You're in Love" (1985), cracked the country Top Ten. Their next single, "I Fell in Love Again Last Night," hit Number One. And that was only the beginning of an impressive string of 15 Top Ten singles for the sisters (including five Number Ones). One of their most well-known was "Men"—a humorous diatribe against the opposite sex. The sisters also recorded two hit duets with The Bellamy Brothers. They left Warner Bros. in 1993.   —R.P.

Foster & Lloyd

BORN: Foster, July 20, 1959, Del Rio, Texas
       Lloyd, December 6, 1955, Fort Hood, Texas

This dynamic, youthful duo, comprised of Nashville songwriters Radney Foster and Bill Lloyd, recorded only three albums in the late 1980's before disbanding. Yet their provocative musical mix—strong co-written original songs, Everly Brothers-style harmonies, and a penchant for mid-tempo rockabilly—stands the test of time well and reveals that they were on the cutting edge of Nashville's late 80's talent explosion.

Foster was born in Del Rio, Texas, in 1959. Lloyd, born in 1955, was an Army brat who grew up in Louisville, Kentucky, and made minor critical waves in 1987 with a pre-Foster & Lloyd solo album called *Feeling the Elephant*. The two of them met as staff songwriters for the now defunct MTM Music Com-

pany, in Nashville. They quickly became friends, then co-writers, turning out tunes that were covered by Ricky Van Shelton, Sweethearts of the Rodeo and Marshall Crenshaw. "It turned out that when we wrote together, it meshed better than what each of us was doing apart," Foster recalled in a 1990 interview in *Country Music Magazine.*

When the duo pitched RCA a demo tape of themselves harmonizing on some of their co-written tunes, their hope was to get the songs cut by The Judds. They were surprised, and a trifle hesitant, when RCA countered by offering them a recording contract of their own. "At that point," Lloyd recalled, "we were both headlong into our separate careers."

Foster & Lloyd, the duo's 1987 debut album, was a minor masterpiece, giving them Top Ten hits with "Crazy Over You" and "Sure Thing." However, *Faster and Louder* (1988) and *Version of the Truth* (1989) both lacked the first album's sharp focus. Two more Top Tens came with "What Do You Want From Me This Time" and "Fair Shake." The duo broke up in 1991.

Radney Foster released a noteworthy 1992 debut solo album on Arista, *Del Rio, Texas, 1959,* that bodes well for his future. Bill Lloyd returned to songwriting and occasional A&R work before releasing his own solo album in 1994, *Set to Pop,* on the East Side Digital label. (See also, Radney Foster.)   —B.A.

Radney Foster

BORN: July 20, 1959
BIRTHPLACE: Del Rio, Texas

After several years of critical and commercial success in the late 1980's as half of Foster & Lloyd, the duo split, both pursuing solo careers. Radney Foster was first out of the chute with his Arista Records debut, *Del Rio, Texas 1959*, in 1992. Named for his place and year of birth, that album—an intelligent mix of Texas-folk and straightforward country—spawned five hit singles, including "Nobody Wins" and "Just Call Me Lonesome." Foster co-produced with renowned roots-country producer Steve Fischell. (See also, Foster & Lloyd.) —G.F.

The Four Guys

This stalwart vocal quartet, which has undergone numerous personnel changes over the years, had minimal chart success for RCA and other smaller labels in the late 1970's and early 80's with maudlin numbers like "Made in the U.S.A." and "Mama Rocked Us to Sleep (With Country Music)."

They worked on WWVA's *Wheeling Jamboree* before joining the Grand Ole Opry in 1967, where they are still members. —B.A

Wally Fowler

BORN: February 15, 1917
BIRTHPLACE: Bartow County, Georgia
DIED: June 3, 1994

To modern country fans, composer-singer Wally Fowler is best known as the founder of The Oak Ridge Quartet, which was the first incarnation of The Oak Ridge Boys. But to gospel fans, Fowler was an important high-profile promoter who took gospel music singing into the modern age by inventing a package stage show called the "All-Night Sing" in 1948. Born as John Wallace Fowler in Bartow County, Georgia, in 1917, Fowler gained his early experience with The John Daniel Quartet, a popular group then on the Grand Ole Opry. In 1944 he relocated to Knoxville, where he moved into mainstream country, organizing a popular band called The Georgia Clodhoppers and writing hit songs like "That's How Much I Love You" for Eddy Arnold.

A move to Nashville in 1946 led to his further work on the Opry, as well as to the establishment of Wallace Fowler Publications, a publishing company second only to Acuff-Rose among early Nashville publishers. Starting in 1948, and for some 20 years thereafter, he organized the "All-Night Sings," in which as many as a dozen quartets or groups would appear in one concert that would often run from six to eight hours. He died in June 1994, after falling from his fishing boat on a lake near Nashville. —C.W.

Curly Fox and Texas Ruby

BORN: Curly, November 9, 1910, Graysville, Tennessee
    Ruby, June 4, 1910, Wise County, Texas
DIED: Ruby, March 29, 1963

Curly Fox was a flamboyant, innovative fiddler whose sense of showmanship and style won him national popularity in the 1930's and 40's. Born Armin LeRoy

Fox in Graysville, Tennessee, on November 9, 1910, Fox began his career working and recording with pioneer bands like The Roane County Ramblers and The Shelton Brothers. In 1939 he married Texas Ruby Owens, and as a duo they worked the *Boone County Jamboree* and later the Grand Ole Opry. By 1948 they were booking out of New York and playing venues like the Hollywood Bowl. A series of Columbia recordings in 1945-46 featured Ruby's husky vocals on hits like "Blue Love" and "Don't Lie to Me," but it was Curly's 1947 fiddle version of "Black Mountain Rag" on King that became their biggest hit—and the biggest instrumental of the decade. In later years the pair returned to Nashville, where Ruby died in a house fire in 1963. Curly continued to play occasionally through the 1980's, often featuring his comic numbers like "Whoa Mule."   —C.W.

J.L. Frank

BORN: April 15, 1900
DIED: May 4, 1952

J.L. "Joe" Frank, a pioneering country music promoter, helped shift country music into an entirely new phase, moving country entertainers up from rural school houses and other similarly modest venues to big-city auditoriums during the 40's and 50's. Along the way, Frank helped develop the careers of notables like Gene Autry, Pee Wee King, Roy Acuff, Eddy Arnold, Minnie Pearl, Ernest Tubb and many more. (Frank's daughter was married to Pee Wee King.)

Beloved throughout the country music community of his time for his compassion and kindness, Frank was posthumously elected to the Country Music Hall of Fame in 1967.   —B.A.

Janie Fricke

BORN: December 19, 1947
BIRTHPLACE: South Whitney, Indiana

This singer (who later changed the spelling of her name to Frickie, since everyone mispronounced it anyway) possessed a technical brilliance that made her one of the most in-demand studio backup singers in Nashville in the 1970's. Her splendid harmony vocals graced the records of stars of the day like Dolly Parton, Elvis Presley, Ronnie Milsap, Vern Gosdin and Johnny Duncan, among others. However, the same versatility and polish that made Fricke so effective in a supporting role (one fellow singer used to tease her by asking, "Which of the 16 voices of Janie Fricke are you going to be tonight?") always came across as a bit lacking in personality when thrust into the lead role.

Fricke was born in South Whitney, Indiana, on December 19, 1947. Before coming to Nashville, she worked as a jingle and studio singer in Dallas and Memphis (where she was also in a group called Phase II, along with Judy Rodman and Karen Taylor-Good) and collected a degree in elementary education from the University of Indiana.

The big break that took Fricke up from the doo-wops to a solo career came in 1976 when she sang an impressive uncredited duet with Johnny Duncan on his Top Five rendition of Kris Kristofferson's "Stranger."

Fricke signed with Columbia Records in 1977 and had a fairly credible run in the charts over the course of the next few years, hitting the Number One spot with songs like "Don't Worry 'Bout Me, Baby," "It Ain't Easy Bein' Easy," "On My Knees" (a duet with Charlie Rich), "He's a Heartache (Looking for a Place to Happen)" and "Tell Me a Lie." It was as much a sign of the fallow times between the Urban Cowboy era and the emergence of the New Traditionalist movement in the mid-1980's that Fricke managed to walk away with the Country Music Association's Female Vocalist of the Year award in 1982 and 1983, yet never really attained the sort of grassroots popularity or consistent record sales which sustain solo careers.

Her final chart entry came in 1989.   —B.A.

Kinky Friedman

BORN: December 31, 1944
BIRTHPLACE: Palestine, Texas

Born in Palestine, Texas, in 1944, Richard "Kinky" Friedman served in the Peace Corps before settling in Austin and assembling his band, The Texas Jewboys. The name alone, a takeoff on Bob Wills' Texas Playboys, was too much for many audiences in the country bars the band played during the late 1960's. Country fans were also taken aback by

Friedman's lyrics, which poked fun at everything from the Vietnam war to his own Jewish background.

While Friedman's onstage profanity and off-color humor got The Texas Jewboys kicked off the stage more than once, it also got them plenty of publicity, helping "The Jew from Palestine" land a contract with Vanguard Records in 1973. Their first album, *Sold American*, included such titles like "Ride 'em Jewboy" and "Let Saigons Be Bygones." Another song, "We Reserve the Right to Refuse Service to You," described the experience of a long-haired Jew at a Southern redneck cafe. Friedman cut a second album and, to the surprise of many, was invited to perform on the Grand Ole Opry in 1975. That same year The Jewboys began touring with Bob Dylan's Rolling Thunder Review. In 1976 they signed with Epic Records; their first Epic album, *Lasso from El Paso*, included "Asshole from El Paso," "Dear Abbie" and "Men's Room L.A." In perhaps the least likely ending for a country music singer, Kinky went on to become a successful mystery novelist—*A Case of Lone Star* is one of his several successful titles—in which he turned his Texas Jewboy character into a sleuth.   —M.B.

David Frizzell

BORN: September 26, 1941
BIRTHPLACE: El Dorado, Arkansas

The younger brother of country legend Lefty Frizzell, David toured with Lefty in his teen years, then worked with Buck Owens before striking out on his own. Through the 1970's his recording career yielded few hits, but later singles on Warner and Viva in the early 80's charted better, especially his series of duets with his then sister-in-law, Shelly West. (She was married to Allen Frizzell, the youngest of the three Frizzell brothers.) Among their Top Ten duet hits were "You're the Reason God Made Oklahoma" (Number One in 1981), "A Texas State of Mind" and "I Just Came Here

to Dance." Frizzell also scored a Number One on his own in 1982 with "I'm Gonna Hire a Wino to Decorate Our Home." His final chart entry came in 1987. (See also, Shelly West and Lefty Frizzell.)   —G.F.

Lefty Frizzell

BORN: March 31, 1928
BIRTHPLACE: Corsicana, Texas
DIED: July 19, 1975

A singer who defined the honky-tonk sound, and one of the most influential country vocalists of all time, Lefty Frizzell was among country music's most noted vocalists. Merle Haggard, John Anderson and, later, Randy Travis all had heavy overtones of Lefty in their own singing styles, and readily, even proudly, admitted as much. William Orville Frizzell was born in Corsicana, Texas, in 1928. As a youngster he was entranced by the records of Jimmie Rodgers. He got his start in music when, at age 12, he landed his own radio show over KELD in El Dorado, Arkansas, where the Frizzells settled briefly. His nickname of "Lefty" came as a teenager, after he punched out a schoolyard bully. From then on, even in his days playing local bars, he was known as a hell-raiser. By the mid-1940's he was entranced by the honky tonk music of artists like Ted Daffan, Floyd Tillman and Ernest Tubb. They had become the next phase beyond Jimmie Rodgers, singing earthy, real-life songs about lost love, drinking and other subjects appropriate for the barroom. By 1947 he was on the radio in Roswell, New Mexico, singing Ernest Tubb and Jimmie Rodgers songs, as well as original material. After winding up in jail in Roswell, he wrote the song "I Love You a Thousand Ways."

By 1950 he was developing a following at the Ace of Clubs, a dancehall in Big Spring, Texas. By then he had developed his own vocal style. His phrasing, inspired by Floyd Tillman, involved "stretching" certain words in a way to put the lyric across. As word of his popularity spread, he attracted the attention of Dallas recording studio owner Jim Beck. Beck's studio had become a home base for younger talent, including many artists signed to Columbia like Marty Robbins. Beck brought Frizzell in to cut some demo recordings and took them to Nashville, playing them for Columbia A&R man Don Law. Beck wanted Law to hear the songs, but Law, captivated by Frizzell's

voice, went to Big Spring and offered him a contract. He recorded Frizzell singing his original "If You've Got the Money, I've Got the Time" and "I Love You a Thousand Ways" in July. The record was issued in September, and within two months had sold two and a half million copies. Each side of the single remained Number One for three weeks.

Every Frizzell record released through 1952, including classics like "Always Late," "Mom & Dad's Waltz," "Don't Stay Away," "Forever" and Jimmie Rodgers' "Travelin' Blues," made it to the Top Ten. Over time his vocal style influenced many, including a young fan named Merle Haggard. Frizzell toured the country as his hits came in waves, but never created a home base except for a brief period when he moved to California, There he joined *Town Hall Party*, a barn dance TV show in the Los Angeles area. With "Run 'Em Off" in 1954 he had his last Top Ten record for five years. Rock 'n' roll set back the hard country style of Frizzell and others like him. His next big record came in 1959 with Marijohn Wilkin's mysterious, folk-flavored ballad, "The Long Black Veil." Then in 1964 came the story-song, "Saginaw, Michigan," which became his last Number One record. He spent the remainder of the 1960's looking for another hit: He recorded a few masterpieces, like "Honky Tonk Stardust Cowboy," which didn't even chart. Frizzell remained with Columbia until signing with ABC records in 1973. In 1974 he had respectable hits with "Lucky Arms" and "I Never Go Around Mirrors." But his hard-living lifestyle was wrecking his marriage. Plagued by high blood pressure, he refused to take his prescribed medication, preferring to drink. As he was preparing to leave on tour in 1975 he suffered a massive stroke, and died hours later.

In 1982 he was inducted into the Country Music Hall of Fame. A year later his song, "It Hurts to Face Reality," a tune he never recorded commercially, became the theme song for the Academy Award-winning film, *Tender Mercies*. —R.K.

Hank Garland

BORN: November 11, 1930
BIRTHPLACE: Cowpens, South Carolina

Walter Louis Garland, influenced by Maybelle Carter, became a guitar prodigy at an early age. By 1945, when he was 15, he was playing in a band around

Spartanburg. In 1945 he met Grand Ole Opry artist Paul Howard, leader of the Western swing oriented Arkansas Cotton Pickers. Howard hired Hank later that year (though by law he had to leave the band until he turned 16). By 1947 he'd graduated to Cowboy Copas' band. Both Billy Byrd and Harold Bradley helped him learn about jazz guitar. In 1949 Owen Bradley and Paul Cohen began using him on sessions, and Bradley even signed him to Decca as a singer-guitarist. He recorded an instrumental, "Sugarfoot Rag," which Red Foley recorded with lyrics in 1950, with Garland playing the guitar solo. After an early 1950's stint backing Eddy Arnold, Garland became a fixture in the Nashville studios, working on such classics as Patsy Cline's "I Fall to Pieces," Elvis' "Little Sister" and various rockabilly and country hits. He also became a formidable jazz guitarist, with his 1960 Columbia album, *Jazz Winds from a New Direction,* revealing the depth of those talents. A near-fatal 1961 automobile accident north of Nashville resulted in brain damage that impaired his playing skills and ended his active musical career. —R.K.

Larry Gatlin and The Gatlin Brothers

BORN: Larry, May 2, 1948, Seminole, Texas
Steve, April 4, 1951, Olney, Texas
Rudy, August 20, 1952, Olney, Texas

Larry Gatlin and his brothers, Steve and Rudy, were one of the more prolific country acts of the mid-to-late 1970's and early 80's. The brothers were surrounded by music during their early years. Their father, an itinerant oil driller who eventually settled the family in Odessa, Texas, played guitar. Their mother was an accomplished pianist. Family sing-alongs were quite common, and on weekends they would often attend local concerts that featured their favorite musical acts, including gospel groups like

The Statesmen Quartet and The Blackwood Brothers. The boys' first public performance was at a talent show at Hardin-Simmons University in Abilene, Texas. Larry was seven, Steve was four and Rudy two. They walked away winning first place. During their elementary and high school years, the brothers continued singing, and Larry began woodshedding his songwriting skills.

When Gatlin entered the University of Houston as an English major, it marked the first time he and his brothers parted company. While still in college he heard that The Imperials, a gospel group scheduled to open up for Elvis Presley on The King's upcoming tour, were holding auditions for a baritone. He tried out for the slot, and although he didn't get the gig, the group was nevertheless impressed with his singing. They asked him to join them for a month of performances with singer Jimmy Dean in Las Vegas.

Gatlin jumped at the opportunity. It was there that he met Dottie West, who was on the same bill. She heard some of his songs, and asked him to send some of his tapes to her office in Nashville when the Vegas engagement was over. He sent eight songs, and she recorded two of them, "Once You Were Mine" and "You're the Other Half of Me." She also sent Gatlin plane fare to come to Nashville to continue his writing.

When he arrived, West continued opening doors for him. She played one of his tapes for Kris Kristofferson, who in turn passed the recording on to Monument Records president Fred Foster. Foster was impressed, and offered Gatlin a record deal in 1972. Before it was finalized, Gatlin had invited his brothers to come to Nashville to put together a group. The timing couldn't have been more perfect. All three wound up playing on Gatlin's Monument debut, *The Pilgrim* (1974), which yielded a country hit, "Penny Annie."

Gatlin's next two Monument releases also contained hit singles. *Rain Rainbow* featured the hit single, "Delta Dirt," and his third album, *Larry Gatlin With Family and Friends*, furnished "Broken Lady," which climbed to Number One on the country charts and won a Grammy in 1976. That same year, the brothers were made members of the Grand Ole Opry, which they remain today.

The brothers formally reunited as a band on Larry's fourth album, *High Time*, which contained the Number One single, "Statues Without Hearts." From that point on, the brothers continued rolling out chart-toppers such as "I Wish You Were Someone I Love" (1977), "All the Gold in California" (1979), "Take Me to Your Lovin' Place" (1980), "What Are We Doin' Lonesome" (1981), "Houston" (1983) and "The Lady Takes the Cowboy Everytime" (1984).

In 1992 the brothers, with their "Adios Tour," bid a fond farewell to the rigors of 17 years of traveling 220 days a year doing one-night performances. The brothers, however, continued to record and pursue other projects, individually and as a group. Larry made his Broadway debut as the lead in *The Will Rogers Follies*, Rudy oversaw the openings of a couple of Gatlin Brothers Music City Grilles (combination Texas-style eateries and nightclubs), and Steve recorded an album of Christian country music.

The brothers moved to the Branson Entertainment label, which released *Moments to Remember* in 1993 and *Cool Water* in 1994.   —R.P.

Connie B. Gay

BORN: August 22, 1914
BIRTHPLACE: Lizard Lick, North Carolina
DIED: December 4, 1989

Connie B. Gay was an immensely influential promoter, broadcaster and business entrepreneur who built an entertainment empire in the Washington, D.C., area. Gay played a central role in the growth of country music throughout the 50's and 60's and in the widening of its popularity to reach a more demographically diverse audience during those decades.

He did much of this through *Town and Country Time*, a series of radio and television shows aimed at country's growing cosmopolitan market. There is hardly a major country star of the 50's and 60's—from Patsy Cline to George Jones—whose career was not at least to some extent shaped by Gay. Gay's influence was such that it even went beyond music: he was even an advisor to several Presidents. The founding President of the Country Music Association and later President of the Country Music Foundation, he was one of a relative handful to be elected to the Country Music Hall of Fame before his death. He was inducted in 1980. (See also, Country Music Association.)　　　　　　　　　　　　—B.A.

Crystal Gayle

BORN: January 9, 1951
BIRTHPLACE: Paintsville, Kentucky

Crystal Gayle, Loretta Lynn's little sister, was born Brenda Gail Webb on January 9, 1951, in Paintsville, Kentucky. She was the youngest of eight children born to a hard working coal mining family that liked to relax by singing and listening to country, folk, pop and gospel music.

As a youngster, Brenda Gail dreamed of stardom. She began singing in her church choir and at school functions. When she was 16, she accompanied Loretta and Conway Twitty on a tour. At the time she changed her name to Crystal, receiving her inspiration from the Krystal hamburger chain.

In 1970 Gayle recorded her first single for Decca Records, "I've Cried the Blue Right Out of My Eyes." The song was written by Loretta, and it climbed to Number 23 on the country charts. Gayle then moved over to United Artists Records, and with crackerjack producer Allen Reynolds at the boards, rolled out a string of chart toppers in the contemporary country vein—"Wrong Road Again" (1975), "Somebody Loves You" (1975) and "I'll Get Over You" (1976). The latter became her very first Number One song.

In 1977 Gayle had a monster hit with "Don't It Make My Brown Eyes Blue." The song enjoyed widespread success on the pop as well as country charts, and subsequently earned her a Grammy for Best Country Vocal Performance-Female. Three additional Number One songs followed in 1978: "Ready for the Times to Get Better," "Talking in Your Sleep" and "Why Have You Left the One You Left Me For."

In 1979, Gayle became the first country artist to tour China, and during the 1980's she continued to crank out at least 10 chart-toppers, such as "Too Many Lovers" for Columbia, "'Til I Gain Control Again" for Elektra, and "Our Love Is on the Faultline" and "Baby, What About You" for Warner Bros. During this period Gayle also logged some hit duet performances, especially "You and I" with Eddie Rabbit and "Makin' Up for Lost Time" with Gary Morris. She and Morris also performed the theme for the TV soap opera, *Another World*.

During the 1990's Gayle's recording career was relatively quiet, although she did manage to squeeze out a minor hit for Capitol in "Never Ending Song of Love," which reunited the singer with producer/friend Allen Reynolds. As the 90's progressed, she signed on with the Branson Entertainment label.　　—R.P.

Bobbie Gentry

BORN: July 27, 1944
BIRTHPLACE: Chickasaw County, Mississippi

Barely 23 years old, Mississippi-born Bobby Gentry (born Roberta Streeter) was completely unknown when she recorded a song she'd written, "Ode to Billie Joe," in July 1967. Within weeks the song topped both the country and pop charts, and Bobbie Gentry was an international celebrity. Her debut album of the same name went Gold, and Gentry won three Grammys: Best Female Vocal Performance and Contemporary Female Solo Vocal Performance, as well as for the Best New Artist of 1967.

The following year she cut a duet album with Glenn Campbell; like everything else Bobbie Gentry touched in the late 1960's, the album went Gold. Over the next few years she toured extensively in the U.S. and Europe.

She hosted a BBC-TV series and the weekly *Bobbie Gentry Show* on Armed Forces Radio. Gentry began the 1970's with two more duets with Glen Campbell: "Let It Be Me," which won a Country Music Association award, and a remake of The Everly Brothers' "All I Have to Do Is Dream."

All things considered, though, she never even came close to the furor that the somewhat enigmatic lyrics to "Ode to Billie Joe" created; practically everyone from that era still wonders what the song's protagonist lobbed off the Talahatchee Bridge after Billie Joe jumped to his death.

A movie was even made, following the song's storyline. In the early 90's, Reba McEntire covered another of Gentry's hits, "Fancy."   —M.B.

Terri Gibbs

BORN: June 15, 1954
BIRTHPLACE: Augusta, Georgia

Blind from birth, Terri Gibbs learned to play piano at age three, and wanted a music career for as long as she could remember. After several attempts to catch Nashville's ear, she gained the attention of MCA Records. Her first single, "Somebody's Knocking," catapulted her to instant fame, reaching the Top Ten on both the pop and country charts in early 1981. Awards from the Academy of Country Music and Country Music Association followed and Gibbs, with her blues background and truly original style, seemed destined for success.

But later hits failed to make the Top Ten, and in 1985 Gibbs moved on to Warner Bros. where she released three more singles.   —G.F.

Gibson

It's hard to imagine 20th-century American music without Gibson instruments. From the mandolin orchestras of the early 1900's and the Dixieland banjos of the 1920's, to the archtops of the 1930's and the brash electric rock 'n' roll guitars of the 1950's and beyond, Gibson has always been at the forefront.

The first Gibsons were made by Orville H. Gibson. The son of English immigrants, he was born in Chateaugay, New York, in 1856 and moved to Kalamazoo, Michigan. As a young man, he worked in various businesses, including a shoe store and restaurant. Interestingly, Gibson's hobbies included whittling and woodworking, and in the 1880's he set up shop as a musical instrument maker. What was unique about Gibson's craftsmanship was his belief in the superior vibrating characteristics of unstressed wood. When constructing mandolins and guitars, for example, rather than bending strips of wood, as was the practice in those days, he would carve the sides and arched tops from solid slabs.

As Orville Gibson's reputation spread, demand for his ornate instruments began to outpace production. In 1902, five businessmen from Kalamazoo pitched him with the idea of organizing the Gibson Mandolin-Guitar Manufacturing Company, Limited. He gave the go-ahead. For a fee, Gibson gave the company his one and only patent, and the right to use his name. After that, he was not actively involved with the company, and in 1918 he died in Ogdensburg, New York, of chronic endocarditis.

After World War I, the banjo replaced the mandolin as the instrument of choice, and the Gibson Company hopped on the bandwagon. Then in 1927, after a man named Ralph Peer discovered and subsequently recorded The Carter Family in Bristol, Tennessee, the guitar began to rise steadily in popularly. In fact, the guitar Maybelle Carter played during the historic Bristol sessions was a Gibson L-1 flat top guitar. Gibson seized the moment.

To compete against the popular "dreadnought" flat tops designed by C.F. Martin and Company—and endorsed by Jimmie Rodgers and Gene Autry—Gibson introduced the Jumbo and the mahogany-body J-35. Hank Williams played a J-35 when he was a teenager. The bigger and boomier J-200 followed in 1937, and was popularized by Ray Whitley, who helped design the model, and Tex Ritter.

In 1944 the Chicago Musical Instrument Company, a large distribution firm, acquired controlling interest in Gibson. After World War II, the company began moving into the electric guitar and amplifier arena—rolling out the Les Paul model and its various off-

shoots. The Les Paul later became popular among the Southern rock bands of the late 1960's and early 1970's.

During the mid-1950's, Gibson played a major role in kicking off rock 'n' roll. Bill Haley played an L-7 on "Rock Around the Clock," and Scotty Moore, Elvis Presley's lead guitarist, first played a hollowbody ES-325, later graduating to an L-5. In 1955, guitarists Billy Byrd and Hank Garland designed the Gibson Birdland Electric. In 1957, Gibson bought the New York-based Epiphone Company and moved its production operation to Kalamazoo, Michigan. The folk and country-rock boom of the 1960's pushed Gibson to its highest production level. During that period flat tops such as The Hummingbird, The Dove and The Everly Brothers models were added to Gibson's hefty acoustic roster.

In 1969 ECL, an Ecuadorian company, acquired controlling interest in Gibson. In 1970 the parent company changed its name to Norlin, and in 1974 a second plant was built in Nashville. In 1984 Gibson closed its Kalamazoo facility and moved its headquarters to Nashville. In 1986 the company was sold to Henry Juskiewicz, David Berryman and Gary

Zebrowski (who eventually left the partnership), and in 1987 the company bought the Flatiron mandolin company of Bozeman, Montana. After leaving Gretsch, Chet Atkins signed on as an endorser, introducing the Chet Atkins CEC (Classical Electric Cutaway), a nylon-stringed solidbody electric that sounded like an acoustic. The steel-stringed Chet Atkins SST followed in 1987. During the late 1980's and 1990's, Gibson instruments continued to play an important role in country music. Endorsers included Travis Tritt, Clint Black, Emmylou Harris, Alan Jackson, Mary-Chapin Carpenter, Hal Ketchum, Dolly Parton and Brooks & Dunn.   —R.P.

Don Gibson

BORN: April 3, 1932
BIRTHPLACE: Shelby, North Carolina

Donald Eugene Gibson grew up the son of a railroader. He started playing guitar and eventually formed a band with some local boys, called The Sons of the Soil. When Don was 16, they were popular enough to play over the local radio station. That show led to a Mercury recording contract for the band in 1949; no hits emerged. Gibson started a new band called The King Cotton Kinfolks and landed an RCA recording contract in 1950, again with no success. He finally left his home area and wound up at WNOX in Knoxville, where he became popular on the station's country shows. A second RCA session, yielding only minimal notice and one record, led to a Columbia recording contract in 1952. That, too, went nowhere, and he continued as a singer and sideman at WNOX and started writing songs.

Around 1955 he wrote the ballad, "Sweet Dreams," which impressed Wesley Rose of Acuff-Rose enough to sign Gibson as a songwriter. He recorded the song for MGM in 1955, and it became his first hit, reaching Number Nine nationally. Faron Young's version became the big hit, however (until Patsy Cline re-recorded it in 1963). Gibson was writing more of his own material in light of this success, and in 1956 Chet Atkins re-signed him to RCA. His first recordings were standard fiddle and steel honky tonk, but Gibson didn't stand out with that arrangement. The advent of the Nashville Sound that Atkins helped develop proved his salvation, as did two new original songs he wrote: "Oh Lonesome

Raven's "Country Green" became a Top Ten in 1971. His own "Woman (Sensuous Woman)" was his final Number One in 1972, though he had three more Top Tens with the label and recorded duets with Sue Thompson. Gibson also had to confront serious problems with drug abuse that nearly destroyed him and his career in the late 60's and early 70's. He continued recording after leaving Hickory, doing a greatest hits album for K-Tel and some private sessions. Ray Charles made "I Can't Stop Lovin' You" a pop hit in 1962 and recorded superb versions of several other Gibson hits that demonstrated their durability. This was further proven in 1993, when Mark Chesnutt had a hit with a cover of Gibson's "Woman (Sensuous Woman)." In recent years, however, Gibson has remained semi-retired.

—R.K.

Vince Gill

BORN: April 12, 1957
BIRTHPLACE: Norman, Oklahoma

Vince Gill's winning of the Country Music Association's 1993 Entertainer of the Year award was not only a case of lofty recognition that was a long time coming; it also seemed to send a message of belated poetic justice. Gill's triumph at the CMA ceremonies served as a reminder that in the trendy 90's, tried and true talent, and integrity, sometimes do get their just rewards, and nice guys occasionally do finish first.

The son of an Oklahoma attorney and appellate judge, Gill was born in 1957 and had his first band together by the time he was in his teens. By the mid-70's, Gill, barely out of high school, graduated up to professional music's big leagues. His first significant musical association was as a member of The Blue Grass Alliance, a progressive bluegrass (newgrass) ensemble that included other virtuosos like Sam Bush, Dan Crary and Tony Rice. Gill's next stop was the West Coast, where he sang and played guitar with noted newgrass fiddler Byron Berline.

It's a tribute to Gill's talent as a singer and songwriter and to his mastery of various stringed instruments that he next ended up as lead singer for the pop harmony group, Pure Prairie League. He sang lead on that band's 1980 hit, "Let Me Love You Tonight." (Gill is such a phenomenal guitar player that in the early 90's, his friend, British rock star Mark

Me" and "I Can't Stop Lovin' You." Atkins stripped the fiddles and steel away, added The Anita Kerr Singers to a small rhythm section, and the two songs on one single became a double-sided smash. "Oh Lonesome Me" remained Number One for eight weeks on the country charts and crossed over to become a pop Top Ten as well. "Lovin'" was a country Top Ten. He followed it with another original: "Blue Blue Day," a Number One record in 1958. "Give Myself a Party" and "Look Who's Blue" followed that same year, as did Grand Ole Opry membership. Other hits included "Who Cares" and "Don't Tell Me Your Troubles" in 1959, a hit remake of "Sweet Dreams" in 1960 and "Sea of Heartbreak" in 1961.

Though some felt the Nashville Sound watered down hard country, it gave Gibson great punch as a vocalist. He and Atkins continued to experiment with Gibson's sound. In 1963, the same year the Opry fired Gibson for lateness, he and Atkins recorded *Girls, Guitars and Gibson.* The album featured Gibson with jazz guitar virtuoso Johnny Smith, Harold Bradley playing nylon string guitar and The Anita Kerr Singers. In addition to recording many albums for RCA, he had additional hit singles through the mid-60's, including "Funny, Familiar Forgotten Feelings" and "Rings of Gold."

After leaving RCA in 1969, he signed with Acuff-Rose's Hickory label, where his version of Eddy

Knopfler, invited him to accompany Dire Straits on the road.)

When Prairie disbanded, Gill put his own band together for a while before getting a call from Rodney Crowell, another future country star, who was then just beginning to embark on his own solo career. For several years, Gill was lead guitarist/harmony singer in Crowell's now-legendary band, The Cherry Bombs.

By 1984, when he made his own solo recording debut on RCA with an album called *Turn Me Loose*, Gill had relocated to Nashville, along with his wife, Janis Gill (who would later make her own mark, teaming up with her sister, Kristine, as The Sweethearts of the Rodeo). Though his RCA releases garnered critical acclaim, they resulted in only a couple of lukewarm hits. For the next four or five years he had to content himself with writing songs for more commercially viable artists and playing guitar and singing background on records of friends like Rosanne Cash, Emmylou Harris, Bonnie Raitt, Sissy Spacek, Guy Clark and Reba McEntire (a fellow Okla-

homan with whom he recorded the Number One duet, "The Heart Won't Lie," in 1993).

It was in the late 80's that Gill finally went across the street to MCA Records and began making records with producer Tony Brown, his former bandmate in The Cherry Bombs (and also, ironically the A&R man who'd first brought him to RCA). And that's when everything finally began to fall into place for him. Since then, the hits—"When I Call Your Name," "Pocket Full of Gold," "I Never Knew Lonely," "Look at Us," "Liza Jane"—and the platinum albums—*When I Call Your Name, Pocket Full of Gold, I Never Knew Lonely*—have kept right on coming.

Gill's warm, vibrato-laden tenor is a bit of a stylistic change-up from country's usual sea of growling, tortured baritones, and has made him one of the most effective balladeers in the business. Above all, his singing conveys a tenderness and warm accessibility—which, to those who know him, seems to accurately reflect the personality of the man, who is one of Nashville's best-loved musicians. The Grand Ole Opry made him a member in 1991.   —B.A.

Mickey Gilley

BORN: March 9, 1936
BIRTHPLACE: Natchez, Louisiana

Mickey Gilley, symbol of the Urban Cowboy era, grew up in Ferriday, Louisiana, with his famous cousins, Jerry Lee Lewis and Jimmy Swaggart, all three playing the same blues and boogie woogie piano style. When Gilley was 17, he moved to Houston. In addition to working construction jobs, he started playing music in the area and began recording even before Jerry Lee. When rock 'n' roll took off, the resemblance to Jerry Lee's style stood him well. His cousin helped him land record deals with various small labels. By 1964 Gilley had his own record company, Astro Records, and started to gain some regional notice. In 1968 "Now I Can Live Again" became his first country hit, issued by the larger Paula label. In 1971 he became part owner of Gilley's, a huge Houston nightclub. Three years later his Astro recording of the old George Morgan hit, "Roomful of Roses," was picked up by the short-lived Playboy label (owned by the magazine), and wound up a Number One record. Gilley began successfully remaking oldies (something he did throughout his peak years). He had Number One records with versions of "I Overlooked an Orchid," "City Lights" and "Window Up Above" in 1974 and 1975. His 1976 Number One hits included "Don't the Girls All Get Prettier at Closing Time" (more in the Jerry Lee mold), and a remake of Sam Cooke's "Bring It on Home to Me." In 1977 came his biggest hit, "She's Pulling Me Back Again." His Top Ten streak continued after he joined Epic Records in 1978, with "Here Comes the Hurt Again." After the smash 1980 movie, *Urban Cowboy,* was filmed at Gilley's, the club became a worldwide tourist attraction, and Gilley, who appeared in the film, found his career peaking with nearly back to back Number One singles in a row from 1980-1983, including "True Love Ways,"

"Stand By Me," "That's All That Matters," "A Headache Tomorrow (Or a Heartache Tonight)," "You Don't Know Me," "Lonely Nights," "Put Your Dreams Away" and "Talk to Me." Gilley's success continued until the Urban Cowboy fad ended around 1986-87. By 1989 the Gilley's club was closed amid various business problems; it was subsequently destroyed by fire. Gilley left Epic in 1988 for the tiny Airborne label. Today much of his performing activity is centered in Branson, where he owns a theater and a restaurant, and his recordings appear on labels favoring Branson artists. (See also, Gilley's.)   —R.K.

Gilley's

A brief history of Gilley's nightclub in Pasadena, Texas, a suburb of Houston, is in many ways an amusing parable about trends and fads, and the tumultuous fad-driven boom and bust that the country music industry endured (often at the expense of good taste) in the early 1980's. For strange as it may seem, this dingy, airplane-hanger sized dance and juke joint actually inspired a brief national obsession with country music (or at least some people's notion of what country music was).

Gilley's opened for business in 1971. The club was started by Houston businessman Sherwood Cryer, who also happened to manage Mickey Gilley, the journeyman singer and first cousin to Jerry Lee Lewis

who'd hit the big time in 1974 with a surprise hit remake of the country classic, "Room Full of Roses." Cryer, in a move beneficial to both himself and his main artist/client, named his new club after Gilley, who bolstered its popularity by often performing there.

For several years, Gilley's was just a popular, giant-sized Houston watering hole where local dudes and dudettes came to strut their stuff, dress and dance Western, and try their luck on a mechanical ride that emulated the gyrations of a bucking rodeo bull. As time went on, the nightclub's popularity grew, and it was expanded—eventually to 48,000 square feet—to accommodate demand.

In 1978, everything changed when *Esquire Magazine* writer Aaran Latham descended on Gilley's and wrote a tongue-in-cheek feature story about the club, the mechanical bull and the weird little Urban Cowboy lifestyle that had grown up around it all. Hollywood came calling a year or two later with a feature film, starring John Travolta and Debra Winger, based on Latham's article. *Urban Cowboy*, directed by the late James Bridges, was something less than a great movie. It took the same tongue-in-cheek stance as Latham's piece and mainly told a predictable story about some sassy, air-headed kids with nice butts, nice hats and fancy Western dance moves who mainly drank too much beer, made out a lot, ran around in their pick-up trucks and rode the mechanical bull. *Urban Cowboy* proved a resounding box office smash and gave the always fad-hungry American public a new trend to chase: country music. Soon even city-dwelling dental technicians and financial planners across the country—people who, just a year or two earlier, wouldn't have been caught dead singing a Roy Acuff song in the shower—were flocking to Western dance clubs (most of them complete with mechanical bulls), sporting Stetsons, and tuning their car radios to the local country station. For a year or two, the Urban Cowboy boom was a tide that lifted everybody's ship. Gilley's became a national tourist attraction (and, accordingly, the prices in the club went up, and the service and cleanliness went down). Gilley, the singer, despite his less than monumental talent, began commanding superstar concert fees. His even more modestly talented former warm-up act at Gilley's, a good ol' boy named Johnny Lee, who could almost carry a tune on a good day, got a hit out of the deal with a song called "Looking for Love."

Alas, despite its impressive crossover sales, much of the music spawned by the Urban Cowboy craze, does not stand the test of time particularly well—Johnny Lee's theme song being a not-so-shining example. All in all, most of it was even mediocre enough to make true-blue country fans nostalgic for that bleak era in the early 70's when folks like John Denver and Olivia Newton-John reigned supreme at the Country Music Association awards.

And nobody was really surprised when, after the fad had worn off, Gilley's closed, and Mickey Gilley and Sherwood Cryer parted ways in a flurry of nasty, protracted lawsuits. The building was eventually destroyed by fire. (See also, Mickey Gilley, Urban Cowboy.)
—B.A.

Jimmie Dale Gilmore

BORN: May 6, 1945
BIRTHPLACE: Amarillo, Texas

Jimmie Dale Gilmore's father, who played electric guitar in a Western dancehall band, named his son after Jimmie Rodgers. The family eventually settled in Lubbock, where young Gilmore fell sway to a host

of musical influences ranging from fellow Texans Bob Wills, Lefty Frizzell and Buddy Holly to Hank Williams, Little Richard, Elvis Presley, Johnny Cash and Bob Dylan.

In the late 1960's, Gilmore started writing and performing in Lubbock, and in the early 1970's, along with singer-songwriters Joe Ely and Butch Hancock, he formed The Flatlanders. The band went to Nashville to record what would be their only album, for Shelby Singleton's Plantation label. The record, an interesting combination of acoustic country and bluegrass, sold next to nothing. (Rounder Records re-released the album on CD in 1991, retitling it *The Flatlanders: More a Legend Than a Band.*)

The band soon broke up, and Gilmore moved to Denver, where he immersed himself in Oriental philosophy and the beat writings of Jack Kerouac and Allen Ginsberg, a move that would have a profound effect on his own writing. In the early 1980's, Gilmore resumed his musical career in Austin, Texas. By the late 80's, he had released two country-meets-rockabilly rave-ups—*Fair and Square* and *Jimmie Dale Gilmore*—for the independent, Oakland-based HighTone label.

A few tours abroad followed, and in 1989, at the Cambridge Folk Festival in England, Elektra Records executive David Bither was bowled over by Gilmore's performance with Butch Hancock. After the show, Gilmore gave Bither an encore performance at his trailer. Within weeks, Bither signed him to Elektra. In 1991, Gilmore released the critically acclaimed album, *After Awhile. Spinning Around the Sun*, Gilmore's second major label release, followed in 1993, with the critics again mesmerized by the cosmic cowboy's poetic spirituality and country roots.   —R.P.

Johnny Gimble

BORN: May 30, 1926
BIRTHPLACE: Tyler, Texas

Perhaps the best-known exponent of Western swing fiddle and electric mandolin playing, Johnny Gimble got his start working with his brothers, Jerry, Gene and Dick, in a band called The Rose City Swingsters.

By 1943 he was working in Shreveport with The Shelton Brothers before joining the Army at the end of World War II. After his return, he joined a Texas group called The Rhythmairs. In 1949 he joined Bob

Wills' Texas Playboys and quickly stood out for his superb fiddle and electric mandolin work (best exemplified on Wills' MGM recording of "Boot Heel Drag").

He also developed a trademark of scat-singing along with his fiddle licks. Gimble remained a Texas Playboy until 1951, when he settled in Dallas and did session work at Jim Beck's studios. After Western swing's popularity began to wane, he became a barber in a veterans' hospital to make a living. But eventually he returned to music, traveling to Nashville where he became a part of the A-Team of studio pickers in the late 60's.

The Western swing revival gave him greater prominence as a former Texas Playboy, and in 1974 he won the Country Music Association's Instrumentalist of the Year award. He's recorded on his own and played on various recordings by a variety of artists, including George Strait, Asleep at the Wheel and Willie Nelson.

He later moved back to Texas but remains active and vital, working on record sessions and as part of Playboys II, a group of former Texas Playboys featuring steel guitarist Herb Remington, guitarist Eldon Shamblin and other swing greats.   —R.K.

Tompall Glaser and The Glaser Brothers

BORN: Tompall, September 3, 1933
BIRTHPLACE: Spalding, Nebraska

Though the three Glaser Brothers would eventually go their separate ways and make their separate and individual marks on country music, they began their career as a tightly-knit vocal trio. The brothers hail from Spalding, Nebraska, where Tompall was born in 1933, Chuck in 1936, and Jim in 1937. Their rancher father got them started singing and playing guitar early in life, and by the late 1940's they had their own local TV show.

An appearance on the nationally televised *Arthur Godfrey's Talent Scouts* led the Glasers to a meeting with Marty Robbins, who quickly put the brotherly trio to work singing harmonies on his 1959 Number One hit, "El Paso." In 1963, the Glasers also contributed backup vocals to Johnny Cash's immortal "Ring of Fire." By then, they were touring with Cash and had become members of the Grand Ole Opry. "The Streets of Baltimore," one of many songs written by Tompall, has since become a modest country-folk classic, having been recorded by Bobby Bare and numerous other artists.

Working with producer Owen Bradley, and later with "Cowboy" Jack Clement, The Glaser Brothers cast themselves and their airy, gentle harmonies in a folk mode and had sporadic 70's chart success with songs like "Rings" (a Top Ten 1971 cover of a pop hit by the group Cymarron) and Kris Kristofferson's "Lovin' Her Was Easier (Than Anything I'll Ever Do Again)," which reached Number Two in 1981.

But the Glasers' various ambitious side pursuits, as song publishers, managers, and as aspiring solo artists, eventually pulled them apart as a trio. They disbanded in 1973, and regrouped only briefly six years later. The windfall that they earned from their publishing ventures—specifically from the copyrights they held on John Hartford's resoundingly popular "Gentle on My Mind" and the top five Gary Puckett & The Union Gap pop hit, "Woman, Woman" (which was also written by Jim Glaser)—eventually enabled the Glasers to open their own recording studio on Nashville's 19th Avenue South, a couple of blocks off Music Row's main drag. Dubbed "Hillbilly Central" by veteran country music columnist Hazel Smith,

Girls of the Golden West

BORN: Millie, April 11, 1913, Mt. Carmel, Illinois
      Dolly, December 15, 1915, Mt. Carmel, Illinois
DIED: Dolly, November 12, 1968
      Millie, May 2, 1993

Country music's leading female duo in the 1930's and 40's, The Girls of the Golden West, were in fact two sisters named Millie and Dolly Good. Though the publicity writers of their radio station home, Chicago's WLS *National Barn Dance*, insisted the pair was from Muleshoe, Texas, they were in fact from Mt. Carmel, Illinois. They did specialize in Western and cowboy songs, such as "Cowboy Jack," "Lonely Cowgirl" and "There's a Silver Moon on the Golden Gate," and they were among the first women singers to adopt full-scale Western costumes (which they made themselves). Their singing style featured incredibly tight harmony and high, wordless keening that enchanted radio listeners at WLS and, later, at WLW in Cincinnati. Dolly later married Prairie Ramblers fiddler Tex Achison; Millie married announcer Bill McCluskey. The group retired in 1949, after making a long series of Bluebird and Vocalion records. Dolly died in November 1968, at age 52. Millie died in May 1993, just after her 80th birthday. —C.W.

their studio became an informal gathering place for the Glasers' restless kindred spirits and fellow musicians: well-known Music Row anti-establishment, counter-cultural types, Waylon Jennings, Willie Nelson and Kris Kristofferson among them. Typical members of this set went against Nashville's grain by wearing their hair long and shaggy in that land of crew cuts and flat tops while dreaming of a new day on Music Row when artists, as opposed to producers and publishers, would call the creative shots. Eventually, they would come to be collectively known as The Outlaws—a revolutionary early 70's musical movement that ultimately coalesced out of their iconoclastic, anti-music business establishment visions. And Tompall Glaser, in the very early 70's, was right at the center of all this.

Because of his close association with Jennings (some of whose early 70's records he produced), Tompall quickly became the most high profile of the Glaser siblings. Before his Outlaw phase, he'd scored brief solo chart success with singles like "T for Texas" (a re-titled 1976 cover of Jimmie Rodgers' 1927 "Blue Yodel") and 1975's "Put Another Log on the Fire (Male Chauvinist National Anthem)," and he'd received particularly strong critical acclaim for his introspective 1973 album, *Charlie*. Superstar status briefly struck when "T

for Texas" and "Put Another Log" by Tompall and His Outlaw Band were included on the multi-million-selling compilation album, *Wanted: The Outlaws*. The album also included selections by Nelson, Jennings and Jennings' talented and lovely wife, Jessi Colter; it proved a real cornerstone in launching Jennings and Nelson to superstardom, and giving strong public identity to the Outlaw movement. Tompall toured briefly with Nelson and Jennings. However, Tompall—unlike Nelson and Jennings—did little to follow up in terms of building a hit solo career, and has since spun off on a number of his own eccentric musical and business pursuits.

While brother Chuck opted to stick to the business side of country music, Jim Glaser eventually proved himself a talented—if only sporadically commercially successful—singer in his own right. He had his first solo chart successes as early as 1968 and 1969 with modest hits like "God Help You Woman," "Please Take Me Back," "I'm Not Through Lovin' You" and "Molly." But Jim never really scored big until his early 1980's album, *The Man in the Mirror*, resulted in a string of Top Ten singles and the 1984 Number One hit, "You're Gettin' to Me Again." Over the years, Jim was also in demand as a backup singer, embellishing hits by Sylvia, Ronnie McDowell and numerous other artists with his studio harmonies.   —B.A.

Lonnie Glosson

BORN: February 14, 1908
BIRTHPLACE: Judsonia, Arkansas

Lonnie Glosson's first professional experience came in St. Louis. Later, he worked in Shreveport before eventually joining the WLS *National Barn Dance* and other Chicago radio programs. He made his first record in 1930 for a label owned by Sears (who also owned WLS). He worked around the country and taught Wayne Raney much of his early harmonica skills. The two even worked together on and off beginning in the late 30's.

He played harmonica on some of Raney's vocal recordings for King Records and hosted his own television show in Atlanta late in the 40's. He and Raney continued their partnership through most of the 50's. Glosson, in his mid-80's, continues to perform both in the U.S. and Europe.   —R.K.

Gold Record

A Gold record is a sales achievement award issued by the trade group, Recording Industry Association of America, indicating that an album has sold 500,000 units (or $1,000,000 based on 1/3 the suggested retail price). A record company makes a request for certification, then provides sales figures to the RIAA, which audits them for accuracy. Once the investigation is complete, a Gold record is awarded. The process began in 1958, in a slightly different manner. Then, the award was based solely on the dollar amounts. In 1976, the current system began: Gold certifications for albums were based on sales of 500,000 units *or* $1,000,000, and a new category, platinum, for album sales in excess of 1,000,000 units *or* $2,000,000. Gold awards are also issued for singles and music videos, using only unit sales (no dollar figures): 500,000 units for singles; 50,000 units for videos. (See also, Platinum Record.)   —G.F.

Bobby Goldsboro

BORN: January 18, 1941
BIRTHPLACE: Marianna, Florida

Bobby Goldsboro was born January 18, 1941, in Marianna, Florida. He learned to play guitar by imitating Elvis Presley and Carl Perkins. He moved to Dothan, Alabama, at age 15, where he and friends formed a band, The Webs. After two years of college, from 1962 to 1964, he toured with Roy Orbison.

In 1968, he reached the Number One position on *Billboard*'s pop and country charts with the maudlin "Honey," and entered the Top 20 on each chart with further hits of that ilk—"Autumn of My Life" and "Watching Scotty Grow," among them. His other Top 20 country singles include "Muddy Mississippi Line" (1969), "Goodbye Marie" (1980), "Love Ain't Never Hurt Nobody" (1981) and "Alice Doesn't Love Here Anymore" (1981). In addition to his responsibility for these hits, he also hosted a syndicated television show in the mid-70's.   —S.W.

Charlie Gore

BORN: October 4, 1930
BIRTHPLACE: Chapmanville, West Virginia

Charlie Gore was one of many truly talented performers whose followings were regional and who, despite making records, never had the opportunity to hit the national scene with a decent hit.

As a teenager he worked on radio in Logan, West Virginia, then at stations in Huntington and Worthington. His biggest break came when he joined the WLW *Midwestern Hayride* cast and began recording for Syd Nathan's King label. Backed by Zeke Turner, Jerry Byrd and other gifted musicians, he made some excellent singles, but not a one ever broke into the charts. By the late 50's, Gore had returned to West Virginia and put aside his singing career for one spinning records. He later became involved in local politics.   —R.K.

Vern Gosdin

BORN: August 5, 1934
BIRTHPLACE: Woodland, Alabama

The nickname, "The Poor Man's George Jones," which Vern Gosdin has been called more than once, does not do justice to this Alabama native's exquisite country voice. It's a voice which has been showcased vividly on hits like "Set 'Em Up, Joe" and the 1989 Country Music Association Song of the Year, "Chiseled in Stone," as well as on quasi-chart-toppers of yesteryear like "Yesterday's Gone," "(Just Enough To) Keep Me Hangin' On" (both of which featured duet accompaniment from Emmylou Harris) and "Break My Mind."

Gosdin was born in Woodland, Alabama, on August 5, 1934, and has been singing since childhood. He and his brother, Rex, began working together as a duo in the early 50's, performing at local schoolhouses and on Radio WVOK in Birmingham. After brief musical stints in Atlanta and Chicago in the 50's,

Gosdin ended up on the West Coast in the 1960's. In California, he worked as a welder and later played in a bluegrass band with Rex and a third brother, Ray. A few years later, he and Rex teamed up and recorded as The Gosdin Brothers, opening shows for everyone from Merle Haggard to The Byrds. The Byrds, at one point, recorded an original song of Gosdin's called "Someone to Turn To" that ended up in the soundtrack of the Dennis Hopper/Peter Fonda/Jack Nicholson film, *Easy Rider*. Gosdin also participated in sessions for The Byrds' classic album, *Sweethearts of the Rodeo*. His original compositions have since been recorded by everyone from George Jones and Merle Haggard to George Strait and the late Keith Whitley. In California, Vern and Rex also worked in The Golden State Boys, a bluegrass outfit that included Chris Hillman, a founding Byrd and more recently leader of The Desert Rose Band.

Gosdin ended up back east, in Atlanta, where he founded his own business, The Arrowhead Glass Company. He prospered in the Atlanta building boom, and decided to give Nashville one more try. In 1976, he landed a contract with Elektra Records. The company seemed rather lukewarm on him until he talked Emmylou Harris' manager into talking Emmylou herself into singing on a couple of his records. He had three Top Tens at Elektra, then continued touring and recording for various independent labels, many of which had a habit of going out of business right when he seemed to get things rolling. He had a particularly good run in the mid-1980's on Compleat Records, where he scored his first Number One, "I Can Tell By the Way You Dance (You're Gonna Love Me Tonight)." But, as had too often been the case in Gosdin's long but checkered recording career, Compleat soon bit the bullet, too.

"There I was with a Number One record, and I couldn't tell a bit of difference," he lamented in a 1990 interview with *Country Music Magazine*'s Bob Allen. "I wasn't making any more money. It wasn't long afterwards that I found out the only reason Compleat had signed me was for a tax write-off. I was trying to get a Number One record, and they didn't even want one! After 20 different labels, I decided it was either time to get a major label or get the hell out of Nashville."

Gosdin's next stop, of course, was with Columbia, the label for which he recorded *Chiseled in Stone*, and for which he still records today.

Gosdin has never quite re-attained the all-time artistic high watermark he achieved with that Gold-certified album in 1987. Yet he has been consistently turning out noteworthy music in the years since and has already earned himself a place in country music's pantheon of great veteran singers. —B.A.

Billy Grammer

BORN: August 28, 1925
BIRTHPLACE: Benton, Illinois

Singer-guitarist Billy Grammer had only one big hit, but it was one whose origins went back at least a century. His earliest work was done at WARL radio in Arlington, Virginia, just outside Washington, D.C., beginning in 1947, on a show produced by Connie B. Gay. He made his first recordings in 1949. He also worked the road with T. Texas Tyler and Hawkshaw Hawkins, and was in demand for recording session work. Beginning in 1955 he was featured on Jimmy Dean's Washington-based TV program, *Town and Country Time*, which also launched Patsy Cline's and Roy Clark's careers and appeared on the CBS network. When Grammer signed with Monument in 1958, he found almost immediate success with "Gotta Travel On," a British song that first surfaced in the 1800's. Its strong folk flavor—just as interest in folk music revived across the nation—made it a huge crossover hit, reaching both the country and pop Top Five. Grammer joined the Grand Ole Opry that year. In 1963, his Top 20 version of "I Wanna Go Home" was actually the first hit version of "Detroit City," which became a bigger hit that year for Bobby Bare. Grammer was always a formidable guitarist and designed the Grammer Guitar, an acoustic flattop model that enjoyed some popularity. He also did extensive session work. —R.K.

Grand Ole Opry

The Grand Ole Opry, which holds the distinction of being the world's oldest continuous running live musical radio show, is to country music what the Vatican is to the Catholic Church. There is simply no metaphor quite strong enough to convey the Opry's immense importance in the growth of country music's national popularity over the decades, or its central role in the parallel blossoming of Nashville as an international recording center.

The Opry (whose rich history is detailed in Chet Hagan's 1989 book, *The Grand Ole Opry*) came into being in early 1926 when it was first broadcast over WSM-AM, a Nashville radio station that took to the air in October 1925. Events leading to the start of Opry began on November 28, 1925, when a preacher missed his radio show, and WSM station director George D. Hay, who had been hired away from the WLS *National Barn Dance*, drafted local fiddler Uncle Jimmy Thompson to fill in. The response from listeners was overwhelming, and on December 26, the show became a regular feature, starring Thompson and banjo player Uncle Dave Macon. As the show progressed, more local musicians were added, including the harmonica playing DeFord Bailey and the stringband music of Humphrey Bate's Possum Hunters and The Crook Brothers. The show became known as the WSM *Barn Dance;* it was in 1927 that Hay coined the name Grand Ole Opry.

In style and substance the Opry owed much to similar "barn dance"-style country music variety shows like the *Louisiana Hayride* in Shreveport, and WLS' *National Barn Dance*, in Chicago, both of which predated it. However, the Opry soon emerged with a format and flavor all its own. One of those most singularly responsible for this was station director—and show emcee—Hay. Known to his listening audience as the "The Solemn Old Judge," Hay continued to add new talent to the show's roster. But the live Saturday night radio show's growing popularity and singular identity in its listeners' imaginations was cemented by Uncle Dave Macon, who became one of the Opry's first stars by parlaying his huge repertoire of folk songs, his mastery of the banjo and his comic gifts as a former vaudeville and minstrel performer into massive popularity. By the early 1930's, WSM had boosted its signal to 50,000 watts, a clear-channel frequency which, by night, reached 30 states and

parts of Canada. New talent added to the cast in this era included The Vagabonds, The Delmore Brothers, Pee Wee King and His Golden West Cowboys, Fiddlin' Arthur Smith, Roy Acuff (1938), Bill Monroe (1939) and Minnie Pearl (1940).

As the Opry's three-hour-long Saturday night broadcasts burgeoned in listenership, the show was moved to bigger and bigger halls to satisfy the ever increasing demand for tickets. In the early 1940's, the Opry troupe took up residence in the Ryman Auditorium, a hallowed old tabernacle in downtown Nashville (often referred to as "The Mother Church of Country Music").

As the 40's progressed, the Opry began to overtake the WLS *National Barn Dance* as the dominant barn dance show nationally. The addition of superstars Roy Acuff and Ernest Tubb to their line-up, as well as the growing popularity of Minnie Pearl's comedy and Bill Monroe's bluegrass music, gave the Opry an edge. Camel Cigarettes sent their "Camel Caravan" out on tour featuring Pee Wee King with his vocalist Eddy Arnold, Ernest Tubb and other Opry stars. Other acts joining the show were singer-songwriter Zeke Clements, the Western swing-oriented Paul Howard and his Arkansas Cotton Pickers and Curley Williams and The Georgia Peach Pickers. The Opry segment sponsored by Prince Albert Tobacco was carried live over NBC, hosted by Acuff. After Acuff left the Prince Albert segment in a dispute, Prince Albert hired Red Foley from WLS as his replacement. The Opry's rise continued and its success led directly to the development of the recording and country music business activities using Nashville as a headquarters. Most Opry acts were booked through WSM's Artists Service bureau, and the requirements that all cast members appear a specified number of Saturdays a year were strictly enforced. One of the first artists to quit the show, feeling his stardom would be stifled by the Opry, was Eddy Arnold, who'd become a solo vocalist in 1944, went on to superstardom, and quit in 1947. In the late 40's, Hank Thompson had a chance to join the cast and decided not to, due to the appearance requirement and poor money (musician's union scale). Hank Williams, who joined in 1949, was a major boost to the show, as were later additions like Canadian Hank Snow, George Morgan, Little Jimmy Dickens and Hank's friend Moon Mullican, the first pianist to become a singing star. The "wholesomeness" of the show continued, as most references to liquor were taboo for years. Ironically, Williams, comic Rod Brasfield and other artists all battled serious problems with liquor. (Mom's, later known as Tootsie's Orchid Lounge was right across the alley from the Opry's backstage entrance.)

By the early 50's, the Opry's popularity continued. though some younger artists, most notably Lefty Frizzell, felt they didn't need the Opry to establish themselves; yet others, like Carl Smith, were among the final generation of stars directly built by the Opry itself. Some old-timers continued on the show, but others, like Uncle Dave Macon, were dying off. West Coast artists had proven they, too, didn't need the Opry to become successful. Hay's role gradually diminished as his physical and mental health faltered,

and as his successors, managers Jack Stapp and Jim Denny (both of whom eventually left the Opry when their outside music publishing activities were deemed a possible conflict of interest) sought to "modernize" the show by easing back on the mountain stringbands and bringing aboard younger rhinestone-suited recording stars. This often caused intense resentment among older castmembers, and intramural squabbling among Opry members was routine. For instance, Bill Monroe, angry at former bandmembers Flatt and Scruggs' success at emulating a style of music (bluegrass) he considered his own, was successful in keeping them off the Opry, even though the duo had their own WSM radio show until 1955. The incursion of rock 'n' roll also hurt the Opry badly. Denny had suggested Elvis Presley go back to truck driving after his 1954 Opry appearance singing "That's All Right (Mama)." Gradually, however, younger artists were added to the cast including Bobby Helms, Charlie Louvin, Porter Wagoner, Stonewall Jackson, Roy Drusky, Jean Shepard, Jimmie C. Newman, Johnny

Cash (briefly) and Don Gibson. Still, into the 1960's, the Opry went out over WSM's 50,000 watt clear channel every Saturday night, with Acuff, Monroe, Tubb and the others on board every week. More younger talent, Bill Anderson, Connie Smith and David Houston came into the cast in the late 60's, as did George Jones, Dolly Parton, Jack Greene. Jeannie Seely and Charlie Walker. As Nashville's reputation as the country music capitol of the world grew, tourists continued to flock to the Opry.

But the Ryman Auditorium had never been built for such a crowds. The building was not air-conditioned; the original straight-backed church pew seats remained. The dressing rooms were cramped and uncomfortable and the antiquated building less than safe. In the late 60's, National Life, the owners of WSM and the Opry, decided to move the show to a larger, more modern, air-conditioned facility and began planning what became Opryland. On March 9, 1974 the final show took place at the Ryman. A week later, on March 16th, the premiere show at the new Opry House at Opryland took place, with a politically beleaguered President Richard Nixon, in the final days of Watergate, on hand as Roy Acuff played "Wabash Cannonball" to open the first show in the new auditorium.

In recent decades, the Opry's influence has diminished somewhat. Today, the show has become less a barometer of country music's mainstream and more of a living museum devoted to its past glories. To its credit, the Opry has, all through the years—even as the country music industry has again and again weathered eras of heavy pop/crossover influence—remained a stolid, purist bastion of genuinely rural strains of country music of yesteryear. And it is just this sense of tradition, timelessness and nostalgia that has endeared it in millions of listeners' hearts.

Quite a few of today's superstars are Opry members—Dolly Parton, Emmylou Harris, Ricky Skaggs (a particularly devout Opry cast member), Randy Travis, Vince Gill, Alison Krauss, Clint Black, Garth Brooks, Hal Ketchum, Barbara Mandrell, Joe Diffie and Alan Jackson, among them. However, present-day membership rules do not require these artists to perform there on a regular basis. Moreover, today, though it's quite possible to have a successful country career without the exposure afforded by Opry membership, it is still one of the most sought-after and exclusive badges of prestige in the business: one of the most genuine stamps of authenticity a country singer can have bestowed on him.)

In 1983, the Opry became the anchor for The Nashville Network cable channel, which is owned by Gaylord Broadcasting, the Opry's present-day parent company. Today, the televised portion of the Opry shown on TNN is one of the network's most heavily viewed broadcasts. Bill Monroe, an Opry member since 1939, has the distinction of having the longest tenure of any current member. (Minnie Pearl is close behind, having joined in 1940, though she was recently incapacitated by a stroke.)

It was Garrison Keillor—who was inspired by the Opry to create his own popular radio musical/comedy radio show, The Prairie Home Companion—who vividly captured The Grand Ole Opry's enduring appeal in a lengthy profile of the show which he wrote in *The New Yorker* in the 1970's: "You listen to the Opry, and pretty soon you have a place in mind—a stage where Uncle Dave sang and told jokes and swung the banjo, where the Great Acuff wept and sang 'The Great Speckled Bird,' where Hank Williams made his Opry debut with 'Lovesick Blues'....where Cousin Minnie Pearl calls out 'Howdee! I'm just so proud to be here!' And eventually, you have to go and be there, too." (See also, Ryman Auditorium.)   —B.A.

Mark Gray

BORN: October 24, 1952
BIRTHPLACE: Vicksburg, Mississippi

With Mark Gray, a former member of the band Exile, Columbia/ Nashville must have thought it had another Kenny Rogers, or maybe even a country-flavored Billy Joel, on its hands. In 1983, on the eve of Gray's first album release, the record label flew several hundred members of the music press and the radio industry to Chicago where they staged a lavish showcase for this gifted country-pop piano pounder, even giving away hundreds of free hats

identical to the one the semi-balding singer/songwriter wore.

It was a lot of pressure to put on a young artist. And Gray, who was born in Vicksburg, Mississippi, October 24, 1952, almost predictably, didn't live up to it. Between 1983 and 1985, he did make it into the Top Ten a few times with singles like "Left Side of the Bed," "If All the Magic Is Gone," "Diamond in the Dust" and "Please Be Love." He and Tammy Wynette also had a glossy remake of Dan Hill's pop hit, "Sometimes When We Touch" in 1985, which reached Number Six, thus becoming Gray's best ever chart showing.

But by 1988, Gray had vanished from Columbia Records and from the charts, not to be heard from again. At last sighting, he was still popping up on Music Row occasionally writing songs for various publishing companies.   —B.A.

Jack Greene

BORN: January 7, 1930
BIRTHPLACE: Maryville, Tennessee

Jack Greene began playing guitar at age eight and did his first radio appearances while still in his youth. He also learned to play drums. However, much of his early career was spent working in various bands in the Atlanta area. From the late 40's on, he was with The Cherokee Trio and in 1950, he joined The Rhythm Ranch Boys. After two years in the Army, he returned to Atlanta in 1952 and joined The Peachtree Cowboys. Ten years later, Ernest Tubb hired him as The Texas Troubadours' drummer and warm-up vocalist. (For a time both Greene and Cal Smith worked as Texas Troubadours.) Since Tubb's band had its own separate recording contract with Decca, Greene got a chance to record, and by 1965 had his own Decca contract. He finally went solo after his 1966 version of Dallas Frazier's ballad, "There Goes My Everything," hit Number One for several weeks and earned him two Grammy nominations. The follow-up single, "All the Time," was another Number One hit. Greene became a member of the Opry on December 23, 1967. Through the late 60's, Greene had several more Top Tens, including "You Are My Treasure," "Until My Dreams Come True" and "Statue of a Fool" (the latter revived by Ricky Van Shelton, who took it to the top of the charts in 1989). He and Jeannie Seely teamed as duet partners and their single, "Wish I Didn't Have to Miss You," reached Number Two in 1969. Greene continued to have hit records with Decca and then with MCA until fading sales left him label-less in 1975. He recorded for the small Frontline and EMH labels through 1984 and remains an Opry member.   —R.K.

Lee Greenwood

BORN: October 27, 1942
BIRTHPLACE: Southgate, California

Country music's own "Mr. Las Vegas," Melvin Lee Greenwood actually established a career in the gambling mecca—both as an entertainer and a casino employee—before signing with MCA Records in 1980.

With a deep, raspy voice (a la Kenny Rogers), Greenwood started out promisingly enough with "It Turns Me Inside Out," his gripping, almost haunting first single in 1981. While that song reached the Top 20, Greenwood went on to far greater success as he moved into the crossover realm with saccharine, country-lite material that kept him high on the charts (19 Top Tens) throughout the mid-80's. Among his Number One singles are "Somebody's Gonna Love You," "Going, Going, Gone," "Dixie Road," "I Don't Mind the Thorns (If You're the Rose)," "Don't Underestimate My Love for You," "Hearts Aren't Made to Break (They're Made to Love)" and "Mornin' Ride." Worst of all though, is the song he's most identified with, the bombastic, jingoistic "God Bless the USA," a 1984 Top Ten that seems to have a life of its own, resur-

facing each time there's a war, or a Republican convention. After leaving MCA in 1989, Greenwood signed with Capitol, producing one more Top Ten, "Holdin' a Good Hand," in 1990. He was last seen heading for Branson.   —G.F.

Gretsch

Like Martin guitars, Germany contributed Friedrich "Fred" Gretsch to the development of American guitars. In 1883, after arriving from Mannheim, Germany, Gretsch began a small instrument shop in Brooklyn. When he died suddenly in 1895, his son, Fred Jr., took over the company while still a teenager. The company's reputation for banjos and guitars grew so that by 1916, he'd built a ten-story factory in Brooklyn. When Duke Kramer was added to the staff, he was able to sell the company's instruments by incorporating customers' suggestions and desires into their products. By the time Fred Jr.'s sons took over in 1942, the company was established solidly, though behind Gibson, Epiphone and Martin in terms of market share. Merle Travis' first decent guitar was a $30 Gretsch Model 30 archtop. Gretsch was not a widely used instrument by country pickers, except for Red River Dave, until the 50's. It was Gretsch's Jimmie Webster, a guitarist himself, who approached Chet Atkins about designing a signature model guitar. When the "Chet Atkins" CA 6120 was introduced in 1954, and the 6121 solidbody followed in 1955, Atkins' popularity among guitarists and his use of the hollowbody model on records and onstage made the latter model an instant hit among country pickers. The candy apple red finish, "G" brand on the top and western decorations made it extremely appealing, leading to an entire line of Atkins Gretsch guitars. A number of other country and rockabilly pickers, most Atkins admirers, adopted the CA 6120, including Duane Eddy and Eddie Cochran. The Beatles' George Harrison, another Atkins fan, also used Atkins guitars through the group's peak years. Atkins worked closely with the company on models like the "Country Gentleman," the "Tennessean" and, in 1973, the elaborate "Super Chet." Also in 1954, Gretsch introduced their solidbody model 6130 "Round Up" electric (styled similar to an Atkins model) and the acoustic "Town and Country" and

"Rancher," all aimed at country singers. In 1955 Eddy Arnold and Hank Garland were featured in a Gretsch endorsement advertisement, though neither man ever used the instruments much. Gretsch was sold to Baldwin Piano and Organ in 1967, and Atkins continued working with the company through the 70's. His last major projects were the solidbody "Atkins Super Axe" and "Atkins Axe" models, introduced in 1978. Roy Clark also used one. Atkins gradually grew dissatisfied with the company and moved on to work with Gibson. The company went through complicated ownership changes until they quit making guitars for a time in 1981 before restarting modestly. In 1985, Fred Gretsch, great grandson of the founder, purchased the company and began building instruments that reproduced the company's best known models of the past. —R.K.

Nanci Griffith

BORN: July 16, 1954
BIRTHPLACE: Austin, Texas

For quite a few years before she made a brief, uneasy foray into Nashville's major-label mainstream in the late 1980's, Nanci Griffith was already a revered singer/ songwriter in Texas and on the national folk circuit. In fact, her first successes in country came as a songwriter—when Kathy Mattea had a hit with her "Love at the Five & Dime." Mattea has since covered other Griffith originals, as have Suzy Bogguss and other mainstream women singers. Griffith spent most of her life around the Houston and Austin areas of Texas before hitting the national folk circuit, then later relocating to Nashville. Her earliest, as well as some of her best, recording was done on the independent, Massachusetts-based Rounder label.

Griffith has never been shy about the fact that her influences spring more from folkies like Carolyn

Hester and early Bob Dylan, and from literary figures like Eudora Welty and fellow Texan Larry McMurtry than they do from country's pantheon of greats. "'Folkabilly' is what I've always called my music," recalled Griffith in a *Country Music Magazine* interview with Bob Allen."When I first started out, the folk community had a hard time accepting me, because at the time it was very much entrenched in this 'granola' business and there was a lot of very mediocre music.

"On the other hand," adds the singer/songwriter, who possesses an unconventionally shrill, little-girlish, but thoroughly compelling singing style, and who writes brilliant, emotionally layered, lyrically sophisticated ballads and story-songs, "I really didn't consider myself country either, because I don't dress in sequins and I'm not out there doing flashy stage moves in cowboy boots."

Evidently country radio didn't think Griffith was country either, since her brief stint with MCA resulted in no significant hits. (None of her singles have gone higher than Number 36 in the country charts.) It did, however, enlarge upon her already glowing reputation in the contemporary folk world, and she's since gone on to greater glory. Leaving MCA for Elektra, in 1992 she released *Other Voices, Other Rooms,* an inspired collection of duets that featured contributions by everyone from Bob Dylan, Odetta and The Indigo Girls, to neo-country folkies like Emmylou Harris, Iris DeMent, John Prine, John Hartford, Arlo Guthrie and Guy Clark. Besides bringing an added dimension of "community" to country's often-neglected folk fringes, *Other Voices, Other Rooms* also helped solidify Griffith's much-deserved reputation as an artist whose tastes, perceptions and—God forbid!—sense of literacy go well beyond the often predictable pale of the country mainstream. —B.A.

David Grisman

BORN: March 23, 1945
BIRTHPLACE: Hackensack, New Jersey

Originally a bluegrass mandolin virtuoso, David Grisman became a pioneer of what's become known as "New Acoustic Music," an instrumental form fusing bluegrass styles and techniques with various styles of ethnic music, as well as blues and the free-form improvisations of jazz. In the late 1960's he played in

Earth Opera, a Boston-based band formed by fellow New Acoustic/newgrass star Peter Rowan. His classic 1977 album on the Kaleidoscope label, *The David Grisman Quintet*, which featured guitarist Tony Rice and fiddler Darol Anger, became a landmark in that field. Grisman, whose group has continued with various personnel changes (Mark O'Connor was a later addition) has gone on to work in a variety of contexts, including sessions and appearances with the late western swing mandolinist Tiny Moore, legendary jazz violinist Stephane Grappelli, The Grateful Dead's Jerry Garcia (he, Garcia, Rowan and Vassar Clements were in a short-lived group called Old and In The Way, which made an album), and more recently, a second jazz violin legend, Svend Asmussen. The controversial "new age" music may or may not be a spin-off of this, but there is no question Grisman remains one of the great acoustic music innovators of his generation, yet still plays traditional bluegrass with enthusiasm. —R.K.

Guitar

The guitar arrived in America with early European settlers, and gradually European guitar makers like Christian Freidrich Martin emigrated to America and began building the stringed instruments. Guitars were difficult to mass-produce, however, until the Industrial Revolution of the late 1800's. The appearance of the louder steel string guitars improved things somewhat, but fiddle, mandolin and banjo remained dominant among white stringbands. Black southern musicians were quicker to adopt the guitar, and it became an integral part of rural black music. White musicians noticed this and began using guitars, which started showing up more often in white stringbands by the early 1900's. Grand Ole Opry musician Sam McGee, for example, learned much about guitar picking from black railroad workers who played during their lunch breaks near his Tennessee home. As cheaply produced guitars appeared in mail order catalogs, and more high quality guitars came on the market, they gained greater favor.

As the guitar became popular in stringbands, a number of guitarists began creating their own innovative styles, such as Roy Harvey, who worked with Charlie Poole, and Riley Puckett, who worked with Gid Tanner. Each created rhythmic bass runs that

enhanced their bands' sounds and formed the basis for the later guitar styles of bluegrass. Jimmie Rodgers also helped sell many guitars in the late 1920's and early 1930's by his use of the instrument. He appears to have been the first country singer to have a guitar model named for him, when Weymann created their "Jimmie Rodgers Special" model in 1930. In 1932 WLS *National Barn Dance* singer, Arkie the Arkansas Woodchopper, had Martin guitars build him one of their large D-2 "dreadnought" guitars with a herringbone wood trim. It became the classic Martin D-28. In 1933 his fellow *Barn Dance* star, Gene Autry, had Martin build him an elaborate pearl inlaid version of "Arkie's" guitar that became the D-45. Sears Roebuck began marketing its inexpensive "Gene Autry" guitars in the 1930's, and these were the first guitars many young future guitar stars owned. Other musicians, including Ray Whitley, preferred Gibson acoustics (the company built their classic J-200 jumbo acoustic for Whitley in 1937).

The electric guitar had been around in varying forms since the late 1920's and Grand Ole Opry group The Vagabonds had even experimented with some sort of amplification early on. But the first real amplified guitars were steel guitars. In 1936, Gibson introduced their ES-150 electric guitars. Most southeastern country musicians rejected them, but the Western swing bands of the Southwest were quick to adopt them, most notably the Light Crust Doughboys' Muryel "Zeke" Campbell and Eldon Shamblin.

After complaints that Ernest Tubb's early acoustic Decca recordings were inaudible, Tubb had guitarist "Smitty" Smith use an electrified guitar on his 1941 "Walking the Floor Over You." It established Tubb's style and helped end the Opry's ban on electric guitars when Tubb came to the show. Still, few country singers used electrics, one exception being Floyd Tillman.

The first true guitar stylists were a varied lot. Maybelle Carter's famous "drop thumb" guitar style, epitomized by her solo work on "Wildwood Flower," inspired generations of country pickers. Karl Farr's acoustic guitar work with The Sons of the Pioneers combined country with a bit of jazz. California guitarist Porky Freeman had a huge regional hit with his amplified version of "Boogie Woogie on the Strings" in 1943. After the war, Zeb Turner used a similar style on his "Zeb's Mountain Boogie."

The syncopated Western Kentucky thumb and index finger picking style pioneered by Kennedy

Jones, featuring a thumb pick, formed the basis for the picking of Ike Everly and Mose Rager, who taught the style to Merle Travis. Travis' playing over WLW in the late 30's and early 40's inspired young Chester Atkins to develop his own version of the style. Jazz guitarists like Belgian Django Reinhardt and black electric guitarist Charlie Christian also influenced country guitar players. Harold Bradley and Billy Byrd were both Christian disciples, as were Bob Wills/ Spade Cooley guitarist Jimmy Wyble and pioneer Nashville studio musicians, Hank Garland and Grady Martin. Nashville guitarists, a group that included Ray Edenton and later Reggie Young, could usually play in any style required.

Though Rickenbacker had introduced a solidbody model in the 1930's, it never caught on. In 1950 Leo Fender introduced the Fender Broadcaster (changed to Telecaster—see Fender for more information), the first successful solidbody guitar, and its success largely came from country pickers. Other gifted soloists also appeared, including Jimmy Bryant, who played dazzlingly fast country jazz and whose playing was much in demand in L.A. recording studios in the 50's, and Joe Maphis, a pioneer in flatpicking fiddle tunes on guitar, who played the first doubleneck "Mosrite" brand electric guitar made by Semie Moseley. Gretsch's Chet Atkins line and Gibson's Byrdland, designed by Billy Byrd and Hank Garland, also caught on.

But acoustic stylists hadn't stagnated during this period. Lester Flatt, building on the styles of earlier players like Roy Harvey, created a punchy guitar style combining chords and bass runs that he used with Bill Monroe's Blue Grass Boys and then with his partner, Earl Scruggs. Other fine bluegrass guitarists included The Stanley Brothers' George Shuffler, who "crosspicked" his instrument like a mandolin, as did guitarist Bill Napier. Blind guitarist Doc Watson also picked up the idea of finger picking fiddle tunes as Joe Maphis had. Hank Snow, who often soloed on his records, showed the influence of Karl Farr. Like Snow, singer Billy Grammer was another superb guitar soloist.

In the 60's, the Fender Telecaster stylings of country-rockabilly guitarist James Burton, singer Buck Owens (who played guitar on many Capitol rock and country releases), Owens' lead guitarist Don Rich and Merle Haggard's guitarist Roy Nichols all had considerable impact, as did the nylon string playing of Jerry Reed, who expanded the Travis-Atkins style

to use all the fingers of the right hand. Owens, Reed, Roy Clark and Glen Campbell were among the best-known singers of the 60's who were also formidable guitarists. In the 70's, Telecasters symbolized the Outlaw movement through Waylon Jennings' prominent use of the instrument. British Telecaster ace Albert Lee's work with Emmylou Harris' Hot Band had considerable influence in the late 70's, as did that of his fellow Brit Ray Flacke. In the 80's the Telecaster stylings of Dwight Yoakam guitarist Pete Anderson, Jerry Donohue and Desert Rose Band guitarist John Jorgenson proved the instrument as durable as ever.

In acoustic music, Willie Nelson's gut-string guitar work, influenced equally by Django Reinhardt and Grady Martin, became a trademark of his stage and recorded performances. In bluegrass, Eddie Adcock's playing revealed the influence of Jimmy Bryant and other electric players. Tony Rice, a veteran bluegrasser, epitomized a more complex style combining jazz influences, as did Merle Haggard's young electric guitarist Clint Strong. In the 1990's, though, the technology has changed, no country guitar style, acoustic or electric, is truly out of date, and new ideas continue to flow.
—R.K.

Jack Guthrie

BORN: November 13, 1915
BIRTHPLACE: Olive, Oklahoma
DIED: January 15, 1948

Leon Jerry "Jack" Guthrie's career didn't endure like that of his more famous cousin, Woody Guthrie. Yet in the mid 1940's, Jack was the one enjoying nationwide popularity. Though Oklahoma-born, he grew up in Texas and Oklahoma. Like many Oklahomans during the Depression, the Guthries relocated to Southern California in 1932. There Jack worked at various jobs. In 1937, after briefly co-hosting a Los Angeles radio show with Woody, Jack began a modest local solo career along with day jobs that included rodeo work. By 1944, he'd connected with Capitol Records, where producer Lee Gillette was impressed by both Guthrie's distinctive voice and by "Oklahoma Hills," a song of Woody's that Jack wrongly said he wrote. Released by Capitol in 1945, Jack's swinging version stayed at Number One on *Billboard's* Folk Music Charts six weeks, along with the flipside, "I'm

Brandin' My Darlin' with My Heart." By the time of the release, Jack had been drafted and stationed in the Pacific. Woody challenged Jack's appropriation of "Oklahoma Hills," and both shared composer credits. Health problems, eventually diagnosed as tuberculosis, ended his Army hitch, and after one last hit in 1947 with "Oakie Boogie" (an early country boogie hit), his condition worsened. He died in a Livermore, California hospital.   —R.K.

Woody Guthrie

BORN: July 14, 1912
BIRTHPLACE: Okemah, Oklahoma
DIED: October 3, 1967

Born in Okemah, Oklahoma, in 1912, Woody Guthrie is America's most legendary folk singer. His Dustbowl ballads in many ways made him the musical conscience of the nation in the 1930's and 40's. His "This Land Is Your Land" (which was written in angry response to Irving Berlin's jingoistic "God Bless America"), has since been recorded by everyone from Pete Seeger to Bruce Springsteen, and is only one of his many original compositions that have endured as popular American folk anthems.

Guthrie—whose life has been documented not only in his own autobiography, *Bound for Glory* (which inspired a feature film of the same name in 1977, starring David Carradine), but in an award-winning biography, as well—was born into relative comfort and grew up listening to both white and black folk musicians in his native Oklahoma. But a series of catastrophes devastated the family. His father's real estate business failed. His sister was killed in a coal stove accident, and his mother was committed to the state asylum. When his father moved back to his native Texas, young Woody left home with a harmonica at 14, beginning a series of journeys that inspired many of his greatest songs. After settling briefly in California, where he worked as a painter and saloon singer, Woody spent the Depression traveling across the Southwest, performing for union groups, migrant workers and others whose suffering and populist discontent found voice in his songs. During these years, he wrote hundreds of songs—often as many as one or two a day—quite a few of which have been recorded by country artists over the years.

In the late 1930's, Guthrie moved to New York where, after a stint in the Merchant Marines, he quickly fell in with other folk singers, including Leadbelly, and his life-long friend and fellow union organizer, Pete Seeger. He performed on the eastern U.S. folk circuit and sang on numerous radio shows during these years.

The first recordings of Woody's music came out of a chance meeting with music collector Alan Lomax (who also discovered Leadbelly) in the late 1930's. Lomax invited him to Washington, D.C., to record his songs for the Library of Congress' Archive of Folk Songs. The resulting 12 records remain the best testament of Woody's songwriting vision.

With Seeger, Leadbelly and on his own, Woody also recorded a number of singles for Folkways Records, including now immortal songs like "Tom Joad," "The Ballad of Pretty Boy Floyd," "Goin' Down the Road (Feelin' Bad)," "Pastures of Plenty," "Deportee (Plane Wreck at Los Gatos)," "Hobo's Lullaby," "Oklahoma Hills," "I Ain't Got No Home in this World Anymore," "Billy the Kid" and "Sharecropper Song."

Woody's career was cut short in the 1960's by Huntington's chorea, the degenerative muscle disease that eventually killed him. Among those who visited him during his long convalescence was a young Bob Dylan, who was immensely influenced by Guthrie's legacy and has continued to keep his memory alive since his death in October 1967. His son, Arlo Guthrie, followed in his father's footsteps with a folk music career, including a Top 20 version of "City of New Orleans." In 1988 Columbia released *Folkways: A Vision Shared—A Tribute to Woody Guthrie and Leadbelly.* It is a testimony to the magnitude of these two men's lasting influence that the project featured guest appearances by everyone from Willie Nelson, Emmylou Harris and Doc Watson to Bob Dylan, Bruce Springsteen and the rock group, U2.   —M.B.

Merle Haggard

BORN: April 6, 1937
BIRTHPLACE: Bakersfield, California

Merle is one of country music's Elder Statesmen, that select group whose music, past and present, serves as a musical role model for younger artists. Haggard created music as compelling as any ever written. His songs evoke vivid scenes of the rough life of Dust Bowl immigrants who traveled from Texas and Oklahoma to Northern California during the 1930's. He drew on his own troubled youth and prison days to draft telling, dramatic miniatures of life's less savory side. His songwriting skills created exquisite love ballads, anthems of blue collar pride and honky tonkers that stand with the best.

He also reminds us of where it all came from. In his way, Hag was a New Traditionalist 20 years ahead of his time, paying homage (as he still does) to Jimmie Rodgers, Bob Wills and Lefty Frizzell, men whose music influenced his very being. Indeed, his recorded tributes reintroduced these greats to many new fans and, in the cases of Wills and Lefty, triggered a vast reawakening of interest in their music.

He has influenced numerous younger singers too, including Emmylou Harris and the late Gram Parsons, as well as Randy Travis, John Anderson, Alan Jackson, the late Keith Whitley and even the more pop-oriented K.T. Oslin.

Merle Ronald Haggard's route to stardom was anything but simple. Like Johnny Cash, he lived through the hard times many singers sing about but few actually experience. In 1934 his parents, Jim and Flossie Haggard, lived on a farm in Oklahoma with two of their children when a fire caused by lightning destroyed their barn, taking much of their livestock,

and livelihood, with it. Shortly afterward they moved west and settled near Bakersfield, California.

Merle was born April 6, 1937, in a home built from an old railroad refrigerator car. Merle's childhood was mundane until his father died following a series of strokes in 1946. His mother went to work to support the family. By the time Merle was in his teens, he'd fallen in love with the music of Hank, Lefty, Ernest Tubb and Bob Wills. He was also playing guitar, trying to emulate his idols. His high-spiritedness led him to skip school and wind up in a reform school from which he escaped at one point. From there, his rebellion against authority grew. And so did his rap sheet. From 1952 to 1958, he was arrested for everything from auto theft to burglary in the Bakersfield area. Flossie Haggard's best efforts weren't enough to control him. He even married and had two children while continuing his life of crime.

When he tried to burglarize a restaurant that was still open, he was again apprehended. Convicted and sentenced, he wound up in California's legendary San Quentin prison in 1958. Even there he resisted authority and wound up serving seven days in isolation. That seven-day stretch gave Merle the chance for some brutal self-examina-

tion, and when it ended, he decided to work toward a parole. A live performance by Johnny Cash at San Quentin while Haggard was incarcerated there helped keep his musical dreams alive.

Paroled in 1960, he dug ditches and picked guitar on the side in a Bakersfield club. The club work turned into a full-time job and transformed him into one of the principal pickers in Bakersfield's local music scene. He then signed on as a bass player with Wynn Stewart, one of Bakersfield's pioneer country stars, then playing in Las Vegas.

Wynn Stewart had written "Sing a Sad Song" and planned to record it himself, until Merle begged Wynn to let him try it. Merle recorded it for the tiny, Bakersfield-based Tally label. Late in 1963, it went to Number 19 nationwide. His next single, "Sam Hill," barely broke the Top 50. Then he found a song by Liz Ander-

son, Lynn Anderson's mother and a formidable songwriter in her own right. The song was "(My Friends Are Gonna Be) Strangers." Released by Tally late in 1964, it crashed into *Billboard's* Top Ten early in 1965, prompting Capitol Records to sign him. Capitol had already gotten several successful Bakersfield singers under contract: first Tommy Collins, then Buck Owens and now Haggard and Wynn Stewart, whom they picked up around the same time. In 1965, his first marriage ended, he formed his band, The Strangers, and married singer Bonnie Owens, Buck Owens' ex-wife, who became part of Merle's act.

In 1966 he had three Top Ten records, all of them now classics: "Swinging Doors" and "The Bottle Let Me Down" (both Haggard originals) and "The Fugitive" (another Liz Anderson tune). Despite their shared Bakersfield background, Haggard's singles differed greatly from those of Buck Owens, in whose band, The Buckaroos, Haggard briefly served. Buck's were jovial, while Merle's outlook was darker, more sobering, based on his own troubled past. The quality and integrity of his music was immediately obvious. He won his first awards from the West Coast-based Academy of Country Music in 1965.

The year 1967 brought "Branded Man" and "Sing Me Back Home," both Haggard originals that are classics today. Not all of his singles during this time became classics, however. "The Legend of Bonnie and Clyde," Number One for two weeks in 1967, has been overshadowed by its flipside, "Today I Started Loving You Again" which became a classic though it wasn't a hit. By then, Haggard's excellent band, The Strangers was staffed by top Bakersfield pickers—guitarist Roy Nichols (formerly of The Maddox Brothers and Rose) and steel guitarist Norm Hamlet. His first hit of 1968 was "Mama Tried," another confessional about his past. He paid tribute to blue collar workers in 1969 with "I Take a Lot of Pride in What I Am" and "Workin' Man Blues," then honored his mother again with "Mama's Hungry Eyes." Even the anti-hippie "Okie From Muskogee"—written by Merle and Stranger Eddie Burris more as a laugh than a reprimand—and "Fightin' Side of Me" didn't diminish Merle in the eyes of Gram Parsons and other long-haired, country-rock musicians. "Okie" was the Country Music Association's Single of the Year in 1969.

In 1969 he cut a two-LP tribute to Jimmie Rodgers, *Same Train, A Different Time,* and in 1970, combined The Strangers with former Texas Playboys for *A Tribute to the Best Damned Fiddle Player in the World,*

his influential Bob Wills tribute. He did two live albums, one of which, *Okie From Muskogee*, won the CMA's Album of the Year Award. That same year the CMA named him both Top Male Vocalist and Entertainer of the Year.

The hits continued through the 70's—from "Daddy Frank" and "Carolyn" to "Grandma Harp" to "If We Make It Through December," to name just a few. He dabbled in Dixieland music, adding horns to The Strangers. Ironically his final Number One with Capitol, in 1976, was a re-creation of Bob Wills' "Cherokee Maiden." In 1977, when he joined MCA Records, he recorded a tribute single to Elvis Presley and followed it up with an entire tribute album, *From Graceland to the Promised Land.*

With MCA and later with Epic, he continued to cut acclaimed recordings. His 1979 MCA album, *Serving 190 Proof*, remains one of his greatest successes and produced two classics, "Red Bandana" and "My Own Kind of Hat." After his move to Epic Records, he released his 1981 album, *Big City*, which was on the *Cashbox Magazine* Top Country Album charts for nearly two years. When his marriage to Bonnie Owens ended in divorce, he married singer Leona Williams, who worked with The Strangers, in 1978.

There were more hits in the early 80's, like "Misery and Gin," "Big City," "Are the Good Times Really Over" and a few quirky ones like "Let's Chase Each Other Around the Room." He had hit duets with Clint Eastwood, Janie Fricke, George Jones and Willie Nelson and even made a few film appearances.

He eventually added ex-Texas Playboys Tiny Moore, Jimmy Belken and Eldon Shamblin to an expanded version of The Strangers. They remained with him several years. By 1983 his marriage to Leona Williams had ended. Meanwhile, his son Marty was pushing his own solo career and worked both with his sister, Dana, and as part of The Strangers. Though Bonnie Owens and Merle haven't remarried, she again tours with The Strangers.

His records have occasionally lost their edge, yet after a miss or two, Merle always seems to come back with a big hit. After a relatively fallow period in the early 1990's, during which he left Epic, signed with Curb, fell many millions of dollars in debt to the IRS and went back to playing clubs, he rebounded with *1994*, an album which brought renewed critical acclaim, though no hits.

It is only a matter of time until he winds up in the Hall of Fame next to his idols.　—R.K.

Hal Lone Pine Breau and Betty Cody

BORN: Hal, June 5, 1916, Pea Cove, Maine
      Betty, August 17, 1921, Auburn, Maine
DIED: Hal, March 26, 1977

This husband-wife team consisted of Harold (Hal) "Lone Pine" Breau and his wife, Rita Cote Breau, best known as "Betty Cody." They worked both in Maine and at the *WWVA Jamboree* in Wheeling, West Virginia. Their son, Leonard, known as "Lenny," became an excellent guitarist who toured with his parents and recorded on his own. Betty had a major hit on RCA in 1953 with "I Found Out More Than You Ever Knew," an answer to The Davis Sisters' "I Forgot More Than You'll Ever Know." In the summer of that year they joined WWVA. Hal died in 1977. Eventually Leonard Breau, who finger picked in the Travis-Atkins style, became friendly with Chet Atkins, who signed him to RCA in the late 1960's. He became a renowned jazz guitarist, though plagued by drug and alcohol abuse. He was murdered in August 1984. Betty has remarried, becoming Betty Binette. As of the mid-90's, she was still living in Maine.　—R.K.

Roy Hall

BORN: January 6, 1907
BIRTHPLACE: Waynesville, North Carolina
DIED: May 16, 1943

Roy Hall headed one of the Southeast's leading show bands in the years before World War II. Although rooted in stringband traditions, Hall's Blue Ridge Entertainers embraced the contemporary country sound of Gene Autry, Jimmie Davis and early Western swing bands. Many historians mark the band as a transitional link between older and modern country music styles.

Hall was a cotton mill worker in 1937 when he began singing professionally with his younger brother, Jay Hugh Hall. The brothers briefly worked over WSPA in Spartanburg, South Carolina, when Jay Hugh joined Clyde Moody in Wade Mainer's Sons of the Mountaineers. Roy remained at WSPA, assembling The Blue Ridge Entertainers, featuring influential fiddler Tommy Magness. In fall 1938 the band moved to Winston-

Salem; that November it began recording for Vocalion.

The Entertainers' greatest success came after moving to Roanoke in 1939. Hall's Saturday night WDBJ radio show, *The Blue Ridge Jamboree*, attracted such a huge following throughout western Virginia that by 1941, Hall kept two separate bands of the same name on the road. After a session for Vocalion, he secured a Bluebird contract and recorded such best sellers as "Don't Let Your Sweet Love Die" and "Can You Forgive." World War II brought an end to the band. After Hall's death in an auto accident, Jay Hugh Hall and another brother, Rufus, reorganized The Entertainers and kept the band going until 1947.　　—D.S.

Roy Hall

BORN: May 7, 1922
BIRTHPLACE: Big Stone Gap, Virginia
DIED: March 2, 1984

James Faye "Roy" Hall, a stomping hillbilly boogie pianist in the style of Moon Mullican, never became a star in his own right, but his influence on another singer-pianist had major implications. He learned piano, it's said, from an elderly black man, and in the late 40's formed his first band, The Cohutta Mountain Boys. They recorded three singles for the Fortune label of Detroit in 1949 including "Dirty Boogie," and he played a part in discovering The Davis Sisters and bringing them to Fortune before they joined RCA. In 1950 Hall recorded for Bullet, then a thriving independent Nashville label. He also opened an after-hours honky tonk catering to musicians in Nashville. Webb Pierce brought Hall into his organization in 1954 as a pianist and got him a Decca recording contract. The recording that immortalized Hall was his version of "Whole Lotta Shakin' Goin' On," recorded for Decca in 1956 with Hank Garland on lead guitar (Garland had listened to rhythm and blues radio stations to pick up enough blues feel for the session.) Hall always insisted he and a black musician wrote the song, but others have debated this. What is known is that Hall's recording, with a slower, loping beat, was heard by Jerry Lee Lewis at a point when Jerry Lee, still unknown, was playing at the club Hall owned in Nashville. Jerry Lee took the song in a different, wilder direction.

Meanwhile, Hall did some excellent rockers on Decca, among them his version of Bobby Charles'

"See You Later Alligator" in 1955, his own "Three Alley Cats" (co-authored with Jimmy Rule) and the wild "Diggin' the Boogie," in 1956. He later recorded for Webb Pierce's Pierce label as "The Hound." Hall was a heavy drinker who eventually managed to sober up in the late 60's. He did extensive work with Alcoholics Anonymous while working behind the scenes in Nashville. He also found enough rockabilly fans in Europe and America interested enough to record him again in the years before his death in 1984.   —R.K.

Tom T. Hall

BORN: May 25, 1936
BIRTHPLACE: Olive Hill, Kentucky

Like so many leading artists of the 1970's, Tom T. Hall parlayed his success as one of Nashville's most celebrated songwriters into an eminently successful recording career.

Yet Hall (dubbed "The Story Teller" by his contemporaries) has, unlike many of his contemporaries, always remained a writer at heart. (In addition to the many hit songs he has penned for himself and other artists, he has also authored several books.) And his original songs (the best of which were written in the late 60's and early 70's) often had an unusual narrative or philosophical spin of some sort. While another country singer-songwriter might spin yet another ode to lost love or wasted days and nights, Hall would be more apt to compose a character sketch that reflects on old age ("Old Dogs, Children, and Watermelon Wine"), a painfully nostalgic reminiscence of a childhood hero and his tragic death ("The Year That Clayton Delaney Died"), a darkly comic recollection of a country funeral ("The Ballad of Forty Dollars") or a snide polemic on small-town hypocrisy ("Harper Valley P.T.A.").

Hall's best and most enduring work has always been informed by the journalist's acute eye for quirky detail, and a vivid sense of everyday pathos. For instance, Hall once wrote a haunting song called "It Sure Gets Cold in Des Moines," which, on its face, is about nothing more than a lonely traveler stranded in a Iowa hotel in the dead of winter. The man in the song sits in the hotel bar and watches a woman crying, alone at a table. We never find out why she's crying, but the desolate scene that Hall sets tells us a world about sadness, isolation and the

human condition—as do so many of his songs.

Hall, the fourth son of a brick plant worker who was also an ordained Baptist preacher, was born in rural Olive Hill, Kentucky, May 25, 1936. He was still a teenager when his mother died and his father was disabled in a hunting accident, and he was compelled to leave school at age 15 and take a job in a garment factory to help the family make ends meet.

But Hall—who today is one of country music's true closet intellectuals, hobnobbing with novelists William Styron and Kurt Vonnegut—was drawn to the world of music and the written and spoken word, even as a youngster. He began writing poetry—often about the loneliness and despair of his relatively isolated and semi-impoverished Appalachian upbringing—when he was eight, and songs shortly thereafter. By his teens, he already had his own bluegrass band and was performing for a guy who went from one small Kentucky town to the next, showing western movies with a projector and screen placed on top of his '47 Chevy.

Hall went on to work as a DJ at a small station in Morehead, Kentucky. Later, he spent several years in Germany with the U.S. Army. Back in civilian clothes, he returned to radio, put another band together, ran a country store for a while and attended college in Roanoke, Virginia, on the G.I. Bill. All the while, he was turning out country songs. When a friend took some of them to Nashville and "pitched" them around, Jimmy C. Newman and David Dudley became the first of dozens of artists to record his original compositions. In 1964, Hall moved to Nashville, "scared stiff, with 46 dollars in my pocket.

"For one long year, I wrote eight hours a day, for five days a week," he recalled of his early time in Nashville. "I really didn't know any other approach. I was determined to be a songwriter."

Even after his songs had made him a relatively wealthy man, Hall would continue to return to his native rural Kentucky again and again, in search of renewed inspiration. In fact, one of his classic albums of the early 70's, *In Search of a Song*, was borne of one such songwriting expedition.

"In searching for songs, I'd found something I was not aware I was searching for—me," he recalled in his book, *The Storyteller's Nashville*. "I'd told the untellable and dragged the past into the present, word by word. I was, at the same time, proud and ashamed....I had escaped my environment, and yet I longed for the simplicity and the independence that was demonstrated by the people that I had left behind. I had to learn that we never escape who we are."

Hall has been a member of the Grand Ole Opry since 1980. —B.A.

Stuart Hamblen

Born: October 20, 1908
Birthplace: Kellyville, Texas
Died: March 8, 1989

Carl Stuart Hamblen, the son of a minister, was attending college in Abilene, Texas, when he got his chance to expand his singing hobby into something more. He was just 20 when he went to New Jersey and recorded for Victor. By the 1930's he moved to California, where he became a major player in the fledgling West Coast country music scene. He began performing on numerous stations there, often with the pioneer California band, The Beverly Hillbillies. He also appeared in Western movie roles. His radio popularity increased and by the 1940's, he hosted the *Covered Wagon Jubilee.*

A hard drinker, Hamblen's first hit single for Columbia "(I Won't Go Huntin', Jake) But I'll Go Chasin' Women" reflected that lifestyle, which

changed after he attended a Billy Graham rally and became a dedicated Christian. His next hit, "(Remember Me) I'm the One Who Loves You" (also recorded by Ernest Tubb in 1950) was a decidedly more conservative love song. In 1951 his original hymn, "It Is No Secret (What God Can Do)," became a Top Ten at a time few hymns ever did. In 1952 his religious fervor ran so strongly that he ran for president on the anti-alcohol Prohibition ticket. His final hit, another original gospel song, "This Ole House," was a country hit for him and a huge pop success that same year for Rosemary Clooney. He later recorded for Coral and Kapp, and in 1971 began hosting a Sunday morning religious program, *The Cowboy Church*, over KLAC in Los Angeles. —R.K.

George Hamilton IV

Born: July 19, 1937
Birthplace: Winston-Salem, North Carolina

George Hamilton IV had several pop hits ("A Rose and a Baby Ruth," "High School Romance") before moving to Nashville and signing with RCA Victor in 1959. The singer-songwriter churned out a number of hit singles in the 1960's, including "If You Don't Know I Ain't Gonna Tell You," "Truck Driving Man" and the Number One hit, "Abilene." He became an Opry member in 1960.

In the mid-1960's George discovered folk music, recording two albums, *Folk Classics* and *Folksy*, in 1967, and the folk-inspired *Canadian Pacific* in 1969. In addition to his own recordings, George is remembered for his major role in bringing country music to international audiences. A regular performer at England's Wembley country music festival, he also hosted the first internationally syndicated country music show, seen in eight countries. In 1974 he became the first country music performer to perform in the Soviet Union, and in 1976 he hosted the first International Festival of Country Music, held in Sweden. In the late 1970's George resumed recording for American audiences, with the albums *Fine Lace and Homespun Cloth* (1978) for ABC/Dot, and *Forever Young* (1979) on the MCA label. Though he doesn't record these days, he's still an Opry regular. —M.B.

Butch Hancock

BORN: July 12, 1945
BIRTHPLACE: Lubbock, Texas

This Dylan-esque, raspy-voiced, Lubbock-born singer/ songwriter first recorded in 1971 in a group called The Flatlanders, which also included fellow Lubbockites and long-time musical compatriots, Joe Ely and Jimmie Dale Gilmore. (*The Flatlanders: More a Legend Than a Band*, music from this short-lived alliance, was re-released on CD in 1991, by Rounder Records, some 20 years after it was recorded.)

Lacking the persuasive vocal dexterity of either Ely or Gilmore (who have both recorded quite a few of Hancock's original songs), Hancock has, over the years, distinguished himself more as a songwriter ("West Texas Waltz," "Own And Own," "Fools Fall in Love," "Nothing of the Kind," etc.). Yet he has occasionally recorded for various independent labels (including Sugar Hill which, in 1991 released *Own And Own*, a collection of his vintage work) while actively touring the international coffeehouse circuit. Hancock is also a Texas Tech-trained architect, and an accomplished still photographer and video producer. —B.A.

Buddy Harman

BORN: December 23, 1928
BIRTHPLACE: Nashville, Tennessee

Drummer Murrey M. "Buddy" Harman has been one of the leading Nashville session musicians since the 1950's. Though he is best known as the drummer who replaced D.J. Fontana in Elvis Presley's studio bands, his greater importance lies in the fact that he was one of the first and most influential drummers on the Nashville scene. Born in Nashville on December 23, 1928, he grew up listening to swing era giants Gene Krupa and Buddy Rich. After a hitch in the Navy and some study at a percussion school, he

returned to Nashville. His first recordings were done in 1952 for Moon Mullican, and two years later he became a regular member of Carl Smith's band, The Tunesmiths. By 1957, as drums became more a part of country, Harman became a regular studio musician; by the 1960's he was averaging 600 sessions a year, including backing pioneer rock 'n' roll acts like Presley and The Everlys. In the 1980's, as session work thinned out due to the advent of a new generation of studio musicians, he worked with Floyd Cramer and Jerry Lee Lewis. Later, he worked at the Nashville chapter of the American Federation of Musicians. —R.K.

Harmonica

The modern harmonica as we know it was developed in Germany in the 1800's. It became popular around the time of the Civil War, especially among rural musicians. It was commonly called the "French harp," "mouth harp" or "mouth organ." The first truly great country harmonica player was black musician DeFord Bailey, a pioneer Grand Ole Opry performer. Another harmonica player, Lonnie Glosson, had a style that inspired Wayne Raney, who worked with The Delmore Brothers and later became a hit recording artist. Raney also sold harmonicas by mail on his Cincinnati radio program in the late 40's.

Another musician, "Harmonica" Frank Floyd, deeply influenced by the blues, was the first white man to record for Sam Phillips' Sun Records. Singer-harmonica player Onie Wheeler recorded country and rockabilly in the 50's for Columbia before joining Roy Acuff's Smoky Mountain Boys. He replaced Acuff's harmonica player Jimmie Riddle, another talented player, who'd moved to piano. Blues harmonica players like Little Walter Jacobs and Sonny Boy Williamson also influenced country players, most notably Charlie McCoy, who came to Nashville in the 60's. Country-R&B star Delbert McClinton plays blues-style. Noted player Mickey Raphael has been a part of Willie Nelson's band for yearly 20 years. Some younger musicians continue to use the harmonica: Clint Black plays the instrument on several of his hits. Though not as widely used now as it once was, the harmonica remains an essential component of certain types of country for both its lonesome feel and, on upbeat songs, its expressive and even humorous overtones. —R.K.

Emmylou Harris

BORN: April 2, 1947
BIRTHPLACE: Birmingham, Alabama

Nobody in the music business has aged as gracefully as Emmylou Harris. Born in Alabama on April 2, 1947, her career has both spanned and spawned musical genres. Yet her low-key, private lifestyle and understated, almost shy, public personality convey the message that Emmylou is a dedicated artist and a class apart from many of today's celebrity-conscious performers.

After graduating as valedictorian of her high school class, Emmylou spent a couple of years in various colleges (University of North Carolina, Boston University) and pursued an acting career. During that time she began singing and waitressing, and eventually realized that music was her real love. More than 25 years after she headed for New York to follow that star, Emmylou still confessed to being consumed by her passion for music.

The earlier years nearly burned out that ardor, as waitressing, hostessing in a model home development and raising a daughter as a single mother (after her first marriage to songwriter Tom Slocum ended in divorce) often took precedence over her other aspirations. She played in clubs from New York to Washington, D.C., and, while performing in the D.C. area, met Gram Parsons, then part of The Flying Burrito Brothers and looking for a female singer. Parsons followed up a year of promises by sending her a plane ticket to Los Angeles. There, she sang on his *GP* and *Grievous Angel* albums and joined his 1973 tour and, through it all, came heavily under the influence of Parsons' eclectic brand of music, a country-rock fusion that was both innovative and inspired.

Emmylou was devastated when Parsons, her friend and mentor, died of a heart attack in September 1973. His untimely death (he was 26) served as a catalyst for her career, however, since in an effort to hold her life together, she formed her own band, the now-famous Hot Band, which included Rodney Crowell and Ricky Skaggs and, later (though not actually during the classic Hot Band era), Vince Gill. Her first major label album, 1974's *Pieces of the Sky*, with Warner Bros., took off, with "If I Could Only Win Your Love" (her revival of an old Louvin Brothers chestnut) reaching Number One. She followed this up with *Elite Hotel*, earning a Grammy nomination. Her producer at this time was Brian Ahern, whom she eventually married. (She and Ahern had a daughter, and eventually divorced.)

Throughout two decades of recording, Emmylou's pure voice has cut through traditional country ballads and contemporary rock, earning five Grammy awards—three for Best Country Vocal Performance Female (*Elite Hotel*, *Blue Kentucky Girl* and "In My Dreams") and two for Best Country Vocal Performance by a Duo or Group ("That Lovin' You Feeling Again" with Roy Orbison, and the album, *Trio,* with Dolly Parton and Linda Ronstadt).

Of her later albums, 1987's *Trio* generated the most recognition and critical acclaim. In 1991, she recorded *Live at the Ryman*, a tribute to Nashville's venerable music hall and yet another demonstration of Emmylou's unabashed disregard for sticking to any one musical category. *Live at the Ryman* also showcased Emmylou's new band, The Nash Ramblers, an acoustic ensemble she formed in 1990, which has included a stellar line-up of musicians, including such notables as mandolin-player Sam Bush, Carl Jackson (an occasional member), guitarist Randy Stewart (who now records for RCA as Jon Randall) and bass player Roy Huskey Jr. Harris' decision to switch to all-acoustic backing came after continuing throat problems served as a warning that her voice could no longer compete with the high-decibel electric magic of the still-great Hot Band.

The former East Coast, then West Coast, singer became a Nashville transplant in the early 1980's when she married songwriter Paul Kennerley and moved herself and her two daughters to Music City (they divorced in 1992).

She has served as president of the Country Music Association's board of directors for several years, and in January 1992 was named a member of the Grand Ole Opry.   —M.B.

Freddie Hart

BORN: December 21, 1926
BIRTHPLACE: Lochapoka, Alabama

Fred Segrest grew up dirt poor, the son of a sharecropper. He did hard farm labor from childhood on and began playing on homemade guitars in between his field work. So desperate was he to escape poverty that he ran away from home several times until his parents sent him to a Civilian Conservation Corps Camp, in 1938. As a teenager, he faked his age to join the Marine Corps and served in the Pacific during World War II. After arriving home, he did various jobs throughout the South, including a stint working as a nightclub bouncer in Phoenix City, Alabama. His desire to play music never ended, and he hung out for a time with Hank Williams in Nashville and began writing songs. Eventually George Morgan and Wayne Raney recorded some of his songs, and Raney introduced him to Lefty Frizzell. Frizzell took Hart under his wing as a sideman.

Afterwards, Hart started working extensively in California, and appeared on Cliffie Stone's *Hometown Jamboree,* later becoming a regular on *Town Hall Party.* His Capitol recordings weren't successful, but by 1959 he'd moved to Columbia, where he had a number of moderate hits, most notably his 1959 "Chain Gang" and, in 1960, "The Key's in the Mailbox." In the mid-60's, still based in California, he recorded some more modestly successful hits for Kapp, then signed with Capitol Records again. As before, his records didn't sell, and he was on the verge of being dropped again when an Atlanta DJ began playing the syrupy love ballad, "Easy Loving." In 1971 it topped the country charts for three weeks and enjoyed crossover success in the pop field. Hart's heavily sentimental, romantic musical valentines remained popular through the early 70's; he had three Number One records: "My Hang-Up Is You" (six weeks at the top), "Bless Your Heart" and "Got the All Overs for You (All Over Me)." In 1973 "Super Kind of Woman" and "Trip to Heaven" both reached the top of the charts. In 1974, "Hang in There Girl," "The Want-To's" and "My Woman's Man" were his biggest successes. In 1975 more Top Tens came with "I'd Like to Sleep Till I Get Over You" and "The First Time." He had his final Top Ten in 1976 with "Why Lovers Turn to Strangers."

Hart recorded for Capitol with less success through the rest of the decade before joining Sunbird in the early 80's. His final two chart singles appeared on the El Dorado and Fifth St. labels. Today, Hart spends much of his time running his trucking company and a school for handicapped kids.　　　—R.K.

John Hartford

BORN: December 30, 1937
BIRTHPLACE: New York, New York

John Hartford achieved considerable success in the late 60's as a mainstream country singer/ songwriter before re-establishing himself as an innovative entertainer in traditional country music. Born December 30, 1937, in New York City and raised in St. Louis, John Harford (Chet Atkins added the "t" in 1966) was exposed to old-time music and bluegrass at an early age. He learned banjo, guitar, mandolin and fiddle while in his teens; by 1958 he was the banjo player with Don Brown and The Ozark Mountain Trio. Hartford also played with Doug and Rodney Dillard; during the early 60's he frequently played fiddle with The Bray Brothers in Champaign, Illinois.

Hartford moved to Nashville in 1965 to work a late-night disc jockey shift over WSIX. His early attempts at songwriting impressed The Glaser Brothers, who signed him to a publishing contract; Chuck Glaser soon persuaded RCA Victor to record him. An introspective love song from Hartford's second RCA album, "Gentle on My Mind," generated considerable airplay and some chart success in 1967; Glen Campbell's cover version for Capitol was a Top 40 pop hit. The song also steered country music songwriting into a significant new direction. Moving to California in 1968, Hartford became a writer and performer on *The Smothers Brothers Comedy Hour* and the *Glen Campbell Goodtime Hour;* he also played banjo on The Byrds' landmark country-rock album, *Sweetheart of the Rodeo.*

By 1970 he decided to return to his primary love: acoustic music. The following year, Hartford relocated to Nashville and assembled a backup band that included guitarist Norman Blake and two bluegrass veterans: fiddler Vassar Clements and dobro player Robert "Tut" Taylor. Bluegrass purists had little patience for the band's loose, modern rhythms and Hartford's quirky lyrics. But open-minded younger listeners were captivated; the band's only album, *Aereo Plain* (on Warner Bros.), was a precursor of "newgrass" music.

Since the mid-70's Hartford has primarily entertained audiences as a one-man show, drawing upon both traditional music and his own compositions.

He occasionally retreats from music to work as a riverboat pilot. He's also planning to reunite several members of his Aereo-Plain band for performances and recording.   —D.S.

Hawkshaw Hawkins

BORN: December 22, 1921
BIRTHPLACE: Huntington, West Virginia
DIED: March 5, 1963

Today Harold Franklin "Hawkshaw" Hawkins has been unfairly relegated to the status of a footnote: one of the stars killed in the plane crash that also took the lives of Patsy Cline and Cowboy Copas. But his contributions to country music go deeper than that.

Hawkins began playing and singing early in life, and by his late teens landed a $15 a week job at WSAZ in Huntington, West Virginia. He worked at various stations before being drafted in 1942. Discharged in 1945, Hawkins

finally made it to WWVA. In July 1946 he made his first recordings for King Records, and in 1947 had modest success with "Sunny Side of the Mountain."

His first hit record was a cover of Hank Williams' train song, "Pan American," which charted in 1948, followed by "Dog House Boogie."

Though Hawkins' recording career was fitful, he was a star via radio and personal appearances. Records were only beginning to define an artist's success.

In 1949 Hawkins had a minor hit with "I Wasted a Nickel," but returned to the Top Ten with a 1951 cover of Lefty Frizzell's hit, "I Love You a Thousand Ways," followed by "I'm Waiting Just for You" and another cover version of the Pee Wee King hit, "Slow Poke." In 1955 he joined the Grand Ole Opry and signed with RCA Victor, where he had no success. In 1959, briefly signed to Columbia, he found success with "Soldier's Joy," a Revolutionary War song in the style of Johnny Horton's hit, "Battle of New Orleans." He married singer Jean Shepard, also an Opry cast member, in 1960, and in 1962 he re-signed with King. His biggest hit, "Lonesome 7-7203," an upbeat honky tonk shuffle, was climbing the charts in early 1963. After his death, it remained at Number One for four weeks.   —R.K.

George D. Hay

BORN: November 9, 1895
BIRTHPLACE: Attica, Indiana
DIED: May 8, 1968

Known to Grand Ole Opry fans for decades as "The Solemn Ole Judge," George D. Hay, a former Memphis newspaperman turned radio announcer (he did a stint at Chicago's WLS *National Barn Dance* before his arrival at Nashville's Radio WSM in 1925), is generally acknowledged as the originator of the Grand Ole Opry.

It was Hay who was central to shaping the entire concept and format of what has since become the world's longest continuously running live radio show. For nearly 30 years, he was also the Opry's master of ceremonies and played a huge role in deciding who got on the Opry and who did not.

Hay was elected to the Country Music Hall of Fame in 1966. (See also, Grand Ole Opry.)   —B.A.

Roy Head

BORN: January 9, 1941
BIRTHPLACE: Three Rivers, Texas

Growing up, Roy Head was enamored of the R&B/rockabilly/rock sounds of the day, and his early career followed that route. He had a moderately successful pop career in the mid-1960's, including the Number Two hit, "Treat Her Right." But personal problems, including drinking and vocal cord trouble, stifled his career as the 60's wore on. By the mid-70's, in a comeback attempt, he focused on country music, scoring chart hits on ABC, Elektra and other smaller labels. His biggest country hit was 1977's "Come to Me." He never really left his roots behind, often doing country versions of rock and pop hits, and he never really found long-term stardom. His final chart entry came in 1985.   —G.F.

Jimmie Heap

BORN: March 3, 1922
BIRTHPLACE: Taylor, Texas
DIED: December 4, 1977

Texas honky tonk singer/composer/bandleader Jimmy Heap, leader of The Melody Masters from 1948 until 1958, worked extensively on the *Big D Jamboree* in Dallas. In 1950 or '51 he recorded the original version of "The Wild Side of Life" for Imperial, before Hank Thompson's version made it a massive hit in 1952. "Release Me," a Heap original, was The Melody Masters' sole hit record. Their 1954 version for Capitol launched it as an American standard recorded by everyone from R&B singer Esther Phillips to Englebert Humperdinck. Heap and his vocalist, Perk Williams, recorded and performed for many years in Texas. Heap died in 1977.   —R.K.

Hee Haw

In the late 1960's, the fast-paced NBC-TV program, Rowan and Martin's *Laugh-In*, with brief skits and rapid-fire one-liners, dominated network TV. In Canada, a similar show with a rural motif, titled *Hot Diggety*, enjoyed popularity. In 1968, several people

involved with the Canadian show succeeded in selling CBS-TV on an American version. They recruited the day's top country singers, Buck Owens and Roy Clark, as co-hosts with Grandpa Jones, Minnie Pearl, Stringbean and Archie Campbell as second-level stars, along with Canadian comics Gordie Tapp and Don Harron from *Hot Diggety*. Other charter members were rotund storyteller Junior Samples and Lulu Roman, along with Buck's band (The Buckaroos), The Hager Twins, Cathy Baker and Gunilla Hutton.

The show was a replacement for CBS' politically controversial *Smothers Brothers Comedy Hour*, premiering on June 13, 1969. It featured plenty of comedy (and scantily dressed women) in a barnyard setting, so much so that it briefly sparked controversy in Nashville, where some considered the show's "hillbilly" stereotypes (including a donkey cartoon as a mascot) bad for country. When CBS, seeking to appeal to younger viewers, canceled it in 1971, the producers syndicated it, and its popularity boomed, making the cast household names. The shows were taped in Nashville twice a year in marathon sessions, the routines pasted together to create a complete program. Actors, singers, comedians, evangelists and even a few politicians appeared, as did many vocalists. In 1978 it briefly spawned a spin-off sitcom, *Hee Haw Honeys*. The cast changed as individuals came and went, and Stringbean, Samples and Campbell died. Owens quit in 1986, feeling the show stereotyped him as a comic. Clark continued with guest co-hosts. In 1990 the show's producers decided to "update" the show by dumping the rural stage sets, only to find that they lost viewers. In 1992 *Hee Haw* ended, though the "classic" shows remain immensely popular in reruns on The Nashville Network. Grandpa Jones and other veteran castmembers still perform in a *Hee Haw* stage show at Opryland.   —R.K.

Bobby Helms

BORN: August 15, 1933
BIRTHPLACE: Bloomington, Indiana

This early country-pop crossover singer was, briefly, a national sensation in the mid-1950's. In 1957, Helms' rendition of "Fraulein" peaked at Number One and stayed in the country charts for nearly a year. That same year, "My Special Angel" not only topped the country charts but also rose to Number Seven in the national pop charts. Helms scored big again in late 1957 with "Jingle Bell Rock," which not only eased into the pop Top Ten, but has remained a Yuletide playlist favorite ever since. Not surprisingly Helms, who continued to be a minor presence in the country charts into the early 1970's, was named by *Cashbox Magazine* as the Top Country Singer of 1957.   —B.A.

Don Helms

BORN: February 28, 1927
BIRTHPLACE: New Brockton, Alabama

Don Helms is memorable for his work as steel guitarist with Hank Williams' Drifting Cowboys. His high-register steel guitar licks made Hank's records instantly identifiable. Helms started working with Hank in 1943; they played Alabama honky tonks together until Helms joined the service. Later, in Nashville, Hank and Helms rebuilt The Cowboys around Helms, fiddler Jerry Rivers and guitarist Bob McNett. They backed Hank on the road, but didn't initially record with him until Fred Rose, Hank's producer, felt they were ready to. Rose himself suggested the high-note chords Helms played on the recordings. After Hank was fired from the Opry in 1952, Helms joined Ray Price's band. He worked with Price for a while, then became a sideman on the Opry and on records. He played steel on Price's "I'll Be There (If You Ever Want Me)" and Patsy Cline's "Walkin' After Midnight," and later made his own album for Smash Records. He also became a partner with Doyle and Teddy

Wilburn in Nashville's Wil-Helm talent agency. Helms and members of The Cowboys frequently reunite for recordings and shows, including performances with Hank's daughter, Jett Williams.   —R.K.

The Hi-Flyers

The Hi-Flyers were one of the early Western swing units in the Fort Worth area to follow Milton Brown's early Musical Brownies. A number of talented musicians worked with the group when it recorded in the 1930's. The leader was guitarist Elmer Scarborough; among the other musicians in the group were fiddler Darrell Kirkpatrick (who moved to accordion), guitarist Buster Ferguson, clarinetist Butch Gibson and steel guitarist Andy Schroeder. Later, Sheldon Bennett, fiddler for Hank Penny's Radio Cowboys, joined the band. They disbanded in 1941.   —R.K.

Highway 101

Named for one of the main north-south highways along the Pacific Coast, Highway 101 created a new generation of California country-rock with a hard edge and strong traditional slant; the group was influential even though it did not come together on its own. Manager Chuck Morris conceived it as a quartet in

1986, and first hired drummer Scott "Cactus" Moser. Next came bass player Curtis Stone, son of Country Music Hall of Famer Cliffie Stone, founder of the old *Hometown Jamboree* and a bass player himself. Next came guitarist Jack Daniels and then female vocalist Paulette Carlson, whose demo recordings had impressed Morris.

The group got a record deal with Warner Bros., and made a strong start with "The Bed You Made for Me" in 1987, followed by "Whiskey, If You Were a Woman." "Somewhere Tonight," Number One for two weeks in the fall of 1987, was followed by two more Number One's: "Cry, Cry, Cry" and "(Do You Love Me) Just Say Yes." Next came several Top Tens, "All the Reasons Why," "Setting Me Up" and "Honky Tonk Heart," and one more Number One, "Who's Lonely Now," in 1989. In 1990 they revived the Roger Miller-Justin Tubb composition, "Walkin', Talkin', Cryin', Barely Beatin' Broken Heart," as well as "This Side of Goodbye" and "Someone Else's Trouble Now."

In 1991, Paulette Carlson saw a stronger career as a solo singer.

The group replaced her with Nashville singer Nikki Nelson, but later hits never charted as highly. The group signed with Liberty in 1992, but after minimal chart success, left the label in '94.   —R.K.

The Highwaymen

Given their interlocking friendships and artistic collaborations, the eventual coming together of The Highwaymen, an on-again-off-again quartet consisting of Johnny Cash, Waylon Jennings, Willie Nelson and Kris Kristofferson, seemed not only natural but almost inevitable.

Waylon & Willie are, of course, for better or worse, branded into the annals of country music history together. Kris Kristofferson was not only a central figure with W&W in the Outlaw movement, but also a close friend and former protégé of Cash, who was one of the first to have hits with Kristofferson's songs.

Cash and Jennings were roommates and partners in petty mayhem back in the 1960's and also recorded a few hit duets. The connections go on and on.

For all that, The Highwaymen was a long time coming—an idea that had been tossed around for years but really wasn't physically possible until all four men's separate careers had cooled off enough for them to record an album together, called *Highwayman*, in 1985. The album's title track hit Number One that same year, and when they got around to touring, it was big-time box office boffo—on stage, side by side, these four giants of the industry sort of resemble country music's Mt. Rushmore.

Highwayman, the album, had its moments, and was certainly strong enough to put aside speculation that the entire enterprise was merely concocted to breathe life into the individual recording careers of Nelson, Cash, Jennings and Kristofferson. Yet its strength and appeal lay very much in the way it recollected the rugged individualism of the Outlaw era when songs did matter. It took nearly five years for the fabulous foursome to stand still long enough at the same place to make a second album, entitled (predictably enough) *Highwayman 2*. Though it didn't have the focus of the first album, it too had its high points. Among them were the foursome's stirring rendition of Lee's "Ladies Love Outlaws" Clayton's "Silver Stallion," some brilliant vocals from Jennings, some vintage Willie Nelson performances (even if he did cheat and do them on his own in his Pedernales studio), and a typically stoic performance by Cash on the enigmatic Kristofferson original "Anthem '84." The Highwaymen also teamed up for a quickie movie: a TV remake of the Western classic, *Stage Coach*. (See also, entries on individual artists.)　　　　　　　　　　　　　　—B.A.

Faith Hill

BORN: September 21, 1967
BIRTHPLACE: Jackson, Mississippi

Faith Hill was born in 1967 in Mississippi, and has been singing ever since she was three years old. While in high school she was inspired by the vocal deliveries of female country artists such as Patsy Cline, Reba McEntire and Emmylou Harris.

She formed her first band when she was 17, playing at rodeos and fairs, but the lure of bigger and better things kept beckoning. When she was 19, she headed for Nashville.

Her first job in Music City was selling T-shirts at Fan Fair. She continued to look for work as a singer, but

wound up taking a job as a receptionist at singer Gary Morris' publishing company. Morris encouraged her, but her break came singing harmony with singer-songwriter Gary Burr at Nashville's famous Bluebird Cafe. Martha Sharp, Warner Bros. A&R's senior vice president, heard them and offered Hill a recording contract.

Her first single, "Wild One" (1994), reached the Number One position on the *Billboard* country chart and stayed there for four weeks. What's more, Hill's debut album, *Take Me As I Am*, went Gold. Her second single, a countrified re-working of Janis Joplin's gut-wrenching "Piece of My Heart," also soared to Number One.　　　　　　　　　　　　—R.P.

Goldie Hill

BORN: January 11, 1933
BIRTHPLACE: Karnes County, Texas

Agolda Voncile "Goldie" Hill got her start around 1952 when she joined the *Louisiana Hayride*. Dubbed the "Golden Hillbilly," she soon landed a Decca contract. Her first hit was "I Let the Stars Get in My Eyes" in early 1953, an answer to the hit single for Slim Willet and Skeets McDonald, "Don't Let the Stars Get in Your Eyes," that was Number One for three weeks. In 1954 she and Ernest Tubb's son, Justin, had a top hit with "Looking Back to See." The follow-up duet, 1955's "Sure Fire Kisses," reached Number 11. Her next duet, "Are You Mine," was with fellow *Hayride* singer and Decca artist, Red Sovine, and it made the Top 20. Her next hit was in 1959, two years after she married singer Carl Smith, when "Yankee, Go Home" was a solo single (it included a recitation by Sovine).

She made four albums for Decca, and in the late 1960's signed with Epic for two more. She had one minor hit single as Goldie Hill Smith in 1973 before she and Smith both scaled down their careers to devote more time to raising horses. Now retired, she and Carl Smith live in Nashville.　　　　　　—R.K.

Stan Hitchcock

BORN: March 21, 1937
BIRTHPLACE: Pleasant Hope, Missouri

Stan Hitchcock began his career as a radio DJ in Springfield, Missouri, before moving to Nashville to try his hand at recording. He signed with Epic in the mid-1960's and had a few minor hits, along with one Top 20, 1969's "Honey, I'm Home." Later he recorded for several smaller labels, with little chart success. He also hosted his own local TV series in the 60's, an experience he drew on later as program director for Country Music Television, a position he held until the cable network was sold to Gaylord Entertainment in 1991. —G.F.

Becky Hobbs

BORN: January 24, 1950
BIRTHPLACE: Bartlesville, Oklahoma

Despite critical acclaim and being at least once on the verge of a breakthrough, Becky Hobbs, one of the few female singer-keyboard players in the business, has yet to find lasting success. She began working in an all-girl band while attending the University of Oklahoma, was active for a time as a pop songwriter in Los Angeles, then moved to Nashville, where she wrote songs that were recorded by Alabama, Emmylou Harris and Conway Twitty (his Number One, "I Want to Know You Before We Make Love"). She began recording for Mercury in 1978 with no success until her 1983 duet with Moe Bandy, "Let's Get Over Them Together." Things weren't much better with Liberty or EMI America, though her 1988 honky tonk album, *All Keyed Up*, released by MTM Records just before the label folded, gained ample praise. It included the Top 40 single, "Jones on the Jukebox." When MTM folded, RCA picked up Hobbs and reissued the album, releasing the single, "Do You Feel the Same Way Too?" The

RCA deal was short-lived, as was a deal with Curb Records that produced two singles, "A Little Hunk of Heaven" and a cover of "Talk Back Trembling Lips." Nonetheless, she tours extensively around the world, and, in 1994, released the album, *The Boots I Came to Town In,* on the Intersound label. —R.K.

Adolph Hofner

BORN: June 8, 1916
BIRTHPLACE: Moulton, Texas

Adolph Hofner, with his brother, Emil, grew up in the area of Texas settled heavily by Germans. His father was German, his mother Czechoslovakian. He took to guitar, and Emil became a steel guitarist. He had the freewheeling approach to music that's marked all great Texas musicians, and loved everything from polkas to Bing Crosby and Milton Brown. By 1936, Adolph Hofner was a member of Jimmie Revard's Oklahoma Playboys. Though he worked in music part-time, he played and recorded both with Revard and another group called The Showboys. One recording with the latter group, a version of "It Makes No Difference Now," attracted enough attention that by 1939, Hofner had started his own band, The San Antonians, with Emil (dubbed "Bashful" or "Bash") playing electric steel. They landed a recording contract with Columbia and did well on uptempo songs like "Sometimes," combining energetic vocals with J.R. Chatwell's outstanding swing fiddling. Hofner's band also played polkas, reflecting his popularity in the Texas German community. He later recorded for Decca. By the late 1940's the band obtained sponsoring from Pearl Beer and renamed themselves The Pearl Wranglers. Hofner continued performing with the band into the 1990's. —R.K.

Homer & Jethro

BORN: Homer, July 29, 1917, Knoxville, Tennessee
    Jethro, March 10, 1923, Knoxville, Tennessee
DIED: Homer, August 7, 1971; Jethro, February 4, 1989

Though they both grew up in Knoxville, teenage guitarist Henry "Homer" Haynes and Kenneth "Jethro" Burns auditioned separately for a 1935 radio amateur show sponsored by Knoxville station WNOX.

Hometown Jamboree

In 1946, Cliffie Stone, who hosted a number of radio shows in the Los Angeles area, began hosting a radio show with a regular cast over KXLA Radio in Pasadena. Known as the *Dinner Bell Round-Up*, its cast included Wesley Tuttle, Cliffie's father (Herman the Hermit), Merle Travis, Red Murrell, Tex Ann Nation, KXLA disc jockey and announcer-turned-singer Tennessee Ernie Ford, Eddie Kirk and several instrumentalists. Stone felt that since it had evolved into a barn dance radio show, the program needed a new name. The result was *Hometown Jamboree;* Merle Travis wrote its theme.

In 1948 the show premiered on KCOP-TV on Saturday nights, broadcast from the El Monte Legion Stadium. Sponsored locally, it featured music, comedy (some with Tennessee Ernie) and a crack band eventually including fiddler Harold Hensley, accordionist Billy Liebert and the guitar-steel team of Jimmy Bryant and Speedy West. Later cast additions included teenage female singers Molly Bee and Bucky Tibbs. Because of Cliffie's connections with Capitol, many *Hometown* performers recorded for Capitol, including Tennessee Ernie, Eddie Kirk, Bryant and West, Gene O'Quinn and Molly Bee. The show later moved to KTLA, preceding Spade Cooley's popular Saturday night show. Cliffie also managed Ernie Ford as the singer moved from country to mainstream network TV. Stone continued hosting the show until KTLA canceled it in the late 1950's. Stone occasionally revives *Hometown* as a live stage show in Southern California, featuring new talent and veterans like Molly Bee and Western singer Eddie Dean.   —R.K.

They jammed together backstage, and the station immediately hired them as staff musicians. They worked there with a jazz string band known as The Stringdusters. By the early 1940's they'd started singing pop songs in an exaggerated hillbilly style and joined Kentucky's *Renfro Valley Barn Dance*. After World War II military service they reunited at WLW in Cincinnati and recorded for King Records. In 1948, RCA producer Steve Sholes signed them, suggesting they start writing and performing parodies of country and pop songs. Their first RCA hit (with June Carter) parodied the pop tune, "Baby, It's Cold Outside." "(How Much Is) That Hound Dog in the Window," their 1953 takeoff on Patti Page's saccharine pop hit, also did well. Jethro's brother-in-law, Chet Atkins, used the duo as studio musicians in Nashville in the 1950's, and Hank Williams once said he never felt a song was a hit until it had been "butchered" by the pair. They continued into the 50's; their 1959 hit, "Battle of Kookamonga," spoofed "Battle of New Orleans." Both superb musicians, they did two fine jazz albums for RCA. They were also featured in Kellogg's Corn Flakes' famous early 1960's "Ooh! That's corny!" TV commercials. After Homer's death from a heart attack, Jethro performed as a solo instrumentalist until he died of cancer in 1989.   —R.K.

CLIFFIE STONE'S HOME TOWN JAMBOREE
compliments of: Howard Dameron's **Hub City Mattress Co.**

Honky Tonk

If the earliest days of country music relied heavily on traditional British and Southern ballads and gospel songs, honky tonk music opened the music up to chronicling a side of life less idyllic. Built around love denied, love pursued, hell-raising, cheating, drinking, desolate sorrow and violence, it emerged in the 1930's in the South and Southwest. The term "honky tonk," around since the turn of the century, gradually came to refer to the small Southern taverns and beer halls, particularly in Texas, that attracted farmers and laborers, and became centers of drinking and violence. Jimmie Rodgers sang numbers that strongly hinted at the sound, including "Gambling Polka Dot Blues," "Pistol Packin' Papa" and the traditional number, "Frankie and Johnny." By the mid-30's, honky tonk began to take on a more cohesive identity, much of it (though not all) from Texas. Some of Jimmie Davis' early, double-entendre recordings hinted at a more explicit type of music. In 1936, Al Dexter recorded "Honky Tonk Blues," a number he wrote with James B. Paris about the women that hung around these beer joints. A year earlier, The Shelton Brothers' Decca recording of "Deep Elem Blues," an old blues referring to a wild section of New Orleans, also pointed to a new, rawer type of country lyric.

The music's more sorrowful side was characterized by "The Last Letter," Rex Griffin's recording of his own song of suicide over lost love. It became a country standard. Decca Records, with its extensive recording activities in Texas, took excellent advantage of this new style by recording The Shelton Brothers, Buddy Jones, Jimmie Davis and many of the Western swing bands, like Cliff Bruner's Texas Wanderers, Bob Dunn's Vagabonds (who recorded a 1939 instrumental "Stompin' at the Honky Tonk"), Leon's Lone Star Cowboys and others. These bands all played both instrumentals and vocals, and helped establish the fiddle, guitar and steel instrumentation that still dominates honky tonk.

But the Decca honky tonk artists with the most impact in the late 30's and early 40's were Floyd Tillman and Ernest Tubb. Tillman's "It Makes No Difference Now" became an early hit of the genre when recorded by Cliff Bruner. Tillman became a master singer and composer with numbers like "A Precious Memory." Jimmie Rodgers disciple Ernest Tubb became the second major Texas honky tonker when

he signed with the label in 1940. His first recordings didn't go over in the noisy taverns, so he added an electric guitar when he recorded his own "Walkin' the Floor Over You" in 1941. It became a classic and made Tubb a star of the idiom with numbers like "I'll Get Along Somehow," "I Ain't Goin' Honky Tonkin' Anymore" and "You Nearly Lose Your Mind."

By 1941, Decca wasn't alone. Columbia had Texas steel guitarist-songwriter Ted Daffan and his band, The Texans, under contract. His songs, including "Worried Mind," "Born to Lose" and "Headin' Down the Wrong Highway," became some of the biggest honky tonk hits of the World War II years. Al Dexter, who hadn't done that well on the national level, changed all that with his rollicking song of barroom violence, "Pistol Packin' Mama," one of the first big country hits to "crossover" to equal success in the pop field. By the war's end, many singers were heading the same direction as Tubb, whose stardom continued unabated. Both Tubb and Floyd Tillman had hits with Texan Jerry Irby's cocky drinking song, "Drivin' Nails in My Coffin." Merle Travis' early hits, "Divorce Me C.O.D." and "So Round! So Firm! So Fully Packed!," were snappy, syncopated honky tonkers. Even Red Foley, who normally excelled on ballads, was recording numbers like the boogie woogie "Tennessee Saturday Night."

Hank Williams, who got his start in Alabama honky tonks, took honky tonk music—including compelling lyrics like "Honky Tonkin'" and "Honky Tonk Blues" (not the Al Dexter song)—to a new level with his original compositions and a raw, heartfelt vocal style. Texan Lefty Frizzell, whose unique vocal style was influenced by both Tubb and Floyd Tillman, became a huge star in 1950 with another anthem, "If You've Got the Money, I've Got the Time" and "I Love You a Thousand Ways." From Louisiana, Webb Pierce emerged in the early 50's with a stark, nasal vocal style that excelled on numbers like "There Stands the Glass" and "Back Street Affair," both standards of the genre today. New talents like Ray Price, Carl Smith and Little Jimmy Dickens all did some of their greatest work as honky tonk singers. Moon Mullican, around in the earliest days of Texas honky tonk, enjoyed popularity in the 50's. Hank Thompson used a Western swing accompaniment to enhance his vocals. Few women attempted the style initially; exceptions included Rose Maddox and Charline Arthur. Kitty Wells' "It Wasn't God Who Made Honky Tonk Angels" opened both country music and honky tonk to female singers. In

California, Johnny Bond, Tommy Collins and Wynn Stewart excelled in the field.

Honky tonk gradually fell out of favor after rock 'n' roll surged in the mid-50's. By the late 50's fiddles and steel guitars were no longer as accepted, and many artists took on the new, smoother Nashville Sound accompaniment. Patsy Cline, nonetheless, did some excellent honky tonk numbers despite smooth backing, including "Walkin' After Midnight" and "Crazy." Johnny Horton's honky tonk numbers were free of fiddles and steel but no less raw. Tubb, Dickens, Tillman and Ray Price continued on. So did a new, gifted Texas singer named George Jones who—along with Tubb and Price—remained resolute in his use of fiddles and steel. On the West Coast, the early Bakersfield singers like Tommy Collins and Buck Owens stuck close to fiddles and steel. Owens gradually stripped away the fiddles, much as Johnny Horton had, but his and Don Rich's twanging Telecaster heralded a new and highly successful form of honky tonk music from Bakersfield. Owens and Merle Haggard both carved out stardom for themselves with this guitar-driven sound. Ironically, by the late 60's, Ray Price abandoned honky tonk in favor of lush pop crossover music.

The twin fiddle and steel sound never completely died. Mel Tillis used it on his early hits, and Merle Haggard remains stubbornly dedicated to it, becoming as much a legend in the field as Tubb or Frizzell. In 1973, Texan Moe Bandy brought the sound back to the charts a time when many despaired that it was about to be forgotten. Even with Billy Sherrill's symphonic "Sherrillized" arrangements, George Jones remained one of the greatest of all honky tonk singers, his stardom continuing unabated. Willie Nelson never quit singing honky tonk, from the time he recorded his song, "Night Life," in the late 50's, until the present. By the late 70's, Hank Williams Jr.'s music, with strong overtones of Southern rock, spoke to the younger honky tonk crowd, while in the early 80's, John Anderson's Lefty Frizzell-influenced voice and George Strait's undiluted Texas honky tonk sound stood tall during the Urban Cowboy period. New Traditional artists like Randy Travis, Dwight Yoakam and Ricky Van Shelton combined youth with homage to the music's past. In the 90's, Strait inspired artists like Tracy Byrd and Clint Black as well as Joe Diffie and Marty Brown, and female vocalists like Bobbie Cryner make it clear that after a half-century, honky tonk music remains alive and well.   —R.K.

Hoosier Hot Shots

Though primarily a comedy musical act, The Hoosier Hot Shots did much of their performing on country barn dance programs. The group, consisting of a trio of Indianans (Gabe Ward and Ken and "Hezzie" Trietsch) met when they were teenagers and started playing music together in the 1920's. Hezzie Trietsch became the washboard and sound effects master, Ken Trietsch the clarinetist, and Ward the banjoist and guitarist. They started working in an orchestra, then went on their own to WOWO in Fort Wayne in 1932. Their popularity there soon led to an invitation to join Chicago's WLS *National Barn Dance* in 1933. They joined WLS act Uncle Ezra, and stayed with him when he landed an NBC radio show. A number of bass players worked with the group, and Hezzie's washboard included whistles, bells, pie pans and other noisemakers. They recorded for ARC (later absorbed by Columbia) from 1935-42. Produced by Uncle Art Satherley, their novelty records became favorites. They did films from the late 1930's into the 40's, after leaving WLS and heading to Hollywood. The group continued to work until Hezzie Trietsch died in the 1970's. Ken and Gabe continued to work on and off, until Ken died in the 1980's. Ward continued performing until he died in 1992.   —R.K.

Johnny Horton

BORN: April 30, 1925
BIRTHPLACE: Los Angeles, California
DIED: November 5, 1960

Born into a family of transplanted Texans, Johnny LaGale Horton never aimed at a musical career, and through young adulthood drifted through tries at college and various jobs. By the early 1950's, ready to try something new, he used his fishing skills to construct a musical persona. As "The Singing Fisherman" he began making guest appearances on Cliffie Stone's *Hometown Jamboree*. These led to his own local TV shows and recordings for the Cormac and Abbott labels, yet gained him little attention.

Around 1952 Horton started appearing on the *Louisiana Hayride* in Shreveport and recording (without success) for Mercury. He became popular on the *Hayride*, and in 1953 married Billie Jean,

Hank Williams' widow. He also connected with Tillman Franks, the veteran *Hayride* bass player who became his manager.

In 1956 Franks got Horton a record deal with Columbia, where he started recording rockabilly-flavored country material, including his first hit, "Honky Tonk Man" (revived by Dwight Yoakam in 1986). He had several more hits in that style, including "I'm Coming Home" and "I'm a One Woman Man."

Though he toured nationally, Horton kept his home base in Shreveport. By the late 1950's, he and producer Don Law stumbled across the idea of doing historical saga songs. The first, "When It's Springtime in Alaska," a Horton original, did well in 1959, but its success was eclipsed by his explosive version of Jimmie Driftwood's "Battle of New Orleans" (the melody based on the fiddle tune, "The Eighth of January") that same year. "Battle" topped the country and pop charts and helped make historical saga songs a craze. Horton had a string of similar hits, including "Johnny Reb," "Sink the Bismarck" and "North to Alaska."

Just as the latter song was being released, Horton's career abruptly ended early one morning on a highway near Milano, Texas. He was traveling with Franks and guitarist Tom Tomlinson when a drunk driver hit their car head-on. Franks and Tomlinson were injured; Horton died instantly. He'd had premonitions of his death, and had discussed them with several friends.   —R.K.

Roy Horton

BORN: November 5, 1914
BIRTHPLACE: Broad Top, Pennsylvania

This former coal miner grew up in the Allegheny Mountains of Western Pennsylvania, but later became a key figure in early country music, first as a recording specialist and then as a top music publishing executive with the vast Peer-Southern organization.

As chairman of the CMA's board, it was Horton who cut the ribbon for the opening of the Country Music Hall of Fame in 1967. He himself was elected to its hallowed annals 15 years later, in 1982. He continued to work for Peer-Southern (now called Peer Music) into the 90's.   —B.A.

David Houston

BORN: December 9, 1938
BIRTHPLACE: Bossier City, Louisiana
DIED: November 30, 1993

A descendant of both Robert E. Lee and Sam Houston, Louisiana-born singer-songwriter David Houston got his start on the *Louisiana Hayride* while still a teenager.

It was while working on the popular radio show that he met talent manager Tillman Franks, who was instrumental in signing him with Epic Records in the early 1960's. Houston's first single, "Mountain of Love," was one of the smash hits of 1963, leading several trade magazines to name him the Most Promising Country Performer of 1964.

His next single, "Livin' in a House Full of Love," was an even bigger hit, and his theme song, "Almost Persuaded" (co-written and produced by producer Billy Sherrill), went Gold—then rare for a country single—in 1966. Yet, like many young artists who achieve early success, Houston, who made a steady living through the years with his catfish farm in Louisiana, found the momentum impossible to maintain.

His next several efforts attracted little attention, and his name was conspicuously absent from the charts in the late 1960's. He scored a Top 20 hit in 1974, a duet with Barbara Mandrell titled "I Love You, I Love You," and resurfaced four years later at Elektra/Asylum. The following years were hit-and-miss, although he had some success in the 1980's with two moderately successful singles, "You're the Perfect Reason" and "Sad Love Song Ladies."

"Almost Persuaded," though, remains the classic husband-who-walked-the-line song, and has probably been played in as many barrooms as any George Jones weeper, and covered by about as many artists (including Jones). Houston died of a brain aneurysm in Louisiana in 1993.   —M.B.

Harlan Howard

BORN: September 8, 1929
BIRTHPLACE: Lexington, Kentucky

Born in Kentucky in 1929, Harlan Howard is among the greatest country songwriters of all time, considered by his peers to be in a class with Hank Williams, Don Gibson and Floyd Tillman. He grew up in Detroit, and, after moving to California in the 1950's, set his sights on becoming a recording artist. By then he'd married Lula Grace Johnson, better known as Jan Howard. He also became a close friend of Buck Owens, and together they started Blue Book, a music publishing firm. Howard later turned it over to Owens, and it became a multi-million dollar concern, publishing Owens' and Merle Haggard's classic songs of the 1960's. Howard later recorded on his own, though with little success, for Monument, RCA and Nugget. Among his classic compositions are "Heartaches by the Number," "Pick Me Up on Your Way Down," "Mommy for a Day," "Streets of Baltimore,"

"I Fall to Pieces," "Tiger by the Tail," "Heartbreak USA," "No Charge" and "Busted." The Howards moved to Nashville and later divorced. Howard lives in Nashville today, where he still writes songs and is often interviewed about the earlier days of country music, providing pithy and witty commentary on happenings past and present. —R.K.

Jan Howard

BORN: March 13, 1930
BIRTHPLACE: West Plains, Missouri

Born Lula Grace Johnson in West Plains, Missouri, Jan Howard enjoyed country music as a child, but it wasn't until after her marriage to the up-and-coming hit songwriter, Harlan Howard, that she considered a career as a singer.

Early in their marriage, Harlan used Jan to sing demos of his songs; it was these tapes that brought her voice to the attention of Challenge Records, who signed her in the late 1950's.

While Jan scored a couple of hit singles—"Yankee Go Home" and "A World I Can't Live In"—her career continued to take a back seat to raising her children. In the early 60's she appeared on the Grand Ole Opry, and within a few years she signed a new contract with Decca Records.

Her debut album, *Evil on Your Mind*, appeared in 1966; the title single, written by Harlan, became a Top Ten hit. She made the charts again the following year with the single, "Roll Over and Play Dead," and cut a second album, *Bad Seed*. Her next release, "Count Your Blessings, Woman," also made the charts in 1968.

In the late 1960's and early 70's Howard was known for her duets with Bill Anderson, which gained them two Country Music Award nominations for Best Vocal Duo in 1968 and 1970.

Jan and Harlan divorced in the mid-70's, though she continues to work under the name Howard. She's been an Opry member since 1972. —M.B.

Paul Howard

BORN: July 10, 1908
BIRTHPLACE: Midland, Arkansas
DIED: June 18, 1984

Paul Howard's 1940's Western swing band, The Arkansas Cotton Pickers, was not only one of the few Western swing bands working in the Southeast, it boasted a formidable roster of talent, including fiddler Harold Hensley, guitarists Hank Garland, Grady Martin, and Jabbo Arrington, steel player Billy Bowman and drummer Joe Morello, a future jazz legend. Yet Howard didn't set out on a musical career. He left home in 1923 and moved to Kansas. From there, he did manual labor around the Southwest and picked up a guitar for the first time while working at a copper mine. He started playing and singing in earnest, performing in Arizona, and by the mid-1930's, did a Jimmie Rodgers-style act back in Arkansas. By 1940 he felt confident enough to audition for the Grand Ole Opry. Hired as a vocalist, he soon formed a band called The Arkansas Cotton Pickers that expanded into a full-blown Western swing unit. He stuck to a Western swing sound on his 1940's Liberty and Columbia recordings. He quit the Opry in 1949 and moved to Shreveport, Louisiana. He promoted dances and continued working with The Cotton Pickers until the 1970's. After disbanding his group, he returned to Little Rock and played gospel and bluegrass until his death. —R.K.

Con Hunley

BORN: April 9, 1945
BIRTHPLACE: Luttrell, Tennessee

After showcasing for music business executives at a nightclub in Nashville in 1977, piano-playing Conrad Logan Hunley found himself being pulled between five different record labels all wanting his services. He settled on Warner Bros. where, from 1978

through 1982, he had a string of 11 Top 20 songs, though none reached the Top Ten. He was sometimes compared to fellow piano player Ronnie Milsap, on account of their penchant for blues, rock and soul-laced country music. Milsap, though, found his groove and long-term success. Hunley didn't: Later singles on MCA, then Capitol, failed to heat up radio or the record-buying public. His final chart hit, in 1986, was titled "Quittin' Time." —G.F.

Ferlin Husky

BORN: December 3, 1925
BIRTHPLACE: Flat River, Missouri

Ferlin Husky is not often perceived as a pioneer of the Bakersfield Sound—that distinction is usually reserved for Tommy Collins, The Maddox Brothers and Rose, Wynn Stewart, Buck Owens and Merle Haggard—but he was definitely a part of the movement. He is also one of the only country singers of the past few decades to record under three names: his own; his first stage name, Terry Preston; and his comic alter ego, Simon Crum. As a child he played guitar and dreamed of a music and film career. After a five-year stint in the Merchant Marines during World War II, he wound up in California, where he worked in Salinas with local performer Big Jim DeNoone, then did some bit parts in Western films. In 1950 he signed with Four Star Records and worked on Cliffie Stone's *Hometown Jamboree*. Stone brought him to Capitol Records in 1952, where he recorded initially as Terry Preston. Bakersfield artist Tommy Collins played guitar on his first records, including a ballad titled "Gone." Five records into the contract, he reverted to his given name of Ferlin Husky (then spelled "Huskey").

Still, he had no success until 1953 when his duet with Jean Shepard on "A Dear John Letter" became the first hit for both, remaining Number One for six weeks. Their follow-up, "Forgive Me John," also went to the Top Ten before they each went back to concentrating on solo recordings. Husky's next big hit came in 1955 with "I Feel Better All Over (More Than Anywhere's Else)" and the flipside, "Little Tom." As Simon Crum, his "Cuzz You're So Sweet" made it to Number Five in the spring of 1955. He joined the Opry during that period. He also acted in film and on stage, appearing in a dramatic role on TV in 1958 and in various films, including *Mr. Rock and Roll* (1957) and *Country Music Holiday* (1958). In 1957 Husky again recorded "Gone," this time in a near-operatic style with neutral Nashville Sound backing. Some country disc jockeys considered it too uptown, but it became his biggest hit ever, remaining at Number One for ten weeks on the country charts, and reaching the Top Five on the pop charts. Late in 1958 Simon Crum had another hit with "Country Music Is Here to Stay." In 1960 his gospel number, "Wings of a Dove," did as well as "Gone": ten weeks at Number One. After that, he had a number of lesser hits, the biggest being "Once" in 1966. He also appeared in the film *Country Music on Broadway.*

He left Capitol for ABC in 1972, with modest success, remaining there until 1975. He had open heart surgery in 1977, but returned to the road. Later, he had a museum at Conway Twitty's Twitty City, but it was lost in 1989's Hurricane Hugo. —R.K.

Frank Hutchinson

BORN: March 20, 1891
BIRTHPLACE: Raleigh County, West Virginia
DIED: November 9, 1945

West Virginia native Frank Hutchinson is generally considered the first white country bluesman to record. Between 1926 and 1929, Okeh issued 32 sides featuring his distinctive singing and guitar playing; some titles also featured his harmonica.

Hutchinson's reputation primarily rests upon a relatively small number of slide guitar specialties, notably "Coney Isle," "The Train That Carried the Girl from Town" and "Worried Blues." Even after his death in 1945, Hutchinson's records particularly appealed to musicians: Cowboy Copas reworked "Coney Isle" for his 1960 hit, "Alabam'," while Doc Watson introduced the other two songs to Northern folk music audiences in the mid-60's. —D.S.

Alan Jackson

BORN: October 17, 1958
BIRTHPLACE: Newnan, Georgia

When he made his recording debut in 1989, Alan Jackson seemed almost too good to be true. He was a veritable publicist's dream. It just seemed improbable that a guy so young, and as ruggedly handsome as the hirsute blond young studs in Winston advertisements, could also sing and write vintage country tunes with such sheer, tortured maturity and conviction.

Yet a half a decade later, Jackson not only continues to live up to all the rush of hype that accompanied his debut, but has repeatedly exceeded expectations. Like George Strait, he has thus far proven to be amazingly consistent; all the delightful promise of his first album, *Here in the Real World*, has been maintained and enlarged upon. His growing list of hits (many of them self-written) includes "Here in the Real World," "Wanted," "Chasin' That Neon Rainbow," "Don't Rock the Jukebox," "Someday," "Midnight in Montgomery," "Tonight I Climbed the Wall," "Chattahoochee" and "She's Got the Rhythm (I've Got the Blues)." They have established him as a stylistically sure-footed straight country singer, heavily steeped in the traditions of an earlier generation of vocal masters like Vern Gosdin, Cal Smith and George Jones.

"When I came to Nashville, I wanted to carry on the tradition of real country music," Jackson explained around the time of the release of *Here in the Real World*. "And I'd like to stay that way....You know that George Jones song, 'Who's Gonna Fill Their Shoes,'" he added, referring to a recent Jones hit that laments the passing of greats like Hank Williams and Lefty Frizzell, and poses the question of whether or not their legacy will be carried on. "Well, I don't know whether I can fill their shoes, but I'd sure like to try."

Jackson, for all his immense talent, was raised in a distinctly non-musical family, and never even attended his first country concert until he was 20. (He recalls it was The Kendalls.) "It's not like I was born with a guitar in my hand," he said of his growing up years in the small city of Newnan, Georgia, where he was born October 17, 1958, the youngest of five children—except for him, all girls. "I was far more interested in cars and girls for the whole rest of my early life than I was in writing songs."

Jackson, in fact, tried his hand at just about everything—driving a forklift, selling cars, painting cars, clerking in a shoe store, waiting tables in a barbecue restaurant—before finally deciding, in 1985, to make a run at a music career.

Moving from Newnan to Nashville with his wife, Denise, was a big jump, but Jackson landed on his feet. He got a job in the mail room at The Nashville Network, and eventually was signed to a modest draw as a songwriter for Glen Campbell's publishing company. Though he's since become one of the hottest and most drooled-over country "hunksters" on the contemporary scene, Jackson emphasizes that stardom did not come easily. He was turned down by every major record label at least once, and twice by some, before finally striking Gold (and platinum) with the relatively new country division of the Arista label. Nowadays, he can even laugh when he recalls the high-level recording executive who once showed him the door, assuring him his quest was a lost cause: that he simply didn't have star potential. "Things like that are hard to swallow," Jackson remembered with a complacent shrug. "But a lot of times you've just got to realize that's only one man's opinion, and not let it stop you from keepin' right on trying."

Jackson became a member of the Grand Ole Opry in 1991. In 1994, he was one of the top three concert grossers in country music, running neck and neck with Reba McEntire and topped only by Garth Brooks.

He's scored more than seven Number One records and sold over nine million albums and still counting.

—B.A.

Stonewall Jackson

BORN: November 6, 1932
BIRTHPLACE: Tabor City, North Carolina

Singer/songwriter Stonewall Jackson made his first trip to Nashville at the age of 24, driving a log truck. His plan was to record demos of his original songs, hoping to convince Grand Ole Opry luminaries to record them, but when Wesley Rose heard them, he quickly signed Jackson to Columbia Records. He was made a member of the Grand Ole Opry that same year. Two years later, in 1958, Jackson had his first Number One single, "Life to Go." His next single, "Waterloo" (1959), also made it to Number One on the country charts and went Top Five on the pop charts as well.

(In fact, it was hard to escape the "every puppy has its day, everybody's got to pay" refrain.) Thus began a string of Top Ten hits, including "Why I'm Walking" (1960), "A Wound Time Can't Erase" and "Leona" (both 1962), "Old Showboat" (1963), his own "Don't Be Angry" and the Number One, "B.J. the D.J.," both in 1964. Several more Top Tens followed, the last coming in 1971. He left Columbia in 1973, recording briefly for MGM. These days, Jackson performs on the Opry, and runs several businesses (including his own restaurant).
—M.B.

Tommy Jackson

Born: March 31, 1926
Birthplace: Birmingham, Alabama
Died: December 9, 1979

One of the original "Nashville Cats," fiddler Tommy Jackson played on hundreds of hit records in the 1950's and 60's. His straight, clean, driving style and distinctive, well-rounded tone helped accentuate hits ranging from Hank Williams' "Lovesick Blues" to Ray Price's "Crazy Arms." A native of Birmingham, Alabama, born March 31, 1926, Jackson actually grew up in Nashville, and won his spurs playing on the Opry in the bands of Curley Williams, Paul Howard and Milton Estes. His work with Red Foley's band, The Cumberland Valley Boys (which included steel player Jerry Byrd and lead guitarist Zeke Turner), eventually led to a stint in Cincinnati in the late 1940's. After returning to Nashville and establishing himself as a session man, he began a series of "square dance" albums for Dot under his own name; these contained definitive versions of many old fiddle tunes, and were

much sought after by fiddle fans and younger fiddlers. By the 1970's Jackson had lost his place as Nashville's top studio fiddler, and was working to help his son Mychael establish a career. Jackson died in December 1979.
—C.W.

Wanda Jackson

Born: October 20, 1937
Birthplace: Maud, Oklahoma

Though Wanda Jackson's biggest hits were in the country field, her impact on early rock 'n' roll was every bit as important. Born 50 miles southeast of Oklahoma City, she got her first guitar during the period her family lived in California from 1941-49. When the Jacksons moved back east, to Oklahoma City, Wanda, still in high school, won a local talent contest and landed her own show on KLPR Radio. After Hank Thompson moved his home base to Oklahoma City, he heard Wanda's show and invited her to sing on weekends with his Brazos Valley Boys. He wanted Capitol Records' Ken Nelson to sign her, but Nelson, remembering legal problems he'd had signing an under-age Jean Shepard a few years earlier, declined. Instead, Wanda went with Decca, who re-

corded her in a duet with Thompson's bandleader, Billy Gray, on "You Can't Have My Love." It became a Number Eight country hit in 1954. After she recorded 14 other songs for Decca, Nelson relented, signing her to Capitol in 1956. That year, working on country package shows in the South, Wanda met Elvis Presley, who encouraged her to try doing rockabilly. She did, putting "I Gotta Know" into the Top 20 that fall. Unlike most female singers, who presented a demure image, Wanda wore silk fringe outfits, tight dresses and high heels. Ernest Tubb once insisted she cover up a shoulder-baring gown she wore when working the Opry. (Angered, she never returned.) Though she recorded raging-hot rockers like "Honey Bop" and "Fujiyama Mama" using top-flight studio musicians like Buck Owens and Joe Maphis, the idea of a raw, female Elvis was ahead of its time.

Meanwhile, she had great bands, including one that featured Roy Clark and Big Al Downing, a talented black musician who later had a brief run in the country charts. After she married Wendell Goodman in 1961, she began to tone down somewhat, putting more emphasis on her country sound (though some rockers ended up on the B-sides of her singles). In 1961 two ballads, "Right or Wrong" and "In the Middle of a Heartache," went Top Ten. She also did an early version of "Silver Threads and Golden Needles." Through the 60's, she had modest hits, the biggest being the 1968 Top 20, "A Girl Don't Have to Drink to Have Fun." Wanda finally left Capitol in 1972, a year after she became a born-again Christian. Her main reason for leaving was that the label wouldn't let her record a gospel album. Though many believe she quit country for gospel, she never intended to, and found frustration on the gospel-oriented Myrrh records when they, in contrast, refused to let her record secular music. And today, though she remains involved in religious activities in Oklahoma, she still sings her country and rockabilly hits here, and in Europe, where she remains a revered figure. —R.K.

Sonny James

BORN: May 1, 1929
BIRTHPLACE: Hackleburg, Alabama

Sonny James was born Jimmie Loden in Hackleburg, Alabama, on May 1, 1929. After serving as a soldier in the Korean War, he played his guitar and sang in country night clubs and at county fairs, often performing the original songs he had written while serving in Korea. Somewhere along the way he made the acquaintance of Chet Atkins, who introduced him to Capitol Records producer Ken Nelson in the early 1950's. James quickly signed with the label, but took several years to come up with his first hit. When he finally made it to the charts in 1957 with "First Date, First Kiss, First Love," the record sounded a lot more like pop than country. The follow-up single, the now classic "Young Love," made it to Number One on the pop charts and broke the country Top Ten as well.

James kept up a hectic schedule of live perfor-

mances through the early 1960's, but except for a 1962 Dot album titled *First Love*, failed to place a record on the charts. That began to change around 1964, when a song he co-wrote with Bob Tubert called "You're the Only World I Know" reached Number One on the country charts. He scored a second hit later that year with a song by Boudleaux and Felice Bryant titled "Baltimore." In addition to three Grammy nominations, 1965 also brought James two more hits, the Number One, "Behind the Tear," and the Top Ten, "I'll Keep Holding On."

In the latter part of the decade James' name was rarely absent from the album charts. Among his most popular titles were *Behind the Tear*, *True Love's a Blessing*, *World of Our Own* and a live album titled *Astrodome Presents Sonny James in Person*. Around the same time James also tried his hand at acting, appearing in a handful of films like the Jayne Mansfield vehicle, *Las Vegas Hillbillies*, and 1967's *Hillbillies in a Haunted House*.

James began the 1970's with a string of Number One singles: "It's Just a Matter of Time," "My Love," "Don't Keep Me Hangin' On" and "Endlessly." Meanwhile, as the decade went on, he became increasingly involved in producing and music publishing. Nevertheless, the Number One hits kept on coming, among them "Empty Arms," "Bright Lights, Big City" and "Here Comes Honey Again" in 1971, "That's Why I Love You Like I Do" and "When the Snow Is on the Roses" in 1972 and "Is It Wrong for Loving You" in 1974. Later hits include the Top Ten "When Something Is Wrong with My Baby" and "Come On In" in 1976, and a cover of Jimmie Rodgers' "In the Jailhouse Now." James remained on Capitol Records until 1972; the later hits were on Columbia. After 1978, James moved over to a series of smaller labels, scoring few chart entries. As of the early 1990's, he was still residing in middle Tennessee, but was no longer active as a recording artist.   —M.B.

Waylon Jennings

BORN: June 15, 1937
BIRTHPLACE: Littlefield, Texas

It didn't take Waylon Jennings long to figure out what he wanted to do, and he's been doing it ever since. By the time he was 12, he'd gotten his first job: as a DJ on a radio station in his Littlefield, Texas, hometown. In 1955, after dropping out of high school, he moved to Lubbock, Texas, for another radio job, and met Buddy Holly. In 1958, he became the bassist for Holly's band, The Crickets. In turn, Holly produced and played guitar on Waylon's first record, "Jole Blon," that same year. A year later Waylon gave up his seat on Holly's tour plane to J.P. Richardson, "The Big Bopper." The plane crashed, killing all passengers on board, including Holly.

Waylon worked in Phoenix for six years with his band, The Waylors, becoming a popular local act. He recorded briefly for Herb Alpert at A&M Records on the West Coast before Chet Atkins signed him to RCA in 1965 and brought him to Nashville. His first single release, "That's the Chance I'll Have to Take," charted in the Top 50. His first appearance in the Top Five came with "Walk on Out of My Mind" in 1968, followed by "Only Daddy That'll Walk the Line," which reached Number Two.

Like many artists with staying power (measured in decades, not years), Waylon's strength and success as an artist came with his determination to do things his way. In 1972, after years of having his records produced by unsympathetic staff producers, he convinced RCA to let him use The Waylors on his recordings.

He recorded *Honky Tonk Heroes*, consisting of songs written almost entirely by Texan Billy Joe Shaver. (Unlike compatriots Willie Nelson, Johnny Cash and Kris Kristofferson, Waylon did not write the bulk of his own material—though he has composed some memorable songs.) The album produced no hits, but is considered a landmark, and songs like "Old Five and Dimers, "Lonesome, Orn'ry and Mean," "Black Rose" and the title tune are regarded as Waylon trademarks, as well as Shaver standards. Two years later, "This Time" brought Jennings his first Number One.

Waylon married recording artist Jessi Colter in 1969, his fourth wife, and six years later the couple collaborated with Willie Nelson and Tompall Glaser, producing the first country album to be certified platinum—*Wanted: The Outlaws*. (There were other country million-sellers prior to this, but platinum certifications had not yet come into existence.)

Different people give different origins for the categorizing of Waylon's music as Outlaw music. Some say it's because he and the other performers known as outlaws rebelled so strongly against the prevailing Nashville Sound; others say it was because Waylon and the others rebelled against the establishment itself, refusing to buy into the unfair-to-artist contractual dealings of the major labels (which not only deprived artists of any sort of say-so in artistic decisions regarding their music but also paid them a mere pittance in royalties); still others say it was the lifestyle of the group—drugs, alcohol, no-shows, long hair and all around hell-raising—things that the youthful post-Vietnam, post-hippie audience that still existed

out there in the 70's obviously related to: they bought his records by the millions.

Most likely, it was a little of all the above, and Jennings himself—much like Willie Nelson—always had mixed feelings toward the Outlaw label, which sometimes came out in his music. *I've Always Been Crazy* (which became the first country album to ship Gold, and whose title tune hit Number One in 1978) and early bravado-laced anthems like "Ladies Love Outlaws" contrasted with the misgivings expressed in "Don't You Think This Outlaw Bit's Done Got Out of Hand" (another Number One single which followed hard on the heels of Jennings' arrest on drug charges—something that no doubt stemmed from his increasing notoriety and the dark rumors of drug use and debauchery that swirled around him).

Whatever the Outlaw tag meant, and whatever consequences it brought, there's still no question that Waylon paved the way for others who wanted to do it their way, to choose their own material, produce their own records and live their lives without consideration for some record label-generated publicity scheme. And his massive record sales from the late 70's and early 80's showed that he succeeded: His *Greatest Hits* album sold more than four million copies alone. (His first Gold single, ironically was the rather lightweight theme song for the *Dukes of Hazzard* TV show, "Good Ol' Boys.")

Some of Waylon's best music over the years has been the duets he's performed with longtime friend Willie Nelson, including "Mamas, Don't Let Your Babies Grow Up to Be Cowboys," "Luckenbach, Texas (Back to the Basics of Love)" and "Good Hearted Woman." He and wife Jessi also had a hit duet with "Suspicious Minds" in 1976.

After a long run with RCA, Jennings moved over to Epic in the early 80's. In 1985 he surfaced as one of The Highwaymen, the multi-million-dollar quartet consisting of Waylon, Willie, Kris Kristofferson and Johnny (as in Cash). The title song from the album *Highwayman* became a Number One hit in '85, and the group re-formed again five years later with another hit album, *Highwayman 2*, and another top-grossing tour.

Like Johnny Cash before him, Waylon underwent successful heart bypass surgery in 1988, and, like Cash, bounced back to top form quickly. A natural comedian and raconteur, he turned his delightful 1987 autobiographical album, *A Man Called Hoss*, into a one-man show and, with Willie Nelson, developed a club on Memphis' Festival Island, Waylon & Willie's Cafe. In 1993, Waylon returned to the label of his greatest successes, RCA, with a two-CD boxed set, and plans for new material.

Of all Waylon's awards (including two Grammys and the Horatio Alger Award, given to people from humble origins who have attained success), one stands out. In addition to becoming a vehement anti-drug advocate since kicking his own habit a number of years ago, he has become a spokesperson for GED, the adult education equivalent of a high school diploma. After years of bopping through life as a high school dropout, Waylon got his own GED and now actively encourages others to do the same.   —M.B.

Jim & Jesse

BORN: Jim, February 13, 1927, Coeburn, Virginia
Jesse, July 9, 1929, Coeburn, Virginia

Partners in one of bluegrass' greatest "brother" acts, Jim and Jesse McReynolds grew up in rural Virginia as part of an extended musical family. Their grandfather, Charles McReynolds, had a substantial musical reputation in western Virginia; his work included recordings for Victor with his Bull Mountain

Moonshiners at the famous 1928 Bristol Sessions. Jim & Jesse, playing guitar and mandolin respectively, debuted in 1947 on WNVA. Things looked promising when they signed with Capitol, but the Korean War intervened and Jesse was drafted. After his discharge in 1954 they continued, leading their own backup band, The Virginia Boys (with banjoist Bobby Thompson and Vassar Clements among its members). Their next major label was Epic, with whom they signed in 1962. Their hard traditional sound was made unique by Jesse's much-copied mandolin "crosspicking."

In 1964 they joined the Grand Ole Opry. The group was adventurous enough to record *Berry Pickin' in the Country* in 1965, the only existing bluegrass album made up wholly of Chuck Berry numbers. Their biggest chart hit came in 1967 with "Diesel on My Tail." Today they remain Opry members, and one of bluegrass music's most respected traditional duos.   —R.K.

Johnnie and Jack

BORN: Johnny, May 13, 1914, Mt. Juliet, Tennessee
      Jack, May 13, 1916, Columbia, Tennessee
DIED: Jack Anglin, March 8, 1963

The memorable but relatively short-lived duet team of Johnny Wright and Jack Anglin, known as Johnnie and Jack, would no doubt have had greater impact on country music if its existence had not been cut short by Anglin's untimely death in an automobile accident in 1963, at age 46. (He died, ironically enough, en route to funeral services for Patsy Cline, who was killed in a plane crash on March 5th.) Still, Johnnie and Jack's 1950's and very early 1960's recordings—including hits like "Poison Love," "Cryin' Heart Blues," "What About You" and "Ashes of Love"—stand the test of time beautifully.

Johnnie Wright was born in 1914 in Mt. Juliet, Tennessee, just outside Nashville. (He later changed the spelling of his name to Johnny.) His family included several generations of gifted old-time banjo and fiddle players. Jack Anglin was born in nearby Franklin, Tennessee, in 1916, and by 1936 was performing with his two older siblings as The Anglin Brothers on WSIX in Nashville.

Beginning in 1937, Wright and Anglin played together and separately in various bands under various names (often with Wright's wife, Kitty Wells, who would eventually go on to solo fame). Finally, in the mid-1940's they joined the Grand Ole Opry as Johnnie and Jack and The Tennessee Mountain Boys. In 1948 they moved to the *Louisiana Hayride* in Shreveport, and in 1949 were signed to RCA Records by Chet Atkins. A year later they had their first hit, "Poison Love."

Through the years since Anglin's death, Johnny Wright has continued recording (12 chart entries between 1964 and 1968, including his 1965 Number One single, "Hello Vietnam"). As of the mid-1990's, he is still touring and performing with his wife, Kitty Wells, and their son, Bobby Wright.   —B.A.

Bob Johnston

BORN: May 14, 1932
BIRTHPLACE: Unknown

Bob Johnston, a producer at Columbia Records in Nashville, played an instrumental role in bringing country music to a younger, hipper audience during the late 1960's.

For starters, he produced folk-rock icon Bob Dylan's back-to-the-country classic, *Nashville Skyline*

(1969), which featured Nashville session stalwarts Charlie McCoy on harmonica, Pete Drake on pedal steel, Norman Blake on dobro and a young Charlie Daniels on bass. Johnston's trademark was adding heavier rhythm to recorded tracks by incorporating extra rhythm guitars and drums—a technique later adopted by other Nashville producers such as Billy Sherrill and Allen Reynolds. He also had a knack for finding good songs by other writers. In 1970 he produced Johnny Cash's *Hello, I'm Johnny Cash*, which included Tim Hardin's "If I Were a Carpenter" and Kris Kristofferson's "To Beat the Devil."

Johnston's formula for broadening country music's audience also extended to the bluegrass arena. In the late 1960's and early 70's he produced Flatt and Scruggs' *Changin' Times* and *Nashville Airplane*, which featured "contemporary" material, including a couple of Bob Dylan tunes.   —R.P.

George Jones

BORN: September 12, 1931
BIRTHPLACE: Saratoga, Texas

In a world increasingly informed by global communications, creeping suburbanization and the omnipresence of FM rock radio, George Glenn Jones may be among the last pure country singers. Today he is, in many ways, a link to a long-gone era; even after nearly 40 years as a recording artist, he is still musically, and emotionally, anchored in a time when Hank Williams, Lefty Frizzell and Roy Acuff ruled the jukebox, and the Pentecostal church, the beer joint down the road and the stand-up AM radio in the parlor (tuned to Nashville's clear channel WSM) were still the true cement of community and family life. He was born in a log cabin in the East Texas region called the Big Thicket, a hard-living area of oil fields and lumber camps. He was the eighth child of a hard-drinking laborer and his wife.

George Glenn grew up loving music and singing.

When he began listening to the Grand Ole Opry on the family's first radio in the late 30's, Roy Acuff became his idol, along with Bill Monroe. When the Joneses moved to Beaumont, young George had a guitar and sang in the city streets for tips. As a teenager he began working with local performers, initially imitating Acuff and later Hank Williams. After his first marriage foundered, he joined the U.S. Marines and performed while stationed in Southern California. Following his 1953 discharge, he returned to Beaumont, soon connected with the newly founded Starday Records and met the label's co-founder, Harold "Pappy" Daily. Though his first record, "No Money in This Deal," attracted little notice, George caught on with the *Houston Jamboree* barn dance show and took a second job as a Beaumont DJ. During this period, he married again and, in 1955, recorded "Why, Baby Why."

The song gave George his first Top Ten success, though Webb Pierce and Red Sovine's duet version charted higher. He had three Top Tens in 1956, and his career momentum grew after that with hits like "Just One More" (1956) and "Color of the Blues." Pappy Daily also, in light of Elvis' success, had George record some rockabilly titles issued under the name "Thumper Jones," a name George took from the cartoon character Thumper Rabbit. In 1958 the crazy moonshine number, "White Lightning," written by pioneer rock 'n' roller J.P. "The Big Bopper" Richardson, became his biggest hit yet, followed by the similar-sounding "Who Shot Sam." By the time he did "The Window Up Above" in 1960, he was starting to develop the intense ballad style that would inspire so many imitators. "Tender Years," in 1961, further revealed his growth as a singer, as well as being a Number One record for seven weeks. By this time Jones was on Mercury, still produced by Pappy Daily, who had George under contract, and moved his Number One singer with him when he when he moved from label to label. In the early 60's he brought George to United Artists where he had several more hits. The biggest was "She Thinks I Still Care." In 1962, DJ's voted it their favorite single and *Billboard* gave George its Favorite Male Country Vocalist award. In 1963 he had another major hit, the more up-tempo "The Race Is On," and he and hard-country female vocalist Melba Montgomery teamed for the bluegrass-flavored duet, "We Must Have Been Out of Our Minds." His vocal influence on singers like Buck Owens was strong during these years.

Daily moved George to Musicor Records in 1965, where he recorded over 300 songs of varying quality, including duets with pop singer Gene Pitney. Among his major hits with Musicor were "Love Bug" (revived by George Strait in 1993). In 1967 George recorded his biggest hit with Musicor: Dallas Frazier's "Walk Through This World With Me." It was his first Number One record since 1961. Meanwhile, George's hard-drinking lifestyle was already attracting notice. It led him to miss concerts and get himself into various scrapes. His second marriage ended in 1968, and he soon met Tammy Wynette, whom he married in 1969, the same year he joined the Grand Ole Opry. The two couldn't record together until George's Musicor contract ended in 1970. At that point Tammy's Epic Records producer, Billy Sherrill, brought George to his label, ending Jones' 15-year association with Pappy Daily. Sherrill was a different type of producer, who routinely used symphonic strings and pop ideas on his records, but he and George were able to work together. Over the next several years with Epic, George enjoyed hits both alone and with Tammy. Solo, his biggest were "Loving You Could Never Be Better" (1972), "Once You've Had the Best" (1973), "The Grand Tour" and "The Door" (1974). With Tammy he scored with "Take Me" (1971), "The Ceremony" (1972) and "We're Gonna Hold On" (1973). If the latter title indicated problems, it was so. The song appeared around the time Tammy filed for divorce. George's drinking was driving a wedge between the couple, and Sherrill was shrewd enough, knowing that the couple's domestic woes were making headlines, to gear the recorded material to capitalize on what was fast becoming a real-life Nashville soap opera of separations and reconciliations. George and Tammy finally divorced in 1975, though they continued recording together and, ironically, in 1976 had two Number One records with "Golden Ring" and the 1947 Francis Craig Orchestra hit, "Near You."

George's greatness began to be noticed outside the country media when he performed at a Willie Nelson Fourth of July picnic in 1976 and galvanized an audience of both old-line and younger fans. In 1978 he had a Top Ten record with pop singer James Taylor's "Bartender's Blues" (with Taylor singing harmonies). He recorded a hot rockabilly version of Chuck Berry's "Maybelline" that year with Johnny Paycheck. All the while his drinking, aggravated by cocaine abuse, was sending his personal and financial life into a spin. He became a frequent topic of the tabloids as his no-shows at performances escalated. Tammy and George, once again recording together, had their final Top Ten duet in 1980 with "Two Story House."

It took George and Sherrill nearly a year to complete the song that in 1980 became George's greatest triumph, the Bobby Braddock ballad, "He Stopped Loving Her Today," a song Johnny Russell had recorded unsuccessfully. Jones thought little of it, but Sherrill kept pushing it. Its combination of symphonic backing and a raw, emotional vocal earned it a Number One spot, but more importantly, a Grammy as Country Song of the Year. It also won a Country Music Association award for both Song of the Year and Single of the Year. George won Male Vocalist of the year as well. The album containing the song, *I Am What I Am*, won Jones his first Gold record. Songs like "I'm Not Ready Yet" (1980), "If Drinkin' Don't Kill Me (Her Memory Will)" and "Still Doin' Time" (1981) were outstanding, from-the-heart performances that underscored his personal crises, which continued to worsen. Doubts about how long Jones would survive grew. A videotape of him being pulled over by Tennessee lawmen for drunken driving was seen nationwide. Still, his records continued to do well as the media dubbed him country's greatest singer. In 1982 he had a hit duet with Merle Haggard on Willie Nelson's song, "Yesterday's Wine."

After Tammy, he had a number of relationships with women, few of them lasting. That changed when he met Louisiana native Nancy Sepulveda, whom he married in 1983. Though he continued to drink for a time, he and Nancy left Nashville for George's home area of Texas, settling near Colmesneil, where, after being instutionalized numerous times, he gradually began to recover, even to the point of cutting his liquor intake and ending his drug dependency. Meanwhile he continued making hits, including, in 1983, a duet with Ray Charles on "We Didn't See a Thing." Solo, he had a Number One with "I Always Get Lucky With You." He also recorded duets with Brenda Lee and Lacy J. Dalton. Over the remainder of the 80's, he restored his credibility with concert audiences and became a virtual miracle: a singer who'd traveled Hank Williams' road every bit as fast and hard as Hank but lived to tell about it. As music critic Jack Hurst of *The Chicago Tribune* once noted, "George Jones could well prove to be the Last Country Singer, if that is taken to mean the last spiritual descendant of the field's archetypal demigod, Hank Williams....But

Williams' lanky body couldn't stand the pressure long enough to see its 30th birthday. Self-abusing just as viciously, Jones has outlived his role model by 20 years. He sings better too."

By the late 80's, Jones was ready to leave Epic. By then, Billy Sherrill had left the label and was producing Jones independently, but the sound had run its course and the singer needed a change. His final Epic hit in 1988 was a remake of Johnny Horton's 1957 honky tonker, "One Woman Man." He signed with MCA Records in 1991 where he recorded several albums of varying quality. In 1992 he recorded "I Don't Need Your Rocking Chair," which featured virtually the entire new generation of country singers, most of whom openly professed their admiration and musical debt to Jones. On the record were Vince Gill, Mark Chesnutt, Garth Brooks, Travis Tritt, T. Graham Brown, Clint Black, Joe Diffie, Pam Tillis, Alan Jackson and Patty Loveless. (Others who show his more obvious vocal influence are Sammy Kershaw and David Ball.) In recent years, Jones, the former quintessential hillbilly hellion, has become a sort of country "gray eminence," as well as a musical role model for Nashville's latest generation of hard country virtuosos (who, for all their artistry and dedication to the form, still seem a generation removed from the music's true sources). In 1992, in belated recognition of his primitive vocal genius, Jones was elected to the Country Music Hall of Fame and featured in such unlikely places as *The New York Times Magazine*. Today, Jones is almost universally hailed as the Sinatra of hardcore traditional country music. Though he continues to show vitality as a singer, his releases have, ironically, been more or less crowded out of the charts by the same "Young Country" crowd (Alan Jackson, Randy Travis, Sammy Kershaw, Mark Chesnutt) that so reveres him. In 1994 he did an extensive schedule of stage shows at Opryland, prepared to write his autobiography, and began formulating plans to record a new duet album with Tammy Wynette. He remains an Opry member as well.

Throughout his career Jones has never strayed from his hard country roots, even as his distinctly unreconstructed sound has fallen out of vogue and back in again. Country music is, after all, the only music he knows; it's as much a part of him as the blood in his veins and the grit under his nails. "If you're gonna sing a sad song or ballad, you've got to have lived it yourself," Jones once stated as he struggled to make some connection between the angst of his music and his own years of personal turmoil. "You can think back on anything that made you sad—anything. Maybe your little dog died. And you think about that while you're singing, and pretty soon, it makes you sad. You become lost in the song, and before long, you're just like the people in the song." —B.A.

Grandpa Jones

BORN: October 20, 1913
BIRTHPLACE: Niagara, Kentucky

Though much of America first discovered Grandpa Jones as a regular on the cast of TV's *Hee Haw*, he'd been in the music business 40 years by the time that show began in 1969. Louis Marshall Jones, son of a tobacco sharecropper, was the youngest of 10 children. At age 16 he landed his own radio show in Akron, Ohio, and during the mid-1930's he worked with singer Bradley Kincaid, who once chided him for moving too slow, "like an old grandpa." From that, the "Grandpa Jones" character evolved, complete with false mustache and costume. In 1937 Jones joined Wheeling's *WWVA Jamboree*, where singer-banjoist Cousin Emmy taught him the old-time "frailing" banjo style she used (Uncle Dave Macon did not influence Jones' music, though both had similar styles). In 1942 he joined Cincinnati's WLW *Boone County Jamboree* and he, Merle Travis and The Delmore Brothers formed the gospel quartet known as The Brown's Ferry Four. In 1943, he and Travis made the first recordings ever done for King Records.

After two years in the Army, Jones resumed his career in 1946, recording "Eight More Miles to Louisville" and "It's Raining Here This Morning" for King, and joining the Opry with his wife Ramona, a former WLW fiddler. His 1947 King recordings of "Mountain Dew" and "Old Rattler" did well. In 1958 Jones had a modest hit for RCA with "All American Boy." He joined Monument Records in 1960 and had his biggest hit in 1962 with Jimmie Rodgers' "T For Texas."

A charter cast member of *Hee Haw*, he remained until its end in 1992. In the 1970's and early 80's he recorded albums for CMH Records, and in 1978 became a member of the Country Music Hall of Fame. His autobiography, *Everybody's Grandpa*, appeared in 1984.

Though he no longer tours and needs no "Grandpa" makeup, he continues to work at the Opry and at Opryland, including a starring role in the Opryland *Hee Haw* stage show.   —R.K.

The Jordanaires

The Jordanaires were for many years the Grand Ole Opry's top gospel quartet and have sung on hundreds of Nashville recording sessions and near-countless TV shows and radio shows. The Grammy-winning group, which was originally founded in Springfield, Missouri, in 1948 as a barbershop quartet performing gospel material, included Gordon Stoker, Hoyt Hawkins, Neal Matthews and Hugh Jarrett. They

made their first Opry appearance in 1949. Just a year later they were featured on Red Foley's million-selling gospel recording, "Just a Closer Walk with Thee."

In July 1956 the group joined Elvis Presley for some sessions in New York; from then on they turned up frequently on Presley's most successful albums. They backed numerous artists through the years, including Patsy Cline, Don Gibson, Kitty Wells, Patti Page and Tennessee Ernie Ford, Johnny Horton and Jimmy Dean. Also, in the 60's, they released several of their own albums. In 1977, they backed up Merle Haggard on "From Graceland to the Promised Land," a tribute recorded after the death of Elvis Presley. Most recently, they sang backup on tracks on Billy Ray Cyrus' second album, *It Won't Be the Last.*   —M.B.

Wynonna Judd

BORN: May 30, 1964
BIRTHPLACE: Ashland, Kentucky

When Wynonna Judd (who recently dropped her last name for professional reasons and today is simply known as "Wynonna" to her legion of fans) first contemplated a solo career after her mother fell ill with a liver ailment, her fears and doubts were almost traumatic in their magnitude.

"I can't deal with it right now," Wynonna told long-time *Country Music Magazine* contributor Bob Allen in the midst of The Judds' emotional 1991 "Farewell Tour," when she was asked about the daunting challenge of stepping out on her own. "There's just this incredible fear that I have, of, will I be able to survive on my own?...I really wish I could imagine going on by myself. I wish I could, but I just can't. There are days when I think, what do you do when you've already had the best?"

Wynonna's worries, as it turned out, were largely for naught. *Wynonna*, her 1992 debut album, was one of the most critically acclaimed releases by a country artist so far in the 90's. (*Rolling Stone:* "Easily the most important release by a country artist so far this decade...powerful, stirring, ennobling music." *USA Today*: "The year's most anticipated country album....It's magic.") *Wynonna* yielded three Number One singles in 1992 ("She Is His Only Need," "I Saw the Light" and "No One Else on Earth") and ultimately sold more than three million copies, thus cementing the reputation of the woman whom many consider the most talented female vocalist to hit Nashville since Patsy Cline.

Taking her solo career on the road in 1992, Wynonna met with similarly overwhelming acceptance. Yet the self-doubts still lingered. But by the time of the 1993 release of *Tell Me Why*, her second album, Wynonna seemed to have found her solo wings and was standing on somewhat less shaky ground. "With this album I feel energized and excited," she said shortly after the release of *Tell Me Why*.

Though a little more self-consciously crossover than her first album, *Tell Me Why* was nearly every bit the commercial and critical success. *Tell Me Why* also drew more heavily from the younger Judd's rock 'n' roll and blues influences. "My influences—and I thank God for this now—were records from the old record shops, the used bins. Bluegrass was my first influence, and the mountain harmonies, the mountain soul of Hazel and Alice, the harmonies of the family from The Delmore Brothers, The Stanley Brothers and The Louvin Brothers. Then I started listening to Bonnie Raitt. She's been one of the biggest influences of my vocal style. Instead of Top 40 I was listening to big band, and I was listening to the stuff that my grandparents were going dancing to on weekends. I was pretty eclectic."

Today, Wynonna is not just one of the leading female singers on the country scene; she's a diva of popular culture with whom the national media seems to have as much fascination as it does with a Mariah Carey or a Gloria Estefan.

But Wynonna herself has seemingly changed little from the days when she shared the spotlight with her mother, Naomi (who has since written songs for her daughter and contributed the occasional vocal harmony on Wynonna's albums). She still resides on a Nashville farm (with three horses, seven dogs and 22 cats at last count) not far from the home she used to share with Naomi. More often than not, she tools around on her turquoise Harley-Davidson motorcycle or in her '57 Chevy—the same car that brought her to Music City with her mother more than a dozen years ago. And she's still constantly counting calories and—much like Oprah Winfrey or the late Elvis Presley—

fighting a very public battle with her weight.

In the spring of 1994, the unmarried Wynonna, at work on a third album and touring extensively, threw the country world for a loop by revealing she was pregnant and unsure if she'd marry the child's father, thus possibly preparing herself for membership, along with Tanya Tucker, in country's growing club of unwed mothers.

Ashley Judd, Wynonna's sister, though not a singer, has, in the 1990's, made a mark for herself as an actress, with a recurring role in the TV show, *Sisters*, star billing in the critically acclaimed film, *Ruby in Paradise,* and other primo Hollywood roles. (See also, The Judds.)
—B.A.

The Judds

BORN: Naomi, January 11, 1946, Ashland, Kentucky
Wynonna, May 30, 1964, Ashland, Kentucky

The Judds— Naomi and Wynonna—a vastly talented mother-daughter vocal team from Ashland, Kentucky (by way of Hollywood), deserve a lot of credit for helping usher in country music's mid-1980's New Traditionalist movement. Their recording debut came at a time when Nashville was still in a period of creative bankruptcy, hung over from the Urban Cowboy era when the country-pop plasticity of "Leisure Suit Age" crooners like Kenny Rogers, John Denver and Olivia Newton-John ruled the roost.

The Judds' secret—if there was one—was their utterly natural ability to combine the Appalachian authenticity of duet teams of yesteryear like The Delmore Brothers and The Boswell Sisters with the cosmopolitan panache and fluidity of a pop harmony combo like The Andrews Sisters. Their organic harmonies also rose from the stylistic tension between Naomi, who had grown up in northeastern Kentucky under the influence of their heroes of bluegrass and mountain music, and Wynonna, who spent a lot of her formative years in California grooving to the more contemporary sounds of Bonnie Raitt, Joni Mitchell and Linda Ronstadt. (These influences would became far more apparent once Wynonna embarked on a gloriously successful solo career in the early 1990's.)

Naomi Judd was born Diana Ellen Judd; her daughter Wynonna was born Christina Ciminella. They began perfecting their harmonies years before they ever set foot on Music Row in search of a deal. They

started out singing around the kitchen table and on the back porch, often practicing with a rinky-dink little K-Mart tape recorder. So when they did start making the rounds in Nashville, they already had a pretty good idea of the sound they were after.

"I was looking for a producer who could develop the unique sound we had in our hearts and minds," Naomi recalled in a 1984 interview with *Country Music Magazine*. "We wanted to make sure that nobody messed with our sound. We needed somebody who realized that our voices were the main instruments, and that all the rest was just decoration."

They found what they were looking for in producer Brent Maher and guitarist/session leader Don Potter. With their help The Judds were able to preserve their natural vocal magic amidst the often daunting setting of studio technology. Frequently this was accomplished by using all-acoustic, or nearly all-acoustic, arrangements.

The Judds were soon riding high with early hits like "Had a Dream (For the Heart)," "Why Not Me," "Grandpa (Tell Me 'Bout the Good Old Days)" and "Rockin' with the Rhythm of the Rain." Their reign in the charts lasted for nearly eight platinum-studded years, until 1990, when Naomi was sidelined with a serious liver ailment and Wynonna forged ahead with a solo career. Though their duet sound became a bit more stylized (their later hits, like "Love Can Build a Bridge," featured far more sophisticated arrangements) and their stage show became increasingly glitzy as time went on, they never completely lost the innocence and soulful effervescence that had been the key to their success at the outset, and had made them such sentimental favorites with country fans. Ashley Judd, Naomi's other daughter and Wynonna's younger sister, has also recently made a mark as an actress—most notably in the film *Ruby in Paradise* and in NBC-TV's *Sisters*. (See also, Wynonna Judd.) —B.A.

Karl and Harty

BORN: Karl, December 17, 1905, Mt. Vernon, Kentucky
Harty, April 11, 1905, Mt. Vernon, Kentucky
DIED: Harty, October 18, 1963
Karl, May 30, 1975

Though they were not really brothers, the close harmony duet singing of Karl Davis and Hartford Taylor in many ways helped define the genre of "brother"

duet singing of the 1930's and 1940's. Born in Mt. Vernon, Kentucky, near Renfro Valley (Karl on December 17, 1905, Harty on April 11, 1905), the pair were childhood friends who learned traditional songs from singers in the rugged eastern Kentucky foothills. In the late 1920's, together with a number of other local musicians, they were coaxed by John Lair into coming to Chicago, where they appeared on the WLS *National Barn Dance* as part of The Cumberland Ridge Runners, a band that included Lair, Red Foley, Slim Miller, Hugh Cross and Linda Parker. They became immensely popular over the air, and in 1934 recorded what would be their signature song, "I'm Here to Get My Baby Out of Jail." Throughout the 1930's the pair made a long series of records for ARC (later Columbia) that included "Prisoner's Dream," "I Need the Prayers of Those I Love" and, in 1941, their most enduring original song, "Kentucky." In 1937 they moved from WLS over to rival WJJD's *Suppertime Frolic*, where they continued to hold forth until the 1950's. Harty died in 1963, while Karl lived on into the 1970's. —C.W.

Toby Keith

BORN: July 8, 1961
BIRTHPLACE: Clinton, Oklahoma

When Toby Keith's debut single, "Should've Been a Cowboy," made it to Number One, and became an anthem for the NFL's Dallas Cowboys, a circle was completed: Keith actually was a professional football player (as well as a rodeo hand and an oil field worker) before embarking on a music career. But music was his calling, and he and his band, Easy Money, made a living for more than five years on the Western club circuit before Nashville came calling in 1992. And Keith was ready with, as one *Country Music Magazine* writer put it, a batch of "stylistically wide-ranging, sometimes pop-inflected original songs." His debut album on Mercury Records yielded four Top Ten singles in the neo-honky tonk vein. In mid-1994, Mercury/PolyGram, moved Keith over to sister label, Polydor.   —G.F.

The Kendalls

BORN: Royce, September 25, 1934, St. Louis, Missouri
      Jeannie, November 30, 1954, St. Louis, Missouri

Born in Missouri on September 25, 1934, Royce Kendall grew up playing guitar and singing with his brother Floyce. He and Floyce pursued a desultory musical career that included some television work, calling themselves "The Austin Brothers." Royce also worked with Hank Cochran in the late 1950's. He never considered music a serious career until he began singing for fun with his teenaged daughter, Jeannie (born November 30, 1954, also in St. Louis), in the 1960's. In 1969, when she was 15, they did a demo recording in Nashville that impressed steel guitarist-producer Pete Drake. The Kendalls were signed to Drake's Stop label and had a minor hit with the pop-folk tune, "Leaving on a Jet Plane." Success with Dot Records and United Artists in the early 70's was only minor; then in 1977 their close harmony version of the honky tonk number, "Heaven's Just a Sin Away," went to Number One for four weeks...the start of a roll of hits like "It Don't Feel Like Sinnin' to Me," "Pittsburgh Stealers," "Sweet Desire," also a Number One record, and "I Had a Lovely Time." In the early 80's they continued to do well with "You'd Make an Angel Wanna Cheat," "I'm Already Blue" and Dolly Parton's "Put It Off Until Tomorrow."

After signing with Mercury in 1981, their success continued with "Teach Me to Cheat," "If You're Waiting on Me," and their final Number One, "Thank God for the Radio," in 1984. After that they began to chart lower, and they accomplished little with MCA/Curb in the mid-80's, with Step One in the late 80's, or with Epic after that.   —R.K.

The Kentucky Colonels

Despite the name, The Kentucky Colonels was actually a California bluegrass band formed in the mid-50's by three young brothers from Maine. Originally known as The Country Boys, the group consisted of Roland White on mandolin, Clarence White (1944-1973) on guitar and Eric White Jr. on tenor banjo and bass; their father and sister occasionally played with them. In 1958 the brothers adopted a full bluegrass sound after hiring banjo player Billy Ray Latham. The following year The Country Boys were booked at the Ash Grove, a Los Angeles folk club, and appeared several times on Cliffie Stone's famed West Coast TV show, *Town Hall Party*. Dobroist Leroy Mack joined in 1960, and Roger Bush replaced Eric White in 1961. About this time the band recorded for Capitol with Andy Griffith; they also appeared on his popular CBS-TV show. When Roland was drafted, Clarence began filling in the band's instrumental sound with an astounding lead guitar style that seemed to defy conventional space and time.

With the release of their first album in 1962, The Country Boys adopted the name "The Kentucky Colonels" to avoid confusion with Mac Wiseman's backup band. The group added fiddler Bobby Slone in 1963 and, after Roland's return, began a tour of Midwestern and East Coast folk clubs. The following year they played the Newport Folk Festival and cut an influential instrumental album, *Appalachian Swing*, for World Pacific. The band hit a creative peak in 1965 when Scotty Stoneman replaced Slone. Unfortunately, jobs began drying up as the folk boom faded; the group formally disbanded later that year. Clarence assembled former members and other musicians for occasional Kentucky Colonels jobs through 1967.   —D.S.

The Kentucky HeadHunters

"We're a blues band that grew up on Southern rock and somehow slipped through the cracks and ended up as the band of the year," Kentucky HeadHunters rhythm guitarist Richard Young once confided to *Country Music Magazine* after the band won a prestigious Country Music Association award. "I dunno how it happened, I'm just sure as hell glad it did," he commented.

The Kentucky HeadHunters, a ragged-looking, wild-haired band of veteran Southern rockers with a blues-country disposition, came storming out of south-central Kentucky and through Nashville's back door with their surprise million-selling 1989 album, *Pickin' on Nashville*, most of which they'd recorded themselves, with $4500 in borrowed money, before they even had a label deal. Around that same time, of course, other left-of-center artists like Lyle Lovett, Steve Earle and Nanci Griffith were also making a mark in the country scene. It was an all-too-brief era marked by an open door policy of risk-taking and experimentation by the major labels—the right time for The HeadHunters.

The Kentucky HeadHunters' musical specialty was their canny but quite natural fusion of boondock rock & raunch, blues swagger, country sentimentality and low-brow camp. They struck Gold—and platinum at least once—by revving up country oldies by folks like Bill Monroe, Waylon Jennings and Carl Perkins with a driving Southern rock back beat and brash electrification. They rounded their repertoire out with their own high-spirited, often tongue-in-cheek, original songs written in a characteristically irreverent vein.

Looking back, the fact that The HeadHunters were twice recipients of the Country Music Association's Group of the Year award (1990 and 1991), yet just two years later were without a real label deal, tells us less about the band's staying power or lack of it than it does about the fickleness of a younger generation of country fans and the radical swing back toward conformity and predictability that country radio and the record industry has taken since the late 1980's.

To wit: By the time The HeadHunters released their second album, *Electric Barnyard* (1991), they were already paying the price for their uncouth originality in the form of a backlash from country radio. The arguments for pulling the plug on airplay for the band revolved around their warm-hearted but irreverent novelty remake of "The Ballad of Davy Crockett." The forces at country radio deemed the record too controversial. Thus the welcome mat that greeted The HeadHunters during the late 80's stylistic free-for-all turned into a slamming door in the utter conformist atmosphere of the early 90's.

The pressure proved a bit much for the band.

In 1992, brothers Ricky Lee and Doug Phelps, the lead singer and bass player, respectively, left to pursue a solo career. Their first solo album, *Let Go* (1993), under the name Brother Phelps, received generally warm reviews and revealed a brotherly flair for harmony that somehow had gone unnoticed in the high-decibel HeadHunters musical mix.

But the HeadHunters' founding members—brothers Richard and Fred Young and their first cousin, guitarist extraordinaire Greg Martin—quickly regrouped. All of them hailed from around Edmundton, Kentucky, and had grown up playing in bands together; one ensemble had been called Itchy Brother. They added another cousin, former Itchy Brother bass player Anthony Kenney, and lead singer Mark S. Orr, a longtime friend and Itchy Brother alum, and re-emerged with a new, improved, and slightly more blues-oriented sound. As the 90's progress, The HeadHunters were still out there burning up the concert circuit and had found a new niche for themselves in the blues and R&B charts, having recorded a straight-ahead blues album with former Chuck Berry piano player, Johnnie Johnson. —B.A.

197

Doug Kershaw

BORN: January 24, 1936
BIRTHPLACE: Tiel Ridge, Louisiana

The best-known half of the Cajun team of Rusty
and Doug, Doug Kershaw's flashy fiddling style,
competent vocals and onstage flamboyance made
him a hit with rock audiences in the 1970's and
one of a handful of Cajun artists to enjoy success
in the country mainstream over the years. His first
successes came locally, in the Louisiana area. He
backed his mother, Rita Kershaw, and by 1948 he
and younger brother Rusty were leading The Continental Playboys, along with a third brother, Pee
Wee. They hosted their own TV show in Lake
Charles in 1953 and began recording for the local
Feature label. By the mid-50's they'd signed with
Wesley Rose's Hickory label. In 1955 Rusty and
Doug had their first hit with "So Lovely Baby";
they hit again in 1957 with "Love Me to Pieces."
Their most successful record was their version of
Doug's composition, "Louisiana Man," in 1961, a
song that's since become a Cajun and country stan-
dard. After the duo separated in 1964, Doug re-
corded for various labels before catching on at
Warner Bros. in the late 60's. Though he never
sold many records, and though his solo work was
seldom as inspired as the records he made with
Rusty, he was a popular and flamboyant live act.
He appeared on the *Louisiana Hayride* and was a
member of the Grand Ole Opry for a while. He
has continued recording sporadically, his most
recent chart entries being a 1988 duet with Hank
Williams Jr., and a 1989 solo single.   —R.K.

Sammy Kershaw

BORN: February 24, 1958
BIRTHPLACE: Kaplan, Louisiana

There's hardly a country singer on the face of the
earth who doesn't bear at least some trace of the
George Jones influence. But Louisiana-born Sammy
Kershaw sounds so much like Jones, it's uncanny.
Only part of the similarity can be traced back to
the early 80's when Kershaw was an occasional
Jones protégé of sorts. "When I was five, my mama
got her first George Jones record," he recalled. "I
remember a little later I heard 'Things Have Gone
to Pieces,' an old Jones hit. My mother bought the
record, and I used to sit in the living room by
myself and just play that song over and over. I've
been hooked ever since."

Born in Kaplan, Louisiana, Kershaw began singing in local clubs when he was 12. He kept on
playing all through his 20's, while occasionally
making ends meet in a variety of day jobs, including DJ, rice mill worker, dry cleaning manager,
carpenter and stand-up comedian. It was only after years of near-misses in the music business that
Kershaw finally hooked up with Mercury Records
in Nashville in the early 1990's. (At the time, he
was working as a contractor, building Wal-Mart
stores all through the South.) His debut 1991 album, *Don't Go Near the Water*, with its bedrock
Jones-style hard country appeal, mixed with
Kershaw's own quirky musical disposition (captured vividly in the smash hit, "Cadillac Style"),

made Kershaw an instant favorite with conservative country audiences. With *Haunted Heart*, his second album (which, like his first, was certified Gold), Kershaw stepped out a little from the George Jones shadow with his own stylistic nuances, scoring a Number One hit with "She Don't Know She's Beautiful," and several other Top Tens.

"I can't sing a song unless I've lived it, and at one time or another I've lived 'em all," Kershaw once noted of his musical style and his years of personal storms. His third album, *Feelin' Good Train*, was released in 1994, featuring Kershaw in a slightly more obvious blues and R&B vein. —B.A.

Clark Kessinger

BORN: July 27, 1896
BIRTHPLACE: South Hills, West Virginia
DIED: June 4, 1975

Clark Kessinger was probably the most technically proficient country fiddler to record during the late 1920's. Kessinger's skill, timing and precision led many listeners to believe he was classically trained; he actually was self-taught.

Kessinger was born July 27, 1896, in West Virginia. He began playing fiddle at age five. An early influence was Ed Haley, a blind musician noted for his smooth, long-bow approach; Kessinger also listened to records by Fritz Kreisler and other classical violinists. In 1919 he teamed up with his guitarist nephew, Luches Kessinger, to play dances in the Charleston, West Virginia, area. Between 1928 and 1930 the duo made 35 records for Brunswick as The Kessinger Brothers; in the late 30's they appeared at the National Folk Festival in Washington, D.C. Kessinger cut back on personal appearances after Luches' death in 1943.

In 1964 Kessinger was playing local dances and competing at fiddlers' conventions when Ken Davidson recorded him on his small Folk Promotions label. The resulting album, *The Legend of Clark Kessinger*, is considered a classic American fiddle album. Appearances on NBC-TV's *Today*, CBS-TV's *To Tell the Truth* and the Grand Ole Opry, along with major folk festivals, soon followed. In July 1971 Kessinger suffered a stroke and never regained his dexterity. He died June 4, 1975, in St. Albans, West Virginia. —D.S.

Hal Ketchum

BORN: April 9, 1953
BIRTHPLACE: Greenwich, New York

If each of the many new artists who have arrived on the country scene in the early 90's were to be typecast, Hal Ketchum's role would be that of the "Thinking Woman's Heartthrob." Handsomely graying and given to writing introspective, sensual ballads which he serves up in a smoldering, new-age, Texas folk-country style, Ketchum is one of the more recent "graduates" of the Texas school of folk-country song poets. His debut 1991 album on Curb, *Past the Point of Rescue*, added a

compelling, slightly dark and artsy tone to the contemporary country scene.

Ketchum cemented his popularity with a string of Top Ten hits from that album: "Smalltown Saturday Night" (which hit Number Two in 1991), "I Know Where Love Lives," "Five O'Clock World" (a remake of the old Jay & The Americans Top 40 pop hit), and the haunting title song, "Past the Point of Rescue," which got to Number Two in 1992. *Sure Love*, Ketchum's 1992 album, enlarged upon his popularity, with three more Top Tens: the title track, "Hearts Are Gonna Roll" and "Mama Knows the Highway." In 1994, he was made a member of the Grand Ole Opry and his *Every Little Word* album was released. Ketchum was born in Greenwich, New York, in 1953, and almost accidentally fell into the Texas singer/songwriters' scene around historic Gruene, Texas, when he moved from New England to the Lone Star State in the early 80's, in search of carpentry work and a warmer climate. —B.A.

Merle Kilgore

BORN: September 8, 1934
BIRTHPLACE: Chickasha, Oklahoma

Raised in Shreveport, Louisiana, Merle Kilgore first entered the music business as a DJ on Shreveport's KENT Radio, in 1950. As an aspiring recording artist, Kilgore made appearances on both the Grand Ole Opry and the *Louisiana Hayride* in the 1950's. On the *Hayride*, he was drawn to the legendary Hank Williams and enjoyed a brief association with him. During the later 1950's and the 1960's, Kilgore earned prominence as a country songwriter with classic titles like "Wolverton Mountain" (a big hit for Claude King), "Johnny Reb" (a hit for Johnny Horton) and "Ring of Fire" (immortalized by Johnny Cash). He also made appearances in several Hollywood feature films.

As a recording artist, Kilgore had a few sporadic showings between 1960 and the early 1990's. His only Top Ten single, "Love Has Made You Beautiful," came in 1960; one of his most fascinating chart outings was with an intriguing song called "Mr. Garfield" (1982), which featured supporting vocals from his friends, Johnny Cash and Hank Williams Jr. After serving as Hank Jr.'s warm-up act for years, Kilgore was promoted to the post of Hank's personal manager.   —B.A.

Bradley Kincaid

BORN: July 13, 1895
BIRTHPLACE: Lancaster, Kentucky
DIED: September 23, 1989

Bradley Kincaid, The Kentucky Mountain Boy, was never a country star in the traditional sense of the word. His ties were to the folk ballads of earlier centuries and to Tin Pan Alley numbers of his own era which he interpreted and enlivened with his clear tenor. He studied traditional Appalachian ballads while attending Berea College in Kentucky, then moved to Chicago in the 1920's with his wife. She worked for the YMCA; Kincaid enrolled in the YMCA College (later George Williams College) at night, and auditioned for WLS Radio. He joined their *Chicago Barn Dance* (later the *National Barn Dance*) where his popularity was such that during the four years he was there (during the late 1920's), he received more than 100,000 fan letters a year. He began recording in 1928, the year he graduated from college. Many of his recordings appeared under pseudonyms. During the 1930's he continued recording and worked one-year stints at a number of different radio stations. While at WBZ in Boston, he worked with a young man named Louis Marshall Jones. Kincaid gave Jones his famous "Grandpa" stage personality and a pair of 100-year-old leather boots. Kincaid worked briefly at WLW's *Boone County Jamboree* in the 1940's and at the Grand Ole Opry. He owned a radio station in Springfield, Ohio, for a time and continued

to record into the 70's; he later owned a music store. He still performed, until seriously injured in an automobile accident. He died in 1989. —R.K.

Claude King

BORN: February 5, 1932
BIRTHPLACE: Shreveport, Louisiana

Louisiana-born Claude King took up the guitar at age 12, and was soon playing music with his lifelong friend, Buddy Attaway, in the Shreveport area. After serving in the Navy from 1942 to '46, he and Attaway recorded for the tiny President label in 1947. In 1948 they joined KWKH's *Louisiana Hayride* in Shreveport and recorded for Webb Pierce's Pacemaker label.

In the 50's, King recorded solo for the Specialty and Dee-Jay labels before signing with Columbia in 1961. "Big River, Big Man" and "The Comancheros" were Top Ten records that year, followed by the 1962 smash hit, "Wolverton Mountain," which stayed nine weeks at Number One and became a Top Ten pop record as well.

His Civil War song, "The Burning of Atlanta," made the Top Ten that fall. In 1965 he had another big hit with "Tiger Woman" and in 1969 scored again with a remake of his late friend Johnny Horton's "All for the Love of a Girl." By 1972 he'd left Columbia. Later records for small labels went nowhere, and King eventually retired from music. —R.K.

Pee Wee King

BORN: February 18, 1914
BIRTHPLACE: Abrams, Wisconsin

Frank Anthony Kuczynski was encouraged to be a musician by his father, who led a local polka band in dairy country in Wisconsin. Frank learned to play

the accordion and around 1933 joined the cast of Milwaukee's WRJN *Badger State Barn Dance* and formed his own band. Gene Autry, then a star of the WLS *National Barn Dance*, heard the group and asked them to back him in Chicago. Autry gave Kuczynski, who was five-foot-seven, the name "Pee Wee"; the "King" part came from saxophonist Wayne King, popular in the 1930's. Pee Wee and his boys went with Autry to WHAS in Louisville, Kentucky, in 1934. Autry didn't last long; within eight months he was off to Hollywood. Pee Wee worked briefly with a local Kentucky band, Frankie More's Log Cabin Boys, then formed his own group in 1936. In tribute to The Girls of the Golden West, he called them "The Golden West Cowboys," and set about developing their sound, a blend of Autry-style Western music and the sophisticated string band sounds of groups like Clayton McMichen's Georgia Wildcats and Louise Massey and The Westerners. In 1937, they joined the Opry, bringing a hard-driving professionalism and sense of the showy to that staid, still largely local show. J.L. Frank, the pioneer country music promoter, was Pee Wee's father-in-law. The two of them did much to revolutionize and upgrade the presentation of country music in the late 30's and 40's. (Among other things, Frank designed Pee

Wee's promotional posters—they were striking.)

The band left the Opry briefly, but returned by the early 40's, now featuring singer Eddy Arnold and fiddler Redd Stewart. In the early years of World War II, Pee Wee King and The Golden West Cowboys toured military bases in the U.S. as part of the hugely successful Camel Caravan. When Arnold left the band in 1944, Cowboy Copas replaced him, before he too went out on his own (and Stewart began handling most vocals). Pee Wee began recording for RCA in 1946, the year he and Stewart wrote lyrics to an instrumental waltz they had been playing since 1941. The song became "The Tennessee Waltz," a country and pop standard that is now the official state song of Tennessee. Pee Wee and Redd recorded it in December 1947; it was a hit record for them in 1948. When Patti Page recorded it in 1950, she had one of the biggest hits of the decade. Other hits for King and his band included "Tennessee Polka" (1949), "Bonaparte's Retreat" (1950) and, in 1951, their biggest, "Slow Poke," which remained at Number One for 15 weeks.

In 1948, King returned to Louisville, drawn away from the Opry by the lure of TV. From 1948 through the early 60's he hosted a variety of radio and TV shows in Louisville and elsewhere throughout the central Midwest, and continued touring until 1968. A member of the Country Music Hall of Fame since 1974, and active on various boards and committees, King, now semi-retired, performs only on special occasions. —R.K.

King Records

Before Sam Phillips ever produced a record, an asthmatic, cigar-chewing, bespectacled Cincinnatian named Syd Nathan was doing what Phillips later got credit for: mixing black and white songs and styles among black and white artists. Born in 1906, Nathan worked in a number of fields, including running a used record store. With the WLW *Boone County Jamboree* in town, Nathan got to know some of the show's performers, including Grandpa Jones and Merle Travis. In September 1943, he took the two to a Dayton radio station to make the first discs for his new label, to be called King Records—"King of 'em all," said Nathan. Since WLW barred their performers from recording, Jones and Travis used pseudonyms on the

two 78 rpm discs. Two duets were released on one disc as "The Sheppard Brothers" and two Travis solo performances as "Bob McCarthy." Issued in November 1943, they were King's debut and remain among the rarest country records.

Nathan continued to push the label by signing new artists including Hank Penny, Lloyd "Cowboy" Copas, Moon Mullican, Hawkshaw Hawkins, Bill and Evalina and The Delmore Brothers. The label's first big hits came in 1946 with Copas' "Filipino Baby," The Delmores' "Freight Train Boogie" and Penny's "Steel Guitar Stomp." To take advantage of the burgeoning country scene in California, Nathan recruited Merle Travis, who'd moved to Los Angeles, as his West Coast A&R man. Travis signed a number of artists, none of them successful. In 1947 Moon Mullican's "New Pretty Blonde (Jole Blon)" became a Top Ten record, and recordings by The Delmores, Grandpa Jones and others also did well.

By the late 40's, King had become a major independent label, recording pop, country and R&B as well as gospel, with their own studio and manufacturing facility in Cincinnati. Clyde Moody, Bonnie Lou, The Bailes Brothers and Jimmie Osborne were additional King artists.

Though known for his foul temper, iron-clad contracts, hassles over song publishing and disputes with the Musicians' Union, Nathan had a true pioneering spirit, which led him, in 1949, to hire black musician Henry Glover as a producer. Glover worked routinely with white country artists, including Moon Mullican and The Delmore Brothers; he played a major role in creating and producing The Delmores' 1949 hit, "Blues Stay Away from Me." Nathan and Glover had Wynonie Harris cover Hank Penny's country hit ,"Bloodshot Eyes," giving Harris a huge R&B hit. Such crossovers became common at King. In the 50's, the label's rhythm and blues and rock successes surpassed their country hits, though King still recorded such bluegrass legends as The Stanley Brothers and Reno and Smiley. In the early 60's two veteran artists who had left King returned to give it its last major country hits: Cowboy Copas had "Alabam'" with them in 1962; Hawkshaw Hawkins had "Lonesome 7-7203" in 1963. But King's biggest artist became R&B legend James Brown. After Nathan died of heart disease in 1968, Nashville's Starday Records acquired the business. In the 70's, both Starday and King were acquired by Nashville's Gusto Records, now known as IMG (International Marketing Group). —R.K.

Pete "Oswald" Kirby

BORN: December 26, 1911
BIRTHPLACE: Sevierville, Tennessee

Pete "Oswald" Kirby (real name Beecher) was a guitarist, banjoist and dobro player who rode to fame as Bashful Brother Oswald of Roy Acuff's legendary Crazy Tennesseans.

One of ten musically inclined children, Kirby grew up in Sevier County, Tennessee.

His earliest musical influence was his father, who was proficient on guitar, fiddle and banjo.

As a young man, Kirby worked in a sawmill and cotton mill before moving to Chicago to take a stab at a music career.

While in Chicago, he played guitar in a number of beer joints at night, and during the day worked in a restaurant part time.

In the early 1940's he moved back to Tennessee, establishing himself in Knoxville, where he hooked up with Acuff and subsequently joined his Crazy Tennesseans on radio station WRL. While with Acuff he became known as Bashful Brother Oswald, and usually appeared on stage in bib overalls.

Although having earned his keep as a skilled guitarist, Kirby became well known for his exceptional dobro playing during his stint with Acuff.

In 1971 he appeared on The Nitty Gritty Dirt Band's masterpiece album, *Will the Circle be Unbroken.*

During the 1970's Kirby put out a series of critically-acclaimed solo recordings for Rounder Records, including *Don't Say Aloha* and *That's Country,* the latter with fellow Smoky Mountain Boy Charlie Collins. In 1994 he published his autobiography, and, even after Acuff's death, continued to perform at the Opry.   —R.P.

Eddie Kirk

BORN: March 21, 1919
BIRTHPLACE: Greeley, Colorado

Born in Colorado in 1919, this smooth-voiced ballad singer—a boxer earlier in his life—was a veteran of the early California country music scene, first as a part of the band, The Beverly Hillbillies, and then for a time with Gene Autry. After World War II he joined Capitol Records and became a regular member of Cliffie Stone's organization, which developed into the *Hometown Jamboree,* a popular West Coast radio and TV show.

Though popular on the show and a sought-after rhythm guitarist on recording sessions, Kirk's solo success on Capitol was minimal. His smoother style was much in the mold of Eddy Arnold. His only big hits included "The Gods Were Angry" in 1948, and a cover of George Morgan's "Candy Kisses" in 1949.   —R.K.

Alison Krauss

BORN: July 23, 1971
BIRTHPLACE: Decatur, Illinois

In addition to possessing a heavenly vibrato, this contemporary bluegrass vocalist is also one fine fiddle player. Alison Krauss was born on July 23, 1971, and grew up in Champaign, Illinois, where her parents encouraged her to play an instrument.

At five, young Alison took a liking to the violin, and within a few years she began taking away armloads of prizes at Midwestern fiddle contests. At 14, Rounder Records owner Ken Irwin heard a tape and was stunned by her sweet and smooth voice, as well as her virtuoso fiddle playing.

Krauss made a huge splash at the prestigious Newport Folk Festival, and, in 1987, she recorded her first album for Rounder, *Too Late to Cry.* It featured some top-notch bluegrass session players, including Sam Bush on mandolin and Jerry Douglas on dobro, and subsequently won rave reviews. Krauss' follow-up album, *Two Highways*, introduced her band Union Station, and again demonstrated her uncanny knack for making traditional bluegrass seem utterly contemporary.

The year 1992 was a banner one for Krauss. In addition to releasing *Every Time You Say Goodbye*, which further showcased her mellifluous vocals and Union Station's stellar musicianship, Krauss became a member of the Grand Ole Opry. At the ripe young age of 21, she was the first bluegrass artist in 19 years to be inducted into the Opry. Krauss' honeyed voice has also graced recordings by Dolly Parton, Vince Gill, Mark Chesnutt, Lionel Cartwright, Patty Loveless, Nanci Griffith, Michael McDonald, Michelle Shocked and The Desert Rose Band. In 1993 Krauss produced an album, teaming her with the gospel-singing Cox Family. —R.P.

Kris Kristofferson

BORN: June 22, 1936
BIRTHPLACE: Brownsville, Texas

There was a brief season, back in the late 1960's and early 70's, when the country singer/songwriter was king on Music Row. This was the era when starkly original grassroots musical poets like Tom T. Hall, Billy Joe Shaver and country-folkies John Prine and James Talley injected the music with the sort of informed irony, pointed social commentary and political consciousness that is, for the most part, painfully missing today.

Kris Kristofferson, more than any one single writer, came to personify this golden age of the country lyric. His best and most memorable songs—"Help Me Make It Through the Night," "Lovin' Her Was Easier," "Sunday Mornin' Comin' Down," "For the Good Times," "Me and Bobby McGee"—combined the melodic simplicity of 50's and 60's country with the ethereal, darkly romantic vernacular of impressionistic poetry. Along the way, Kristofferson also imbued country with a fresh dimension of individual expression and sexual candor that was unusual for the times.

Not surprisingly, Kristofferson's colorful personal background was a far cry from the traditional "up-to-Nashville-from-the-barn-dance" biographies of so

many of his predecessors. Born in Brownsville, Texas, June 22, 1936, Kristofferson was an Army brat, the son of a two-star Army general.

He graduated from Pomona College, a liberal arts institution in Southern California, and later attended Oxford University in England as a Rhodes Scholar. Along the way, he was a Golden Gloves amateur boxer, an Army captain and helicopter pilot and an aspiring novelist.

Stationed in the Army in Germany in the early 1960's, Kristofferson became so disillusioned with the military life there that he volunteered for a tour of duty in Vietnam. Instead, he ended up as a candidate to teach English at West Point.

Back in the States, though, he bailed out of the service and opted instead for a crash course in country music songwriting in Nashville, where he endured six starvation years on Music Row, barely making ends meet as a bartender, construction worker and janitor at Columbia recording studios. It was at Columbia that he met Johnny Cash, who would later become one of dozens of leading country artists to storm the charts with Kristofferson compositions.

Due to his gruff singing style (more talking than singing, actually), Kristofferson never made much headway as a recording artist in his own right in the country charts; yet his albums sold well with the 70's college/post-Woodstock crowd. Kristofferson came to their attention in a blitz of media fascination that arose from his unusual background as an Oxford-educated hillbilly songwriter.

In the mid-70's he became a sort of fellow traveler in the Willie Nelson/Waylon Jennings-inspired Outlaw movement, appearing regularly at the Willie Nelson Picnic. Kristofferson's brooding, charismatically handsome looks and his macho-intellectual persona—along with his starkly original songs—coupled with the media's fascination with his background—earned him a berth as a popular performer throughout the decade. (He frequently toured with his then-wife, singer Rita Coolidge.)

Kristofferson's stage presence also led to an uneven career as a film star. (He still pops up in the occasional made-for-cable movie opus or Willie Nelson celluloid caper.) He starred in more than a dozen films, including *A Star Is Born* (in which he co-starred with Barbra Streisand), *Alice Doesn't Live Here Anymore, The Sailor Who Fell from Grace with the Sea, Heaven's Gate, Pat Garrett and Billy The Kid* (with Bob Dylan), *Cisco Pike, Rollover* and *The Songwriter* (with Willie Nelson).

Though Kristofferson has continued to record sporadically in the years since his 1969 debut on Monument Records, he never managed to recapture the sheer breathtaking poetry of his earliest compositions. In fact, it seems like the bloom started falling off his songwriting once he escaped the constraints of the hard times and despair that inspired so many of those earlier compositions; they are the pedestal upon which his reputation rests. In the 80's and early 90's he recorded and toured as a member of The Highwaymen, with Willie, Waylon and Johnny Cash, and has remained active in political and humanitarian causes. His 1990 *Third World Warrior* album took on such unlikely topics as U.S. involvement in El Salvador   —B.A.

Sleepy LaBeef

BORN: July 20, 1935
BIRTHPLACE: Smackover, Arkansas

Few rockabillies better exemplify the music's wild and varied roots than Thomas Pausley LaBeff, better known as the deep voiced rocker "Sleepy LaBeef." Sleepy became a minor-league rockabilly favorite in the 1950's. Some of his early musical activities as a teenager were in Smackover's Holiness Church. He also found inspiration in the intense singing and guitar work of black gospel singer Sister Rosetta Tharpe. In 1953 he began working in Beaumont as a gospel sideman and then moved to the *Houston Jamboree*, a barn dance show. As rockabilly began to spread throughout the South via Elvis, LaBeef moved into that field. He recorded for Starday in 1956, with little success. LaBeef recorded country and rock for a variety of labels, having two minor chart hits with "Every Day" on Columbia in 1968 and "Blackland Farmer" in 1975. But the revived interest in rockabilly and LaBeef's love of performing kept him going. Peter Guralnick profiled him in his book *Lost Highway*. LaBeef, based in New England, signed with Rounder Records in 1979. He continues touring in the U.S. and Europe, and, in 1994, Guralnick and his son Jake produced the rocking *Strange Things Happening* album for Rounder.   —R.K.

k.d. lang

BORN: November 2, 1961
BIRTHPLACE: Consort, Alberta, Canada

"Torch-and-twang" balladeer k.d. lang was born in the little town of Consort, Alberta, Canada, on November 2, 1961. While growing up, k.d. (real name Kathy Dawn) took an instant liking to music, especially country music. At seven she started taking pi-

and Roger Miller's "Lock, Stock and Teardrops." The following year, she released *Absolute Torch and Twang*, which went platinum, and picked up a Grammy for Best Country Vocal Performance Female.

She was featured in the Canadian art house film *Salmonberries*, and, in 1990, she caused controversy among cattle ranchers and the beef industry when—as a vegetarian—she publicly denounced meat eating. In addition, she came out of the closet and openly declared that she was a lesbian.

In 1992 lang released *Ingenue*, a torchy pop album done with her longtime co-writer and co-producer Ben Mink. It won commercial and critical acclaim, achieved platinum sales and yielded the hit, "Constant Craving." In 1993 she was involved in the soundtrack to the Gus Van Zant film, *Even Cowgirls Get the Blues.*   —R.P.

Don Law

BORN: February 24, 1902
BIRTHPLACE: London, England
DIED: December 20, 1982

This pioneering country producer and Nashville Sound pioneer was born in London, England, in 1902. He was a member of the London Choral Society and worked in Poland as a cashier for a timber company before emigrating to the U.S. in 1924. Once in the States, Law sold etchings in New York and even tried his hand as a farmer in Alabama before entering the music business as a bookkeeper for Brunswick Records in Dallas. Law was working with Columbia Records under fellow Englishman Art Satherley recording country and blues music throughout the South. Satherley, with Law's assistance, built a country roster at Columbia that was second to none. Satherley retired from Columbia in the early 50's and Law took over, strengthening Columbia's already-strong country presence. He was not among the producers who initially favored Nashville. For several years he concentrated Columbia's recording activities at the Jim Beck Studio in Dallas. Among those he brought to the label were Ray Price, Johnny Cash, Flatt & Scruggs, Lefty Frizzell, Johnny Horton, Carl and Pearl Butler and others. After Beck's death, Law began recording extensively in Nashville, and became a major player in the development of the more neutral Nashville Sound which resulted in various coun-

ano lessons, and by 10 she had moved on to the guitar. As a teenager lang began writing songs, and in 1983 she formed a band called The Reclines in deference to country legend Patsy Cline, one of her idols. The band earned a cult-like following in Alberta, and, in 1984, they released an album on the independent Bumstead label titled *A Truly Western Experience*, which caught the attention of Sire Records and led to a recording contract with the label.

Lang's 1987 Sire debut, the country-rocking ("cowpunk") *Angel with a Lariat*, was produced by British pub-rocker Dave Edmunds and won a number of rave reviews. That same year, she hit the country charts with a moving duet with Roy Orbison on a remake of his "Crying." For her next release, lang coaxed veteran producer Owen Bradley to come out of retirement and work the boards. The result was *Shadowland*, a potpourri of musical styles ranging from rockabilly, country and Nashville Sound pop to big band. The record featured an all-star lineup of Bradley-produced legends—Kitty Wells, Loretta Lynn and Brenda Lee—on "The Honky Tonk Angels Medley." In 1988 lang hit the country charts again with Harlan Howard's "I'm Down to My Last Cigarette" try records achieving pop success. He extensively used the Bradley Recording studio on 16th Avenue South, which Columbia purchased in 1962. From the mid-to-late 60's until his retirement, Frank Jones was his assistant. By the early 70's, Billy Sherrill epitomized the next generation of Columbia producers. Law, who has been frequently nominated but not yet elected to the Country Music Hall of Fame, died in 1982. (See also, Art Satherley.)　　　—R.K.

Tracy Lawrence

BORN: January 27, 1968
BIRTHPLACE: Atlanta, Texas

Tracy Lawrence's rural Arkansas tenor established him as one of the leading purveyors of honky tonk balladry during the early 1990's. Born in Atlanta, Texas, on January 27, 1968, Lawrence and his family moved to Foreman, Arkansas, when he was four. He sang at church, studied guitar and was playing in jamborees by the time he was 15. Two years later he began playing the honky tonk circuit around Louisiana, Arkansas, Texas and Oklahoma with various bands. He moved to Nashville in 1990, entered and won a number of singing contests and landed a regular spot on *Live at Libby's*, a Nashville radio show. Within seven months, Lawrence had a record deal with Atlantic.

But in May 1991, right after completing his major label album, Lawrence stepped into the middle of an armed robbery attempt and was shot four times. Atlantic held up the album's release while he recuperated. Five months later, when Lawrence returned and the record was finally released, his career skyrocketed. The album, *Sticks and Stones*, sold more than 800,000 copies. The title track became a Number One single, followed by two more Number Ones: "Today's Lonely Fool" and "Runnin' Behind." Lawrence's follow-up album, *Alibis*, proved to be just as successful as the first. In 1993 Lawrence won the Academy of Country Music's New Male Vocalist award.　　—R.P.

Chris LeDoux

BORN: October 2, 1948
BIRTHPLACE: Biloxi, Mississippi

After years of a hand-to-mouth existence singing on the rodeo circuit, Chris LeDoux is well on his way to becoming the most popular singing cowboy of the 1990's. His success is well measured with hits like "Cadillac Ranch," "Under This Old Hat" and "What'cha Gonna Do With a Cowboy"—the latter a duet recorded with his friend and chief supporter, Garth Brooks, which hit Number Seven in 1992.

LeDoux was born in Biloxi, Mississippi, in 1948, but moved with his family to Austin, Texas, in 1960. It was in Texas that he began riding in rodeos. He was still at it in 1976, and became world bareback champion. LeDoux also studied sculpting (an avocation he still pursues) at Eastern New Mexico State University. He began his recording career in the late 1970's and early 80's, making records on small labels and peddling them at his rodeo performances.

It was with Garth Brooks' help that LeDoux finally landed a major label deal with Liberty Records a few years ago. Good things have since followed, including major award nominations from both the Country Music Association and the Academy of Country Music. His album titled *What'cha Gonna Do With a Cowboy* went Gold.　　—B.A.

Albert Lee

BORN: December 21, 1943
BIRTHPLACE: Herefordshire, England

This influential country and rock guitarist of the 1970's, best known for his work with a Fender Telecaster and similar instruments, began his career working with British rock performers like Jackie Lynton and Chris Farlowe. However, his interest in country grew when he began listening to records by the American team of guitarist Jimmy Bryant and steel player Speedy West. In the late 1960's he joined a British country band called Country Fever, before working with the rock band Heads, Hands and Feet. In the late 70's he replaced James Burton in Emmylou Harris' Hot Band and lent his Fender Telecaster to a number of songs, including her versions of "How High the Moon" and "Luxury Liner." His precise, fiery rapid-fire picking on the records of Ricky Skaggs, Rodney Crowell and others inspired an entire school of country Telecaster players. With several excellent solo albums for A&M, Polydor and MCA under his belt, Lee joined rock legend Eric Clapton's band for a time in the early 1980's. Based in California, he still does extensive recording and solo work, in addition to regular tours as The Everly Brothers' lead guitarist.   —R.K.

Brenda Lee

BORN: December 11, 1944
BIRTHPLACE: Lithonia, Georgia

Brenda Lee, born Brenda Mae Tarpley, got her career underway when she was five years old, winning a talent contest in her native state with her brassy version of "Take Me Out to the Ballgame." In 1953 her father, a carpenter, died in a freak accident (a hammer, dropped by someone working above him on a job site, hit him in the head). From then on, her remarkable voice—which led to her nickname, "Little Miss Dynamite"—became her family's ticket to survival.

By 1955, with the help of Red Foley, she appeared on the nationally televised *Ozark Jubilee*, which Foley hosted. Soon she was also booked for appearances by Steve Allen, Ed Sullivan and Perry Como on their popular musical variety shows. In 1956, Lee, at age 11, signed with Decca Records. Teamed up with producer Owen Bradley, she was soon on her way to stardom.

Depending on the perspective with which you look back on Brenda Lee's heyday in the 1960's—when she helped sing the soundtrack for the puppy love era of the early years of that decade with million-selling Nashville-produced hits like "Sweet Nothin's," "I'm Sorry," "I Want to Be Wanted," "Dum Dum," "Fool #1," "Rockin' Around the Christmas Tree," "All Alone Am I" and "Break It to Me Gently"—Brenda Lee is either one of the best women rock 'n' roll singers, or one of the best country singers, of all time. Actually, she qualifies for either category, and her music has effortlessly transcended both. In the late 60's, as pop trends changed, Brenda, now a married mother of two, cut back to spend time with her children, but continued recording. In the 1970's Lee was back on the country charts with a string of hits, including versions of Kris Kristofferson's "Nobody Wins" and Shel Silverstein's "Big Four Poster Bed." She has continued recording sporadically into the 90's (with Warner Bros.), and has sold some 100 million records worldwide. —B.A.

Dickey Lee

BORN: September 21, 1943
BIRTHPLACE: Memphis, Tennessee

Born Dickey Lipscomb, Dickey Lee began playing country music as a teenager, and first recorded for Sun Records in Memphis in 1957. But it was another five years before he came into his own as a performer and songwriter of maudlin pop-country fare.

He placed a handful of singles on the pop charts in the late 1960's, including "I Saw Linda Yesterday," "The Girl from Peyton Place" and "Patches" (a Number Six pop hit in 1962). He signed with RCA Records in 1971 and cut his debut album, *Never Ending Song of Love*, the following year.

Throughout the 1970's Lee placed at least one

song on the country charts every year. Hits like "Rocky" (a Number One song in 1975), "9,999,999 Tears" (a 1976 Top Five written by Razzy Bailey) and "Peanut Butter" (1977) helped him maintain his popularity with audiences. His original songs were recorded by both pop and country artists, including Connie Francis, George Jones and Jerry Lee Lewis. Lee and RCA parted company in the late 1970's. He signed with Mercury Records and recorded such chart singles as "Don't Look Back," "Lost in Love" and "I Wonder If I Care As Much."

When last heard from, Lee was still hard at work, cranking out future country hits. —M.B.

Johnny Lee

BORN: July 3, 1946
BIRTHPLACE: Texas City, Texas

Johnny Lee (born J. L. Hamm, in Texas City, Texas, in July 1946) grew up on a dairy farm in Alta Loma, Texas, just south of Houston. His one big claim to fame is his smash crossover hit single, "Lookin' for Love (In All the Wrong Places)," which was the theme song to the hit 1980 movie, *Urban Cowboy*.

Lee started out as a Houston area rock musician in the early 1960's, and ended up in the Navy later that decade, spending some time in Vietnam. Back in the U.S., he landed a spot in Mickey Gilley's band. Minor chart hits on GTR and ABC/Dot Records eventually earned him a promotion to Gilley's warm-up act.

After "Lookin' for Love" made Lee an *Urban Cowboy*-era cult hero, he continued touring with Gilley for several years before eventually striking out on his own. He gained a bit of further distinction by marrying TV actress Charlene Tilton, of *Dallas* fame.

Lee never came close to recapturing the across-the-board success of "Lookin' for Love." He has not been heard from in the charts or on a major label for quite some time, though he does still pop up on the touring circuit.

(See also, Gilley's and Urban Cowboy.) —B.A.

Jerry Lee Lewis

BORN: September 29, 1935
BIRTHPLACE: Ferriday, Louisiana

"The Killer," one of the founders of rockabilly and rock, whose vast repertoire has also spanned pop, country, gospel, rock and blues, owes much of his music to black blues pianists and hillbilly boogie greats Moon Mullican and Merrill Moore. Lewis grew up with his cousins, Mickey Gilley and Jimmy Swaggart, around Ferriday, Louisiana. At age nine his parents bought him a piano and he taught himself to play, inspired by the music he heard at a local black nightclub. Swaggart and Gilley also learned similar piano styles.

As a teenager, Lewis married twice, briefly studying for the ministry before a boogie version of a hymn got him expelled. Few in the music business noticed him until he went to Memphis in 1956, first impressing Sun Records producer Jack Clement, then owner Sam Phillips. His first hit single, "Whole Lotta Shakin' Goin' On," launched his career in 1957. The huge hit in both the country and rock fields was followed by another smash, "Great Balls of Fire." "Breathless" and "High School Confidential" were country and rock hits in 1958. His career faltered after his controversial third marriage that year to his under-aged teenage cousin, Myra Gail Brown.

He signed with Smash records in 1963, but didn't do well until he and producer Jerry Kennedy decided to focus on country ballads in 1967. Hits like "Another Place Another Time," "What's Made Milwaukee Famous," "She Still Comes Around" and "To Make Love Sweeter for You" (all 1968) revived him in a big way. This revival continued in 1969 with "One Has My Name." In 1970 his singles—released on Mercury—"Once More With Feeling," "I Can't Seem to Say Goodbye" and "There Must Be More to Love Than This"—were his biggest; the latter reached Number One. Fol-

lowing it were "Chantilly Lace" (1972), "Sometimes a Memory Ain't Enough" (1973), "He Can't Fill My Shoes" (1974), "Let's Put It Back Together Again" (1976), "Middle Age Crazy" (1977), "Come On In" and "I'll Find It Where I Can" (1978). In 1979 he signed with Elektra, and in 1980 reminded everyone of his versatility by having a Top Ten with the pop standard, "Over the Rainbow." His final big hit came in 1981 with "Thirty Nine and Holding."

Hard drinking and drug use took its toll, and, in 1981, he nearly died of stomach ailments. Nonetheless, his recording career continued, though more modestly, on MCA and smaller labels. In addition to run-ins with the police and the IRS over back taxes, controversy surrounded the mysterious death of his fifth wife in 1983 (one of two of his many ex's to die under accidental circumstances). However, nothing has truly tamed The Killer. He was inducted into the Rock 'n' Roll Hall of Fame in 1986. The 1989 film *Great Balls of Fire*, starring Dennis Quaid, chronicled Jerry Lee's early days. Today, though still dogged by tax problems, Lewis resides part-time in Ireland, and continues to tour the world.   —R.K.

Texas Jim Lewis

BORN: October 15, 1909
BIRTHPLACE: Meigs, Georgia
DIED: January 23, 1990

Texas Jim Lewis was one of many country artists who identified with Texas, despite not being born there. He lived there for a time in 1928, but later began working in New York City with his band, The Lone Star Cowboys. He made his first records in 1937, the same year he appeared in his first Western film. He also toured the Midwest for promoter Larry Sunbrock in the late 1940's. During World War II, Lewis relocated to Los Angeles, where he led some modestly successful Western swing units. He recorded for a number of labels including Decca, where he had one big hit with Al Dexter's "Too Late to Worry, Too Blue to Cry," in 1944. Lewis eventually left music, relocating to Seattle where he hosted a local children's TV show for seven years. His brother, Rivers Lewis, better known as "Jack Rivers," worked as a guitarist in the post-World War II L.A. country scene.   —R.K.

Liberty Records

Liberty Records was founded in 1945, and among its first country artists were Paul Howard and the Arkansas Cotton Pickers. Over time, owner Al Bennett expanded the label, though its early emphasis was primarily on pop music. By the late 50's, Bennett hired former disc jockey Joe Allison to create a country division. By the early 60's, the label had a number of acts including, most notably, Bob Wills, Floyd Tillman, Gordon Terry, Warren Smith and Willie Nelson. Among their country-oriented rock singers were Johnny Burnette and Eddie Cochran. Liberty's country catalogue was later acquired by EMI, the entertainment conglomerate that also owns Capitol Records. After years of dormancy, Liberty arose as a powerful force in mainstream country during the 1990's: When ubiquitous producer/executive Jimmy Bowen assumed the position of president of Capitol Records/Nashville, he promptly renamed the Capitol country division Liberty (mainly in order to distance himself from Capitol's lackluster recent history in the country field and its traditionally shoddy and second-rate Nashville operations). "The name has meaning for me on two levels," Bowen explained of the change. "Al Bennett, who owned and ran Liberty in its heyday, was a dear friend of mine....But the name Liberty also means something broader. If there's a word for what's happening in the world in the 90's, it's the hope of, and the chance for Liberty." The name trade, along with Bowen's assumption of power, seems to have done the trick. Former Capitol (now Liberty) artists like Garth Brooks, Willie Nelson, Tanya Tucker, Suzy Bogguss and Chris LeDoux have flourished in the 1990's, and given the label a new lease on life in the country music world.   —R.K.

The Light Crust Doughboys

The Light Crust Doughboys were the original, embryonic Western swing band. This trio, led by Bob Wills on fiddle, Herman Arnspiger on guitar and Milton Brown on vocals, was hired by Burrus Mills to advertise Light Crust Flour. Wilbert Lee O'Daniel, general manager of Burrus Mills, hired the band and acted as their master of ceremonies on the show, which became so popular that an entire network of

Texas radio stations broadcast it. Eventually Durwood Brown joined as second guitarist. They recorded for RCA Victor in 1932 (the record was released under the name, "The Fort Worth Doughboys") before Brown left that year, replaced by Tommy Duncan. Wills' brother, Johnnie Lee, also joined as banjoist. When Bob Wills left in 1933, Burrus continued the group. Subsequent line-ups included steel guitarist Leon McAuliffe, singer Leon Huff, guitarist Muryel "Zeke" Campbell and pianist John "Knocky" Parker. The group did extensive recording for ARC, continuing even after Burrus Mills fired O'Daniel in 1935 (he founded The Hillbilly Boys). Many of their ARC Recordings were lifeless stabs at pop songs; others were excellent, particularly "Gin Mill Blues" featuring John "Knocky" Parker and the double entendre, "Pussy, Pussy, Pussy." In the late 1940's they recorded for King, both as The Light Crust Doughboys and as Mel Cox and His Flying X Ranch Boys. The band has continued, with numerous personnel changes, into the 1990's.   —R.K.

Little Texas

A six-man group well noted for their soaring harmonies and tight instrumental work, Little Texas cracked the country Top Ten in late 1991 with their debut single, "Some Guys Have All the Love." The group originated in 1984 when lead vocalist Tim Rushlow (whose father sang in a 1960's band called Moby Dick and The Whalers) teamed up with guitarist/vocalist Dwayne O'Brien. The pair played the Arlington, Texas, club circuit for about a year before hooking up with lead guitarist Porter Howell and bassist Duane Propes.

The four formed a band, hit the road and, while playing at a fair in Springfield, Massachusetts, met keyboardist/vocalist Brady Seals (nephew of songwriter Troy Seals and cousin of singers Jim and Dan Seals), and drummer Del Gray.

Warner Bros. Records executives in Nashville were impressed with the band, and signed them to a development and record deal in 1988. During that period the band chose its unusual name, which is actually the name of a hollow south of Nashville where people on the run from the law used to hide during the 1920's. The band was sent on the road for two years, and at the end of 1990 they cut "Some Guys." The song took nearly a year to crack the Top Ten, but when it did it firmly established Little Texas as a high-energy, tightly knit group in the tradition of country-rock giants such as Poco, The Eagles and Alabama.

On the heels of "Some Guys," Little Texas recorded their debut album, *First Time for Everything*, which yielded four Top 20 hits: the title song, "You and Forever and Me," "What Were You Thinkin'" and "I'd Rather Miss You." The album went Gold, and in the spring of 1992 the group appeared on the Grand Ole Opry.

The hits kept on rolling in 1993 when Warner Bros. released the group's second album, *Big Time*. Three singles from the album, "What Might Have Been," "My Love" and "God Blessed Texas" reached Number One.   —R.P.

Hank Locklin

BORN: February 15, 1918
BIRTHPLACE: McLellan, Florida

Hank Locklin had roughly a decade and a half of success; but two songs, both now country standards, have really defined him: "Please Help Me, I'm Falling" and "Send Me the Pillow That You Dream On." Born Lawrence Hankins Locklin, he began playing music as a child and in 1942 appeared over a Pensacola station. He worked with various acts in the 1940's, including Jimmy Swan's band, and hooked up with the *Louisiana Hayride* in the late 40's.

His first hits came on Four Star Records in 1949 with "The Same Sweet Girl," and the Number One record, "Let Me Be the One," in 1953. In 1956, he signed to RCA and had a hit cover version of George Jones' "Why Baby Why," and an even bigger hit in 1957 with "Geisha Girl." But his first enduring record came in 1958 with the ballad, "Send Me the Pillow That You Dream On," which went to Number Five. "It's a Little More Like Heaven" peaked at Number Three that year, but his biggest hit was yet to come. "Please Help Me, I'm Falling" was Number One for 14 weeks in 1960, and crossed over to the pop Top Ten as well. It also featured the first recorded example of the "pedal piano" style popularized by Floyd Cramer. That same year, he was made a member of the Grand Ole Opry.

Though RCA continued to release numerous singles and albums, Locklin had only three more big records: "Happy Birthday to Me" (1961), "Happy Journey" (1962) and "The Country Hall of Fame," which made it to Number Eight in 1967.

One of the early country artists to tour Europe, Locklin then worked around Houston and Dallas, but hasn't done much recently, save for Opry appearances.　　　　　　　　　　　　—R.K.

Hubert Long

BORN: December 3, 1923
BIRTHPLACE: Poteet, Texas
DIED: September 7, 1972

Hubert Long got his first taste of the music business working in the record department of a Texas five and dime store. By the end of his days he'd built a virtual music empire.

His Hubert Long Talent Agency was both one of the first and one of the biggest talent promotion and development organizations in Nashville, and in 50's and 60's country music.

Long was a founder of both the Country Music Association and the Country Music Foundation. He was also the first person to serve as both President and Chairman of the CMA. He was elected to the Country Music Hall of Fame in 1979.　　　　　　　　　　　　—B.A.

Longhorn Ballroom

The Longhorn Ballroom in Dallas, Texas, began its existence as the Bob Wills Ranch House, an elaborate dancehall owned by the legendary father of Western swing, which opened in 1951. Elaborately furnished, with leather decorations and a massive dance floor, it opened to much fanfare.

Wills, despite bringing in top talent, was never a strong businessman and left the management in the hands of unscrupulous parties who destroyed the enterprise and seriously damaged Wills' finances.

After Wills pulled out, Dewey Groom, leader of the Western swing band, The Texas Long-

horns, took the facility over in 1947. He renamed it the Longhorn Ballroom, retaining much of the look it had with Wills. Groom also founded Longhorn Records, which had some modest national success.

The Longhorn became a staple of country music in the Dallas area into the 1980's. Groom eventually sold the Longhorn, but in its day it hosted top country artists whenever they were in the area.　　　　　　　　　　　　—R.K.

Lonzo & Oscar

BORN: Lonzo, July 7, 1917, Edmonton, Kentucky
　　　　Oscar, January 19, 1919, Edmonton, Kentucky
DIED: Lonzo, June 5, 1967

This country comedy team was popular on the Grand Ole Opry for many years, and was best known for novelty and comedy hits, including the 1948 million-seller, "I'm My Own Grandpa." The duo originally consisted of Lloyd "Lonzo" George (a.k.a. Ken Marvin) and Rollin "Oscar" Sullivan.

Sullivan was born in Edmonton, Kentucky, in 1919 (he was nicknamed Oscar as a youth), and met George when they were both members of Eddy Arnold's band. Noting their shared propensity for hillbilly buffoonery, Arnold not only gave the two of them a format for their cornpone comedy as his warmup act, but also came up with their goofy stage name. George was replaced by John Rollins (1917-1967) in 1945, two years before the comedy team joined the Grand Ole Opry cast. The act survived several more personnel changes over the coming years, and had several more modest chart records, including "Country Music Time" (1961) and "Traces of Life" (1974). George died on June 5, 1967.　　　　　　—B.A.

John D. Loudermilk

BORN: March 31, 1934
BIRTHPLACE: Durham, North Carolina

John D. Loudermilk, first cousin to the legendary Louvin Brothers (whose real last name was Loudermilk), was one of the most prolific and celebrated Nashville songwriters of the 1950's and 60's. It's a tribute to his vast talent that a goodly number of Loudermilk's compositions were pop and even rock 'n' roll hits, as well as country chart-toppers.

"Tobacco Road" (first recorded by The Nashville Teens in 1964, and since recorded by dozens of other country, pop and rock artists), "Talk Back Trembling Lips" (a Number One for Opry star Ernie Ashworth in 1963), "Waterloo" (first popularized by Stonewall Jackson in 1959), "Abilene" (made famous by George Hamilton IV in 1963), "Ebony Eyes" (one of several Loudermilk compositions turned into hits by The Everly Brothers) and "Then You Can Tell Me Goodbye" (an Eddy Arnold Number One in 1968) are just a few of Loudermilk's many well-known titles.

Loudermilk was born in Durham, North Carolina, on March 31, 1934. He was still a student at Durham College when his "Rose and a Baby Ruth" (which he was inspired to write after listening to a melody from a Crisco shortening commercial) became a hit for George Hamilton IV in 1956.

Through the years, Loudermilk often recorded on his own (occasionally under the pseudonyms of "Johnny Dee" and "Ebe Sneezer"), though his own chart releases—"Bad News" (1963), "Blue Train of the Heartbreak Line" (1964), "Th' Wife" (1964) and "It's My Time" (1967)—met with only minimal chart success. —B.A.

Louisiana Hayride

This long-running live country music radio show, which commenced broadcasting from the Shreveport, Louisiana Municipal Auditorium over Radio KWKH on April 3, 1948, rivaled Nashville's Grand Ole Opry in popularity for the better part of a decade, even earning the nickname "Cradle of the Stars."

Hank Williams, Elvis Presley, Johnny Cash, Webb Pierce, George Jones, Jim Reeves, Johnny Horton, Faron Young, Sonny James, Mac Wiseman, Leon Payne, Slim Whitman, Floyd Cramer, Jimmy C. Newman, The Bailes Brothers, The Blue Sky Boys, Red Sovine, Goldie Hill, The Maddox Brothers and Merle Kilgore were just a few greats for whom the *Hayride* proved a stepping stone from regional to national fame. Much of the *Louisiana Hayride*'s sustained popularity had to do with manager Horace Logan's sharp eyes and ears for raw talent with star potential.

The *Louisiana Hayride*'s power, prestige and influence was boosted further in 1950 when its weekly Saturday night broadcasts began going out over the "Hayride Radio Network," which included 27 stations in four states.

The *Hayride*'s gradual decline, however, had to do with the fact that no music industry (recording, publishing, management or booking companies and other support services) took shape around the *Hayride* the way it had in Nashville around the Opry in the 40's and 50's. Thus, eventually the *Hayride* became a mere Triple-A farm team for the Opry, as more and more of its headlining artists eventually jumped ship for the greater career opportunities that existed in Nashville. —B.A.

The Louvin Brothers

Born: Ira, April 21, 1924, Rainesville, Alabama
      Charlie, July 7, 1927, Rainesville, Alabama
Died: Ira, June 28, 1965

A generation after The Blue Sky Boys, The Louvin Brothers remain one of the defining close-harmony acts in country music, their echoes remaining strong in the music of The Everly Brothers and in numerous bluegrass acts. Lonnie Ira and Charlie Elzer

Loudermilk grew up in Henegar, Alabama, not far from Rainesville, where they were born. They started singing together as boys, developing their close harmony style by listening to the records of Alabama's Delmore Brothers, The Blue Sky Boys and The Monroe Brothers. Both played guitar, but Ira decided to switch to mandolin so he and Charlie could copy the guitar/mandolin they heard on The Blue Sky Boys' and Bill and Charlie Monroe's records.

They started performing in their home area as teenagers and then worked around Chattanooga, landing their own radio show there on WDEF in 1942 as "The Radio Twins." Ira and Charlie continued working in the area as The Foggy Mountain Boys from 1943 until Charlie joined the Army in 1945. Ira briefly worked with Charlie Monroe until the brothers reunited in 1946 as The Louvin Brothers. The duo worked in Knoxville in the late 40's, recording one song for the New York based Apollo label in 1947, and one single for Decca in 1949. In 1951 they signed with MGM, recording 12 songs through 1952. Still not successful with their records, they joined Capitol in 1952, recording heavy doses of gospel that didn't sell well. Finally moving to secular music, while retaining their distinctive bluegrass- and gospel-flavored harmonies, they joined The Grand Ole Opry in 1955 and had a Top Ten record that same year with the ballad "When I Stop Dreaming."

Their first Number One came in early 1956 with "I Don't Believe You've Met My Baby." That year the brothers had three more hits with "Hoping That You're Hoping," "You're Running Wild" and the semi-rocking "Cash on the Barrel Head." After two Top 20's in 1957, they had another Top Ten in early 1959 with "My Baby's Gone."

They remained active, though Ira, a heavy drinker, had a volatile temper and a reputation for occasionally smashing his mandolins. The brothers recorded a number of outstanding albums for Capitol, including magnificent album-length salutes to The Delmore Brothers in 1960 and to Roy Acuff in 1962.

The two went their separate ways in 1963. Charlie began recording for Capitol, having hits in 1964 and 1965 respectively with "I Don't Love You Anymore" and "See the Big Man Cry." Ira, who could fix and build instruments as adeptly as he broke them, also had one minor solo hit in 1965. Ira, who'd moved back to Henegar, was returning from a show date when his car was struck head-on near Williamsburg, Missouri, killing him, his wife and two other occupants instantly.

The Louvin legacy lives on with Charlie Louvin, and with other artists who've continued recording and performing Louvin Brothers material, in the years since Ira's death. These include many bluegrass acts as well as Emmylou Harris. In 1992 Bear Family Records reissued the Louvins' complete recorded legacy in a CD boxed set. (See also, Charlie Louvin.)   —R.K.

Charlie Louvin

BORN: July 7, 1927
BIRTHPLACE: Rainesville, Alabama

Right before Ira Louvin's death in 1965, Charlie Louvin decided to launch a solo career, continuing on the Opry and remaining on Capitol Records. His early solo years were his biggest. "I Don't Love You Anymore" was a Top Ten in 1964, while "See the Big Man Cry" did similarly well in 1965. He had moderate chart success over the next seven years, including some duets with Melba Montgomery, the most successful of which was the Top 20 "Something to Brag About." He also appeared in two films, *Music City U.S.A.* and *Golden Guitar*. After leaving Capitol, Louvin recorded for United Artists and Little Darlin' records.

He recorded a 1979 duet with Louvin Brothers fan Emmylou Harris on the Soundwaves label, and in 1989 recorded a rare duet with Roy Acuff on the Acuff favorite, "The Precious Jewel."

For a brief time in the early 1990's he worked with Charles Whitstein (of The Whitstein Brothers, a modern-day bluegrass duo that did much to keep the Louvin vocal tradition of yesteryear alive) before returning to a semi-active solo career.

Charlie Louvin also continues to be active on the Opry, where he's appeared since 1955.

(See also, The Louvin Brothers.)   —R.K.

recording contract in 1985, as the New Traditional movement was just beginning. Loveless had a number of hits in that hard country style with MCA, produced by Tony Brown and Emory Gordy Jr. After several minor successes, "If My Heart Had Windows" became her first Top Ten record in 1988, the same year she was made a member of the Grand Ole Opry. Another Top Ten followed with "A Little Bit In Love." "Blue Side of Town," "Don't Toss Us Away" and "Timber, I'm Falling In Love" (her first Number One) all followed in 1989. That year she married Emory Gordy.

In 1990, "Chains" became her second Number One, followed by "On Down the Line" and, in 1991, "I'm That Kind of Girl" and "Hurt Me Bad (In a Real Good Way)." She left MCA for Epic in 1992, but her first album was delayed by major surgery to repair bleeding vocal cords. After her recovery, she made a strong return with the 1992 Epic album *Only What I Feel.* —R.K.

Patty Loveless

BORN: January 4, 1957
BIRTHPLACE: Pikeville, Kentucky

One of the late 1980's finest young female singers, Patricia Ramey, a distant cousin of Loretta Lynn, grew up in a country music-loving family. At age 14 she started singing with her brother, Roger, and began writing songs. Roger took her to Nashville where she landed a songwriting contract with Owepar, Porter Wagoner's and Dolly Parton's publishing company. When she met The Wilburn Brothers, they were impressed enough to add her to their tours (just as they had added Loretta Lynn some years earlier, before her solo career took off) during her summer vacations from high school.

After Wagoner released her from the Owepar contract, she signed as a writer with The Wilburns' Sure-Fire Music. From 1975 on, she worked around North Carolina with her new husband, former Wilburn drummer Terry Lovelace, singing in rock bands. After the marriage ended, she returned to country. Roger Ramey became her manager and she became a writer for Acuff-Rose. A demo tape she made led to an MCA

Lyle Lovett

BORN: November 1, 1956
BIRTHPLACE: Klein, Texas

Lyle Lovett was born November 1, 1956, in Klein, a tiny Texas town named for Lovett's grandfather, town founder Adam Klein. He began singing and writing songs while studying journalism and German at Texas A&M. Around the same time, Lovett met singer Nanci Griffith while interviewing her for the school newspaper. It was her encouragement that got him started playing small nightspots in Austin, Houston and Dallas.

It was while playing a folk festival in Luxembourg that Lovett met The J. David Sloan Band. The band was to back him on the demo tape that landed Lovett a contract with MCA Records in the mid-1980's, after songwriter Guy Clark gave the tape to producer/executive Tony Brown.

His critically acclaimed debut album, *Lyle Lovett,*

(most of which was culled from those same demo recordings, with a few tracks added in Nashville) appeared in 1986 and yielded Lovett his first chart entry, "Farther Down the Line." He cut a second album, the blues-influenced *Pontiac*, before hooking up with an 11-piece touring combo he appropriately called his Large Band. His third album, *Lyle Lovett and His Large Band*, went Gold and earned Lovett a 1989 Grammy for Best Country Vocal Performance Male. The album included such chart singles as "I Married Her Just Because She Looks Like You" and "Here I Am." His cover of Tammy Wynette's "Stand by Your Man," though not a chart hit, was the focus of much attention.

His fourth album, *Joshua Judges Ruth*, was released in March 1992. Though only one of Lovett's dozen or so single releases between 1986 and 1989 dented the country Top Ten ("Cowboy Man," in 1986), Lovett has survived by garnering a large musical following from outside the country mainstream—the same sort of listeners who, no doubt bought Tom Waits and Jesse Winchester albums in earlier times. This widespread popularity, along with the sardonic wit and trenchant sarcasm of many of his songs, also landed him a spot as opening act on the rock supergroup Dire Straits' world tour.

Lovett has also achieved minor notoriety as a film actor, playing a supporting role in the Robert Altman film, *The Player*. Lovett married famous actress Julia Roberts in 1993. The bride was barefoot.   —M.B.

Lulu Belle & Scotty

BORN: Lulu Belle, December 24, 1913, Boone, North Carolina
     Scotty, November 8, 1909, Spruce Pine, North Carolina
DIED: Scotty, February 1, 1981

Lulu Belle, born Myrtle Eleanor Cooper on December 24, 1913, in Boone, North Carolina, grew up in the South and moved to Illinois. Her love of singing led to an audition at WLS, which she passed. It was on the WLS *National Barn Dance* that she got her stage name and met Scotty Wiseman. Though Lulu Belle originally sang with Red Foley, she and Scotty soon became a team, both offstage and on. Scotty Wiseman, born November 8, 1909, in Spruce Pine, North Carolina, got his start in music playing harmonica, fiddle, guitar and later banjo and developing a taste for The Carter Family and Bradley Kincaid.

While still attending college, he'd begun singing over WRVA in Richmond in 1927 and, after graduating, worked as a radio program director in Fairmont, West Virginia, before moving to Chicago. All along, he'd also felt an affinity for traditional folk music of the South.

By 1933, he'd been signed to Victor Records' Bluebird division as Skyland Scotty (a play on his mountain home) and joined the WLS *National Barn Dance*. Lulu Belle and Scotty married in 1934 and remained with the show until 1958, except for their brief World War II move to WLW in Cincinnati. They also toured and recorded throughout those years for ARC, the short-lived Vogue label, and for Starday.

After leaving WLS in 1958 (Scotty had meanwhile earned a master's degree) they semi-retired to North Carolina, doing selected appearances; Scotty also did some teaching. Lulu Belle became a North Carolina state legislator. Following Scotty's death in 1981, she remarried and in 1986 recorded an album for the Old Homestead label.   —R.K.

Bob Luman

BORN: April 15, 1937
BIRTHPLACE: Nacogdoches, Texas
DIED: December 27, 1978

Bob Luman was a 1960's and 70's country star who got his start playing rockabilly. Bobby Glynn Luman grew up in a musical family and by the mid-1950's was a *Louisiana Hayride* cast member, having been inspired by Elvis Presley's success on the show—and by having seen Presley in person. He moved to California in 1957, where he joined the cast of the *Town Hall Party* TV show. Luman's guitarist, James Burton, wound up joining Rick Nelson there. After recording rockabilly for Imperial and Capitol, his frustration mounted when his initial Warner Bros. recordings failed to click. The Everly Brothers encouraged him to record Boudleaux Bryant's "Let's Think About Living," and in 1960 it became a Top Ten country and pop hit.

After a four-year Army stint he returned and refocused on country, eventually joining the Grand Ole Opry. He signed with Epic in 1968 but the hits remained minor until his 1972 cover of the pop tune, "When You Say Love," hit the Top Ten, followed in 1973 by "Lonely Women Make Good Lovers," "Neither One of Us" and "Still Loving You." He suffered a severe illness in 1976, and though he resumed his career in 1977, a year later he was stricken by pneumonia, this time fatally.   —R.K.

Loretta Lynn

BORN: April 14, 1935
BIRTHPLACE: Butcher's Hollow, Kentucky

As a child Loretta Webb grew up much as the legendary movie *Coal Miner's Daughter* depicted her early life. Living in Butcher's Hollow (she calls it "Butcher Holler") Kentucky, her father worked in the Van Leer coal mines. Their poverty was assuaged somewhat by listening to the Grand Ole Opry. Loretta particularly admired the singing of Molly O'Day and the music of Bill Monroe. She took care of her younger brothers and sisters until she met Oliver Vanetta Lynn, nicknamed both "Doolittle" and "Mooney." She married him at age 14, in 1949. Mooney took her to Custer, Washington, where she raised their children, and in her spare time sang and wrote songs.

Mooney, unlike many husbands of that era, actively encouraged his wife in her musical ambitions. She soon had a guitar, and by the late 1950's began singing at local clubs and on a local TV show in Tacoma, hosted by Buck Owens, who lived there at the time. By 1959 a local admirer, businessman Norm Burley, had befriended the Lynns and started Zero Records specifically to record Loretta. The Lynns traveled to Los Angeles so she could make her first record. There she met steel guitarist Speedy West, who produced her first single, "Honky Tonk Girl," with some of L.A.'s top musicians backing her. The Lynns went on the road, meeting disc jockeys to promote the single. It paid off when it broke into the Top 15. In the fall of 1960, she accepted an invitation to sing on the Grand Ole Opry.

Feeling confident, the Lynns moved to Nashville where her songwriting impressed The Wilburn Brothers, who signed her to their Sure-Fire music publishing company. Their influence helped her land a Decca recording contract in 1962. She also became a regular cast member of the Wilburns' syndicated TV show. Patsy Cline also took Loretta under her wing and not only helped in her early career, but became one of

her best friends. By 1962 "Success" broke into the Top Ten, and that year she was made an actual member of the Grand Ole Opry. In 1963 she began a steady occupancy of the Top Ten with songs like "Before I'm Over You," "Wine, Women and Song" and "Blue Kentucky Girl." Her songs took on a tougher, harder edge by the mid-1960's, with an in-your-face attitude epitomized by "Don't Come Home A-Drinkin' with Lovin' on Your Mind," "You Ain't Woman Enough" and "Fist City." She also enjoyed success recording with Ernest Tubb, particularly on songs like "Mr. and Mrs. Used to Be" and "Sweet Thang."

Loretta was a country superstar by the early 70's, her tours and recordings consistently successful. No one expected she would falter—or break through to the mainstream. But that's exactly what she began to do with songs like "Coal Miner's Daughter" and "You're Lookin' at Country." Her gut bucket country style reflected her lack of interest in attracting pop listeners, even though her longtime producer, Owen Bradley, was an architect of the Nashville Sound. She also stood up for women's rights with Shel Silverstein's "One's on the Way," a blunt chronicle of glamour versus working class life. At the same time, she had an equally successful duet career with Conway Twitty. From 1971 to 1975 they racked up five Number One records including "After the Fire Is Gone," "Lead Me On," "Louisiana Woman—Mississippi Man," "As Soon as I Hang Up the Phone" and "Feelins'."

During the 1970's the media caught on to her blunt yet thoroughly lovable personality, with not a hint of polish or packaging. She began to be featured on TV talk and variety shows. She also appeared in TV commercials. Her 1975 record, "The Pill," a candid celebration of the liberation brought on by birth control, proved that country music had traveled far from its more sedate days. In 1976 she published her autobiography, *Coal Miner's Daughter*, which quickly became a best-seller, because co-author George Vecsey made sure that her straight-talking personality came through on every page. The book became a popular film biography in 1980, starring Sissy Spacek, who managed to capture not only Loretta's personality, but also sang Loretta's songs authentically. As Lynn's riches grew, she bought much of Butcher Holler and also the entire town of Hurricane Mills, Tennessee.

In the early 1980's, while her younger sister Crystal Gayle's pop-country career began to take off, Loretta's records began to falter, as she lost her direc-tion. Part of this came from a personal and business break with The Wilburn Brothers, who up till this point still had a stake in her career. She quit writing her own material while they battled in court. The loss of her own voice in her music was a blow from which she never quite recovered. She also tried recording more pop-oriented country material. By 1988 her records were far less successful, and that year she recorded her final MCA album. Also that year, she was elected to the Country Music Hall of Fame. She still tours, but began appearing in Branson in the early 1990's. In 1993 she, Tammy Wynette and Dolly Parton recorded together on the Gold-selling album, *Honky Tonk Angels*. —R.K.

Shelby Lynne

BORN: October 22, 1968
BIRTHPLACE: Quantico, Virginia

Shelby Lynne grew up in Jackson, Alabama. She began singing with her sister and her father, who led bands in the area and also owned a nightclub. Her musical tastes ran the gamut from jazz and mainstream pop music of the 1940's and 50's, to country and Western swing. In 1986 her life was shattered when her father, a heavy drinker, murdered her mother at their home and then killed himself. Her grief and immense sense of loss drove her to focus even more on her music, and Lynne went to Nashville. She got a chance to do a demo tape, which showcased her powerful voice (it had much the same wallop as the young Patsy Cline).

An appearance on the TNN show, *Nashville Now,* in 1987 led to offers from several major labels, and she finally signed with Epic. Her first chart record, though not a huge success, was "If I Could Bottle This Up," a duet with none other than George Jones, a big fan of hers, with whom she also toured. Her Epic recordings didn't sell, but other singers, including Willie Nelson, were taken by her throaty voice.

Her biggest hit on the label came in 1990 with "Things Are Tough All Over." She won the Country Music Association's Horizon Award in 1991, but after the modest success of her singles and three acclaimed albums for Epic, she signed in 1993 with the tiny Morgan Creek label, distributed by Mercury. Her album, *Temptation,* may have yielded only one minor hit, "Feelin' Kind of Lonely Tonight," but with its emphasis on big band Western swing, the album enjoyed universal praise from critics. In the spring of 1994 she recorded an album with Willie Nelson and jazz guitarist Jackie King, which has yet to be released.   —R.K.

Mac and Bob

BORN: Mac, February 2, 1902, Gray, Kentucky
        Bob, March 16, 1897, Oliver Springs, Tennessee
DIED: Bob, 1978; Mac, July 25, 1984

In the early days of country radio, listeners to WLS in Chicago preferred to hear the sweet, well-crafted harmonies of a duo comprised of two blind singers named Lester McFarland and Bob Gardner—known familiarly as Mac and Bob. Both came from the hills north of Knoxville, Tennessee, and both learned their music at the Kentucky School for the Blind in Louisville. Though they started their career singing over WNOX in Knoxville, it was the spectacular success of their Brunswick records that won them their fans. Their 1926 hit, "When the Roses Bloom Again," made them the masters of the sentimental duet, and later hits like "The Knoxville Girl" and "You're as Welcome as the Flowers in May" solidified this. Later

acts like The Monroe Brothers, The Delmore Brothers and The Louvin Brothers all learned from Mac and Bob. The duo retired from full-time radio in 1950, and both returned to rural Tennessee to live out their last days. Bob died in 1978, Mac in 1984.   —C.W.

Warner Mack

BORN: April 2, 1938
BIRTHPLACE: Nashville, Tennessee

Warner Mack is best known for his 1965 Number One country single, "The Bridge Washed Out." Born Warner MacPherson, his name change was due to a clerical error rather than a conscious choice, but he decided to keep it. He grew up in Vicksburg, Mississippi, listening to country music and became a regular on the KWKH *Louisiana Hayride* after high school. He appeared on Red Foley's *Ozark Jubilee* in the 1950's and had his first country hit in 1957 with "Is It Wrong (For Loving You)" on Decca Records. He moved to Nashville in the 1960's.

His other Top Ten hits, all of them on Decca, include "Sittin' in an All Nite Cafe" (1965), "Sittin' on a Rock (Crying in a Creek)" (1965), "Talkin' to the Wall" (1966), "It Takes a Lot of Money" (1966), "Drifting Apart" (1967), "How Long Will It Take" (1967), "I'm Gonna Move On" (1968), "Leave My Dream Alone" (1969) and "I'll Still Be Missing You" (1969).   —S.W.

Uncle Dave Macon

BORN: October 7, 1870
BIRTHPLACE: McMinnville, Tennessee
DIED: March 22, 1952

On the front of his instrument case was painted "Uncle Dave Macon, World's Greatest Banjo Player." "The Dixie Dewdrop," as Uncle Dave was fondly called, was the first star of the Grand Ole Opry and one of country music's first recording stars. He was a consummate entertainer and great banjoist, and an important preserver of folk songs and music from the turn of the century. Through his many reissued recordings, he remains one of the most influential early country musicians.

David Harrison Macon was born near McMinnville, south of Nashville, Tennessee, on October 7, 1870. When he was 13 years old, his parents moved to Nashville. At 15, he was inspired to take up the banjo after hearing banjoist-comedian Joel Davidson performing in Sam McFlin's Circus Show. Before long he developed into a first-rate banjoist, playing both a hard-driving frailing style and a complex, old-time finger style.

Shortly before the turn of the century, he settled near Readyville, Tennessee, married Matilda Richardson and started farming. In 1900 he formed the Macon Midway Mule and Wagon Transportation Company, hauling freight, vegetables and liquor between Murfreesboro and Woodbury, Tennessee. He always carried his banjo with him and performed informal shows for folks, collecting new songs along the way. By 1920 the route that took two days to travel by wagon could easily be covered in a day by truck, but Uncle Dave refused to learn to drive. The mule could not compete with the Model-T and his company folded.

In 1923 Uncle Dave played at a party for a wealthy farmer in Nashville. A manager of the Loew's Theater circuit was in the audience and invited Macon to play at his theater in Birmingham, Alabama. The run was so successful that he was booked at Loew's Theaters throughout the country on the vaudeville circuit. Until this time Uncle Dave had performed just for fun, although his exuberant personality always made him the life of the party. Now, as a professional entertainer, he began to hone his skills before a variety of audiences and take home several hundred dollars a week. At 53 he had started an exciting new career, and there was no holding him back.

Within a year he had made 20 records for Vocalian. Over the next 14 years he would make more than 175 commercial recordings, many of them solo, others with sidemen including Sid Harkreader and the great Sam and Kirk McGee. In all of them his vitality and charisma shine through. He knew how to win over a live audience, and he used the same vaudeville tricks to hold the record buyer's attention. There was no predicting what Uncle Dave would do. He

would often tell a joke, recite a poem, make a dedication or play a banjo solo before starting to play the main song. He started his recording of "Comin' Round the Mountain" by saying, "I'm gonna play with more heterogeneous constipolicy, double flavor and unknown quality than usual," and then launched into the song. It was his way of making the records personal, lively and real.

His many recordings include "Keep My Skillet Good and Greasy," "She Was Always Chewing Gum," "Way Down the Old Plank Road," "Death of John Henry," "On the Dixie Bee Line," "I Got the Morning Blues" and "Sail Away, Ladies." By the time the Grand Ole Opry started in 1925, Uncle Dave Macon was a seasoned, 56-year-old, professional entertainer and the only member of the cast with a national reputation. As historian Charles Wolfe has noted, "He was perhaps the only member of the early Opry cast that didn't need the Opry as much as it needed him." For the next 15 years he was the undisputed star of the show. In 1939, when Hollywood decided to make a film titled *The Grand Ole Opry*, Uncle Dave was chosen to star in it along with Roy Acuff. During his career he toured with many country music greats, among them The Delmore Brothers, Roy Acuff and Bill Monroe. Everyone who worked with him, or even saw him, has a story about Uncle Dave. These countless anecdotes have helped make Uncle Dave Macon a legendary figure in country music.

He was 83 when he died in 1952. He performed right up to the end. In 1966, he was elected to the Country Music Hall of Fame. Uncle Dave Macon brought the music, humor and spirit of rural, 19th century America into the 20th century. With his irrepressible personality, ability as an entertainer and skillful use of the media, he created a vast audience for traditional old-time music, a devoted audience that will undoubtedly take his music with them into the next century. —D.H.

Rose Maddox

BORN: August 15, 1925
BIRTHPLACE: Boaz, Alabama

The Maddox family exemplified the tens of thousands of Southerners who headed west during the Dust Bowl years of the 1930's. Rose was the youngest of six children of a sharecropper. Fleeing poverty, they moved west in 1933, eventually settling in California's San Joaquin Valley where the family did farm work. What rescued them from a life of hard labor was their love of music, and their talents.

In 1937, Rose and her brothers began working at KTRB Radio in Modesto, mixing hillbilly songs with pop tunes and gospel. Their popularity grew until World War II forced Rose's brothers into the service. After the war, they reunited, this time taking on a wild new image, with costumes designed by N. Turk and a heavy reliance on electric instruments and bass-slapping that predated rockabilly. The group landed a contract with Four Star Records, Rose's wild vocals becoming a major attraction in the band and on records ("Philadelphia Lawyer" being the best known). They next began recording for Columbia and worked as regulars on the *Louisiana Hayride*. In 1956 the group disbanded and Rose continued as a solo per-

former. Her Columbia material included some fine moments, but she found her biggest success on Capitol, where she began recording in 1959 (her brothers still accompanied her on records). Her biggest hits there included three duets with Buck Owens, "Mental Cruelty" and "Loose Talk" in 1961, followed by "Sweethearts in Heaven" in 1963. Alone, her biggest successes came with "Sing a Little Song of Heartache" in 1962. Her 1962 Capitol album, *Rose Maddox Sings Bluegrass*, featured backing by Reno and Smiley's band, with Bill Monroe sitting in (uncredited) for five songs. Rose continued working, and in the late 60's was part of Buck Owens' package show. As the 70's wore on, she began to find greater recognition for her and her brothers' musical contributions. She continued working here and overseas, singing bluegrass and hard country, despite serious heart problems in the 1980's. In the 1990's, nearing age 70, she continues to tour. —R.K.

J.E. Mainer

BORN: July 20, 1898
BIRTHPLACE: Weaversville, Indiana
DIED: June 12, 1971

Another country string band pioneer, J.E. Mainer, who'd worked in the cotton mills from his teenage years, first played banjo. But in 1913 he recovered the fiddle of a drunken musician he'd seen get killed by a train, rebuilt it and learned to play on it. He soon became a formidable fiddler and formed a string band in 1923 with his

brother Wade, guitarist "Daddy" John Love and mandolinist-guitarist Zeke Morris. They flourished in the 1930's after joining WBT Radio in Charlotte, North Carolina, as The Crazy Mountaineers. After four years in Charlotte they moved to New Orleans, then to Raleigh, North Carolina and WPTF. Mainer's early recordings were done for Bluebird, and included such classics as "Maple on the Hill," recorded in 1936. The group worked in Tennessee through the 1940's, and recorded for King after World War II. Mainer recorded for the Library of Congress and the Rural Rhythm label prior to his death. (See also, Wade Mainer.) —R.K.

Wade Mainer

BORN: January 21, 1907
BIRTHPLACE: Weaverville, North Carolina

Wade E. Mainer pioneered banjo picking with the thumb and one finger (as opposed to the old-time, "drop thumb" style). His innovation was later copied and refined by bluegrass artists as the three-finger style of picking. He and his brother, J.E., formed The Crazy Mountaineers (later called Mainer's Mountaineers), playing at local dances. In 1934, they started working at WBT in Charlotte, North Carolina, sponsored by Crazy Water Crystals. In 1935, they recorded some of their popular radio songs for Victor's Bluebird label, including one of the top-selling discs of the 30's, "Maple on the Hill." Crazy Water Crystals soon sent the brothers to another station, WPTF in

Raleigh, North Carolina. After a run-in with a Crazy Water executive, Wade and band member Zeke Morris decided to quit working for the company. J.E. and the fourth band member, John Love, decided to stay on. The radio station hired Wade and Zeke independently; they called themselves The Sons of the Mountaineers. After Zeke decided to leave music, Wade and various musicians traveled the South, playing at various radio stations and making occasional recordings for Bluebird and, later, King. In 1942, he played for President Franklin D. Roosevelt at the White House. Wade left music in the late 40's, working for General Motors in Detroit, but returned to performing after his GM retirement in 1972. In 1987, he won the National Endowment for the Arts Heritage Award and, in 1990, the Bluegrass Music Association's Lifetime Achievement Award. Several recordings have appeared on Old Homestead Records. (See also, J.E. Mainer.) —G.F.

Barbara Mandrell

BORN: December 25, 1948
BIRTHPLACE: Houston, Texas

Barbara Mandrell's contribution to 70's and 80's country music was primarily her introduction of the smooth, mainstream refinements via her popular network television variety show in 1981 and 1982. But the gift came with a price: Country music purists reviled the show, bashing Barbara and her sisters for portraying country in a Las Vegas-style context, taking the twang and the *Hee Haw*-ness out of the music in order to get it into millions of living rooms.

Yet Mandrell would be the first to say, "That's entertainment." And, above all, she—like most of her critics—considers herself an entertainer first, a singer second.

She was born December 25, 1948, in Houston, to Irby and Mary Mandrell, a music store owner and music teacher, respectively. The family later moved to Oceanside, California, where she spent most of her formative years. Her parents' vocations provided her with both instruments and the discipline and guidance to learn to play them. As a child she became proficient on several different instruments, and made her first public appearance as an accordionist at age five, and also quickly mastered the pedal steel and saxophone. At 11 she traveled with Irby to a music trade show in Chicago, where Chet Atkins and "Uncle" Joe Maphis heard her demonstrate several instruments. Impressed, Maphis and his wife, Rose Lee, took her along as a steel player for their show in Las Vegas. From that point on, Mandrell and her entire family were hooked on show business, with special ties to Las Vegas and its style. Still a youngster, she made television appearances on *Town Hall Party* and Red Foley's *Five Star Jubilee*, then toured with the Johnny Cash troupe, along with Patsy Cline, George Jones and June Carter.

Upon returning home, The Mandrell Family Band—including drummer Ken Dudney—toured the country, specializing in entertaining at military installations and for various civic groups. When Dudney joined

the Navy, he and Mandrell—just 18, and two weeks shy of high school graduation—married, on May 28, 1967, and she retired to become a housewife.

Less than a year later, after a visit to the Grand Ole Opry, Barbara decided to come out of retirement. She moved to Nashville in 1968 and got a recording contract a year later. By 1972 she had four chart records, including "Tonight My Baby's Coming Home," her first Top Ten single. Mandrell received the Academy of Country Music's 1971 award for Top New Female Vocalist, and was invited to join the Grand Ole Opry, which she remains a member of today

After that her hits kept coming, unexpectedly groundbreaking cheating songs from a straight-and-narrow suburban-looking country girl next door:

"Burning the Midnight Oil," "Standing Room Only," "Married But Not to Each Other," "Woman to Woman." Then came her first of six career Number Ones, "Sleeping Single in a Double Bed," followed by "(If Loving You is Wrong) I Don't Want to Be Right," "Crackers," "The Best of Strangers" and "One of a Kind of Pair of Fools."

Along the way, Mandrell also racked up dozens of awards: The ACM's Female Vocalist of the Year (1978 and 1981) and Entertainer of the Year 1980; the CMA's Female Vocalist (1979, 1981) and Entertainer of the Year (1980, 1981); and a 1982 Grammy for Inspirational Performance for "He Set My Life to Music."

She also launched her own television show, *Barbara Mandrell and The Mandrell Sisters* (which also featured her younger and more modestly talented sisters, Louise and Irlene), which was redolent with the slick Las Vegas influence long evident in her live shows: big-productions glitzy dance routines, lavish costume changes, silly skits, high-powered and eclectic guest stars, and even some music now and then. In fact, the show was so demanding and the schedule so exhausting, that it eventually took its toll on Mandrell's voice; in 1982 she was forced to cancel after just two years.

In the meantime, all the considerable energy that had gone into her TV show had become noticeably missing from the records she made during this same time frame. She kept up the hits pretty steadily throughout much of the 1980's, but as the decade moved on and a new breed of musicians commandeered the charts, her brand of slick uptown country (much of it produced by Tom Collins, perhaps the most modestly talented producer to ever get a record in the country Top Ten and one of a handful of those personally responsible for some of the gloppiest music to come out of Nashville in the late 70's and early 80's) began to sound stale, pretentious and contrived.

Then in 1984, back home in Tennessee, Mandrell and her two older children, Matthew and Jaime, were involved in a serious automobile accident in which the driver of the other car, headed the wrong way on a Tennessee highway, was killed and all three Mandrells were seriously injured.

She did not perform again until nearly 18 months after the accident. And although she maintains a much lower profile than she did before the accident, she's still active, performing and making television appearances. Her autobiography, *Get to the Heart: My Story*, released in 1990, was on the *New York Times* bestseller list for six months. She continues to fill her shelves with awards, earning *Music City News'* 1985 Living Legend, and TNN/MCN's Minnie Pearl Award in 1991. And though her records no longer sell, she has been successful with a new cash cow: as a TV spokesperson for a wide variety of name brand products, from prunes to polyesters.

She's also active in the Nashville sports community, and has been inducted into the National Association for Sports and Physical Education and the Tennessee Sports Halls of Fame because of her sponsorship of teams and benefit activities.

Mandrell continues to take a lot of flak from country music historians who tend to disdain her brand of show-biz-style country—if they bother to remember it at all. Ironically, one of her best-known songs that addressed this very issue doesn't even show up in most critic's all-time Top Ten: "I Was Country (When Country Wasn't Cool)" caught a lot of flak, even when she received the vocal support of George Jones; but it came out at a time when country was being embraced by a generally non-country crossover audience—a phenomenon which, ironically, Barbara Mandrell herself had a whole lot to do with. (See also, Louise Mandrell.) —M.B.

Louise Mandrell

BORN: July 13, 1954
BIRTHPLACE: Corpus Christi, Texas

Louise Mandrell's greatest talent is one she has usually borne gracefully: the ability to stand in her more talented older sister, Barbara's, imposing shadow.

Born in Corpus Christi, Texas, on July 13, 1954, Louise joined Barbara's touring show at age 15. In 1974, she left and first joined Opry star Stu Phillips' band, then graduated to singing backup for Merle Haggard, who also gave her a small solo slot on his show. On Epic Records in the late 70's and early 80's, she

had a run of modest chart records, including a number of duets with her then-husband, songwriter R.C. Bannon. (Together, they recorded a handful of forgettable albums: *Me and My RC, You're My Super Woman, You're My Incredible Man,* etc.) In 1974, Louise moved over to RCA, where she managed a handful of Top 10 hits between 1978 and 1988, including the Top Five, "I Wanna Say Yes," in 1985 and the Number Six, "Save Me," in 1983.

Louise's greatest exposure came when she was part of *Barbara Mandrell and The Mandrell Sisters*, a popular early 80's national TV show that lasted for two seasons. The show co-starred Barbara, Louise, and Irlene Mandrell (the third Mandrell sister). The modestly talented Louise has continued performing and recording, and is currently a big hit in Branson, Missouri. (See also, Branson and Barbara Mandrell.) —B.A.

Manuel

BORN: April 23, 1938
BIRTHPLACE: Coalcoman, Michoacan, Mexico

Tailor Manuel Cuevas is the man who dresses the stars—from boots to hats to everything in between. He's become the premier Western tailor, designing stagewear for the likes of Dwight Yoakam, Marty Stuart, Porter Wagoner, Johnny Cash, Alan Jackson, Randy Travis, Hank Williams Jr., Linda Ronstadt, Elvis and many others, both rock and country.

He's also had his hand in wardrobe for various Hollywood movie and television productions. Mexican-born Manuel (he uses only the first name) started tailoring at age eight. After college, he immigrated to the United States and settled in Los Angeles, working as a designer for Nudie. After 14 years, he opened his own shop in L.A. In 1989, he moved to Tennessee, opening a new shop in Nashville. He closed the L.A. store in 1990. —G.F.

Joe and Rose Lee Maphis

BORN: Joe, May 12, 1921, Suffolk, Virginia
      Rose, December 29, 1922, Baltimore, Maryland
DIED: Joe, June 27, 1986

Otis Wilson Maphis was among the fastest, flashiest and most flamboyant country guitarists in the business. As a teenager he was deeply influenced by Maybelle Carter's playing. He then taught himself to flatpick fiddle tunes on the guitar—if he didn't actually pioneer this innovation, he was certainly among the first. Along the way, he learned to play fiddle, mandolin and banjo as well. He worked around Virginia through the 1930's and caught on at WRVA in Richmond with Sunshine Sue Workman and her Rangers. When they moved

to WLW in 1942, Maphis went with them. There, he began his close friendships with Merle Travis and Grandpa Jones. Maphis spent two years as an entertainer in the Army before returning to Richmond where Sunshine Sue had founded the WRVA *Old Dominion Barn Dance.* There he met and married singer Rose Lee Schetrompf, and in 1952 the two moved to California. Soon the Maphises became regulars on *Town Hall Party* and began recording for Columbia. Joe became a busy session guitarist, working on several early Ricky Nelson hits and on the soundtrack to the Robert Mitchum film, *Thunder Road* (the title track of which became a minor pop hit in 1958). In the late 50's, the Maphises hired a teenaged steel guitarist named Barbara Mandrell to play Las Vegas with them, giving her a professional start in music. Joe recorded and toured with Rosie until shortly before his death from lung cancer in 1986. June Carter Cash had him interred in the Carter family burial plot not far from his idol, Maybelle Carter. After working for a time backstage at the Grand Ole Opry, Rose Lee Maphis returned to Maryland, where she was born.　　—R.K.

Martin

In 1833, guitar maker Christian Fredrich Martin left his home in Markneukirchen, Germany, for America. He settled in New York and opened C.F. Martin and Company. Six years later, he moved his business to Nazareth, Pennsylvania, on the northern edge of what's known as "Pennsylvania Dutch" country. Martin made guitars throughout the rest of the century, the business remaining in family hands. Their guitars were known for high quality craftsmanship, a reputation that kept the company expanding into the 1900's. As the guitar became more a part of country music, Martins were considered top of the line along with Gibsons. Jimmie Rodgers used Martins. In 1932, WLS' Arkie the Arkansas Woodchopper ordered one of Martin's widebodied D-2 "dreadnought" guitars with his name inlaid on the fingerboard. In 1933, Gene Autry who had long favored Martin guitars, had an elaborate Martin Dreadnought custom-built in their fancy, pearl-and-ivory inlaid Style 45. It became the company's first D-45. Some musicians favored Martin Hawaiian guitars. Bob Dunn, the first electric steel guitarist in country music, used a Martin steel-string acoustic with the strings raised and a commercially made "Volu-Tone" pickup and amp as the first electric steel guitar used in country music. Bluegrass musicians like Lester Flatt also favored Martins, and the D-28 "herringbone" (nicknamed for the elaborate wood trim around the edges) became the quintessential bluegrass guitar. Hank Williams used his Martin dreadnoughts most of the time. Merle Travis had his 1938 D-28 fitted with a custom neck by P.A. Bigsby. When he played a guitar onstage, Eddy Arnold favored a smaller Martin acoustic, as did Marty Robbins. One of Chet Atkins' early guitars was a Martin archtop. Elvis Presley used a Martin D-18 on the Sun recordings, later adding his name with stick-on letters. Johnny Cash has generally used Martin dreadnoughts, often a D-45. Tony Rice now owns Clarence White's Martin D-28. Martins have remained so much in demand that vintage models routinely fetch five-figure amounts from collectors. At times demand for certain Martins have required customers to put their names on waiting lists. The company features their classic models and a wide variety of variations, including acoustics with special amplification. The company's current management includes Christian Fredrich Martin IV.　　—R.K.

Benny Martin

BORN: May 8, 1928
BIRTHPLACE: Sparta, Tennessee

Of all the fiddlers who emerged during the early years of bluegrass, no one was more imaginative or dynamic than Benny Martin. Born May 8, 1928, in Sparta, Tennessee, Martin began playing professionally while in his early teens. By 1942 he was fiddling on WNOX's *Mid-Day Merry-Go-Round* in Knoxville; two years later he moved to Nashville to join Big Jeff and The Radio Playboys on WLAC. Between 1947 and 1951 he was a fiddler for Bill Monroe, Robert Lunn and Roy Acuff; he also played guitar for Curly Fox. Martin launched his own singing career in 1951; two excellent MGM releases failed to sell, so he resumed work as a sideman. His finest recorded moments came in 1952 during his stint with Lester Flatt and Earl Scruggs.

While touring with the Kitty Wells/Johnnie and Jack show in 1954 and 1955, Martin resumed his singing career. Sessions for Mercury, RCA Victor, Decca and Starday followed, but he failed to establish himself as a recording artist. Martin's reputation was hampered by a well-publicized drinking problem that often affected the quality of his performances. In 1965 Martin and Don Reno formed a promising partnership; the team split after releasing an excellent single for Monument. Martin recorded frequently during the 70's, but the results were often indifferent. Some albums were misguided attempts to appeal to a younger "newgrass" crowd; others rekindled some of his brilliance as a fiddler.   —D.S.

Grady Martin

BORN: January 17, 1929
BIRTHPLACE: Chapel Hill, Tennessee

Thomas Grady Martin began his professional odyssey in 1944 as a 15-year-old fiddler with Big Jeff Bess and His Radio Playboys. Two years later he became one of the twin lead guitars in Grand Ole Opry artist Paul Howard's Arkansas Cotton Pickers, moving with other former Howard sidemen to Little Jimmy Dickens' original Country Boys after Howard left the Opry.

Martin's gritty electric leads also stood out on Red Foley's 1950 pop and country smash, "Chattanoogie Shoe Shine Boy," and helped launch his studio career. He also led the backup band on the ABC-TV show, *Ozark Jubilee*, hosted by Foley.

Like all studio musicians, he worked for all labels. He also recorded pop instrumentals for Decca as the leader of a studio band known as The Slew Foot Five.

Martin's throbbing, muscular leads helped define Johnny Horton's 1956 hit single, "Honky Tonk Man." He was among the first to use nylon string guitar on country records, most notably on Marty Robbins' "El Paso" (1959) and Lefty Frizzell's "Saginaw, Michigan" (1964). His stinging electric licks also enhanced Conway Twitty's "Linda on My Mind" and Jeanne Pruett's "Satin Sheets." When a new generation of studio players took over, Martin's session work fell off, despite his skills. After teaching Merle Haggard to play lead guitar, he did some work on the soundtrack to Willie Nelson's film, *Honeysuckle Rose*. That led to a permanent slot in Nelson's backup band, where he remained until retiring in 1994.   —R.K.

Jimmy Martin

BORN: August 10, 1927
BIRTHPLACE: Sneedville, Tennessee

Like so many other bluegrass stars, singer-guitarist Jimmy Martin got his start working with Bill Monroe's Blue Grass Boys from 1949 to 1953. The singer-guitarist also recorded with The Osborne Brothers for RCA in 1954. However, for over 30 years Martin has led his own band, The Sunny Mountain Boys . More novelty-oriented than most bluegrass artists, he managed to hit the charts four times (two more than Bill Monroe) in the late 1950's and early 60's with songs like "Rock Hearts" (1958) and the trucker song, "Widow Maker" (1963). However, some some bluegrass purists have frowned on his use of a drummer. Martin's band has also nurtured a new generation of talent, including J.D. Crowe, Alan Munde and Vic Jordan. —R.K.

Kathy Mattea

BORN: June 21, 1959
BIRTHPLACE: Cross Lanes, West Virginia

One of the most successful "third generation" women singers, Kathy Mattea is like many country singers of her times in that she is a product of the suburbs (the greater Charleston, West Virginia, area) and was a straight-A student for at least some of her semesters at West Virginia University before dropping out and heading for Nashville.

Mattea made her entry into the music business by the conventional route: playing in Music City clubs and singing on countless demo records for several years, until her growing reputation as a vocalist with a rich, mid-range alto (not unlike Anne Murray's) landed her a contract with Mercury, the label she still records for today.

Mattea's first two Mercury albums—*Kathy Mattea* (1984) and *From My Heart* (1985) neither generated much chart action nor showcased her as much more than just another girl singer cast heavily in an Murray-ish, middle-of-the-road stance that ill suited her. Her real artistic—and commercial—breakthrough came with 1986's *Walk the Way the Wind Blows*. On this and her subsequent *Untasted Honey* (1987) and *Willow in the Wind* (1989), she brought a newgrass edge to her sound (partly with the help of fellow West Virginia artist, newgrasser Tim O'Brien, who wrote the title song from *Walk the Way the Wind Blows*, Mattea's second Top Ten hit, and duetted with her on a few tracks from this era).

Mattea's first Number One single came with 1987's "Goin' Gone," a cover of a Nanci Griffith tune that demonstrated the folkish direction that Mattea's music was by now beginning to take. She swung back toward a more mainstream country sound and scored her first "career" record with the Number One, "Eighteen Wheels and a Dozen Roses," which won the Country Music Association's Single of Year in 1988. Another major breakthrough came in 1989 with "Where've You Been," a lovely ballad co-written by Mattea's songwriter husband, Jon Vezner, and noted Nashville tunesmith Don Henry (who made his own noteworthy album debut a year or two later with *Wild in the Backyard*). A Top Ten hit, "Where've You Been" became a crowd favorite and a show-stopper in Mattea's live performances. It also resulted in her first Gold album, a CMA Award for Song of the Year and a Grammy Award. For two consecutive years— 1989 and 1990—she also won the CMA's Female Vocalist of the Year Award.

Always musically adventurous, Mattea, despite these commercial successes, opted to "push the envelope," recording an eclectic and even more folk/ "New Age"-informed album titled *Time Passes By* (1991). *Time Passes By* was, like much of the work of country diva Emmylou Harris, an intensely personal work, a collection of Mattea's most important influences. The album represented a major creative risk for Mattea, and ultimately resulted in just one Top Ten. Her more recent albums—*Lonesome Standard Time* (1992) and *Walking Away a Winner* (1994) have put her back on a slightly more mainstream footing and are gradually recapturing the career momentum lost during her *Time Passes By* phase.

The bluegrass influence heard so often in Mattea's music is something she comes by honestly. Before arriving in Nashville in 1978, she was in a college bluegrass band called Pennsboro. She made her living during her first couple years in Music City as a waitress and as a tour guide at the Country Music Hall of Fame before establishing herself as one of the town's most in-demand demo and jingle singers. She also toured as a backup singer for Bobby Goldsboro, Don Williams, The Oak Ridge Boys and Gary Morris. In 1988, she married songwriter Jon Vezner, who co-wrote "Where've You Been" about an actual event in his grandparents' lives.

"What you create comes from yourself," Mattea once observed of her intensely personal approach to music making. "But there's some level that isn't fulfilled unless other people get it... That's the zen of it, sort of."   —M.B.

The Mavericks

This Miami-based band debuted in 1992 with *From Hell to Paradise*, a stunning self-produced musical collection that brilliantly melded the stone country soul of Hank Williams with moving social commentary on urban issues like poverty, homelessness, and a generation of Cuban-Americans' desperate cultural transplantation from Castro's Cuba to Miami.

Raul Malo, the band's lead singer/songwriter and the son of Cuban émigrés, is the real force behind The Mavericks. He's not only an accomplished songwriter with a strong social awareness, but a remarkable singer in the Roy Orbison tradition as well.

From Hell to Paradise, which has a power reminiscent of early Creedence Clearwater Revival, showcased all the above-mentioned strengths. *What a Crying Shame*, the band's 1993 follow-up,

was produced by mainstream Nashville producer Don Cook, and placed more emphasis on casting Malo's powerful vocals and his talents as a songwriter in a less interesting but still compelling mainstream country vein. They record for MCA Records. Bandmember Robert Reynolds married Trisha Yearwood in May 1994.   —B.A.

MCA/Decca Records

Established in 1934, Decca Records (today part of the MCA Entertainment conglomerate) quickly became a pioneer in the country music field. The label's co-founder, Dave Kapp, did much to widen the label's country base by making numerous early field recordings throughout the southern U.S. Jimmie Davis was one of Decca's first significant country signees, joining the label in 1934. During the next decade and a half, the label's roster expanded to include many of the most influential artists of the times: Ernest Tubb (who signed in 1940), Bill Monroe (1949) and Kitty Wells (1952), among them.

Another early Decca executive, Paul Cohen, was largely responsible for the label's eventual emergence as on of country's "Big Three" (RCA-Victor and Columbia being the other two). Cohen, who took over country A&R in 1945, helped guarantee Decca's future dominance when he hired Owen Bradley, pianist, dance bandleader and WSM music director, as his assistant in 1954. When Cohen moved on to head Coral Records, Bradley took over all of Decca's Nashville production work. Over the course of the next two decades Bradley rose to become one of the most influential country producers of his era. Patsy Cline, Webb Pierce, Buddy Holly, Brenda Lee, Loretta Lynn, Conway Twitty, Bill Anderson and Jack Greene were just some of the artists whom Bradley brought to the label and/or produced.

In more recent years, as Decca was absorbed by MCA (which also acquired the catalogue of the former ABC/Dot label), the merged company became an even more formidable presence in the country charts, due to dynamic latter-day Nashville chiefs like Jim Fogelsong, Jimmy Bowen and Tony Brown. MCA's roster continues to grow, making it an even more towering presence. George Strait, Wynonna Judd, Reba McEntire, George Jones, Trisha Yearwood, Vince Gill, Rodney Crowell, Marty Stuart, Mark Chesnutt,

Patty Loveless, Lyle Lovett, Nanci Griffith, The Mavericks, Marty Brown, Joe Ely, Kelly Willis, Waylon Jennings, John Anderson, McBride & The Ride, Mark Collie, Tracy Byrd and The Desert Rose Band are just a few of the hit artists who've been associated with MCA in the past decade. In 1994, MCA re-launched the Decca label, as a subsidiary, signing Dawn Sears and transferring Mark Chesnutt over from the parent label.

—B.A

Mac McAnally

BORN: July 1, 1959
BIRTHPLACE: Belmont, Mississippi

Singer-songwriter Lyman "Mac" McAnally Jr. was born in Belmont, Mississippi, on July 1, 1959. As a youngster he was heavily influenced by his mother's gospel piano playing. McAnally began playing that instrument, as well as the guitar, and at 13 performed his first gig at a bar on the Tennessee-Mississippi border.

A few years later he moved to Muscle Shoals, Alabama, to work in the recording studios there. He began writing songs, and at 18 cracked the pop Top 40 with "It's a Crazy World." The song went to Number Two on the adult-contemporary charts, firmly establishing Mac as a talented songwriter with a knack for combining sensitive lyrics and wry humor with pop-flavored melodies. His songs have since been recorded by dozens of country's leading artists, including Alabama ("Old Flame"), Shenandoah ("Two Dozen Roses"), Sawyer Brown ("Cafe on the Corner"), Ricky Van Shelton ("Crime of Passion"), Jimmy Buffet ("It's My Job"), Steve Wariner ("Precious Thing") and Ricky Skaggs ("Simple Life").

Mac signed with Warner Bros. in 1989 and released the critically-acclaimed *Simple Life*, which featured guest appearances by Vince Gill, Tammy Wynette, Mark O'Connor and Ricky Skaggs, among others. In 1992 he signed with MCA and recorded another well-received album, *Live and Learn*, which

was produced by session whiz Tony Brown. Besides being in constant demand on sessions for his smooth vocals and outstanding guitar work, McAnally has also excelled as a producer in recent years, having co-produced Ricky Skaggs' critically acclaimed 1991 album, *My Father's Son* and Sawyer Brown's recent hit albums.

—R.P.

Leon McAuliffe

BORN: January 3, 1917
BIRTHPLACE: Houston, Texas
DIED: August 20, 1988

William Leon McAuliffe, Bob Wills' best-known instrumentalist, began his career as a protégé of Western swing steel guitar pioneer Bob Dunn, and worked with The Light Crust Doughboys before joining Wills in 1935. In 1936 his adaptation of black guitarist Sylvester Weaver's "Guitar Rag" became the classic steel guitar instrumental, "Steel Guitar Rag," after he recorded it with The Playboys. Wills' spoken introduction "Take it away, Leon!" became as well known as the song itself.

McAuliffe and Playboy guitarist-arranger Eldon Shamblin later created the twin guitar ensemble within The Playboys, playing sophisticated harmonized parts on their respective instruments ("Bob Wills Special" and "Twin Guitar Special" are examples of this). McAuliffe was also one of Wills' most effective vocalists, aside from Tommy Duncan. He remained with The Playboys until 1943—even appear-

ing with them in several Hollywood westerns—when he left to serve as a civilian naval flight instructor.

In 1946, he formed his own Western swing band and made some superb recordings for Majestic Records before signing with Columbia in 1949. His instrumental, "Panhandle Rag," became a huge hit, and the band played extensively in the Southwest during the 1950's and 60's, recording for Cimarron records.

Eventually McAuliffe retired to Rogers, Arkansas, where he bought a radio station. The Western swing revival of the early 1970's brought him back to active performing, first on Bob Wills tributes held before Wills' death, then as leader of The Original Texas Playboys. This group of Wills alumni, which included original Playboy drummer Smokey Dacus, guitarist Shamblin and pianist Al Stricklin, recorded three albums for Capitol and toured extensively. An agreement to disband when any "original" member died, came to pass upon Stricklin's death in 1987. —R.K.

Martina McBride

BORN: July 29, 1966
BIRTHPLACE: Sharon, Kansas

Martina Schifft McBride is one of those new women singers whose urbane beauty pageant good looks at first overshadowed her formidable talent when she emerged with her impressive 1992 RCA debut album, *The Time Has Come.*

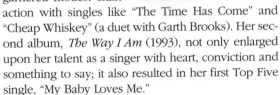

McBride's first album garnered modest chart action with singles like "The Time Has Come" and "Cheap Whiskey" (a duet with Garth Brooks). Her second album, *The Way I Am* (1993), not only enlarged upon her talent as a singer with heart, conviction and something to say; it also resulted in her first Top Five single, "My Baby Loves Me."

McBride, the daughter of a farmer/storekeeper/country band leader, got her start singing around her home territory of south-central Kansas in her father's band, The Schiffters, and later in the clubs of Wichita, as well as with various touring bands. She moved to Nashville in 1989 with her husband, John McBride, who ended up working as a sound man for Garth Brooks. Soon she was accompanying John on the road, selling Garth Brooks T-shirts as a concessionaire.

After circulating demo tapes far and wide, McBride landed a contract with RCA. Brooks gave McBride a chance as his opening act. She has since gone on to headline her own show. —B.A.

Terry McBride & The Ride

Originally a trio known as McBride & The Ride (assembled by MCA Records executive Tony Brown), the band became a six-piece ensemble under the moniker Terry McBride & The Ride in 1994, reflecting Terry McBride's heightened status as the act's lead vocalist and primary songwriter.

The new Ride consists of Gary Morse on steel, Rick Gerken on keyboards, Keith Edwards on drums (who replaced Billy Thomas of the original trio), Bob Britt on guitar (replacing Ray Herndon of the original line-up) and Randy Frazier on bass.

Terry McBride (born September 16, 1958, in Austin, Texas) got his start performing with his father, independent label artist Dale McBride (who scored a few minor chart records in the 70's), then spent two years as Delbert McClinton's bass player. He also worked with Lee Roy Parnell and Rosie Flores before signing with MCA.

Among the singles on the band's first three albums were the Top Ten hits "Sacred Ground," "Going Out of My Mind," "Just One Night" and "Love on the Loose, Heart on the Run." A fourth album, *Terry McBride & The Ride,* featuring the new line-up, was released in late 1994. —G.F.

C.W. McCall

BORN: November 15, 1928
BIRTHPLACE: Audubon, Iowa

William Fries, the given name of C.W. McCall, found a niche for himself during the 1970's C.B. (Citizens' Band) radio boom and the concurrent rise of car-and-truck chase movies like *Smokey and the Bandit*. Adopting the persona of a trucker in his singing and songwriting, McCall hit paydirt on MGM and Polygram Records with Top 20 singles like "The Old-Home Filler-Up and Keep-On-A-Truckin' Cafe," "Wolf Creek Pass," "Convoy" (a country and pop Number One in 1975, which later spawned a movie of the same name, starring Kris Kristofferson) and "Roses for Mama." But as America's fascination with truckers and C.B.'s faded, so did McCall's chart action. His final single appeared in 1979. In the 80's he ran for—and was elected—mayor of Ouray, Colorado.　　—G.F.

Charly McClain

BORN: March 26, 1956
BIRTHPLACE: Jackson, Tennessee

Charly McClain is best known for her string of country-pop hits which began in the late 1970's and continued through the 1980's. She had three Number One hits during her time with Epic Records: "Who's Cheatin' Who" (1980/1981), "Radio Heart" (1985) and "Paradise Tonight" (1983), a duet with Mickey Gilley. Born March 26, 1956, in Memphis, Charlotte Denise McClain began by singing taped messages with her two siblings to give to her hospitalized father. Soon after, she formed a band with her brother which lasted into the 1970's. She then became a cast member of the *Mid-South Jamboree* (1973-75) and later toured with O.B. McClinton. While most of her singles were solo efforts, she did record several duets with fellow Epic/Columbia artists Johnny

Rodriguez (1979) and Mickey Gilley (1984).

After her marriage to actor/singer Wayne Massey in July 1984, she also recorded several duets with him. Her last Top Five hit was "With Just One Look In Your Eyes" (1985). After that, her hits began to trail off, and she moved over to Mercury Records, placing her last single on the charts in 1989.　　—S.W.

Harry "Mac" McClintock

BORN: October 8, 1882
BIRTHPLACE: Knoxville, Tennessee
DIED: April 24, 1957

One of the most colorful figures in early country music, Harry McClintock (known as Haywire Mac, Radio Mac or simply Mac) recorded a number of early cowboy and hobo songs for RCA Victor. A native of Knoxville, Tennessee, where he was born on October 8, 1882, he roamed the country as a railroad boomer, a hobo, a cowboy, union organizer, set designer, reporter, seaman—and singer. By the 1920's he had settled on the West Coast, and started to record for Victor in 1928. Though he claimed authorship of numerous traditional songs, he did have genuine hits with "Hallelujah, I'm a Bum," "The Bum Song," "Ain't We Crazy" and his most enduring piece, "The Big Rock Candy Mountain"— all dating from 1928 Victor sessions. Mac later did bit parts in Gene Autry films, did radio and TV shows, and wrote for *Railroad Magazine*. He died in San Francisco in April 1957.　　—C.W.

Delbert McClinton

BORN: November 4, 1940
BIRTHPLACE: Lubbock, Texas

A veteran Texas rocker and former leader of The Ron-Dels, McClinton played drums on a number of 1950's rockabilly recordings and worked extensively in rhythm and blues groups. His first national exposure came with his famous harmonica solo on Texas rocker Bruce Channel's 1962 pop hit, "Hey Baby." (On an English tour that year, McClinton inspired The Beatles' John Lennon to play harmonica, which he did on "Love Me Do.") Returning to Texas, McClinton worked locally, be-

fore gaining national attention with his 1976 ABC album, *Victim of Life's Circumstances*, a brilliant fusion of country and R&B. Though critically acclaimed, the album did not sell, nor did equally worthy follow-up albums on ABC. Emmylou Harris later had a huge hit with his "Two More Bottles of Wine." Several more fine efforts for MCA and Capricorn followed, and in 1980 he managed a Top Ten pop hit with "Giving It Up for Your Love" on Capitol. Though less prominent in the 1980's, McClinton continued recording and performing. In 1993 he had a hit duet with Tanya Tucker on "Tell Me About It." And recently, Lee Roy Parnell featured McClinton in a duet role on one of his albums—Parnell's way of tipping his hat to McClinton, who's been such a huge influence on his music.   —R.K.

O.B. McClinton

BORN: April 25, 1940
BIRTHPLACE: Senatobia, Mississippi
DIED: September 23, 1987

O.B. McClinton honed his skills as a performer while serving in the Air Force. After his discharge he wrote songs for R&B artists like James Carr and Otis Redding before turning to country. Inspired by the success of Charley Pride, a rare role model for a young black country

singer, McClinton played some tapes of his country songs for Stax/Volt executive and R&B legend Al Bell, who signed him first as a staff songwriter, then as an artist, in 1971. He recorded his debut album, *Country McClinton*, in 1972. After switching to Epic Records, O.B. made the country charts with the singles, "Yours and Mine," "Hello, This Is Anna" and "Natural Love." While O.B. never became a household name, he shared with Charley Pride the distinction of achieving acceptance in a field where black performers are few and far between. He was a galvanizing performer, a virtual necessity for touring in the South in the early 1970's—and it was a considerable loss to country music when he died of abdominal cancer in 1987 at age 47.   —M.B.

Del McCoury

BORN: February 1, 1939
BIRTHPLACE: Bakersville, North Carolina

Since 1971, Del McCoury has been one of traditional bluegrass music's strongest adherents. Although his style and repertoire remain distinctly his own, McCoury's music comes closest to capturing the essence of Bill Monroe during his vintage years in the late 1940's and early 1950's.

Delano Floyd McCoury was born on February 1, 1939, in Bakersville, North Carolina, and raised in York County, Pennsylvania. In February 1963, he was playing banjo with a local bluegrass band when Bill Monroe offered him a job in his band. Upon arriving in Nashville, Monroe shifted McCoury to guitar and encouraged him to sing lead. After a year with Monroe's Blue Grass Boys, McCoury and fiddler Billy Baker briefly worked in Los Angeles with The Golden State Boys.

In 1967 he formed Del McCoury and The Dixie Pals. *High on a Mountain*, a 1972 album for Rounder, firmly established McCoury's reputation on the bluegrass circuit. Never a prolific songwriter, McCoury recorded sporadically for Rebel and other labels through the 1970's and early 80's.

In 1987 he renamed his group The Del McCoury Band and began recording with Rounder on a regular basis; his sons Ronnie and Robbie also joined the group. As age takes its toll on bluegrass music's pioneers like Monroe, McCoury's confident, dynamic tenor and tight ensemble work assures that the tradition that they forged will be carried on. In recent years, he's gained greater notice from critics and the mainstream media.   —D.S.

Charlie McCoy

BORN: March 28, 1941
BIRTHPLACE: Oak Hill, West Virginia

Charlie McCoy learned to play the mouth harp at the age of eight. When he was a teenager, he began playing in a number of country and rock bands, and, during the late 1950's and early 60's, was a frequent performer at country and rock clubs in Florida. While performing on a country show known as the *Old South Jamboree*, he met Mel Tillis. McCoy soon moved to Nashville and found work through Tillis' agent, Jim Denny. He signed his first recording contract in 1961. In the next few years, nine of his singles made the country Top 40. But McCoy's greatest successes came as a session player. He was a sought-after session harmonica player for such big-name artists as Elvis Presley, Tom T. Hall, Bob Dylan and Joan Baez. He also toured with the bands of a number of Grand Ole Opry stars, including Stonewall Jackson.

He continued to produce his own albums, and an album he made in 1969 with an all-star group of session players called *Area Code 615* was widely acclaimed. He didn't attract a following until 1972, when a Florida DJ gave Charlie's harmonica rendition of "Today I Started Loving You Again" so much airplay that other local stations began to do the same. The four-year-old cut was released as a single and quickly hit the Top Ten. Seizing the moment, Monument, his label, released McCoy's cover of the Hank Williams classic "I'm So Lonesome I Could Cry," which also became a major hit. His single, "The Real McCoy," won him the 1972 Grammy for Best Country Instrumental Performance. He also won the Country Music Association's prestigious Musician of

the Year award for both 1972 and 1973.

McCoy continued to make country charts in the mid-1970's with singles like "Release Me" in 1973, "Boogie Woogie" in 1974 and "Fair and Tender Ladies" in 1978. He also cut a number of successful albums, including *Harpin' the Blues*, *Charlie McCoy's Greatest Hits*, and *Appalachian Fever*.

In 1977 he was named musical director of the popular TV series *Hee Haw*. —M.B.

Neal McCoy

BORN: July 30, 1963
BIRTHPLACE: Jacksonville, Texas

As a child Hubert Neal McGauhey Jr. was exposed to a variety of musical styles, from country and big band to pop and Motown. In 1981 the half-Irish, half-Filipino McCoy won a talent contest at a Dallas country nightclub, which led to a contract with Charley Pride's management firm. He ended up opening for Pride for six years, and word of mouth about his dynamic, boisterous stage show made it to the ears of Atlantic Records' Rick Blackburn, who signed McCoy in 1990. After two albums and several singles that were stylistically all over the map and achieved little chart success, McCoy found his groove in 1994 with two Number One singles, "No Doubt About It" and "Wink." Both are from his third album, also titled *No Doubt About It*. —G.F.

Mel McDaniel

BORN: September 6, 1942
BIRTHPLACE: Checotah, Oklahoma

After working the Oklahoma clubs during his teen years, Mel McDaniel hit Nashville in 1969. After almost two years of trying to make it in Music City, he moved his family to Alaska. A couple of years of club gigs there, and he was ready to try Music City again. This time things clicked: he worked as a demo singer for Combine Music, and got a recording contract with Capitol in 1976—though it took him five more years to score his first Top Ten hit. A few scattered Top Tens sprinkled throughout the 80's ("Louisiana Saturday Night," "Big Ole Brew," "Baby's Got Her Blue Jeans On" and "Stand Up," among them) kept him in the charts until 1989. Though he lists Elvis, Johnny Cash, Jerry Lee Lewis and Chuck Berry as his influences, his sound treaded much closer to mainstream country radio fodder. McDaniel has been a Grand Ole Opry member since 1986.   —G.F.

Skeets McDonald

BORN: October 1, 1915
BIRTHPLACE: Greenway, Arkansas
DIED: March 31, 1968

Enos William "Skeets" McDonald got his start working in the Michigan area. His vocal on the 1950 "Mean and Evil Blues," by Johnny White and His Rhythm Riders, was among his early recordings. In the early 1950's he relocated to California, and his 1952 cover of Slim Willet's "Don't Let the Stars Get in Your Eyes," recorded for Capitol, hit Number Two nationally. He also helped give Wynn Stewart his start in country music, and became a regular on the popular Southern California TV show, *Town Hall Party*. He later moved into a rockabilly-flavored sound with his 1958 Capitol album, *Goin' Steady with the Blues*. As trends changed, however, McDonald moved to Columbia. He managed several hits for them from 1959 to 1967, and had a Top Ten hit with "Call Me Mr. Brown" (1963) and a Top 30 hit with "Mabel" (1967). In 1968 he died of a heart attack.   —R.K.

Ronnie McDowell

BORN: March 26, 1950
BIRTHPLACE: Fountain Head, Tennessee

While growing up in Portland, Tennessee, Ronnie McDowell was a huge fan of Elvis Presley, and could mimic his singing exceptionally well—something that later became the basis for most of his career. After high school McDowell joined the Navy, and it was there that he decided on pursuing music full-time.

After his discharge he brought some of his songs to Nashville. He landed a non-musical job at Scorpion Records. When Elvis died, McDowell wrote "The King Is Gone" in tribute, and Scorpion released it. It became a huge hit on both the pop and country charts, and led to McDowell singing the soundtrack to the 1979 movie, *Elvis*. From there he signed with Epic, scoring 11 Top Ten hits, including the Number Ones "You're Gonna Ruin My Bad Reputation" and "Older Women." Though McDowell received much praise for his vocals—especially when he wasn't being an Elvis clone—critics pointed out that he was often hampered by weak songs (some of them self-penned) and overwrought production. Later singles for Curb were less successful, and the most recent McDowell sightings have been in Branson.   —G.F.

Pake McEntire

BORN: June 23, 1953
BIRTHPLACE: Chockie, Oklahoma

Reba McEntire's older brother began his musical career singing with Reba and their sister Susie in a little trio that their mother (also a gifted vocalist) booked into local clubs and community centers as The Singing McEntires. Their fledgling career came to an end when Reba went solo and hit the big-time. Pake, a third-generation Oklahoma cattle rancher and rodeo rider (his father and grandfather were both national rodeo champions), was in his early 30's before he ventured to Nashville to seek his own fame and fortune.

McEntire's debut RCA album, *Too Old To Grow Up Now*, was greeted with modest chart success, but enough positive critical reaction to prove to the world he had more than just his famous last name going for him. Even *Country Music Magazine*'s veteran reviewer, Rich Kienzle, predicted good things for McEntire based on *Too Old To Grow Up Now:* "Imagine Norman Petty getting hold of Buddy Holly last January, instead of 30 years ago," Kienzle raved, "and you'll have an idea of what McEntire sounds like. Pake's fresh viewpoint gives us another giant in the New Wave of the 80's."

Unfortunately, this prophecy did not come to pass for this McEntire. His later releases were greeted with indifference. Pake, with three daughters at home and a successful cattle operation to look after, tired of the tour grind and returned to Oklahoma.   —B.A.

Reba McEntire

BORN: March 28, 1954
BIRTHPLACE: Chockie, Oklahoma

Reba McEntire has been cranking out solid chart-topping hits for more than a decade in her own inimitable style, which has gradually drifted from hardcore, Oklahoma-style country to polished country-pop, finding an ever wider audience along the way. McEntire conveys an image of strength, drive and determination, both on and off stage—strength as a woman, which she's bringing more into play in her songs ("Is There Life Out There"), and strength as an artist and business-woman who has always stood up for her own way of doing things.

McEntire rode into the world on March 28, 1954, in Chockie, Oklahoma, the daughter of a school-teacher, Jacqueline, and a rancher and world champion steer roper, Clark. Reba, sister Susie and brother Pake (also a country music singer) traveled the rodeo circuit as The Singing McEntires, while, at the same time teenage Reba competed as a barrel rider. When Red Steagall heard McEntire sing the National Anthem at 1974's National Finals Rodeo, he was so impressed he arranged for her to go to Nashville and cut a demo, which resulted in Mercury/Polygram signing her. Steagall also managed her for a time early in her career.

Although McEntire had her first chart song ("I Don't Want to Be a One Night Stand") in 1976, it took six more years before she began to find her own voice with her first Number One, "Can't Even Get the Blues," in 1982. Much of the time in between was spent with producers who tried to take her distinctive, roots-derived country sound in a pop direction, a move she fought, largely with the support of her mother, who urged her to develop her own style. The stubbornness paid off, especially when Reba moved to MCA Records, where, along with producer Harold Shedd (of Alabama fame), she made *My Kind of Country* (1984), the first album to capture her back-to-

basics country vision and one of her best ever. Teaming next with producer Jimmy Bowen, she made *Have I Got a Deal For You* (1985), which was yet another breakthrough, and another hard country classic. That same year, McEntire was made a member of the Grand Ole Opry.

"It seemed like back when I did *My Kind of Country*, nobody was doing that kind of thing, and it really did feel like country music was slipping away," McEntire told *Country Music Magazine* in a 1987 interview. "The old Ray Price-type songs are something that I'll never get away from," she added, when asked about her later drift toward a more uptown song. "Western swing: that's my roots, that's my heritage....I'm just trying to find a balance and not get too far one way or the other."

Whoever's in New England (1986), her next album, was another masterpiece. It leaned a little more heavily towards the subtle, uptown pop influence that has informed McEntire's music more overtly in the nearly dozen albums she's made since. In the early 1990's, she changed producers again, working with superstar producer Tony Brown.

The result of all this has been a continuous string of big hits, making Reba one of the hottest and most consistent stars in country music. "Whoever's in New England" (Number One in 1986) brought her first Grammy, and "Little Rock," "What Am I Gonna Do About You" and "One Promise Too Late," all culled from the same album, also went Number One. More recent Number Ones include "The Last One to Know," "New Fool at an Old Game," "Cathy's Clown" (a 1989 remake of a 1960 Everly Brothers hit), "You Lie" (1990), "For My Broken Heart" (1991), "Is There Life Out There" (1992), "The Heart Won't Lie" (a 1993 duet with Vince Gill) and "Does He Love You," a 1993 duet with Linda Davis.

McEntire's personal life has not always followed the same steady path as her recording career: Her first marriage to rodeo champion Charlie Battles ended in 1987 after 11 years. Two years later, she married her steel player-turned-manager, Narvel Blackstock, and their son, Shelby Stephen, was born on February 23, 1990. One year later, March 16, 1991, a plane crash took the lives of her road manager, Jim Hammon, and seven members of her band. The group was leaving San Diego, where they had performed at a private show for IBM; the plane crashed soon after take-off. McEntire threw herself into work as therapy, performing a few weeks later on Hollywood's

Academy Awards show, and a month afterwards on the Country Music Association Awards show. She released *For My Broken Heart* as a tribute to the friends who were killed. Putting together a new band, McEntire got on with her life with a healthy attitude—she neither blamed God nor herself; and when *For My Broken Heart* went double-platinum, she refused to apologize for its success, observing that the album, a result of tragedy and heartbreak, had helped to heal not only her, but many others who heard it.

Reba's comfort with herself and her musical style has earned her an uncountable number of awards from the major country music awards organizations—Country Music Association, Academy of Country Music and *Music City News*/TNN. In 1986 the CMA named her Entertainer of the Year. And she stretches the envelope—successfully—acting to good reviews: Her performance in *Tremors* (1990) as a gun-toting monster-killer was hysterical; and she also starred in *The Gambler IV* with Kenny Rogers and has more recently continued making successful forays into cinema.

Under the guidance of Blackstock, the always ambitious multi-media star has also parlayed her musical successes into a formidable business empire, called Starstruck Entertainment, which includes a management arm (Joe Diffie, Linda Davis, Aaron Tippin and Brother Phelps are all managed by Starstruck), as well as a publishing division, horse farm, jet charter service and a huge new Music Row headquarters. In 1994 her autobiography, *Reba*, entered *The New York Times* bestseller list. Still, some longtime fans have despaired of her strong moves from traditional country to pop. —M.B.

with fiddler Arthur Smith in a trio they called The Dixieliners, and toured extensively. As trends changed, The McGees endured as favorites on the Opry. (Sam played the first electric steel guitar on the Opry, only to be told not to bring it back by Opry boss George D. Hay.) In later years, they were also popular at folk festivals. In 1975, Sam died in a tractor accident on his farm. Kirk continued working on the Opry until his death in 1983. —R.K.

Sam and Kirk McGee

BORN: Sam, May 1, 1894, Franklin, Tennessee
        Kirk, November 4, 1899, Franklin, Tennessee
DIED: Sam, August 21, 1975
        Kirk, October 21, 1983

Sam and Kirk McGee, a guitarist and banjoist-fiddler respectively, were among the first generation of Grand Ole Opry performers. Sam was particularly influenced by the fingerpicking guitar styles of local black railroad workers. The McGee brothers began working with Uncle Dave Macon in 1924, and in 1926 joined him on the WSM *Barn Dance*, which soon became the Grand Ole Opry. In 1930 the brothers linked up

Tim McGraw

BORN: May 1, 1967
BIRTHPLACE: Delhi, Louisiana

The son of professional baseball player Tug McGraw (who, in a 20-year career, pitched for the New York Mets and the 1980 World Series champion Philadelphia Phillies), McGraw's self-titled debut album on Curb Records in 1992 spawned three singles, none of which did much on the charts. But that all changed in 1994 with the release of the novelty single, "Indian Outlaw." While its references to wigwams, tom-toms and peace pipes, raised the ire of Native American groups, McGraw nevertheless found himself with a Number One single, as well as a Number One album (*Not a Moment Too Soon*) on both the pop and

country charts. That success continued with another Number One, the follow-up single, "Don't Take the Girl." Critics have pointed out McGraw's over-reliance on novelty numbers like "Indian Outlaw" as a weakness, which in time he may or may not overcome.   —G.F.

Clayton McMichen

BORN: January 26, 1900
BIRTHPLACE: Allatoona, Georgia
DIED: January 4, 1970

No instrumentalist dominated country music like fiddler (and also guitarist) Clayton McMichen did in the 1920's and 30's. He was one of the genre's first great studio musicians, dominating the recording scene of the 1920's the way musicians like Chet Atkins and

Mark O'Connor would in later years. Coming into the Atlanta music scene from Allatoona, Georgia, where he was born in 1900, McMichen became a key figure in the famed string band, The Skillet Lickers. At the same time that he appeared on many of their hot fiddle breakdowns, he had his own band called McMichen's Melody Men that had huge hits of the day with "Sweet Bunch of Daisies" and others. He also sang duets (under the pseudonym Bob Nichols) with Riley Puckett, scoring one of the biggest hits of the decade with "My Carolina Home." He composed songs and recorded with Jimmie Rodgers as well. In the 1930's, upset with the failure of The Skillet Lickers to "modernize" their sound, he formed The Georgia Wildcats and began to play his own brand of Western swing and what he called "hillbilly jazz." In the 1940's he was a popular fixture over WHAS radio in Louisville, where he led a Dixieland band with horns and drums. He died in 1970 in Battletown, Kentucky.   —C.W.

Mercury Records

Mercury was one of the most important of the half dozen or so powerhouse independent labels to pop up during the post-war era (in this case in Chicago, in 1945) as the demand for records surged among the American public.

Under executive Murray Nash, Mercury's early artists included cowboy star Rex Allen, Flatt and Scruggs, The Carlisles, The Hoosier Hot Shots, Faron Young, and pop singer Patti Page (who gave Mercury a tremendous boost with her phenomenally successful version of "Tennessee Waltz"). The company opened its first Nashville office in 1952, under the leadership of D. Kilpatrick. Don Pierce and Shelby Singleton were two other executives to play significant roles in the label's early Nashville years.

The label (now part of the international entertainment conglomerate, PolyGram) has remained a vital force in country music all through the years. The Statler Brothers, Tom T. Hall, Reba McEntire, George Jones, Johnny Cash, Hank Williams Jr., Kathy Mattea, Toby Keith, Sammy Kershaw and Billy Ray Cyrus are among the many artists to record under the Mercury logo in more recent decades. In 1994, parent company PolyGram launched a Nashville division of Mercury's sister label, Polydor.   —B.A.

MGM Records

A direct spin-off of the Loews Corporation, owners of the Metro-Goldwyn-Mayer film studios, MGM records was founded in 1945. The company's first president, Frank Walker, was formerly with Columbia and RCA Victor Records and had extensive experience recording all types of music, including country. Walker's experience gave the company credibility, though they didn't actually commence operations until late 1946. Early artists signed were Texas Western swing artist, Sam Nichols, and singer-songwriter Carson Robison. But its first major country signings came in 1947 with Hank Williams that spring and that fall, Bob Wills, who had just left Columbia. Hank and, to a lesser extent, Wills became the company's flagship country artists. Though other artists like Texas honky tonker Jerry Irby joined the label in the late 40's, none had Hank's stature. The Louvin Brothers, Marvin Rainwater and Red Sovine, along with The Osborne Brothers, were all MGM artists in the 50's. Conway Twitty's early rock hits were all done for MGM in the 60's, as were all of Tompall and The Glaser Brothers' hits. Hank Williams Jr. became one of the company's major artists, as did Eddy Arnold (very briefly) and Mel Tillis in the 70's.

In the late 70's, MGM briefly ran a country label called MGM/South, but by the mid-70's, the entire label ceased operations. The label had been narrow-minded in the country field, failing to promote Tompall Glaser's groundbreaking solo albums. It also mistrusted Hank Williams Jr.'s increasing reliance on Southern rock as part of his sound. Problems with its handling of the album, *Hank Williams Jr. And Friends,* led Williams to leave the label not long before it shut down. MGM's catalog was eventually purchased by PolyGram, who also own Mercury Records and the Smash Records catalog. —R.K.

Mid-Day Merry-Go-Round

The *Mid-Day Merry-Go-Round* was a popular and influential radio show over WNOX in Knoxville, running from the mid-1930's until the 1950's. Though some considered it a "farm club" for the Grand Ole Opry—and though dozens of *Merry-Go-Round* stars did move on to the Opry's greener financial pastures—the show had its own distinct personality and musical style. Much of its approach was defined by the show's announcer and emcee, Lowell Blanchard, who welcomed all sorts of music, from hillbilly jazz to gospel. In the early days of the show, personnel included a young Chet Atkins, Homer and Jethro, a young Roy Acuff and Archie Campbell. After the war the show was a major launching pad for the talents of Bill and Cliff Carlisle, Martha Carson, Johnnie and Jack, Don Gibson, Smilin' Eddie Hill, Kentucky Slim, The Maybelle Carter Family, Claude Boone and many others. —C.W.

Jody Miller

BORN: November 29, 1941
BIRTHPLACE: Phoenix, Arizona

Born Myrna Joy Miller, Jody Miller gained her fame on Capitol Records with "Queen of the House," a 1965 answer song to "King of the Road," a hit by another Miller—Roger (no relation). The song won her a Grammy that year, but no further hits came along until 1971's "He's So Fine" on Epic Records. Other big hits included "There's a Party Goin' On," "Baby I'm Yours" and "Good News." Her country/pop style kept her on the charts through 1979, though none of her singles reached the Top Ten after 1973. These days, she owns a ranch in Blanchard, Oklahoma, where she raises quarter horses. —G.F.

Ned Miller

BORN: April 12, 1925
BIRTHPLACE: Raines, Utah

Ned Miller never aspired to a full-time musical career. He played on the side while working at laboring jobs in Utah, then California. He started recording for the Fabor label around 1956. Among his releases were his original ballad, "From a Jack to a King." He also wrote Bonnie Guitar's 1957 hit, "Dark

Moon." Yet Miller had no real success with Fabor or with Capitol until 1962, when Fabor re-released "From a Jack to a King." By early 1963 it had spent four weeks at Number Two. Miller's subsequent hits were modest, except for his 1965 Top Ten single, "Do What You Do Do Well." Miller never liked performing, and after recording with minimal success for Capitol and Republic Records, he retired to Las Vegas in the 1970's. Ricky Van Shelton had a Number One single with "From a Jack to a King" in 1989.   —R.K.

Roger Miller

BORN: January 2, 1936
BIRTHPLACE: Fort Worth, Texas
DIED: October 25, 1992

Roger Dean Miller, one of country's great singer-songwriters, did not have an easy life. Shortly after his birth, his father died and his mother became ill. Miller and his three brothers were separated and sent to live with various relatives. In 1939, Roger went to Erick, Oklahoma, to live with an aunt and uncle. Growing up, he met his first musical role model: future star Sheb Wooley, his cousin's husband. Wooley gave the boy a fiddle, and Roger picked cotton to earn enough money for a guitar.

After quitting school in the eighth grade he worked on area ranches. After two years in the Army he went to Nashville, and recorded unsuccessfully for Mercury. For a time he worked in Nashville as a bellhop, and gained experience playing fiddle behind Minnie Pearl and drumming for Faron Young. In 1958 he signed a songwriting contract with Nashville's Tree Music, and though his Decca recordings went nowhere, in 1958 several of his songs, recorded by more established artists, took off. Ray Price had a smash with "Invitation to the Blues." Ernest Tubb did well that year with "Half a Mind," and Jim Reeves took "Billy Bayou" to Number One. Chet Atkins signed Miller to RCA, and "You Don't Want My Love" made

the Top 20 in 1961, followed by his Top Ten recording of "When Two Worlds Collide," a song he co-wrote with Bill Anderson.

By 1963, frustrated with recording, he decided to try acting. To make extra money, he recorded some of his novelty songs for Mercury. He expected little, since he sang these songs only for friends and didn't put much commercial stock in them. But in mid-1964 "Dang Me," released on Mercury's Smash label, reached Number One on the country charts, staying there for six weeks, and became a pop hit as well. The next single, "Chug-a-Lug," also became a crossover hit. In 1965 his modern hobo tune, "King of the Road," became one of the year's biggest records, winning him six Grammys. Other hits followed that year including "Engine, Engine #9," "Kansas City Star," "England Swings" and "Husbands and Wives." Miller's loony, hip persona became a national rage.

In 1966 he hosted his own NBC variety show, and later was part owner of Nashville's King of the Road motel. In 1973 he was inducted into the Nashville Songwriters' Hall of Fame. After his recording career wound down, he retired to New Mexico. But in the mid-1980's he re-emerged to write the score for the Broadway musical, *Big River*, based on Mark Twain's novel, *Huckleberry Finn*. It won him Broadway's highest honor, the Tony Award. Miller, always known for his quick wit, even maintained his sense of humor as he fought throat cancer, which eventually claimed his life. Old friends Ralph Emery, Buddy Killen and Glen Campbell have all included colorful "Roger Miller stories" in their autobiographies.   —R.K.

Ronnie Milsap

BORN: January 16, 1946
BIRTHPLACE: Robbinsville, North Carolina

Though the bulk of his success has befallen him in the country field, country music is merely one hue on Ronnie Milsap's varied musical palette. In fact, his earliest successes as a recording artist were as a white rhythm and blues singer/pianist on the New York-based Scepter label. "I grew up in a time when it was all right to like all kinds of music," recalls Milsap, who was born in the small North Carolina Smoky Mountain community of Robbinsville, and lost his sight at an early age due to congenital glaucoma. "I remember in the 1950's, a lot of stations in the South would play Ray Price, Jim Reeves and Patsy Cline, and would mix a little Little Richard and Fats Domino right in there with them. Maybe that's why, later, I was a little disappointed after several years of being in Nashville, that there was such criticism of anybody who might want to record a song that had a little bit of blues or a little bit of rock 'n' roll in it."

Milsap initially stormed the country charts in the mid-70's with a string of conventional enough country hits: "The Girl Who Waits on Tables," "Day Dreams About Night Things," "I'm a Stand By My Woman Man," "Please Don't Tell Me How the Story Ends" and others.

But always a restless and innovative soul, Milsap, in the years since, has proceeded to wander all over  the musical map. There have been champagne-smooth crossover hits ("It Was Almost Like a Song," "Only One Love in My Life"), 50's nostalgia (the 1985 Number One, "Lost in the Fifties Tonight," and a Number One 1986 remake of The Weavers' big 1957 pop hit, "Happy, Happy Birthday Baby"), full-blown rock ("She Loves My Car," which, in the video format, even made it to MTV), and even a quasi-disco hit called "Get It Up." All in all, Milsap's eclectic taste translated into 35 Number One singles between 1974 and 1989. It's worth noting that nearly all of the above-mentioned musical explorations were commercial successes, netting Milsap Grammy awards and platinum albums.

All in all, it's been a long journey for this son of a sawmill worker, who was shipped off to the Governor Morehead School for the Blind in Raleigh, North Carolina, when he was six. Life at Morehead was lonely and, at times, full of abuse and deprivation; but it was there that he began a rigorous study of both the piano and violin. Later, Milsap turned down an opportunity to study pre-law on scholarship, and instead opted to play sessions at Chip Moman's American Studios in Memphis. There, he backed everyone from Dione Warwick to Elvis Presley. Presley, in fact, became so fond of Milsap that he even hired him to play several private parties at Graceland, The King's palatial Memphis home.

Milsap turned his back on a lucrative living playing Memphis nightclubs to come to Nashville, where he went to work for a fraction of the pay at The King of the Road, a motel owned by the late Roger Miller which was then a popular nightspot for the Music Row set. Milsap eventually signed with RCA, and by 1974, scored three Number One records ("Pure Love," "A Legend in My Own Time" and Kris Kristofferson's "Please Don't Tell Me How the Story Ends") and won the first of his many Country Music Association awards. Milsap has been a member of the Grand Ole Opry since 1976. —B.A.

Bill Monroe

BORN: September 13, 1911
BIRTHPLACE: Rosine, Kentucky

One of the stories they don't tell about the time Elvis tried out for the Grand Ole Opry was what happened when he ran into bluegrass great Bill Monroe backstage. Monroe recalls: "He come around and apologized for the way he'd changed 'Blue Moon of Kentucky.' I told him that if it would help him get his start and give him a different style, I was for him a hundred percent." Elvis was sincere; a few years later, during the so-called "Million Dollar Quartet" jam session at Sun, where Elvis was joined by Jerry Lee Lewis and Carl Perkins, Elvis and Lewis sang no less than four of Monroe's old songs. Another Sun alumnus, rockabilly singer Charlie Feathers, made the connection even more explicit: "Bill Monroe's music and colored artists' music is what caused rock 'n' roll."

For a singer whose music, bluegrass, is supposed to have merely a cult following, Bill Monroe has had an amazingly broad influence over the last 50 years. His 1985 album, *Bill Monroe and Friends*, had some of Nashville's biggest names actually fighting to get on it; the winners included obvious choices like Ricky Skaggs and Emmylou Harris, but also mainstream figures like Johnny Cash, Willie Nelson, Barbara Mandrell, Waylon Jennings, Mel Tillis, Larry Gatlin and The Oak Ridge Boys. In a city full of "legends in their time," Monroe still stands unique, in all kinds of ways. He's actually had only a handful of certified chart hits, preferring to work through a long series of steadily-selling albums. And, unlike many of his age

and tenure, he refuses to rest on his laurels by remaking old favorites for TV packages and restricting his touring to a few big shows. His albums continue to break new ground, featuring new songs, new performing ideas and new sidemen. In 1986, to celebrate his 50th year in the music business, Monroe took off on a grueling 50-state tour—traveling, as he always has, by bus and car. Next to the late Roy Acuff, Monroe has been on the Opry longer than any other singer, but his career shows no signs of slowing down. He is still building his legend.

And legend it is; there's no doubt about that. Monroe doesn't just attract fans; he creates disciples. People name their children after him; amateur mandolin players bring their instruments to him to bless;

families build their vacations around his annual gathering at Bean Blossom, Indiana. And Monroe is refreshingly free of false modesty about all this. When asked how he feels when he is called "The Father of Bluegrass Music," he answers, "Well, I don't mind that. That's really the truth, you know. I accept that, I guess, as well as any man could. I think it's a great honor to originate a music—something to be proud of." In other conversations, he talks fondly of "his" music, and reviews with pride the various other "students" who have graduated from his school—everyone from Flatt and Scruggs to Ricky Skaggs.

Monroe hails from the rich farmland in western Kentucky, near a little town called Rosine. In one direction was Muhlenberg County, where Merle Travis

would develop his influential guitar style; in another was Louisville, home of a thriving black music culture that merged ragtime, blues, jazz and string band music. The radio station of choice was WLS in Chicago, where the Monroe family listened to singers like Bradley Kincaid and bands like The Prairie Ramblers and The Hoosier Hot Shots. There were two churches in Rosine, a Baptist church and a Methodist church, and regular rural "singing conventions," where young Bill learned to sing the tenor parts to songs like "Beautiful Life" and "He Will Set Your Fields on Fire." And there was Bill's uncle on his mother's side, Pen Vandiver, an old-time square dance fiddler; after the older boys had left home, young Bill would ride horseback to dances with "Uncle Pen" to back him on mandolin or guitar. "We'd go out in the country maybe four or five miles and play for a square dance at somebody's home; they'd clear a room out and me and him would play the dance. We'd make three or four dollars apiece." Years later, in 1950, Bill would write "Uncle Pen," one of his best known songs, in tribute to these times.

As the Depression hit western Kentucky, many local farm boys fled north into the industrial centers looking for work; Bill's older brothers, Birch and Charlie, had already left, and soon Bill joined them. For five years he worked at a Sinclair Oil refinery in East Chicago and played dances with his two brothers in his spare time. Then, in 1932, the three Monroes got their first professional jobs in music—not as musicians, but as buck dancers in the WLS *Barn Dance* touring troupe. It was good work, and in 1934 Bill and brother Charlie decided to strike out on their own, doing full-time music as The Monroe Brothers. Bill played mandolin, Charlie guitar, and they specialized in sentimental songs like "Little Red Shoes" and "What Is a Home Without Love" and up-tempo gospel songs like "Drifting Too Far from the Shore." In some ways, they were like many other brother duets of the time, such as The Delmore Brothers or The Blue Sky Boys, but they liked to play songs faster and dazzled people with their intricate mandolin and guitar runs. For a time, they were sponsored by a curious product called Crazy Water Crystals (which apparently promoted "regularity") at stations in the Midwest, but in 1935 they moved down south to the Carolinas, where their radio career really took off.

In fact, the brothers were doing so well on radio that when the first letters came offering them a recording contract with RCA Victor, they threw them away. Finally, on February 17, 1936, in a warehouse in Charlotte, North Carolina, RCA's Eli Oberstein corralled the Monroes for their first session. It yielded five records on the company's budget-line Bluebird label, including hits like "What Would You Give in Exchange for Your Soul," "Nine Pound Hammer," "Foggy Mountain Top" and "New River Train." Over the next two years, the brothers would record some 60 songs for Bluebird—about half of them gospel, many of them from older generations like The Carter Family, and most of them arranged by Charlie. They had success, but each brother wanted more, and in 1938 they decided to split.

Charlie kept the RCA contract, and for a time was doing better than Bill. "I didn't sing a solo until I was 27 years old," Bill recalls. "I'd always sung tenor to Charlie. But with that training, to get up and hit those high notes, there wasn't any trouble for me to sing high, so I did." Finding the proper backup combination was a different matter. The first group he actually called The Blue Grass Boys—in Atlanta—consisted of a fiddle, a guitar and a jug. He soon substituted the string bass for the jug, but still did not add a banjo. By 1939 he felt he was ready. "I went into Nashville on a Monday morning, and went up to the Opry office. Judge Hay and Harry Stone and David Stone were all going out to get coffee. After they came back, I played 'Mule Skinner Blues' for them, and 'Bile Them Cabbage Down' and 'John Henry.' And they said I had the kind of music National Life needed, and they said, 'If you ever leave the station, you'll have to fire yourself.'" Monroe joined the Opry that fall, and during the next two years made his first solo recordings for RCA Victor—including such classics as "Orange Blossom Special," "Dog House Blues," "In the Pines" and "Tennessee Blues."

During the 1940's Monroe carefully built his band and crafted his sound—in between grueling tent shows he performed for the Opry and a series of exhibition baseball games that his boys played. By 1942 he had added David "Stringbean" Akeman on banjo, completing the basic bluegrass band line-up. By 1946 he had created what many call the greatest bluegrass band of all time—Earl Scruggs on banjo; Lester Flatt on guitar and vocals; Chubby Wise on fiddle; and Howard Watts (Cedric Rainwater) on bass. It was this band that really defined bluegrass music, in 28 sides recorded for Columbia between September 1946 and October 1947. This was Elvis' source for "Blue Moon of Kentucky" as well as "Molly and Tenbrooks," "Will You Be Lovin' Another Man" and "I'm Going Back to Old Kentucky." The Blue Grass Boys were the hottest thing on the Opry, and when Monroe and Scruggs took their driving instrumental solos, the Ryman Auditorium went wild. By the early 1950's, as band after band sought to copy the Monroe style, the term "bluegrass" was being used to describe a type of music, not just a band.

In the early 1950's, as former Blue Grass Boys Flatt and Scruggs saw their own careers take off, Monroe's career seemed to falter. His new label, Decca, tried to push him toward mainstream country, and even saddled him with sessions using electric guitars and Nashville studio sidemen like Grady Martin. Monroe shook this off, though, and was soon producing new masterworks: "Footprints in the Snow" (1952), "I'm Working on a Building" (1954), "Gold Rush" (1967), "Linda Lou" (1961) and "Lonesome Moonlight Waltz" (1970). His instrumentation grew more and more complex—at one point he was using three fiddlers—and through the 1950's and 1960's The Blue Grass Boys band became what Monroe calls "his school." His graduates were sent out to carry on the tradition, and they included Jimmy Martin, Sonny Osborne (of The Osborne Brothers), Hubert Davis, Bill Keith, Del McCoury, Roland White, Vassar Clements and dozens of others. In the 1960's, with help from his new manager Ralph Rinzler, Monroe began to expand his music into the "folk revival" circuit of the North and West, and onto college campuses. He found a national audience and even today has fans in places where even the most sophisticated mainstream country acts have trouble. In 1970, he was elected to the Country Music Hall of Fame.

In the early 1980's there were rumors that Monroe was about to retire. In his *Master of Bluegrass* album appeared the haunting, melancholy hit with the cryptic title, "My Last Days on Earth." He underwent major surgery. He even made his peace with the Gibson company over a long-running dispute about his mandolin. But then came a new surge of creativity, and soon Monroe was back, as strong as ever, appearing in a video with Ricky Skaggs and doing a wild buck dance on the Country Music Association Awards show. He continues to play the Opry regularly. In a recent interview, he summed up his work by saying, "I just wanted a style of music of my own." Such a pronouncement was, and continues to be, one of country music's great understatements.

(See also, Charlie Monroe and Bluegrass.) —C.W.

ing Chair" and "Down in the Willow Garden."

Monroe retired from music in 1957, but in 1972 he re-emerged and began appearing at concerts and bluegrass festivals, often with Jimmy Martin. He died on September 27, 1975. (See also, Bill Monroe.) —D.S.

Patsy Montana

BORN: October 30, 1912
BIRTHPLACE: Hot Springs, Arkansas

Singer and fiddler, sometime songwriter and virtuoso yodeler, Patsy Montana was one of the most popular acts in country music throughout the 1930's and 40's— and the first solo female country music star. Born Rubye Blevins in 1912 outside Hot Springs, Arkansas, Patsy studied the violin at the University of the West (now UCLA) and played fiddle for a few Jimmie Davis sessions before forming her own group, an all-female trio called The Montana Cowgirls. In 1933 Patsy joined a male quartet, The Prairie Ramblers, which performed regularly on the WLS *National Barn Dance* in Chicago. Two years later she had her first hit song, "I Wanna Be a Cowboy's Sweetheart," on ARC Records. It became the first million-selling record by a woman, paving the way for generations of female performers from Patsy Cline to Reba McEntire,

Charlie Monroe

BORN: July 4, 1903
BIRTHPLACE: Rosine, Kentucky
DIED: September 27, 1975

Although Charlie Monroe was the dominant figure in the original Monroe Brothers, his music and accomplishments have been overshadowed by the fame of his younger brother Bill. Charlie's tenor voice was warmer and slightly richer than his brother's. The two recorded together during the 1930's. Later, heading his own band, The Kentucky Pardners, Charlie fused old-time music with the emerging honky tonk sound. Lester Flatt, Curly Seckler, Red Rector, Slim and Wilma Martin, Tex Isley and Ira Louvin were band members at various times.

During the 1940's Monroe ran one of the Southeast's most successful tent shows. His popularity led to a solo RCA Victor contract in 1946; for the next five years he recorded such enduring songs as "I'm Coming Back, But I Don't Know When," "Bringing in the Georgia Mail," "Red Rock-

to Suzy Bogguss—who's always been a particularly big Montana fan and, in fact, covered "Cowboy's Sweetheart" in 1988.

Patsy continued to record and tour with The Prairie Ramblers, scoring such hits as "Sweetheart of the Saddle" (1936), "There's a Ranch in the Sky" (1937), "Singing in the Saddle" (1939) and "Shy Little Ann from Cheyenne" (1940). She also appeared in several Gene Autry movie serials. Though Patsy pretty much stopped recording in the early 1950's, except for occasional independent releases, she continues to perform into the 1990's. (See also, The Prairie Ramblers.) —M.B.

John Michael Montgomery

BORN: January 20, 1965
BIRTHPLACE: Danville, Kentucky

With the platinum success of his debut album, *Life's a Dance*, this crowd-pleasing Kentucky boy—who was discovered by Atlantic Records' Rick Blackburn while playing a club in Lexington, Kentucky—moved right to the head of the class of 1993. He was the only one of that year's newcomers to score a million-selling album. He one-upped that in 1994 when his sophomore album, *Kickin' It Up*, landed at the top of both the pop and country album charts—a feat usu-

ally reserved for the likes of a Garth Brooks or Billy Ray Cyrus. It's Montgomery's contemporary ballads that have attracted the most radio attention, though his albums mix them with doses of Southern rock and neo-honky tonk. In addition to Merle Haggard, he cites Lionel Richie, Bob Seger and Lynyrd Skynyrd as shaping his musical style. —G.F.

Melba Montgomery

BORN: October 14, 1938
BIRTHPLACE: Iron City, Tennessee

Raised in Florence, Alabama, singer-songwriter Melba Montgomery got her start with a four-year stint as a member of Roy Acuff's Smoky Mountain Boys in 1958. She cut her debut album, *Melba Montgomery*, on the United Artists label in the early 1960's and had her first chart success with "Hall of Shame" and "The Greatest One of All." Montgomery found a fan in industry executive Pappy Daily, who signed her to the Musicor label, where the chart action continued, including "Baby, Ain't That Fine," a 1966 duet with fellow Musicor artist, pop singer Gene Pitney. Daily also teamed Montgomery up for a series of duets with his earlier discovery, George Jones, including "We Must Have Been Out of Our Minds" (Melba's own composition, which made it to Number Three in 1963) and "Don't Keep Me Lonely too Long." In the early 70's, Montgomery signed with Capitol, recording a series of duets with Charlie Louvin ("Something to Brag About" and "Did You Ever" among them). Next, Montgomery moved on to Elektra, making the charts in 1973 with "Wrap Your Arms Around Me," a song she co-wrote with her husband, musician Jack Solomon. A year later she recorded "No Charge," a sentimental number that became her biggest hit ever, reaching Number One on the country charts, and becoming a Top 40 pop hit. After a few more minor hits, she went back to

United Artists in 1977, putting two more singles onto the charts, including a Top 20 cover of "Angel of the Morning." Later recordings came on smaller labels. Her last chart entry appeared in 1986.   —M.B.

Monument Records

During the 1960's and early 70's, Monument Records held the distinction of being the most powerful independent label in Nashville, as well as the only Nashville-based label to achieve success not only in the country field, but in pop and R&B as well. Monument was originally established in 1958 in Washington, D.C., by long-time proprietor Fred Foster. Foster's label hit pay dirt that same year with its very first single release: Billy Grammer's "I Gotta Travel On," which was a million-seller.

Foster moved Monument's operations to Nashville in 1960. In the ensuing years the label signed and recorded a slew of artists who would go on to fame (sometimes on Monument, sometimes on other labels). Among them were Roy Orbison, Willie Nelson, Dolly Parton, Kris Kristofferson, Ray Stevens, Larry Gatlin, Connie Smith, Billy Walker, Charlie McCoy and Boots Randolph.

Meanwhile Monument's publishing arm, Combine Music, prospered under the stewardship of Foster's partner, Bob Beckham, who signed writers like Kris Kristofferson, Larry Gatlin, Chris Gantry and Vince Mathews, and built the company into a formidable publishing operation. By the early 1980's, however, Monument's influence had faded and the company fell into a quagmire of bankruptcy and litigation. In 1983 the label's impressive back catalog of master tapes was sold at auction (most of them to a division of CBS Records).   —B.A.

Ralph Mooney

BORN: September 16, 1928
BIRTHPLACE: Duncan, Oklahoma

Ralph Mooney is one of the all-time masters of playing the pedal steel guitar in the high-pitched West Coast style that was the underpinning of the Bakersfield Sound., Mooney started out in the late 1940's in Western swing bandleader Merle Lindsay's group, The

Oklahoma Night Riders. Later in the 40's, he built his own mechanism to raise and lower strings like the other early pedal steels. Leo Fender borrowed Mooney's instrument to study it and gave him a Fender model. Mooney graduated to touring with Skeets McDonald in the early 50's, then joined Wynn Stewart in the mid-50's. Around that same time, he and Chuck

Seals wrote the country standard, "Crazy Arms," a 1957 hit for Ray Price, since recorded by several dozen different artists. Mooney worked extensively with Stewart into the early 60's; he also played on countless country sessions backing Stewart, Buck Owens, Merle Haggard and Wanda Jackson. He created his own distinct sounds for each artist he worked with. In 1968 he and guitarist James Burton recorded the Capitol album, *Corn Pickin' & Slick Slidin'*. In the 70's and 80's, "Moon" became a fixture in Waylon Jennings' band.   —R.K.

Bob Moore

BORN: November 30, 1932
BIRTHPLACE: Nashville, Tennessee

A Nashville native, Bob Moore did much of his early work with acts on the Opry and over various WSM radio programs in the early 50's. After bassist Ernie Newton began to pull away from session work, and after a brief period working with Red Foley on the *Ozark Jubilee* in the 50's. Moore became the major studio bassist in Nashville. He was part of the A-Team, which in the 50's included guitarists Hank Garland, Harold Bradley, Ray Edenton, Grady Martin, pianist Floyd Cramer, drummer Buddy Harman and fiddlers Dale Potter and Tommy Jackson. Moore worked hundreds of sessions and had a chance to join Hank Garland, Chet Atkins, Boots Randolph and other Nashville session players to perform at the 1960 Newport Jazz Festival. In 1961 he had a Top Ten pop instrumental hit with "Mexico" on Fred Foster's Monument Records. Moore also played a major role in

defining the sound of Roy Orbison's classic Monument recordings. As session leader, he received—and got— billing on Roy's Monument hits as "Bob Moore, His Orchestra and Chorus." Moore, playing primarily string bass, continued to be among the most in-demand session players in the 60's and 70's. As the 80's began, Moore's session work began tapering off as a new generation of Nashville session musicians moved in. After a hand injury limited his playing, Moore moved to Florida, where he now owns a nightclub. His daughter, Linda, was part of the early 80's Nashville group, Calamity Jane.   —R.K.

Tiny Moore

BORN: May 12, 1920
BIRTHPLACE: Port Arthur, Texas
DIED: December 15, 1987

Like many former Texas Playboys, fiddler and electric mandolinist Billie "Tiny" Moore endured many years of obscurity between the 1950's and the 1970's, when Western swing became fashionable again. Moore was particularly influenced by Leo Raley, who played an amplified mandolin in the 1930's. Tiny, nicknamed for his size, worked as a fiddler for Happy Fats and his Rayne-Bo Ramblers and later with the Port Arthur Jubileers.

After World War II military service, he auditioned for Wills' Texas Playboys in a Texas restaurant. Despite the fact that Bob Wills disliked mandolin (his father, fiddler Uncle John Wills, made Bob play it as a child), he hired Tiny in 1946. He remained with The Playboys, based in Sacramento, California, until 1949, when Wills moved back to Texas, assigning Tiny to remain in Sacramento as mandolinist and arranger for Bob's brother, Billy Jack Wills, and his Band. Tiny's sophisticated arranging gave the band a modern focus, though they never achieved more than local fame. Married in 1948 to Dean McKinney of The McKinney Sisters, a vocal duo that worked with Wills in the 40's, Tiny settled in Sacramento, eventually becoming a children's TV show host and opening a music store. Merle Haggard used him for his 1970 Bob Wills tribute album, and soon Tiny was performing at Western swing concerts. Eventually he joined Merle Haggard's Strangers, and recorded a solo album with Jethro Burns and another solo album, both for the Kaleidoscope label, before returning to his Sacramento home. He was to join Playboys II, a new Texas Playboy alumni band, when he died of a heart attack.   —R.K.

George Morgan

BORN: June 28, 1925
BIRTHPLACE: Waverly, Tennessee
DIED: July 7, 1975

Opry singer George Morgan was born June 28, 1925, in Waverly, Tennessee, and raised in Barberton, Ohio. After a brief Army stint during World War II, he began playing in bands and working on radio stations in Ohio. In the late 40's he landed a spot on WWVA's *Wheeling Jamboree*. A demo tape he sent to RCA found its way to the Grand Ole Opry, which requested that he audition.

He joined the Opry in 1948 and landed a recording contract with Columbia, scoring a Number One hit with his first single, the self-penned "Candy Kisses," in 1949. A string of Top Ten hits followed that year, including "Please Don't Let Me Love You," "Rainbow in My Heart," a cover of Eddy Arnold's "Room Full of

Roses" and "Cry-Baby Heart." But after that, his hits became sporadic, with only three Top Tens throughout the 50's and one in the 60's. Morgan ran into the same problem that others in the country field faced—the rise of rock 'n' roll. Morgan was a traditionalist, uncomfortable with rockabilly or even the countrypolitan Nashville Sound that others turned to in response. He generally stuck with his traditional sound and continued as a popular Opry member right up until his death (except for a brief period in the late 50's when he left to host a television show on Nashville's WLAC).

In 1966, Morgan left Columbia Records, recording for a number of labels—Starday, MCA/Decca and 4 Star among them—scoring two Top 20's in the 70's: "Lilacs and Fire" and "Red Rose from the Blue Side of Town." His later records, including 1974's "Red Rose," featured Little Roy Wiggins, the steel player left behind in the wake of Eddy Arnold's switch from traditional country to countrypolitan. In May of 1975, Morgan suffered a heart attack. He died on July 7, 1975, following open heart surgery. His daughter, Lorrie Morgan, is currently a top country star—and, like her father, an Opry member.   —M.B.

Lorrie Morgan

BORN: June 27, 1959
BIRTHPLACE: Nashville, Tennessee

The daughter of Opry singer George Morgan , Loretta Lynn Morgan is living proof that nepotism doesn't guarantee celebrities' kids quick and easy success. Though Lorrie made her first appearance on the Opry stage as a teenager, it is only now, 20 years later, that she has reached superstardom.

After her father's death in 1975, Lorrie kept his band together and toured with them. She sang (bluegrass, of all things—her least favorite music) at the Opryland theme park and did a two-year tour as George Jones' backup singer. After joining the Opry in 1984, Lorrie signed briefly with MCA Records, only to lose the contract when the label demanded she quit the show. She refused to do so and continues as an Opry member today.

After a few years of playing clubs and singing on demos, she signed with RCA Records in 1988; her first RCA single, "Trainwreck of Emotion," became a major hit the following year. Her debut album, *Leave the Light On*, was released in the spring of 1989, and topped the million sales mark. Around the same time Lorrie's husband, singer Keith Whitley, who became her second husband in 1986, died from alcohol poi-

soning. That same year Lorrie scored her first Top Ten hit, "Dear Me," followed by a string of successful singles including "Out of Your Shoes" and "Five Minutes" (both in 1989). The following year Lorrie recorded "Til a Tear Becomes a Rose," a studio-engineered duet with her late husband that was later named Country Music Association Vocal Event of the Year.

Her three more recent albums, *Something in Red* (1991—also on RCA), *Watch Me* (1992, on the RCA-affiliated label, BNA) and *War Paint* (1994, also on BNA), have all met with favorable reviews and brisk sales and displayed a musical talent that can range from easy-going pop-flavored balladry to hard country soulfulness. And no doubt, Lorrie's got a lot to sing about: In 1991 she married Brad Thompson, former driver of Clint Black's tour bus; they've since divorced. In 1994, Lorrie moved back to RCA Records after a time on BNA, both of which are owned by the same company, BMG. —M.B.

Gary Morris

BORN: December 7, 1948
BIRTHPLACE: Fort Worth, Texas

Before moving to Nashville and signing with Warner Bros. in 1979, Gary Morris put in his time playing the clubs, and was even involved in Jimmy Carter's presidential campaign. A consistent hitmaker from 1983 to 1987, Morris' best-known hit is probably 1983's "Wind Beneath My Wings." Though it didn't reach Number One, it was typical of Morris' country/pop style and it earned Song of the Year awards from both the Country Music Association and the Academy of Country Music. (Later, the song became a Number One pop hit for Bette Midler.) While making hit records, Morris also took a detour into acting. Using his deep, rich voice to good effect, he starred opposite Linda Ronstadt in the Puccini opera, *La Boheme*, at the New York Public Theater in 1984;

landed a role in the prime-time soap, *The Colbys*, in 1986, and had a starring role in the Broadway production of *Les Miserables* in 1988. *The Colbys* wasn't his only soap connection: he and duet partner Crystal Gayle had Number One hits with "Another World," the theme to the daytime drama, and "Makin' Up for Lost Time," which was featured on *Dallas*. Morris left Warner Bros. in 1988, recording for Universal in '89 and Capitol in '91. —G.F.

Moon Mullican

BORN: March 27, 1909
BIRTHPLACE: Corrigan, Texas
DIED: January 1, 1967

Aubrey "Moon" Mullican, "King of the Hillbilly Piano Players," influenced Jerry Lee Lewis, Roy Hall and other country boogie pianists. Born in Polk County, Texas, Aubrey Mullican first learned blues guitar from a black sharecropper, then taught himself to play blues on the family's pump organ. Around 1925 he moved to Houston, where he began playing in clubs. His nickname "Moon" may have been shortened from "Moonshine." In the late 30's he sang and played piano with Western swing fiddler Cliff Bruner's Texas Wanderers, doing the vocal on Bruner's 1939 recording of Ted Daffan's "Truck Driver's Blues." He led a touring band for his friend Jimmie Davis' 1943 campaign for Louisiana governor and performed extensively around his home base of Beaumont, Texas. Around 1946 he signed with King Records and a year later had his first hit with "New Pretty Blonde (Jole Blon)." Several other hits followed from 1948-51, among them "Sweeter Than the Flowers," "Mona Lisa," "Goodnight Irene" and "Cherokee Boogie." His friendship with Hank Williams helped Mullican land a spot on the Grand Ole Opry and led to a rumored collaboration on Hank's composition, "Jambalaya," though Moon received no composer credit. Moon left the Opry in the mid-50's and left

King around 1956. He found no further success on records until his 1961 hit recording of "Ragged But Right" for Starday. Moon suffered a heart attack onstage in Kansas City in 1962. He continued recording and performing locally until a fatal heart attack at his Beaumont home on New Year's Day of 1967. Moon's old friend, former Louisiana Governor Jimmie Davis, delivered the eulogy.   —R.K.

Earl "Joaquin" Murphey

BORN: December 30, 1923
BIRTHPLACE: Hollywood, California

Earl Murphey began playing the steel guitar at his parents' insistence as a teenager, and in the early 40's auditioned for Spade Cooley's band. He amazed the band members who heard him audition, and he soon became an integral part of the Cooley organization. Among his most dazzling numbers was "Oklahoma Stomp," the showcase instrumental he recorded with Cooley's original band for Columbia in 1945. He received his nickname because promoter Foreman Phillips, for whom Cooley worked, felt some of the band members should have nicknames that reminded their audiences of the South and Southwest. (Many of California's country music fans had moved from those regions to work in World War II defense plants.) While Jack Williams became "Tex" Williams (despite being from Illinois), Murphey was named to remind fans of the San Joaquin Valley. Murphey quit Cooley in 1946 to join Andy Parker and The Plainsmen, where he did some outstanding solo work on Parker's vocal recordings and on various swing instrumentals the group recorded. Murphey, who also played on Merle Travis' first Capitol recording date, next joined Tex Williams' Western Caravan, where he appeared on "Smoke! Smoke! Smoke! (That Cigarette)" and other numbers. In 1947 he became the first musician to play a Bigsby steel guitar. After leaving Williams in the late 40's, he recorded with T. Texas Tyler and others and worked again with Cooley. Murphey's career tapered off by the mid-50's. Though steel guitar promoter DeWitt Scott coaxed him out of retirement in 1976 and recorded a Murphey album for his Mid-Land label, Murphey, who refuses interviews, remains a mysterious and somewhat eccentric yet admired figure. He was elected to the International Steel Guitar Hall of Fame in 1980.   —R.K.

Michael Martin Murphey

BORN: March 14, 1942
BIRTHPLACE: Dallas, Texas

One of the most successful rock-to-country crossovers, Michael Martin Murphey has weathered the perilous shoals of 1970's California soft rock to emerge as a minor—but solidly entrenched—country star. Though he toured briefly in the 1960's as part of a group called The Lewis & Clark Expedition, Murphey is perhaps best known for his 1975 hit, "Wildfire," which catapulted him to rock stardom during the Southern California country-rock golden era. After a few more pop hits ("Carolina in the Pines" and "What's Forever For"—which also crossed over in reverse, going from the pop charts to become a Number One country song), Murphey disappeared from the scene, but re-emerged as a country artist, with hits like "Still Taking Chances" (1982), "A Face in the Crowd" (a Number Four duet with Holly Dunn in 1987), "A Long Line of Love" (a Number One in 1987) and "Talkin' to the Wrong Man" (a duet with his son Ryan that reached Number Four in 1988).

Murphey has, in more recent years, become an avid student and devotee of Western cowboy music. His Westfest concerts have brought together the best of Western arts and artisans, including cowboy poets, country music singers with a Western flavor, cowboy and cowboy movie performers and Western and Native American artists. In 1990 he recorded an album of cowboy music that, while not commercially successful, marked an important watershed.   —M.B.

Jimmy Murphy

BORN: October 25, 1925
BIRTHPLACE: Birmingham, Alabama
DIED: June 1, 1981

Jimmy Murphy was a singer and composer best known in the Knoxville, Tennessee, area during the period 1950-1970, and best remembered for his unusual guitar playing and his song, "Electricity." Born in Birmingham in 1925, Murphy followed his father's trade as a brick mason, playing music only in his spare time. He moved to Knoxville in 1950, working first on WROL with Archie Campbell, then later on WNOX's *Mid-Day Merry-Go-Round*. In 1951 he signed a contract with RCA Victor, eventually cutting eight sides (including "Electricity" and other originals), and signing with Acuff-Rose as a songwriter. By 1955 he was doing rockabilly for Columbia, often with Onie Wheeler; but these, like the Victor sides, produced no real hits. In the 1960's he did some admirable sides for several minor independent labels, including K-Ark, REM and Loyal. A Library of Congress researcher "rediscovered" him in 1976, and this led to *Electricity*, a 1978 album on the Sugar Hill label, on which Murphy was backed by a set of stellar bluegrass musicians, including Ricky Skaggs.   —C.W.

Anne Murray

BORN: June 20, 1946
BIRTHPLACE: Springhill, Nova Scotia, Canada

Anne Murray has adroitly walked the fine line between pop and country for more than 20 years. The Canadian-born singer scored her first Top Ten country hit for Capitol in 1970 with "Snowbird," which also reached the pop Top Ten. Her first country Number One came from "He Thinks I Still Care," a gender-bending rewrite of the George Jones hit, in 1974. (It's indicative of her broad appeal that the flip side was a version of The Beatles' "You Won't See Me," which made it into the pop Top Ten.) Her string of chart busters would continue right through 1990: She had a Gold single with "You Needed Me" in 1978; three Number Ones in 1979 ("I'll Just Fall in Love Again," "Shadows in the Moonlight" and "Broken Hearted Me"); further Number Ones with "Could I

Have This Dance" in 1980 and "Blessed Are the Believers" in 1981; and on and on. Her platinum-selling albums include *Greatest Hits* in 1980 and *Christmas Wishes* a year later.

Murray continued the streak with her 1984 album, *A Little Good News*. After hitting Number One on the country charts, the title single won Murray both a Grammy (for Best Country Vocal Performance—Female) and a Country Music Association award for Single of the Year. The album also won the CMA's Album of the Year award that year and produced two other Number Ones: "Just Another Woman in Love" and "Nobody Loves Me Like You Do." Her most recent Number One came in 1986, "Now and Forever (You and Me)." Murray continued recording for Capitol through 1991. Many of her hits, particularly "Snowbird," "Danny's Song" and "You Needed Me," remain staples of both country and adult contemporary radio, and Murray continues to record and perform, now signed to SBK/ERG Records. She released *Croonin'* in 1993, an album of 50's pop classics (from the likes of Patti Page, Peggy Lee, Rosemary Clooney and Eddy Arnold) that had inspired her musically in her early years.   —M.B.

Red Murrell

BORN: June 17, 1921
BIRTHPLACE: Willow Springs, Missouri

Ozark-born Joyce Wayne "Red" Murrell started play-ing music when he was eight, and learned a number of instruments while attending school. He was in-spired by various musicians, including fiddler Wade Ray. He started working in Missouri, but by 1940 had moved to the West Coast, working first in Northern California before settling in Los Angeles just before World War II. There he started playing with a small band and moving toward a Western swing sound. He worked for a while with Texas Jim Lewis before start-ing his own band, called The Ozark Playboys. Murrell recorded for a number of small labels in the late 1940's, and worked around California into the 50's.　—R.K.

Music City News

Music City News, the oldest Nashville-based country music fan magazine, was founded in 1963 by singer Faron Young, mainly as a newsletter for country art-ists, who tended to be on the road so much that they seldom saw one another.

The premier issue of *Music City News* hit the presses in July of 1963, with features on Elvis, Ralph Emery and Audrey Williams. One of the first ten sub-scribers was George Jones. Over the years, *MCN*'s small, localized readership gradually expanded to its current level—a circulation of about 200,000 a month. In 1979, it was acquired by Multi Media Corporation, which owns and operates it today.

Music City News initiated its annual awards in 1967, initially calling them the "Popularity Polls." The awards show was first televised in 1978; in 1990 it was merged with The Nashville Network's Viewers' Choice Awards, and re-named the *TNN/Music City News Country Awards*.　—B.A.

Nashville

Nashville, popularly known as Music City, is the capi-tal of Tennessee, and sits in the north-central region of the state. The first permanent settlement around

Nashville was established on Christmas Day in 1779 by James Robertson, who had led a group of 400 settlers on a 300-mile trek from North Carolina across the frozen Cumberland River. The settlers erected a fortress called Fort Nashborough, and, within a few years the settlement began to prosper, primarily be-cause the Cumberland provided easy access to the Mississippi, Ohio and Tennessee rivers, and their at-tending avenues of trade. In 1796 Tennessee joined the union, and in 1806 Nashville was incorporated. By 1810, the thriving frontier town had nearly 2,000 inhabitants.

Nashville's best-known citizen during the early 19th century was Andrew Jackson, the seventh president of the United States, who was nicknamed "Old Hickory," and whose home, The Hermitage, is today one of the Nashville area's most popular tourist at-tractions. Another prominent figure was James K. Polk, the expansionist 11th president, who was affection-ately dubbed "Young Hickory." During the Civil War, Nashville served as a strategic Confederate supply depot before falling under Union occupation and was bitterly fought over by the two Armies.

During the rest of the 19th century Nashville pros-pered as both a business and education center. Ma-jor colleges were founded in Nashville—Vanderbilt, Fisk, Peabody College and Meharry. Many consider Fisk University's Jubilee Singers, who were organized to raise money for the fledgling college in 1871, to be the first musical act to emerge from the city.

It was the insurance industry—the city's second-largest industry—that served as the catalyst in estab-lishing Nashville as the music capital of the United

States. In 1925, the National Life and Accident Insurance Company established radio station WSM (which became Nashville's third radio station), the home of the Grand Ole Opry, and the following year, the Life and Casualty Insurance Company of Tennessee established WLAC.

The Grand Ole Opry was actually the brainchild of George D. Hay, a native of Attica, Indiana, who served as a columnist for the *Memphis Commercial-Appeal* and later as a popular radio announcer—"The Solemn Old Judge"—for WLS in Chicago. While with WLS, he had injected some authentic humor and a homey atmosphere into the station's *Barn Dance* program. Soon after WSM took to the air, Hay was hired as station director. (See separate entry on Grand Ole Opry.)

Although the Nashville-based radio stations familiarized listeners with country music on the airwaves, most of the artists' records were recorded in Cincin-

nati or Chicago. That changed, however, in 1944 when RCA recorded Eddy Arnold, and in 1945 when Paul Cohen, of Decca Records, recorded Red Foley in WSM's Studio B. Later during the same year two WSM engineers, Aaron Shelton and Carl Jenkins, formed a commercial recording company called Castle Recording Company. Its studio was located in Nashville's famous Tulane Hotel. Cohen was the first record executive to use the studio, and among the early Decca country artists who recorded there were Foley, Ernest Tubb and Kitty Wells. Nearly every major record label took advantage of the Castle studio, and within a couple of years companies like RCA and independent producers like Owen Bradley began opening their own studios in Nashville.

The late 1940's and early 50's saw a plethora of independent labels located in the city: Bullet, Dot, Tennessee, Nashboro, Excello and Republic among them. Many of them served not only country music,

257

but the rich blues and R&B sound that was also developing in the city. WLAC DJ's, like Hoss Allen, played a pivotal role in spreading black R&B and soul music across the country, and Nashville-based non-country artists like Francis Craig, Pat Boone and The Fairfield Four had important records in the 1950's.

With this increased recording activity in Nashville, and the growing reputation of the Opry, came a number of other music-related entrepreneurial businesses—booking agencies, music publishing houses (most notably Acuff-Rose, see separate entry), A&R offices. A relatively small, several-block section on the southwest side of the town near Vanderbilt (around 16th and 17th Avenues South) gradually came to be a center for these growing concerns. This area aptly came to be known as Music Row. Over the course of the next few decades, the city became established as the country music capital of the world—though, in fact, banking, insurance, publishing (of religious materials) and tourism are "Music City's" leading industries.

Since the 1920's, the city has actually had a hot-cold relationship with the music industry. When WSM first opened, Nashville saw itself as "The Athens of the South," a cultural and educational center symbolized by the replica of the Parthenon. The "old money" residents of the West End and Belle Meade were embarrassed by the Opry and its singers, their prejudice lasting well into the 50's. One effect of this was that Nashville failed to develop more than one live performance venue of any consequence, and for years—until the mid-1990's—tourists had to content themselves with attending the Grand Ole Opry if they wanted to hear live music. Early singers tended to be relegated to an area of East Nashville; by the 40's, many were living in the Brentwood area south of downtown; by the 50's, many performers had moved north of town to the Madison and Goodlettsville suburbs.

A significant change was the removal of the Grand Ole Opry from its downtown location at the Ryman Auditorium. In the late 60's, 406 acres east of the Nashville area were purchased by NLT (National Life Insurance's, and WSM's, and the Opry's, parent company). From that deal sprang Opryland USA— a complex that includes a musical entertainment theme park that opened in 1972 and the new Opry House (which opened in 1974). Also part of the complex are the Opryland Hotel, The Nashville Network's studios and offices, and the studios of WSM-AM and FM. The whole thing was purchased by the Gaylord Broadcasting Co. in late 1983. This area, known as Music Valley, has grown into a major tourist area, with the addition of nightclubs, shops, hotels and the like. The Music Row area, on the other hand, also continued to grow, with tourist attractions like the Country Music Hall of Fame and Museum and souvenir shops owned by numerous country stars.

By the 1990's, the music industry was centralized in three locations: the original Music Row, the Music Valley area, and, most recently, the downtown Second Avenue strip of renovated clubs and dance halls, like the Wild Horse Saloon (owned by Opryland). The studio business has also expanded to accommodate the production of television and radio commercials, as well as a rich variety of musical types. It has been estimated that some 60% of the recording taking place in Nashville is non-country.   —R.P.

Nashville (The Movie)

This 1975 feature film by director Robert Altman did a lot to cast national light on Music City, though not necessarily the kind of light it wanted. *Nashville* starred Keith Carradine, Henry Gibson and Ronee Blakley, who played an addle-brained, over-the-edge character who was a very thinly veiled composite of Loretta Lynn and Tammy Wynette. Rather than glorifying country as "music of the people," Altman (known for satirical films like *M*A*S*H* and *The Player*) instead chose to focus—much in the spirit of *Hollywood Babylon*—on the behind-the-scenes pettiness,

hypocrisy, crass anti-intellectualism and affluence that insulated country stars from the blue collar audience they professed to represent. This disturbing insider's portrayal stung the country record business: Nashville hated *Nashville*. The movie even drew a front-page condemnation from Music City's cheer-leading afternoon newspaper, *The Banner*. Yet the controversy only served to help Altman's cause. The movie received considerable critical acclaim, and Keith Carradine even won an Academy Award for "I'm Easy," a lightweight but touching ballad he performed in the film, which became a pop hit in 1976.

Such a graphic look at the sleaziness and shadows behind the down-home celebrity image had only been done with such devastating effectiveness once before: by director Daryl Duke in his low-budget 1973 film, *Payday*, a gritty country & western film noire that depicted an out-of-control, self-destructive honky-tonk singer (based heavily on a Waylon Jennings-like character) in his last days of a fatal pill- and booze-induced rampage. —B.A.

The Nashville Network

When The Nashville Network (TNN) debuted on March 7, 1983, the cable network was picked up by some 800 cable operators, giving it a reach of seven million households. By 1994, the network, owned by Gaylord Broadcasting (also owners of Opryland and the Grand Ole Opry—all of which the company purchased in late 1983), was available to almost 59 million households. TNN's shows cover country news, music, lifestyles and sporting events through a com-bination of original and syndicated programming. The prime-time anchor show from TNN's debut until late 1993 was *Nashville Now*, hosted by Ralph Emery. Popular offerings include *The Statler Brothers Show*, *Grand Ole Opry Live*, *BASSMasters* and reruns of *Hee Haw*. —G.F.

Nashville Sound

This somewhat ubiquitous and ill-defined term most often refers to music made in Nashville from the late 1950's through the 1980's by artists and producers who were intent on widening country music's appeal to a larger, more urban audience. The reason for this was simple. Rock 'n' roll sent country record sales into a tailspin, hurting recording artists, country radio stations and the entire industry. By the late 50's, it was clear that something had to be done. The impetus came from three producers: RCA's Chet Atkins, Decca's Owen Bradley and Columbia's Don Law. The idea was to strip off the fiddles and steel guitars, which limited the appeal of many country records, and "neutralize" the sound, using rhythm sections, vocal choruses and later string sections to refine—in some cases, obliterate—traditional, hard-core country music's innate twang and stridence. "Country-pop," "Lite Country," "Suburbanite Country," "Easy Listening Country," "Countrypolitan," and "Crossover Country" are a few other terms that have become synonymous with Nashville Sound. Many artists actually became more effective, freed of the fiddles and steel. Among them were Jim Reeves and Don Gibson. It didn't hurt others, like Eddy Arnold and Connie Smith. Another essential part of the Nashville Sound was the use of session musicians able to work up innovative ideas on the spot. The so-called A-Team included bassist Bob Moore, pianist Floyd Cramer, guitarists Hank Garland, Grady Martin, Harold Bradley and Ray Edenton, drummer Buddy Harman and saxophonist Boots Randolph. Adding sound effects to records such as the hammer sound on "Big Bad John" (actually Floyd Cramer hitting two pieces of a microphone boom) also became essential, though sometimes overdone. During the 1970's, producer Billy Sherrill took the style to its pinnacle (or some would say, excess) with immensely successful country-to-pop crossover artists like Charlie ("Behind Closed Doors") Rich as well as Tammy Wynette,

David Houston and even some music of George Jones.

Ever since the advent of the Nashville Sound, a certain tension has existed between artists who cling to traditional country stylings (mountain music, honky tonk or grassroots ethnic) as their inspirational wellspring and those who have found their muse, and in many cases, made fine music, by incorporating elements of pop. This tension, along with inevitable cyclical shifts in public taste, has caused the stylistic pendulum of mainstream country music to swing back and forth between the traditional and the more urbane. In the mid-60's, hard country epitomized by Buck Owens, Merle Haggard and Loretta Lynn made a strong comeback, though in the early 1970's crossover country—controlled mainly by producers—was still healthy. Much of the mid-70's Outlaw movement was a backlash against the power of producers and advocated a return to artists controlling the sound of their recordings. The Urban Cowboy sound of the early 1980's was a newer version of the Nashville Sound, since it pursued pop record sales. When it fell from favor, the New Traditionalism of the mid-1980's brought things back to basics. During the 1990's, the influence of pop—and rock—music on mainstream country has become so pervasive as to have virtually rendered the term Nashville Sound archaic in modern music terminology. It's indicative of the changing times that many of the artists who thrive in 1990's country charts would have been simply classified as pop artists a decade or two ago.   —B.A.

National

The National String Corporation was a leading manufacturer of metalbody and woodbody resonator guitars. During the 1920's, some musical instrument builders were experimenting with different ways to boost the sound of an acoustic guitar so that it could hold its own against the much louder banjo. One such individual was John Dopyera, one of six children of a Czechoslovakian family living in Los Angeles.

Dopyera invented a guitar whose top featured a bowl-like aluminum cone which acted like a resonator. When the strings were plucked, the vibrations from the resonator created a volume level that could overpower any other stringed instrument. He named his resonator guitar and manufacturing company National; his brothers—Rudy, Emil (Ed), Louis and Robert—were also involved in the business in various financial and production roles. He left the company in 1928 and founded the offshoot Dobro Corporation, Limited.

Throughout the next 50 years, National employees would either actually design or exert a profound influence on the manufacture of other guitars such as Rickenbacker, Barth, Magnatone, Supro, Regal, Sho-Bro (Gretsch), Mobro (Mosrite), Hound Dog and Original Musical Instruments (O.M.I.). Although strong family bonds held the company's vision intact, behind-the-scenes financial wheeling and dealing and subsequent mistrust ultimately led to at least six different ownerships. In 1988, two former O.M.I. employees, Don Young and MacGregor Gaines, formed the National Resophonic Company and began making woodbody as well as metalbody guitars in the tradition of the Dopyera brothers.

Among the more popular country musicians who played either National or Dobro guitars were Pete Kirby (Bashful Brother Oswald) of Roy Acuff's band, Flatt & Scruggs' dobroist Uncle Josh Graves and Mike Auldridge.   —R.P.

Ken Nelson

BORN: January 19, 1911
BIRTHPLACE: Caledonia, Minnesota

It was Capitol Records' country A&R man Lee Gillette, with whom Ken Nelson had earlier worked at Radio WJJD in Chicago, who brought the former guitarist to the label to manage Capitol's transcriptions division in the late 1940's. After Gillette moved over to pop record production at Capitol in 1950, Nelson took his place as head of country A&R. In this capacity, Nelson brought a number of major new talents to the label—Faron Young, Sonny James, Jean Shepard and Wanda Jackson among them. His signings of Ferlin Husky and Tommy Collins helped set in motion the Bakersfield Sound in the early 1950's. He also discovered Buck Owens when Owens came to play guitar on a Tommy Collins session, and he subsequently used Owens as a guitarist on various other sessions. Nelson, a silent partner in the Central Songs publishing company, also worked extensively with rock artists like Gene Vincent and satirist Stan Freberg.

But Nelson's peak years came late in his career at Capitol, when he produced Buck Owens' massive string of hits through the 1960's, and in 1964 signed Merle Haggard to the label. Working out of the Capitol tower in Los Angeles he produced most of Capitol's country artists (though other Capitol producers worked out of Nashville). Nelson retired from Capitol in the early 1970's.

As a producer he stood apart in that he did not believe in trying to dictate a "style" or "sound" to an artist, preferring to let the artist rely on his own musical instincts. Nelson now lives in retirement in Northern California.   —R.K.

Rick Nelson

BORN: May 8, 1940
BIRTHPLACE: Teaneck, New Jersey
DIED: December 31, 1985

Rick Nelson was born May 8, 1940, in Teaneck, New Jersey. The son of 1950's TV icons Ozzie and Harriet Nelson, he was endeared to an entire teenaged generation by his co-starring role (along with his brother David) on their popular TV show. Additionally, the show gave young Ricky Nelson (it was later that he became "Rick" in an attempt to shed the teen idol image) an extraordinary platform for performing his music for a national audience. His first record, a cover of Fats Domino's "I'm Walkin'," which he recorded to impress a girl, sold over a million copies on the West Coast indie label, Imperial Records. For the next six years, Nelson was one of the top selling rock performers in America, with a string of Top Ten pop hits including "A Teenager's Romance," "Be-Bop Baby" and "I Got a Feeling," to name a few. Other Nelson hits like "Hello Mary Lou" and the Number One, "Poor Little Fool," sounded more like country than pop.

However, Nelson's rockabilly records with James Burton on lead guitar were as raw as anything coming from Memphis. After the smash success of Nelson's own composition, "Travelin' Man," which sold over five million copies worldwide, he signed with Decca Records in 1963 and cut a series of pop-influenced albums: *For You* and *The Very Thought of You, Spotlight on Rick* and *Best Always*, in 1965.

When *Ozzie and Harriet* ended its long run in the mid-1960's, Nelson was faced with a difficult career choice: his albums were selling poorly and he had never really gotten comfortable with the soft, Johnny Mathis-style material he was doing in his Decca sessions. Nelson assembled a country band, The Stone Canyon Band, and went to work on the 1967 album, *Country Fever*. The album yielded a moderately successful single, "You Just Can't Quit," and Nelson, encouraged, cut three more country albums: *Another Side of Rick* in 1968, plus a live album (*In Concert*) and *Rudy the Fifth*, in 1969. The latter included an original song by his idol, Bob Dylan, "She Belongs to Me," which became the first of Nelson's songs to turn up on country charts.

While Nelson was trying to break into country, he also performed at occasional rock nostalgia concerts. It was one of these performances—a particularly disillusioning show at Madison Square Garden in October 1971—that inspired him to write a song called "Garden Party" that went on to become his greatest hit. While Nelson was trying to move in a new direction and gain acceptance as a country performer, fans were only interested in hearing him sing his old 1950's pop hits: "When I got to the Garden Party/They all knew my name," he lamented in the lyrics of "Garden Party." "But no one recognized me/ I didn't look the same."

Throughout the rest of the decade, contractual disputes temporarily stalled Nelson's career as he struggled to void a 20-year pact he'd signed with Decca/MCA. During that time Nelson had a few minor hits, "One Night Stand" (MCA, 1974) and "Dream Lover" (Epic, 1979) and continued to perform on college campuses, where he remained a popular draw. His legal woes resolved, Nelson singed with Capitol Records in 1979 and released a new album, *Playing to Win,* soon after. He was winning new respect in the music industry, and his career seemed headed for an upturn when he was killed in a plane crash on December 31, 1985, at the age of 45.   —M.B.

Willie Nelson

BORN: April 30, 1933
BIRTHPLACE: Abbott, Texas

Few country music stars have engendered as much good will as Willie Nelson, despite his label as one of the original Outlaws. It's also safe to say he is one of the most durable artists and one-of-a kind personalities to ever come rolling down the country music turnpike. Born in the tiny hamlet of Abbott, Texas, Nelson was raised by his grandparents, "Mama" and "Daddy" Nelson. He and his sister, Bobbie Lee, both loved music. In 1939 at age six, his grandfather gave him a guitar and taught him some chords. After his grandfather's death, the family had a tough economic period. But Willie continued his musical obsession when the family got a radio. Not only did he love the sounds of the Grand Ole Opry, he loved Southwestern acts like Bob Wills and Ernest Tubb. He also found himself drawn to mainstream pop music including big bands and jazz, as well as the German polkas that were a part of Texas' huge German settlement, Nelson has paid tribute to nearly all of these influences in the course of his career. He started writing his own songs, and, at age 10, started playing guitar with a local band, John Raycjeck's Bohemian Polka Band. After Bobbie married musician Bud Fletcher, Willie joined his brother-in-law's Western swing band, The Texans. He also had the chance to see Bob Wills in person. After graduating from high school in 1951 he wound up spending nine months in the Air Force until discharged due to back problems.

Back home, he met a carhop, Martha Matthews, who became his first wife in 1952. A year later they left Abbott for San Antonio, where Willie worked in a band until they moved on. At radio stations in Pleasanton and Fort Worth Texas, Willie worked as a DJ, playing music on the side. By 1956 Willie and Martha moved to Vancouver, Washington, where Willie's mother lived. He landed a morning radio show on KVAN there, and made his first record, which he sold over his radio show. When the station wouldn't give him a raise, Willie took his family back to Texas where he played music and supported himself with various odd jobs. After moving to Houston—by this time deeply involved in songwriting—he continued playing, working in radio and, for a time, teaching guitar at a school owned by mandolinist Paul Buskirk. He also recorded for D Records, owned by former Starday owner Pappy Daily. He sold one song, a gospel tune titled "Family Bible," to Buskirk, Buskirk's business partner Walt Breeland and singer Claude Gray. Willie sold Buskirk half of another song: "Night Life," a song Daily felt was too bluesy, so Willie recorded it under a pseudonym. When Gray's recording of "Family Bible" made the Top Ten in 1960 Willie realized he had to go to Nashville, and arrived there late that year.

After meeting songwriter Hank Cochran at the legendary Tootsie's Orchid Lounge, Cochran got him a writing contract with Pamper Music.

There, he wrote "Hello Walls," which became a huge Number One record for Faron Young. Billy Walker had a hit with Willie's "Funny How Time Slips Away." As Willie's songwriting gained him notice, Liberty Records signed him as an artist. Over the next several years, Willie, Hank Cochran, Mel Tillis, Roger Miller and Harlan Howard spearheaded a new generation of Nashville composers able to create more complex, true-to-life songs than anyone had previously written. His first hit record in 1962 was "Willingly," a duet with Shirley Collie, followed by "Touch Me," a Willie solo recording that went Top Ten that same year. He joined Ray Price's Cherokee Cowboys as bass player and singer, and in 1963 Patsy Cline recorded Nelson's "Crazy," making it a Number Two country single. Divorced by 1963, Willie married Shirley Collie. He left the label in 1964 and on November 28, joined the Grand Ole Opry cast. He also joined the cast of his idol Ernest Tubb's half-hour syndicated TV show, appearing as a regular with Tubb and his Texas Troubadours. He briefly recorded for Monument Records, then signed with RCA. Chet Atkins knew his potential, but over the next six years, he had only two big hits. Still touring, he replaced drummer Johnny Bush with Paul English in 1967.

Still, the lack of wider success frustrated Willie, and by then problems were brewing between Shirley and him. By late 1970, Shirley was gone and Willie was in personal turmoil. His marriage had unraveled, he had no hit records, and his main popularity was still centralized in Texas. When a fire destroyed his home outside Nashville on December 23, he moved back to Texas. RCA finally dropped his contract, but playing around Texas, Willie saw a new trend: Young long-haired people in the area who loved rock 'n' roll and blues were gravitating to country music. At Austin's huge rock and country showcase the Armadillo World Headquarters, Willie and his progressive music were welcomed by young and old alike. In late 1972 he met Atlantic Records executive Jerry Wexler, known for recording classic R&B but well versed in country music, too. A longtime admirer, he signed Willie as the flagship artist for Atlantic's new country music division. In early 1973 he and a group of Texas and New York musicians recorded the *Shotgun Willie* album in New York. At the same sessions they recorded the gospel album *The Troublemaker* (issued in 1976 on Columbia). Though he had no big hits from it, *Shotgun Willie* sold well. Later that year he threw his first Willie Nelson Fourth of July Picnic in Texas. That fall he recorded the now-classic concept album *Phases and Stages*. But when Atlantic's country experiment failed, he moved to Columbia, where he was guaranteed creative control.

Creative control had become a point of contention in Nashville, and was a bone of contention shared by Waylon Jennings, Willie and Tompall Glaser, all of whom felt they had a better idea of how to produce their records than most Nashville producers did. After Willie finally gained this creative control on Columbia, he produced his first album, *Red Headed Stranger,* for the label and the hit single, Fred Rose's old song, "Blue Eyes Crying in the Rain," proved him right in 1975 by becoming his first Number One hit. He'd spent only $20,000 to do the album, completing it in a few days in a small Texas jingle studio; and Columbia was nervous, feeling it was too under produced (minus strings and elaborate arrangements) to sell. When it did, eventually topping the million sales mark, Willie found true vindication, and finally earned the success that had so long eluded him. Over the next several years Columbia released other high quality recordings, all done his way. Meanwhile, *Wanted: The Outlaws*, an RCA album featuring new and old recordings by Willie, Waylon, his wife Jessi Colter and Tompall Glaser was also taking off and would eventually sell a million copies and feed the Outlaw image.

Willie never lost his boyhood love of classic American pop songs by George and Ira Gershwin, Hoagy Carmichael, Irving Berlin and other legendary composers. In 1977 he decided to do an entire album of such songs. The result was *Stardust*, released in 1978. It remained on *Billboard's* Top Album charts for over two years and was certified quadruple platinum (four million copies sold). Three songs, including "Georgia on My Mind," "Blue Skies" and "All of Me" became country hits in 1978, the first two going to Number One. Willie Nelson's music now transcended categories. He was now a major star of American popular music. That Texas eclecticism that had for years puzzled Nashville now earned the respect of jazz, rock, pop, blues and country fans around the world.

In 1979 his film career began with a starring role with Robert Redford in the film *The Electric Horseman*, which yielded his 1980 hit, "My Heroes Have Always Been Cowboys." Also in 1979 the Country Music Association—epitomizing the Nashville establishment—honored him as Entertainer of the Year. By 1982, when "Always on My Mind" became another crossover hit (the album of the same name went triple platinum), Willie Nelson records were everywhere. Old material was repackaged in covers with new photographs, even though some of the music inside, which had been ignored in its own time, wasn't that different from the music he now made. He had hit duets with Waylon, with Leon Russell, with Julio Iglesias, Merle Haggard, actress Mary Kay Place, Kris Kristofferson and Roger Miller. He, Waylon, Kris Kristofferson and Johnny Cash, a proto-Outlaw himself, recorded together as the Highwaymen. In honoring his roots, Willie did more than talk. He recorded a magnificent album of classic Texas honky-tonk music with his former boss Ray Price and recorded similar albums with past legends like Webb Pierce, Hank Snow and Faron Young, his way of paying homage to country's past.

Fame, including sold-out concerts and record sales gave Willie wealth, but never diminished his social consciousness. His support of the embattled family farmer has never ended since he began his star-studded Farm Aid in 1985 to raise money to assist them. Willie's greatest tribulations involved severe tax difficulties with the IRS, which claimed more than $16 million in back taxes, taking nearly everything he owned, and forcing Willie on the road again to help pay off his debt. He even released an album, *The IRS Tapes*, to help pay off his massive tax burden, which finally ended when they reached a settlement in 1993.

He continues to tour heavily; the Farm Aid concerts have become an institution; and his 1993 album, *Across the Borderline*, featuring contributions from such eclectic performers as Paul Simon, Sinead O'Connor, jazz singer-pianist Mose Allison and other pop stars, introduced him to a new audience. Ironically it also concluded his relationship with Columbia, which refused to release a subsequent pop standards album, *Moonlight Becomes You*. He released the album on the small Justice label. His concerts still sell out, and he's become a regular at Branson, Missouri's Ozark Theater. He also dabbled in nightclub ownership: starting a club in Memphis with old friend and co-hort Waylon, and, briefly, owning another club in Nashville near Opryland. He also holds a long-term contract with the Desert Inn in Las Vegas. He signed a new contract with Jimmy Bowen's Liberty Records in 1994. Now in his early 60's and still going strong, he disdains the idea of slowing down his recording and concert schedule.   —R.K.

New Grass Revival

The New Grass Revival was founded in 1972 by fiddle and mandolin virtuoso Sam Bush, a long-haired native of Bowling Green, Kentucky, and former Bill Monroe bandmember with a passion for traditional bluegrass music and a flair for innovation. The initial lineup consisted of Bush, Courtney Johnson on banjo, Curtis Burch on guitar and Ebo Walker on bass. Walker left and was replaced by Butch Robbins, who was soon replaced by Beatles freak and R&B-inflected singer John Cowan.

Playing at bluegrass festivals, concert halls and clubs across the country during the mid-1970's, the band stamped itself as one of the most talented of the modern bluegrass—or "newgrass"—ensembles, freely serving up rhythm & blues, rock and even reggae influences in its super-charged brand of bluegrass music. During this period, the group also began its recording career with the release of *New Grass Revival* on the Starday-King label, which featured songs by Jerry Lee Lewis, Leon Russell and Vassar Clements. The band later moved on to Flying Fish and came out with *Fly Through the Country*, followed in the late 1970's by *When the Storm Is Over, Too Late to Turn Back Now* and *Barren County*.

By the time the 1980's rolled around, New Grass

Revival was making TV appearances and touring 42 weeks out of the year. The group reached its heyday beginning in 1981, however, when guitarist Pat Flynn and banjoist Bela Fleck replaced Burch and Johnson respectively. Flynn was an exceptionally gifted guitar player, and Fleck contributed an uncanny knack of stretching the banjo beyond its traditional bluegrass role, embracing jazz fusion, New Age and rock in the process. The result was a powerhouse bluegrass band with a distinctive hard-edged sound (boosted not only by Cowen's powerhouse vocals but also his substitution of electric bass for the traditional bluegrass stand-up bass) and an almost surrealistic penchant for musical fusion. The group toured with Leon Russell, and in 1984 signed with the Sugar Hill label. The band's first Sugar Hill release, *On the Boulevard*, featured diverse material such as reggaeking Bob Marley's "One Love" and soul man Curtis Mayfield's "People Get Ready."

In 1986 the group signed with EMI-America and had some minor country hits with "Ain't That Peculiar" and "Unconditional Love," but ultimately proved a little too eclectic for mainstream country radio. The group formally disbanded, however, in 1991 when

Emmylou Harris recruited Bush to head up her all-acoustic backup band, The Nash Ramblers. Fleck continues to take the banjo to new heights with a bluegrass-jazz-rock ensemble called Bela Fleck and The Flecktones. Flynn and Cowan (who has recorded lat east one solo album—an all R&B outing) remain active as Nashville session men, as do Bush and Fleck on those rare occasions when not preoccupied with their other various and sundry musical involvements. Bush, Cowan, Fleck, and Flynn continue to record together occasionally—either as a foursome or in various smaller configurations. All four recently came together when superstar Garth Brooks requested The New Grass Revival's backing for a song on his best-selling *In Pieces* album.   —R.P.

New Traditionalism

Ever since Elvis Presley's success knocked the country market back on its heels and led to the smoother Nashville Sound, country music has moved back and forth between uptown pop-influenced sounds and hard-edged traditionalism. The success of the 1980 film, *Urban Cowboy*, spawned a new style of country music that played heavily to fans who had been attracted to the dance atmosphere as portrayed at Gilley's (Mickey Gilley's famed Houston-area club) in the John Travolta film. An entire school of artists emerged, playing music with more pop than country overtones. Yet even at the peak of that fad, a number of new, young performers were emerging whose influences went back to the heart of country. Many had grown up on rock 'n' roll, but found their way to George Jones, Merle Haggard, Patsy Cline, Hank Williams Sr., Bob Wills and Buck Owens.

Though Emmylou Harris had successfully established herself with such a sound in the mid-70's, the next of these to make an impact was John Anderson, who had his first hits in the early 80's. The second was ex-bluegrasser Ricky Skaggs, who committed himself to playing traditional country and bluegrass with a modern edge. Next came Texan George Strait, whose music was solidly in the style of Hank Thompson and Bob Wills and hardcore Oklahoma singer Reba McEntire. All these artists were rising in popularity, and by 1985, the Urban Cowboy sound had fallen so far from public favor that *The New York Times* ran a page one story on the panic in Nashville.

The feeling that Skaggs, McEntire, Strait and the others were on to something grew. Warner Bros. signed Randy Travis, who sang like another hard-edged hero, Lefty Frizzell. Warner Bros. sister label, Reprise, signed Dwight Yoakam, a college-educated Kentucky native who made his name playing hard country in punk-rock clubs and who idolized Buck Owens. Epic signed Ricky Van Shelton, another hard country vocalist. The success of Travis, Yoakam and Shelton, followed by the acoustic duo, The O'Kanes, and the sister-act, Sweethearts of the Rodeo, and other back-to-basics singers like Patty Loveless made it clear that the sound had a following. Critics dubbed the music's exponents "New Traditionalists." Though Anderson's career flagged (later to be revived), Strait, Yoakam, Travis and McEntire eventually emerged as major lights. Strait's cowboy hats were copied by other male vocalists, who were dubbed "hat acts." The success of Garth Brooks, himself a Strait devotee, and the infusion of more rock and pop music attitudes into country in the early 90's effectively ended the New Traditionalist era, while some of its leading practitioners like McEntire have moved toward a more middle-of-the-road sound. Yet Travis, Strait, Anderson and Yoakam continue to be major stars, faithful to their New Traditionalist origins.   —R.K.

Mickey Newbury

BORN: May 19, 1940
BIRTHPLACE: Houston, Texas

Mickey Newbury began reading his poetry in Houston coffee-houses, where the folk music revival of the early 1960's inspired him to learn the guitar and set his poetry to music. He moved to Nashville and within a few years saw his songs become hits for country performers like Don Gibson and pop stars like Tom Jones, both of whom recorded successful covers of Mickey's "Funny Familiar Forgotten Feelings." After trying for four years to get the song recorded, Newbury's "Just

Dropped In (To See What Condition My Condition Was In)" became a smash hit for Kenny Rogers and The First Edition. Newbury's "American Trilogy" was also a hit for Elvis Presley.

He cut a number of disastrous albums for several different labels before signing with Elektra in the late 1960's; his Elektra albums sold somewhat better than his previous attempts. He became something of a cult figure in the Kristofferson singer/songwriter era (garnering write-ups in *Rolling Stone*), and major artists continued to record his songs through the 70's and 80's, including Waylon Jennings, Ray Charles, Willie Nelson and Joan Baez. In 1981 Newbury cut an album on Mercury Records titled *After All These Years*. The record included songs he'd written over a period of nearly 20 years, many of which had been major hits for other artists. —M.B.

Bob Newman

BORN: October 16, 1915
BIRTHPLACE: Macon, Georgia
DIED: October 8, 1979

With brothers Hank and Slim, singer-songwriter Bob Newman was one-third of the fine Western vocal group, The Georgia Crackers, which performed in California before and after World War II. A gifted composer, Newman wrote the ballad, "The Leaf of Love," recorded by both Gene Autry and Tex Williams. In the early 1950's The Crackers relocated to Ohio, where Newman recorded solo material for King, including originals like "Phfft! You Were Gone" (later popularized by the cast of *Hee Haw*), "Lonesome Truck Driver's Blues" and "Haulin' Freight." In the early 50's Newman performed and worked as a DJ in Arizona. Tragically, he signed away many of his songwriting royalties, including those to "Phfft!," which could have left him financially comfortable. —R.K.

Jimmy C. Newman

BORN: August 27, 1927
BIRTHPLACE: Big Mamou, Louisiana

Along with Doug Kershaw, Jimmy C. Newman was one of country's pre-eminent performers of Cajun music and one of only a handful of Cajun artists to

have an impact in the country charts. Born in Big Mamou, Louisiana, on August 27, 1927, Newman got his start singing with a hometown band at age 19; he quickly moved to hosting his own show on radio station KPLC in Lake Charles, Louisiana. Before long he was performing on Shreveport's *Louisiana Hayride*.

It was largely thanks to his work on the *Hayride* that Newman landed a contract with Dot Records in the early 1950's. His first single, co-written with J. Miller, was a song called "Cry, Cry Darling." It made a healthy showing on country charts in 1954 and paved the way for other popular singles like "Seasons of My Heart," "Blue Darling" and "Daydreaming." His biggest hit was 1957's "A Fallen Star."

Newman joined the Grand Ole Opry in 1956 (he remains a member today) and toured extensively through the U.S. and Canada. By the end of the decade he had switched to MGM and scored another handful of hits, including "You're Making a Fool Out of Me" in 1958, "Grin and Bear It" in 1959 and "A Lovely Work of Art" in 1960.

He left MGM in the mid-1960's and signed with Decca, where he recorded still more hits—"Alligator Man," "Big Mamou," "Bayou Talk" and "Louisiana Saturday Night." He continued to tour extensively through the 1960's and 1970's, performing a repertoire of bayou-influenced songs like "Back in Circulation," "Alligator Man," "D.J. for a Day" and "Blue Lonely Winter." These days, he continues to tour and perform on the Opry. —M.B.

Juice Newton

BORN: February 18, 1952
BIRTHPLACE: Lakehurst, New Jersey

After kicking around California's country/folk/rock scene for much of the 1970's, singer Judy Kay Newton (or Kaye Cohen), born in New Jersey and raised in Virginia, rose to fame in the early 80's era of pop/

country crossover music. In fact, her biggest hits were as successful on the pop charts as they were on the country charts. Known for her strong, identifiable voice, her top hits—some of them cover versions—include "Queen of Hearts," "Angel of the Morning," "The Sweetest Thing," "Break It to Me Gently," "You Make Me Want to Make You Mine," "Both to Each Other" (with Eddie Rabbitt) and "Hurt." Newton recorded for Capitol until 1984, then RCA. Her most recent chart hit appeared in 1989. —G.F.

Olivia Newton-John

BORN: September 26, 1948
BIRTHPLACE: Cambridge, England

English-born, Australian-raised Olivia Newton-John was somewhat of a reluctant country singer at the start: She knew very little about American country music (her background was in pop and folk), but her record company (MCA) decided to market her mellow music to both audiences. It worked—from 1973 to 1978, she epitomized the successful crossover artist, with as high a profile on the country charts as she had on the pop charts—but it led to a backlash by Nashville's old

guard artists, who were offended by her Best Female Vocalist win at the 1974 Country Music Association awards, not to mention her millions of record sales. A new group, the Association of Country Entertainers (with members like George Jones, Dolly Parton, Hank Snow and George Morgan) sprang up to fight against the "pop infiltration" of country music. Founded mostly on sour grapes, the group didn't last long, and Newton-John established herself with such hits as "Let Me Be There," "If You Love Me (Let Me Know)," "I Honestly Love You," "Have You Never Been Mellow" and "Please Mr. Please." As the 70's wore on she landed movie roles (*Grease*, *Xanadu*) and moved further into the pop and dance realm, leaving country behind in 1979. Her pop hits continued through 1988. In 1992 she battled breast cancer, and in 1993 MCA released a greatest hits package that included many of her early country hits. —G.F.

The Nitty Gritty Dirt Band

Since its inception back in Long Beach, California, in 1966, The Nitty Gritty Dirt Band has undergone a gradual but dramatic evolution. The band—whose membership, as of the mid-1980's, included Jimmy Ibbotson, Jeff Hanna, Jimmie Fadden, Bob Carpenter, and John McEuen (the latter of whom left the band a few years ago and has since taken a number of fascinating solo excursions)—started out as a long-haired, teen-age, back-to-the-earth country/folky jug-rock band (rock singer Jackson Browne was an early member) that initially found success with late 60's and early 70's hippy era anthems like "House on Pooh Corner" and their massively popular rendition of Jerry Jeff Walker's "Mr. Bojangles."

The Dirt Band is perhaps best remembered for its landmark three-album set, *Will the Circle Be Unbroken*, released in 1972. This critically heralded and exceedingly ambitious project was recorded in Nashville at a time when The Dirt Band was still, by and large, a fixture on the California country-rock scene. Yet it included contributions by many of country's most revered veterans and traditionalists: Roy Acuff, Mother Maybelle Carter, Earl Scruggs, Vassar Clements and Doc Watson, among them. For that reason, and on account of the stylistic and aesthetic fusion it represented, *Circle* did much to break down the "corn barrier," awakening the interest of 70's youth in coun-

try music. The album also opened a floodgate of "West Coast-meets-Music City" musical cominglings, which have continued unabated in the years since.

But by the early 1980's, The Dirt Band, by then in early middle age, and having undergone a number of personnel changes, found new life in the country charts with hits like "Long Hard Road," "Modern Day Romances" and "American Dream."

Along the way, The Nitty Gritty Dirt Band has taken any number of other interesting musical side trips. The band worked on the soundtrack to the long-ago Clint Eastwood film, *Paint Your Wagon*; they've duetted with Linda Ronstadt, provided the instrumental accompaniment to Steve Martin's novelty pop hit, "King Tut"; and were one of the first American bands ever to tour the former Soviet Union.

"It seems like people, all through the years, have tried to categorize us," Fadden added with a laugh. "You know: 'What are you guys? Folk? Rock? Country?' It seems like everybody worries about that but us!" Country, folk or whatever, they continued to have a good run on the country charts during the mid- to late 80's, with 15 Top Ten records for Warner Bros., including the Number Ones "Fishin' in the Dark," "Modern Romance" and "Long Hard Road."

In 1989, they updated the classic *Circle* with *Will The Circle Be Unbroken, Volume II*, including such guests as Johnny Cash, The Carter Family, Roy Acuff, Earl Scruggs and many others from the traditional, neo-traditional and newgrass scenes. Next, they were briefly signed to MCA and then to Liberty in 1992.

"This band," singer Jimmie Ibbotson pointed out with a wink and a grin, "has outlived most of our marriages."   —B.A.

Norma Jean

BORN: January 30, 1938
BIRTHPLACE: Wellston, Oklahoma

Singer/guitarist Norma Jean was born Norma Jean Beaser near Wellston, Oklahoma, on January 30, 1938. She learned to play guitar from an aunt, and by the age of 13 had her own radio show on station KLPR in Oklahoma City, where the family had moved when Norma was five. At 20 she joined the cast of Springfield, Missouri's *Ozark Jubilee*, where she performed for the first time under the name Norma Jean.

Norma Jean moved to Nashville in 1960 where she soon met country star Porter Wagoner, who invited her to join the cast of his syndicated TV show. Thanks to her association with Wagoner, she also had the chance to perform at the Grand Ole Opry, making her one of the few country artists in recent times to perform on the Opry stage before ever signing a recording contract.

It wasn't long, though, before Norma Jean signed with Columbia and cut a few records, none of which attracted much attention on the charts. In 1963 she switched to the RCA/Victor label and promptly had a Top Ten hit with "Let's Go All the Way." Her name was rarely absent from the charts through the rest of the decade. In 1964 she scored a Top Ten hit with "Go Cat Go" and later that year cut her RCA debut album, *Norma Jean*. Another Top Ten followed in 1965, "I Wouldn't Buy a Used Car from Him." Norma Jean made the Top Ten again the following year with a collaboration with Bobby Bare and Liz Anderson titled "Game of Triangles." That was her last Top Ten record, and in 1971, she left RCA, continuing to record for small labels. She still performs into the 90's.   —M.B.

Jim Ed Norman

BORN: October 16, 1948
BIRTHPLACE: Fort Edwards, Florida

Jim Ed Norman is largely responsible for making Warner/Reprise a leading Nashville record label. During the mid-1970's he earned high marks as a string arranger for recordings by Linda Ronstadt and the country-rocking Eagles. Clive Davis, president of the Arista Records and former head of CBS Records, was so impressed with Norman's arranging that he persuaded him to become a producer.

Taking Davis' advice, Norman learned the production ropes and subsequently went on to produce a string of hit singles and albums for artists such as Jennifer Warnes, Kenny Rogers, Crystal Gayle, Johnny Lee, Michael Martin Murphey, Anne Murray, The Forester Sisters, Mickey Gilley and Janie Fricke during the late 1970's and early 80's.

In 1983 he became vice president of A&R (artists and repertoire) with Warner/Reprise in Nashville. The following year, when Jimmy Bowen exited as Warner/Reprise's president, Norman stepped in. It was all uphill after that. To establish Warner/Reprise as a wild duck among Nashville's more mainstream record companies, he signed hip country artists such as Dwight Yoakam, The Texas Tornados, the acappella group Take 6, and jazz banjoist Bela Fleck. Norman also signed and developed two of Warner/Reprise's hottest country superstars—Randy Travis and Travis Tritt. In 1992 he founded the Warner Western label, a Warner/Reprise offshoot devoted strictly to American Western music and culture.   —R.P.

Nudie Cohen

BORN: November 8, 1908
BIRTHPLACE: Brooklyn, New York
DIED: May 10, 1984

The creation of one of country music's most memorable visual trademarks—those brightly-colored stage costumes—was largely the work of Paul "Nudie"

Cohen, a short, Jewish, ex-boxer from Brooklyn. Shortly after Word War I, Nudie, the son of a cobbler, bounced back and forth between both coasts as a semi-professional flyweight boxer, Hollywood movie extra and struggling tailor.

While in Los Angeles in the early 1940's, and nearly broke, he befriended country singer Tex Williams and convinced him he could sharply outfit Tex and his band. The costumes ended up either too short or too long and had to be altered at the last minute before a show, but, nevertheless, Tex liked Nudie's style. The word spread, and before long, Nudie was outfitting a host of cowboy singing stars, including Gene Autry, Roy Rogers and Rex Allen.

Nudie's business thrived during the 1940's and 1950's, and over time his costumes became more colorful—and more outlandish. His idea was to come up with a gimmick that corresponded with an artist's name or personality. For example, he designed a suit for Porter Wagoner that was decorated with wagon wheels. His most excessive creation was a 25-carat gold lame tuxedo for Elvis Presley. The late country-rocker Gram Parsons sometimes sported a Nudie suit emblazoned with marijuana leaves.   —R.K.

Mark O'Connor

BORN: August 5, 1961
BIRTHPLACE: Seattle, Washington

Eight-year-old Seattle native Mark O'Connor was studying classical guitar when he happened to catch Cajun fiddler Doug Kershaw performing the foot-stompin' "Diggy Liggy Lo" on TV's *Johnny Cash Show*. From that moment on, young O'Connor knew he wanted to be a fiddler. At 11, his parents bought him a fiddle, and after learning a few tunes, he performed at a local square dance. More engagements followed, and soon Mark began experimenting with different rhythms. He also began winning fiddle contests, and, in the process, attracted the attention of Texas fiddle virtuoso Benny Thomasson, who had relocated to Washington State.

When he was 12, O'Connor's mother brought him to Nashville, where he was befriended by Tut Taylor, the well-known dobroist and musical instrument dealer. Taylor told the owner of The Pickin' Parlor, a popular Music City bluegrass club, all about

O'Connor's hot playing. So one night the owner invited Mark to sit in with Charlie Collins and Brother Oswald of Roy Acuff's Smoky Mountain Boys. The young fiddler tore the place up. What's more, within four days he was invited to play at the Grand Ole Opry and was subsequently offered a record deal. At 15, O'Connor fronted a stellar instrumental trio with Norman Blake on mandolin and Charlie Collins on guitar. His flair for improvisation during this period also played a significant role in spurring on new-wave bluegrass—the so-called newgrass movement of the early 1970's.

By the age of 22, O'Connor had won four National Fiddle Championships, had toured with The David Grisman Quintet and The Dixie Dregs and had recorded three critically-acclaimed albums for Rounder Records—*Mark O' Connor* (1974), *Markology* (1978) and *On the Rampage* (1979). He also became a steady session man, performing on more than 450 recordings by artists such as Randy Travis, Michael Martin Murphey, The Nitty Gritty Dirt Band, Mary-Chapin Carpenter, Willie Nelson, James Taylor and Paul Simon.

During the mid-1980's, Mark began to devote more attention to his solo career. He signed with Warner Bros. Records, and in 1993 released *Heroes*, a potpourri of fiddle music in which he pairs up with some of his idols, including jazz artists Jean-Luc Ponty and Stephane Grappelli, classical violinist Pinchas Zukerman and Nashville session stalwart Buddy Spicher. —R.P.

Molly O'Day

BORN: July 9, 1923
BIRTHPLACE: Pike County, Kentucky
DIED: December 5, 1987

Born La Verne Lois Williamson—a coal miner's daughter—Molly O'Day possessed a compelling and influential vocal style which, in her heyday, earned her the title of "The Female Roy Acuff." After singing on various radio stations throughout the South—in Charleston and Beckley Springs, West Virginia, among many other places—O'Day landed a spot on the *Renfro Valley Barn Dance*, a live country radio show broadcast out of central Kentucky via a powerful 50,000-watt clear-channel signal. During the World War II years, the *Renfro Valley* broadcasts were often transmitted

overseas for the American troops, and General Douglas MacArthur later acknowledged that he was a big fan of O'Day's.

O'Day began recording for Columbia in 1946. The music she made for the label over the next four years—including songs like "Tramp on the Street," "Six More Miles," "When God Comes and Gathers His Jewels" (the latter two songs written and sent to her by her friend, Hank Williams), "Don't Sell Daddy Any More Whiskey" and "The Drunken Driver" (a particularly big radio hit)—has influenced many singers through the years, and today O'Day is acknowledged as one of the greatest woman vocalists country music has ever produced. O'Day was stricken by tuberculosis in 1952, and had part of a lung removed. She recovered, however; and from then until her death in 1987, she devoted herself to religion. For years, she hosted *Hymns from the Hills*, an inspirational program broadcast on WEMM-FM out of Huntington, West Virginia. —B.A.

The O'Kanes

When Nashville songwriter Jamie O'Hara teamed up with fellow tunesmith and some-time recording artist Kieran Kane, the idea was to have fun and keep it spontaneous. After all, both had already enjoyed considerable success: O'Hara was best known for penning The Judds' hit, "Grandpa (Tell Me 'Bout the Good Old Days)"; Alabama's "Gonna Have a Party" was one of many well-known Kane originals, and Kane had his own Top 20 hits—"It's Who You Love" and "You're the Best" on Warner Bros. in 1981. In fact, when Kane and O'Hara made their first duet recordings in Kane's attic demo studio (the same recordings that would eventually become their first Columbia album), they weren't at all sure they'd even come up with anything that the Nashville labels would be interested in. "It just wasn't quite as mainstream as what we'd been hearing on the radio," Kane, the son of a sausage maker and a Queens, New York, native told

Country Music Magazine in a 1987 interview. "And we felt we might end up shipping it to an overseas label. We felt it was just sort of traditional and off-center enough that a European audience might be interested in it."

But when Rick Blackburn, then head of CBS/Nashville and eager to make his label a player in the "New Traditionalist" movement, heard the tapes, he quickly signed The O'Kanes, and those attic recordings were released more or less intact. The response to Kane's and O'Hara's neo-Everly Brothers-style harmonies and their ultra-minimal, acoustic-flavored arrangements was immediate and overwhelmingly positive. "Oh Darlin'," the first single from *The O'Kanes*, their debut album, hit the Top Ten. "Can't Stop My Heart," their second single, reached Number One.

But by their second album, *Tired of Running*, released in 1987, the elusive, spontaneous innocence of The O'Kanes debut platter had already slipped through their fingers. By their third and final album, *Imagine That* (a full-blown studio outing, produced by Allen Reynolds and released in 1990), Kane and O'Hara realized they weren't having fun anymore. So they amicably parted ways and went back to their respective individual careers as songwriters.

In early 1994 Kane and O'Hara each emerged with solo albums. O'Hara's is called *Rise Above It*; Kane's is entitled *Find My Way Home*. Both records, to some extent, managed to recapture hints of The O'Kanes' prime-time magic, while mining fresh musical and thematic ground. —B.A.

The Oak Ridge Boys

The Oak Ridge Boys, whose most current lineup consists of Duane Allen (born April 29, 1943, Taylortown, Texas), Joe Bonsall (May 18, 1948, Philadelphia, Pennsylvania), Richard Sterban (April 24, 1943, Camden, New Jersey) and Steve Sanders (September 17, 1952, Richland, Georgia), have actually been around in name for decades.

Right around the end of World War II, a country-gospel quartet called The Country Cut-Ups formed in Knoxville, Tennessee. One of the group's early performances was at an atomic research center in nearby Oak Ridge. The band (which, in one of its early gospel incarnations, in 1945, joined The Grand Ole Opry) changed its name to The Oak Ridge Quartet, and subsequently established themselves as a gospel group. The quartet went through personnel changes (more than 40 members have come and gone in the group's half century or so of existence), disbanded and then resurfaced in 1957. In 1964 the group became known as The Oak Ridge Boys.

In 1965, William Lee Golden (born January 12, 1935, Browton, Alabama) joined the band, followed by Allen two years later. Together the two of them played a crucial role in moving the group away from traditional gospel music and into more mainstream country. When Sterban joined in 1972, and Bonsall came on board the following year, the transformation of the group's musical direction was complete. In 1975, The Oaks had a minor hit with "Family Reunion." Additional secular exposure came in 1977 when singer-songwriter Paul Simon employed them as backup singers on his hit single, "Slip Slidin' Away." With some encouragement from Johnny Cash, who asked them to open some of his shows in Las Vegas and occasionally recorded with them (Cash and his wife June Carter backed them on their very first chart entry, 1973's "Praise the Lord and Pass the Soup"), the group persisted in the country arena, and was signed by ABC-Dot. in 1977.

The Oaks' ABC debut album, *Y'All Come Back Saloon*, spawned two Number One country singles—the title track and "You're the One." In 1978, the Academy of Country Music voted the recording Album of the Year and named The Oaks Vocal Group of the Year.

Throughout the late 1970's and into the early 80's, The Oaks, with their gospel-tinged country-pop laced with smooth, soaring harmonies and tight instrumentation, rolled out a slew of best-selling hits such as "Crying Again" (1978), "I'll Be True to You" (1978), "Sail Away" (1979), the Rodney Crowell-penned "Leaving Louisiana in the Broad Daylight" (1979), "Trying to Love Two Women" (1980) and "Beautiful You" (1980). In 1978, they also won the Country Music Association's Vocal Group of the Year award.

Their biggest hit came in 1981 when "Elvira," their good-timey remake of Dallas Frasier's novelty 1966 pop hit, became a major pop hit as well as a Number One country single. More chart-toppers continued throughout the 1980's with "Bobbie Sue" (1982), "American Made" (1983), "I Guess It Never Hurts to Hurt Sometimes" (1984), "Make My Life With You" (1985) and "Come On In (You Did the Best You Could)" (1986).

In 1987, Golden was asked to leave the band due to personality clashes and artistic differences with other members of the group. He subsequently recorded several modestly successful solo albums. Golden was replaced by Steve Sanders, who had previously served several years as the band's rhythm guitarist. With Sanders attempting to fill Golden's shoes, the band roared back with three more Number One singles between 1987 and 1990—"This Crazy Love," "A Lot of River" and "No Matter How High." But as time went on, The Oaks seemed to be spending more time and energy on their wardrobes and various business ventures than on their music; and their gospel-rooted, country-pop quartet sound, which seemed so vital in the late 1970's and early 80's, came across as contrived and slightly archaic

when seen in the light of the ultra-hip late 1980's.

In 1991, The Oaks signed with RCA, where they had another Top Ten hit with "Lucky Moon" and made several more albums. They remain an energetic and popular touring band and recently guested on a Billy Ray Cyrus album.   —R.P.

Old Dominion Barn Dance

This popular live Saturday night country radio show was broadcast on WRVA Radio, from the WRVA Theater in Richmond, Virginia, in the 1940's and 1950's. Like Shreveport's *Louisiana Hayride*, it was also carried nationally for a while on the CBS Radio Network. Sunshine Sue Workman was the *Barn Dance*'s major star and main attraction for years. Noted Washington, D.C., area country music promoter/impresario Carleton Haney was also a guiding force behind the show for much of its duration. Lester Flatt, Grandpa Jones, Joe Maphis, Clyde Moody and Red Smiley are just a few of the many artists who were at one time or another associated with the *Old Dominion Barn Dance*.   —B.A.

Old-Time Music

One of the Northern folk music revival's most enduring legacies has been an appreciation for "old-time" or "old-timey" music—the vital backwoods sound that marked country music's earliest recordings.

The golden era of old-time music was between 1924 and 1931. After Okeh Records' surprising success with Fiddlin' John Carson's first release in 1923, field representatives from major labels traveled the South looking for outstanding regional talent. Two independent labels, Gennett in Indiana and Paramount in Wisconsin, recorded numerous stringbands, solo singers, duet acts and gospel groups in their Midwestern studios. Styles within the old-time genre varied from region to region. Performers in isolated portions of western Virginia and eastern Tennessee often produced a pure, folk-based sound that seemed untainted by modern popular music. Others, like Clarence Ashley and Uncle Dave Macon, reflected minstrel and medicine show traditions. Some younger musicians embraced elements from semi-classical music and Tin Pan Alley hits; Clayton McMichen, Lowe Stokes and Riley Puckett of North Georgia's Skillet Lickers respectively recorded works by W.C. Handy, Jerome Kern and Oscar Hammerstein II.

As the Depression eroded record sales, surviving labels shifted from the old-time sounds to intimate country stylists like Jimmie Rodgers, Jimmie Davis and The Delmore Brothers. Nevertheless, during the late 1930's the older string band styles still had Southeastern adherents; Mainer's Mountaineers, Fiddlin' Arthur Smith and His Dixieliners, The Coon Creek Girls and others put a fresh spin on earlier traditions. The arrival of Bill Monroe and bluegrass music further distanced old-time music from the country music mainstream.

In 1958 three New York-based folk musicians formed The New Lost City Ramblers, the band that sparked the 1960's old-time music revival. John Cohen, Tom Paley and Mike Seeger studied and carefully recreated the sounds of old-timey artists Charlie Poole, The Carter Family, Uncle Dave Macon, Ernest Stoneman and dozens of other pioneering rural recording artists. Folkways released the trio's first album in 1959. While not strong sellers, The Ramblers' early albums inspired many young folk musicians to take up the fiddle, banjo, guitar, mandolin and autoharp. The trio's musical scope expanded in 1963 when bluegrass and Cajun music enthusiast Tracy Schwarz replaced Paley.

The Ramblers verified the validity of old-time music as a vital, durable musical form and reawakened interest in the artists who had originated it decades earlier. Through their efforts, older musicians such as Clarence Ashley, Dock Boggs, Jimmie Tarlton, Frank Profitt, Roscoe Holcomb, Cousin Emmy and others found eager audiences in larger cities and college towns. A young New York duo, The Holy Modal Rounders (which, for a time, included celebrated playwright/actor Sam Shepard), used old-time music as a platform for its whimsical satires.

Two influential Durham, North Carolina, groups, The Hollow Rock String Band (1966-68) and The Fuzzy Mountain String Band (1967-73), specialized in rarely heard instrumentals collected from regional fiddlers. Both groups offered a precise, studied sound that reflected their members' academic backgrounds. The Highwoods Stringband (1971-78) rejected this dry instrumental approach, forging the driving, rhythmic style that remains the model for most contemporary old-time bands. Sporting twin fiddles, a guitar,

clawhammer-style banjo and a bass, the band placed as much importance on vocals as on instrumentals.

The Red Clay Ramblers, a group formed in 1973 by former Hollow Rock and Fuzzy Mountain String Band members, evolved from a straight old-time group into a versatile show band. The group, which remains active today, has included everything from Carter Family numbers and Stephen Foster classics to clever original tunes and traditional jazz pieces in its recorded repertoire. The Ramblers' versatility led to its appearance on Broadway in the Sam Shepard play, *A Lie of the Mind*, and they have provided the soundtrack music for one of his films.

Today, the appeal of this music extends beyond the United States and Canada into Europe and Japan. Old-time bands exist in virtually every major city and town, and they frequently gather at regional festivals to swap tunes and instrumental techniques.   —D.S.

Roy Orbison

BORN: April 23, 1936
BIRTHPLACE: Vernon, Texas
DIED: December 6, 1988

Roy Kelton Orbison, son of an oil field worker, began his career as a Texas country singer, evolved into a rockabilly without prolonged success, and finally found himself as one of the great rock balladeers of the 1960's, his greatest records all produced in Nashville with the cream of Nashville's session musicians. He spent most of his youth in the tiny hamlet of Wink, Texas. Idolizing Texas honky tonk legends like Ernest Tubb and Lefty Frizzell, he started The Wink Westerners while still attending high school. The band played mostly honky tonk and, in typical Texas fashion, some pop dance music as well. After high school, he attended North Texas State University, then Odessa Junior College. Meanwhile he became captivated by the new sounds of rockabilly and formed a band called The Teen Kings. By 1955 they had their own local TV

show in Odessa, Roy once hosting Elvis as a guest artist. The group had recorded a 45 r.p.m. disc including "Ooby Dooby," a song Orbison picked up from its composers, two Texas college students. After Johnny Cash made an appearance, on Orbison's TV show, he approached Sam Phillips at Sun Records with the disc. After rejecting it, Phillips reconsidered and the band came to Nashville and re-recorded the song for Sun in 1956. It became a modest hit, and Orbison made other Sun recordings, including "Rockhouse" and wrote songs for other Sun artists. His "Go! Go! Go!" became better known as Jerry Lee Lewis' ferocious "Down the Line." By 1957 with no more success and a feeling Sun didn't know what to do with him, Orbison moved on. The Everly Brothers recorded "Claudette," Orbison's original song about his new wife, and it did well enough that he was signed as a songwriter with Acuff-Rose, the Nashville publishing company with which the Everlys were closely associated. When his Sun contract expired, Wesley Rose, of Acuff-Rose, helped Orbison secure an RCA contract in the late 1950's that also went nowhere. In 1960 he signed with Fred Foster's new, independent Monument Records, and that year finally found his voice—as a pop ballad singer. (Ironically, Sun's Jack Clement had discouraged Orbison from singing ballads at Sun.) He had no country hits during this period; but in 1960, "Only The Lonely" went to Number Two on the pop charts, followed by the Top Ten "Blue Angel"; and in 1961, the atmospheric, melodramatic "Running Scared" reached Number One. Later that year the majestic "Crying" reached Number Two and the rocking flipside, "Candy Man," made the Top 30. Foster used Nashville's finest studio pickers to back him. The band, led by bassist Bob Moore, included such legends as Harold Bradley, Hank Garland, Floyd Cramer, Buddy Harman and The Anita Kerr Singers. In 1962 the loping rocker, "Dream Baby," was his biggest hit. Orbison was popular in America and overseas, where he did one British tour with the Beatles. In 1963 came "Mean Woman Blues" (the flipside was "Blue Bayou," a Top 30 hit then, now recognized as a classic and since recorded by Linda Ronstadt and others). In 1964 came the symphonic "It's Over" and the now-classic rocker, "Oh Pretty Woman." In 1965 Orbison joined MGM and a year later, Claudette Orbison died in a motorcycle ac-

cident in Tennessee. In 1968, two of his sons died in a house fire. He remarried Barbara Wellhonen, a native of Germany. After leaving MGM in 1973, where he had only modest success, he signed briefly with Mercury and returned to Monument in 1976. By the late 70's, however, Orbison's career was clearly on the upswing, and not as an oldies act. His duet with Emmylou Harris on "That Lovin' You Feelin' Again" became a Top Ten country hit. His song, "In Dreams," was featured in the film *Blue Velvet*. He and rock legends Bob Dylan, George Harrison, Jeff Lynne and Tom Petty formed a supergroup called The Traveling Wilburys. In 1987, the same year he was inducted into the Rock and Roll Hall of Fame, he had a hit remake of "Crying," sung as a duet with k.d. lang. A cable TV special, *A Black and White Night,* featured Orbison performing at Los Angeles' Coconut Grove nightclub, backed by an all-star band that included k.d. lang, James Burton and rock legend Bruce Springsteen. The future looked highly promising for Orbison. Then, while stopping off at his mother's home in Madison, Tennessee, in late 1988, a sudden heart attack killed him. *King of Hearts*, a posthumous album of predominantly unissued material, was released on Virgin Records in 1993.   —R.K.

The Osborne Brothers

BORN: Bobby, December 7, 1931, Hyden, Kentucky
      Sonny, October 29, 1937, Hyden, Kentucky

Brothers Bob and Sonny Osborne were born in Hyden, Kentucky (tenor vocalist/mandolinist Bob on December 7, 1931; baritone/banjo player Sonny on October 29, 1937). The brothers grew up on bluegrass, making their radio debut on Knoxville's WROL in 1953 and recording with Jimmy Martin in the mid-1950's. Within a short time the brothers moved first to station WJR in Detroit, then to Wheeling, West Virginia, where they joined the cast of the popular *WWVA Jamboree*. In 1956, shortly after moving to Wheeling, the brothers signed with MGM Records. Within a few years they added a third member, guitarist/banjoist Benny Birchfield.

With the explosion of interest in bluegrass in the late 1950's and 60's, The Osborne Brothers became a popular act on college campuses. While they scandalized bluegrass purists by occasionally integrat-

Jimmie Osborne

BORN: April 8, 1923
BIRTHPLACE: Winchester, Kentucky
DIED: December 26, 1957

Jimmie Osborne had a brief career, one that stressed somber ballads and recitations. He signed with King Records, and his first hit was the Top Ten, "My Heart Echoes," in 1948. His biggest hit, drawn from a true story, was 1949's "The Death of Little Kathy Fiscus," based on the tragic death of a child in an accident. During the Korean War he recorded a number of equally somber numbers like "Thank God for Victory in Korea" and "God Please Protect America," a Top Ten record in 1950. Though he made appearances on the Grand Ole Opry, the *Louisiana Hayride* and the WLS *National Barn Dance* through the years, overall his success was modest. He took his own life in 1957.   —R.K.

K.T. Oslin

BORN: May 15, 1941
BIRTHPLACE: Crossitt, Arkansas

Can a never-married, over-40, former Broadway actress and New York jingle singer find happiness as a country singer? In the case of K.T. Oslin, the answer is probably not. But for the span of two or three albums, Oslin did offer a frank, socially conscious and forthright new mature woman's perspective to the country charts. Unlike anyone before her, she spoke out clearly for all those older woman out there who are forced to cope with such middle-aged reality adjustments as diminishing expectations for romance, weight problems, menopause and crow's feet.

Oslin's anthem is the title song from her 1987 RCA debut album, *80's Ladies*, which won her a Grammy in 1988, at least briefly redefined the image of women in mainstream country music, and sold more than a million copies (as did her second album, *This Woman*). She's since gone to the top of the charts several times, with hits like "Do Ya" (1987), "I'll Always Come Back" (1988), "Come Next Monday" (1990) and "Hold Me" (1989), the last of which won her two more Grammy awards. Oslin was also the

ing drums and electric guitars into their songs, they found an enthusiastic young audience for their distinctive renditions of tunes like "Banjo Boys," "Take This Hammer," "Mule Skinner Blues" and "Each Season Changes You." They scored one Top 20 country hit in 1958 with "Once More."

The Osbornes stayed with MGM for seven years, during which time they recorded a number of albums, including *Voices in Bluegrass* (1965), *Up This Hill and Down* (1966), *Modern Sounds* (1976), *Ru-Be-eeee* and *Country Roads* (both 1970). In the mid-1970's they had a number of releases on the Decca/MCA label, including two well-received double-record sets: *The Best of The Osborne Brothers* and a collection of Felice and Boudleaux Bryant material titled *The Osborne Brothers: From Rocky Top to Muddy Bottom*. Though not their biggest country chart hit (it only reached Number 33 upon its 1968 release), their best-known song is the oft-covered "Rocky Top." Their modest entries in the country charts (including 1979's "Shackles and Chains," recorded with Mac Wiseman) continued until 1980. They continue as Grand Ole Opry members today, having joined the cast in 1964.   —M.B.

ing hits for other artists like Gail Davies, Dottie West, Judy Rodman and actress Sissy Spacek. But the country world at that point was not yet ready for her outspokenness, as later heard in "80's Ladies" and "Didn't Expect It to Go Down This Way." In fact, some of these hits were at first deemed too radical to be released. "Women were still supposed to be quiet, demure, and sing a sad song, and I just wasn't like that," she later recalled.

In recent years, Oslin's star has cooled somewhat as she herself has grown weary of the constant demands of touring and being a celebrity. She did appear as the owner of the Bluebird Cafe in the film, *The Thing Called Love,* in 1993.

In retrospect, though, there's a whole lot more to Oslin's songwriting than just the travails of datelessness and over-30 angst. She has consistently shown a deep, telling insight into the human condition that more often than not transcends the usual battle of the sexes. "I write from a personal point of view," Oslin explained in a recent interview. "I see what my friends are going through, how they react to relationships. I learn from watching people and try to put it in terms that music fans would find interesting." In 1993 she released a greatest hits package called *Songs from an Aging Sex Bomb,* which included some new material.
—B.A.

Marie Osmond

BORN: October 13, 1959
BIRTHPLACE: Ogden, Utah

Marie Osmond was born in Ogden, Utah, in 1959, around the same time as her older brothers formed a pre-pubescent barbershop quartet. By the time Marie began performing in the early 1970's, The Osmond Brothers were known around the world. Though Marie herself went on to build a career as a pop singer, her earliest hits, produced by Sonny James, were unmistakably country. In 1974 she cut her first single, "Paper Roses," which rose to the top of country and pop charts alike. She made the country charts again in 1975, with a slightly twangy duet version of the standard, "Make the World Go Away," sung with her brother, Donny. In between ice-skating routines, Marie also sang country songs on the siblings' late-1970's ABC variety program, *The Donny and Marie Show.* While most of Marie's late 70's and early 1980's

Academy of Country Music's 1989 Top Female Vocalist.

Oslin's real appeal was rather fundamental: more than any other late 80's country diva, she was probably close, demographic-wise, looks-wise and lifestyle-wise, to the average female country fan. These fans heard her lovelorn and often angry commentaries on loneliness and discontent in a male- and youth-dominated world and felt like they were hearing their own innermost dissatisfactions being played back to them in three-quarter time. Tom T. Hall once told Oslin, "You're everybody's screwed-up sister." Oslin's laughing reply: "That's one of the best descriptions of me, ever!"

Oslin was born in 1941, and grew up in various locales in Arkansas, Alabama and Texas. Heading to New York in her 20's, she appeared in various Broadway shows (including a production of *Hello Dolly* that starred Betty Grable in 1967). She sang commercial jingles and studio backup vocals and starred in TV commercials. She first came to Nashville in 1981 and recorded briefly for Elektra Records, while writ-

releases included at least a smattering of country material, she re-focused her attention on country in the mid-1980's, signing with Curb/Capitol. She was rewarded with three Number Ones, her first since "Paper Roses." These included a 1985 duet with Dan Seals titled "Meet Me in Montana." The song won them a Country Music Association award for Duo of the Year and proved that Marie had what it took to win country audiences. The following year brought two more Number One hits: "There's No Stopping Your Heart" and a duet with Paul Davis, "You're Still New to Me." Her final chart entry came in 1990.   —M.B.

The Outlaws

More than anything, it was the Outlaws' attitude that was different. The entire Outlaw movement of the early and mid-70's, when you get down to it, was less an outright musical rebellion than it was a search for some alternative to the creeping cosmopolitanism of mainstream Nashville music— something which had alienated artists like Waylon Jennings and Willie Nelson by the early 70's. The advent of The Outlaws was a reaction to a conformist studio system which had denied stardom to a brilliant eccentric like Willie Nelson who had

been cutting records in Nashville since the late 1950's; it was a response to a system which had all but beaten down an iconoclast like Waylon Jennings who had spent the 1960's trying to both buck Nashville's mainstream and flow with it.

"The thing is, they always told me they knew better," Waylon Jennings complained bitterly in a 1978 interview with Robert Hillburn of *The Los Angeles Times.* "They wouldn't let me pick my own songs. They didn't want me to even use my own band. They'd bring in their buddy musicians and listen to their advice on a record, but not mine. I'd cut a basic track on a record, and by the time they got through adding stuff to it, I wouldn't even recognize it. They also complained about the way I dressed and that my hair was too long. And it was pretty short in those days."

The first documented use of the term "outlaws" to label the group of rebels who would later comprise "the outlaw movement" was in the January 1974 issue of *Country Music Magazine* in a classic piece of New Journalism by Dave Hickey, titled "In Defense of the Telecaster Cowboy Outlaws."

The Outlaw moniker was formally hung on Jennings, Nelson and their various musical compatriots by a cleverly packaged 1976 album compilation called *Wanted: The Outlaws,* which also included music from Jessi Colter and Tompall Glaser. (Glaser's contributions to the early Outlaw movement as a producer, musical guru, ren-

egade influence and merely by dint of his chaotic personality, is not accurately reflected by his relatively meager recorded output.) The cover art of *Wanted: The Outlaws* depicted a "Wanted" poster with the above-mentioned musicians' pictures on it, and it proved a wonderful marketing tool. Most of all, it captured the fancy of post-Vietnam, anti-establishment American youth who had grown increasingly alienated from the bouffants, rhinestones and general conservatism of mainstream Nashville music, and who'd already turned on to Southern rock and California country-rock in huge numbers. *Wanted: The Outlaws* eventually sold a million copies (the first Nashville-produced country album to do so), even though most of the music on it had been previously released. It also jump-started Nelson's and Jennings' careers into the platinum realm, and the two of them virtually swept the CMA awards in 1976—the CMA being a staid organization which, up until then, had virtually ignored them.

Even so, Willie Nelson (whose biggest legal transgressions, up until the time of his IRS problems, were some speeding tickets and a couple of minor pot busts) has never been completely comfortable being stuck with the Outlaw handle: "I don't really like the term 'Outlaw,'" he insisted in a 1976 interview. "I always thought it was corny. All the term means is something that lives outside a working system. I like to sing. Titles are made to merchandise and distribute."

Waylon & Willie (their names are now forever inseparable), of course, went on to become superstars, while most of the other Outlaws eventually drifted off into their own distinct musical bags or faded back into the woodwork of Texas.

Looking back, Jennings has made it clear that what the whole Outlaw theme was really about artistic freedom: having the right to do your own thing. "I never went out to set a style of any kind, just to do it," Jennings insisted. "It just came naturally, I guess, because I don't know anything about music. I just know about my music. I have to do it like I feel it." —B.A.

Ovation

Ovation—the guitar with the trademark roundback body—was invented in 1965 by Charles Kaman, an aeronautical engineer/inventor/guitarist who was also the chairman and chief executive officer of Kaman Corporation, a diversified company that serves the defense, industrial and commercial markets.

Kaman was working on ways to improve the performance of helicopter blades by using a combination of spruce and composites, when he noticed that the materials had outstanding vibration-enhancing characteristics. Being a guitarist (he was offered a job with Tommy Dorsey's band in the late 1930's), he had a hunch the synthetics would make an excellent guitar body.

And so the Ovation "roundback" was born. The dense surface of the guitar's Lyrachord bowl coupled with its parabolic shape focuses sound waves through the soundhole, creating a bright sound and projection. The company, which is headquartered in Bloomfield, Connecticut, quickly became America's largest producer of acoustic guitars.

In the mid 1970's, Ovation rolled out the Adamas, a top-of-the-line acoustic guitar that featured a thin top made of carbon-graphite and birch veneer. Among the many country music artists who have played Ovation and Adamas guitars are Glen Campbell, Eddie Rabbitt, The Bellamy Brothers and Billy Ray Cyrus. —R.P.

Paul Overstreet

BORN: March 17, 1955
BIRTHPLACE: Newton, Mississippi

To date, Paul Overstreet is best known as a songwriter. His original compositions—"Diggin' Up Bones," "On the Other Hand," "Forever and Ever, Amen," "Deeper Than the Holler," "No Place Like Home"—almost single-handedly jump-started the early career of Randy Travis. "Same Ole Me" (George Jones), "When You Say Nothing at All" (Keith Whitley), "Battle Hymn of Love" (Kathy Mattea), "A Long Line of Love" (Michael Martin

Murphey) and "One Love at a Time" (Tanya Tucker) are just a few more of the better-known compositions of this man who was voted Songwriter of the Year by the Nashville Songwriters' Association in 1987.

In recent years, Overstreet has also made a modest but significant mark as a recording artist. In this capacity, he's steadfastly followed the rather singular path of writing and recording material that reflects his devout Christian beliefs and his deep faith in bedrock family values. This has resulted in hits like "Love Helps Those," "Sowin' Love," "Seein' My Father In Me," "Daddy's Come Around," "All the Fun" and "Richest Man on Earth."

"I came to a place that, spiritually speaking, was a new birth to me," explains Overstreet, who arrived in Nashville in 1973, with no job and no place to live. (He spent his first few nights sleeping in a church and eventually found work as a welder before infiltrating the music industry as a writer.)

"I was conditioned to write about misery," adds the singer/songwriter, who was briefly married to Stella Parton, and who admittedly drank and drugged profusely during his early years in Music City, but long ago came clean. "So it was more of a challenge for me to say, 'No, I'm not gonna write like that. I'm gonna wait till I get an idea that's worth sharing with people.'"

He briefly recorded as part of the trio, Schuyler, Knobloch and Overstreet, which scored a Number One with "Baby's Got a New Baby" (written by Overstreet).

He also had a Number One which he recorded in trio with Tanya Tucker and Paul Davis: "I Won't Take Less Than Your Love" (1988), a song which Overstreet co-wrote with his frequent songwriting partner, Don Schlitz.   —B.A.

Tommy Overstreet

BORN: September 10, 1937
BIRTHPLACE: Oklahoma City, Oklahoma

Born on September 10, 1937, in Oklahoma City and raised in Houston, singer/guitarist Tommy Overstreet—cousin of 1920's pop singer, Gene Austin—got his first guitar at age 14. After graduating high school, Overstreet moved to Nashville and

landed a recording contract with Dot Records in 1967. While he placed a few singles on country charts in the late 1960's ("Rocking a Memory," "Games People Play"), it wasn't until 1971, with the release of "Gwen (Congratulations)," that Overstreet found chart success. The song went on to become the first of six Top Ten singles he would record through 1977. The others were "I Don't Know You (Anymore)," "Ann (Don't Go Runnin')," "Heaven Is My Woman's Love," "(Jeanne Marie) You Were a Lady" and "Don't Go City Girl on Me." During this time Overstreet toured extensively with his band, The Nashville Express. They became a popular act overseas, especially in Germany, where a version of "Heaven Is My Woman's Love," sung entirely in German, became a Number One hit. Overstreet remained on the charts throughout the decade, though with less success. Overstreet recorded a total of 17 albums for Dot (later ABC/Dot) before switching to the Elektra/Asylum label in 1979. In the 80's he recorded for smaller labels, with his final chart entry appearing in 1986. In 1994, he signed with independent label DD&M.   —M.B.

Buck Owens

BORN: August 12, 1929
BIRTHPLACE: Sherman, Texas

The statistics speak for themselves: Buck Owens had 15 consecutive Number One records between 1963 and 1967, a total of 20 between 1963 and 1974. And 26 other singles made it to the Top Ten, including both sides of his 1964 single, "My Heart Skips a Beat" and "Together Again," which switched Number One and Number Two positions at one point. He epitomizes the "Bakersfield Sound" of the 1960's, a form of honky tonk music that originated with the Texas and Oklahoma refugees who relocated to California during the Depression.

Bakersfield produced other stars aside from Buck and fellow Bakersfield giant Merle Haggard. Rose Maddox, Ferlin Husky, Tommy Collins and Wynn Stewart were among them, but Buck's guitar-driven music helped define country in the 1960's.

Alvis Edgar Owens Jr. was born outside Sherman, Texas, not far south of the Red River, on August 12, 1929. He was the second child and first son of sharecropper Alvis Owens and his wife Maicie. Their life was not easy. The Depression was on, and they were literally living in the Dust Bowl chronicled in the John Steinbeck novel, *The Grapes of Wrath*. "Buck" was a mule on the Owens farm, and after young Alvis Jr. announced his name was "Buck," the name stayed with him.

Doing farm work in the midst of all this left its impact on Buck, who vowed as a boy that he'd never be poor, hungry or without decent clothes when he grew up. Everything he became stemmed from that resolve. In November 1937, the Owens family and other relatives (ten in all) piled into a 1933 Ford pulling a trailer and headed west. They settled just outside Phoenix, Arizona, started working on local farms and on occasion traveled to California to harvest fruit.

By this time a teenaged Buck was soaking up bluegrass, Western swing and the music of artists like Eddy Arnold, Cowboy Copas and others. His mother showed him some guitar chords, and he was soon playing in local honky tonks, first in a duo with a friend, then with a band called Mac's Skillet Lickers. There he met Bonnie Campbell, whom he married in 1948. His parents disliked the idea of Buck playing honky tonks (he drove a truck to make a living), but Buck saw clubs as a training ground.

In 1951 when Buck and Bonnie moved to Bakersfield, California, the Owens family soon followed. There he became lead singer and guitarist in Bill Woods' Orange Blossom Playboys, the house band at the popular Blackboard Club. Guitarist Joe Maphis wrote the honky tonk anthem, "Dim Lights, Thick Smoke (and Loud, Loud Music)," after watching Buck in action at the club.

Bakersfield-based singer Tommy Collins used Buck as his lead guitarist on his 1954 hit, "You Better Not Do That," on Capitol, and Capitol producer Ken Nelson liked Buck's playing enough to use him as a studio musician on various country, rock and pop recording sessions from then on. Buck never took all his cues from country; he admired Elvis and Little Richard, incorporating both hardcore honky tonk and rock in his music. Buck's first recordings for the Pep and Chesterfield labels were honky tonk, except for one rockabilly record done under the name Corky Jones. But Ken Nelson, feeling Buck lacked a vocal style, resisted signing him as a singer until 1957.

When his early Capitol releases didn't sell, Buck moved to the Tacoma, Washington, area in 1958. He played clubs, owned part of a radio station and hosted a local TV show that gave a local amateur named Loretta Lynn her first exposure. In 1959 he scored his first success with the single "Second Fiddle," which made the Top 30. That fall, "Under Your Spell Again," another Texas style shuffle of the sort Ray Price made popular, became his first Top Ten. Buck returned to Bakersfield. Soon he was touring the country with a young guitarist and fiddler he met in Washington, Don Ulrich, better known as Don Rich.

By 1963 Buck connected with Jack McFadden, who remains his manager today. That same year Buck had his first Number One record with "Act Naturally" and expanded his backup band, which one of the bass players—Merle Haggard—dubbed "The Buckaroos." The driving sound of "Act Naturally" was part of its success: Buck called it the "freight train" sound, because of its churning speed. His twanging guitar style gave his records a spare, stringing, trebly sound that he and Ken Nelson deliberately emphasized to cut through on AM radio.

Buck was hitting a peak by the mid-60's with a near-unprecedented string of Number One's: "Love's Gonna Live Here," in 1963; "Together Again," "My Heart Skips a Beat" and "I Don't Care" in 1964; "I've Got a Tiger by the Tail," "Before You Go," "Only You" and "Buckaroo" in 1965; "Waitin' in Your Welfare Line," "Think of Me" and "Open Up Your Heart" in 1966; "Sam's Place" and "Your Tender Loving Care" in 1967. He was on top; The Beatles' recording of "Act Naturally" affirmed the appeal of his work beyond the country audience. Buck raised some eyebrows among country fans and music business types by praising The Beatles' music at a time when few others agreed.

Buck also became an astute businessman even while concentrating on his music. He'd taken over the tiny Blue Book music publishing company in the 50's. Founded by his friend, songwriter Harlan Howard, it published Buck's and fellow Bakersfield star Merle Haggard's biggest songs. He had a booking agency, bought a Bakersfield radio station and started another, and later bought two stations in Phoenix and opened his own recording studio. In 1966 he started hosting *The Buck Owens Ranch Show*, a syndicated show seen in over 100 markets.

His professionalism was legendary, with stage shows going on longer than his contract specified; drinking and drug abuse were nearly nonexistent in The Buckaroos. Don Rich became his alter ego, handling problems on the road and contributing immensely to Buck's music. In 1966 they played Carnegie Hall, with Capitol recording the show. In '68 he and Roy Clark started co-hosting CBS' *Hee Haw*. Buck and his red, white and blue guitar became one of the show's symbols.

Through the late 60's and early 70's, the hits continued, including "Tall Dark Stranger" (Number One in 1969) and several Top Tens that marked the end of the "freight train" sound, including "Bridge Over Troubled Water" and two bluegrass numbers: "Ruby" and "Roll in My Sweet Baby's Arms." His final Number One, "Made in Japan," came in 1972. With *Hee Haw* in syndication after CBS canceled it, Buck was still riding high. He signed his last Capitol contract, this one giving him ownership of all his recordings after 1980. But bad times were looming.

The death of Don Rich in a 1974 motorcycle crash devastated Buck. When his Capitol contract ended

in '75, he signed with Warner Bros., producing albums in the country-pop sound he always disliked; few of them sold. He added fiddler Jana Jae to The Buckaroos, and in 1977 married her, only to leave her days later. Always proud of his straight-arrow reputation compared to other stars, Buck suddenly found himself facing embarrassing publicity. The couple divorced.

By 1980 he was at a crossroads. Unable to take the pain and stress that began with Rich's death, he quit touring except for a few appearances. Though *Hee Haw* paid well, he began feeling that the show overexposed him and that he'd allowed its comedy to trivialize his reputation as a masterful honky tonk singer. He finally quit in 1986 and concentrated on his businesses. At times he was wistful about his career, wondering if his music would ever be noticed again.

The New Traditionalists of the mid-80's answered that question. His influence on Dwight Yoakam, Marty Stuart and the late Keith Whitley was immense, as it was on the very first New Traditionalist, Emmylou Harris. The Desert Rose Band and Highway 101 also acknowledged Buck's influence, as did dozens of other artists. One day in 1987, Yoakam showed up in Buck's Bakersfield office when he came to play the Kern County fair, and coaxed him out of retirement. The two later sang "Streets of Bakersfield," a song Buck first cut in 1972, on a TV special in 1988. Response was so strong that they recorded it. The duet reached Number One that fall. He toured briefly, and recorded two underrated albums for Capitol and a mediocre country-pop album for Curb.

In the mid-90's, Buck (who underwent successful throat cancer surgery that saved his voice), takes it easy doing only selected show dates, spending the rest of the time overseeing his companies, which are run by his family. His music, his records, business empire and 160-acre ranch outside Bakersfield, are proof that a poor farm kid from Texas with guts, determination and vision can succeed.   —R.K.

Vernon Oxford

BORN: June 8, 1941
BIRTHPLACE: Benton County, Arkansas

Born near Rogers, Arkansas, in 1941, and raised in Wichita, Kansas, Vernon Oxford was an ultra-hard, old-time country singer who had the misfortune to pop up in Nashville in the late 70's, during an era when the town was far too preoccupied with Outlaws like Waylon & Willie and crossover hipsters like Kenny Rogers to pay much attention to him.

With singles titles like "Redneck Roots" and "A Good Old-Fashioned Honky Tonk Barroom Brawl," it was pretty easy to tell where—both stylistically and ideologically—Vernon Oxford was coming from. Other Oxford-recorded chart-skimmers like "Shadows of Your Mind," "Clean Your Own Tables" and "Your Wanting Me Is Gone" were only a little more subdued. (To say that Oxford was the Marty Brown or the Aaron Tippin of his generation does not began to do justice to the strident "twang factor" in his music.) Though Oxford garnered a fair amount of critical attention for his back-beyond-the-basics approach, country radio never really paid him much attention either. His sole trip to the country Top 20, in fact, came with his raucous 1976 novelty tune, "Redneck (The Redneck National Anthem)."   —B.A.

Ozark Jubilee

Founded in Springfield, Missouri, by KWTO executive Si Siman, the *Ozark Jubilee*, an Opry-style barn dance radio program, evolved out a local show called *Korn's A-Crackin'*. The *Jubilee* went on the Mutual Broadcasting System in the early 50's as part of Siman's new RadiOzark production company that produced transcribed syndicated shows. By 1954, the show was successful enough that Siman decided to expand it into a TV show. Siman formed a new company, Crossroads Television Productions, and convinced Red Foley to leave the Grand Ole Opry to become the show's host. They signed a deal with ABC-TV, and the cast, which included regional talent like Aunt Sap and Uncle Cyp Brasfield, bandleader Slim Wilson and others, went on the air on January 1955. Based in Springfield, and broadcast on ABC from the Jewell

Theater, via KTYV in Springfield, it attracted top-notch stars of the era as guests. It also nurtured new artists who became stars, most notably Porter Wagoner and Brenda Lee. The show was one of several that helped give country music major national exposure in the 50's, and its Missouri roots predated the phenomenon of Branson by several decades. The show continued until ABC canceled it in 1960, largely due to Foley's indictment on tax fraud charges (a jury acquitted him). In 1961 the show ran briefly on ABC once again, as *Five Star Jubilee*, co-hosted by Tex Ritter, Carl Smith, Rex Allen, Jimmy Wakely and former *Your Hit Parade* singer Snooky Lanson, before going off the air for good.   —R.K.

Patti Page

BORN: November 8, 1927
BIRTHPLACE: Muskogee, Oklahoma

Though Patti Page made her name in pop music, her roots were in the country music scene of Oklahoma. Born Clara Ann Fowler, she was one of 11 Fowler children who grew up in Tulsa. Dropping her first name, she began working with Al Klauser and His

Oklahomans in the late 40's. During those days in radio, sponsors often owned "names" which were taken by performers who appeared on given shows. The Page Milk Company sponsored a show over KTUL Radio in Tulsa, hosted by a singer given the name "Patti Page." Ann Fowler took this name when she replaced the original "Patti Page," and the name stuck. She became popular with Jimmy Joy and His Orchestra, and by the late 40's had a Mercury recording contract and began having pop hits. Her 1949 version of "Money, Marbles and Chalk" crossed over to the country charts, and she was also one of the first singers to harmonize with herself on record. Her 1950 recording of Pee Wee King's "The Tennessee Waltz" also crossed over to country success, though most of her success remained in the pop world. She did an excellent album of country songs in Nashville, titled *Country Hits*, with Hank Garland and other Nashville pickers. Her occasional country recordings throughout her career include "Hello We're Lonely" with Tom T. Hall in 1972.　　　—R.K.

Andy Parker

BORN: Born March 17, 1913
BIRTHPLACE: Magnum, Oklahoma
DIED: October 2, 1977

Parker was just 16 when he began broadcasting over a tiny radio station in Elk City, Oklahoma. By 1937 he was in San Francisco, portraying, appropriately enough, a singing cowboy on the NBC radio series *Death Valley Days*. During the early years of World War II, Parker worked outside music in defense plants in California. After relocating to L.A. in 1944, he formed Andy Parker and The Plainsmen, and worked at KNX in Los Angeles. He and the group, whose members changed, did a number of western films. They recorded for several labels, although some of their best work was done for the Coast label in 1946 when the group included Parker on guitar, fiddler Harry Sims, accordionist George Bamby, steel guitarist Joaquin Murphey and bassist Clem Smith. They recorded for a time for Capitol, but with groups like The Sons of the Pioneers enjoying far greater success, Parker could never really stand out. None of his records charted nationally, and he remained primarily a West Coast act. Parker eventually was forced to retire due to heart problems.　　　—R.K.

Lee Roy Parnell

BORN: December 21, 1956
BIRTHPLACE: Abilene, Texas

Born on December 31, 1956, in Abilene, Texas, singer/ songwriter/guitarist Lee Roy Parnell hit his stride by combining an eclectic blend of country and rhythm and blues that made him stand out amidst the "hat acts" of the late 1980's and early 90's.

Lee Roy traces his affinity for American roots music to his childhood on a cattle ranch near Fort Worth. He grew up listening to the music of Merle Haggard and Western swing king Bob Wills, who happened to be a friend of his father. In fact, at the age of six, young Lee Roy sang "San Antonio Rose" with Wills on WBAP Radio in Fort Worth.

During his mid-teens, Lee Roy began playing and writing music in earnest and formed his first band at 19. It was during this period that he fell under the spell of Southern rocker Duane Allman's snarling slide guitar work and also apprenticed with Delbert McClinton, to whose 70's country/soul/blues style Parnell admittedly owes a lot. Lee Roy spent nearly

10 years honing his singing and guitar-playing skills in the honky tonks of Texas before relocating to Nashville in 1987.

When he began a series of Monday night performances at Music City's famous Bluebird Cafe, Nashville insiders began to take note, including Tim DuBois of Arista Records, who offered him a contract. His debut for Arista, titled *Lee Roy Parnell* (1990), became a critical as well as a modest commercial success. Lee Roy's tough rhythm and blues edge, soulful voice and stinging slide, the critics said, brought a refreshing diversity to Nashville. Subsequent releases, *Love Without Mercy* (1992) and *On the Road* (1993), firmly established Lee Roy as a clever country stylist with a rock 'n' roll sensibility.   —B.A.

Gram Parsons

BORN: November 5, 1946
BIRTHPLACE: Winter Haven, Florida
DIED: September 19, 1973

Gram Parsons never had a hit record, nor were any of his songs ever played on country music radio. Not a likely country hero, he was a charismatic figure whose best songs are laced with haunting fundamentalist Christian imagery that ran counter to his own free-wheeling, excessive lifestyle, not to mention that of the late 60's counter-culture crowd that made up his audiences. Yet his accomplishments and his impact on country music remain both indelible and profound.

During his brief tenure with The Byrds, Parsons played on *Sweetheart of the Rodeo*, a pure country album that caught the California rock band's followers by surprise. In the process, Parsons opened new musical pathways to young rock fans who previously closed their ears to country music. (His Nudie suits, emblazoned with marijuana leaves, were symbolic of his unique musical path.) Parson's landmark recordings and haunting songs won followers from Rodney Crowell and Dwight Yoakam to The Rolling Stones and Elvis Costello. His music inspired such future country-rock bands as Poco, The Eagles and New Riders of The Purple Sage, who in turn influenced many country singers of the 1990's. Parsons' singing partner and musical protégée, Emmylou Harris, continued to build her own successful career after his untimely death at age 26.

Born Cecil Ingram Connors on November 5, 1946, in Winter Haven, Florida, Parsons grew up in Waycross, Georgia. In the early 1960's he sang in a folk group with Jim Stafford and Kent "Lobo" Lavoie. After dropping out of Harvard University he formed the International Submarine Band, basically a honky tonk country group that could deliver a Beatles-inspired sound when needed. The band recorded its sole album in Los Angeles in December 1967; Parsons left to join The Byrds two months later. After recording *Sweetheart of the Rodeo*, Parsons suddenly quit the band; later that year he and another Byrd, former bluegrass mandolinist Chris Hillman, formed The Flying Burrito Brothers. He recorded three albums with The Burritos; the first, *The Gilded Palace of Sin*, is a country-rock classic.

After an extended recuperation from a 1970 motorcycle accident, Parsons recorded *G.P.*, his first solo album, working in a style that he now called "cosmic American music." He had just completed his second album on September 19, 1973, when he died in Joshua Tree, California, of heart failure stemming from a drug and alcohol overdose.   —D.S.

Dolly Parton

BORN: January 19, 1946
BIRTHPLACE: Sevier County, Tennessee

Dolly Parton, an artist who launched her career in country music, but has since transcended the field in terms of her music and the scope of her celebrity, was born January 19, 1946, in Sevier County, Tennessee, the fourth of 12 children. Her humble origins would later inspire some of her all-time best music—specifically, her early original songs like "Coat of Many Colors" (Number Four in 1971), "My Tennessee Mountain Home" (a Top 20 in 1973) and "Joshua," which in 1970 became her first of more than 20 Number One hits. She sang throughout childhood, and headed for Nashville the day after high school graduation. There she went through the typical few years of paying dues—waitressing and making the rounds—before signing with Monument Records in 1966 (the same year she married her intensely private husband, contractor Carl Dean). She debuted inauspiciously on the country charts with "Dumb Blonde" in 1967, which peaked at Number 24. But her pairing with Porter Wagoner on his television show in 1967 was the beginning of her true rise to superstardom, as the duo began a string of consistent hits between 1967 and 1980, including "The Last Thing on My Mind" (a Top Ten in 1967), "We'll Get Ahead Someday" (Top Five in 1968), "If Teardrops Were Pennies" (Number Three in 1973) and "Please Don't Stop Loving Me" (Number One in 1974).

Parton's solo career, since her somewhat acrimonious split with Wagoner (she was actually recording her own records all during their duet days) has run the gamut of pure country to mainstream pop (vacillating between the extremes of sublime to awful along the way). Her venture into films has been similarly and spectacularly uneven, spanning the extremes between the magnificent (*Steel Magnolias* and *9 to 5*) and the abysmal (*Rhinestone*, *Best Little Whorehouse in Texas*). She also hosted an em-

barrassingly bad television series, *Dolly*.

Parton's music in recent years has never come close to equaling her vintage early 70's recordings; and the truth is, her willingness to become a big-busted parody for the mass market TV audiences has actually done much to trivialize the immense musical talent so evident in that early work. Yet amidst the drek she's released in the past decade, there have been a few gems (*White Limozeen*, a 1989 album produced by Ricky Skaggs, which was certified Gold, *Eagle When She Flies*, which in 1991 became her second million-selling album, and *Honky Tonk Angels*, a 1994 collaboration with Tammy Wynette and Loretta Lynn). Particularly inspired was her quality union with Emmylou Harris and Linda Ronstadt (the three have been friends and occasional collaborators for years) that resulted in both an unfettered television show and a fine album, *Trio*, which won Grammys for Best Country Vocal Performance by a Duo or Group, and Album of the Year in 1987. (She also earned Grammys in 1978 for "Here You Come Again" and 1981 for "9 to 5.")

Her early hits, including "Jolene," "Coat of Many Colors" and "The Bargain Store," were pure country, some of the best music she's ever made, and perhaps that's one reason she took such a critical hit when she moved towards pop with more urbane chart-toppers like "Here You Come Again" (which admittedly sold far better and first introduced her to the huge crossover audience that has since taken her to its collective heart). By the time she started on the crossover route, Dolly had already become a highly visible symbol of country music. She had, in fact, become a self-invented caricature of sorts by extravagantly accentuating her natural attributes to play for the belly laughs and off-color jokes, and mainly, to make sure audiences would have no trouble remembering who she was. Busty, dizzy and bouffanted, country music fans loved her and country music detractors laughed. It made her a superstar, and a multi-multi-millionaire; but to music insiders, it also presented a portrait of an artist out of touch with her inspirational roots.

Ironically, Dolly is anything but dizzy, anything but rootless. She's a strong woman and gifted businessperson, who owns two production companies responsible for successful movies, like *Father of the Bride* and *Shining Through*. She has written more than 3,000 songs, owns five music-publishing houses and is said to have personal wealth well in excess of

30 million dollars. She fulfilled yet another dream when she opened her own theme park, Dollywood, not far from where she was born, in Sevier County, Tennessee, in 1986. In conjunction with the park and in cooperation with the National Foundation to Protect America's Eagles, she also opened Eagle Mountain Sanctuary in 1991. She also founded the Dollywood Foundation, a non-profit organization to support education and reduce the dropout rate in Sevier County.

Big bust and blonde bouffant notwithstanding, *Ms. Magazine* recognized Dolly as Woman of the Year in 1986.

Meanwhile, her legacy of good music continues, and in 1992 she and another duet partner, Ricky Van Shelton, took Vocal Collaboration and Video of the Year from The Nashville Network/Music City News Country Awards for "Rockin' Years." And her life story in book form hit the stands in late 1994 and headed right for the best-seller lists. Dolly has been a member of the Grand Ole Opry since 1969.   —M.B.

Johnny Paycheck

BORN: May 31, 1941
BIRTHPLACE: Greenfield, Ohio

Born Don Eugene Lytle in southern Ohio on May 31, 1941, Johnny Paycheck began playing guitar and writing songs as a teenager. In the late 1950's and early 1960's he played bass guitar in the bands of such country luminaries as Porter Wagoner, Faron Young, George Jones and Ray Price. His strong voice also made him a sought-after backup singer for major country acts, while his original compositions gained him a reputation as an up-and-coming songwriter. It was Johnny's demo tape of one of his songs that caught the attention of record executive Aubrey Mayhew, who helped get him into the studio to cut his first single, "Don't Start Countin' on Me," in 1965. The song wasn't a hit, nor was the follow-up single, "The Girl They Talk About." Around the same time Johnny was hired as the opening act for George Jones; in the 1965-66 season they played all 50 states and made a whirlwind 20-day tour of Europe. It was while Johnny was touring with Jones that his third single, "A-11," made the country Top 40. Encouraged by this early success, Johnny and Aubrey Mayhew formed their own label, Little Darlin' Records, and were re-

warded with Top Ten single, "The Lovin' Machine," in 1966. That same year Tammy Wynette cut Paycheck's "Apartment #9" as her first single. But while Johnny seemed to be headed for country stardom, his drinking and drug habits were getting further and further out of control. He was asked to leave the Jones tour after his drunken antics at a Los Angeles performance. In the early 1970's, veteran producer Billy Sherrill agreed to work with Johnny on the condition that he clean up his act. The collaboration produced a succession of chart hits including "Song and Dance Man" and "Mr. Lovemaker" (1973), "For A Minute There" and "All American Man" (1975) and "Gone at Last" (1976).

Johnny and Sherrill had a brief schism as Johnny suffered a relapse of heavy drinking. Perhaps sensing that his big breakthrough was just around the corner, Johnny declared bankruptcy and begged Sherrill for a second chance. In the summer of 1976, Johnny released "11 Months and 29 Days," which he'd co-written with Sherrill, followed by the Top Ten hit, "I'm the Only (Hell Mama Ever Raised)." Not long after, he headed into the studio to record a single whose title would become a permanent fixture on T-shirts, coffee mugs and in TV sitcom punchlines. The song, of course, was "Take This Job and Shove It," written by fellow Columbia artist David Allan Coe. The song reached Number One in 1978 and spent 18 weeks on the charts, cementing Paycheck's identity as a hit-maker, but also marking the zenith of his checkered career. Paycheck quickly scored two more hits with "Me and the I.R.S." and the Top Ten, "Friend, Lover and Wife," co-written with Sherrill.

The 80's brought a few hits in the form of duets with George Jones and Merle Haggard, though by now, his low-life ways and rampant egotism and unpredictability had even worn out his welcome with his fellow artists. Similarly, his limitations as a singer and his lack of artistic vision (which seemed to hardly go beyond his chronic penchant for the low-life themes in his music) began to wear thin with audiences. It became clear that Paycheck's's outlaw image had gone too far, and that old habits really do die hard when he was convicted in 1986 of a barroom shooting in Ohio.   —M.B.

Leon Payne

BORN: June 15, 1917
BIRTHPLACE: Alba, Texas
DIED: September 11, 1969

Born in Alba, Texas, June 1917, this blind singer and distinguished songwriter appeared in various Southwestern bands in the 1930's (including Bill Boyd's Western swing band) before becoming a cast member of the *Louisiana Hayride* and the *Grand Ole Opry*, which he joined in 1949.

Payne, who died in 1969, achieved some notoriety as a crooner with his recordings of self-written ballads like "I Love You Because" (a Top Five single which stayed in the charts eight months in 1949), "They'll Never Take Her Love From Me" and various

other sides he recorded for the Bullet and Capitol labels. Yet Payne is most indelibly remembered for "Lost Highway," which he wrote and recorded several years before Hank Williams covered the song and took it to immortality.   —B.A.

Minnie Pearl

BORN: October 25, 1912
BIRTHPLACE: Centerville, Tennessee

November 1940: The Grand Ole Opry's powers-that-be weren't sure that the 28-year-old female comic they were auditioning would fit in. She lacked the raw, rural background of most Opry acts. College educated, she was well-versed in drama, classical literature and classical music. She wasn't even that familiar with the show; yet here she was, trying to take a made-up stage character and make it work.

The Opry, then broadcast from the War Memorial Auditorium in Nashville, slotted her as a guest performer. Sarah Colley walked on the Opry stage, nervous. After her spot, she asked her mother, who was in the audience, how she did. Her mother replied that "Several people woke up." It was a tentative beginning for Minnie Pearl, but within two years she was a Nashville institution. For the next 51 years, Minnie's simple, innocent (and authentic) country humor created an unforgettable character who performed in a variety of settings.

Her roots were far removed from that. Born in 1912 in Centerville, Tennessee, southwest of Nashville, Sarah Ophelia Colley was the fifth daughter of Tom Colley, a well-to-do owner of a lumber business. It was an urbane, educated household she grew up in. Her mother, Fannie Colley, was well-educated and steeped in the virtues of propriety. But like her father, Sarah had a feeling for earthy humor. She enjoyed vaudeville shows and attended local tent shows.

Sarah's dramatic aspirations continued through her

teens. In 1930, after she graduated from high school, she enrolled in Ward-Belmont College in Nashville. Bear in mind, the Nashville of the 1920's was not Music City U.S.A. but the "Athens of the South": a center of high culture, education and refinement, and a far cry from the blue-collar, rural roots of much of the rest of Tennessee and the South. Ward-Belmont, an exclusive women's school, produced polished, proper Southern women.

After graduation, Colley taught dramatics, dance and piano in Centerville. Then in 1934 she joined the Wayne P. Sewell Production company as a show director. This Atlanta firm produced amateur theater, mostly musical comedies, in the South. Sewell directors went into towns and supervised productions which featured local citizens playing the roles and raised funds for local organizations such as Lions Clubs. The job put Sarah Colley in touch with the other side of the South. As she directed these shows, she was able to observe rural Southerners closely and, with her dramatic training, capture their essence.

During one trip in 1936 she spent time with an Alabama family. An elderly woman in the home told her stories, local folk tales, and had a colorful way of explaining things in rural dialect. Sarah drank it in. She saw a potential character she could portray, and as time went on, she added ideas of her own to flesh out the character concept, including childhood memories of a railroad switching station near Centerville known as Grinder's Switch. That colorful locale would provide the name for her fictitious hometown. She named her character Minnie Pearl.

In 1937, when Tom Colley died at age 80, Sarah went home to be with her mother. She ran a government-funded recreation center in Centerville and in 1940 produced a show for a local banker's convention. When a speaker was late, Minnie filled in the time, and went over well enough that a Nashville banker suggested WSM recruit her for the Opry.

Her first audition at WSM's offices didn't go well, and she made only $10 her first time onstage at the Opry. But George Hay called her the following Wednesday and asked her to come back the next Saturday. When she arrived, she found 300 pieces of fan mail waiting for her, and was offered a permanent slot on the Opry. Minnie had touched on something that the show needed.

Her pure country humor, in the form of the innocent country spinster who is not quite sure about anything but *so* proud to be there, struck a chord in people. There was something lovable, common and universal in the character of Minnie Pearl that transcended class considerations and everything else. Roy Acuff was one of Minnie's first supporters. He added her to his touring show, which often performed in tents. She was able to polish and refine the character even further there, and by 1943 she was on the road with other Opry stars, entertaining the troops at U.S. military bases as part of the Camel Caravan.

Shortly after the war ended, Rod Brasfield—also from Centerville—joined the Opry as a comedian. Soon Brasfield and Minnie, though they each did separate routines, also began to perform together. Brasfield, a largely forgotten figure in Opry history, took on a naive, hillbilly personality and could get away with racy (for that time), double-entendre humor that anyone else couldn't have gotten on the air. Minnie, who played the straight man to Brasfield, was in awe of him. She would work with Brasfield until he became ill and died in 1958.

In 1947, the same year she appeared at Carnegie Hall with an Opry troupe, Sarah Colley married Henry Cannon, a former Army Air Corps captain and pilot who became her right hand, chauffeuring Minnie and other Opry stars on their tours. Minnie's career continued through the 1950's. She even appeared on *This Is Your Life* in 1957. And though Minnie wasn't really a recording artist, she made some records for King, RCA and Starday, among others. In 1967 she lent her name to a chicken franchise that lasted a few years before going under, one of her few failures. On the other hand, she had success with a straight dramatic role as an evangelist in the otherwise horrible 1967 B-movie, *That Tennessee Beat*, which featured Merle Travis and other Nashville singers making hilarious attempts at "acting," hobbled by an awful script.

Offstage, Sarah Cannon was an urbane, well-educated Southern lady, as she'd been raised to be. Intelligent and well-read, she had no trouble deciding where Minnie left off and Sarah began. In 1968 she was nominated for membership in the Country Music Hall of Fame, but because so many singers and pioneers were still being inducted into the then-new Hall, it took seven years, until 1975, for her to finally win the award.

As Nashville grew as a music and entertainment capital, Minnie continued to work. Though she didn't tour as often, she found herself doing more network TV and occasional shows in Las Vegas. A regular on

Hee Haw almost from the show's beginning, and still an Opry regular (often trading quips with old friend Roy Acuff, who helped her polish her act years before), she became an inspiration to women when she successfully won a battle with breast cancer.

The success of The Nashville Network also kept her busy until 1991 when, at age 78, she suffered a serious stroke that curtailed her performing activities permanently.   —R.K.

Pedal Steel

The pedal steel guitar evolved from the original steel guitars. Among the first ones were Gibson's six-pedal "Electraharp," introduced in 1939. The concept was straightforward: to permit the musician to create chords that might be difficult, if not impossible, to play on a non-pedal instrument. This was done with a mechanical mechanism in the body of the instrument, operated by foot pedals, to alter the pitch of the guitar's strings in order to create these chords. Initially, pedal steels did not catch on with country performers. A California Western swing player named Dick Roberts built his own pedal mechanism, but used it on a limited basis.

The first country pedal steel player to take the instrument's potential seriously was Speedy West. In 1947, West, based in Los Angeles, was impressed by a non-pedal steel that Paul Bigsby built for Joaquin Murphey. He had Bigsby build him a pedal steel, taking delivery in February of 1948. The first session on which he used the instrument was Eddie Kirk's recording of "Candy Kisses," in 1949. Over the next several years, West used the instrument on hundreds of country and pop recording sessions and on his own recordings with guitarist Jimmy Bryant. Others followed Speedy's example. Ralph Mooney improvised a pedal mechanism for his non-pedal steel; Wayne Burdick, with Tex Williams' band, used the Gibson Electraharp (though few others did).

Though West was the first true country pedal guitarist, Bud Isaacs (who also played a Bigsby pedal guitar) introduced the instrument to Nashville, and the impact of his playing with Webb Pierce's band in the early 50's was summed up on Pierce's 1954 hit recording of "Slowly," which inspired steel guitarists all over the nation to save enough money for a Bigsby. (Bigsby had a lengthy waiting list in those days.)

Though non-pedal players were still dominant, the versatility of pedal guitars meant the non-pedal steel's days in country music were numbered. But the first pedal steel virtuoso to fully explore the instrument's possibilities was Buddy Emmons, who first came to prominence as a member of Little Jimmy Dickens' Country Boys. In 1955 Emmons and Shot Jackson began building a steel (in a chicken coop owned by another steel player, Howard White) and created their first Sho-Bud pedal guitar. Though Fender began making pedal steels in 1957, Sho-Bud quickly became the dominant favorite among country pedal steel players, in part because their mechanisms were more responsive and better-built. Emmons had a strong jazz influence in his music, and this was particularly obvious in his solo recordings, as well as his work with Little Jimmy Dickens' Country Boys and Ray Price's Cherokee Cowboys. Jimmy Day also became a major name in pedal steel. Even a few non-pedal players, Don Helms and Western swinger Herb Remington, came to embrace pedal steels, as did country-jazz virtuoso Curly Chalker. Emmons' country-jazz playing inspired a number of other players, most notably Buddy Charleton of Ernest Tubb's Texas Troubadours and Nashville's Doug Jernigan.

Of all the Nashville pedal players, however, Pete Drake came to epitomize the Nashville style of playing. Another member of Nashville's A-Team of studio musicians, Drake even recorded a pedal steel instrumental hit of his own in 1964 with "Forever." Drake's notoriety on the instrument was such that he was even called on to work on Bob Dylan's *John Wesley Harding* and *Nashville Skyline* albums in the late 60's, and later recorded in separate projects with Ringo Starr and Paul McCartney.

Lloyd Green gained fame after his impressive pedal work on Warner Mack's 1965 hit, "The Bridge Washed Out."

Since pedal steels generally have two separate necks, two tunings dominated pedal steel in Nashville: the E9 (considered suitable for most commercial country records) and C6 (favored for Western swing or jazz). Only one West Coast pedal player truly stood out after Speedy West moved to Oklahoma in the mid-50's: Ralph Mooney. Buck Owens, who often featured steel prominently on his records, found his own gifted steel soloist when Tom Brumley replaced Jay McDonald in The Buckaroos around 1963, remaining until he joined Rick Nelson's Stone Canyon Band.

Other steel guitar makers also emerged. After

Emmons ended his partnership with Shot Jackson, he and Ron Lashley began building "Emmons" brand pedal steels. In Texas, Maurice Anderson founded his MSA company to manufacture steels. Sho-Bud changed ownership. Other companies have come and gone over the years and the instrument itself has undergone many improvements. Steel guitarist DeWitt Scott, owner of Scotty's Music in St. Louis, has run the International Steel Guitar Convention in that city for years. On Music Row today, though the pedal steel's status tends to rise and fall with changing musical trends, it remains a staple and fundamental ingredient in modern country music. Paul Franklin, veteran Sonny Garrish, Bruce Bouton and Dan Dugmore are part of the current A-Team who appear on most of the records produced in Nashville. In Texas, Tom Morrell and Herb Remington are among the greats still playing there. And though technology will undoubtedly change the instrument over time, the pedal steel's distinctive whine will remain an integral part of country music for the foreseeable future. —R.K.

Ralph Peer

BORN: May 22, 1892
BIRTHPLACE: Kansas City, Missouri
DIED: January 19, 1960

One of the most important executives in the early history of country music, Ralph Sylvester Peer was born in Kansas City, Missouri, May 22, 1892.

After working for the Columbia Phonograph Company, Peer became recording director for Okeh Records in 1920 and was responsible for recording many of that legendary label's early "race" records ("race" then being a euphemism for blues) with giants like Mamie Smith. He had also, by the mid-1920's, released "old time" tunes on early country artists like Ernest V. Stoneman, Fiddlin' John Carson, The Jenkins Family, Roba Stanley and Henry Whitley's Virginia Breakdowners.

In the mid-20's, Peer went to work for the Victor Talking Machine Company and began scouring the southeastern U.S. on field recording trips as he searched for talented new rural and mountain performers—artists for whom he coined the phrase "hillbilly" musicians. On one of these trips, to the city of Bristol, on the Tennessee-Virginia border, in August 1927, Peer discovered and made the first recordings of two future giants of early country music: Jimmie Rodgers and The Carter Family. Peer went on to oversee many of the ensuing recordings made by these two legendary acts.

Sensing the glorious future that lay head for country music, Peer also shrewdly formed his own Southern Music Publishing Company, the cornerstone of which was Jimmie Rodgers' compositions. In the ensuing years, Peer also added to Southern Music's burgeoning song catalogue dozens of other early country classics ("Muleskinner Blues," "Wabash Cannonball," etc.). Thus the company, now known as Peer Music, eventually grew to be one of the true multi-million-dollar cornerstones of the modern country music industry. Ralph Peer died on January 19, 1960. In 1984, he was elected to the Country Music Hall of Fame. —B.A.

Hank Penny

BORN: August 18, 1918
BIRTHPLACE: Birmingham, Alabama
DIED: April 17, 1992

Herbert Clayton "Hank" Penny, born and raised in Alabama, got his start as a teenager in Birmingham as a banjoist-comic with Happy Hal Burns. By 1936, entranced by the Western swing music of Bob Wills and Milton Brown, he formed The Radio Cowboys, one of the few Western swing oriented bands working east of the Mississippi. They worked in Birmingham, Chattanooga and Atlanta, and, in 1938, began recording for the American Recording Company. The Cowboys dissolved in 1940, and by 1942 Penny was at WLW's *Boone County Jamboree* in Cincinnati. He began recording for King Records in 1944 and a year later moved to Los Angeles. There, he worked as a comic and led top-flight Western swing bands. His hit records for King included "Steel Guitar Stomp" (featuring Noel Boggs and Merle Travis) and "Get Yourself a Red Head" in 1946 and "Bloodshot Eyes" in 1949. Penny also co-founded L.A.'s legendary country nightclub, the Palomino.

Penny's contentious attitude hurt his career. Later recordings for RCA and Decca didn't sell, and by 1954 he left Hollywood with his third wife, singer Sue Thompson. They relocated to Las Vegas, among the earliest country performers based there. Penny

and Thompson divorced in 1963 (their son, Greg Penny, has produced k.d. lang). Penny later married singer Shari Bayne. After a brief period in Nashville in the late 60's, Penny returned to California in the 70's, remaining there until his death.   —R.K.

Carl Perkins

BORN: April 9, 1932
BIRTHPLACE: Tiptonville, Tennessee

One of rockabilly music's founding fathers, Carl Perkins was, some would argue, more talented than his former Sun labelmate, Elvis Presley. Many of the songs he wrote or arranged became rock 'n' roll classics, inspiring cover versions by The Beatles and countless other acts. His "Blue Suede Shoes" has been called the first true rock 'n' roll record. It topped *Billboard*'s country charts, and reached Number Two on both its pop and R&B charts in 1956. It might have reached the top pop spot if a serious auto acci-

dent en route to a *Perry Como Show* appearance hadn't derailed Perkins' momentum. It was his former labelmate Elvis Presley's version of the song, which went Top 20 in the pop charts in '56, just weeks after Perkins' version peaked, that is most often remembered today.

Perkins was born on April 9, 1932, near Tiptonville, Tennessee. Exposed to country, blues and gospel music at an early age, he began learning guitar before he was a teenager. By the early 1950's he recruited his two brothers to form The Perkins Brothers Band. Primarily performing in Jackson, Tennessee, honky tonks, the band played country hits of the day, infusing them with a strong backbeat. Perkins, who grew up a bluegrass fan, also loved the blues and enjoyed putting the churning upbeat rhythms of bluegrass behind a blues number, or playing stinging blues guitar licks on a country tune. A 1954 audition with Sam Phillips led to two releases on his Flip and Sun labels; released under Perkins name, neither record generated much action.

"Blue Suede Shoes" was Perkins' third release. Phillips promoted the record hard, using the capital he received from selling Presley's contract to RCA

Victor. His efforts paid off when "Blue Suede Shoes" became Sun's first million-selling record. Three follow-up singles were strong in the country market, but failed to generate interest among pop buyers—Perkins' music ultimately proved too raw and southern to appeal to youthful Northern audiences.

Perkins jumped to Columbia in January 1958, but none of his Columbia masters captured the excitement of his Sun sides. "Pink Pedal Pushers" was a Top 20 country hit in 1958. Succeeding records went nowhere. By 1964 his career appeared over. Alcohol problems further complicated his life. But Perkins agreed to appear with Chuck Berry on a package tour of Britain, and was surprised at the adulation he received. Perkins eventually joined Johnny Cash's touring show, along with The Carter Family and The Statler Brothers.

Once back in America, Perkins resumed his career as a country singer. "Country Boy's Dream," a 1966 single on Dollie, provided his first chart success in eight years. Perkins eventually succeeded in controlling his alcoholism and remained an integral part of Cash's show. He wrote Cash's 1968 Number One hit, "Daddy Sang Bass," and was a regular on Cash's ABC-TV show. These factors led to a second Columbia contract, which produced a superb 1969 single, "Restless," and an outstanding album, *On Top*. A series of indifferent albums appeared on various labels through the 1970's and 80's. In 1986 he was honored by a Cinemax special featuring George Harrison.

Today Perkins remains a revered figure in America, Europe and Japan. He often performs on the road with his sons, Gregg and Stan, although, in the 90's he's cut back on personal appearances after a life-threatening bout with throat cancer.   —D.S.

Sam Phillips

BORN: January 5, 1923
BIRTHPLACE: Florence, Alabama

Memphis native Sam Phillips is primarily known for nurturing and developing such major recording artists as Elvis Presley, Carl Perkins, Johnny Cash, Roy Orbison and Jerry Lee Lewis. While most of them achieved greater fame and fortune after leaving Phillips' Sun label, few ever recaptured the raw vitality and innovation of the rockabilly records they made in his small Memphis studio.

Phillips was a popular radio announcer in January 1950 when he opened his custom studio, Memphis Recording Service. That summer he began recording both country and blues artists and selling the masters to established labels. In March 1951 he recorded "Rocket 88," a raucous R&B tune by singer/sax player Jackie Brenston; it became a top R&B hit for Chicago's Chess label. Successes by Howling Wolf

and Rosco Gordon led Phillips to start Sun Records in March 1952.

Sun concentrated on serving black markets until Elvis Presley's groundbreaking single, "That's All Right, Mama," achieved regional success in July 1954. From that point, Phillips concentrated on what would later be called "rockabilly," a raw, infectious hybrid of country and blues (often called "race") music recorded with a spacious, slapback echo. In November 1955 Phillips sold Presley's contract to RCA Victor for $30,000, which gave him the capital he needed to break Sun's first national hit, Carl Perkins' "Blue Suede Shoes."

In 1956 and 1957 Sun hit the country and pop charts with songs by Perkins, Johnny Cash, Jerry Lee Lewis and Roy Orbison.

By 1958, Phillips had virtually abandoned record production to concentrate on his expanding business interests. (He was one of the original investors in Holiday Inn.) Most Sun and Phillips International recordings made after that date lack the edge that made the earlier productions so vital and appealing. In 1969 Phillips sold the Sun label to Shelby Singleton, but maintained his lucrative broadcasting and music publishing interests.   —D.S.

Piano

From the beginning of country music, pianos have been an intergal part of its sound. When available, pianos would play with rural stringbands performing for dancers. Its percussive rhythms made the dance beat more definable. One early country piano recording was done in 1927, when Virginia's Shelor Family String Band was recorded by Ralph Peer at the legendary Bristol Sessions (which also saw the first records by Jimmie Rodgers, Ernest Stoneman and The Carter Family). However, many early country performers thought little of using piano. Charlie Poole was once ejected from a recording session when he wanted to use one; his New York producers felt it wasn't country-sounding. But this was not the case with early Opry star Sam McGee, who learned some of his instrumentals from a player piano roll. Pianist Lillian Armstrong even backed Jimmie Rodgers on the session where her husband, Louis, played trumpet.

When a very young Bob Wills was playing fiddle for dances in Texas, pianos were a common part of the accompaniment. After Milton Brown left the Light Crust Doughboys to form his Musical Brownies in 1932, he hired a jazz pianist named Fred "Papa" Calhoun, the first pianist in Western swing. When Bob Wills started the Playboys in 1933, he went through several pianists before he found Al Stricklin. The Western swing scene in Texas spawned other pianists, including Moon Mullican, who worked with Cliff Bruner, and the crazed, stomping, pot-smoking singer-pianist John "Smokey" Wood, who worked with The Modern Mountaineers and his own band, Smokey Wood and His Wood Chips. On the West Coast in the 1940's, pianists were a common part of most groups. The talented Vic Davis, blind pianist Jimmy Pruett and Billy Liebert worked with various country and Western swing acts.

During World War II, the influence of black boogie-woogie piano became substantial on country acts. Moon Mullican signed with King Records in 1946, and became the first singer-pianist to become a major star, with hit recordings like "New Pretty Blonde (Jole Blon)" and in the early 50's, "Cherokee Boogie." In Nashville, Owen Bradley did extensive piano work on country records, as he did with his Nashville-based dance band. Bradley sometimes played behind Ernest Tubb, who referred to him as "Half Moon" Bradley (because he only played halfway like Moon Mullican). Fred Rose played piano on some Hank Williams sessions (he can be heard briefly at the end of Hank's 1952 "Half as Much"). Del Wood's 1951 hit, "Down Yonder," made her a part of the Opry until her death in 1989. In California, San Diego pianist Merrill Moore did an excellent series of country boogie recordings for Capitol, while Roy Hall did likewise from the late forties on. Hall and Mullican were both influential

on Jerry Lee Lewis' style, which was based so indelibly on his piano-pounding. (Though bluegrass king Bill Monroe didn't use a piano on the road, for a time he had Sally Ann Forrester playing accordion with The Blue Grass Boys during World War II.)

Floyd Cramer, who began as a pianist on the *Louisiana Hayride* and later became a Nashville studio musician (his spooky piano licks on Presley's "Heartbreak Hotel" remain classic today) began making successful instrumental recordings in 1958 with "Flip, Flop and Bop." In 1959 Chet Atkins played him a demo of a song titled "Please Help Me, I'm Falling." The next day, Atkins planned to have Hank Locklin record it. Chet liked songwriter Don Robertson's style on the song's demo, using chromatic grace notes to recreate the changing pitches of a pedal steel, so he told Cramer to learn what later became known as the "slipnote" style for the Locklin session. Cramer's piano figures became an integral part of the song and led to his own composition in that same slipnote style: "Last Date." Cramer, and later blind pianist Hargus "Pig" Robbins, became the top keyboard players in the Nashville studios. Jerry Lee Lewis, of course, had a profound influence with his over-the-top piano playing; though when he became a successful country singer in the late 60's, he showed restraint, taste and grace when playing on his ballads. Charlie Rich's piano work, understated on his big hits of the 1970's, always reflected the influence of jazz. Even a hardcore traditionalist like Roy Acuff routinely featured the piano in The Smokey Mountain Boys, with Jimmie Riddle doing the honors. Jim Reeves would cancel a show if his pianist, Dean Manuel, wasn't provided a decent instrument. Other singers, like Ronnie Milsap, Mickey Gilley, Becky Hobbs and Gary Stewart all use piano as their primary instruments. Today, electronic keyboards and synthesizers have become an intregal part of country recordings, some well-played, others used to excess.

—R.K.

Webb Pierce

BORN: August 8, 1921
BIRTHPLACE: West Monroe, Louisiana
DIED: February 24, 1991

Webb Pierce will forever be remembered for his guitar-shaped swimming pool and silver dollar-inlaid Pontiac. But there was much more to him than those extravagant symbols of his success. Only six country singers top him in total number of records sold, and in his heyday, his records hung in the Number One spot for months at a time. (Few artists keep a song at Number One for more than a week or two today.)

In addition, Webb was among the handful of artists who defined honky tonk music, and several of his performances, most notably "Back Street Affair" and "There Stands the Glass," are some of the best and most definitive of the genre. He, along with Carl Smith, Lefty Frizzell and others, truly carried the torch after Hank Williams died.

Then there's the voice: keening like a steel guitar, cutting and achingly expressive on ballads, cocky on upbeat numbers. Webb is one of a handful of truly memorable country vocalists, up there with Jimmie Rodgers, Lefty Frizzell, Hank Williams or Willie Nelson. The edge makes him instantly identifiable. The remark Waylon Jennings once made about himself—that he "couldn't go pop with a mouthful of firecrackers"—applied doubly to Webb. Nashville's later crossover trends would not be kind to him.

Webb Pierce was born in West Monroe, Louisiana, on August 8, 1921. He started singing and playing as a youth. During his stint in the Army just after World War II, he sang, and after his discharge in 1948, he returned home to pursue a musical career. In nearby Shreveport, the *Louisiana Hayride* was just getting started over radio station KWKH.

Though he managed to land a local show on station KMLB in Monroe, the salary wouldn't pay the bills. So he went to work at the Sears, Roebuck store in Shreveport, eventually ending up manager of the men's wear department. Meanwhile, he took every radio appearance he could get. "We used to put Webb on our radio shows," recalls Teddy Wilburn of The Wilburn Brothers, then based in Shreveport.

Webb set his sights on the *Hayride*. When he finally made it onto the cast, he connected with regional record distributor Pappy Daily, who later took George Jones to fame. Daily got Webb a contract with Four Star Records in 1949, and Webb's "Panhandle Rag," the Leon McAuliffe steel guitar hit with lyrics added, became a regional hit in Arkansas, Louisiana and Texas. Pacemaker Records was another of Webb's projects. Owned by Webb and *Hayride* boss Horace Logan, the label recorded mostly local talent. Webb sang occasionally on numbers like "Hayride Boogie" by Tillman Franks and The Rainbow Boys. Two other Hayride artists who went on to greater

fame started with Pacemaker: Faron Young and Claude King. Teddy Wilburn of The Wilburn Brothers was also a Pacemaker artist for a time.

Webb signed with Decca Records in late 1951; early in 1952 he coasted to his first Number One hit with his version of Joe Werner's 1936 Cajun song, "Wondering." Webb's record topped the charts for four weeks. In June "That Heart Belongs to Me" spent three weeks at Number One, and the brilliant "Back Street Affair" was there for four.

Webb had a virtual lock on Number One chart positions during those years. In 1953 "It's Been So Long" spent eight weeks as the top country song. That fall, "There Stands the Glass," one of the starkest, most moving drinking songs of all time, was Number One for 12 weeks. The flipside, "I'm Walking the Dog," Webb's version of a song he originally produced on Pacemaker artist Tex Grimsley in 1951, followed "Glass" at Number Three.

Another of Webb's hits was one of the first recordings to feature the pedal steel guitar. (Non-pedal, "Hawaiian" steel, as played by Don Helms and the great Jerry Byrd, was common in Nashville—until Bud Isaacs brought his Bigsby pedal steel to town.) Webb wrote the ballad, "Slowly," with songwriter Tommy Hill to feature the new instrument. When he recorded it late in 1953 with Isaacs, everyone knew they had something new. "Slowly" stayed 17 weeks at Number One in 1954. The flipside, "Even Tho," followed it for two. Pedal steels were suddenly the rage. Non-pedal players bought pedal guitars or tried rigging up homemade pedal mechanisms for their instruments.

Webb's grip on the charts seemed positively ironclad. June 1954 saw him co-found Cedarwood Music with ex-Grand Ole Opry manager, Jim Denny; Cedarwood became one of Nashville's major song publishing operations. That same summer, however, Webb ran into something that spelled trouble. He was in Memphis headlining at the Overton Park Shell. A teenaged Elvis Presley was slated to appear at the bottom of the bill—Presley had just cut his first record for Sun. According to several accounts, the crowd's reaction to the young, inexperienced Presley infuriated Webb, though the youngster was hardly a real threat at the time.

That year Webb's "More and More" hung ten weeks at Number One, and in 1955 his jumping version of Jimmie Rodgers' "In the Jailhouse Now" spent 21 weeks—five months—at the top of the charts. "I Don't Care" followed it for a whopping 12 weeks. "Love, Love, Love" came next: 13 weeks before it slipped out of Number One.

Webb left the *Hayride* and moved to Nashville in 1955 to join the Grand Ole Opry. He and *Hayride* buddy, Red Sovine, had a Number One duet that year with their version of George Jones'-penned hit, "Why Baby Why." (Jones' own version of the song, released around the same time, made it into the Top Five.)

But the winds of change Elvis had kicked up were blowing through Nashville. Pierce's intense ballad, "Yes I Know Why," spent seven weeks at Number Two in 1956. Next Webb tried injecting rock into the old song, "Hayride Boogie." Titled "Teenage Boogie," it only made Number 10 and did not cross over to the pop charts. In 1957 Webb covered The Everly Brothers' "Bye Bye Love;" but it was the The Everly original, not Pierce's version, that topped the charts.

That year he found a new and gifted source of quality material in Air Force veteran and aspiring songwriter, Lonnie Melvin Tillis, from Pahokie, Florida. Webb's first success with a Tillis song was "I'm Tired," Number Three in 1957. Tillis signed with Cedarwood Music and wrote hit after hit for Pierce. Through 1957, 1958 and 1959, the Pierce/Tillis string included "Honky Tonk Song"—Number One in 1957, "Tupelo County Jail"—Number Seven in 1958 and "I Ain't Never"—nine weeks at Number Two in 1959. "I Ain't Never" even became a pop hit, reaching Number 22.

By 1960, Webb had peaked. Decca released *Webb With a Beat!*, an album designed to underscore his willingness to rock. But it didn't wash. As things turned out, Tillis' "Honky Tonk Song" was his last Number One hit. The rock boom took some of the steam out of his career, as it did for other hardcore singers, and Webb's raw voice and anything-but-subtle delivery did not adapt particularly well to the other alternative, the Nashville Sound.

However, he was far from out of the running, for he was immensely wealthy. He went in for the trappings of stardom, building the famous $35,000 guitar-shaped swimming pool at his home and dressing in some of the loudest sequined suits ever made by the legendary Hollywood Western tailor, Nudie. Meanwhile, the Tillis-penned Top Tens continued: "Alla My Love"—Number Five, "Crazy Wild Desire"—Number Eight, co-written by Pierce and Tillis and "Take Time," a Number Seven hit written by Tillis, Marijohn Wilkin (composer of "Long Black Veil") and Harry Hart. Webb and Tillis also cut several duets; "Sands of Gold" and "Those Wonderful Years" were both Top Ten in 1963. But Webb's success had begun to pale. "Memory #1" got to Number Two for two weeks in 1964, but other attempts hung in the lower reaches of the *Billboard* charts. His last Top Ten was "Fool, Fool, Fool" in 1967.

Webb continued working the road and the Opry, and he cashed in on Nashville's growing tourist trade, opening his home, just up the street from the Governor's Mansion, in the posh Nashville suburb of Oak Hill, to tourists, selling souvenirs and showing off his guitar-shaped pool. The traffic sparked a feud with his next-door neighbor, Ray Stevens, and then a lawsuit. Webb lost, the buses were banned and he built another pool on Music Row.

During the 1970's Webb and Decca split. Webb signed with Plantation Records in 1977; there he had minimal success. Longtime admirer Willie Nelson, who'd cut his teeth on Pierce's classics, cut a duet album with him in 1982, and one single, a remake of "In the Jailhouse Now," made it to Number 72. Webb, for all his immense past achievements, appeared to be forgotten. Pierce spent his final years tending to his business interests, obliterating his legend with a reputation for hard-drinking surliness and finally, waging a battle with cancer that he lost on February 24, 1991. But one quick listen to his old hits will tell you Webb Pierce did much more than make a contribution to his chosen field—he was one of its true pillars. —R.K.

Ray Pillow

BORN: July 4, 1937
BIRTHPLACE: Lynchburg, Virginia

Though he's been a Grand Ole Opry regular for years—since 1966, to be exact—Virginia-born Ray Pillow's recording career never really took off. After a four-year hitch in the Navy, Pillow finished college and began his career in country music. He signed with Capitol Records in 1964, having his most successful record, and only Top Ten, in 1966: "I'll Take the Dog," a duet with Jean Shepard. Unable to duplicate that success, Pillow left Capitol in 1967, label-hopped throughout the 70's, and released his final single to date in 1981 on the independent label, First Generation. —G.F.

Pirates of the Mississippi

Not quite as redneck as Confederate Railroad and not quite as cornpone (or musically adventurous) as The Kentucky HeadHunters, this Alabama-based band found success with the 1991 ballad, "Feed Jake." Accompanied by a hit video, the song told a moving tale of the death of a childhood friend

(Jake being the dead friend's dog). It brought the band its first Top Ten. Over the course of four albums on Liberty Records, the band has yet to match that success, but they've received a substantial amount of critical acclaim, and took home the Academy of Country Music's Top New Group award in 1991. The Pirates' sound incorporates Southern rock, country, boogie and soul. The band's line-up includes lead singer/songwriter Bill McCorvey, guitarist/songwriter Rich Alves, bassist Dean Townson, drummer Jimmy Lowe and steel player Pat Severs. —G.F.

Platinum Record

Like the Gold record, the platinum record is a sales award provided by the Recording Industry Association of America, a trade organization. A record company requests an audit for platinum status if an album has sold over 1,000,000 units, or has $2,000,000 in sales (based on 1/3 the suggested retail price). The platinum award began in 1976. In 1984, the multiplatinum award was created for albums selling over 2,000,000 copies or having dollar-sales of more than

$4,000,000 (again based on 1/3 suggested retail price). Platinum awards are also issued to singles and music videos, using only unit sales: 1,000,000 units is a platinum single; 100,000 units is a platinum video. (See also, Gold Record.) —G.F.

Charlie Poole

BORN: March 22, 1892
BIRTHPLACE: Randolph County, North Carolina
DIED: May 21, 1931

Charlie Cleveland Poole only lived to age 39, but in those years he created a body of work that lives on. Born in the textile mill country of North Carolina, he grew up in an area that, unlike most of the rural Southeast, was every bit as wild as the Texas oil country, full of drinking, fighting, gambling and every other kind of mayhem. That begat the hard lifestyle that would eventually kill Poole.

Growing up, he began playing banjo and learning the rural songs of his native region. By the 1920's he was performing extensively, not only in the South, but in the Northeast and Midwest as well. He still worked on and off in the textile mills, finally quitting in 1925 when he and his band, The North Carolina Ramblers, started recording for Columbia.

The Ramblers consisted of guitarist Norman Woodleiff (replaced later by Roy Harvey) and fiddler Posey Rorer. "Don't Let Your Deal Go Down" and "Can I Sleep in Your Barn Tonight, Mister" were two of their early big sellers which went on to become country standards. Poole's and his band's eclectic repertoire included many other songs which, decades later, would become popular all over again with folk singers and even a few jazz artists.

Poole continued performing, but his erratic lifestyle and a gradual decline in record sales didn't help matters. He wanted to try different styles of rural music, including a twin-fiddle, but Columbia insisted he stick with the old formulas of his early work. Over time, Poole's drinking worsened and he became musically inactive, and after one drinking binge too many, his body gave out. He died of a heart attack. —R.K.

Sandy Posey

BORN: June 18, 1947
BIRTHPLACE: Jasper, Alabama

After two years of doing background vocals at the American Recording Studio in Memphis, Sandy Posey did a demo of a song called "Born a Woman" that attracted the attention of MGM Records. She signed with them and cut a single of the song that climbed the pop charts in 1966.

After taking time off from 1968 to '70, Sandy signed with Columbia Records and had a Top 20 hit with the Vietnam era ballad, "Bring Him Home Safely to Me," the result of her collaboration with legendary producer Billy Sherrill. Her cover of the Elvis Presley hit, "Don't," also rippled briefly through the country charts in 1973.

After signing with Warner Bros. Records in 1977, Sandy had a few more modest chart singles, including "Born to Be With You" in 1977, and a year later, her successful medley of two pop standards,

"Chapel of Love" and "Love, Love, Love." Her final single appeared in 1983. Perhaps her biggest claim to fame is that her hit, "Born a Woman," joins "Dreams of an Everyday Housewife" as one of the two songs modern women singers—maybe modern women in general—would like to blot out of their minds.   —M.B.

Dale Potter

BORN: April 28, 1929
BIRTHPLACE: Puxico, Missouri

Allen Dale Potter became one of the earliest Nashville studio fiddlers in the 1950's. Potter's fiddling became influential with other fiddlers, particularly through his dynamic "Fiddle Patch" (a fiddle version of Spade Cooley's "Oklahoma Stomp") and the boogie woogie number, "Fiddle Sticks," recorded with The Country All-Stars in 1952. Potter began playing fiddle at KWOC in Poplar Bluff, Missouri, and later moved to Arkansas, where he worked with Butterball Paige.

He later recorded with Paige for Bullet Records. Potter first came to Nashville with Milton Estes and The Musical Millers, a WSM act sponsored by Martha White Flour, and first appeared on the Opry in 1948. Potter also got into the early Nashville country recording scene; his heavy-bowed fiddle can be heard on Hank Williams records like "Lost Highway" and "May You Never Be Alone."

He also did extensive sessions with Red Foley (his fiddle can be heard on Foley's 1950 hit, "Sugarfoot Rag") and Webb Pierce, among others. After Korean War military service, he returned to Nashville and the recording scene.

By the mid-50's he'd joined Carl Smith's band, The Tunesmiths, and continued doing sessions, including the classic 1954 Chet Atkins album, *A Session With Chet Atkins*. He worked on the road extensively with the Philip Morris country shows, along with Smith. By the late 50's, he was recording (and on occasion, performing) with Bill Monroe. Potter eventually left Nashville, working for a time with Vegas country queen, Judy Lynn. He later worked in Hawaii before moving to Dallas, and then back to his native Missouri. —R.K.

The Prairie Ramblers

A hot, versatile stringband best known for backing singer Patsy Montana and for its long tenure with the WLS *National Barn Dance*, The Prairie Ramblers were formed in 1932 as The Kentucky Ramblers; original members included: Shelby David "Tex" Atchison, fiddle; Floyd "Salty" Holmes, harmonica, guitar and jug; Charles "Chick" Hurt, mandola; and Jack Taylor, guitar and bass. The Prairie Ramblers' name was adopted the following year when the band moved to Chicago's WLS, then owned by Sears (hence the station's call letters: an abbreviation for "World's Largest Store"), which published a magazine called *The Prairie Farmer*. The group made its first records for Victor that December.

Noted for its quick tempos and jazzy instrumental solos, the early Prairie Ramblers sounded much closer to latter-day bluegrass than it did to its own era's old-time stringband music. In 1935 the band signed with ARC and cut dozens of popular records in a more Western style, including such slightly risqué material as "The Sweet Violet Boys." Atchison and Holmes departed by World War II; later band members included Alan Crockett, George Barnes, Wade Ray, The Fiddlin' Linvilles and Ralph "Rusty" Gill. The Ramblers left WLS in 1949 to work at other Midwestern stations; Hurt and Taylor disbanded the act in 1956. (See also, Patsy Montana.)   —D.S.

Elvis Presley

BORN: January 8, 1935
BIRTHPLACE: Tupelo, Mississippi
DIED: August 16, 1977

The most popular and revered recording artist in modern history, Elvis Presley remains an enduring American icon years after his untimely death, in 1977, at age 42.

Elvis Aron Presley was born into poverty. His twin brother, Jesse Garon Presley, died at birth. His father, Vernon Presley, briefly went to prison for altering a check, leaving young Elvis and his mother alone for a time. Looking for new employment opportunities, the Presley family moved to Memphis in 1948. The Mississippi River town was already a major musical center, and Elvis grew up listening to virtually every type of popular music heard in the South: urban rhythm and blues, black vocal groups, honky tonk country music, bluegrass, black and white gospel music and popular vocalists of the era.

In 1953 Presley made a demonstration record for his mother at Sam Phillips' Memphis Recording Service. Phillips and his assistant, Marion Keisker, thought the youth had potential to be a recording artist on Phillips' Sun label, so they brought him back to the studio the following summer. At first Presley produced unexceptional ballads that owed a debt to Dean Martin and Ink Spots tenor Bill Kenny. During an unproductive session on July 5, 1954, Presley cut loose with a manic version of Arthur "Big Boy" Crudup's "That's All Right, Mama." Lead guitarist Scotty Moore (influenced by Merle Travis and Chet Atkins) and bassist Bill Black quickly picked up on Presley's driving rhythm guitar. For a B-side they recorded Bill Monroe's "Blue Moon of Kentucky" with a similarly frenzied spirit, vastly different from the waltz tempo of Monroe's original. Other rock 'n' roll records may have preceded Sun 209, but none sounded anything like this. Rhythm and blues fans thought it was too country (the influence of upbeat bluegrass rhythms was strong) and country fans believed it sounded too black; but teenagers in West Tennessee, Arkansas, Louisiana and Texas couldn't get enough of the record. Presley became a *Louisiana Hayride* regular, and appeared on package tours with Hank Snow and other country acts. Many country artists simply didn't want to follow Presley onstage—his live act was already a hard one to beat. His early repertoire included such country favorites as The Shelton Brothers' "Just Because," as well as R&B numbers.

After releasing five singles, a cash-strapped Phillips sold Presley's contract to RCA Victor for $30,000. Around this time, Presley's new mentor, Colonel Tom Parker, became his manager—though in years to come, Parker would often seem far more interested in Presley as a commodity than as an artist. At the same time, RCA producers Steve Sholes and Chet Atkins eased Presley away from the edgy, distinctly Southern sound of his Sun recordings. Presley's first RCA Victor single, the moody "Heartbreak Hotel," shot to the top of both country and pop charts, bolstered by a heavy publicity blitz from the savvy Parker. Other Presley successes followed, notably "Hound Dog," "All Shook Up," "Don't Be Cruel," "Love Me Tender" and "(Let Me Be Your) Teddy Bear." Presley also completed four films before the Selective Service called his number in 1958. At this time, though country music remained part of his repertoire, and though many of his hits did extremely well on the country charts, he emphasized rock and pop. Nevertheless, several prominent Nashville studio musicians, including Hank Garland, began working on his recordings. After a 13-month Army tour in Germany, Presley resumed his career in March 1960 with an outstanding series of sessions in Nashville that produced three Number One pop singles and the album, *Elvis Is Back*. Two additional Nashville sessions in October 1960 resulted in the chart-topping "Surrender" and a superb gospel album, *His Hand in Mine*.

With his marquee value at its peak, Presley withdrew from live performances to concentrate on his movie career. As a result, while he spun out a string of second-rate films, his recording career suffered; much of what he cut between 1961 and 1968 was indifferent material associated with his even more indifferent movies. Presley also ceased playing gui-

tar at his sessions—the last important link to his rockabilly roots. Yet he often recorded in Nashville, and found some country songs to his liking, such as Jerry Reed's semi-rockabilly compositions, "Guitar Man" and "U.S. Male."

By 1968 Presley needed a jolt out of the doldrums of mediocre movies and waning record sales. A riveting December 1968 NBC-TV special proved the solution: It rejuvenated his career. A high point of the show was Presley's reunion with Scotty Moore and other long-time Memphis musical cronies. The show was literally Presley's finest hour; it was followed by a year-long creative burst. Fourteen sessions held at Chips Moman's Memphis studio in January and February 1969 produced five million-selling singles, including the chart-topping "Suspicious Minds," and the critically acclaimed album, *From Elvis in Memphis.* Later that year Presley launched a series of Las Vegas appearances with a new band that included lead guitarist James Burton. Five marathon Nashville recprdoing sessions in June 1970 produced 34 masters, including 12 country, bluegrass and rock 'n' roll standards that appeared on the superb 1971 album, *Elvis Country,* his first real return to that field in years. During the next six years Presley's popularity soared with old fans and new ones alike, in-

cluding rock, pop and country music lovers.

Yet his creative rejuvenation eventually gave way to flagging inspiration, overproduced recordings and formulaic live shows, which soon became as dull as his movie appearances—all of which was as frustrating to Elvis himself as it was to his huge following.

In 1973 Parker and Presley attempted to recapture the winning combination of five years earlier: a television special followed by new sessions in Memphis. *Aloha from Hawaii,* telecast throughout the world in January, captured Presley as the flamboyant entertainer that many of his fans seem to remember most fondly. But two series of sessions cut at the Stax Studios later that year produced few memorable sides. The youthful spark in his voice had gradually given way to a vibrato-laden and somewhat tired-sounding baritone. Weight problems and longtime abuse of prescription painkillers and other types of powerful narcotics began to sap his strength; and onstage, his deterioration became painfully obvious to everyone except his most adoring and naive fans. Presley died August 16, 1977, after suffering a heart seizure at his Memphis home, most likely brought on by his years of drug abuse. Nonetheless, a decade and a half after his death, Presley is even more revered and exalted than ever; he remains an American cultural icon and the idol of millions, including many generations of country performers.   —D.S.

Frances Preston

BORN: August 27, 1934
BIRTHPLACE: Nashville, Tennessee

Frances Williams Preston began her Music Row career as a receptionist and has since gone on to become one of the most influential and powerful executives in modern country music—in all of popular music, for that matter.

Preston became southern area manager of the ubiquitous Broadcast Music Association (BMI), the influential world-wide music performance licensing organization, in 1958. All though the years, as she has risen, step by step, to her present position as world-wide president and chief executive officer of BMI, she has been a tireless advocate of country music and staunch protector of the rights of country songwriters. Though she spends far less time in Nashville since assuming the world-wide reins of BMI, Preston, during her many years there, was not only Music Row's foremost pioneering woman executive; she was also one of the Music City record industry's most popular and well-liked figures.

Preston was elected to the Country Music Hall of Fame in 1992—not only while still very much alive, but at the ripe young age of 58.   —B.A.

Kenny Price

BORN: May 27, 1931
BIRTHPLACE: Florence, Kentucky
DIED: August 4, 1987

Kenny Price, known as "The Round Mound of Sound," was a singer and instrumentalist (guitar, banjo, drums and bass fiddle) best known for his appearances on *Hee Haw*, beginning in 1976. Born in Florence, Kentucky, he had his first Top Ten single in 1966 with "Walking on New Grass," on the Boone label. By then, he had appeared on the *Midwestern Hayride* for almost 10 years, beginning in 1957.

Price originally got headed in a musical direction way back when he got his first guitar at age five. Even so, his career goal as a youth was to become a farmer, not a musician. During the Korean War he entered the service and performed on war-time USO shows. After he returned to civilian life in 1954, he appeared on the *Hometowners* show on Cincinnati's WLW-TV. He signed with RCA before joining *Hee Haw* in 1976, and had more than 20 chart singles on that label between 1969 and 1976. His biggest career records were the Top Ten hits, "Happy Tracks" (1967), "Biloxi" (1970) and

"The Sheriff of Boone County" (1970-71).

Later, Price, Grandpa Jones, Roy Clark and Buck Owens came together to form the *Hee Haw* Gospel Quartet. He continued recording for RCA until 1976, then moved over to smaller labels like MRC and Dimension. Price died of a heart attack in 1987.   —S.W.

Ray Price

BORN: January 12, 1926
BIRTHPLACE: Perryville, Texas

Few other artists ever swam against the prevailing current as often as Ray Price did. When rock turned Nashville on its ear, Price, Hank Williams' protégé, ignored both it and the Nashville Sound to create some of the rawest, most wrenching emotional honky tonk music ever made—a style and a sound that lives on today in George Strait's music.

Price's band, The Cherokee Cowboys, was a training ground for many legendary artists and musicians, among them Willie Nelson, Roger Miller, Johnny Paycheck, Johnny Bush, steel guitar master Buddy Emmons, fiddler Wade Ray and others. It was easily one of the best country bands of the 1950's and 1960's.

Then in the mid-1960's, Price finally drifted toward the lushly arranged country-pop ballads that he'd previously ignored—songs with which so many of his peers were having big hits. It was a controversial move, to be sure. But even so, Price was right—his softer sound broadened his audience.

Ray Noble Price was born in Perryville, Cherokee County, Texas, January 12, 1926. As a boy, he worked on the family farm before leaving the rural East Texas area for Dallas as a teenager. Although he'd cultivated an interest in music, the early days of World War II found him studying veterinary medicine at North Texas Agricultural College in Abilene. It wasn't long before he joined the Marines and was shipped out to serve in the Pacific.

In 1946 he resumed his studies, playing music on the side, most notably on Abilene's KRBC *Hillbilly Circus* radio show. Already billing himself "The Cherokee Cowboy," he let veterinary studies take more and more of a back seat. to his music. In 1949 he returned to Dallas and landed a spot on the prestigious *Big D Jamboree*. His first national exposure came when portions of the *Jamboree* were broadcast over the CBS Radio Network. Price also discovered

Jim Beck's recording studio in Dallas. Beck was a brilliant electronics engineer who built much of his own equipment from scratch. The studio was so popular with Columbia Records in the late 1940's that it even briefly threatened Nashville as a country recording center. (Tragically, in 1956, just when Beck was about to establish Dallas as a recording capital, he died a horrible death by carbon tetrachloride poisoning when he accidentally inhaled the vapors while cleaning the recording heads in his studio. After that, Dallas's rising glory in the country record business faded fast.)

In 1949 Price signed with the Nashville-based Bullet label (the same label Chet Atkins began his career on) and cut "Jealous Lies," a morose ballad. Still, he had little hint of what lay in store. His singing lacked confidence. Nevertheless, his reputation grew, and in March of 1951 he was signed to Columbia. Not long afterward he moved to Nashville where he and Hank Williams became fast friends. Together they co-wrote "Weary Blues from Waitin'," and Williams' clout got Price his first appearance on the Opry. Price did shows with Williams and occasionally covered for him when Williams was too drunk to perform. After Williams and Audrey separated, Williams and Price shared a house until Price, tired of Williams' constant partying, moved on.

In July 1952 Ray Price had his first hit, "Talk to Your Heart," which hit Number 11 on the *Billboard* charts. Two months later his version of Slim Willet's "Don't Let the Stars Get in Your Eyes" hit Number Four. Some people say Price inherited Williams' Drifting Cowboys after his death; but country music historian Charles Wolfe, who has studied Price's early career, maintains he actually took over the band in August of 1952 after the Opry fired Williams, four months before his death.

The following year was a dry one for Price, but in February 1954, "I'll Be There" reached Number Two, followed quickly by "Release Me," which went to Number Six just a couple of months later. With Hank gone, Price was the logical person to pick up his mantle. His voice had matured into an incredible instrument—his phrasing and control would impress an opera singer—and the raw backing provided by the band was the perfect foil for it.

By 1954 he'd organized a new band, The Cherokee Cowboys, a conscious attempt on his part to find musicians better able to bring a Western swing element to his music. Another dry year, 1955, followed. But in 1956, as Elvis burst on the scene, "Crazy Arms," Price's first Number One record, climbed onto the charts during the summer and stayed there a phenomenal 45 weeks. "I've Got a New Heartache" came right behind at Number Three.

At a time when many hard-country artists, frightened of losing their audience, tried recording rockabilly with varying degrees of enthusiasm, Price ignored all that and stuck to his famous "shuffle" beat, something he had developed in the Nashville studios with drummer Buddy Harman and bassist Bob Moore. His instincts paid off again. In 1958 he took Bill Anderson's song, "City Lights, " to Number One. A more heavily-bowed fiddle, the shuffle beat and a keening steel dominated subsequent Top Five classics such as "Heartaches By the Number" (40 weeks on the charts in 1959), "The Same Old Me" (1959), "Heart Over Mind" (1961), "Soft Rain" (1961) and "Pride" (1962).

No one complained when Price first used strings and vocal choruses on his 1960 *Faith* album, a collection of sacred songs. In 1963 he recorded "Make the World Go Away," which went to Number Two. (Eddy Arnold's hit version of the same song, released two years later, was nearly identical to Price's.) From that point on, Price used string sections more and more, upsetting many of his hardcore fans in the process. With "Burning Memories" in 1964 and "Danny Boy" in 1967, he made the crossover transition complete.

Certainly he had a right to change. He once said, "Nothing can survive without expansion." But was he "expanding" himself out of country music, abandoning a distinctive style for a nondescript pop-country approach? In some ways, yes. He could handle pop material, but Perry Como and Jerry Vale sang the same things and sang them better. When Price took string sections on tour, the controversy became red hot.

But he stuck to his guns, and in 1970, his slick version of Kris Kristofferson's ballad, "For the Good Times," hit Number One country and Number 11 pop. The album of the same name was just as successful as the single, and the Cherokee Cowboy got what he'd wanted: a crossover hit. In 1971, "I Won't Mention It Again," even more pop, also went Number One, followed by "I'd Rather Be Sorry" (another Kristofferson ballad) that same year, which reached Number Two. He'd snared a new audience, even though his follow-up songs were dull and pompous. In 1972 "The Lonesomest Lonesome" hit Number Two, and "She's Got To Be a Saint" reached Number One. In 1973 "You're the Best Thing That Ever Happened to Me" followed suit.

After 23 years, Price and Columbia finally parted ways in 1974. He joined the Myrrh label, where "Like Old Times Again" hit Number Four in 1974, and "Roses and Love Songs," a song that sounds just like you'd expect it to, reached Number Three. From there he went to ABC/Dot Records. During this period, he cut back on touring to spend more time raising horses on his ranch near Dallas. The ABC material was uniformly awful. His 1975 *Say I Do*, an album of Jim Weatherly songs, was easily the worst he ever made. The hits, predictably, became few and far between. His biggest in 1976 was a remake of Hank's "Mansion On the Hill" that made it to Number 14.

In 1977 Price reunited with Emmons and other ex-Cherokee Cowboys for *Reunited*, a partially successful attempt to recreate the spirit of the old band. Though he himself still favored strings, he recognized that a goodly percentage of his audience still loved the old sound. Although he turned up two Top 20 hits with Monument in 1978, Price's elevator music was clearly wearing thin—he even had problems getting a recording contract. However, he and Willie Nelson had remained friends (they lived near each other in Nashville for years), so when Ray suggested they record together in 1980, Willie agreed.

Willie captured the old Cherokee Cowboys sound intact, using Emmons, Johnny Gimble and other musicians to create the magnificent 1980 album, *San Antonio Rose*, based on a 1962 Price album by the same name. Ray and Willie, both in superb voice, sang the old numbers without missing a beat, proving a rare exception to the rule that you can't go home again.

The album hit Number Three on *Billboard*'s country charts and stayed in the running for 47 weeks. The single, "Faded Love," hit Number Three, and "Don't You Ever Get Tired of Hurting Me," a remake of Price's 1965 hit, made it to Number 11. Price went on to enjoy considerable success with the Dimension label. In 1981 "It Don't Hurt Me Half as Bad" and "Diamonds in the Stars" both went Top Ten.

Today, Ray Price lives in Texas and records for Nashville's Step One Records, for whom he's done several albums, including three re-recorded albums of his biggest hits. He seems content to do show dates and sing his hits of old, still favoring the string sound. If that's what he prefers, so be it. But one thing is certain: Ray Price's greatest contributions to country music have been—and will be—as the Cherokee Cowboy.

—R.K.

Charley Pride

BORN: March 18, 1938
BIRTHPLACE: Sledge, Mississippi

Charley Pride is certainly not the only black country artist to come stumbling down country's largely segregated pike; but he is the only black American to attain superstar status in the field and sustain it over the better part of a decade and a half.

Working mostly with producer Jack Clement, between 1969, when he first hit the top of the charts with "All I Have to Offer You Is Me," and 1984, when he made his last trip to Number One with the hit single, "Every Heart Should Have One," Pride had 29 Number One singles (19 of them consecutive), making him one of the all-time top country chart artists in history. "Kiss an Angel Good Morning" (1971), "Is Anybody Goin' to San Antone" (1970), "Amazing Love" (1973) and "Mississippi Cotton Delta Town" (1974) are just a few of the many songs he turned into classics with his hearty, fulsome baritone.

Pride insists it was never his intention to break down the color barrier. "It wasn't until I got to Nashville that it was pointed out to me, 'Hey, you're the first,'" he explained to Bob Millard in an interview with *The Journal of Country Music*. "Before that, it had eluded me. I had been singing country music for so long for just the love of it...but the point is, once it got to that magnitude—I hadn't thought about it until somebody pointed it out to me."

Pride was born in rural Sledge, Mississippi, in 1938, one of a sharecropper's eleven children. Instead of being drawn to the black delta blues which were then prevalent in rural Mississippi, Pride instead grew up listening to the Grand Ole Opry on his father's Philco radio and fell in love with the sounds of Roy

Acuff, Ernest Tubb and Bill Monroe.

By age 14, Pride was already singing along with the Opry, accompanying himself on a ten dollar Sears, Roebuck guitar he bought with his proceeds from picking cotton. But as a youngster, he was also consumed by baseball. And after a stint in the armed services, he ended up pitching and playing outfield for the Memphis Red Socks in the old Negro American League. "I managed to strike out Gene Baker and Roy Campanella," he recalled. "But Willie Mays, I never could get him out." After a brief, undistinguished call-up by the California Angels, and a failed spring training tryout with the New York Mets, Pride abandoned his baseball dreams. Yet, ironically, it was baseball that ultimately opened the door to his musical career. In the mid-60's Pride ended up playing ball in the semi-pro Pioneer League for a team in Montana, where he made ends meet working in a zinc-smelting plant. When he began singing country songs at half-time during the games, he became such a hit with the crowds that he soon branched out and began performing in local clubs, as well. That's where he was spotted by touring Opry stars of the day, Red Foley and Red Sovine, who, in turn, brought him to the attention of RCA/Nashville producer/executive Chet Atkins.

Pride's RCA debut came in 1965 with a single called "Snakes Crawl at Night." The label was so skittish that they shipped the record without enclosing any sort of liner or promotional photo of Pride. The plan— and the hope—was to let the record catch on, then break the news to country fans and see how they reacted to the shattering of country's color barrier.

Though there were some tense moments along the way, country listeners' acceptance of Pride was immediate, and immense. They were not only enamored of his rich, confident vocal style, which rather effortlessly coalesced the scarred-knuckle drawl of a Hank Williams or a Roy Acuff with the gentlemanly crooning of a Jim Reeves or Eddy Arnold; they also fell in love with his relaxed, expansive stage presence and personal charm. Pride went on to win three Grammy awards, earn several platinum albums, and receive the Country Music Association's 1971 Entertainer of the Year award, while setting attendance records around the nation.

Pride, who is one of RCA Records' top sellers of all time, was with the label right through 1986, when he moved over to 16th Avenue Records. He scored a few more singles there, including the Top Five "Shouldn't It Be Easier Than This," before the label folded. He's now on the Intersound label, and, in 1992, was finally made a member of the Grand Ole Opry.
—B.A.

John Prine

BORN: October 10, 1946
BIRTHPLACE: Maywood, Illinois

Though the pointed social commentary of many of his most well-known songs ("Illegal Smile," "Paradise," "Sam Stone," "Angel From Montgomery," etc.) has tended to earn him a closer association with folk than country, John Prine's music—particularly that of his early vintage years, as captured on albums like 1971's *John Prine* and 1972's *Diamonds in the Rough*—has a strong country element, as well. His songs from that era may have embraced the left-of-center politics of America's Vietnam-era youth (exemplified by the graphic anti-war imagery of "Sam Stone" and the sly endorsement of marijuana use in "Illegal Smile"); yet Prine's familiar three-chord melodies, gruff vocals and flair for droll punnery were ripped right from the bluegrass and country influences of his family roots, which went back many generations in rural Kentucky. His early memories of family trips back to the Bluegrass State culminated in "Paradise (Muhlenberg County)," a song which lambastes the Peabody Coal Company's rampant environmental destruction in the name of progress, and which has since become a staple in the repertoires of a thousand and one bluegrass bands.

Prine, the son of a steel worker and local union president, grew up in a blue collar suburb of Chicago. He wrote many of his now classic songs while trudging through the snow, delivering letters for the U.S. Postal Service.

Everything changed when his friend and fellow Chicago songwriter, the late Steve Goodman (who wrote "The City of New Orleans," a Number One country hit for Willie Nelson and a pop hit for Arlo Guthrie, and "You Never Even Call Me By My Name," the 1975 novelty Top Ten that kicked off David Allan Coe's career) introduced Prine to Kris Kristofferson. With Kristofferson's help, Prine was soon on Atlantic Records. (Kristofferson wrote the liner notes to Prine's debut album and introduced Prine to the world when he brought him up to do a few songs at Manhattan's Bitter End Cafe; Bob Dylan jumped up and backed Prine on harmonica.) Kristofferson's own songwriting was so influenced by Prine's lyrical brilliance that he later wrote and recorded a song called "Jesus Was a Capricorn (Ode to John Prine)."

The same folk-rock crowd that has sustained the careers of artists like Tom Waits and Randy Newman over the years has also kept Prine afloat. (His metaphors are a little too arcane, his sense of irony a little too finely honed, and his voice a little too unadorned and beer-soaked to make it with mainstream country audiences.) Yet Prine is a long-time Nashville resident, and for quite a few years has run his own Oh Boy Records out of Music City. Dozens of mainstream country artists have covered his songs over the years— Johnny Cash, Lynn Anderson, Tanya Tucker, Jack Clement, Tammy Wynette, John Anderson and Jim and Jesse among them.

Prine's critically acclaimed 1991 album, *Missing Years*, seemed to bring his recording career back to life after a period of relative dormancy. The album, on which he was joined by notables like Bruce Springsteen, also won him a Grammy Award.   —B.A.

Jeanne Pruett

BORN: January 30, 1937
BIRTHPLACE: Pell City, Alabama

Alabama-born Jeanne Pruett (born Norma Jean Bowman) landed her first job in Nashville in the mid-1960's writing songs for Marty Robbins Enterprises. In her seven years there, her songs were recorded by, among others, Nat Stuckey, Bill Phillips and Conway Twitty. It was Pruett's demo tape, intended to interest other artists in recording her songs, that landed her a recording contract with Decca Records in the early 1970's. After MCA took over Decca in 1973, Jeanne had her first big hit, the Number One "Satin Sheets," which also reached the Top 40 on the pop charts. That same year she became a member of the Grand Ole Opry. Her charted MCA singles include the Top Ten, "I'm Your Woman" in 1973, "You Don't Need to Move a Mountain" in 1974, and "Just Like Your Daddy" and "Honey on His Hands," both in 1975. She also broke the Top 30 in 1975 with her own composition, "A Poor Man's Woman." In the late 1970's, Jeanne left MCA for IBC Records, where she had further Top Tens through 1980 with "Temporarily Yours," "It's Too Late" and "Back to Back." Later she recorded for several smaller labels. She remains a popular Opry member today.   —M.B.

Riley Puckett

BORN: May 7, 1884
BIRTHPLACE: Alpharetta, Georgia
DIED: July 13, 1946

Riley Puckett was an enormously influential blind singer and guitarist active during country music's earliest years of commercial recording. A doctor's incorrect treatment of an eye infection robbed Puckett of his sight at age three months. He at-

tended the Georgia Academy for the Blind, began singing, and eventually learned to play guitar. His idiosyncratic picking style included the use of a special type of bass string runs that would later become a staple of the bluegrass guitar style. He got his start as a performer playing on Atlanta street corners, and, in 1924, was discovered by Columbia Records talent scouts looking for musicians who played rural Southern music. His recorded repertoire, which mixed both hillbilly songs and pop tunes, sold well, as did those of his friend, fiddler Gid Tanner. By 1926, Puckett's records were selling so briskly that Columbia president Frank Walker created an all-star unit combining Puckett on guitar and vocals, fiddlers Tanner and Clayton McMichen and banjoist Fate Norris, known as The Skillet Lickers. Their records sold in the hundreds of thousands, including classics like "Bully of the Town" and "Watermelon on the Vine." Their hit comedy recordings such as "A Corn Likker Still in Georgia" pioneered the country comedy genre. One of Puckett's recorded songs that later became a country standard was "Ragged But Right," a staple

of George Jones' early repertoire. He continued to record even after The Skillet Lickers disbanded in 1930, and performed on radio stations around the South during the 1930's and 1940's, though his career gradually ebbed as newer styles took hold. He died of blood poisoning in 1946 and was buried in College Park, Georgia.   —R.K.

Eddie Rabbitt

BORN: November 27, 1944
BIRTHPLACE: Brooklyn, New York

Born in Brooklyn, New York, on November 27, 1944, Eddie Rabbitt was raised in East Orange, New Jersey. His first exposure to music came from his dad, a refrigeration engineer who played fiddle and accordion. Rabbitt started playing guitar at 12, and when he was in high school he began winning talent contests. He dropped out of school and worked a number of jobs—soda jerk, truck driver, fruit picker, mental hospital attendant, local country performer—and shopped his original tunes around New York City's publishing houses before heading to Nashville in 1968 with $1,000 to his name.

Rabbitt began writing and hanging out with songwriters such as Kris Kristofferson and Billy Swan, and found relatively early success when Roy Drusky hit number 33 on the country charts with his "Working My Way Up to the Bottom" (a song Rabbitt later claimed to have written while sitting in a hotel bathtub on his first night in Nashville). He then became a staff writer with music publishers Hill and Range, earning a meager $37.50 a week.

All that changed, however, in 1970 when Elvis Presley copped a Gold record with Rabbitt's "Kentucky Rain." Three years later Ronnie Milsap went to the top of the charts with another Rabbit track, "Pure Love." Elektra Records took notice and signed Eddie the same year.

His first single for the label, "You Get to Me" (1974), did fairly well, and by 1975 Rabbit's songs began cracking the country Top 20. "Drinkin' My Baby (Off My Mind)" went to Number One, followed by Top Ten entries "Rocky Mountain Music" and "Two Dollars in the Jukebox."

This was only the tip of the iceberg. Throughout the remainder of the 1970's and well into the early 80's, Rabbitt continued to deliver solid chart-toppers, including "You Don't Love Me Anymore," "I Just Want to Love You," "Every Which Way But Loose," "Suspicions," "Gone Too Far," "Drivin' My Life Away," "I Love a Rainy Night," "Step By Step" and "Someone Could Lose a Heart Tonight." The galvanizing neo-rockabilly sound of songs like "Drivin' My Life Away" and "I Love a Rainy Night" (both of which were Number Ones in 1980) that he recorded around the turn of the decade made him one of the closely watched artists in Nashville for a brief time.

More hits continued in the mid-1980's, most notably "Warning Sign" and "Repetitive Regret," even though Rabbitt's music had by now cooled into more predictable chart fare. In 1985 tragedy struck; his two-year-old son, Timothy, died following a liver transplant. Rabbitt retreated temporarily from the music scene, but returned in the late 1980's with a new band and a new label. Though he's not had a hit in quite a few seasons, Rabbitt as of the early 90's, is still out there, still crankin' it out. —R.P.

Marvin Rainwater

BORN: July 2, 1925
BIRTHPLACE: Wichita, Kansas

Popular with both country and rockabilly fans, Rainwater, who is of Cherokee Indian heritage (his mother's maiden name was Rainwater—his real name is Marvin Karlton Percy), didn't enter the music business seriously until after World War II. His early performing experience came on Red Foley's *Ozark Jubilee,*

and his first recordings were done for Four Star and Coral. Roy Clark briefly worked for him as his guitarist. It wasn't until he scored big on the CBS-TV show, *Arthur Godfrey's Talent Scouts,* that he signed with MGM and wrote "Gonna Find Me a Bluebird." The song found nationwide success on both the pop and country charts in the spring of 1957. He tried recording rockabilly, doing well with "Whole Lotta Woman" a year later—though it did better on the country charts than in pop, where there were reservations about the song's lyric content. In 1959 he recorded John D. Loudermilk's "Half Breed," his last chart record. After that he moved around from label to label and battled health problems. In the early 90's he was back, actively performing both in Europe and the U.S., based out of Minnesota. —R.K.

Boots Randolph

BORN: June 3, 1927
BIRTHPLACE: Paducah, Kentucky

Homer Louis Randolph III, one of Nashville's original group of session musicians, didn't set out to build a career in country music. His father got him a trombone by swapping a pistol for it—he didn't want the gun in the house. Homer picked up the nickname "Boots" as a kid. The family moved to Evansville, Indiana, during World War II, where at age 16, Boots decided to switch to tenor saxophone. Again, his father got him the instrument. Since his brother played big band jazz, Boots' early listening concentrated in that area, his idols being tenor sax legends Ben Webster, Lester Young, Flip Phillips and Coleman Hawkins. He also grew to enjoy the modern 1940's jazz styles like bebop.

After graduating high school in 1945, he was drafted into the Army where he became a musician. After being discharged in 1946, he focused on music, returned to Indiana and got married. He spent several years with an Illinois band called The Copycats before returning to Evansville. In early 1958, country finger picker Spider Rich, who lived in the area, asked Boots to work with him on some demos Rich wanted to play for Chet Atkins. Atkins heard the demos and was impressed by Boots' sax playing on the tape; Atkins' friend and musical associate, guitarist Jethro Burns (of Homer and Jethro fame) knew Boots' work with the Copycats and seconded Chet's enthusiasm. Randolph was recording for RCA in Nashville by that spring. Owen Bradley heard Boots play and used him on a session with Brenda Lee. A sax figure he played in the course of the session impressed Bradley and it evolved into "Yakety Sax." When Randolph recorded the song, session man Floyd Cramer stuffed towels in his piano to make it more percussive. But it wasn't a hit, nor was any of Randolph's RCA material.

Still living in Indiana and playing clubs, he played the Newport Jazz Festival with Hank Garland, Cramer and Atkins in 1960. Boots commuted to sessions in Nashville until 1961, when he finally moved to Music City. As a full-time session player, he also got a chance to record for Monument in 1963. This time, a remake of "Yakety Sax" became a respectable pop hit, enhanced by his appearances on ABC's *Jimmy Dean Show*. In between sessions and stage performances, he worked the road at times with Atkins and Cramer. When he quit session work in the 1970's, he opened Boots Randolph's, a supper club in Nashville's Printer's Alley, where he regularly performed. His final Monument album came in 1982, one of the label's last releases. He closed his club in the summer of 1994.   —R.K.

Wayne Raney

BORN: August 17, 1921
BIRTHPLACE: Batesville, Arkansas
DIED: January 23, 1993

Raney, a singer-harmonica player who learned his instrument from pioneer country harmonica player Lonnie Glosson, met The Delmore Brothers in Memphis during the 1940's. He became a regular with the Delmores and worked extensively on their King Recordings, including their 1949 classic, "Blues Stay Away From Me," the popularity of which sold millions of harmonicas. Based in Cincinnati, Raney is also reputed to have sold millions of harmonicas himself by mail-order though his 1940's radio show over

WCKY. He did his first solo recording session for King in 1947, accompanied by the Delmores. Two numbers, "Lost John Boogie" and "Jack and Jill Boogie," were strong sellers, but it was his 1949 smash, "Why Don't You Haul Off and Love Me," that remained Number One for three weeks. On it, Glosson's harmonica accompanied Raney's vocal. Raney later recorded for Starday. He also formed a family gospel group and founded his own record company, Rimrock Records.   —R.K.

Leon Rausch

BORN: October 2, 1927
BIRTHPLACE: Springfield, Missouri

Rausch is among the few surviving Bob Wills Texas Playboys to remain active in the music business. He worked with Wills as lead vocalist and guitarist from 1958 to 1964, recording with Wills on some of his mid-60's Longhorn recordings. He recorded for various Texas labels, but the Bob Wills revival of the early to mid-70's brought him his greatest success. He began working with the revived Original Texas Playboys, led by Leon McAuliffe, as lead vocalist in the mid-70's. At the same time he was making honky tonk records for the Texas-based Derrick label. Rausch continued working with The Playboys until they disbanded; today he does extensive freelance recording work and sometimes works with yet another reconstituted Playboy off-shoot group led by ex-Playboys Johnny Gimble and Eldon Shamblin.   —R.K.

Eddy Raven

BORN: August 19, 1944
BIRTHPLACE: Lafayette, Louisiana

Born Edward Garvin Futch, Eddy Raven grew up in Louisiana Cajun country surrounded by Cajun sounds and classic country music. Those early years helped form his style, as did teenage forays into rock. Raven made his first record locally in 1969. It was heard by Cajun country star Jimmie C. Newman, a fellow Louisianan, who urged him to head to Nashville. In 1970, Raven did, and landed a job as a staff songwriter for Acuff-Rose. Throughout the decade, while his songs were becoming hits for Jeannie C. Riley, Don Gibson, Roy Acuff and others, Raven himself bounced around various labels, achieving little chart success. Then, in 1982, The Oak Ridge Boys had a big hit with Raven's "Thank God for Kids." A label deal with RCA followed in 1983, and this time, Raven connected. His first RCA single, "I Got Mexico," went to Number One in 1984, beginning a string of 17 consecutive Top Ten singles, including the Number Ones "Shine, Shine, Shine," "I'm Gonna Get You," "Joe Knows How to Live," "In a Letter to You" and "Bayou Boys." The latter two chart toppers, released in 1989, were on Universal Records. Later hits appeared on Capitol. In 1994, he resurfaced on the Intersound Entertainment label with an album titled *Wild Eyed and Crazy.* —G.F.

Wade Ray

BORN: April 6, 1913
BIRTHPLACE: Evansville, Indiana

Wade Ray, known to some as "Pug" for the shape of his nose, got his start fiddling on the road around the country. In 1931 he joined Pappy Cheshire's National Champion Hillbillies on KMOX Radio in St. Louis, working with Cheshire until joining the Army in 1943. He worked with The Prairie Ramblers on the WLS *National Barn Dance* in the late 40's, before moving to California. In Los Angeles, he formed a hot Western swing unit and briefly owned his own label, Cowtown Records, before signing with RCA. As a recording artist, Ray recorded not only vocals, but driving swing versions of big band favorites like "Dipsy Doodle," and in the early 50's was briefly teamed with steel guitarist Noel Boggs on excellent performances of "It's All Your Fault" and "The Things I Might Have Been." Eventually Ray recorded numbers like "Walk Softly." He also recorded other RCA material with a studio band called The Country Fiddlers, did another album for ABC Paramount and recorded with Ernest Tubb's Texas Troubadours. Wade's singing style heavily influenced Willie Nelson, with whom he worked in the 60's on the album *Country Favorites Willie Nelson Style.* He was also Willie's bass player on the road for a time. In the 1970's he recorded for the Mid-Land label of St. Louis but has recently been afflicted with ill health. —R.K.

Collin Raye

BORN: August 22, 1959
BIRTHPLACE: DeQueen, Arkansas

Over the course of his three albums on Epic, Floyd Collin Wray (as Collin Raye was known the day he was born), has gained fame with a mix of current country music styles from sentimental ballads to

Southern rock boogie to neo-honky tonk novelty numbers: in short, the basic formula for success on 90's country radio. And radio success hasn't eluded Raye either, especially with the ballads: His second single, 1991's "Love, Me," planted itself at Number One for three weeks. Subsequent Number Ones came in 1992 with "In This Life" and in 1993 with "That Was a River." Wary of being viewed primarily as a balladeer, Raye upped the number of Southern rock and novelty numbers on his third album. In concert he's an animated showman who knows how to work a stage and has been known to cover tunes from The Beatles, Rod Stewart and Elton John.   —G.F.

RCA Victor

The Victor Talking Machine Co. was founded in 1901 by Emile Berliner and Eldridge Johnson. Berliner created the flat, lateral-recorded disc, while Johnson developed the spring-driven gramophone to play

them on. Johnson also developed a means of cutting masters on wax, which greatly improved fidelity and surface quality. The label adopted its famous "His Master's Voice" trademark in 1902.

The Victor label issued what many consider the first recordings of jazz and country music. Its first country discs were cut in June 1922 by two unaccompanied fiddlers: Henry Gilliland from Oklahoma and A.C. "Eck" Robertson from Texas. That September Victor issued "Arkansas Traveler" and Robertson's magnificent solo of "Sally Goodin" as a violin novelty; the record was primarily marketed to Northern urban audiences. In 1923 Victor reportedly sold more than a million copies of "It Ain't Gonna Rain No More" by radio singer Wendell Hall. While hardly a Southern performance, the record has been called the first "hillbilly hit."

While Victor focused on serving Northern audiences, the Okeh label, led by Ralph Peer, opened the rural Southern market in the mid-1920's with rough-hewn, best-selling discs by Fiddlin' John Carson and Henry Whitter. Victor recorded Fiddling Powers and His Family in August 1924. Later that year Victor issued "The Wreck of the Old 97" and "The Prisoner's Song" by Vernon Dalhart (Dalhart's real name was Marion Try Slaughter). A Texas-born, classically trained singer, Dalhart sang both songs with an affected hillbilly twang. The coupling became the biggest selling record in Victor's history.

In 1926 Victor lagged behind Okeh, Columbia and Vocalion in releasing material by rural Southern artists. The company then hired away Okeh producer Ralph Peer (see separate entry) who quickly began making field recordings in the Southeast. Peer's field trips captured the music of outstanding stringbands, folk musicians, blues singers, territory bands, jug bands and gospel groups. His summer 1927 sessions in Bristol, Tennessee, launched the successful, highly influential careers of The Carter Family and Jimmie Rodgers. In September 1928 Peer supervised the first commercial recordings ever made in Nashville; he cut numerous masters of early Grand Ole Opry regulars. Jimmie Davis, whom Peer first recorded in a 1929 Memphis session, became another distinctive country artist for Victor.

In January 1929 Radio Corporation of America acquired the Victor Talking Machine company. RCA's assets enabled the label to survive the Depression and competition from radio and sound films. Like other labels, Victor scaled back its recording activities during the Depression years. In summer 1933 RCA introduced Bluebird, a 35-cent label featuring selected reissues and new recordings. Bluebird's most notable artists included The Delmore Brothers, Fiddlin' Arthur Smith, The Monroe Brothers, J.E. Mainer's Mountaineers, The Blue Sky Boys, Roy Hall's Blue Ridge Entertainers, and the pioneering Western swing bands of Milton Brown and Bill Boyd. Producer Eli Oberstein also bolstered the Bluebird catalog with new recordings by veteran country acts like Fiddlin' John Carson, Narmour and Smith, Bradley Kincaid, Riley Puckett, Uncle Dave Macon, Carson Robison and Gid Tanner and His Skillet Lickers. Bluebird's biggest hit was Elton Britt's sentimental "There's a Star-Spangled Banner Waving Somewhere" in 1942.

In February 1946, country and western recordings returned to RCA's full-priced label, now called RCA Victor. Producer Stephen Sholes leaned toward

smooth-voiced vocalists like Britt and Redd Stewart, the lead singer with Pee Wee King's band. However, RCA Victor's most important country artist was Eddy Arnold, who dominated the country sales charts during the late 40's. In 1947 Sholes signed guitarist Chet Atkins, whom he saw as a potential answer to Capitol's Merle Travis. Atkins later proved to be a valuable production assistant to Sholes.

Besides Arnold and King, key RCA Victor country artists during the early 50's included Johnnie and Jack, Homer and Jethro, Porter Wagoner, The Davis Sisters and Canadian singer Hank Snow. In 1955 Sholes signed two artists who ushered in country music's modern era. Charismatic Memphis rocker, Elvis Presley (whose contract RCA purchased from Memphis-

based Sun Records, where Presley had gotten his start), appealed to youthful listeners; Jim Reeves' smooth Texas baritone found a loyal "middle-of-the-road" audience. Presley's and Reeves' styles marked a polarization of traditional country music audiences; both claimed enormous success with Northern listeners.

In 1957 Atkins became chief of RCA's country division. The hit records he produced with Don Gibson, Hank Locklin, Floyd Cramer, Skeeter Davis and The Browns helped shape the so-called Nashville Sound. (See separate entry.) Atkins signed many other important country artists to RCA, including Bobby Bare, Waylon Jennings, George Hamilton IV, Connie Smith, Dottie West and Dolly Parton. To his credit, Atkins also nurtured many talented singers and musicians who operated outside of country music conventions. Charley Pride and Jerry Reed were two Atkins gambles that paid off. Roger Miller, Charlie Rich, Boots Randolph and Willie Nelson also served stints on the label before achieving success elsewhere.

During the mid-70's RCA benefited from the crossover success of Waylon Jennings, then labeled an Outlaw (see separate entry), who rebelled against the standard Nashville productions and attitudes. In 1976, *Wanted: The Outlaws*, a compilation of tracks by Jennings and fellow Outlaws Willie Nelson (by now on Columbia), Jessi Colter and Tompall Glaser, became the first country music album to achieve platinum for sales of more than one million units. (Earlier albums had sold as much, but the platinum award had not been created.)

Surprisingly, RCA Nashville's most consistently charting act during these years was not part of the Outlaw movement at all. The more middle of the road Ronnie Milsap racked up 49 Top Ten country hits between 1973 and 1991.

RCA's major acts during the 80's were Milsap, Parton, Earl Thomas Conley, Alabama and The Judds. In 1985 General Electric purchased RCA, primarily to obtain the National Broadcasting Company (NBC). The record division was sold to Bertelsmann, a German firm that already had a stake in the business.

Since then RCA Victor and sister Bertelsmann labels, Arista and BNA, have continued to develop important country artists, most notably Clint Black, Alan Jackson, Brooks and Dunn, John Anderson, Pam Tillis, Steve Wariner, Lorrie Morgan, Paul Overstreet, Restless Heart, Aaron Tippin, Martina McBride, Diamond Rio and the late Keith Whitley.   —D.S.

Red River Dave

BORN: December 15, 1914
BIRTHPLACE: San Antonio, Texas

Red River Dave McEnery was a well-known radio cowboy who became the first country TV star when he appeared on an experimental TV broadcast at the New York World's Fair in 1939. He later appeared in numerous Hollywood films with Jimmy Wakely and Rosalie Allen, and after the war gained further fame as a writer of topical songs. His "Amelia Earhart's Last Flight" became a camp favorite in the 1960's, and through the 1960's and 1970's he wrote and recorded on small labels "event ballads" about James Dean, Billy Graham, Emmett Till, Bing Crosby and even Bob Wills. None became hits, but their survival proved that earlier country genres were still alive and well. —C.W.

Jerry Reed

BORN: March 20, 1937
BIRTHPLACE: Atlanta, Georgia

Born Jerry Reed Hubbard, Reed made a name for himself as a Nashville session guitarist and songwriter in the 1960's, turning out songs like "U.S. Male" and

"Guitar Man" for Elvis Presley, and "Crazy Legs" for Gene Vincent. In 1965 guitar legend Chet Atkins, then acting as RCA's A&R executive, signed Jerry to the label. While his first album, *The Unbelievable Guitar and Voice of Jerry Reed*, failed to take Nashville by storm, Jerry's next few efforts, *Nashville Underground*, *Alabama Wild Man* and *Better Things in Life*, gradually won him a modest following. As the decade ended, Jerry continued to turn out award-winning songs, earning four BMI country awards and two BMI pop awards.

In 1970, after 15 years in the music business (he'd recorded briefly for Capitol in the mid-50's) Jerry scored his first hit, the Gold single, "Amos Moses" (1970). That same year he put three albums on the country charts: *Cookin'*, *Georgia Sunshine* and a duet album with Chet Atkins titled *Me and Jerry*, which won Reed a Grammy for Best Instrumental Performance. Reed was also named the Country Music Association's Instrumentalist of the Year in 1970. Jerry continued his streak the following year with the smash hit, "When You're Hot, You're Hot." One of the best-selling songs of 1971, it won Jerry a Grammy for Best

Country Male Performance and another CMA Instrumentalist award. That year Jerry put out an unbelievable five albums: *Smell the Flowers*, *Me and Chet*, *Best of Jerry Reed*, *Jerry Reed* and *Oh What a Woman*.

In 1974 Jerry made his first screen appearance, in Burt Reynolds' movie, *W.W. and The Dixie Dance Kings*. It was the beginning of a second career for Jerry; his collaboration with Reynolds continued with two more films, *Gator* in 1976 and the runaway hit, *Smokey and the Bandit*, the following year, plus the two *Smokey* sequels.

In between making movies Jerry continued to place singles on the country charts, including "Sugar Foot Rag," "Age," "Workin' at the Carwash Blues" and "Texas Bound and Flying," all in 1980, and "Caffeine, Nicotine and Benzedrine (and Wish Me Luck)" in 1981. Though his hits trailed off by the 1980's, he did make it to Number One one last time in 1982 with the novelty tune, "She Got the Goldmine (I Got the Shaft)." He followed it up with another novelty, "The Bird," which hit Number Two later that same year. He remained with RCA right through the end of his hitmaking days in 1983.   —M.B.

Del Reeves

BORN: July 14, 1934
BIRTHPLACE: Sparta, North Carolina

Born Franklin Delano Reeves, in Sparta, North Carolina, in 1934, Del Reeves moved to California while still in his 20's and had his own local country TV show in Southern California for four years and also appeared on *The Chester Smith Show*. He also composed songs that were later recorded by country artists like Sheb Wooley, Rose Maddox and Carl Smith.

Del signed with Capitol in 1956. Later, on Decca, he had a Top Ten hit with "Be Quiet Mind" in 1961. He later signed with United Artists, where he recorded a pair of hits, "The Belles of Southern Bell" and "Girl on the Billboard" (a novelty song that reached Number One) that became two of the most popular country singles of 1965.

Del joined the Grand Ole Opry in 1966 and continued to churn out successful singles for United Artists through the early 1970's, including "Landmark Tavern," "Philadelphia Phillies," "The Best Is Yet to Come" and the 1968 Number Three, "Good Time Charlie," to name but a few. While his recording career gradually slowed down in the mid-70's, he turned up on the charts again in 1976, thanks to a series of duets with Billie Jo Spears. He left UA in 1978, making subsequent recordings for smaller labels.

Del remained a fixture in country music television into the 1980's, hosting a syndicated weekly variety show called *The Del Reeves Country Carnival*. Along the way, he appeared on a number of low-budget country music-related feature films. He also played a role in the discovery of Billy Ray Cyrus. His hitmaking days over, Reeves continues to appear on the Opry into the 1990's.   —M.B.

Jim Reeves

BORN: August 20, 1924
BIRTHPLACE: Galloway, Texas
DIED: July 31, 1964

Jim Reeves exemplified the best of the Nashville Sound. His was crossover music in the finest sense of the word. The recordings he did for RCA from 1957 to 1964 remain some of the most memorable music of that era. The fiddles and steel guitar were gone; voices and a quiet, reflective piano hovered in the background.

The honesty and sincerity remained, with Reeves' voice conveying a warmth and timelessness that few other crossover artists have been able to match, including those of today.

Purists who complain that Reeves "abandoned" country music are kidding themselves. Throughout his career, he never quit recording country songs. One of his last hits during his lifetime was the Werly

Fairburn number, "I Guess I'm Crazy," a tune that was as down-home as anything recorded by Hank or Lefty. Actually, with the dozens of Jim Reeves repackages of RCA material (some of which included a fair amount of Tin Pan Alley pop), it is easy to forget that Reeves was a contemporary of both Williams and Frizzell and began his career singing music not that different from their own.

James Travis Reeves was born in Galloway, Texas. His father died within a year of his birth, and he was raised, along with five other children, by his mother, Beulah. Jimmie Rodgers, not surprisingly, was an early hero, but baseball became his obsession. A baseball scholarship took him to the University of Texas at Austin in 1942, but he quit to work the shipyards of Houston, then took to the minor leagues, where he stayed until he was injured. In 1947 he married Mary White, who would play an important role in his future musical career.

He first moved into music as a disc jockey at KGRI in Henderson, Texas. Feeling that his own voice equaled or surpassed that of Ernest Tubb or Lefty Frizzell, he decided to take a serious stab at recording. In 1949 he cut his first records for a tiny local label in Houston, but they went nowhere. His big break came in April 1953, when "Mexican Joe," a song he'd recorded for Abbott Records, became his first Number One record. He was working as an announcer on Shreveport's *Louisiana Hayride* at the time. Fearing they'd lose him as their emcee, the *Hayride* management insisted that Billy Walker—not Reeves—sing the song on the show. One night Reeves had to fill in as a singer anyway, and the management's injunction went by the boards. He sang "Mexican Joe" and wound up with six encores, at which point *Hayride* staffer Horace Logan forbade any more kudos, lest Reeves beat Hank Williams' previously set record for encores. That was the end of his announcing and the beginning of his two-year stint as a *Hayride* star, as he followed up "Mexican Joe" with "Bimbo," another unvarnished country hit, which hit Number Two.

In 1955 Reeves bought back his Abbott contract and moved on to RCA Victor. Without a hit for two years, he soon came up with three in a row—"Yonder Comes a Sucker," "My Lips Are Sealed" and "According to My Heart," all Top Ten, all in one year and all straight country. However, in the wake of Elvis' success, it looked like audiences were beginning to tire, at least for the moment, of the fiddle and steel style that had held sway for over a decade. Desperate to counteract declining record sales, RCA's Chet Atkins, Decca's Owen Bradley and Columbia's Don Law began trying new ideas in the studio. One particularly popular experiment was to strip off the fiddle and steel, introduce a more neutral rhythm section and use background voices to sing the fiddle/steel fill-ins. Reeves tried this and also lowered the volume of his voice, singing close to the microphone.

Then, early in 1957, Reeves, much to Chet Atkins' surprise, selected a ballad called "Four Walls" for his next session. Atkins had thought of the song as a woman's number, but trusting Reeves' intuition, he went with it. RCA released it in March; it hit Number Two on *Billboard*'s country charts in April and Number Eleven on their pop charts in May. Suddenly Reeves was doing *American Bandstand*. When "Blue Boy" hit Number Four in 1958, Reeves renamed his band The Blue Boys and dropped his fiddler and steel player for good. In December of 1959, he crossed over in a big way once again: "He'll Have to Go," cut as the B-side of a single, hit Number One country and Number Two pop.

Jim Reeves was a perfectionist in his work, a trait which landed him in a few minor but telling scrapes. Once, while doing a promotional tour of record shops without his band, he insisted on singing alone with his guitar instead of using the mediocre backup group provided. During a tour of Ireland he canceled two shows when the pianos provided for Blue Boys' pianist Dean Manuel were too worn out, in his opinion, to play. He quit the Opry in the early 1960's, as did others, in a dispute over the number of appearances he was required to make on the show. "If he was home on the weekend," said Mary Reeves, "he wanted to be home." In April 1964 he went to Europe as part of an RCA all-star tour that included Chet Atkins, Anita Kerr and Bobby Bare. The show drew huge crowds. In a U.S. military enlisted men's club in Germany, Reeves walked off the stage when the boisterous audience got to him. A minor furor ensued, which he did nothing to calm, allowing a GI paper to quote him as saying, "I don't play for animals."

But other than that, things were going well. He was planning to study acting and was trying to reduce his touring in order to work on investments. A land deal took him via private plane (he was a skilled amateur pilot) to Batesville, Arkansas, on July 30, 1964, with pianist Dean Manuel. On July 31, while approaching Nashville on his return, the plane ran into a rainstorm and disappeared from radar. Outside his Brentwood home, Marty Robbins heard something crash. It took two days to locate the wreckage and the bodies. On August 4, after funeral services in Nashville, Reeves' body was returned to Carthage, Texas. In 1967, he was posthumously elected to the Country Music Hall of Fame.

Jim Reeves records still sell, three decades after his death; he remains a legend. But he never saw himself that way when he was alive. "He didn't really discredit himself," said Mary Reeves, "but I think he didn't realize how big he actually was." —R.K.

Mike Reid

BORN: May 24, 1947
BIRTHPLACE: Altoona, Pennsylvania

Much has been made of the fact that Mike Reid was an All-Pro defensive tackle for the National Football League's Cincinnati Bengals before moving to Nashville in the early 1980's to take a job as a $100-a-week staff songwriter.

But unlike a Joe Namath or a Terry Bradshaw, both of whom made short-lived and thoroughly laughable post-football end runs into singing careers, Reid has proven to be a country writer and recording artist of unusual perception and talent. Reid's original songs have been recorded by everyone from The Judds, Bonnie Raitt ("I Can't Make You Love Me") and Tammy Wynette, to Conway Twitty, Jerry Jeff Walker and Ronnie Milsap (who had hits with "Stranger in My House," "Lost in the Fifties Tonight" and "Old Folks," a 1988 duet with Reid that hit Number Two).

Reid made his own impressive recording debut with his 1991 album, *Turning for Home*, which resulted in the Number One single, "Walk on Faith." Like *Turning for Home,* his second album, *Twilight Town*, was only a modest commercial success. Yet it showcased soulful original material and almost reverential vocal interpretations that resonate with a comforting serenity—even when Reid addresses the usual perplexities of troubled marriages and lost romances. —B.A.

Reissues

While many collectors will always prefer the original 78 or 45 r.p.m. singles or first-issue LP's, other enthusiasts prefer the convenience of hearing vintage material on LP or compact disc compilations. The first country music reissue, on Victor—*Smoky Mountain Ballads* (Victor P-79)—appeared in August 1941. Compiled by pioneering folklorist John A. Lomax, this five-album set of recordings by Uncle Dave Macon, The Carter Family, The Monroe Brothers and others was aimed at northern audiences interested in folk music. In 1952 Folkways issued Harry Smith's *Anthology of American Folk Music*, a comprehensive three-volume, six-LP set that helped spur urban interest in pre-war blues and country music.

As 10" and 12" LP's began to grab a greater share of the record market, many labels repackaged popular single releases into long-playing albums. By 1960 every major label except Capitol offered older country product on a $1.98 budget LP line. Important budget labels included Harmony (Columbia), Camden (RCA Victor), Vocalion (Decca), Wing (Mercury), Nashville (Starday) and Audio Lab (King).

Reissues of pre-war country music lagged far behind those in jazz and blues, until New York collector David Freeman launched County Records in 1964. Freeman's compilations of early fiddle, banjo and string band recordings often sported informative liner notes; his pioneering efforts helped open the market for Rounder, Old Homestead and other collectors' labels.

Bear Family, a German label initially modeled on County Records, launched the modern era of country reissues in 1978. As compact discs dominated the market in the late 80's, several major labels began serious country reissue projects, including Columbia's Country Classics series and MCA's Country Hall of Fame releases. Reissue labels like Rhino Records have also aggressively packaged quality sets of vintage country music. Boxed sets, usually containing several CD's and illustrated booklets with historical notes, have become a standard in the reissue market. (See also Bear Family Records.) —D.S.

Renfro Valley Barn Dance

This popular and influential live country radio show flourished in Renfro Valley, Kentucky, for many years. After initially being launched over Cincinnati's WLW in 1937, the show moved to KCKY in Kentucky two years later. John Lair, the show's founder, established the *Barn Dance* in order to provide a showcase for the rural Southeastern music he'd loved in his youth, and which he felt was being displaced in terms of national popularity by Western music. Like the *Louisiana Hayride* and the *Wheeling Jamboree*, the *Renfro Valley Barn Dance* proved a stepping stone for local talent. Red Foley, Molly O'Day and Homer & Jethro are just a few artists who cut their teeth on the show before going on to bigger things. The *Barn Dance* still survives today as a stage show on the original property in Renfro Valley.   —B.A.

Reno & Smiley

BORN: Reno, February 2, 1927, Buffalo, South Carolina
        Smiley, May 17, 1925
DIED: Smiley, 1972; Reno, October 16, 1984

Banjoist Don Reno became Earl Scruggs' replacement in Bill Monroe's Bluegrass Boys in 1948. He learned his very similar style from some of the same pickers

who had inspired Scruggs. Reno, in turn, left Monroe to join fiddler Tommy Magness' band, The Tennessee Buddies, where he met guitarist/vocalist Red Smiley. They started their own band in 1951 and signed with King Records, calling themselves Don Reno, Red Smiley and The Tennessee Cutups; the group was considered one of the top-flight bands of bluegrass' golden era. (Reno, in his day, was one of the few banjo players whose name was often spoken in the same breath as Earl Scruggs'.) They recorded prolifically for King and had two hit singles in 1961, "Don't Let Your Sweet Love Die" and "Love, Oh Love, Oh Please Come Home." Reno and Smiley remained together until 1968. After Smiley died in 1972, Reno teamed up with guitarist Bill Harrell. Reno & Harrell continued to work together until 1978. Reno continued to work solo until his death in 1984.   —R.K.

Restless Heart

Few groups have mined the mellow country-pop legacy of The Eagles as assiduously and relentlessly as Restless Heart. At the outset, Restless Heart seemed a band not built to last, insofar as they were manufactured—pulled together by veteran producer/songwriter Tim DuBois (now head of Arista/Nashville). But they survived the departure of two of their five original members, lead singer Larry Stewart, who left in the early 90's in pursuit of a solo career (his debut album, *Alright, Already,* was released in 1993), and founding member Dave Innis, who departed not long afterward. With hits like "That Rock Won't Roll," "Wheels," "The Bluest Eyes In Texas," "Big Dreams in a Small Town," "Fast Movin' Train" and "When She Cries" (a 1993 hit that had the unprecedented distinction of earning ASCAP's Song of the Year award in both Pop and Country categories), Restless Heart has shown a consistent flair for smooth pop melodies and harmonies and technically sophisticated arrangements. Yet their musical appeal has always been rather one-dimensional, and despite many radio hits, they've never quite been able to rise above the perennial role of opening act to the superstars. As accomplished and "radio friendly" as their music is, it's seldom lingered long enough in listeners' collective memories to give the band a solid identity. —B.A.

Tony Rice

BORN: June 8, 1951
BIRTHPLACE: Danville, Virginia

This brilliant, innovative flat-picking acoustic guitarist and soulful singer has worked both the progressive and traditional extremes of bluegrass and newgrass/new acoustic music with an artistry and innovation that has made him one of the most revered figures on the national bluegrass circuit. Influenced heavily by acoustic country guitar greats like Merle Watson, Norman Blake and the late Clarence White, Rice apprenticed with the cutting edge newgrass ensemble, J.D. Crowe and The New South. Rice worked with David Grisman on his now classic 1975 album, *David Grisman*, and on the 1977 Kaleidoscope release, *The David Grisman Quintet*. The Florida-born Rice moved further into Grisman's eclectic newgrass "Dawg" music and continued in that direction even after he formed his own group The Tony Rice Unit in 1980, playing what he called "spacegrass." Yet Rice has always remained true to his traditional bluegrass roots, as well, even when doing stunning interpretations of songs as far afield as Gordon Lightfoot's "Early Morning Rain" or ancient English seafaring ballads. Aside from recording a collection of gorgeous solo albums over the past decade and a half, Rice has also collaborated with everybody who is anybody in bluegrass and newgrass circles: Ricky Skaggs, Norman Blake, Doc Watson, the late Keith Whitley, Jerry Douglas, Sam Bush, Bela Fleck, Vassar Clements, Jerry Douglas

and many others. He has also recorded occasionally as a member of The Rice Brothers with several of his talented siblings—among them noted recording artist Larry Rice, and Wyatt Rice. —B.A.

Charlie Rich

BORN: December 14, 1932
BIRTHPLACE: Forrest City, Arkansas

A some-time farmer and a regular performer at Memphis clubs in the mid-1950's, Rich was signed as a session player at Sun Records after his wife, Margaret Ann, played a copy of a demo tape for Sun A&R executive Bill Justis. At Sun, Charlie sang backup for singers like Johnny Cash and Roy Orbison before the label began releasing a few of his own recordings late in the 50's, which showcased his unique blend of gospel- and jazz-inflected country blues. Although one single, "Lonely Weekends," made the country charts in the spring of 1960, it would be years before Charlie would score a bona fide hit.

Charlie switched to RCA Records and then to Mercury, where he cut a single called "Mohair Sam" that became a major pop hit. But things fell apart for Rich at RCA when a follow-up hit failed to materialize, so he switched to Hi Records in Memphis (where he recorded an obscure but brilliant album in 1967 called *Charlie Rich Sings Country & Western*) and returned to the club scene, where he used booze and pills to escape the frustration he felt after so many years of near misses.

Charlie was at an all-time low when a few unsuccessful years later he signed with Epic and joined forces with veteran producer Billy Sherrill. While their collaboration failed to yield an immediate hit, within a few years Charlie's career was on an upswing. In 1972 Charlie broke the country Top Ten with a Kenny O'Dell composition titled "I Take It on Home." The following year Charlie recorded another O'Dell tune that would become one of the biggest hits of his career: "Behind Closed Doors" The single made it all the way to Number One and became a huge crossover hit as well, earning Charlie his first Gold record and kicking off a hard-earned winning streak that would last through the decade. His next single, "The Most Beautiful Girl," sold over two million copies and put Charlie in line for a bevy of awards: a Grammy for Best Male Vocalist of 1973 as well as Country Music Association awards for Male Vocalist, Single and Album of the year (for the platinum-selling *Behind Closed Doors*).

In 1974 Charlie scored an impressive five Number One hits: "I Don't See Me in Your Eyes Anymore," "There Won't Be Anymore," "A Very Special Love Song," "She Called Me Baby" and "I Love My Friend." He also won Gold record awards for the albums *There Won't Be Anymore* and *Very Special Love Songs*. And after struggling for nearly 20 years to make a name for himself in country music, Charlie was honored with the Country Music Association's 1974 Entertainer of the Year award. Even so, for Rich, a moody and intensely private man, there was misery amidst his new-found stardom. He occasionally lamented publicly that the easy-listening pop mode with which he and Sherrill had finally hit the jackpot was his lowest musical common denominator and an aesthetic betrayal of the integrity of his original country-blues-rooted instincts. Charlie continued to score hits for Epic through the mid-1970's, including "My Elusive Dreams," "Road Song," "Since I Fell for You" and the Number One, "Rollin' with the Flow." In 1978 he climbed the charts with the Top Ten "Beautiful Woman" and a Number One duet with Janie Fricke he wrote himself, "On My Knees." Charlie left Epic in the late 1970's and signed with Elektra Records, where he recorded hits like "A Man Doesn't Know What a Woman Goes Through" in 1980. In the interim he continued to make the charts with songs like "Spanish Eyes" in 1979 and "Even a Fool Would Let Go" a year later. He also cut successful singles on the United Artists label, such as "I Still Believe in Love" in 1978, "Life Goes On" and "I Lost My Head" in 1979, and the hit, "You're Gonna Love Yourself in the Morning," in 1980. After a long hiatus from recording, Rich re-emerged briefly in 1992 with *Pictures and Paintings*, a wonderful album where he once again touched base with his blues-country roots. The producer was Peter Guralnick, writer and *Country Music Magazine* contributing editor, who had chronicled Rich's ups and downs in print for over a decade. —M.B.

Don Rich

BORN: August 5, 1941
BIRTHPLACE: Olympia, Washington
DIED: July 17, 1974

Though his career, and life, were relatively short, Don Rich, by dint of his decade-and-a-half collaboration with Buck Owens, established himself as one of the most influential guitarists in post-war country music.

As a long-time member of Owens' band, The Buckaroos, Rich forged with Owens a guitar signature sound built around the two men's twin Fender Telecasters. Over the years, this provocative styling has found its way into the music of everyone from the early Beatles to Waylon Jennings and Dwight Yoakam. (Yoakam's long-time producer/guitarist extraordinaire, Pete Anderson, has done as much as anyone to keep the Owens/Rich "Telecaster Country" style alive in the 80's and 90's.)

"Don and I made a sort of synergy where one and one don't make two. The two of us together made three ," Owens recalled to *Country Music Magazine*'s Rich Kienzle a few years ago. "He was half a generation younger than I was. He had a freshness and he loved to pick guitar."

Rich was born Donald Eugene Ulrich, in Washington, in 1941. Owens first met him in the late 1950's, when Rich was still a teen-aged fiddle player and Owens had moved to Washington state to dabble in the radio business and host his own local TV show. Owens hired Rich, who would go on to play (guitar and occasionally fiddle) on most of Owens' signature recordings and help Owens perfect his much-imitated sound.

Now and then, Rich, along with The Buckaroos, even came out from under Owens' wing and cut a few records independently. Recording as "Don Rich & The Buckaroos," they had three country chart records in 1969 and 1970, including "Anywhere, USA" and a version of The Band's "The Night They Drove Old Dixie Down."

But it all came to an end quite suddenly on July 17, 1974, when Rich was killed in a motorcycle accident in California. In a sense, it marked the end of Owens' vintage years as well. "After Don's death, I don't think I ever quite recovered," recalled Owens—to whom Rich was not just a band member, but a close friend and musical alter-ego, as well. "Don was incredibly important as a human being. He was as much a part of the music as I was."   —B.A.

Riders in the Sky

BORN: Ranger Doug, March 20, 1946, Great Lakes,
        Illinois; Too Slim, June 3, 1948, Grand
        Rapids, Michigan; Woody Paul, August 23,
        1949, Nashville, Tennessee

Keepers of the cowboy music flame, this Western vocal trio is led by singer-guitarist "Ranger Doug" Green, former Oral Historian at the Country Music Foundation, Bill Monroe sideman and *Country Music Magazine* contributor. Rounded out by fiddler Woody Paul (who has a doctorate in nuclear engineering) and bassist Fred "Too Slim" LaBour, this Western group has served as an extension of Green's longtime love of formative Western vocal groups like The Sons of the Pioneers. Today many of those ensembles have passed into obscurity or history, but the Riders remain one of a handful of active Western vocal groups, certainly the only one currently getting major media exposure. Together since the early 80's, the Riders' love for Western music and their G-rated humor and tongue-in-cheek skits have earned them slots on the Grand Ole Opry (which they joined in 1982) and The Nash-

ville Network. The Riders have recorded for various labels including Rounder, and briefly had their own CBS-TV children's show, replacing *Pee-Wee's Playhouse*, and also a campy comedy program on National Public Radio network.   —R.K.

New Riders of the Purple Sage

This San Francisco-based country-rock band—whose nucleus consisted of vocalist John Dawson (a.k.a. Marmaduke), guitarist David Nelson and bassist Dave Torbert—got its official start in the early 1970's as the Grateful Dead's warm-up band. Dead fans loved the band because often Jerry Garcia would sit in on pedal steel. But even when Garcia was replaced by Buddy Gage, the group had already developed a widespread cult following and continued to be a popular concert draw. Fans were especially drawn to the band's hippie-cowboy-outlaw posturing, as articulated in songs such as "Louisiana Lady," "Henry" and the dope-smokin' anthem "Panama Red" (written by Peter Rowan—a former member of Old and In the Way, another Jerry Garcia off-shoot band—who's since gone on to bluegrass and newgrass fame).

Famous West Coast artists who at one time or another served as New Riders include Mickey Hart and Phil Lesh of Grateful Dead, Spencer Dryden of Jefferson Airplane and Skip Battin of The Byrds. The band recorded seven albums for Columbia before switching over to MCA in 1977. Some of the original members of the New Riders are still playing club dates across the country, but for the most part the band has simply run out of gas. And material.—R.P.

Jeannie C. Riley

BORN: October 19, 1945
BIRTHPLACE: Anson, Texas

Jeanne Carolyn Stephenson decided that she wanted to be a famous singer after a childhood bout with rheumatic fever that kept her bedridden for months, a radio as her constant companion. At the age of 16, she was performing at high school talent shows and becoming the proverbial "big fish in a small pond" in her hometown. A move to Nashville followed in 1966. There Jeannie found work as a demo singer and a secretary. Nashville entrepreneur Shelby Singleton, the head of Plantation Records, heard one of her demos and thought she'd be perfect for a song he had on hold from a then unknown writer—Tom T.

Hall. The year was 1968 and the song, "Harper Valley PTA," a classic put-down of small-town hypocrisy, was cut in two takes. Jeannie knew she had a hit after hearing the first playback. She had no idea how much of a hit, though: The song shot to Number One on both the pop and country charts in September of 1968, selling nearly five million copies, eager audiences eating up its *Peyton Place/Valley of the Dolls* sentiment. It thrust Riley into a whirlwind of touring and television appearances and won her the Country Music Association's Single of the Year Award as well as a Grammy for Best Female Country Vocal Performance. But after the runaway success of "Harper Valley," Riley found herself recording similar "sassy" songs that gave her a racy mini-skirted image far removed from her own conservative personality. A few of these hit the Top Ten—"The Girl Most Likely" and "There Never Was a Time," among them—but Riley was eager to shed the sultry image. She began recording some of her own self-penned material and, in 1971, left Plantation Records in a dispute over royalties. She signed with MGM, scoring a few minor hits through 1973. She then had brief associations with Mercury and Warner before turning to smaller, independent labels in the late 70's. She eventually turned to gospel material. Riley, now a born-again Christian, continues to tour into the 90's.   —G.F.

Tex Ritter

BORN: January 12, 1905
BIRTHPLACE: Panola County, Texas
DIED: January 2, 1974

Though born in rural East Texas (which far more resembles Appalachia than the Old West), and though his early musical influences were rural and southern rather than purely western, Maurice Woodward "Tex" Ritter was identified early in his career with the Texas cowboy image. That is not, however, how he started out. Ritter's skills as a public speaker and his intellect first became apparent when he attended school in Nederland, where the Ritter family had moved. Though he loved cowboy songs, he decided on a law career and in 1922 began attending the University of Texas at Austin. Active in music and theater there, he soon found two professors at the University doing a serious study of cowboy songs, and learned much from them. In 1928, he traveled to New York City just before graduation and wound up getting a minor role in a Broadway show. After a final stab at finishing law school, he returned to New York in 1931 and landed a featured role in the Broadway play, *Green Grow the Lilacs*. That led to other Broadway parts and radio programs and, in 1932, his first recording session for the American Recording Company. Following Gene Autry's success, Hollywood sought other singing cowboys, and in 1936 Tex landed a Hollywood movie contract. He was on the way to stardom by 1937 and made 85 films through 1945. He married actress Dorothy Fay in 1941. Though he recorded for ARC and for Decca without success, he became the first country or western singer signed to the brand-new Capitol label in 1942 and immediately found success with "Jingle, Jangle, Jingle." He had a string of hit records in the 40's with "I'm Wastin' My Tears On You," "There's a New Moon Over My Shoulder," "Jealous Heart" (1944), "You Two-Timed Me One Time Too Often" (1945), "You Will Have to Pay," "Christmas Carols by the Old Corral" (1945), "Rye Whiskey" and "Deck of Cards" (1948). After making his final films in the mid-40's, he again focused on his singing. His repertoire expanded beyond Western music to include a variety of styles. In 1953, his version of "Do Not Forsake Me," the theme from the classic 1942 Gary Cooper film *High Noon*, became a pop hit. By 1952 he'd become host of the popular Southern California country music TV show, *Town Hall Party*, and also its nationally syndicated counterpart, *Ranch Party*. In 1961 he had a final big hit with "I Dreamed of a Hillbilly Heaven." A founding member of the Country Music Association, he was inducted into the Country Music Hall of Fame in 1964. After moving to Nashville, he began co-hosting Ralph Emery's late-night WSM radio show in addition to working on the Opry. He ran for the 1970 Republican nomination for U.S. Senator. He died of a heart attack in 1974, while bailing one of his musicians out of a Nashville jail. His son John Ritter has become a highly successful actor after Tex's death.　　　　　—R.K.

Hargus "Pig" Robbins

BORN: January 18, 1938
BIRTHPLACE: Rhea County, Tennessee

Though blind since childhood, Hargus Robbins learned piano at the Tennessee School for the Blind. He taught himself to play country from listening to records and over time, was able to create his own distinctively country style. By the time he'd finished school, he was good enough to work in Nashville clubs and resolved to pursue a full-time musical career. Though a Nashville Musicians' Union official, fearing Robbins wouldn't get enough work, discouraged him from joining, the pianist not only joined, but by the late 50's was becoming a sought-after pianist on recording sessions. The swirling, bluesy boogie piano on George Jones' "White Lightning" is just one of his countless contributions to Nashville hits in the years since.

Robbins, whose thick physique earned him the name "Pig," became one of Nashville's A-Team, appearing on countless country hits and many Nashville-recorded pop records as well. He received the 1976 Instrumentalist of the Year from the CMA and in 1978 won a Grammy in the same category. Though he briefly recorded on his own as both vocalist and pianist for Elektra in the late 70's, studio work remained his major stock in trade, though a new generation now dominates Nashville studio work.　　—R.K.

Marty Robbins

BORN: September 26, 1925
BIRTHPLACE: Glendale, Arizona
DIED: December 8, 1982

Think of the singers who excel in one style, then try another and fail. That never happened to Marty Robbins. Not once. He may have been known as "Mr. Teardrop," but whether he sang hard country, Mexican, Western, Hawaiian ballads, blues, gospel, rockabilly, contemporary country or mainstream pop, the man never broke a sweat.

Marty was the most versatile singer in country music. I know such blanket statements are risky, but not this time. Willie Nelson may come close, yet Marty still has the edge. Anyone who saw his open-ended shows at the Opry can attest to the breadth of Marty's talent. He was among the greatest entertainers in any field, and even his earliest records hold up well today. If that's not enough, consider this: in 31 years of recording, he was barely ever off the charts.

Martin David Robinson's early years were a far cry from fame and fortune. Born in 1925 in Glendale, Arizona, he had seven brothers and one sister, all of whom lived in stark poverty. His dad drank too much and later abandoned the family, but his grandfather, "Texas Bob" Heckle, cultivated a lifelong love of the Old West and its lore in Marty. As a kid, Marty idolized Gene Autry and worked to earn the money to see his movies.

When he was 19, he joined the Navy and served in the Pacific at the end of World War II. He returned home in 1947 and started playing guitar and writing songs. He worked day jobs and began performing casually around Phoenix. He changed his stage name several times so his mother wouldn't find out about his activities, and landed a spot over at KPHO radio in Phoenix. Soon he graduated to KPHO-TV's *Country Caravan.*

Little Jimmy Dickens, on tour in the Southwest, guested on KPHO in early 1951. When he met Marty, he was so impressed he suggested Columbia Records sign him, which they did, in May. Robbins' first recording session followed in November in Los Angeles with several of his own musicians backing him, augmented by local sidemen. His producer was Columbia's legendary "Uncle Art" Satherley, who had produced Gene Autry, Bob Wills and Roy Acuff and was nearing retirement. None of Marty's first four recordings were blockbusters despite an appealing, laid-back quality not unlike early Eddy Arnold. Still, they sold well enough to satisfy Columbia.

His second session, recorded at Jim Beck's Dallas studio in 1952, yielded the ballad, "I'll Go on Alone." When it was released in early 1953, it hit Number Ten on the *Billboard* charts, even though Webb Pierce had just taken his own version of the song to Number Seven. Marty's golden era was beginning. His boss at KPHO, ex-Grand Ole Opry head Harry Stone, helped him get a guest appearance on the Opry. The Opry made him a member in 1953. Fred Rose himself signed Marty to Acuff-Rose as a composer. Early in 1955 he covered Elvis' "That's All Right, Mama," taking it to Number Nine on *Billboard's* country charts at a time when Elvis wasn't known outside the Deep South.

In 1955 and 1956 he recorded hot versions of "Maybelline," "Long Tall Sally" and his own "Tennessee Toddy" that stand with that era's best rockabilly recordings. None were hits, but he became a crossover success anyway. In the fall of 1956 his version of Melvin Endsley's song, "Singing the Blues," became his first Number One on the country charts. And though pop singer Guy Mitchell's version was Number One on the pop charts, Marty's version was just 16 slots behind, his first crossover.

That was just the beginning. In April 1957, Marty was Number Two on the pop and Number One on the country charts with the teen ballad, "A White Sport Coat," the first of a series of recordings he made in New York with The Ray Conniff Singers. It gave him his first Gold record and made him a national figure. He would crack the pop charts 11 more times in his career. In the fall of 1957, he recorded his first Hawaiian album, *Song of the Islands.* His singles remained teen-oriented ballads through 1957 and 1958. Both "Story of My Life" and "Just Married" crossed over.

Successful as he was, he never stayed long in one style; by 1959 he was exploring his fascination with the Old West. The result was the classic 1959 album, *Gunfighter Ballads and Trail Songs*, and the hit single from it, "El Paso," a song he'd written while driving through Texas. Despite the song's length, four minutes, 37 seconds—unusual for the late 1950's—it topped both country and pop charts and won him a Grammy. Nearly 30 years later, it remains his most enduring record. If Louis L'Amour had a musical counterpart, Marty was it.

Though he cut several albums' worth of fine Western material, his next big hit in 1961 was the blues-tinged ballad, "Don't Worry." While he was recording it at Bradley Studios in Nashville, guitarist Grady Martin (who played the Spanish guitar licks on "El Paso") soloed on a six-string bass. The recording mixer malfunctioned, distorting his solo. Marty liked the weird sound, insisting the record be released as is, credited to "Marty Robbins and The Bumblebees." The "error" didn't hurt the record's success: Number One country, Number Three pop. Columbia released *Marty After Midnight* in 1962. On it Marty crooned Tony Bennett-style jazz and pop that worked surprisingly well, and this was 18 years before Willie's *Stardust*. That same year he had another crossover with the calypso-flavored "Devil Woman." In 1963 he came out with *Hawaii's Calling Me*, a follow-up to 1957's *Song of the Islands*.

Robbins played as hard as he worked. By 1963 he was deeply involved in stock car racing, despite the risks to life and limb. Over the years nothing, not even accidents, deterred him from pursuing his hobby. He and his wife Marizona had two children; always an intensely private man, he wisely insulated his home life from his career.

His hits weren't as prominent in the mid-1960's, but he still sold records and did well on the road. His Western songs broadened to include more contemporary themes, best evidenced in "Cowboy in the Continental Suit" in 1964. In 1966 he even recorded "Ain't I Right," a song reflecting political beliefs so conservative Columbia didn't release it. That same year he wrote *The Small Man*, a Western novel.

The heart trouble started in 1969 with an attack requiring major open-heart surgery. But he made it back to the Opry, and ran overtime with his return appearance. He even resumed racing. In 1970, "My Woman, My Woman, My Wife" became his first Number One record since 1968, and it, too, earned a Grammy.

Marty's finale at the Saturday night show of the Opry became a tradition. Onstage he had enough energy to power a factory. He sang, hollered, picked his tiny Martin guitar, jumped to the piano, ran through medleys of his hits, and often let fly with an impromptu rockabilly version of "Big Boss Man." He obviously enjoyed himself, laughing at private jokes with his band, cracking up in mid-song. He was just as energetic in dealing with his fans and often answered their letters himself.

In 1973 he left Columbia for MCA, and managed a few hits, among them "Walking Piece of Heaven" and "Twentieth Century Drifter," before returning to CBS in 1976. That year two of his releases hit Number One: "El Paso City," a modern Western number and a sequel of sorts to "El Paso"; and his adaptation of the 1920's pop tune, "Among My Souvenirs," which had been a 1960 hit for Connie Francis. Too many wrecks finally curtailed his racing career, and a mild 1981 coronary slowed him down for a time.

But Marty's heart condition was far more serious than most realized. His body was unable to absorb cholesterol; even on the strict cholesterol-free diet he maintained in his final years, his circulatory system clogged up, straining his heart. Nevertheless, onstage it was business as usual. In May 1982, he had his final hit on CBS, "Some Memories Just Won't Die." When he took the stage to accept his 1982 election to the Country Music Hall of Fame, he quipped, "Others deserve it before I do, but it might not happen to me again. So I'm gonna take it tonight."

He'd returned to Nashville from a Cincinnati appearance early that December when the chest pains struck. Though St. Thomas Hospital cardiologists did all they could, the damage was too much. He died December 8. He was 57. His death was doubly hard, for like Ernest Tubb or Bill Monroe, Marty was irreplaceable. Apart from his long and distinguished career, the sole consolation was that unlike many Hall of Famers, Marty Robbins lived long enough to walk on the Opry stage and accept the award himself.—R.K.

Kenny Roberts

BORN: October 14, 1927
BIRTHPLACE: Lenoir City, Tennessee

Kenny Roberts, known as "America's Number One Yodeler," is one of the last of the breed. Active in country music since the late 1930's, Roberts was raised

in Massachusetts and began his career on New England radio stations. In the late 40's, he relocated to the Midwest, working at radio stations like WLW and WWVA, and in television. His best-known recording is the 1949 million-seller, "I Never See Maggie Alone." He also had success with "Choc'late Ice Cream Cone," "She Taught Me How to Yodel" and "Chime Bells." Roberts was a frequent winner in the National Yodeling Championships from 1956 on. Living once again in Massachusetts, Roberts still tours and releases independent label records, often writing with his wife, Bettyanne.   —G.F.

Eck Robertson

BORN: November 20, 1889
BIRTHPLACE: Delaney, Arkansas
DIED: February 15, 1975

Born in Arkansas and raised in Texas, by the early 1900's Alexander Campbell "Eck" Robertson was considered the premier old-time Texas fiddler, winning many local competitions and gaining fame throughout the state before making his mark nationally—as the first man to make genuine country recordings. (Vernon Dalhart recorded first, but his records weren't "country" in style or intent.)

Robertson learned to fiddle at an early age, and was an early wearer of Western garb for his performances—even before the singing cowboys. In 1922, while playing at a Civil War reunion festival in Virginia, he met up with 74-year-old fiddler Henry Gilliland. The two took a train to New York, went to the Victor Records offices and demanded to make a record. They were allowed to, and those sessions, taking place June 30-July 1, 1922, led to the first real country recordings. Among the six fiddle standards they recorded was Robertson's solo of "Sally Goodin," long-considered one of the all-time great fiddle performances. Robertson returned to Texas, playing again

at competitions and radio stations, recording once more in 1930, with members of his family. He continued as an award-winning fiddle player throughout the Southwest for years, remaining active well into his 80's. Robertson died in 1975.   —G.F.

Carson J. Robison

BORN: August 4, 1890
BIRTHPLACE: Oswego, Kansas
DIED: March 24, 1957

One of the early professional country songwriters, Robison wrote numbers like "Life Gets Tee-Jus Don't It," "Little Green Valley," "Blue Ridge Mountain Blues," "Left My Gal in the Mountains" and "Carry Me Back to the Lone Prairie." He began by working in vaudeville shows and on New York radio.

He didn't become involved in country music until he worked with early country star Vernon Dalhart; he then worked with singer Frank Luther and led various groups of his own. One of his early specialties was musical social commentary songs on current events. During the early days of World War II he wrote "hate songs" against the Axis powers like "We're

Gonna Have to Slap the Dirty Little Jap" and "Mussolini's Letter to Hitler," which reflected America's anger over Pearl Harbor. Robison also managed a Number Three record in 1948 with his novelty, "Life Gets Tee-Jus Don't It." Surprisingly, not long before Robison's death, he recorded a rockabilly number, "Rockin' and Rollin' with Gran'maw," for MGM.   —R.K.

Jimmie Rodgers

BORN: September 8, 1897
BIRTHPLACE: Meridian, Mississippi
DIED: May 26, 1933

The true Father of Country Music, James Charles Rodgers was raised by his father, a railroad worker, after his mother died in 1903. He hung around the streets of Meridian and was singing in amateur contests by the time he was 12. He later worked various railroad jobs. A brief marriage produced a daughter, but soon resulted in divorce. In 1920 he married Carrie Williamson and continued doing railroad work, traveling around the country from job to job. He played mandolin or banjo while traveling and heard plenty of black blues as well as country and popular tunes. His railroading days ended in 1924 when he discovered he'd contracted tuberculosis, in those days an always-fatal disease, sometimes taking years to develop.

By 1927 he and Carrie had moved to North Carolina and fell in with some local performers in a band known as The Jimmie Rodgers Entertainers. They landed a spot over WWNC in Asheville. After hearing that Ralph Peer of the Victor Talking Machine Company was holding auditions for rural acts in Bristol, Virginia, Rodgers convinced the group to travel there (The Carter Family also made the trip) in hopes of recording. The group broke up when they got there, but Rodgers recorded "The Soldier's Sweetheart" and "Sleep, Baby Sleep." They sold well, so Peer brought him to the Victor studio in New Jersey for more recordings, including the first of his "Blue Yodels," also known as "T For Texas," a bona fide million-seller. It kicked off an entire series of Rodgers "Blue Yodels," blues numbers with similar melodies and different lyrics. By 1928 he was suddenly wealthy and successful, touring the country and broadcasting from Washington, DC. He was earning $2000 a month from record sales alone. He would record alone, or

with The Carter Family, Hawaiian musicians, jazz bands (including one session with Louis Armstrong on trumpet) or other musicians like guitarist Slim Bryant, who worked the road with him for a time. Between 1927 and 1933 Rodgers made approximately 111 recordings. Soon other record companies were signing singers who could imitate Rodgers' style. His tours across the nation were selling out. His influence on young singers like Ernest Tubb, Hank Snow, Gene Autry and Jimmie Davis was immense. All used Rodgers' style as the basis to create their own. Even his guitar runs at the beginning of many of his songs were widely imitated, and still remain in use today. Rodgers lived high in those years, and had a casual approach to money and a generosity toward others. Though the tuberculosis was not always affecting him, he knew that it would eventually kill him—he even recorded "T. B. Blues," a song that admitted as much. Doctors' insistence that he slow down meant little to him. He wound up in debt by the early 30's, a result of high living. His condition began to deteriorate badly. In need of money as his health failed, he scheduled a session in New York in May of 1933, and, in between numbers, had to rest on a cot in the recording studio. It took him two weeks to record 12 songs, and he died in his room at New York's Taft Hotel when his lungs gave out, not even two days after his final recording. He was buried in Meridian.

The contributions of Jimmie Rodgers to country music and American popular music in general are immeasurable. Rodgers knew poverty and displacement firsthand. He understood working people, because he was part of that culture from his days hanging around the pool halls and barbershops of Meridian. He began many trends that continue in more sophisticated forms today, such as self-promotion and the creation of a well-defined image (as he became a successful performer, he shrewdly promoted his image as the "Singing Brakeman" in photographs, costumes and his only movie, the 1929 15-minute film, *The Singing Brakeman)*. Rodgers was the first country singer who was marketed through carefully coordinated tours and personal appearances. By all indications, he was the first country singer to endorse an instrument, his name going on a Weymann "Jimmie Rodgers Special" guitar (with his name inscribed on the fretboard) in 1930. He was also featured in company advertising. That tradition of country singers playing customized guitars continues to this day.

Rodgers' "Blue Yodels" helped to expose the blues

to vast numbers of whites who might not have heard the form as quickly. His freewheeling use of jazz musicians and pop performers to back him made it clear that country was a not a style defined solely by the old stringbands and traditional ballads brought to America from the British Isles. His records proved that even in the 1920's, the music was open to change and evolution and was never quite as "pure" as many believed. The high living Rodgers enjoyed during his peak years, complete with a lavish home (known as "Blue Yodeler's Paradise") and fancy cars, reflected the sort of high living that future generations of country singers—many who also escaped poverty—would enjoy. His willingness to chronicle his illness in song, as he did in "T.B. Blues," anticipated the way future country singers would deal with their own personal problems through singing about them.

In the years, and even decades, following his death, Rodgers' music continued to influence others, among them Bill Monroe, Lefty Frizzell, Elton Britt and Merle Haggard. Rodgers' "Muleskinner Blues" remains, after 55 years, the opening number of Bill Monroe and His Blue Grass Boys. Young traditionalist Marty Brown still listens to Rodgers. Ernest Tubb, who'd received encouragement early in his career from Rodgers' widow, Carrie, advertised Jimmie Rodgers records for years on his WSM *Midnight Jamboree* program, broadcast from his famous Ernest Tubb Record Shop. In 1955 Rodgers' version of "In the Jailhouse Now No. 2," with over-dubbed accompaniment by Hank Snow's Rainbow Ranch Boys, became a Top Ten record. Rockabilly artists, including Jerry Lee Lewis, thought nothing of including Rodgers songs in their recorded repertoires. Rodgers became the Country Music Hall of Fame's first member in 1961. Merle Haggard's 1969 album, *Same Train, A Different Time,* interpreted Rodgers' music for a new generation. His mix of blues and white country predated Elvis, one reason the Rock 'n' Roll Hall of Fame inducted him in the category of Forefather of Rock 'n' Roll.   —R.K.

Johnny Rodriguez

BORN: December 10, 1952
BIRTHPLACE: Sabinal, Texas

Born Juan Raul Davis Rodriguez, Tex-Mex singer Johnny Rodriguez was one of the most popular country acts of the mid-1970's and one of country's first

Mexican-American performers. The legend goes that Johnny was discovered as a teenager when the Texas Ranger who arrested him for goat-rustling introduced him to a music promoter named Happy Shahan. Shahan hired Johnny to perform as a singing cowboy at his tourist attraction, Alamo Village, then brought Tom T. Hall to the park to hear Johnny sing. Instead of waiting for Hall to contact him, though, Rodriguez set out on his own for Nashville and, within a week, was playing lead guitar for Hall's sessions. He also briefly toured in Hall's band.

Before long Rodriguez recorded a single, "Pass Me By" (written by Justin Hall, Tom T.'s younger brother), on Mercury Records that made it to Number Four on the country charts. His second single, "You Always Come Back to Hurting Me," made it to Number One in 1973 and spent 16 weeks on the charts, paving the way for his debut album, *Introducing Johnny Rodriguez*, which also went to Number One. Rodriguez went on to record two more Top Ten albums for Mercury and a string of chart-topping singles, including five more Number One hits: "Ridin' My Thumb to Mexico," "That's the Way Love Goes" (a cover of a Lefty Frizzell classic), "I Just Can't Get Her Out of My Mind," "Just Get up and Close the Door" and "Love Put a Song in My Heart." With his dark good looks, Rodriguez was a natural for film; in between hit records he found time to appear in the mid-1970's western, *Rio Diablo*.

In 1979 Rodriguez left Mercury for Epic Records and cut an album, produced by Billy Sherrill, titled simply *Rodriguez*. His most popular Epic singles include "What'll I Tell Virginia?" in 1979, "North of the Border" in 1980 and "I Want You Tonight" in 1981.

He also made the charts with "I Hate the Way I Love It," a 1979 duet with Charly McClain that became one of the biggest country hits of that year.

As of the early 90's, Rodriguez, after a number of years lost to personal problems, was back in Nashville, recording once again, on the Intersound Entertainment label. —M.B.

Kenny Rogers

BORN: August 21, 1938
BIRTHPLACE: Houston, Texas

In his heyday, Kenny Rogers parlayed a modest singing talent, a sharp business acumen, and an ambitious, finely honed flair for self-promotion into one of the hottest careers in country music. Between 1977, when he first hit Number One with the hit single, "Lucille," until the late 1980's, he sold millions of records and was seldom out of the top of the charts.

Born into poverty, Rogers found his ticket out of the projects when he began singing with a local group called The Scholars that had a surprise million-seller with a song called "Crazy Feeling." From there, Rogers went on to play bass in a jazz group called The Bobby Doyle Trio, and was later a member of The Kirby Stone Four and The New Christy Minstrels. In 1967, he formed The First Edition, a group whose sound was a cut or two above bubble-gum country-rock and whose success spanned eight Gold singles, and four Gold albums during the decade or so that he fronted it.

Though the First Edition's chart success came mostly in the rock and pop arenas, the band consistently drew some of its best material from top Nashville songwriters of the day like Mel Tillis ("Ruby, Don't Take Your Love to Town"), Mickey Newbury ("Just Dropped In to See What Condition My Condition Was In") and Alex Harvey ("Reuben James").

Signing with United Artists in Nashville in 1975, Rogers' first modest country chart successes as a solo singer came with songs like "Love Lifted Me," "While the Feeling's Good" and "Laura (What's He Got That I Ain't Got)," all of which fell short of the Top Ten. His first giant step toward superstardom came with "(You Picked a Fine Time to Leave Me) Lucille," which not only became his first country chart-topper in 1977, but also crossed over and made a splash in the pop charts. Hard on "Lucille's" heels came "The Gam-

bler" (penned by Don Schlitz, a then obscure Nashville songwriter for whom the song also kicked off an illustrious career as one of Nashville's most successful tunesmiths). "The Gambler" topped both the country and pop charts shortly after its release in 1978. "She Believes in Me," the easy-listening-style ballad with which Rogers followed up "The Gambler," hit Number One across the board, in the country, pop and easy-listening charts. "You Decorated My Life," "Lady," "Coward of the County," "Love Will Turn You Around," "Islands in the Stream" (a 1983 duet with Dolly Parton), "Real Love," "Tomb of the Unknown Love" and "Every Time Two Fools Collide" (a 1978 duet with Dottie West) were some of the additional Number Ones Rogers enjoyed throughout the late 70's and early 80's. Though no one would accuse him of being Dustin Hoffman, Rogers has, over the years, also dabbled in acting, appearing in made-for-TV and low-budget big screen outings like *The Gambler* (parts one through four), *Coward of the County* and *Six Pack*.

To his credit, Rogers has seldom over-estimated his own talents. ("I've never felt I was a great singer,

I've always felt I had a great ear for hit songs.") Nor has he ever misled anyone about his commercial instincts, which have led him into real estate speculation and other business ventures (including a chain of chicken franchises launched in the early 1990's with John Y. Brown, former governor of Kentucky and ex-CEO of Kentucky Fried Chicken). "I am basically success-oriented," Rogers once conceded when asked about his approach to music-making and everything else. "Money is a way of gauging success. If I make more money, I'm doing more things right. If I make less, I'm not doing as many things right."

—B.A.

Roy Rogers

BORN: November 5, 1911
BIRTHPLACE: Cincinnati, Ohio

The myths created in Hollywood occasionally take funny turns, exposing, even developing, one side of a personality (real or invented) while ignoring others. Roy Rogers is a perfect example: the genial, big brotherly character many of us grew up with is virtually all the public remembers. Rogers' impressive gifts as a singer, yodeler, songwriter, bandleader and musician have been overwhelmed by the force of his benign image as The King of the Cowboys.

As fans and non-fans alike know by now, Rogers was born Leonard Franklin Slye in Cincinnati, Ohio, where second base at Riverfront Stadium now rests (or so the legend goes) on November 5, 1911. His family moved to Portsmouth and then to Duck Run on the Ohio River, where he learned to sing, play the guitar, yodel and ride.

California's employment opportunities during the Depression, rather than its reputation as a center for film or music, is what lured the Slye family there in 1930; but by the following year Len had landed a spot on the radio as a vocalist and guitarist for The Rocky Mountaineers. There he met a young Canadian-born singer and songwriter named Bob Nolan, one of the great composers of our time. It took several tries, but eventually he sweet-talked Nolan and another aspiring singer/songwriter named Tim Spencer into forming a Western trio, featuring trio yodeling. At first they called themselves The Pioneer Trio, but their name was amended by a radio announcer who introduced them as The Sons of The Pioneers

because of their youth. After a shaky start these three young men, soon joined by Hugh and Karl Farr, became extremely popular on stage and in films. They began recording for Decca in 1935, and for the American Recording Corporation in 1937.

When Gene Autry sat out on strike at Republic Pictures in 1937 the studio, which, had created the entire singing cowboy concept, found itself with an opening, and Len Slye jumped at the chance. He auditioned, was hired, and signed a contract with Republic on October 13. He appeared in a couple of support roles billed as Dick Weston before starring as Roy Rogers in *Under Western Stars* in 1938. It took a few pictures for Roy Rogers to establish the genial, thoroughly likable character he made famous. His films were helped enormously by the addition of the superb George "Gabby" Hayes in 1939 and his old saddle pals, The Sons of The Pioneers, in 1941.

Following Gene Autry's departure for the service in World War II, Republic put their full promotion push behind Rogers, now billed as The King of the Cowboys. His films became increasingly extravagant in costume and choreography. Rogers' films of this era were the most lavish singing cowboy films ever made, a trend which continued for several years until the industry returned to more action-oriented formats in the late 1940's. In 1947, Rogers married Dale Evans, whom he'd met in the early 40's and costarred with in numerous films.

Rogers' career with Republic Pictures wound to a close in 1951 with *Pals of the Golden West*. When he and Yates could not agree on a contract, he simply moved to television, returning to the silver screen for a couple of guest shots in the 1950's and a starring role in the unpretentious *MacKintosh and T.J.* in 1975.

Over 100 episodes of *The Roy Rogers Show* were filmed for TV from 1951 through 1957. From then on Roy and Dale Evans concentrated on personal appearances. They moved to Apple Valley, California, in the high desert, in 1964, and opened a Roy Rogers Museum, which they moved down the road to Victorville in 1976. In 1987 they returned to TV to host *Happy Trails Theater* on The Nashville Network. To this day Rogers retains his athletic and healthy looks, seeming, as always, at least 15 years younger than he really is.

Roy Rogers the screen personality overwhelmed Roy Rogers the musician. In fact, Roy Rogers was one of the best yodelers of his time, an excellent

solo and harmony singer, a fine guitarist and a capable comedian. His place in The Sons of the Pioneers was filled not by another singer and guitarist, but by Pat Brady, bassist, comedian and, much later, Rogers' sidekick on TV. Rogers was also a gifted songwriter who wrote several of The Pioneers' best early songs, including "Down Along the Sleepy Rio Grande" and, in collaboration with Tim Spencer, "Curly Joe From Idaho," "Cowboys and Indians," "Song of the San Joaquin" and "South of Santa Fe," among many others.

Rogers began to record on his own as early as 1937. He was also featured on many of the Sons of The Pioneer numbers, and they also backed him on his first solo sessions. But Roy Rogers never became the mega-seller in records that his fellow singing cowboys Gene Autry and Tex Ritter did, though he was popular enough in his era. He moved to RCA in the 1940's. By the 1950's he was recording for their children's label. Since then, except for a brief foray into the country charts in the 1970's, he has been content recording inspirational albums with his wife Dale Evans.

Perhaps it was his relative lack of impact as a recording artist, or perhaps it was simply the awesome power of the Hollywood myth-making apparatus. In any case, Roy Rogers the singer, songwriter and musician has been seriously undervalued, while Roy Rogers the baby-sitter for a generation of Americans—as he himself says with a smile—is the figure we respond to so strongly: the image of boyish strength and fearlessness, of respect for nature, animals and the great outdoors. The Country Music Association, however, did recognize his musical contributions: Rogers was elected to the Country Music Hall of Fame in 1988. In 1991, he was coaxed briefly out of musical retirement to participate in *Tribute*, an album which brought together contemporary stars like Randy Travis, Clint Black, Lorrie Morgan and Riders in the Sky to musically salute him. —D.G.

Linda Ronstadt

BORN: July 15, 1946
BIRTHPLACE: Tucson, Arizona

Born in Tucson, Arizona, on July 15, 1946, Linda Ronstadt possessed a naturally flawless soprano that has enabled her to shift gears between folk, pop,

country, rock, Latin, big band and Broadway in a heartbeat. In 1964, at the age of 18, Linda moved to Los Angeles, where she formed her first band, The Stone Poneys, with guitarist Bobby Kimmel and keyboardist Kenny Edwards. The group made three albums for Capitol Records, and had a Top Ten rock hit with Mike Nesmith's "Different Drum."

The band broke up in 1968, and Ronstadt decided to strike out on her own. In 1969, she recorded *Hand Sown...Home Grown*, which featured the hit "Silver Threads and Golden Needles." Ronstadt's 1970 follow-up, *Silk Purse*, proved equally successful. In 1972, she assembled a new band consisting of Glenn Frey, Don Henley and Randy Meisner, who would later go on to form The Eagles. Ronstadt spent the next year fine-tuning her road act, and in 1973, she signed with Asylum Records and released *Don't Cry Now*. The album met with immediate critical and popular success, and played a pivotal role in bridging the gap between rock, pop and country music.

In 1974, her producer Peter Asher became her manager, and they collaborated on *Heart Like a Wheel*—an album that reached Number One on the pop charts and went platinum. From the album came two country hits—a remake of Hank Williams' "I Can't Help It If I'm Still In Love With You" and Phil Everly's

"When Will I Be Loved." Linda's performance on the former earned her a Grammy in 1975 for Country Vocal Performance-Female. The Asher-Ronstadt combination continued to work throughout the rest of the 1970's and well into the early 1980's. Popular country hits during this period included "Crazy" (her 1976 remake of the Willie Nelson-penned Patsy Cline hit), "Blue Bayou" (1977), "I Never Will Marry" (1978) and "Rambler Gambler" (1980).

One of the best performances of Linda's career came in 1987 when she teamed up with friends Dolly Parton and Emmylou Harris to record the landmark *Trio* album for Warner Bros. The album featured a masterful blend of traditional and contemporary country and met with instant critical and commercial success. Four singles from the album entered the country Top Ten, and one—a moving rendition of Phil Spector's "To Know Him Is to Love Him"—went to Number One.

Since 1987, Linda has recorded a number of diverse best-selling albums, including two Mexican releases, *Canciones De Mi Padre* and *Mas Canciones*, and a pop album, *Cry Like a Rainstorm—Howl Like the Wind*. The latter contained "Don't Know Much," a vocal duet with Aaron Neville that became a huge Top Ten hit in the United States as well as abroad. Ronstadt has inspired a number of today's female country stars—Trisha Yearwood and Martina McBride among the most notable.   —R.P.

Fred Rose

BORN: August 24, 1897
BIRTHPLACE: Evansville, Indiana
DIED: December 1, 1954

In the early 1920's Fred Rose established himself not only as an accomplished pianist, but also as a songwriter—penning hit pop tunes such as "Deed I Do" and "Honest and Truly." At 25 he landed a job as a pianist with Paul Whiteman's band. A chance meeting with Gene Autry, however, pointed Rose in the direction of Hollywood, where he subsequently wrote songs like Autry's hit "Be Honest with Me," which was nominated for an Academy Award. In 1942 Rose moved to Nashville, where he found greater empathy with Southeastern country music than he'd expected. That same year he and country music star Roy Acuff started Acuff-Rose (see separate entry)—one of the most successful publishing companies in American popular (as well as country) music history. Rose also wrote some of country music's most treasured classics, including Bob Wills' "Deep Water," "Blue Eyes Crying in the Rain" (a career-making hit for Willie Nelson in 1975, years after Rose wrote it) "Take These Chains from My Heart" (a Number One for Hank Williams in 1953) and "Tears on My Pillow." He liked collaborating with others, and consequently formed successful songwriting partnerships with artists such as Hank Williams. He heard raw talent when he signed Williams to Acuff-Rose in 1946, and became Hank's collaborator and record producer. Rose produced virtually all of Hank's recordings from his early Sterling discs to his final ones, and got Hank his MGM recording contract. Many friends of Hank's, including DJ Hugh Cherry, credit Rose with doing extensive work on some of Hank's numbers, like "I'm So Lonesome I Could Cry," while other, more direct numbers, clearly revealed more of Hank than the more schooled writing of Rose. Rose also worked closely with writer Jenny Lou Carson. Among the dozens of recording artists whose songs were published by Acuff-Rose were Felice and Boudleaux Bryant, John D. Loudermilk, Roy Orbison, The Everly Brothers and Marty Robbins, Ray Whitley and Hy Heath. Rose, a Christian scientist, did not believe in doctors, and after one heart attack, a second coronary killed him. His son Wesley (see separate entry) took over Acuff-Rose and ran it until his death. In 1961 Fred Rose became one of the first members inducted into the Country Music Hall of Fame.—R.K.

Wesley Rose

BORN: February 11, 1918
BIRTHPLACE: Chicago, Illinois
DIED: April 26, 1990

Wesley H. Rose, along with his father, legendary songwriter/publisher Fred Rose, and Opry king Roy Acuff, co-founded Acuff-Rose Publishing Company. (See entries for Hank Williams, Fred Rose and Acuff-Rose.)

This fledgling concern took a giant step toward becoming one of the most powerful music publishing and recording conglomerates in Music City when, in the fall of 1946, a scraggly-looking singer walked in off the streets and interrupted the elder and younger Rose in the middle of a father-son ping-pong competition to ask if he could pitch them some songs. The singer, of course, was Hank Williams; and he was one of many country greats that Wesley Rose would be associated with in the coming years.

The Chicago-born Wesley hesitated at first about leaving his job as an accountant with the Standard Oil Company when his father requested his presence in Nashville to help get Acuff-Rose under way. But after taking over the executive reins of the company in 1945 (so that Fred could devote more time

to songwriting and break songwriters like Williams), he quickly adapted to the music business. Throughout the next three decades, he matured into one of the most powerful and foresighted executive/ publisher/producers in country music.

Rose is credited with "discovering" The Everly Brothers, Roy Orbison and scores of other notables who ended up having long associations with Acuff-Rose and, in some cases, its ancillary recording arm, Hickory Records (founded in 1954). Along with his father, Rose was also one of the first publishers to exploit the pop/crossover market in a big way, by successfully pitching Acuff-Rose country tunes to pop stars of the day like Mitch Miller, Patti Page, Rosemary Clooney and Tony Bennett. Rose was also— like his father—a gifted "song doctor": he had a knack for taking diamonds in the rough that were brought to him by his various staff songwriters and deftly editing the lyrics and streamlining the melodies until they were polished diamonds. Rose was, for years, active in the leadership of the CMA, and was made a member of the Country Music Hall of Fame in 1986, four years prior to his death. In his later years, he suffered from Alzheimer's disease.   —B.A.

Billy Joe Royal

BORN: April 3, 1942
BIRTHPLACE: Valdosta, Georgia

This Valdosta, Georgia-born singer (whose first paying musical job was opening for Gladys Knight and The Pips, which netted him five dollars) is best known for his country and R&B-flavored pop hits of the 1960's, like "Down in the Boondocks," "Cherry Hill Park," "Hush" and "I Knew You When." After falling off the musical map in the 1970's ("I was almost out in the streets," he has since recalled), Royal re-emerged in the 1980's with a string of pop-flavored country hits—"I Miss You Already," "I'll Pin a Note on Your Pillow," "Out of Sight and Out of Mind," "It Keeps Right on Hurtin'" and "Tell It Like It Is," a 1989 remake of Aaron Neville's 1967 R&B hit, which reached Number Two. He earned a Gold record for his 1987 album, *The Royal Treatment,* and opened the 90's with another flurry of minor chart records.   —B.A.

Johnny Russell

BORN: January 23, 1940
BIRTHPLACE: Sunflower County, Mississippi

Born in Sunflower County, Mississippi, in early 1940, singer/guitarist Johnny Russell spent the better part of two decades trying to break through as an artist. His first success, though, came as a songwriter: His most famous composition, "Act Naturally," became a 1963 Top Ten hit for Buck Owens

and was later recorded by The Beatles. Johnny formed his own music publishing company in the mid-60's; his material yielded hit songs for artists like Burl Ives, Loretta Lynn and Patti Page.

Johnny was 40 years old by the time he landed his own contract with RCA in the early 70's. Perhaps feeling he had no time to waste, he scored a number of early hits, including "Mr. and Mrs. Untrue," "Rain Falling on Me," "The Baptism of Jesse Taylor" and "Rednecks, White Socks, and Blue Ribbon Beer," a Top Five in 1973 and his biggest career record. Johnny moved to Mercury Records in 1977 and made the low end of the charts with "We're Back in Love Again" and "Song of the South." Around the same time he got interested in acting and made guest appearances on several network TV series. He became a member of the Grand Ole Opry in 1985 and has since become a popular host on TNN's *Backstage at the Opry*.　　　　　　　　　　　—M.B.

Ryman Auditorium

Often referred to as "The Mother Church of Country Music," the Ryman Auditorium was the home of The Grand Ole Opry from 1943 until 1974, when the Opry moved to its present headquarters at the Opryland Entertainment Complex, a dozen or so miles outside Nashville.

The Ryman was built by Captain Tom Ryman, the wealthy, hard-living owner of a fleet of "pleasure" (i.e.—drinking and gambling) boats that plied the Cumberland River. When the captain converted to devout Methodism after a lifetime of debauchery, he decided to erect a "gospell [sic] and tempernce [sic] Hall" in dedication to his new-found religious devotion. Construction began in 1889 on the Union Gospel Tabernacle (as it was then called). And when Captain Ryman passed on to his just rewards in 1904, it was renamed The Ryman Auditorium in his memory.

Besides housing the Opry, The Ryman, which was, for years, downtown Nashville's biggest public hall, was also put to other secular uses in the 20th century. In its heyday, the 3,000-seat auditorium hosted performances by everyone from Bob Hope and Tyrone Power to Woody Herman and Margaret Truman (who once gave a piano recital there).

Most important, during the 40's, 50's and 60's, the Ryman, located just off Lower Broadway, near the

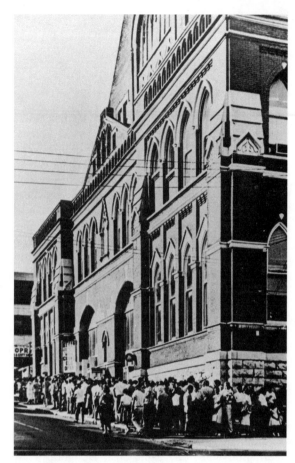

Cumberland River, and around the corner from other venerable country music institutions like Tootsie's Orchid Lounge, Ernest Tubb's Record Shop and Linebaugh's Cafeteria, was the hub and focal point of the nation's fascination with country music.

Over the years, all the greats—from Hank Williams and Minnie Pearl to George Jones and Tammy Wynette—graced the Ryman's stage, and audiences would line up for several blocks to get seats for the Opry's nationally broadcast Saturday night show.

Since the Opry's departure from the hallowed Ryman, the old auditorium (which is on the National Register of Historic Places), has been kept open for tours and has remained a popular tourist attraction. Yet for quite a few years, its dusty old rafters seldom echoed with live music.

But happily, the somewhat down-on-its-luck old edifice has recently undergone renovation, and by mid-1994, was once again hosting a series of live country music shows. (See also, Grand Ole Opry.)　　　　　　　　　　　—B.A.

Art Satherley

BORN: October 19, 1889
BIRTHPLACE: Bristol, England
DIED: February 10, 1986

One of the first great country record producers, Arthur E. "Uncle Art" Satherley's career began far from anything to do with music. At age 23 he came to America and found a job in Wisconsin working for a chair manufacturer. When transferred to another one of the company's plants, in Grafton, Wisconsin, he discovered the company's Paramount Records subsidiary, which recorded many jazz and blues artists. Satherley himself had begun producing artists for the label by 1923. Later in the 20's he joined Plaza Music, which eventually evolved into the better-known American Recording Corporation, or ARC. There, he specialized in recording black blues singers and hillbilly artists. He signed Gene Autry, Roy Acuff, Bob Wills, The Light Crust Doughboys, Al Dexter, Ted Daffan, Hank Penny and The Radio Cowboys, Adolph Hofner, The Prairie Ramblers, The Hoosier Hot Shots, Bob Atcher and Bonnie Blue Eyes and many more, and continued working for the label after ARC was absorbed into Columbia Records in 1939. Satherley produced most of the classic hits of Autry, Wills, Acuff and others, always helping the artists record their music as they played it, without excessive interference. He named a Bob Wills fiddle instrumental "San Antonio Rose" and Wills nicknamed him "Uncle Art."

Satherley continued producing through the 40's and early 50's, signing Marty Robbins to Columbia in 1951. He reluctantly retired in 1952, and in 1971 was inducted into the Country Music Hall of Fame. In the 80's, Satherley still remained in relatively good health. He worked with longtime friend, former Fender Guitar executive Forrest White, to record a memorial album to be issued after his death, featuring some of the classic hits he produced, with his own taped commentary on each. —R.K.

Sawyer Brown

In the mid-1980's, when they first hit the charts, Sawyer Brown earned a somewhat dubious reputation as country music's ultimate party band: a popular touring act that's long on flash and excitement and short on musical substance, yet tremendously popular with the country-oriented fraternity party crowd. But that began to change in the 90's.

Sawyer Brown showed promise when it became the first group to win the Country Music Association's Horizon award for most promising new recording act. And it scored early in its career with chart-topping singles like "Step That Step" and "Leona." Yet, for years, Sawyer never could seem to get more than a modicum of respect from the critics, or from discerning country listeners over the age of 25.

Yet by the early 1990's, Sawyer Brown began surprising people. Though the band clung to its flamboyant, good-timey image, its original songs gradually began to take on a new depth and maturity. The group really turned the corner with its Number One 1991 hit, "The Walk." This song took a poignant and perceptive look at father-son relationships.

The fact that their original material has taken on a deeper resonance has certainly not diminished Sawyer Brown's reputation as country's hardest partiers. In fact, it's gradually earned the band wider commercial acceptance and even begrudging critical respect. In the early 1990's, the band has earned its first Gold albums (*The Dirt Road* and *Cafe on the Corner*) and scored a string of chart-topping hits,

including "Thank God for You," "The Dirt Road," "All These Years," "Some Girls Do" and "Cafe on the Corner."

Sawyer Brown's roots go back to the late 1970's at the University of Central Florida, where founding members Miller and Gregg "Hobie" Hubbard first teamed up to make music. Moving to Nashville in 1981, they eventually added bassist Jim Scholten, drummer Joe Smyth and guitarist Duncan Cameron (formerly of The Amazing Rhythm Aces) to round out their line-up. —B.A.

John Schneider

BORN: March 8, 1954
BIRTHPLACE: Mt. Kisco, New York

Schneider, who rose to prominence as "Bo Duke" on television's *Dukes of Hazzard* series, found a home on the country charts beginning in 1981 with a Top Ten cover of "It's Now or Never." In 1984, he signed with MCA and racked up nine Top Ten hits from '84 to '87, including four Number Ones: "I've Been Around Enough to Know," "Country Girls," "What's a Memory Like You (Doing in a Love Like This)" and "You're the Last Thing I Needed Tonight." The hits trailed off as he tried to balance acting and music, and he returned to acting full-time as the 80's came to an end. In retrospect, Schneider did a credible job for someone who was known primarily as an actor. —G.F.

Earl Scruggs

BORN: January 6, 1924
BIRTHPLACE: Flintville, North Carolina

Earl Eugene Scruggs remains the major innovator of the five-string banjo, who virtually defined its use in bluegrass and other musical forms. The syncopated

finger-picking style created a supercharged feel far beyond that of the "frailing" style in which chords were merely strummed on the banjo. The three-finger picking style on which Scruggs built his style already existed in his area of North Carolina, though he expanded on it dramatically. Earl began playing banjo young and worked on a radio show with The Morris Brothers in his teens. After graduating from high school in 1942, he worked in a defense job making parachutes. He went to Knoxville to join Lost John Miller and His Allied Kentuckians, who soon moved to WSM. Bill Monroe offered Scruggs a job after Monroe and his guitarist, Lester Flatt, heard the young banjoist. But Scruggs declined. After Miller quit touring, Scruggs needed work and joined Monroe in December of 1944. Scruggs' three-finger technique amazed everyone who heard it. He also finger picked guitar superbly.

In 1948 Flatt and Scruggs left Monroe to begin their legendary collaboration, which lasted over 20 years (see Flatt and Scruggs entry). Scruggs' musical interests had always ranged beyond traditional bluegrass. Thus after splitting with Lester in 1969, Earl stretched his horizons by playing with his sons Gary, a bassist, and Randy, a guitarist, in The Earl Scruggs revue. This all-electric band, also featuring former Flatt and Scruggs dobroist Josh Graves and fiddle virtuoso Vassar Clements, had a strong country-rock flavor.

The Earl Scruggs Revue did well for several years, with Steve Scruggs replacing the group's original drummer, Joe Maphis' son, Jody. They did a number of albums for Columbia throughout the 70's before the collaboration wound down. In 1982 Earl and Tom

T. Hall recorded an album together called *The Story Teller and The Banjo Man*. Gary and Randy started a recording studio and have done extensive production work with contemporary artists. After a near-fatal plane crash, Earl briefly collaborated with Rodney Dillard. In July 1994, Scruggs and Bill Monroe performed together for the first time since 1948. —R.K.

Dan Seals

BORN: February 8, 1948
BIRTHPLACE: McCamey, Texas

Dan Seals was born in McCamey, Texas, in 1948 and first came to prominence as half of England Dan and John Ford Coley, a pop harmony duet team that scored a handful of hits in the mid-1970's, including "I'd Really Love to See You Tonight." (Dan's brother, Jim was half of Seals & Crofts, a very popular pop duet team that had its greatest success in that similar time frame; Troy Seals, a prominent Nashville songwriter, is Dan's first cousin.)

Splitting with Coley, Seals eventually went solo and had his first country Top Ten single with "God Must Be a Cowboy," in 1976. To a large extent, he's stuck with the cowboy motif ever since—and with considerable success.

His Number One country hits on EMI and Capitol include: "Let the Good Times Roll," "Love on Arrival," "Big Wheels in the Moonlight," "Addicted," "One Friend," "I Will Be There," "Meet Me in Montana" (a duet with Marie Osmond which won a Duet of the Year award from the Country Music Association) and "Bop." This latter song, a 50's revival-style hit, is one of Seals' biggest career records to date. It won the Country Music Association's 1986 Single of the Year award. He's most recently recorded for Warner Bros.

Asked about the gentle, idealistic quality that permeates so much of his music, Seals explained in a recent interview: "There is a side of me that dreams and hopes for a better world. We're all members of the human race....If we were unified with each other we could knock out the problems of the world a whole lot quicker. We could all get together and make...a beautiful garden." —B.A.

Troy Seals

BORN: November 16, 1938
BIRTHPLACE: Big Hill, Kentucky

Troy Seals, cousin of singers Jim and Dan Seals and uncle of Brady Seals of Little Texas, was born in Big Hill, Kentucky. A prolific Nashville songwriter and an occasional recording artist, he briefly recorded with his wife Joanne, as Joanne & Troy during the 1960's. Seals moved to Nashville in 1969 and has been steadily writing hit songs almost ever since. Some of his biggest titles to date are: "Feelins'," a 1975 Number One for Loretta Lynn and Conway Twitty, "Lost in The Fifties Tonight (In the Still of the Night)," which was a huge crossover hit for Ronnie Milsap, and "I Got a Thing About You Baby," a minor hit for Elvis Presley in 1974. Between 1973 and 1980, Seals also released a few minor chart records of his own on the Columbia and Elektra labels. —B.A.

Jeannie Seely

BORN: July 6, 1940
BIRTHPLACE: Titusville, Pennsylvania

Jeannie Seely was born in tiny Titusville, Pennsylvania, in 1940. As a teenager she had her own weekly regional radio show, then moved to Nashville in the 1960's. She signed with Monument Records and had her first Top Ten hit in 1966, "Don't Touch Me." It was a song that changed Jeannie's life, winning her a Grammy (Best Country Vocal Performance-Female)

and introducing her to her future husband, songwriter Hank Cochran. The following year, Jeannie joined the cast of the Grand Ole Opry and had two more Top Ten hits on Monument, "A Wanderin' Man" and "Welcome Home to Nothing," before switching to the MCA label in 1969. She had a number of hits in the 1970's, mostly written, not surprisingly, by Cochran: "Tell Me Again," "Can I Sleep in Your Arms Tonight Mister" and "I Miss You." Seely remains an Opry member today.   —M.B.

The Seldom Scene

Five Washington, D.C.-area bluegrass musicians conceived The Seldom Scene in fall 1971 as a means to play regularly without sacrificing their day jobs; as a result, the band is "seldom seen." The original band included two veterans of the celebrated bluegrass ensemble Country Gentlemen: mandolinist/tenor singer John Duffey and bassist Tom Gray; and two former members of Cliff Waldron's New Shades of Grass: banjo player Ben Eldridge and Dobroist Mike Auldridge. The only newcomer was guitarist and lead singer John Starling, an army surgeon by profession. Although he was well-versed in traditional bluegrass, Starling's phrasing and repertoire drew more from contemporary pop-folk stylists like James Taylor than it did from conventional bluegrass singers.

Playing weekly at a Bethesda, Maryland, pizzeria, the Seldom Scene quickly developed a loyal following; a series of albums on Rebel brought them ac-

claim outside of the Washington area. The group's folk-influenced vocals, diverse repertoire and occasional free-form, extended instrumental solos, generated controversy within purist bluegrass circles. The Seldom Scene's music was eventually classified as "contemporary bluegrass"; it has since became the genre's predominant style, and they, one of its predominant bands.

The band's personnel remained relatively stable through the years. Singer-songwriter Phil Rosenthal replaced Starling in 1977; Lou Reid replaced him nine years later. T. Michael Coleman replaced bassist Gray in 1988. Starling returned after Reid's departure in 1992. The band remains one of the most popular fixtures on the bluegrass circuit and still performs weekly at the famed suburban northern Virginia listening room, The Birchmere.   —D.S.

Sanger D. "Whitey" Shafer

BORN: October 24, 1934
BIRTHPLACE: Whitney, Texas

One of the kings of the honky tonk songwriting genre, Whitey Shafer's vast catalogue of original material includes some of the true honky tonk anthems of the past 30 years. "All My Ex's Live in Texas" (popularized by George Strait), "That's the Way Love Goes" (covered by the late Lefty Frizzell and more recently by Johnny Rodriguez and Merle Haggard), "I Never Go Around Mirrors" (Lefty Frizzell, Keith Whitley), "Bandy the Rodeo Clown," "Honky Tonk Amnesia," "I Just Started Hatin' Cheatin' Songs Today" (all three hits for Moe Bandy), "I Wonder Do You Think of Me" (Keith Whitley) and "The Baptism of Jesse Taylor" (Johnny Russell) are just some of Shafer's well known titles.

A former turkey farmer from Whitney, Texas, Shafer (who's co-written many of his hits with A.L. "Doodle" Owen, another noted honky tonk song scribe) had the good fortune to have Lefty Frizzell as a neighbor when he first moved to Nashville. "When I met Lefty, he was in a pretty heavy drinkin' phase, and so was I," recalled Shafer, who eventually befriended Frizzell and began co-writing with him.

Recording for Elektra, Shafer had a few minor chart singles of his own in the early 1980's, including such representative titles as "You Are a Liar" and "If I Say I Love You (Consider Me Drunk)."   —B.A.

way ensemble with steel guitarist Herb Remington and electric mandolinist Tiny Moore. Not long before leaving Wills, Leo Fender gave him a prototype Fender Stratocaster, which he used for years. After leaving Wills around 1954, Shamblin returned to Tulsa where he played music on the side and repaired electronic organs. He didn't begin extensive musical work again until after Merle Haggard recruited him to play on his 1970 Wills tribute album. That eventually led to Shamblin joining Merle Haggard's band, The Strangers, in the 1970's. He remained with Haggard until the 1980's, then joined The Original Texas Playboys led by Leon McAuliffe until they disbanded. He continues to work with Playboys II, usually led by veteran Wills sidemen Johnny Gimble and Herb Remington. Shamblin has taught music theory at Oklahoma colleges as well. —R.K.

Eldon Shamblin

BORN: April 24, 1916
BIRTHPLACE: Tulsa, Oklahoma

Seldom do rhythm guitar specialists become legends, but Estel Eldon Shamblin became one long ago. He worked on KTUL in Tulsa, and with the early Western swing band, Dave Edwards and His Alabama Boys, before Bob Wills recruited him for the Texas Playboys. Shamblin's skill at arranging played a major role in improving the sound of the Playboys, particularly as they evolved into a big dance band in the late 30's and early 40's. Just as important was his work as a guitarist. His rhythm guitar playing became the pulse that drove the Tulsa Playboy rhythm section along with Smokey Dacus' drums. By the early 40's Shamblin and steel guitarist Leon McAuliffe began creating guitar-steel guitar ensembles, most notably "Twin Guitar Special."

Shamblin remained with the Playboys until 1942, before entering the Army where he worked in accounting and rose to the rank of Captain. He returned to the Playboys in 1946, becoming the band's road manager as well as guitarist.

Shamblin's role changed as he added more lead guitar to his playing, working for a time in a three-

Billy Joe Shaver

BORN: August 16, 1939
BIRTHPLACE: Corsicana, Texas

An Outlaw singer-songwriter who rose to prominence between the late 1960's and early 1970's, Billy Joe Shaver was born in Corsicana, Texas.

After having been raised by his grandmother, who encouraged his interest in music, Shaver struck out on his own when he was barely a teenager, working a number of jobs ranging from gas station attendant and carpenter to bronco buster, bull rider and sawmill worker (where he lost a couple of fingers in an accident).

Deciding to take a stab at songwriting, he made periodic trips to Nashville where he was greeted by slamming doors. Nevertheless, Shaver persisted; and after several years it finally paid off when Bobby Bare signed him as a writer after he wandered into Bare's office one day without an appointment and played Bare some of his now famous songs. In 1971, Shaver's credentials as a talented tunesmith were carved in stone when Kris Kristofferson included his "Good Christian Soldier" on his album, *The Silver-Tongued Devil*.

His biggest breakthrough, however, occurred in 1973 when Waylon Jennings based an entire album, *Honky Tonk Heroes*, on Shaver's compositions. Around the same time Tom T. Hall used Shaver's "Old Five and Dimers" as the title tune to one of his albums. Since then, Shaver's earthy, hard-hitting and lyrically inspired songs have been recorded by artists such as Elvis Presley ("You Ask Me To"), Johnny Cash ("Jesus Was Our Savior, Cotton Was Our King"), The Allman Brothers Band ("Sweet Mama"), John Anderson ("I'm Just an Old Chunk of Coal"), and also Jerry Jeff Walker, Tennessee Ernie Ford, The Sons of the Pioneers, George Jones and Conway Twitty.

Between 1973 and 1982, Shaver recorded four albums for the Monument, Capricorn and Columbia labels, including his classic Monument debut album, *Old Five and Dimes and Other Rhymes*, which was produced by Kris Kristofferson and featured liner notes from Tom T. Hall. All four albums received widespread critical acclaim, but did little commercially. Throughout the 1980's and into the 1990's, Shaver took a break from recording and focused on writing and playing honky tonks across the U.S.

In 1993, he released *Tramp On Your Street* for Zoo/Praxis. The record, which also featured his son, Eddie, on lead guitar, marked a triumphant return to the bare-bones, stripped-down, rough-hewn music and vividly inspired composition of his earlier works. —R.P.

Ricky Van Shelton

BORN: January 12, 1952
BIRTHPLACE: Danville, Virginia

For the span of a half-dozen or so albums, before he was displaced by a younger wave of crooners who looked better in tank tops, Ricky Van Shelton was country's resident sex symbol.

Though not an outstanding singer, Shelton did at least play a narrow role in the late 80's New Traditionalism surge with his lilting brand of rockabilly/honky-tonk/country boogie, which seemed to owe as much to more obscure 50's and 60's influences like Faron Young and Webb Pierce as it did to Hank, Lefty and the usual crowd.

Raised in the small Pittsylvania County community of Grit, in extreme southern Virginia, Shelton grew up in a hard-shell Pentecostal household where even country music was frowned upon. Maybe that's why, when he reached his teens, it was rock 'n' roll music that he first gravitated toward.

By the mid-70's, however, Shelton had become immersed in country music in a big way. Having taught himself guitar, he took to singing at local get-togethers. (There was a distinct absence of clubs in the Grit area.) It was around this time that he also made the first of many forays down Interstates 81 and 40 to Nashville. In between, he supported himself and his musical obsession by painting houses, refinishing cabinets, doing farm work, managing an appliance store and whatever else it took to keep himself in beer and guitar strings.

It proved fortuitous when, in 1984, Shelton's wife Bettye got a job transfer to Nashville. For the next couple of years, Bettye went off every day to bring home the bacon while Shelton stayed at home, writing songs, rehearsing, and making home-made demo tapes which he passed around town. By night, he'd make the rounds of the Nashville club scene, performing when he could and handing out his little 3-for-$1.99 demo tapes to whoever would take them.

It was actually Bettye's friendship with the wife of

award-winning Nashville author/newspaper columnist Jerry Thompson that ultimately paved Shelton's way to the big time. Thompson himself became so impressed with Shelton's singing that he personally arranged an audition with an acquaintance, Rick Blackburn, then head of CBS/Nashville. Shelton passed the audition with flying colors, and two weeks later was in the studio with producer Steve Buckingham, working on *Wild-Eyed Dream*, his 1987 debut album, which eventually went platinum—the first of a several that would surpass the million sales mark.

Hits from *Wild-Eyed Dream* included chart-toppers like "Crime of Passion" and "Somebody Lied," along with remakes of Roger Miller's "Don't We All Have the Right" and Harlan Howard's "Life Turned Her That Way." They made Shelton an instant hero in an industry that was just beginning to realize the potential that lay in recycling the musical greatness of previous decades. *Loving Proof* (1988), his second album, was similarly propelled up the charts by a string of chart-topping revivalist hits, including "I'll Leave This World Loving You" and a spirited revival of the 1962 Ned Miller jukebox hit, "From a Jack to a King." These albums, as well as *RVSIII* (1990), and others which have since followed, have been studded by worthy remakes of semi-forgotten masterpieces by Hank Cochran, Wayne Kemp, Felice and Boudleaux Bryant, The Wilburn Brothers and other top Nashville tunesmiths of yesteryear.

Shelton's impressive run in the charts continued until well into the 90's—though by then a creeping perception was beginning to take hold that he was merely an idiot savant: a hard worker and a gifted singer who nonetheless seemed satisfied to leave creative decisions to his producer while coasting along on his good looks. It's hard to say which happened first—whether country fans began to cool on his stylistic redundancy or whether he, feeling his age, began to burn out on the rigorous, never-ending demands of touring. Whatever the reason, he took a couple of years' sabbatical from the studio during which he wrote a children's book called *Tales of a Duck Named Quacker*. But by 1993, he was back in the studio and out on the road, full-tilt, once again—though the world now had younger and more vital musical heroes like Garth Brooks and John Michael Montgomery and seemed a lot less interested. He's been an Opry member since 1988.   —B.A.

Shenandoah

Shenandoah has often been referred to as the "other" band from Alabama. With a string of hits based on a soulful gospel-derived harmony style—"The Church on Cumberland Road," "Sunday in the South," "Two Dozen Roses," "Next to You, Next to Me"—this accomplished band has carved a niche for itself in the early 90's country scene.

"If you want to know what we're like, just look at our 'Sunday in the South' video," lead singer Marty Raybon (who has been described as "a cross between Otis Redding and George Jones") once offered. "It says a lot about our beliefs, our backgrounds, what we're all about. I think in the years since we got into this, the five of us have grown, not only as musicians and men, but as fathers and husbands. And I think you can hear that in our music."

Raybon himself hails from Sanford, Florida, where he was born in 1960. He can still recall his parents scraping by and trying to support their five kids, picking oranges and bay leaves for $1.35 an hour. By the time he was in his teens, Raybon was singing in The Bluegrass Alliance, a Florida state champion bluegrass band, which also included his father and brothers.

By the early 80's, Raybon landed in Nashville where he fronted a number of ultimately unsuccessful groups while practically starving to death. In the meantime, Stan Thorn, Mike McGuire, Ralph Ezell, and Jim Seales, the other four musicians who would ultimately comprise Shenandoah, had all descended on Muscle Shoals, Alabama's musical capital, from various locales and were earning comfortable livings as songwriters and session pickers. When they decided to form an impromptu band to play the Muscle Shoals club scene, strictly for pleasure, they came up short a lead singer. Alerted to the opening by a mutual friend, Raybon auditioned, was hired, and promptly relocated from Music City to Muscle Shoals, 120 or so miles to the southeast. "It was $350 a week, which, to me, was a mint at that time," he recalled.

Shenandoah (which actually began recording together when the other members pitched in on some sessions to help Raybon try and land a solo deal) first hit the top of charts in the late 1980's; but just as they were approaching headliner status, the band was hit with a flurry of crippling copyright suits over the ownership of its name. The ensuing litigation virtually hamstrung the band for a couple of years, during which they were kept out of the recording studio by injunction, and what little money they made on the road quickly went toward legal fees.

But in the early 1990's, Shenandoah reemerged and quickly made up for lost time with a pair of strong albums: *Long Time Comin'* (1992) and *Under the Kudzu* (1993).

"As a band, we've been brothers and best friends through the Number One records and Gold albums, and through the worst of times, as well," Raybon explained in a *Country Music Magazine* interview. "I think our recent records really reaffirm what we've been about from the very beginning, which is: 'Point us toward the stage and turn us loose.' Because it's the music that's carried us through this far. And I guarantee you, if you love something as much as we love our music, then folks around you can't help but love it and have a good time, too."   —B.A.

Jean Shepard

BORN: November 21, 1933
BIRTHPLACE: Pauls Valley, Oklahoma

Singer/bassist Jean Shepard was still a teenager when she began performing with an all-girl country band called the Melody Ranch Girls in Bakersfield, California. A few years later, Hank Thompson passed through town while on tour; impressed with Jean's voice, he brought her to the attention of Capitol Records. After signing with Capitol in 1953, Jean recorded "A Dear John Letter," a duet with Ferlin Husky that went on to become a Number One hit. As a solo performer, Jean cracked the Top Ten twice in 1955

with "Beautiful Lies" and "Satisfied Mind." She joined the Grand Ole Opry that same year.

In 1963, in the midst of her professional success, Jean experienced sudden personal tragedy when her husband, Hawkshaw Hawkins, was killed in the same plane crash that claimed the life of superstar Patsy Cline. After Hawkins' death, Jean channeled her grief into her work, scoring a string of Top Ten singles: "Second Fiddle (To an Old Guitar)" in 1964, "I'll Take the Dog" (with Ray Pillow), "If Teardrops Were Silver" in 1966 and "Yours Forever" in 1971. From the mid-1950's to the early 70's, Jean's output had been prolific, averaging one album per year. In 1974, she left Capitol after 21 years with the label. She signed with United Artists and had a number of hits, most notably "Come on Phone" in 1974 and "Another Neon Night" in 1976. Shepard remains a popular Opry member today.   —M.B.

T. G. Sheppard

BORN: July 20, 1944
BIRTHPLACE: Humboldt, Tennessee

Born William Browder, in Humboldt, Tennessee, T. G. Sheppard enjoyed evanescent success in the 1970's and early 1980's with hits like "Try and Beat the Morning Home," "Motels and Memories," "The Last Cheater's Waltz" and "Solitary Man" that straddled the murky musical territory between neo-honky tonk and "easy-listening country."

Sheppard actually began singing professionally in Memphis in his teens and made some early rock 'n' roll recordings (including "High School Days") under the name of Brian Stacy. When these efforts came to naught, he ended up as a record promoter for RCA, sang backup for Travis Womack's band and began writing songs on the side. In 1974, he launched his career by making his own recording of a song everybody else had turned down: Bobby David's "Devil in the Bottle." It was released on Motown's Melodyland label and became one of his biggest hits and his stepping stone to success.   —B.A.

Billy Sherrill

BORN: November 5, 1936
BIRTHPLACE: Phil Campbell, Alabama

Born into modest circumstances, Billy Sherrill rose through the ranks to become the most influential country producer of the 1970's and one of the most significant Nashville record-makers of all time. George Jones (who Sherrill produced for nearly two decades), Charlie Rich, Tammy Wynette, Tanya Tucker, David Allan Coe, Johnny Paycheck, David Houston, Lacy J. Dalton, Johnny Rodriguez, Marty Robbins, Johnny Duncan, Janie Fricke, Ray Charles and even rocker Elvis Costello are just a few of the many artists whose careers Sherrill has helped shape with his uncanny ear for a hit song and his knack for creating distinct musical personas for his artists. Along the way, he's amassed a track record that includes upwards of a hundred Number One records.

Ironically, Sherrill, the son of an evangelist preacher (who often played piano at tent meetings and funerals while his father preached), started out touring the South as a sax player in R&B and rock bands. "Back

then, I was strictly into R&B and B.B. King," he recalled. "I hated country music, and I figured anyone who liked it was a redneck."

Nonetheless, in 1962, when an obscure Nashville artist recorded a song he'd written and he got a royalty check for $4,000, Sherrill eagerly moved to Nashville and ended up working as an engineer in a small studio owned by legendary Memphis producer Sam Phillips. A year later, he hired on with Epic/Nashville, a division of CBS Records, as a "shotgun producer: Ten grand a year and I produced whoever nobody else wanted.

"I still knew about as much about country music as the Shah of Iran," he explained. "So I just decided to do it my way, and screw 'em if they didn't like it. Back then, the musicians had their own repertoire of stock Nashville licks and chord progressions that would work on any song. But I often wanted something different and would make them play it."

Influenced by rock 'n' roll "Wall of Sound" producer Phil Specter and by early Nashville sound pioneer Don Law, Sherrill began experimenting with a bigger, fuller sound in country music and soon pushed the lush Nashville Sound pioneered by 50's and 60's producers like Chet Atkins and his own mentor, Don Law, a step or two further. He hooked up Tammy Wynette (a then unknown Alabama waitress and hairdresser who wandered unannounced into his office one day) with siren songs like "Stand By Your Man" (which he also co-wrote). He paired veteran David Houston up with "Almost Persuaded" (a million-seller, which Sherrill also co-wrote, and which won a Grammy). In the early 70's, Sherrill got hold of Charlie Rich, who'd had only modest success after years as a white blues and R&B singer, and plugged him into a brand-new pop-country sound that resulted in massive crossover hits like "Behind Closed Doors" and "The Most Beautiful Girl."

These are just a few of many Sherrill "success stories" that illustrated his wizardry at teaming obscure recording artists with the right songs and making them superstars.

Over the years, Sherrill has taken his share of critical flack for perpetuating the over-produced Nashville Sound with its pop string and choral stylings. Yet it was Sherrill who, by and large, kept George Jones on the straight-and-narrow hard country/honky-tonk path, even during the early 1970's when that style of music had fallen from favor. And it was with Sherrill at the console that Jones made some of his most all-time memorable recordings.

"A lot of producers can't even carry a tune, and they're great song pickers, and then they turn it over to arrangers and musicians to do it," Sherrill, who, by the mid-1990's, had eased into retirement, explained of his notion of record production in a mid-1980's interview with *Country Music Magazine*'s Bob Allen. "But arrangers with perfect pitch and musicians with doctorates in music can't pick a hit song. They just know what to do with one when they get it. A producer, I guess, is a catalyst between the writer and the artist and the arranger and the public. You have to try to have the ears of the public and recognize what they like." —B.A.

Steve Sholes

BORN: February 12, 1911
BIRTHPLACE: Washington, D.C.
DIED: April 22, 1968

Steve Sholes started with RCA Victor as a part-time messenger boy in 1929, while still a student at Rutgers University in New Jersey. Sholes went to work full-time for the record label six year later, and from then, until his death in 1968, he was a key figure, not only in making RCA a major player in the country field, but also in the parallel growth of Nashville as a recording industry.

Sholes, an inductee into the Country Music Hall of Fame in 1967, began making his earliest field recording excursions into the deep South during the years immediately following World War II. He assumed the position of RCA's head of country A&R shortly thereafter.

Sholes (who never moved to Nashville but spent much time there and was deeply involved in the country music community) began recording his label's country artists in Nashville as early as 1949. (Johnnie and Jack was one of the first acts that he both signed and produced.) At first, he worked out of Brown Radio Productions, a small studio in downtown Nashville.

In 1952-3, he made another propitious move on behalf of the label. He appointed guitarist Chet Atkins, whom he'd signed to RCA as an artist in 1947, as his Nashville production assistant. In the next few years, Sholes and Atkins, working out of various, small Nashville facilities, would record early country stars

like Pee Wee King, Mother Maybelle Carter, The Osborne Brothers and The Davis Sisters.

Sholes gave RCA a major boost when he snapped up Elvis Presley's contract from Sun Records (for a mere $30,000) and produced some of Presley's earliest sessions for the label. He also played a crucial role in signing other early notables like Eddy Arnold, Jim Reeves, Porter Wagoner, Hank Snow, Hank Laughlin, Skeeter Davis and Homer & Jethro.

In 1957, under Sholes' direction, RCA became the first major label to build its own permanent studio facilities in Nashville. With Sholes' former protégé Chet Atkins at the helm, RCA would become a pivotal force in shaping country music in the latter half of the 20th century. Sholes was elected to the Country Music Hall of Fame in 1967, a year before he died of a heart attack while driving his car. —B.A.

Red Simpson

BORN: March 6, 1934
BIRTHPLACE: Higley, Arizona

Though Joseph "Red" Simpson had a brief run of chart action, his greatest success came as a songwriter for fellow Bakersfield singer Buck Owens. Born in Arizona, his family moved to Bakersfield in 1937. In the 50's he began working clubs around Bakersfield, including the legendary Blackboard Club. He wrote numerous songs for (and with) Buck Owens, including hits like "Gonna Have Love," "Sam's Place" and "The Kansas City Song."

In the mid-60's Simpson also recorded for Capitol on his own, including a rare album of police songs: *The Man Behind the Badge*. He also concentrated on trucker songs; his *Roll, Truck, Roll* album is a classic in the genre. His biggest hit was the 1971 novelty, "I'm a Truck." His later trucker recordings for Capitol, Warner and K.E.Y. didn't do as well. Today Simpson still writes and performs in the Bakersfield area. —R.K.

Asher and
Little Jimmie Sizemore

BORN: Asher, June 6, 1906, Manchester, Kentucky
     Jimmie, January 29, 1928, Paintsville, Kentucky
DIED: Asher, 1973; Jimmie, 1985

The most popular of numerous child stars to grace the country airwaves in the 1930's, Little Jimmie Sizemore had the distinction of being the youngest member of the Grand Ole Opry. He and his father joined the show in 1934, when Jimmie was six years old, and was specializing in songs like "My Little Rooster," "Chawin' Chewin' Gum" and "Has Anybody Seen My Kitty." Father Asher Sizemore (born in Manchester, Kentucky, in 1906) was a smooth ballad singer, but a better promoter and showman who pioneered the selling of songbooks by mail, and the use of transcriptions to get his shows into several markets. By the end of the 1930's, Jimmie's brother, Buddy Boy, had joined the act, which by now was heard regularly on the NBC network. Asher and Little Jimmie recorded for Bluebird in 1934. Asher died in Arkansas in 1973, and Jimmie, who had gone into radio management, died in 1985. —C.W.

Ricky Skaggs

BORN: July 18, 1954
BIRTHPLACE: Cordell, Kentucky

Bluegrass wizard Ricky Skaggs, a forerunner of the mid-1980's New Traditionalist boom, came into country music from a bluegrass background during a particularly fallow period in the early 1980's, and helped keep the music on the country straight and narrow. His mandolin & banjo-meets-electric guitar bluegrass-driven rootsy country style produced a string of Number One hits—11 of them in all, including "Crying My Heart Out Over You" (1982), "Heartbroke" (1982),

"Wouldn't Change You if I Could" (1982), "Don't Cheat in Our Hometown" (1983), "Honey (Open That Door)" (1984), "Country Boy" (1985) and his brilliant cover of Bill Monroe's "Uncle Pen" (1984). The Monroe chestnut was one of many traditional country and bluegrass tunes he revved up and retrofitted for the 80's. With his resolutely tradition-flavored recordings from this era he helped pull country music back from the overproduced pop/crossover precipice, at least for a few years.

Skaggs is a Kentucky boy, born into the bluegrass tradition at Cordell, Kentucky, on July 18, 1954. He was a child prodigy who, before he was even out of his teens, was already playing with a number of the bluegrass and country greats. Ralph Stanley (he sang in Stanley's Clinch Mountain Boys for several years, along with his boyhood friend, the late Keith Whitley), J.D. Crowe, Emmylou Harris (whose Hot Band he joined in 1977) and The Country Gentlemen are just of some of the artists he worked with in his formative years. After recording a number of independent bluegrass and newgrass albums (including some with his own band, Boone Creek), he released *Waiting for the Sun to Shine* in 1981. His first major label release, *Waiting for the Sun to Shine* helped redefine country music during a creatively bankrupt era when Nashville was suffering through a post-mechanical bull Urban Cowboy identity crisis. The prickly Skaggs held his ground on production values and stuck to his fundamentalist guns and his love of the older, purer country sounds, which he tastefully updated with wistful vocals and sprightly electrification. Ultimately, record buyers gave him their vote of confidence at the cash register. Skaggs also walked away with the Country Music Association's Entertainer of the Year Award (1985), its Male Vocalist of the Year Award (1982), its Duo of the Year Award (which he won in 1987, along with his wife, singer Sharon White), and its Horizon Award (1982).

He peaked in the early 1980's—after three Gold albums, he grabbed the 1985 CMA Entertainer of the Year Award while his anthemic "Country Boy" single was in heavy rotation at radio stations all over the world. In recent years, the old quilt has become pretty threadbare. He continues performing, often working closely with his wife's group, The Whites. He joined The Grand Ole Opry in 1982 and has been an active member ever since. In recent years, Skaggs, who has recorded much gospel music over the years, has become even more deeply involved in activities stemming from his fundamentalist Christian faith. —M.B.

Jimmie Skinner

BORN: April 27, 1909
BIRTHPLACE: Blue Lick, Ohio
DIED: October 27, 1979

Skinner, who wrote the classic, "Doin' My Time," found his first success on a tiny station in Newport, Kentucky, in the 1940's. He next worked at WNOX in Knoxville as a DJ. He later moved to Ohio and made his early recordings for the Red Barn label. His first hit was a cover version of the hit, "Tennessee Border," in 1949 for a small label. He moved to Cincinnati, and in 1951, in the style of Ernest Tubb, he opened a retail and mail order record outlet, the Jimmie Skinner Music Center in Cincinnati and broadcast a radio show over a station in Kentucky. Skinner signed with Mercury/Starday in the late 50's and was produced by Don Pierce and Pappy Daily, the team who'd had great success with George Jones' earliest releases. Songs like "I Found My Girl in the U.S.A." (a Top Five hit in 1957) and his most well-known song, "Dark Hollow" (Number Seven in 1959), were his most memorable releases. His later Mercury sides charted, but his last chart entry came

in 1969. He subsequently recorded for a variety of labels with no real success, including Vetco, owned by an employee in his music store. —R.K.

Fiddlin' Arthur Smith

BORN: April 10, 1898
BIRTHPLACE: Humphrey's County, Tennessee
DIED: February 28, 1971

Arthur Smith, first of the modern Southeastern fiddlers had a smooth, aggressive style relying on slow bow strokes and slurred, blues-tinged fingering. It greatly influenced Howdy Forrester, Tommy Magness, Curly Fox and the bluegrass musicians who followed. Many Smith arrangements and compositions remain part of today's fiddlers' repertoires. Among the tunes he popularized were "Blackberry Blossom," "Bonaparte's Retreat" and the jazz pieces, "Florida Blues" and "House of David Blues." His original instrumentals include "Red Apple Rag" and "Peacock Rag."

Smith appeared as a solo fiddler on the Grand Ole Opry as early as 1927. In 1932 he formed The Dixieliners with Sam and Kirk McGee; the trio became one of the Opry's most popular acts. In January 1935, Smith began recording for Bluebird, usually backed by The Delmore Brothers. His most popular records were vocals: "Walking in My Sleep," "Pig in the Pen," "There's More Pretty Girls Than One" and "Beautiful Brown Eyes" have become country music and bluegrass evergreens. For a time he worked in California with Western singer Jimmy Wakely. Smith returned to Nashville in 1948, but largely worked outside of music. In the late 1950's and early 60's he recorded for Folkways and Starday; he and The McGee Brothers made a memorable appearance at the 1964 Newport Folk Festival. He died on February 28, 1971, in Louisville, Kentucky. —D.S.

Arthur "Guitar Boogie" Smith

BORN: April 1, 1921
BIRTHPLACE: Clinton, South Carolina

Arthur Smith was a child prodigy on the guitar who at age 18, despite a distinguished high school record that could have gotten him to college, opted for his own radio show over WSPA in Spartanburg (young

Hank Garland, who lived nearby, was a fan). After working briefly in North Carolina he joined the Navy during World War II and was stationed around Washington, D.C. He came up with the idea for the song "Guitar Boogie" around 1944 while playing in his quarters at night. It went over so well with fellow sailors that he perfected the number. He recorded it with his Martin acoustic, backed by rhythm guitar and bass (The Rambler Trio) in Washington, D.C. When released on the New York-based Super Disc label, it sold well, the licks on the record later showing up in the repertoires of various rockabilly bands. MGM bought the Super Disc master, re-released it in 1947 and "Guitar Boogie" quickly became a massive hit nationwide. The financial success led Smith to open a recording studio, recording for MGM and later for Starday and hosting the *Arthur Smith Show* over WBT-TV in Charlotte. In 1973 his banjo instrumental, "Feudin' Banjos," wound up as "Dueling Banjos" in the movie *Deliverance*. Smith successfully sued to establish the song was his.   —R.K.

Arthur Q. Smith

BORN: Unknown
BIRTHPLACE: Grissom, Georgia
DIED: 1963

One of the most mysterious and unsung figures in country music, Arthur Q. Smith was a Knoxville songwriter who wrote some of the best-known pieces in the genre, yet sold them for a pittance to support his drinking habit. Smith's real name was James Pritchett, and though he was born in Grissom, Georgia, he grew up in Harlan, Kentucky. During the 1940's he tried a singing career, recording for Deluxe, King and other labels, as well as appearing on WNOX. For a time he was a staff writer for King and even signed to Acuff-Rose Publishing Company, but most of the time he stood outside radio studios selling songs for $10 to $25 each. His clients included Bill Monroe, Maybelle Carter, Carl Smith, Carl Butler, Hank Williams, Kitty Wells, Lost John Miller, Roy Acuff, Jim Eanes and others. His hit songs, hardly ever appearing with his name on them, included "Rainbow at Midnight," "I Wouldn't Change You If I Could," "I Overlooked an Orchid," "If Teardrops Were Pennies," "Wedding Bells" and "Missing in Action." Smith died in 1963, and in 1991 was the subject of a tribute song

"Be Careful Who You Love (Arthur's Song)," written by his former protégé, Harlan Howard, and recorded by Hank Williams Jr.   —C.W.

Cal Smith

BORN: April 7, 1932
BIRTHPLACE: Gans, Oklahoma

Born in Gans, Oklahoma, in 1932, and raised in Oakland, California, Calvin Grant Shofner (better known as Cal Smith) played in local clubs and worked as a DJ in San Jose before signing with Kapp Records in the mid-1960's. He cut two albums, scoring several minor hits, and in retrospect, is considered one of the most brilliant hard country singers to emerge in the late 60's and early 70's.

In the early 70's, Cal switched to the Decca label and made the Top Ten for the first time with the 1972 single, "I've Found Someone of My Own." The next year, he reached Number One with "The Lord Knows I'm Drinking." Soon after Decca merged with MCA Records, Cal struck Gold with the 1974 single, "Country Bumpkin," from the album of the same name. The album climbed the charts, while the single made it to Number One and won the annual Country Music Association Awards for Single and Song of the Year. It is a classic weeper, charting a woman's path from too much make-up and late nights at the honky-tonk to marriage, kids and, finally, death, while her country bumpkin cries. In the following years, he scored another Number One with "It's Time to Pay the Fiddler," and hit the Top 20 with "She Talked a Lot About Texas," "Jason's Farm" and "I Just Came Home to Count the Memories" (a Top 20 in 1977, which John Anderson revived four years later and took to Number Seven). Later singles charted progressively lower, and he left MCA in 1980.

His final chart entry came in 1986 on independent label Step One Records. During a 1994 appearance on The Nashville Network's *Music City Tonight*, Smith, who has since flourished as a businessman, gave one of his CMA awards to Garth Brooks, who lists "Country Bumpkin" as one of his favorite songs.   —M.B.

Carl Smith

BORN: March 15, 1927
BIRTHPLACE: Maynardsville, Tennessee

Many country music legends remain active in the business right up until the time of their death. Carl Smith is an exception to that rule. When changing times caused his phenomenally successful career to lose its luster, he chose to wind down his career and, finally, to retire with honor. As he explained in 1984, "I just got tired of it...didn't enjoy it and...was just burnt out with it." Six years before that, in 1978, he'd had his last record enter the *Billboard* charts.

A honky tonk giant of the 1950's, the former husband of June Carter and father of Carlene Carter, Smith was once at the top in a big way. In Joel Whitburn's compilation of the *Billboard* charts, *Top Country*

Singles: 1944-1988, Smith is listed as the Number 20 all-time country record seller. From 1951 to 1978 he had a total of 93 singles on the charts; 30 were Top Tens, and five became Number One records. Several of his hits have become standards, and his robust, energetic voice gave his records a distinctive punch different from anything then being done by Hank Williams or Lefty Frizzell.

Smith was born in the late Roy Acuff's hometown of Maynardsville, Tennessee, on March 15, 1927, and grew up taking inspiration from Acuff, Ernest Tubb and Bill Monroe records, copying them and trying to sing. He learned to play a string bass at age 17 and in 1944, he spent a summer vacation working at WROL Radio in Knoxville. After school and a brief stint in the U.S. Navy, he returned home and began pursuing a musical career, working with groups in North Carolina and Georgia before going back to WROL, where he played bass with Skeets Williamson.

(Williamson's sister, Molly O'Day, was just beginning to attract notice for her raw, emotional vocal style.)

He found his niche there, and his singing matured enough by the late 40's to prompt one of his colleagues at the station to send one of his acetate demo recordings to WSM. That demo found its way to Grand Ole Opry officials around 1948 or 1949. Smith, for his part, wasn't particularly concerned about it, as he was quite happy at WROL. He finally traveled to Nashville to do a guest shot on a Hank Williams WSM show that impressed the station sufficiently to sign him. He started out doing a WSM morning show and worked the Opry, and will go down in history as one of the final stars created by the long-gone Opry star-making system.

Producer Don Law at Columbia Records had heard Carl's demos around the same time WSM did and signed him in May 1950. The first hit was "Let's Live a Little," which reached Number Two in the summer of 1951, followed by a two-sided Top Ten—"Mr. Moon" and "If Teardrops Were Pennies"—early that fall, followed quickly again by his first Number One, "Let Old Mother Nature Have Her Way," which stayed at the top of the charts for eight weeks.

His next single, in March 1952, was "(When You Feel Like You're in Love) Don't Just Stand There," a song Ernest Tubb had given him. Like "Mother Nature," it spent eight weeks at Number One. "Are You Teasing Me" also made it to the top that spring.

From then on, it was one Top Ten after another: "It's a Lovely, Lovely World," "Our Honeymoon," "That's Just the Kind of Love I'm Looking For," "Just Wait Till I Get You Alone" and "This Orchid Means Goodbye" (a two-sided single). Smith's cover of Porter Wagoner's "Trademark" (co-written by Porter) and "Do I Like It" (another two-sided hit single) took him through the summer of 1953. Quick on the heels of "Trademark" came the upbeat "Hey, Joe!"—another Number One. In 1981, nearly 30 years later, Moe Bandy and Joe Stampley hit with a parody of this song.

By then he'd married June Carter and formed his own outstanding backup band, The Tunesmiths, which included several top musicians, former Hank Williams Drifting Cowboy lead guitarist, Sam Pruett, and steel guitar ace, Johnny Sibert, among them. In 1954 drummer Buddy Harman, just beginning his distinguished career in country music, joined The Tunesmiths. This former big-band drummer was a revolutionary addition to the group, since few singers at the time were using drums in their bands.

The drums got Smith in trouble. They were acceptable on the road and in the studio, but not on the Opry, and Harman couldn't perform with the group. Although Bob Wills had defied the Opry's demand to hide his drummer in 1944 and freely used drums onstage during a 1948 appearance, the ban still held firm for others, even in 1954. Carl took considerable flak from Opry members Tubb and Acuff, though he did use Harman on his other WSM radio shows, apparently with little problem.

Smith's love for Bob Wills-style Western swing had been ingrained in him as a kid, and at times his music approached rockabilly. His 1954 hit, "Go Boy Go," rocked as much as some of Bill Haley's early work; and since it, too, went Top Ten, with the drums out front, it was clear that country fans weren't quite as rigid in their thinking as many Opry folks thought. Smith also routinely performed "Shake, Rattle and Roll" onstage before anyone had heard of Elvis Presley.

Singer Freddie Hart had written and recorded "Loose Talk," but his recording of it never went anywhere. In 1955, Carl, using a rhumba-like arrangement similar to that used by Johnnie and Jack on "Poison Love," took "Loose Talk" to Number One for seven weeks and made it a standard.

Daughter Carlene (who in recent years has carved out her own impressive career) was born to Carl and June in 1955. Meanwhile, Carl continued to work the road relentlessly. The Top Tens began to taper off a bit, with "You're Free to Go" and the 1956 single, "You Are the One," being his biggest. from that time period. (Daughter Carlene recorded the same song in 1991.)

Smith resigned from the Opry in 1956, made three minor movie appearances, then went on the road for 18 months, headlining a package show sponsored by Phillip Morris. On that show with Carl were Red Sovine, rockabilly Ronnie Self and popular vocalist Goldie Hill. After Carl and June divorced in 1957, he married Goldie. By 1957 the advent of rock 'n' roll had cut into Smith's hits, though he continued touring as heavily as ever. He had only one Top Ten record in 1957 and 1958; and "Ten Thousand Drums," his final one for eight years, came in 1959. From that time on, through most of the 60's, a few of his records reached the Top 20, but most fell short of that. He briefly hosted the ABC-TV country program, *Four Star Jubilee*, and later hosted a Canadian TV show, *Carl Smith's Country Music Hall*.

Into the 1960's, Carl still made great records, though they weren't commercially successful. Many of them gave him a chance to indulge himself in Western swing. Some sessions were virtual jam sessions, with stunning steel guitar by legendary Nashville session musician, Curly Chalker. His last Top Ten record, in 1967, was a cover of the Fred Rose tune, "Deep Water," the last recording Bob Wills made for Columbia 20 years earlier.

From then through the early 1970's, Carl followed a formula of reviving such older gems as "Foggy River," "Good Deal, Lucille," Don Gibson's "Heartbreak Avenue" and Leon Payne's "I Love You Because," done up Western swing style. One single paired Charlie Walker's "Pick Me Up on Your Way Down" with Pee Wee King's "Bonaparte's Retreat." He would do more such songs, including 1971's swinging "Red Door," which anticipated George Strait by a decade. But not one of these gave him anything like a hit.

Finally, in 1974, after nearly a quarter of a century, he left Columbia for Hickory Records, the label owned by Acuff-Rose Publishing. Again, he stuck with older songs. Four subsequent singles and three albums on ABC/Hickory, a short-lived alliance between the two labels, released from 1976 through 1978, barely charted.

It hardly mattered by then, for Carl was starting to drastically scale back his musical career. Goldie had retired from performing long before; the two spent more and more time on their 285-acre horse farm near Franklin, Tennessee. Showing horses became his passion to the point where he quit performing altogether in favor of the life of a gentleman farmer, though he did re-record some of his old hits in the early 80's. It took great determination to make that break. He did some TV through the years, but the desire went out of him, and when it did, he was astute enough not to pursue it further. After a phenomenal run, a run for which he felt enduring pride and gratitude, he knew when the time felt right for him to leave the stage for good.   —R.K.

Connie Smith

BORN: August 14, 1941
BIRTHPLACE: Elkhart, Indiana

Born in Elkhart, Indiana, Connie Smith had settled down to a life as a wife and mother in the early 1960's when country star Bill Anderson discovered

charted singles for Monument Records. Her final chart entry came in 1985, on Epic Records. She continues as an Opry member into the 90's.   —M.B.

Sammi Smith

BORN: August 5, 1943
BIRTHPLACE: Orange, California

Sammi Smith was singing in clubs six nights a week by the age of eleven. She signed with Columbia in 1967 and while she cut several singles with the label, the most important thing that happened to Sammi at Columbia was meeting a janitor at the Columbia studio named Kris Kristofferson.

Sammi toured briefly as the first female vocalist with Waylon Jennings' band, then signed with the small Mega label and recorded a moderately successfully single, "He's Everywhere." It was her second Mega single, however, "Help Me Make It Through the Night," written by none other than her janitor pal Kris Kristofferson, that gave Sammi's career the boost it needed. The song hit Number One on the country charts and broke the Top Ten on the pop charts. It  not only earned Sammi a Grammy for Best Female Country Vocalist of 1972, but also stuck her with an undeserved reputation as a one-hit artist. Actually, Sammi recorded seven more albums for Mega and placed 16 more singles on the charts, including "Today I Started Loving You Again" and "Then You Walk In." On the other hand, she never managed to replicate her earlier success, largely because of the limited promotional and distribution power of a small indie label like Mega, which was plagued by financial problems for years before it went out of business in 1976. In the meantime, Sammi continued to write hit songs for such artists as Waylon Jennings ("Cedartown, Georgia") and Conway Twitty ("Sand-Covered Angels"). She also devoted more and more time to Native American Indian causes. She signed

her singing at a talent show near Columbus, Ohio. Impressed with Connie's voice, Anderson gave a copy of her demo tape to agent Hubert Long, who passed them on to Chet Atkins. With Atkins' help, Connie signed a recording contract with RCA in 1964. The label released her debut single, "Once a Day," late that summer; by November it had reached Number One on the country charts, where it stayed for an incredible ten weeks. By the end of the year, Connie had won the first of two successive *Billboard* awards for Most Promising Country Female Singer.

Connie continued to dominate the country charts for the rest of the decade, with Top Ten hits like "I Can't Remember," "Ain't Had No Lovin'," "I'll Come a-Runnin'" and "Baby's Back Again." She became a regular cast member of the Grand Ole Opry in 1965 and cemented her popularity with frequent appearances on virtually every variety show on television, including *The Jimmy Dean Show, Singin' Country* and *Lawrence Welk*. She recorded over a dozen albums in a five-year period, including *Cute' n' Country Connie Smith Sings Bill Anderson, Downtown* and *I Love Charlie Brown*. She also recorded a number of sacred albums and occasionally performed alongside Billy Graham.

Connie continued to make hits for RCA through the early 1970's, including the singles "Just What I Am" and "If It Ain't Love (Let's Leave It Alone)." In 1973 she moved to Columbia Records and made the charts with singles like "Ain't Love a Good Thing," "Why Don't You Love Me," "('Till) I Kissed You" and "So Sad (To Watch Good Love Go Bad)." In 1977 Connie switched labels again and cut a handful of with Elektra and recorded several albums, including *Mixed Emotions* in 1977 and the excellent *New Winds/All Quadrants* the following year. In 1980 she switched labels again, this time to Sound Factory Records. In the mid-80's, she moved over to indie label Step One. —M.B.

Hank Snow

BORN: May 9, 1914
BIRTHPLACE: Brooklyn, Nova Scotia, Canada

Hank Snow was one of Canada's biggest stars for 13 years before he made it south of the border. And even after he got attention here, his stardom wasn't assured until he racked up three Number One hits in one year.

Nobody sounded quite like him. Hank Williams drawled; Lefty Frizzell and Floyd Tillman slurred; Ernest Tubb slid off pitch; Red Foley and Eddy Arnold crooned. But Hank Snow's singing was built on precise pitch and perfect enunciation. And where most singers simply strummed their guitars, Hank played well enough to record instrumental duets with Chet Atkins.

His main musical influence, like that of Hank Williams, Ernest Tubb and, later, Merle Haggard, was Jimmie Rodgers. Yet he created his own sound, with driving rhythms, clever imagery and occasional Latin flavor. And that sound had repercussions far beyond Nashville. You could hear it in Elvis' Sun singles, and Presley's 1959 hit, "A Fool Such As I," had been a Top Five hit for Hank in 1952. Ray Charles and The Rolling Stones both covered his biggest hit, "I'm Movin' On." Through his music and his 36 years on the Opry, Hank Snow has become a legend on both sides of the Canadian border—but only after plenty of struggle.

Clarence Eugene Snow, born May 9, 1914, in Brooklyn, Nova Scotia, slogged through tough times almost from the beginning. His parents divorced when he was eight. He lived briefly with his grandparents, then went to live with his mother and her new husband, who abused him. He had to grow up fast, and wound up working as a ship's cabin boy at age 12 to get away.

Music wasn't a major factor in his life at first, but after he first got a guitar and then at 16, heard Jimmie Rodgers' version of "Moonlight and Skies," it captured him. He still worked odd jobs as he perfected his Rodgers repertoire but found himself getting real encouragement. A no-pay show on radio station CHNS in Halifax, Nova Scotia, was his first musical employment. He was in the right place at the right time; Canada then had only Montana Slim to call its own. RCA/Canada signed "Hank, the Yodeling Ranger," in 1936.

"Prisoned Cowboy" and "Lonesome Blue Yodel," his first RCA releases, came out, like all his early records, only in Canada. Those records reflected a different Hank Snow. Singing mostly ballads, he not only captured the Rodgers spirit, he improved on it with his outstanding yodeling.

He found the success he sought in Canada, but not in America, where he wanted it most. He didn't cross the border until 1944 when Philadelphia promoter Jack Howard (who later helped Bill Haley get his start), booked him here. Eventually Hank caught on at Wheeling's *WWVA Jamboree*, but after an abortive stab at Hollywood and no hit records, he was failing. His most important encouragement came from fellow Rodgers fan Ernest Tubb.

"If it wasn't for Ernest, I would not be talking to you today," he said after Tubb died. When a Dallas radio station played one of his Canadian records in the late 1940's, it got so much response that RCA in the U.S., after ignoring him for years, finally dropped their blinders and started recording him.

Tubb brought him to the Opry in 1949, the same year his recording of "Marriage Vow" hit Number 11. But his future on the show was uncertain when RCA released "I'm Movin' On" early in 1950. It was different from his other records. Whereas they were all Rodgers-flavored ballads, this one was a sound clearly his own. From the chugging opening fiddle and the train-whistle effects of Joe Talbot's steel guitar to Hank's forceful singing and hot flatpicking, it was a classic even then, and his first American Number One.

His place on the Opry was assured (he became a member in 1950), especially when both "Golden Rocket," a driving train number, and the Latin-flavored "Rhumba Boogie" flew into the Number One

featured by Hank Snow

slot in 1950 and 1951, respectively. Until 1954 every Snow release, 14 in all, went Top Ten.

Among that phenomenal string were "Bluebird Island," "The Gold Rush Is Over," "Fool Such As I" and the surrealistic "Honeymoon on a Rocket Ship." In 1954, he took two ballads, "I Don't Hurt Anymore" (which stayed on the charts 41 weeks) and "Let Me Go, Lover," to Number One and Number Three respectively.

The Presley connection began early. Elvis' disastrous 1954 Opry appearance occurred on Hank's portion of the show. The following year, a 1955 Hank Snow tour orchestrated by his then-manager, Colonel Tom Parker, gave Elvis his first wide exposure beyond the *Louisiana Hayride*. But then, as rock 'n' roll rode roughshod over the Opry, Hank stayed true to his own sound. At the urging of Chet Atkins, Hank moved into the Nashville Sound, without losing his power. By the early 1960's he was, again, racking up huge successes. He made Don Robertson's "Miller's Cave" his own in 1960. Two years later his bluesy, rapid-fire "I've Been Everywhere" appeared and went to Number One, followed in 1963 by "Ninety Miles an Hour (Down a Dead End Street)," which clocked in at Number Two.

He'd become an institution. His spangled Nudie suits, which he wore even at USO shows in Vietnam, and his band, the hard-country Rainbow Ranch Boys, had made him as identifiable as Ernest Tubb. But as the 1960's wore on, hits became fewer and his records wound up lower on the charts. Trends were changing again.

In early 1974, "Hello, Love," a quintessential Hank Snow number, became his first Number One since 1962 and a reaffirmation of the durability of his music. His 104th album, *Still Movin' On*, was issued by RCA in 1977. It tried, with only partial success, to update his sound in the Waylon/Willie context. In 1979 he was inducted into the Country Music Hall of Fame.

He never had another big record, yet with an awesome 35 Top Ten hits, six of them hitting Number One, and more consecutive years on the charts than any other artist, his career has been phenomenal. Not long before he'd have logged a half century with RCA, he quit the label. He hadn't changed; Nashville had. It was not an amicable parting.

Semi-retired today, Snow still performs on the Opry. He spends more time at home these days with his wife, Minnie, and devotes himself to charitable activities on behalf of child abuse victims. Bear Family records has recently chronicled Snow's complete 1936-1980 career on 39 CD's. In 1994, his autobiography, *The Hank Snow Story*, appeared. —R.K.

Jo-El Sonnier

BORN: October 2, 1946
BIRTHPLACE: Rayne, Louisiana

A renowned French-Cajun accordionist, Jo-El Sonnier was born in rural Rayne, Louisiana, on October 2, 1946. He received his first accordion when he was three, and by the time he was six, young Jo-El had his own 15-minute radio spot on a Crowley, Louisiana, station.

When he was seven, he played his first gig at the Crowley Club, and when he was 13, he cut his first record, "Tes Yeaux Bleus" ("Your Blue Eyes"), which became a regional hit. More regional hits followed, and between 1972 and 1980, Jo-El bounced between Los Angeles and Nashville, establishing himself as an impressive songwriter and studio musician. In 1975, he signed with Mercury Records and squeezed out a few minor country hits, such as "I've Been Around Enough to Know," "Always Late (With Your Kisses)" and "He's Still All Over You."

In the 1980's, Jo-El moved back to Louisiana and recorded *Cajun Life*, which was sung entirely in Acadian French and released on the independent Rounder label. In 1982, he hit the road with an all-star band that included musical heavyweights such as Sneaky Pete Kleinow on pedal steel and Albert Lee on lead guitar; and a few years later, he participated in rocker Elvis Costello's *King of America* album, for which he subsequently won numerous accolades for his solid musicianship.

More session work in Nashville followed in the mid-1980's, including performances with Emmylou Harris and Dolly Parton. In addition, Jo-El began re-establishing himself as a songwriter, penning hits for top artists such as George Strait, Johnny Cash, Conway

Twitty, Loretta Lynn, Emmylou Harris and John Anderson.

In 1987, he signed a recording contract with RCA in Nashville, and his first single for the label, "Come On Joe," made the country Top 40. The following year, he hit the Top Ten twice with "No More One More Time" and "Tear-Stained Letter." Throughout the remainder of the 1980's, Jo-El's reputation as a major synthesizer of Cajun, bayou blues and country-rock made his live performances some of the most exciting in country music.

In November 1989, however, tragedy struck. Jo-El's wife, Jamie Talbert, who was also his manager, died unexpectedly of a heart attack. Deeply saddened by her sudden death, Jo-El retreated from the music scene for a few years. He returned in the early 90's, recording for Capitol, and in 1994 released *Cajun Roots*, a Rounder release that featured songs sung in old world French. —R.P.

Sons of the Pioneers

Formed in Los Angeles in 1934, The Sons of the Pioneers (originally called The Pioneer Trio) have held an important place in country music off and on for the past 60 years. Its original members included legendary songwriter Bob Nolan, Tim Spencer and Len Slye (who would later become singing cowboy Roy Rogers after he left the group in 1937). The band also took on musicians Hugh and Karl Farr in 1934, the same year they cut their first hit single, "Tumbling Tumbleweeds." The band continued to score

hits throughout the 1930's and 1940's, even after Spencer departed in '37, and Rogers left the group to concentrate on making movies. Between recording such hit singles as "Cool Water" and "Stars and Stripes on Iwo Jima," the Sons of the Pioneers appeared in a number of Rogers' films.

After the deaths of Tim Spencer in 1974 and Bob Nolan in 1980, The Sons of the Pioneers incorporated new members and continued to perform through the 1970's and 1980's. The band reunited with Roy Rogers in 1979 and made the Top 20 with the single "Ride, Concrete Cowboy, Ride," from the *Smokey and the Bandit 2* soundtrack. In 1980, the original Sons of the Pioneers were elected to the Country Music Hall of Fame. —M.B.

Joe South

BORN: February 28, 1940
BIRTHPLACE: Atlanta, Georgia

Atlanta-born Joe South started out as a session guitarist for artists ranging from Bob Dylan and Aretha Franklin to Conway Twitty and Wilson Pickett.

In 1968, he embarked on a solo career and struck gold with three hit singles, "Games People Play," "Birds of a Feather" and "These Are Not My People." Joe's ability to combine folksy wit with redneck verve made him one of the most sought-after songwriters of the late 1960's, and his material has been covered by artists as diverse as Billy Joe Royal ("Down in the Boondocks"), Lynn Anderson ("I Never Promised You a Rose Garden") and rockers Deep Purple ("Hush"). —R.P.

Red Sovine

BORN: July 17, 1918
BIRTHPLACE: Charleston, West Virginia
DIED: April 4, 1980

Woodrow Wilson Sovine, born in Charleston, West, Virginia, in 1918, was a singer, guitarist and songwriter known for the dramatic recitations that distinguished many of his songs. Red's first band, The Echo Valley Boys, was a regular act on KWKH's popular radio program *Louisiana Hayride*. When Hank Williams left KWKH in 1949, Red took over Hank's ra-

dio show, sponsored by Johnny Fair Syrup. He remained at the station until joining the Grand Ole Opry in 1954. He had a string of hits on Decca in the late 50's, including one with Opry co-star Webb Pierce ("Why, Baby, Why," a Number One in 1955), and "Little Rosa" (Top Five in '56). In the 1960's, Sovine had several hits on Starday, most notably 1965's "Giddy-up Go," a trucker's song which hit Number One. While touring in the 1960's and 70's, Sovine kept an eye out for new talent and helped launch at least one rising star, Charley Pride, whom he heard performing in a Montana club in the early 1960's.

In 1976, Sovine scored another Number One for Starday with the maudlin "Teddy Bear." The song, about a dying child and his C.B. radio, featured Sovine's inimitable style of recitation. Later that year *Cashbox* named him "Best Recitation Performer," a category created just for him. Red next recorded for Starday's parent company, Gusto Records, but had only minor hits for the rest of his career. He died of a heart attack while driving in Nashville in 1980. There was probably no other country performer with the ability to milk schmaltz as well as Red. "Teddy Bear" remains a truck stop classic.   —M.B.

Billie Jo Spears

BORN: January 14, 1937
BIRTHPLACE: Beaumont, Texas

Born in Beaumont, Texas, on January 14, 1937, Billie Jo Spears was first lured to Nashville when a talent scout caught her performance at Yvonne's, a Beaumont area nightclub where, some years earlier, George Jones had gotten his start.

In Music City, Spears was snapped up by United Artists, which was determined to launch her to stardom as "a female George Jones." Ironically, Spears had to move on to Capitol Records before

scoring her first top-five hit, "Mr. Walker, It's All Over," in 1969. But by 1975, she was back with U.A. again when the song that really was the entirety of her career, "Blanket on the Ground" (written by Roger Bowling), went to Number One. Though tame by today's standards, "Blanket on the Ground," with its lyric references to "slippin' around," was actually considered risqué fare for a woman singer in the mid-70's.

Spears continued recording for United Artists and Liberty until the early 80's; but aside from a handful of Top Ten singles—"What I've Got in Mind," "Misty Blue" and "If You Want Me"—she's only rippled the charts since.   —B.A.

Joe Stampley

BORN: June 6, 1943
BIRTHPLACE: Springhill, Louisiana

After a few years spent playing with a rock band in the mid-60's, Louisiana-born singer Joe Stampley "crossed-over" to become a modestly successful country performer in the 1970's. In 1972 he had his first hit single, "If You Touch Me (You've Gotta Love Me)" on the ABC/Dot label. Joe recorded a string of country hits, including "Penny," "Unchained Melody" and the Top 20 "Night Time and My Baby," before switching to Epic Records in 1975. His first Epic single, "Roll on Big Mama," successfully caught the "trucker-as-last-American-hero" wave, and became a Number One hit, followed by Top Tens like "Billy Get Me a Woman," "Whisky Talkin'" and "Baby I Love You So." In 1973 Joe began working with producer Billy Sherrill, turning out hits like "Do You Ever Fool Around." In 1980 he recorded "Holding the Bag," the first of three successful, light-hearted duets with Moe Bandy. The duo went on to cut several albums together, including *Just Good Ole Boys* in 1979 and *Hey Joe (Hey Moe)* in 1981.   —M.B.

The Stanley Brothers

BORN: Carter, August 27, 1925, McClure, Virginia
       Ralph, February 25, 1927, Stratton, Virginia
DIED: Carter, December 1, 1966

Next to bluegrass music's founding father, Bill Monroe, few figures have been as revered in that field as The Stanley Brothers. Noted country music historian Bill C. Malone has praised Stanley's "haunting, almost sepulchral voice," calling him, "one of the most unmistakably rural voices in country music."

Carter Stanley was born in McClure, Virginia, in 1925; Ralph was born in Stratton, Virginia, two years later. For years—from 1946 until Carter's death in 1966—they performed and recorded as The Stanley Brothers. Since Carter's demise, Ralph has carried on with his own band, enlarging upon the Stanleys' legend even further.

Bill Monroe and his former band members, Flatt and Scruggs, may have forged the definitive bluegrass style; but the Stanley Brothers—who were admittedly heavily influenced by the afore-mentioned masters—were close behind. Ralph's three-fingered banjo style was, in great part, inspired by Earl Scruggs' innovations. Yet the Stanleys, with their repertoire of old-time mountain songs, often stood apart with their music's roughhewn simplicity and emotional directness.

The Stanley's vast recorded catalogue (more than 50 albums) includes classics like "Clinch Mountain Backstep," "White Dove," "Little Glass of Wine," "The Fields Have Turned Brown," "Rank Stranger," "Shackles and Chains," "Man of Constant Sorrow" and "Lonesome River." Ricky Skaggs, Keith Whitley, Ron Thomason, Charlie Sizemore, Larry Sparks, Melvin Goins and Curly Ray Cline are some of the bluegrass and country notables who have apprenticed in Ralph Stanley's band in the past three decades.

Today, Ralph Stanley, whose music has veered back more towards its basic Appalachian roots in the three decades since Carter's death, is still making the festival rounds each summer as one of bluegrass' most celebrated éminences grises.

"His perfect phrasing and delicate melodic twists, the product of mountain vocal art, completely untouched for generations, unlike...any form of popular music, are employed for the song, not for the singer," says John Wright in *Traveling the High Way Home*, his acclaimed 1993 biography of Stanley. "It is this stance, and this artistry...that continue to make him 'old time'...and probably America's finest traditional singer."
—B.A.

Jack Stapp

BORN: December 8, 1912
BIRTHPLACE: Nashville, Tennessee
DIED: December 20, 1980

Jack Stapp was barely out of his teens when he went to work for CBS. He quickly rose to become a program director for the broadcast giant's radio network, but eventually opted to be an even bigger fish in a smaller pond when he became director of programming at Nashville's WSM Radio in 1939 and remained in that position until 1957. Stapp's influence was almost immediately felt when he persuaded the NBC Network to accept "feeds" from the Grand Ole Opry's broadcast, thus widening the program's national exposure immensely. Stapp also persuaded NBC to let him produce from Nashville's WSM studios a pop radio show called *Sunday Down South*, which was a showcase for local singers like Dinah Shore, Snooky Lanson and Owen Bradley's Orchestra.

Stapp, along with Jim Denny (see separate entry), his successor as manager of the Opry, also played a major role in re-shaping the entire spirit and content of the Opry during the 1940's, when it evolved from a home-grown presentation featuring stringbands and comedians into a more sophisticated showcase for the rhinestone-studded, chart-topping stars of the day.

Stapp's greatest achievement, however, was founding Tree International Publishing, a company that has since grown to be one of the cornerstones of the Nashville music industry. (He left the Opry when it was agreed that his growing publishing concern represented a conflict of interest with his duties at WSM.) Tree was in recent years acquired by Sony International (around the same time Sony purchased CBS Records) which paid more than a hundred million dollars for the company's vast catalogue, which includes hundreds of country standards.

Stapp was also a founder of the Country Music Association and helped the organization establish its annual awards presentation. He was elected to the Country Music Hall of Fame in 1989.　　—B.A.

Buddy Starcher

BORN: March 16, 1906
BIRTHPLACE: Ripley, West Virginia

Veteran West Virginia country singer Buddy Starcher started performing over radio in Baltimore, Maryland, in 1928, and spent a fair amount of time riding the rails and writing topical songs relating to events of the day, including "Bonus Blues," which chronicled the protests of World War I veterans. Starcher worked for a time over South Carolina radio before returning to the West Virginia area. In 1937 he formed his own band, Starcher's Mountaineers. By 1946 he'd begun recording for Four Star Records, and in 1949 had a national hit with "I'll Still Write Your Name in the

Sand." He also later recorded for Columbia. Throughout this time he remained in West Virginia, and in 1960 began hosting a local morning TV show in Charleston. His biggest national impact came in 1966 when he recorded an original recitation about the parallels between the assassinations of John Kennedy and Abraham Lincoln, "History Repeats Itself," which went to Number Two. In 1970 he briefly managed a Texas radio station before finally returning to his home state and retiring.　　—R.K.

Starday Records

One of country music's more colorful independent labels, Starday Records was founded in 1952 in Houston by Jack and Neva Starnes and Harold "Pappy" Daily. Veteran independent producer Don Pierce purchased a third of the company that October. The label initially concentrated on Texas honky tonk music; Arlie Duff's "You All Come" became its first major success in December, 1953. The Starneses sold their interest in Starday in 1955. At that point Daily and Pierce primarily concentrated on developing George Jones' recording career and that of other Starday artists like Sonny Burns. The label also expanded into rockabilly with Jones, Sonny Burns, Sonny Fisher and others, but their efforts only generated local sales. Pierce's ventures into direct mail sales proved far more successful.

In 1956, Daily and Pierce signed a five-year agreement to produce country records for Mercury Records. Some Starday artists, notably Jones and bluegrass singer Bill Clifton, moved to the larger label; artists with regional appeal remained on Starday. Pierce then shifted the smaller label's primary focus to bluegrass, signing such veteran singers as Jim Eanes, Carl Story and The Stanley Brothers. Pierce also acquired numerous masters from independent producers. In summer 1958, Daily, Pierce and Mercury severed all ties with each other; Pierce retained ownership of Starday.

Under Pierce's leadership, Starday was one of the first labels to place as much emphasis on albums as singles. Pierce also established the first country music record club. During the 60's, Starday successfully revived the waning careers of Johnny Bond, The Willis Brothers and Red Sovine with hit novelty singles.

Pierce's purchase of King Records in 1968 left the firm strapped for cash; Lin Broadcasting bought the operation later that year. Executive moves forced Pierce out of the company in August 1970; the label went bankrupt the following year.

In 1972 Starday reorganized and aggressively re-entered the bluegrass album market with new recordings by major artists. However, a spring 1973, flood damaged its pressing plant and destroyed much of its inventory; the label again sank into in bankruptcy. A reactivated Starday emerged in 1975 under the ownership of Gusto Records. Red Sovine's "Teddy Bear" was its last big hit. In 1977 the Starday name was dropped; future releases appeared on Gusto. —D.S.

The Statler Brothers

Never mind that only two of them are brothers and none of them are named Statler: The Statler Brothers pretty much owned the 1970's. Furthermore they may be the most talented vocal quartet in country music history. Certainly no other group has had such sustained popularity. It's easily measured by their million-selling records, their dozen or so Country Music Association awards, and memorable hits like "Flowers on the Wall" (their very first chart record, which went to Number Two in 1965 and was also a Number Four hit in the pop charts that same year), "The Class of '57," "Do You Remember These" (Number Two in 1972), "Whatever Happened to Randolph Scott," "Pictures," "Bed of Rose's," "I'll Go to My Grave Loving You" (Number Three in 1975), "The Official Historian on Shirley Jean Berrell" (a Top Five in '78), "Elizabeth" (Number One in 1983) and "Hello Mary Lou" (their 1985 Top Five remake of the 1961 Rick Nelson pop hit).

Melding their gospel background with a small-town, nostalgia-tinged brand of secular country music, these hometown boys from the staid Shenandoah Valley city of Staunton, Virginia have served up a brand of musical Americana that harks back to the comfortable "Main Street" familiarity of old-time barbershop quartets. For the better part of two and a half decades, The Statlers have struck a warm chord of recognition in Americans everywhere. Novelist Kurt Vonnegut praised them as "America's poets." It's indicative of The Statlers' immense popularity that they won the CMA's Vocal Group of the Year Award an unprecedented nine times between 1972 and 1984.

They have won the *Music City News* Readers' Poll Awards for more than 25 consecutive years.

"There's most definitely a yearning, people want to go back to the basics," Don Reid (who, like his brother Harold and the rest of the Statlers, has never abandoned his small town roots in Staunton) mused in a 1988 interview with *Country Music Magazine*'s Bob Allen. "I think everybody's scared of what's in the future, and certainly nobody knows. So that's the real comfort: to look back and enjoy the memories.

"People identify with small town life even if they grew up in the slums of a large city," added Harold Reid. "Even if it's not in their background, they can identify with it....Our music has been compared to Frank Capra's movies, and what greater compliment can you get than that?"

The four original Statlers were: the Reid brothers (Don, born June 5, 1945 and Harold, born August 21, 1939), Phil Balsley (born August 8, 1939), and the late Lew DeWitt (born March 8, 1938). DeWitt was replaced in 1982 by Jimmy Fortune after being sidelined by Crohn's Disease, which claimed his life on August 15, 1990. This is the only line-up change that the group has undergone in the 30-some years since its inception.

Some years back, The Statler Brothers bought their old high school in Staunton and turned it into their office and world headquarters. On tours of the school, members of the group are fond of pointing out a little plaque in the school gymnasium where The Statlers (then a gospel group known as The Kingsmen) won their first talent contest. It was over the objections of their practical-minded elders that The Statlers embarked on their professional career in 1963 after they started singing together in Staunton's Lyndhurst Methodist Church. Their big break came one morning when they corralled Johnny Cash at a place called Watermelon Park in Berryville, Virginia, and persuaded him to let them audition as his opening act. (They passed the impromptu audition, but it was months before they were able to track Cash down again and actually open a show for him.)

It was with Cash's help that The Statlers (they got the name off a tissue box in a hotel room at the last minute when in need of a name to record under) landed their first recording contract, with Columbia. But nothing much clicked until they moved down the street to Mercury Records and teamed up with long-time producer Jerry Kennedy. After that, the hits kept right on coming, until well into the late 1980's.

In recent years, as their chart presence has cooled, the Statlers, like many congenial veteran country acts, have found new life hosting their own popular TV show on The Nashville Network. —B.A.

Red Steagall

BORN: December 22, 1937
BIRTHPLACE: Gainesville, Texas

Born in Gainesville, Texas, on December 22, 1937, songwriter Russell ("Red") Steagall taught himself to play guitar and mandolin as a youngster while recovering from polio. He went on to become one of Nashville's most popular songwriters, as well as a recording artist of minor repute.

A former rodeo rider and quarter horse breeder, Steagall turned to songwriting in earnest in the mid-60's when he moved to California. He ended up in Nashville not long afterwards and became a staff writer for (at different times) Combine Music and Tree Publishing Company, two of Music City's powerhouse music publishers.

Some of Steagall's best known hits include: "Lone Star Beer and Bob Wills Music" (this self-written song was a Number 11 hit for him in 1976—Steagall's highest career chart showing), "Party Dolls and Wine" (a minor hit in 1972), "Someone Cares for You" (1974), "Rosie (Do You Want to Talk It Over)" and "3 Chord Country Song." Numerous Steagall originals were also recorded by other hit artists of the 70's and early 80's.

Steagall has recorded for Capital, ABC/Dot and Elektra, and had more than 20 chart records between 1972 and 1980. He's also credited with the "discovery" of Reba McEntire. After hearing McEntire sing

the National Anthem at a rodeo in Oklahoma, he brought her to the attention of Mercury, her first record label, and briefly managed her early in her career. In recent years Steagall has found renewed success as a cowboy singer and presently hosts a popular western music radio show. —B.A.

Steel Guitar

The steel guitar developed in Hawaii near the end of the 19th century, and, after Hawaii became a U.S. territory in 1900, a fascination with Hawaiian culture, including music, swept the United States. Steel guitar became part of numerous vaudeville shows. The instruments themselves differed little from regular guitars, except for the tunings and the raised strings. Door to door salesmen sold steel guitars and instruction courses across the country. Gibson and Martin began building "Hawaiian" guitars. The first country musician known to have used the steel was West Virginia singer-guitarist Frank Hutchinson. Hawaiian players like Sol Hoopii sold records, as did Americans playing Hawaiian guitar like pop musician Nick Lucas. Cliff Carlisle used Hawaiian guitar and several musicians played Hawaiian guitar on Jimmie Rodgers recordings. The Dobro was an improvement on the acoustic Hawaiian guitar.

The first electric Hawaiian guitar appeared in 1931 when the Rickenbacker company of California developed an all-aluminum instrument with a small, round body. These electric steels found favor with some Hawaiian players, but the first country player to use one was Oklahoman Bob Dunn. A former Hawaiian-style guitarist, Dunn, who also loved jazz, joined Milton Brown and His Musical Brownies in 1935, with his Martin acoustic converted to an electric. Dunn's wild solo lines, similar to a jazz trumpet, had an enormous influence on western swing, and inspired Leon McAuliffe before he joined Bob Wills.

Through the 1930's, steel guitar technology evolved as other companies developed and refined electric steels, including Gibson, National and Epiphone. In Texas and Oklahoma, Western swing players like Noel Boggs, Billy Briggs and Ted Daffan forged their own styles. A few of Jimmie Davis' early recordings had featured the steel playing of black guitarist Oscar Woods. Later, he added Charles Mitchell's electric steel to his act. By the 1940's, Pee Wee King, Curly Williams and Ernest Tubb were using amplified steels. Jerry Byrd became popular as part of Tubb's Texas Troubadours, and became *the* steel guitarist in the Southeast. His warm Hawaiian tones and superb touch became common as he did more and more recording sessions in the late 40's, including some with Hank Williams and Red Foley. On the West Coast, Joaquin Murphey, Noel Boggs and Herb Remington became the dominant non-pedal steel players (Remington through his work with Bob Wills and Hank Penny, Boggs through his work with Wills and Spade Cooley). Though Gibson and Rickenbacker steels were common, Leo Fender's steel guitars set the standard among most West Coast players. Jerry Byrd still favored Rickenbackers.

Steel players began to help certain singers define their sounds. Little Roy Wiggins, with his warm Hawaiian-influenced style, became a major component of Eddy Arnold's early hits. Don Helms' high, trebly steel chords (an idea suggested by Fred Rose) helped give Hank Williams' records their distinctive sound. Even after pedal steel broke into Nashville after Webb Pierce's hit "Slowly," many musicians retained non-pedal players in their bands including Carl Smith, who used Johnny Sibert. Gradually pedal steel came to dominate country music, the non-pedal instruments falling from favor. Jerry Byrd, one of several who refused to change to pedals, wound up playing bass on recording sessions, since there wasn't the demand for his non-pedal sound anymore (he eventually moved to Hawaii). Today non-pedal instruments are uncommon, though some more contemporary hits, like Foster & Lloyd's "Crazy Over You," have used them. Asleep at the Wheel's original steel player, Lucky Oceans, plays both pedal and non-pedal guitars while Cindy Cashdollar, the band's current steel player, sticks to non-pedal steel, as does Lee Jeffriess of Big Sandy and The Fly-Rite Boys. The non-pedal steel may be unusual today, but its raw impact can still make a record stand out, or create a mood of the past. —R.K.

Keith Stegall

BORN: November 1, 1954
BIRTHPLACE: Wichita Falls, Texas

In recent years, Keith Stegall has worn quite a few different hats on Music Row. During the 1970's and 80's, his original compositions were recorded by ev-

eryone from Moe Bandy and Becky Hobbs ("Let's Get Over Them Together") to jazz master Al Jarreau ("We're in This Love Together").

"I Think I'm in Love" (recorded by both Conway Twitty and Ed Bruce), "Down in Louisiana" (Charley Pride), "Looks Like Love" (Helen Reddy), "My Heart Will Know" (Con Hunley), "Touch by Touch" (Johnny Mathis), "Sexy Eyes" (Dr. Hook), "Lonely Nights" (Mickey Gilley), "In Love With Loving You" (recorded by both Eddy Arnold and Jerry Reed) and "Texas Heartache" (Juice Newton) are a few more of his well known composer credits. During the 1980's, Stegall had his own on-and-off-again recording career, making occasional forays into the charts. Recording for Capitol in the very early 80's, he had mediocre chart success with songs like "The Fool Who Fooled Around on You," "Anything That Hurts You (Hurts Me), and "Won't You Be My Baby." Moving over to Epic in 1984, he did somewhat better. He reached the Top Ten with "Pretty Lady," and did nearly as well with "California," which hit Number 13 on the *Billboard* charts in 1985.

But more recently Stegall has really come into his own producing other artists. Besides working briefly with Randy Travis (back when Travis was still recording under the name of Randy Traywick), Stegall has been responsible for producing Alan Jackson's long string of Number One records and million-selling albums.

Stegall, a cousin of Johnny Horton, began playing piano at age four, and had his first band, The Pace Setters, at age 12. He recalls making his first public appearance on the *Country Music Shindig Show* in Tyler, Texas. Before turning to country music, he earned a B.A. in Theology at Centenary College in Shreveport, Louisiana, and toured Europe as part of a folk group called The Cheerful Givers. Stegall has also appeared in two feature films: *Killing at Hell's Gate* and *Country Gold*. Stegall recently made history again, signing dual contracts with Mercury's newly formed division, Polydor, as both a producer and an artist. —B.A.

Ray Stevens

BORN: January 24, 1939
BIRTHPLACE: Clarksdale, Georgia

One of the hottest country recording artists and live entertainers of the 1970's, Ray Stevens (born Ray Ragsdale) has distinguished himself as Nashville's "Mad Studio Genius:" a recording artist/songwriter/producer who's had illustrious success over the years with both madcap comedy hits ("Ahab the Arab," "Jeremiah Peabody's Poly-Unsaturated Quick Dissolving Fast Action Pleasant Tasting Green and Purple Pills," "Shriners' Convention," "Turn Your Radio On," "Guitarzan," "The Streak," etc.) and serious songs, as well. (His pop-country best-sellers, "Everything Is Beautiful"—1970, and "Misty"—1975, both won Grammys.)

A native of the Atlanta, Georgia, area, Stevens' formal musical training began at age five and continued through three years at Georgia State University, where he studied musical theory and composition. He moved to Nashville in 1962 and landed a job in the A&R department of Mercury Records. But he soon hooked up with ubiquitous Nashville producer Shelby Singleton, and the hits began.

Though the sharp cutting edge of his manic comedy/social commentary has dulled into a formula for pure belly laughs in recent years, Stevens has continued to flourish. Several of his recent comic videos have been big sellers, netting him millions and, in effect, rejuvenating his career. His live shows have also been some of the most popular on the strip at Branson, Missouri. —B.A.

Gary Stewart

BORN: May 28, 1945
BIRTHPLACE: Letcher County, Kentucky

One of the very best singers to emerge from 70's country music—perhaps even from all of country music history—is a man that relatively few country fans are aware of today: Gary Stewart.

Back in the mid-to-early 1970's, Stewart recorded three classic albums for RCA—*Out of Hand*, *Steppin' Out* and *Your Place or Mine*—which displayed a honky-tonk mania and rockabilly intensity not heard since the salad days of Jerry Lee Lewis. Rock publications like *Rolling Stone* were quick to proclaim this Kentucky-born coal miner's son and life-long Allman Brothers fan the heir apparent to Lewis, and possibly the long missing link between country music and rock 'n' roll. ("Stewart epitomizes rockabilly in the vintage country-boy-gone-crazy mold," a *Rolling Stone* scribe mused in 1976.) Robert Christgau of *The Village Voice* called Stewart's 1975, *Out Of Hand*: "the best regular-issue country album I've heard in five years. The wild urgency of Stewart's voice reminds me of both Hank Williams and Jerry Lee Lewis." *Time Magazine* dubbed Stewart the "king of honky tonk."

Stewart was born in Letcher County, Kentucky. When he was still a youngster, his father was disabled in a mining accident, and the large Stewart family relocated to Fort Pierce, Florida, where Stewart spent his teen years in a local rock 'n' roll band. Later, he took a day job in an aircraft factory and a nighttime musical gig at a club in Okeechobee, Florida, called The Wagon Wheel. Mel Tillis heard him perform there and urged him to come to Nashville. Within two years, he was ensconced in Music City, writing songs for artists of the day like Cal Smith, Jim Ed Brown, Jack Green and Jimmy Dean. He also played piano in Nat Stuckey's and Charley Pride's road bands. His own crack at the big time came when a demo he'd recorded found its way to producer Roy Dea, who landed Stewart a deal with RCA Records.

Stewart's commercial apex came in 1975, when his Jerry Lee-inflected single, "She's Actin' Single (I'm Drinkin' Doubles)" hit Number One. But oddly enough, it was all downhill from there. The unpredictable singer, who was chronically beset by personal problems and a dangerous penchant for the wild side of life, only managed to crack the Top Ten a couple more times with subsequent RCA singles like "Drinkin' Thing" and "Out of Hand." Though he continued turning out records throughout the 1970's they were relatively lack-luster and his heart no longer seemed in it. By the mid-1980's, Stewart was back home in Fort Pierce, without a label deal, and not even wanting one. He spent several years putting his personal life back together (he was dealt a severe blow when his teenage son took his own life) while eking out a living on the Texas dance hall circuit, where his popularity has never faded.

"I never set out to be a country star, or whatever it is," Stewart told *Country Music Magazine's* Bob Allen in a late 1980's interview as he searched for reasons for his premature demise. "I just don't have the itch to be a star."

But in the late 1980's and early 90's, Stewart surprised everyone by teaming back up with Roy Dea, his original RCA producer, and bouncing back with a trio of fine albums—*Brand New, Battleground,* and *I'm a Texan*—for the independent HighTone label, which has also recently re-released some of Stewart's vintage 70's RCA material on CD. These newer albums showcase a different singer: less manic and a bit more weathered, but with new-found maturity. "My voice has gotten lower, and maybe I can't hit all those real high notes like I used to," Stewart, by then a grandfather, observed wryly. "I can't step as high as I used to, but I can still growl as high." —B.A.

Redd Stewart

BORN: May 27, 1921
BIRTHPLACE: Ashland City, Tennessee

Henry Ellis Stewart, who attained fame both as fiddler-vocalist for Pee Wee King's Golden West Cowboys and as co-author of "Tennessee Waltz," grew up in Kentucky. He learned guitar, fiddle and piano, and began writing songs as a teenager. He played in the Louisville, Kentucky, area with bands like The Prairie Riders, and, in the 1930's, met Pee Wee King,

who was based in Louisville and about to join the Grand Ole Opry. He joined King's Golden West Cowboys, working as fiddler throughout the early 40's. While Stewart wound up in the Army (during which time he wrote the song, "Soldier's Last Letter," a hit for Ernest Tubb), vocalist Eddy Arnold left King's band to become a solo singer. Though vocalists like Tommy Sosebee and Cowboy Copas briefly replaced Arnold, and though other band members occasionally sang, Stewart became the Cowboys' principal vocalist. In 1948 he and King put lyrics to a waltz instrumental and created the country and pop standard, "Tennessee Waltz," sung by Stewart on the band's 1948 RCA hit recording. In the early 50's, Stewart briefly recorded as a solo vocalist for King Records. (Though King and the rest of the Cowboys backed him, they weren't credited, due to stipulations in Pee Wee's RCA contract.) Stewart later recorded an album for Hickory Records and still occasionally performs with King. —R.K.

Wynn Stewart

BORN: June 7, 1934
BIRTHPLACE: Morrisville, Missouri
DIED: July 17, 1985

Wynnford Lindsey Stewart, along with Buck Owens and Tommy Collins, was an early pioneer of the stripped-down, West Coast honky tonk style called the Bakersfield Sound. Though Missouri-born, he grew up in Southern California and made his first recordings for the Intro label in 1954 before singer Skeets McDonald brought him to Capitol, where he recorded "Keeper of the Keys" and the Top 20 hit, "The Waltz of the Angels" in 1956. In 1958 he began recording for Jackpot, a subsidiary of the independent Challenge Records and recorded country duets for Challenge with Jan Howard. He had his own solo hits with "Wishful Thinking," which reached Number Five in 1959, and "Big Big Love," a Top 20 in 1961. That same year, he began working in Las Vegas with a band that by 1963 included a bass player with the name of Merle Haggard.

In 1967, re-signed with Capitol, he found his biggest success ever with "It's Such a Pretty World Today," which became his first and only Number One record, having stayed on the charts 22 weeks. After two more Top Tens on Capitol, he recorded for RCA with little success. One single on Playboy Records, "After the Storm," went Top Ten in 1976. Stewart was recording for his own Win Records in 1978. In 1985 he was about to embark on a comeback tour and had a release ready on his Pretty World label when he died of a sudden heart attack.   —R.K.

Cliffie Stone

BORN: March 1, 1917
BIRTHPLACE: Stockton, California

One of the major figures of West Coast country music, Clifford Gilpin Snyder virtually grew up in it. His family moved to Burbank when he was nine months old. His father Herman, whose long hair and beard helped get him movie roles, earned the nickname "Herman The Hermit" when he started working with singer Stuart Hamblen. At 18, Cliffie began playing bass with Hamblen under the name "Cliffie Stonehead," later shortened to Stone. Through the late 30's, he worked as a musician, comedian, DJ and announcer, taking over two of Hamblen's radio shows when he quit them. When Capitol Records began in 1942, Cliffie played bass on some of the label's sessions, and in the mid-40's briefly produced records, which led to his joining Capitol as an A&R assistant and talent scout. He continued working on radio while also playing dances he organized and working session dates. He and Merle Travis co-wrote such classics as "No Vacancy," "Divorce Me C.O.D.," and the lyrics to "Steel Guitar Rag." Cliffie hosted the KXLA *Dinner Bell Round-Up* in 1946 and discovered KXLA staff announcer and disc jockey Ernie Ford, soon to become Tennessee Ernie Ford. In 1948 the show became known as the *Hometown*

Jamboree. Stone also had several hit records on Capitol: "Silver Stars, Purple Sage, Eyes of Blue" (1947), "Peepin' Through the Keyhole" and "When My Blue Moon Turns to Gold Again" in 1948. Cliffie managed Ernie Ford as Ford's fame grew, and continued hosting the *Hometown Jamboree* until its cancellation in the 60's. From then on he still worked on radio and managed his song publishing, which included Central Songs and American Music, later sold to Capitol. In the 70's he worked for ATV Music and later for Gene Autry Music and ran his own label, Granite Records. He was inducted into the Country Music Hall of Fame in 1989. His son Curtis was a founding member of the band Highway 101.   —R.K.

Doug Stone

BORN: June 19, 1956
BIRTHPLACE: Atlanta, Georgia

Arriving on the scene in 1990 with the doleful George Jones-style Top Five tear-jerker, "I'd Be Better Off (In a Pine Box)," Doug Stone dazzled everybody with his resolute flair for neo-honky-tonk balladry. "Pine Box" even earned the fledgling artist a Grammy nomination and his debut album, *Doug Stone,* eventually went platinum. Coming when he did, Stone seemed part of a Georgia-launched "triple threat" also posed by newcomers Travis Tritt and Alan Jackson, who, like Stone, both hailed from the greater Atlanta region. But while Tritt has drifted into Southern rock and matured into a sort of rowdy but amiable successor to Hank Williams Jr., and Jackson has mellowed into the neo-honky-tonk poster boy for the 1990's, Stone has opted for a softer style of romantic balladry: a mellow, country crooning musical bag that seems to have great fan appeal, but often sounds mushy at the center.

Stone has maintained his popularity thus far into the 90's, with a steady string of hits, including "I See You in a Different Light" (a Number One in 1991), "Fourteen Minutes Old," "I Thought It Was You," "A Jukebox with a Country Song" (also Number One in '91), "Warning Labels," "Too Busy Being In Love" (Number One in '92) and "Why Didn't I Think of That" (Number One in '93). His popularity is bolstered by his animated performance style which includes odd dance moves that look like a cross between Michael Jackson, a hillbilly Fred Astaire and John Travolta of the famous "Stayin' Alive" era.

Stone (who was born Doug Brooks, but changed his name to Stone, since there was already a Brooks named Garth in the charts) is fond of saying his career began at age seven, when his mother thrust him out on stage at a concert to sing a duet with Loretta Lynn. By the time he was 15, he was already writing songs, playing five instruments, and performing at local skating rinks around his hometown of Newnan, a distant suburb of Atlanta, with his own band. After high school, he worked as a diesel mechanic while performing in local clubs and tinkering in his home studio by night.

He was "discovered" the old-fashioned way when a Nashville manager, on the advice of a friend who lived in Newnan, journeyed down to Stone's hometown and caught one of his performances at the local VFW hall. The manager later put him in touch with Atlanta producer Doug Johnson, who has produced Stone's records ever since. Stone survived quadruple bypass surgery at age 35 and bounced back with a hit 1992 album entitled *From the Heart*, followed by the aptly titled *More Love* (1993). —B.A.

Stoneman Family

BORN: Ernest V. Stoneman, May 25, 1893
BIRTHPLACE: Monorat, Virginia
DIED: Ernest V. Stoneman, June 14, 1968

Ernest V. "Pop" Stoneman recorded his first test pressings in 1924. However, his first commercial recordings were done for pioneer producer Ralph Peer on Okeh Records in the mid-1920's.

From then on into the 1930's, he and his family recorded prodigiously for a variety of labels, with a variety of musicians. Strong sales of his secular and gospel releases netted him an unheard of $100 a day for recording during the late 20's. However, Pop Stoneman's luck didn't last. He spent money freely, and was forced back into factory work and a meager

existence around Washington, D.C., during World War II. He and his wife Hattie had 23 children, only 13 of whom lived to become adults.

Things changed in the late 40's when Pop and various groups of his children, under the name The Stoneman Family, began playing around the country. The group featured Pop, his sons Scotty (on fiddle), Jim (on bass) and Van (on guitar). Daughters Donna (on mandolin) and Roni (on banjo) rounded the group out. They did not find success easily, though they eventually became popular with folk music audiences after their Folkways album, *Old Time Tunes of the South*, appeared in 1957, during the dawn of the folk music boom. In 1962 the family recorded for Starday. They made their debut on The Grand Old Opry in 1966, and had five minor country hits from 1966 through 1968 on MGM , including "Tupelo County Jail," "The Five Little Johnson Girls" and "Back to Nashville, Tennessee." In 1966 they launched their own TV series, *Those Stonemans*. In 1967 they won the Country Music Association award for Best Vocal Group.

After Pop's death, The Stonemans continued, pursuing a more conventional country sound, and then experimented with a semi-bluegrass sound for RCA. But their success was modest. The best known Stoneman offspring, daughter Roni, became a *Hee Haw* regular and talented country comedian. Her sister, Donna Stoneman, is an evangelist today. —R.K.

Carl Story

BORN: May 29, 1916
BIRTHPLACE: Lenoir, North Carolina

Another major North Carolina-born bluegrass figure, Story began his career as a fiddler. Leading a band in the late 30's, he was evolving musically in much the same direction as Bill Monroe was, albeit on his own. During the World War II years he briefly played fiddle in Monroe's Blue Grass Boys. After the war, now singing and playing guitar, he started recording for Mercury, leading his group, The Rambling Mountaineers, and doing mainly gospel material. He recorded for a time for Columbia in the early 50's before moving to Starday in the mid-50's, during the time its material was being distributed by Mercury. Most of his best work was done for Mercury and Starday, though he also recorded for CMH in the 70's.—R.K.

George Strait

BORN: May 18, 1952
BIRTHPLACE: Pearsall, Texas

No single performer of the 1980's and 90's has done more to preserve the twin-fiddle honky-tonk/swing sound of his native Texas, and prove its continued commercial viability, than George Strait. His trademark white hat, copied by many artists, gave rise to the term "Hat Act," to describe similarly-attired male singers, and his music even inspired superstar Garth Brooks during his formative years. From his debut on MCA in 1981 to the present, he has carried on the spirit of Texas honky tonk and Western swing music in the tradition of Ray Price, Floyd Tillman and particularly Hank Thompson. Strait, who grew up in Pearsall, Texas, was initially interested in rock music during his early days in college. That changed when he married, quit school and joined the Army in 1971. Stationed in Hawaii, he started playing guitar and learned Hank Williams songs, graduating to Bob Wills, George Jones and Merle Haggard, whose 1970 tribute album to Bob Wills, *The Best Damn Fiddle Player in the World*, helped shape his future musical direction. Back in Texas after the service, while finishing his degree in agriculture at Southwest Texas State University, he began playing clubs at night. Though he worked for a time in ranching and was rebuffed by the music industry on his several trips to Nashville, he nonetheless became intent on a musical career. His first recordings were for Pappy Daily's D label. Leading his Ace in the Hole Band, he found a strong regional audience when Erv Woolsey, a former MCA record promotion man and Texas club owner, helped him land an MCA contract in 1981. Woolsey became Strait's manager, and remains so today.

Strait, as it turned out, was in the vanguard of the New Traditionalist movement, which was already stirring even as the Urban Cowboy era of the early 80's peaked. Though MCA Records had its hands full at the time with superstars of the day like Barbara Mandrell and The Oak Ridge Boys, and at first seemed indifferent to Strait's straight country sound, he was soon destined to become one of the biggest superstars of the 1980's and 90's. His first chart single, "Unwound," hit Number Six nationwide in 1981. In 1982 he had three hits, all Top Tens, with "If You're Thinkin' You Want a Stranger" reaching Number

Three. "Fool Hearted Memory" became his first Number One and "Marina Del Rey" reached Number Six in 1983. Beginning with "A Fire I Can't Put Out" in 1983, Strait had a solid streak of Number One records through 1984, including "You Look So Good in Love," a remake of the Bob Wills favorite "Right or Wrong," "Let's Fall to Pieces Together" and "Does Fort Worth Ever Cross Your Mind." In 1985, as New Traditionalism surged in popularity, he embarked on another streak of Number Ones, from "The Chair" to "Ocean Front Property," "All My Ex's Live in Texas" and the driving Western swing number, "Am I Blue." In 1988 he revived Faron Young's 1955 hit, "If You Ain't Lovin,'" as yet another Number One hit. The streak lasted until 1990 when his "Love Without End, Amen" remained Number One for five weeks at a time few singles remained in the top spot for more than a week. In 1989 and 1990 he was named Country Music Association Entertainer of the Year; he'd won the CMA's Male Vocalist of the Year Award in 1985 and 1986.

Through the 1990's, Strait has seldom been out of the Top Five, with such hits as "If I Know Me," "You Know Me Better Than That" (Number One two and three weeks, respectively) and 1993's "Easy Come, Easy Go," which also hit Number One. He had several more hits from the soundtrack of his 1992 movie debut, *Pure Country,* including "Heartland" and "I Cross My Heart," both of which went to hit Number One. As of 1993, he's had 24 Number One singles and still counting. —R.K.

Mel Street

BORN: October 21, 1933
BIRTHPLACE: Grundy, West Virginia
DIED: October 21, 1978

Street—who is best remembered for his self-written 1972 Top Ten hit, "Borrowed Angel," and his subsequent Top Five single, "Lovin' on Back Streets," along with the flurry of a dozen or so other Top Ten and Top 20 hits between 1972 and 1978—was born near Grundy, West Virginia. While dabbling in music, he tried his hand successfully at a number of occupations. He worked construction, climbed tall towers as an electrician for the Niagara Power Project at Niagara Falls, New York, and later owned his own auto body shop in Bluefield, West Virginia.

Street, who'd been singing in nightclubs in Niagara Falls and West Virginia, got his first major career break in 1963 when he became a regular performer on a local Saturday-night TV show called *Country Jamboree*, which was broadcast on WHIS, in Bluefield. "Borrowed Angel," the song for which Street is most often remembered, was actually released twice, both times to resounding indifference, on independent labels before it finally broke into the Top Ten in the summer of 1972, on the small Royal American label.

Though his chart success was sporadic during the years subsequent to "Borrowed Angel's" success, Street earned a handsome living on the road and seemed on the verge of a commercial breakthrough in 1978. He'd only recently escaped the indies and had signed a lucrative deal with Mercury Records, which was planning on giving him a big push. But by late 1978, Street's long-standing battle with alcoholism and depression bested him. He died of a self-

inflicted gunshot wound at age 43 on the morning of October 21, 1978, his birthday. His close friend, George Jones, who admired Street enough to have written liner notes to one of his early albums, braved pending arrest warrants by crossing the Tennessee state line to sing at Street's funeral. —B.A.

Stringbean

BORN: June 17, 1915
BIRTHPLACE: Annville, Kentucky
DIED: November 10, 1973

Born David Akeman, Stringbean was an agile picker and down-home humorist who inherited a special place in the hearts of Opry fans after the death of Uncle Dave Macon in 1952.

The tall, gangly Stringbean began playing professionally on radio station WLAP in Lexington in the mid-1930's and began touring with various country artists, including Ernest Tubb, Red Foley and Uncle Dave Macon. In the 1940's Stringbean

joined Bill Monroe and The Blue Grass Boys, with whom he played until 1945.

He joined the Grand Ole Opry in 1942 and developed an act that featured wild costumes and melded his banjo playing with his comic talents. In between Opry engagements, he appeared on Red Foley's ABC-TV programs off and on for the next 12 years.

It was after joining the Opry that Stringbean struck up a close friendship with legendary banjo player Uncle Dave Macon, who taught the younger player many of his own techniques. Stringbean also picked up on Uncle Dave's burlesque style of comedy; his humorous sketches were a popular Opry attraction throughout the 50's and 60's. During this time Stringbean recorded a slew of albums and singles on a number of different labels.

His best-known albums include *Kentucky Wonder* (1962), *Salute to Uncle Dave Macon* (1963), *Old Time Banjo Picking* and *Way Back in the Hills of Kentucky* (both in 1964). His talents also translated well to television, where he developed a following as a charter cast member of the popular series *Hee Haw*, working with his best friend, Grandpa Jones.

Stringbean (who'd long had a reputation for indiscreetly carrying large sums of cash on his person) was murdered with his wife when they surprised a burglar at their Nashville home on November 11, 1973. Those murders later became grist for a lurid book titled *The Stringbean Murders*. —M.B.

Marty Stuart

BORN: September 30, 1958
BIRTHPLACE: Philadelphia, Mississippi

One of the most well-liked figures in the modern country music industry, Marty Stuart is one of those artists whose importance and contributions to modern country music go far beyond the sum total of his career accomplishments, which include: a Gold album (for his 1992 *This One's Gonna Hurt You*) and a dozen or so hit records, including Top Tens like "Hillbilly Rock" (1990), "Tempted" (1991), "Burn Me Down" (1992), "This One's Gonna Hurt You (For a Long Long Time)," and 1991's Number Two, "The Whiskey Ain't Workin'"—the latter two duets with his friend, Travis Tritt. His presence has also been felt in recent years as an archivist and traditionalist whose love of country music's past heroes borders on religion, and whose fervent artistry (he is also an accomplished guitarist) has done much to keep their influence alive. In the process, he's made some fine music of his own.

John Marty Stuart was a child prodigy of sorts. A native of Philadelphia, Mississippi, he grew up collecting old country records, and for a time was a mandolinist with the gospel-oriented Sullivan family (with whom he collaborated on a fine album called *A Joyful Noise*, on the Country Music Foundation label in 1992). In 1971, at age 13, Stuart began working on the road playing mandolin with Lester Flatt and The Nashville Grass. After Flatt died, he joined Johnny Cash's road band (and was briefly married to Cash's daughter, Cindy). He recorded a now classic 1982 album for the independent Sugar Hill label, called *Busy Bee Cafe*, which brought together Cash, Scruggs and Doc Watson. His first major label break came when he joined Epic in 1986 for one album that didn't sell and another that didn't even get released. (Though, in the wake of his current success, both have since seen the light of day.) In 1990 he signed with MCA, recorded his *Hillbilly Rock* album, and saw things begin to turn around. This time he eased away from the neo-rockabilly bag Epic had pushed him into and instead combined his contemporary "hillbilly rock" with the traditional music he loves. In 1991, his single, "Tempted," became a hit and the above-mentioned hits soon followed.

Stuart's commitment to preserving traditional music is apparent in the many side projects he lends his

time and talents to, as both a producer and sideman. His reverence for the music's past is evident in his extensive collections. He owns vintage guitars that once belonged to Hank Williams, Johnny Cash, Lester Flatt and the late Clarence White; he tours in a bus that once belonged to Ernest Tubb and wears Nudie suits. He was made a member of the Grand Ole Opry in 1992. Additionally, Stuart has written about his idols for *Country Music Magazine* and *The Journal*. —R.K.

Nat Stuckey

BORN: November 17, 1934
BIRTHPLACE: Cass County, Texas
DIED: August 24, 1988

Nathan Wright Stuckey II was born in Texas. After serving as a local DJ, and putting together a band called The Cornhuskers, he gained fame as a *Louisiana Hayride* announcer, then began recording for Sims Records. In the mid-1960's, Nat signed with the Louisiana label, Paula Records, and by 1966, had a Number Four hit with "Sweet Thang." After a few

more Paula singles, RCA picked him up and he scored a Top Ten hit with his first single for them, "Plastic Saddle." He put nine more RCA singles into the Top 20 over the next few years, leaving the label in 1976. That year he switched to MCA Records, managing only two Top 40 hits ("Sun Comin' Up" and "The Days of Sand and Shovels") before leaving the label in 1978.

Though he never attained lasting stardom in the U.S., he was popular in Europe and toured there frequently. He died of lung cancer in 1988 and was buried in Shreveport.   —G.F.

Studio Musicians

The lifeblood of all great country music records is the studio musicians who make their living bouncing from session to session—many of them trained "by ear" as opposed to reading music charts.

One of the first session teams to emerge in Nashville consisted of the members of Red Foley's band—Zeke Turner, electric guitar; Jerry Byrd, steel guitar; Louis Innis, rhythm guitar; and Tommy Jackson, fiddle. All four also wound up on many of Hank Williams' early recordings, and in 1948 they became the house band for King Records in Cincinnati. Other session greats who hit their stride in country music's formative years were electric guitarists Hank Garland and Grady Martin; bass players Ernie Newton, Bob Moore and Junior Huskey; rhythm guitarist Ray Edenton; pianists Marvin Hughes, Owen Bradley and Gordon Stoker; and drummers Farris Coursey and Buddy Harman.

Unlike most pop and rock acts, country artists generally release an album every nine to 12 months, and an entire country album is often recorded in a few weeks, or even a few days, giving plenty of work for the relatively small handful of A-Team studio musicians, many of whom work three or four sessions a day, five days or more a week.   —R.P.

Sun Records

Although it issued many types of music during its 16 years as an active label, Sun Records will forever be associated with rockabilly—the vital, amphetamine-laced fusion of honky tonk country music with raw Southern rhythm and blues so central to the birth of rock 'n' roll.

Sun's genesis dates to January 1950, when radio announcer Sam Phillips opened his custom studio, Memphis Recording Service. That summer he began producing both country and blues artists, selling the masters to established labels like Chess and R.P.M. Early successes by Jackie Brenston, B.B. King, Howling Wolf and Roscoe Gordon led Phillips to establish Sun in March 1952. During the next two years, Phillips primarily recorded Memphis-based blues singers and an occasional country act. In July 1954, Sun released Elvis Presley's fiery "That's All Right, Mama" b/w "Blue Moon of Kentucky." It was a two-sided regional hit with youthful listeners from Tennessee to Texas, and led to a significant change in the label's direction.

In November 1955, RCA Victor bought Presley's contract for $30,000, which gave Phillips the capital to break two other artists: Carl Perkins and Johnny Cash. Perkins' "Blue Suede Shoes," released the following month, became Sun's first major hit, reaching Number One on *Billboard's* country chart and Number Two pop.

Perkins' and Cash's early hits drew many talented young rockers to Sun's Memphis studio, most notably Jerry Lee Lewis, whose manic "Whole Lotta Shakin' Goin' On" and "Great Balls of Fire" were unstoppable pop chart hits in 1957. Other notable Sun rockers were Billy Lee Riley, Warren Smith, Ray Harris, Roy Orbison and Sonny Burgess; most only saw regional success. A subsidiary label, Phillips International, scored pop hits with Charlie Rich, Carl Mann and saxman Bill Justis.

Sun lost much of its momentum in 1958. Carl Perkins and Johnny Cash jumped to Columbia, a scandal derailed Jerry Lee Lewis' career, and Phillips fired his two most talented producer/arrangers, Justis and Jack Clement, over a trivial matter. During the next ten years most Sun records featured indifferent or excessive productions that bore little resemblance to the label's finest moments. In 1969 Phillips sold the label to Shelby Singleton, who repackaged many Sun recordings into sloppily pressed, budget-priced albums which often did the vital importance of the music a great disservice. Singleton also enjoyed chart success with five previously unissued Jerry Lee Lewis masters that sounded similar to Lewis' country hits on Mercury's Smash subsidiary. European interest in American rock 'n' roll led to extensive mining of the Sun vaults; hundreds of unissued Sun blues, country and rockabilly recordings appeared on European and Japanese labels during the 70's and 80's.   —D.S.

Doug Supernaw

BORN: September 26, 1960
BIRTHPLACE: Bryan, Texas

After growing up in Houston, and making a couple of attempts at college, Supernaw went to Nashville in 1987, determined to make it in country music. He spent four years as a struggling songwriter before returning to Texas, assembling a band (Texas Steel) and refining his craft. After attracting the attention of Nashville, he signed with BNA Records in 1992, releasing his debut album, *Red and Rio Grande*, in 1993. With a rich voice and a style that's more traditional country than a lot of the early 90's neo-honky tonkers, Supernaw had a Number One hit with "I Don't Call Him Daddy" and another Top Ten with "Reno," which he co-wrote.   —G.F.

Billy Swan

BORN: May 12, 1942
BIRTHPLACE: Cape Girardeau, Missouri

A long-time band member and compatriot of Kris Kristofferson, Billy Swan is best known for his across-the-board Number One 1974 smash hit, "I Can Help." Swan was born in 1942, in Cape Girardeau, Missouri, and started out in a local band with the improbable name of Mirt Mirtley and The Rhythm Steppers. "Lover Please," a song he wrote at age 16, became a huge

R&B/pop hit for Clyde McPhatter. He later made a name for himself as a record producer, producing several of Tony Joe White's earliest and most critically acclaimed albums.

Though Swan continued recording sporadically until the late 1980's, he never came close to recapturing the one-shot success of "I Can Help" (which was not only by far his biggest career hit, but also his very first major label release). He did, however, have some success in the pop charts with a follow-up, "Everything's the Same." Besides backing Kris Kristofferson for years, Swann also did a stint in Kinky Friedman's band. In 1986, he formed a short-lived band called Black Tie, along with Nashville session man Randy Meisner.   —B.A.

Sweethearts of the Rodeo

BORN: Janis Gill, March 1, 1955, Torrance, California
Kristine Arnold, November 28, 1956, Torrance, California

This sister duet team hit the big time in 1986 with their debut album, *Sweethearts of the Rodeo*, which, like their self-chosen group name, was inspired by the classic 1968 Byrds album of the same name.

rolling, he was also busy talking up the Sweethearts. Thus the time seemed right for Kristine to follow her sister to Nashville. The Sweethearts' first big break came in 1985 when they won the grand prize in the Wrangler Country Showdown competition. The following year their first Columbia album was released. It resulted in four Top Ten hits: "Midnight Girl/Sunset Town," "Chains of Gold," "Gotta Get Away" and "Since I Found You." *Sweethearts of the Rodeo* was rated by *Billboard* as one of the Top Ten albums of 1987 and stayed on the charts for more than 90 weeks.

Unfortunately, Sweethearts of the Rodeo's chart success proved intermittent, at best, despite their noteworthy original songwriting, and Kristine's emergence as a distinctive solo voice within the group. After three more solid albums for Columbia—*One Time, One Night* (1988), *Buffalo Zone* (1990) and *Sisters* (1992), the string ran out. Happily, the Sweethearts found renewed inspiration on the independent Sugar Hill label which, in 1994, released their latest album, *Rodeo Waltz.* —B.A.

Kristine Arnold and Janis Gill (Vince Gill's wife) had already been plying their sisterly duets for many years by the time they had their first chart records—since they were seven and nine years old, respectively, to be more precise. They put their first band together in their mid-teens and began playing in suburban Los Angeles pizza parlors and shopping malls. By the 70's, they were already immersed in the music of the then vital California country-rock scene (Ronstadt, The Eagles, The Byrds, etc.), and were also soaking up every other sort of influence, from The Beatles to Bob Wills—all of which eventually found its way into their distinctive duet sound.

Soon, Janis and Kristine were regulars on California's thriving bluegrass circuit. But for quite a few years afterward, the two sisters drifted out of music and into marriage and motherhood. (Kristine's husband is guitarist John Arnold.) "Janis and I had been beating down doors trying to get somebody interested in our music in L.A. for years," Kristine Arnold later recalled. "And we frankly were burned out, and we thought, 'I don't want to do this anymore. I want to have my family.'"

But then Janis moved to Nashville in the mid-1980's when husband Vince landed a contract with RCA Records. From the moment Vince got his own career

Sylvia

BORN: December 9, 1956
BIRTHPLACE: Kokomo, Indiana

Sylvia (born Sylvia Kirby), a country/pop queen of the early 80's, rode the wave of the Urban Cowboy craze with a string of ten Top Ten hits for RCA. The Kokomo, Indiana, born and raised singer was discovered while working as a secretary for producer Tom Collins, who became her manager and producer.

Country chart hits like "Nobody" (also a Number 15 pop hit), "Like Nothing Ever Happened," "Drifter," "Cry Just a Little Bit" and "Snapshot" propelled her to fame; but by the latter part of the 80's, with the rise of New Traditionalism, Sylvia's brand of glossy pop-country had fallen out of favor. Later, she was a regular on The Nashville Network. —G.F.

James Talley

BORN: November 9, 1944
BIRTHPLACE: Mehan, Oklahoma

A singer/songwriter in the socially-conscious folk vein of Woody Guthrie, Talley also drew his inspiration from Western swing, blues and country, all of which he was exposed to during his childhood in New Mexico. In 1968, he moved to Nashville, gaining employment as a social worker while attempting to make it in music. After an early 70's single on Atlantic, Talley signed to Capitol in 1975. But even with almost unanimous critical praise for his songs covering the plight of the poor and working class—as well as the support of the Carter White House (First Lady Rosalyn called him her favorite singer and had him play at the Inauguration)—Talley found little chart

success. Radio resisted his complex, often depressing tales. After three highly praised but poorly selling albums, Talley was dropped by Capitol in 1977. He's since prospered as a Nashville real estate agent, and his vintage Capitol recordings have been reissued on CD by Bear Family Records in recent years.   —G.F.

Gid Tanner

BORN: June 6, 1885
BIRTHPLACE: Monroe, Georgia
DIED: May 13, 1960

James Gideon Tanner won his place in history as the leader of The Skillet Lickers, the most colorful and well-known stringband in early country music. He was a chicken farmer by trade, and absorbed much of the rural North Georgia fiddling traditions at the turn of the century. He first came to fame prior to World War I when he emerged as a favorite at Atlanta area fiddling contests. In 1924 Columbia records brought him and his friend, Riley Puckett, to New

York as their answer to the popular Fiddlin' John Carson. At this Tanner was not all that successful, but in 1926 the company paired him and Puckett with another young fiddler, Clayton McMichen, and banjoist Fate Norris, to form The Skillet Lickers. This early "supergroup" had dozens of hit records, such as "Watermelon on the Vine," "Bully of the Town" and "Pass Around the Bottle and We'll All Take a Drink." The band broke up in 1931, but Tanner reformed it in 1934 with his son, Gordon, and did a series of sides for Victor/Bluebird, one of which, "Down Yonder," became a country standard. Tanner died in 1960, though Gordon and grandson Phil have kept the Tanner music alive into the present day.   —C.W.

Al Terry

BORN: January 14, 1922
BIRTHPLACE: Kaplan, Louisiana

Besides Jimmy C. Newman and the team of Rusty & Doug Kershaw, Al Terry (a.k.a. Alison Joseph Theriot) was the only Cajun vocalist in the early 50's who had a serious shot at mainstream country success. Though his first recordings were done after World War II for Gold Star and later for the Louisiana-based Feature Records, most of his classic work was done for Acuff-Rose's Hickory Records from 1953 to 1958. His best known recording, the 1953 "Good Deal Lucille," didn't become a big hit, though Carl Smith's cover version did.

The Hickory sides were primarily regional successes, though they featured some of Nashville's best studio musicians (Chet Atkins, Hank Garland, Harold Bradley, Grady Martin, Lightnin' Chance). "Watchdog," however, was a national hit in 1960. After a brief association with Dot, his career slowed down and he returned to the regional labels he began with. Terry, who became handicapped after his recording career tapered off, later worked for the State of Louisiana.　　　　　　　　　　　　　—R.K.

Texas Tornados

The Texas Tornados includes border legend Flaco Jimenez on accordion, Augie Meyers on keyboards, former rock vocalist and general crazy man Doug Sahm and lead singer Freddy Fender, all born and raised in or around San Antonio. The best known of the four, Fender, is remembered for a handful of hits in the mid-70's, including "Wasted Days and Wasted Nights," "You'll Lose a Good Thing" and 1974's "Before the Next Teardrop Falls." Sahm and Meyers played with the 1960's rock band Sir Douglas Quintet (classics: "Mendocino" and "She's About a Mover"), and Jimenez is credited with almost single-handedly bringing the Conjunto accordion to American audiences.

The Tornados got together at Slim's, Boz Scaggs' San Francisco nightclub, in 1989. Warner Bros. liked the idea of a Tex-Mex version of The Traveling Wilburys and signed the group later that year. Their first album, *The Texas Tornados*, was released in 1990. One track, the single "Soy De San Luis," won the group a Grammy for Best Mexican-American perfor-

mance. In 1991, the single "Zone of Our Own" also earned a Grammy nomination for Best Country Vocal Performance by a Group. (See also, Freddy Fender.)　　　—M.B.

B.J. Thomas

BORN: August 7, 1942
BIRTHPLACE: Hugo, Oklahoma

While Billy Joe Thomas was raised in Texas with a country and gospel background, his middle-of-the-road, easy-listening musical style put him firmly in the ranks of the pop-country crossover artists of the1960's and 70's. His very first chart entry came on the Scepter label in 1966 with his version of Hank Williams' "I'm So Lonesome I Could Cry," which was a Number Eight pop hit. He had further pop success in the mid-to-late 60's, most notably with "Hooked on a Feeling" (1968) and "Raindrops Keep Fallin' on My Head" (which was featured in the movie, *Butch Cassidy and the Sundance Kid,* and hit Number One in 1969). His 1975 "(Hey Won't You Play Another) Somebody Done Somebody Wrong Song," marketed as a crossover, reached Number One both pop and country. It was also his last big pop hit. Plagued by personal problems throughout his career, he label-hopped quite often and became a born-again Christian, recording some gospel albums along with secular music. Two more country Number Ones followed in 1983: "Whatever Happened to Old-Fashioned Love" and "New Looks from an Old Lover." By the late 80's, he had re-focused on gospel music.　　—G.F.

Hank Thompson

BORN: September 3, 1925
BIRTHPLACE: Waco, Texas

Before George Strait, before Clint Black and definitely before Garth Brooks, there was Hank Thompson. It was Hank who, during a ten-year period in the late 1940's and 50's, created a sound that paved the way for Strait and company today.

Fusing Texas' most important musical styles, Western swing and honky tonk, he created a highly commercial sound with appeal far beyond The Lone Star State. The two styles differed; except for a few numbers like "San Antonio Rose" and "Faded Love," Western swing was primarily dance music in which lyrics took second place, while honky tonk was oriented toward lyrics and moods. Hank's voice was more polished than Ernest Tubb's, but it conveyed much of the same feeling, and, like Tubb, Hank knew how to put across a lyric. The proof? Twenty-nine Top Ten records between 1948 and 1974. One of them, "The Wild Side of Life," spent 15 weeks at Number One in 1952.

Born in Waco, Texas, in 1925, Henry William Thompson grew up listening to all types of music—including records owned by a neighbor who sold bootleg liquor during Prohibition. His collection of 78's by Carson Robison, Vernon Dalhart and other favorites inspired Hank. He got a guitar for Christmas, and by 1942, while a high school senior, he landed his own show over WACO Radio (the town was actually named for the radio station), billed as "Hank the Hired Hand."

He graduated from high school in 1943 and joined the U.S. Navy, serving as a radioman in the Pacific. During his off hours he wrote songs and sang for his shipmates. After his discharge in 1946 he returned to Waco, set up shop at KWTX radio, assembled his original Brazos Valley Boys and started playing local dance halls.

He soon had a record deal with the Los Angeles-based Globe label and recorded his first single, "Whoa Sailor" (with "Swing Wide Your Gate of Love" on the B-side), in Dallas in 1946. It was a hit in the Southwest and in Texas, thanks largely to the enthusiasm of Dallas disc jockey Hal Horton, whose radio show on 50,000-watt KRLD gave the song nationwide exposure. Hank then cut "A Lonely Heart Knows" and several other singles for the Bluebonnet label in Dallas. At this point, his sound was still evolving; the smoothness of the mature Brazos Valley Boys was yet to come.

In 1947 Capitol Records signed Thompson on the strength of Tex Ritter's recommendation. Ritter had heard Hank while touring Texas and put in a good word for him. That October, at a Dallas radio station, Hank recorded his first nationwide hit, "Humpty

Dumpty Heart." A bouncy number, it was released on Capitol's Americana label (a short-lived subsidiary devoted to country artists) and reached Number Two on the *Billboard* charts early in '48. Hank had two more Top Tens in 1949, "What Are We Gonna Do About the Moonlight" (Number Ten) and "Green Light" (Number Seven). He also re-recorded "Whoa Sailor." This time it went to Number Six nationwide. The follow-up single, "Soft Lips," also reached Number Six.

However, it wasn't until 1952 that Thompson found the song that would truly cement his reputation: "The Wild Side of Life." The song itself was a fusion of old and new—new lyrics added to the melody of The Carter Family tune, "I'm Thinking Tonight of My Blue Eyes." It hit Number One on May 10, 1952, staying there for 15 weeks. Ironically, it was the B-side of the record and not expected to be a hit.

One line in "The Wild Side of Life" gave rise to another classic. The words "I didn't know God made honky tonk angels" inspired J.D. Miller, owner of a record company in Crowley, Louisiana, to write an answer song titled "It Wasn't God Who Made Honky Tonk Angels." Miller produced a recording of it by an obscure female singer named Al Montgomery; it went nowhere. But when Kitty Wells recorded her version in 1952, it went to Number One on August 8th, stayed there six weeks and made her a star as well.

Meanwhile, Hank was on a roll. "Waitin' in the Lobby of Your Heart," with its unusual steel guitar "wah-wah" peaked at Number Three in the summer of '52. The follow-up, "The New Wears Off Too Fast," made it to Number Ten. In May 1953, "Rub-A-Dub-Dub," another nursery rhyme-based song like "Humpty Dumpty Heart," stayed three weeks at Number One. "Wake Up, Irene," his novelty answer to the then-current pop hit, "Goodnight, Irene," spent two weeks at Number One in early 1954. This recording was the first Thompson hit to feature Merle Travis' distinctive guitar picking. Travis would record (and tour) with Hank for many years after that. That same year Hank had several more hits. "A Fooler, a Faker" and "Honky Tonk Girl" were both Number Nines. "The New Green Light," a follow-up to his 1948 hit, reached Number Four. He also did a bit of his own star-making when he discovered Wanda Jackson in Oklahoma and added her to the band.

Praise for The Brazos Valley Boys was understandable. This simple backup group had evolved into a sleek big band, combining the best of Bob Wills' buoyant beat and Spade Cooley's smooth, tight, multiple-fiddle arrangements. A good deal of credit for this creation goes to Hank's early musical director, guitarist Billy Gray. The Brazos Valley Boys even recorded three albums themselves in the 1960's and 70's. Steel guitarist Lefty Nason, an early member, created little accents and punctuations that every Brazos Valley steel player after him used.

Hank employed steel guitar legends Pee Wee Whitewing, Curly Chalker, Bob White, Bobby Garrett and Bert Rivera (at one point the band had twin steels!). He also had fiddle greats Keith Coleman and Curly Lewis. And when Travis wasn't available, Hank did his own Travis-style picking on a Gibson Super 400 electric guitar identical to Merle's.

In 1955 Merle gave Hank and the band a hit with an instrumental version of The Carter Family's "Wildwood Flower." In 1956, Hank had one Top Ten record, "The Blackboard of My Heart." That year, to capitalize on the rock 'n' roll craze he wrote and recorded "Rockin' in the Congo." In 1957 it became a Number 13 hit, but gave Elvis no nervous moments.

Hank's good nature always carried the band through. The late Keith Kolby, who served for a time as Hank's drummer, recalled a time when one of The Brazos Valley Boys, having had too much honky tonkin' the night before, got sick all over Hank's Gibson guitar before a show. Hank simply laughed it off and cleaned up the guitar. They were on the road constantly and became one of the first successful country acts to play Las Vegas.

By 1958 they were back in the Top Ten with "Squaws Along the Yukon," which hit Number Two, and "I've Run Out of Tomorrows," which peaked at Number Seven. At this point, Hank had two "firsts" with Capitol. In 1958 he recorded the first country stereo album—his now-classic *Songs for Rounders*, one of the greatest honky tonk albums ever made. And in 1959 he discovered a song he would make one of the greatest drinking songs of all time, the brash, buoyant "A Six Pack to Go." He first heard it performed in Arizona by a local band that included the song's composer. By the spring of 1960 he'd made it a Number Ten hit.

The next year he had yet another "first" with Capitol, becoming the first solo country artist to record a live album. *Hank Thompson at the Golden Nugget* remains a classic of its kind. Also in 1961 he created a superb version of the Jack Guthrie classic, "Oklahoma Hills," which went to Number Seven. By 1964 his records were hanging lower in the charts, though he still had some fine ones, including "Hangover Tavern," another boozy classic.

He signed with Dot in 1968; it remained his label for nearly a decade. His first two Dot recordings, both honky tonkers, returned him to the Top Ten. "On Tap, In the Can, Or In the Bottle" reached Number Seven; "Smoky the Bar" peaked at Number Five. Hank had a steady stream of singles after that, the biggest being "I've Come Awful Close," a Number 11 in 1971. He worked with a smaller group of Brazos Valley Boys and recorded album-length salutes to pop acts like The Mills Brothers and Nat "King" Cole; 1974 saw his last two Top Ten records, "The Older the Violin, the Sweeter the Music" (Number Eight) and "Who Left the Door to Heaven Open" (Number Ten). After a brief time with MCA, he recorded a bit for Churchill Records, a label owned by legendary manager, Jim Halsey, who got his start managing Hank in the early 50's.

Hank Thompson's legacy is clear every time George, Garth or Clint sing. He kept Western swing alive and broadened its audience. His Capitol recordings remain monuments to his own musical power and vision, as does his status as a member of the Country Music Hall of Fame to which he was elected in 1989.　　—R.K.

Sue Thompson

BORN: July 19, 1926
BIRTHPLACE: Nevada, Missouri

Though Eva Sue McKee was Missouri-born, she grew up in California and began singing there as a child. Her child-like singing voice helped her stand out in the early 50's when she joined California country singer Dude Martin's Round-up Gang and she first recorded with Martin's band for Mercury. She and Martin married, moved to L.A., and for a time had their own TV show on the West Coast. Her recordings for Mercury weren't successful. After she divorced Martin, she married bandleader Hank Penny, a former comic on Martin's show, and recorded with him on Decca in the mid-50's. She and Penny moved to Las Vegas around 1956 and worked there together until their divorce in 1963. In the 60's she signed with the Hickory label, concentrating more on pop material. She had Top Five pop hits with "Sad Movies" in 1961, "Norman" in 1962 and "Paper Tiger" in 1965 before returning to country, recording solo records and doing duets with Don Gibson for Hickory.   —R.K.

Mel Tillis

BORN: August 8, 1932
BIRTHPLACE: Pahokee, Florida

Mel Tillis was born Lonnie Melvin Tillis in Pahokee, Florida, on August 8, 1932. A bout with malaria at age of three left him with a chronic stutter. Instead of treating it as a handicap, though, Tillis found ways to capitalize on his stuttering, making a whole schtick out of it in his performances.

For years, in fact, his speech impediment was a trademark that endeared him to millions of country fans and was the source of continued inspiration—including the title for an album (*M-M-Mel Live*) and a candid 1985 autobiography (*Stutterin' Boy*).

After quitting the University of Florida and being discharged from the Air Force, Mel worked on the railroad for a while, then moved to Nashville in 1957 and began a highly successful career as a songwriter. One of his early compositions, "I'm Tired," became a Number One hit for Webb Pierce—one of many chart-toppers he wrote for Pierce. He went on to write a number of other major hits, including "Ruby, Don't Take Your Love to Town," recorded by Kenny Rogers and The First Edition, and "Detroit City," a smash hit for Bobby Bare.

After building an impressive reputation as a songwriter, Tillis found it difficult to break into performing. Although he had a moderately successful single, "The Violet and the Rose," in 1957, it would take him eight more years in Nashville to break the Top Ten with "Wine" (1965).

Tillis had a number of hits though the 1970's and early 80's, including six Number Ones: "I Ain't Never"(1972), "Good Woman Blues" (1976), "Heart Healer" (1977), "I Believe in You" (1978), "Coca Cola Cowboy" (1979) and "Southern Rains" (1981). The Country Music Association named him Entertainer of the Year in 1976.

Tillis' interest in entertainment is not limited to music. In the mid-70's he hosted a short-lived TV

variety series, *Mel and Susan Together*, with actress Susan Anton. More recently, he co-produced and co-starred (with Roy Clark) in the 1985 film, *Uphill All the Way*. He also appeared in various other films, including *W.W. and The Dixie Dance Kings* with Burt Reynolds and Jerry Reed.

In recent years, Tillis has flourished as a businessman and music publisher and is going strong in Branson, where he recently opened his own theater. His daughter, Pam, is also a country singer.   —M.B.

Pam Tillis

BORN: July 24, 1957
BIRTHPLACE: Plant City, Florida

For years, Pam Tillis was perceived around Nashville as a wild rich kid—the immensely talented but hopelessly spoiled and dissolute progeny of country star Mel Tillis who seemed to routinely blow every chance she got at a recording career of her own. Even the quirky, delightfully idiosyncratic Tillis has herself conceded in so many words that privilege and its accompanying excesses are not the best breeding ground for ambition.

"My dad grew up in rural Florida during the De-

pression, when he worked in the fields and everybody went to bed with the chickens," Tillis recalled a few years ago. "I grew up in suburban Nashville with a new Cadillac every year, listening to Southern rock."

Pam Tillis was herself actually born in Plant City, Florida, on July 24, 1957. Music was obviously in her blood; she made her first stage appearance at age eight, singing with her father on The Grand Ole Opry. As a teenager, she also sang for a while in the elder Tillis' road band.

At age 16, she was sidelined for a while by a serious auto accident that required plastic surgery. Yet, as Pam, the oldest of Mel's five children, reached college age, her interests turned elsewhere; Southern rock and country-rock became her music of choice, and she even moved to California and was briefly in a jazz fusion band.

But later, back in Nashville after a number of "lost years," the responsibilities of single parenthood (she has a son, Ben, and just a couple of years ago married noted Nashville songwriter Bob DiPiero) caused Tillis to gradually buckle down and take her own talents a little more seriously.

She initially found success as a songwriter, her tunes having been covered by Conway Twitty, Highway 101, Barbara Fairchild, Gloria Gaynor, Juice Newton and others. Her searing, yet oddly little-girlish soprano also made her a much-in-demand demo singer. Along the way she dabbled in disco and new wave.

Thus all the building blocks were there; yet, for some strange reason, during the five years of her first major label record deal, with Warner Bros., she came up with nothing that reached higher than Number 55 in the country singles charts.

But, at long last, when Tillis signed with the fledgling Arista label in 1990, the success so long predicted for her finally became a reality. Her fine Arista debut album, *Put Yourself In My Place* (1991) resulted in three memorable hits: "Don't Tell Me What to Do," "One of Those Things" and "Maybe It Was Memphis." *Homeward Looking Angel* (1992), her second Arista album, carried the momentum of its predecessor forward, spawning two Top Five hits, "Shake the Sugar Tree" and "Let That Pony Run," and two additional Top 20's: "Cleopatra, Queen of Denial" and "Do You Know Where Your Man Is." Her third Arista album, *Sweetheart's Dance*, was released to much critical acclaim in 1994.   —B.A.

Floyd Tillman

BORN: December 8, 1914
BIRTHPLACE: Ryan, Oklahoma

One of country music's greatest composers and a major contributor to the rise of honky tonk, Floyd Tillman's unique vocal phrasing influenced both Lefty Frizzell and Willie Nelson. His songs also had a pop flavor that made them palatable to pop singers as well. After growing up in Post, Texas, Tillman worked around Houston with bandleader Adolph Hofner and later with a pop orchestra before joining Leon "Pappy" Selph's Blue Ridge Playboys in 1936. With Selph, he wrote the classic honky tonk ballad, "It Makes No Difference Now," selling it to singer Jimmie Davis for $300 (he later reclaimed the rights). The first known country singer to accompany himself on electric guitar, Tillman began recording for Decca in 1939 but didn't have any hits until World War II. His first big one was "They Took the Stars out of Heaven," which became a Number One record in 1944. Later that year his sentimental war-time ballads, "Each Night at Nine" and "G.I. Blues," also became hits.

After Columbia signed him in 1946, his first hit came with Jerry Irby's drinking song, "Driving Nails in My Coffin." In 1948 his own ballad, "I Love You So Much It Hurts," became a Top Five hit. In 1949 Tillman wrote the song that would define his career: "Slippin' Around," one of the first songs to deal head-on with adultery. Tillman's version was a hit, and that fall Margaret Whiting and Jimmy Wakely's duet version on Capitol topped both the country and pop charts. Tillman also had a country hit that year with "I Gotta Have My Baby Back." After leaving Columbia in 1954, Tillman recorded for various labels. In 1976 he was inducted into the Nashville Songwriters Hall of Fame, and in 1984, the Country Music Hall of Fame. He rarely appears in public, though a 1993 appearance on TNN's *The Texas Connection* revealed his gifts had barely been affected by age. —R.K.

Aaron Tippin

BORN: July 3, 1958
BIRTHPLACE: Pensacola, Florida

Aaron Tippin's anthemic 1990 hit, "You've Got To Stand For Something," which was also his debut single and the title tune to his debut album, not only reached Number Six on the country charts, it also set the tone for this South Carolina-raised singer's still-young career. While other stars of the day have gained mass popularity with a country style that embraces the mellow accessibility of subtle pop or country-rock influences, Tippin's charm and distinctiveness lie in his resolute—at times, almost defiant—twanginess. Much like Kentuckian Marty Brown, Tippin (especially on his early recordings) seemed to even one-up the New Traditionalists.

Born in Pensacola, Florida, on July 3, 1958, Tippin grew up on a 120-acre farm in South Carolina's mountainous northwestern-most "Dark Corner" region, best known for its bootlegging and other nefarious activities. His hard country musical journey started when

he was in his early teens and stumbled across an eight-track tape of Hank Williams' greatest hits. He quickly fell in love with the style and has been ever since.

Tippin worked has a welder, truck driver, heavy equipment operator, raised hogs, flew small aircraft, competed in semi-professional body building contests, sang in local bands, married, had a daughter, and divorced before finally landing in Nashville at age 28. Armed with a video of an appearance he'd made on The Nashville Network show, *You Can Be a Star*, he began making the rounds. But he found his initial success as a songwriter. (He and Mark Collie co-wrote Collie's hit, "Somethin' With a Ring to It," and his songs have also been recorded by Charley Pride, David Ball, The Kingsmen and various other gospel artists.) He balanced songwriting with working in a Kentucky rolling mill for several years before a demo tape he'd made came across the desk of Joe Gallante, then head of RCA/Nashville, who signed him to his first recording contract.

As of the mid-90's, the Tippin juggernaut is still rolling boldly along. With each album he's widened his audience. (His 1992 album, *Read Between The Lines,* was a certified million-seller and *Call of the Wild*, his most recent, seems headed in the same direction.) His radio friendly 1992 hit, "There Ain't Nothin' Wrong with the Radio," hit Number One— his only chart-topper to date. More recently, he's beefed up his aggressive hard country vocal delivery with a boisterous stage show and a pounding percussive and rhythmic musical underpinning which he calls his "four-wheel-drive bottom end sound, underneath traditional fiddle and steel."   —B.A

Tootsie's Orchid Lounge

This hole-in-the-wall tavern on Nashville's Lower Broadway first opened for business in March 1960, serving up beer, fried chicken and jukebox music under the proprietorship of Mrs. Hattie Louise Tatum—fondly known as Tootsie by famous patrons like Willie Nelson, Tom T. Hall, Faron Young, George Jones, Kris Kristofferson and dozens of other songwriters and stars who congregated there in the 60's and early 70's.

By dint of the fact that its back entrance was just across the alley from the Ryman Auditorium, long-

time home of the Grand Ole Opry, Tootsie's quickly became the favored watering hole of country stars (who couldn't make any references to alcohol on the stage of the Opry, but weren't above having a couple of cold ones between performances) and the songwriters and executives trying to corral them to do a little business. Thus Tootsie's, for all its down-home formality (the dusty walls were, and still are, plastered with photos, autographs, album covers and every other sort of memorabilia), soon became one of the hubs of the Nashville music industry.

But in the 1970's, as the Opry moved to its new digs at Opryland and the increasingly corporate record industry entrenched itself on Music Row, Tootsie's relevance faded and it survived mainly on the strength of the tourist trade. The fading establishment was dealt another blow when Tootsie died of cancer on February 18, 1978. In the late 80's and early 90's, as the once shabby Lower Broadway district has undergone revitalization, Tootsie's, now a colorful anachronism, still holds on by a thread.   —B.A.

Town Hall Party

In 1952, country music promoter William Wagnon came to Los Angeles and took over the last dance-hall run by promoter-TV show host, Bert "Foreman" Phillips: the old Town Hall building in Compton, California, a Los Angeles suburb. Wagnon started holding western dances in the building, but dances weren't as popular as during World War II. He then shifted instead to a Grand Ole Opry style "Barn Dance" format. Wagnon knew network TV host Art Linkletter, host of CBS' popular afternoon show *House Party*, aimed at housewives. He named his barn dance show *Town Hall Party*. It debuted over KFI Radio, and the early cast included host Tex Ritter, Johnny Bond (who also wrote for the show), Wesley Tuttle, Les "Carrot Top" Anderson, Eddie Dean, Merle Travis and Joe and Rose Lee Maphis. They began broadcasting over a new television station, KTTV Channel 11. It began as a two-hour broadcast with guest performers. Initial response was poor until an hour was added so the show ran from 10 PM to 1 A.M. It quickly became a hit; and since the old Town Hall had a dance floor, dancers were welcomed, as were any Nashville artists passing through—including Patsy Cline, Johnny Cash and Jim Reeves. The show also featured rockabilly, played by Carl Perkins (as a guest) and The Collins Kids and Bob Luman as cast regulars. The show's announcer was Jay Stewart, later the announcer on the popular TV game show, *Let's Make a Deal*.

By the late 50's the show included among its regulars Freddie Hart and Tex Williams. Among the musicians in the show's staff band were its leader, Joe Maphis, blind pianist Jimmy Pruett and two talented female musicians: fiddler Margie Warren and steel guitarist Marian Hall, who replaced Dick Stubbs. Some 39 half-hour versions of *Town Hall,* retitled *Ranch Party* or *Western Ranch Party* were nationally syndicated in the late 50's. *Town Hall Party* finally ended for good in 1960. —R.K.

Transcriptions

In the days of radio, most radio shows, even those featuring music, were done live. But even in the 1930's, the idea of pre-recorded music, "transcribed" onto discs, was gaining favor in all fields of music. In some cases, performers would "transcribe" their shows before going on tour. In other cases, transcription companies would record artists and sell the recordings to radio stations, often to be used as pre-packaged shows. Since the discs were often 16 inches, some performers were able to record longer tunes than they could fit on a 78 r.p.m. (10-inch) shellac disc.

Some live broadcasts of local country shows and of programs like the Grand Ole Opry were "transcribed" for broadcast to the U.S. military through the Armed Forces Radio Service. Some of the best-known transcriptions in the country field are the Bob Wills Tiffany Transcriptions, which were recorded from 1945-47 to be sold as radio shows (the effort was unsuccessful). Hank Snow's Thesaurus Transcriptions, done under the auspices of NBC, were also sold to stations. Various artists recorded for World Transcriptions, including Ernest Tubb, while others recorded for Standard Transcriptions, among them many West Coast artists. Capitol Records even had a Transcriptions division within the company, and at times would release transcription material on commercial singles or albums. Eventually, as DJ's came into favor and tape recording became routine, the concept of "transcriptions" became outdated, but they remain valuable to record collectors and music researchers. —R.K.

Merle Travis

BORN: November 29, 1917
BIRTHPLACE: Rosewood, Kentucky
DIED: October 20, 1983

The year was 1936. Eighteen-year-old Merle Robert Travis, his stint in the Depression-era Civilian Conservation Corps over, traveled to see his brother, Taylor, in Evansville, Indiana. Together, they attended a dance that was being broadcast live over local radio. When Merle got up and finger picked an impromptu version of "Tiger Rag" on his guitar, dazzling the crowd, The Tennessee Tomcats, an area band, immediately hired him. From that day on, Merle Robert Travis was a professional musician.

But he was much more. In a field where many performers played music and did little else, Travis was a brilliant and diversified performer—and individual. True, he popularized the complex guitar finger picking of his native Western Kentucky. Granted, he had his own share of hits and wrote hits for others, among them "Sixteen Tons" and "Smoke! Smoke! Smoke! (That Cigarette)." In addition, he was an accomplished taxidermist, journalist, watch repairman and cartoonist. Like many creative people Travis denied, even ridiculed, his talents. Says longtime friend, Hank Penny, "I used to tell him, 'Merle, don't down yourself'. He'd say, 'Oh, heck, I can't play.... Oh, Lord, what a li'l ol' ticky guitar player I am.'"

Born November 29, 1917, in Rosewood, Kentucky,

he was the youngest of four children. His father, Rob Travis, worked in the local coal mines. The Travises finally settled on a farm near Ebenezer, Kentucky; the house lacked electricity, but the mine work was steady. Rob Travis taught Merle to play five-string banjo. Then in 1929 Merle's brother, Taylor, made him a guitar. From then on his direction was set.

Merle's curiosity developed early. His curiosity drew him to friends of his father's: guitar-playing miners Ike Everly and Mose Rager, who taught him the complex picking style unique to the area. While the right-hand thumb plays syncopated accompaniment on the bass strings, the index finger plays melody on the treble strings. The combination sounds like two guitars playing at once.

After a brief hitch with The Tennessee Tomcats in Evansville, Merle joined legendary fiddler Clayton McMichen and his Georgia Wildcats in 1936. In 1937 he caught on with another group, The Drifting Pioneers, who eventually settled at WLW Radio in Cincinnati, performing on the station's *Boone County Jamboree*.

Merle made friends at WLW, among them Wesley Tuttle, Hank Penny, flatpicking guitar virtuoso Joe Maphis and Grandpa Jones; the friendships with these four turned out to be lifelong. When a foul-tempered, cigar-chewing, Cincinnati record store owner named Syd Nathan started his own record label, King, Merle and Grandpa became his first artists. The year was 1943. Meanwhile, Chet Atkins, living with his dad in Georgia, heard Merle's picking on a broadcast on his homemade radio. Fascinated, the aspiring young guitarist figured out his own version of Merle's style. The rest is history.

Merle joined the Marines late in 1943, but their tough discipline didn't mix with his free spirit. He was back in Cincinnati within a couple of months, his first marriage shot and his drinking heavy—the drinking was a problem that would plague him for the rest of his life. Clearly, it was time for a change. On March 1, 1944, borrowing $10 each from most of the WLW cast, he caught a train to L.A. Wes Tuttle, who had moved there before him, showed him around. Tuttle recalls that musicians were floored by Merle. "A lot...couldn't believe him until they saw him play. If they heard him on radio, they swore there was someone playing rhythm guitar for him."

At first he scuffled, working bars and dance halls and recording for small labels, using his own name and pseudonyms. He worked with cowboy singer Ray Whitley's Western swing band, and his friendship with Tex Ritter led to his being signed to Capitol Records in 1946. At his first session, he cut his first double-sided hit: "Cincinnati Lou" and "No Vacancy," which reached Number Two (for four weeks) and Number Three, respectively, almost simultaneously.

That summer, Capitol producer Lee Gillette suggested he record an album of folk songs. Merle said he didn't know any. Gillette suggested he write some. So, with his songwriting skills growing by leaps and bounds, he dredged up some traditional Kentucky songs from memory and created the rest. He pieced "Sixteen Tons" together from remarks, letters and conversations of family members and friends back in Kentucky. Even the new songs, which included "Dark as a Dungeon" and "I Am a Pilgrim," sounded old. The album, *Folk Songs of the Hills,* four 78 r.p.m. discs in a folio, attracted little notice when it was released.

Wes Tuttle remembers one night in 1947 when he and Merle wrote 20 songs. "I'd say out of the 20 he actually wrote 17. He was fantastic. He could write a new theme song for a radio or television show in ten minutes." When Merle's friend, Western swing bandleader Tex Williams, was in danger of being dropped by Capitol, Merle wrote "Smoke! Smoke! Smoke! (That Cigarette)" while painting a fence at home. The song jump-started Tex's career and gave Capitol its first million-seller.

Merle's honky tonk records had a distinctive sound. His then-girlfriend, Virginia "Ginny" Cushman, often played the sassy trumpet that soared over the rollicking, syncopated beat, fiddle and steel gliding in and out. The trumpet stood out noticeably on his second big hit of 1946: "Divorce Me C.O.D.," Number One for 14 weeks, and the flipside, "Missouri," hit Number Five.

Merle's biggest year on records turned out to be 1947. "So Round, So Firm, So Fully Packed," a song that cleverly used ad slogans of that day (like Coke's "The pause that refreshes") to make its point, remained at Number One for 13 weeks. "Steel Guitar Rag," which featured new lyrics by Merle, reached Number Four in the spring of 1947, as did its flipside, "Three Times Seven." Late that year, "Fat Gal" was a Number Four hit, and the flip, "Merle's Boogie Woogie," went to Number Seven. In 1948, however,

"Crazy Boogie," at Number 11, was his only hit, and by 1949 his hit-making days seemed largely over.

Merle's sensitive, gentle nature contributed to his genius. Yet a dark side, fueled by booze, too often reared its head, the result of his insecurities and self-destructive bent. "When he drank, he was just out of control," says Wes Tuttle. At times he had problems with the law.

He was once escorted from jail to a recording session by an L.A. County Deputy Sheriff after fighting with a cop who'd stopped him for driving his motorcycle drunk. And though he favored flashy Western clothes onstage, performing was often an ordeal for Merle. Harold Hensley, who fiddled on Merle's records and performed with him on Cliffie Stone's *Hometown Jamboree* out of Pasadena, recalled after one night's show, "(Merle said), 'Those people with those little beady eyes, watchin' me all the time. It makes my flesh crawl.'" Hensley remembers his response: "That's part of the game, and I'd tell him that. He was a fine performer, but, boy, he went through the throes doin' it."

In 1953 he landed a cameo role in the film treatment of James Jones' World War II novel, *From Here to Eternity*, starring Burt Lancaster, Frank Sinatra, Montgomery Clift and Donna Reed. Cast as a guitar-picking private, he sang "Re-Enlistment Blues" throughout the film. In June 1955 he had his only instrumental hit: a Number Five version of "Wildwood Flower," recorded with Hank Thompson's Brazos Valley Boys, with whom Merle often performed in the 1950's and 60's. His second marriage, to singer Judy Hayden, came and went.

Tennessee Ernie Ford, another of Merle's friends from the *Hometown Jamboree*, had his own daily NBC-TV program by then. He'd sung Merle's "Sixteen Tons" on the show and in concert and was under the gun. Too busy to record, he had nothing his label, Capitol, could release. He hastily went into Capitol's brand new studios at Hollywood and Vine and laid down "Sixteen Tons." By the close of 1955, it had soared up the country and pop charts and would stay at Number One for ten weeks remaining on the charts well into 1956. Merle, as the song's composer, also attracted national interest.

As "Sixteen Tons" peaked in January 1956, he attracted less favorable headlines when he struck his third wife, Bettie, during a binge, and as she and her sons fled the house, threatened to "kill anybody who comes near." Police surrounded the home, and Joe

Maphis, also an established star on the West Coast by then, finally coaxed him out. The publicity stemming from that incident didn't stop Ebenezer, Kentucky, from honoring him with a special monument on "Merle Travis Day," June 29, 1956. Gene Autry and The Everly Brothers, the sons of Merle's old guitar tutor, Ike Everly, were on hand.

He continued recording for Capitol through the late 50's and early 60's, but without any hits to speak of. Though he and Bettie moved to Nashville, not much happened aside from a minor hit with "John Henry Jr." in 1966 and a role in the horrid, low-budget 1967 film, *That Tennessee Beat*. His Capitol contract ended about 1969. For a time he wrote for Johnny Cash's early 70's ABC-TV show. The love of Americana he shared with Cash helped the show stand out from others like it.

Merle and his disciple (and longtime friend), Chet Atkins, had recorded a Grammy-winning album, *Atkins-Travis Traveling Show*, in 1974, and in 1977 he was inducted into the Country Music Hall of Fame. But, gradually, his health began to suffer from years of drinking and pill abuse, and his music also suffered as a result. Beginning in 1979 he recorded the first of several albums for CMH Records, some good, but others reflecting his age and failing health.

He divorced and married again—this time to Hank Thompson's ex-wife, Dorothy—in 1980 and moved to the Cherokee Indian nation in Eastern Oklahoma, near Tahlequah. Out of Nashville and L.A., he eased off the liquor and began writing richly detailed accounts of his years in the business. *Travis Pickin'*, his 1981 acoustic instrumental album for CMH, was nominated for a Grammy. One of the better episodes of Barbara Mandrell's NBC show featured her longtime buddies, "Uncle Joe" (Maphis) and "Uncle Merle," picking away on a special segment. He had clearly turned a corner.

But it was too late. On the evening of October 19, 1983, he collapsed, the victim of a massive heart attack. He died in an Oklahoma hospital the next morning. He'd have turned 66 the next month. His remains were cremated and scattered around the Travis monument in Ebenezer, Kentucky.

There will not be another artist of Merle Travis' like. Even his worst fears and insecurities could not long suppress that homespun genius. His influence, particularly through his guitar playing and songwriting, will be savored far beyond our own lifetimes.
—R.K.

Randy Travis

BORN: May 4, 1959
BIRTHPLACE: Marshville, North Carolina

If anyone was worried that the George Jones/Lefty Frizzell honky tonk tradition was dying a slow death, their fears were put to rest by Randy Travis' 1986 debut album, *Storms of Life*, which included resolutely hard country hits like "Diggin' Up Bones" and "On the Other Hand."

With *Storms of Life*, as with his half-dozen or so subsequent albums, Travis has demonstrated a masterful, instinctive feel for tradition-flavored country music. His rich, subtle baritone is one of the most amazing and confident voices heard in country since the arrival of George Strait in the very early 80's. As a songwriter he has, again and again, shown a maturity and insight well beyond his years. Though the hard country turf has become crowded in the years since Travis' debut, few, if any, have approached his sheer vocal artistry.

Travis was born Randy Traywick, May 4, 1959, on a farm near Marshville, North Carolina, about 30 miles outside Charlotte. His father, who raised horses and turkeys ("the dumbest animals in the world," Travis once observed), had his own construction company, and was also a hard-core country fan. By the time Randy was eight, the elder Traywick had his son playing guitar and singing along with his old man's Hank Williams and Stonewall Jackson records. By age 10, he and his brother Ricky were singing at local VFW halls, and a few years later he graduated up to the beer joints.

Though the musical influence stuck, Travis' life took a wayward turn by the time he was in his teens. Unhappy at home, he ran away repeatedly, dabbled in drink and drugs, and often landed in jail for assault, breaking and entering, and various and sundry other charges. Afte rmany times violating probation, he was staring at a five-year sentence when a Charlotte club owner named Lib Hatcher heard him sing at a talent contest and quickly got him released to her custody. Hatcher (who became Mrs. Randy Travis on May 25, 1991) put her young charge to work in her club, dish washing, short-order cooking and singing—in no particular order. In 1981, Hatcher, with Travis in tow, moved to Nashville and took over The Nashville Palace, a tourist-oriented night spot near the Opryland complex. Once again, Travis put in his

time, flipping burgers and serving up Jones and Haggard on the bandstand.

It took four years and a gradual industry shift back toward traditional country music before Travis finally managed to catch the ear of Warner Bros. Records. But when he did finally get his foot in, the door swung wide open. *Storms of Life* went platinum within a few months of its release, and Travis won the Country Music Association's 1986 Horizon award. For the next half decade, he was one of the most influential, critically acclaimed and commercially viable artists on the scene.

"I'll tell you what's funny," Travis said in a 1987 interview with *The Washington Post*. "I worked clubs for all those years, from the time I was 14, right on up to last year. And we still work a club date now and then. Doing clubs, you're always singing everybody else's hits. George Jones' hits, Lefty Frizzell's hits, Hank Williams' hits....Then all at once you get to where you're doing Randy Travis hits. That's weird, man," Travis laughed. "That's a big change, for sure."

Though his recording career fell from the multi-platinum heights in the early 1990's, Travis, who became a member of The Grand Ole Opry in 1986, seemed to revive things nicely with *This Is Me*, his back-to-the-basics 1994 album. He has also ventured into films in recent years, including an outing with Rob Lowe in *Jesse James and The Younger Brothers*. —B.A.

Rick Trevino

BORN: May 16, 1971
BIRTHPLACE: Austin, Texas

More of a traditionalist than many of the early 90's newcomers, Columbia Records' young Rick Trevino draws on his Tex-Mex background for inspiration. The half-Mexican Trevino was born and raised in Texas and attended Texas A&M before working toward a country music career. A substantive singer with a distinctive voice, Trevino plays both guitar and piano. His debut album was released in both Spanish and English versions, as was his first single, "Just Enough Rope" ("Bastante Cordon" in Spanish). Also included on his debut were fine covers of Bill Anderson's 1961 hit, "Walk Out Backwards," and Marty Stuart's "Honky Tonk Crowd." Critics view him as a face to watch as the 90's progress. —G.F.

Travis Tritt

BORN: February 9, 1963
BIRTHPLACE: Marietta, Georgia

When Travis Tritt threw his hat in the ring with his surprise 1989 Top Ten hit, "Country Club"—a semi-hokey novelty tune that has been thematically cloned countless times since by Nashville tunesmiths—nobody seemed to take him that seriously.

At least not at first. But Tritt's platinum 1990 debut album (also titled *Country Club*) on Warner Bros. showcased a formidable talent and an entertainer non-pareil whose gilded southern-fried vocal chops not only reflected mainstream country influences, but healthy doses of Southern rock (heard on tracks like "Put Some Drive in Your Country" and "Son of the New South") and rhythm & blues, as well.

It's All About To Change (1991), Tritt's second album, not only enlarged upon his expansive vocal and stylistic range; it also demonstrated his masterful songwriting and resulted in four Number One hits, including "The Whiskey Ain't Workin'"(a spirited duet with Marty Stuart) and "Here's a Quarter (Call Someone Who Cares)," a bitter kiss-off to an ex-lover. *It's All About to Change* eventually sold more than 2 million copies.

On *t-r-o-u-b-l-e* (1992—also a million-seller) and on *Ten Feet Tall and Bullet Proof*, his fourth and most recent album, Tritt managed to hold the line, consistently provoking and delighting listeners with his uncanny ability to walk the narrow path that straddles his country and Southern rock roots.

All the while, he has continued to grow as an entertainer; he is one of those rare showmen who has the knack for achieving intimacy with a roomful of 20,000 people—which is really what separates the great entertainers from the merely good ones.

But at the time of the release of "Country Club," who would have imagined all this? Particularly from an artist who readily admits that his own sense of musical direction was vague in the beginning.

As Tritt explained to *Country Music Magazine*'s Patrick Carr in a 1990 interview: "Warner Bros.' idea of my music and my idea of my music were different in the beginning.

"I really didn't know what direction I was going in—I enjoyed James Taylor and John Denver, and on the other hand I enjoyed Hank Williams Jr., and The Allman Brothers, and Lynyrd Skynyrd—but some of the people at Warner Bros. wanted to make me into a Lee Greenwood, Gary Morris type singer....But I've got a part of me that has 'Southern rock 'n' roll' written all over it, and that has to come out, in my shows and on my records. If it doesn't, I feel like I'm just prostituting myself."

Tritt was born on February 9, 1963, in Marietta, Georgia, where he still resides today. He married and divorced twice and, after graduating from high school in 1981, worked for a while in the heating and air conditioning business and loaded trucks. He remembers being particularly moved by his boss in the air conditioning business who'd had a shot at being a rock 'n' roll guitarist, passed it up, and had regretted it ever since. Tritt resolved to stop dragging his feet, to not let the same thing happen with his own musical dreams. With that in mind, he spent six years playing the local bars and VFW halls until he finally caught the attention of Danny Davenport, a Warner Bros. field representative stationed in Atlanta (he and Davenport made the tapes they later pitched to Warner in Davenport's home studio) and West Coast super-manager Ken Kragen.

More recently, Tritt has also ventured into films and has hosted VH1's *Country Countdown*, the cable network's country music video show. He was also made a member of the Grand Ole Opry in 1992. In 1994, he also published his autobiography, *Ten Feet Tall and Bullet Proof* (co-written with *Country Music Magazine*'s Michael Bane).

Ironically, just as his recording and performing career was coming into full fruition, Tritt stirred up controversy in June 1991, with something that had nothing to do with his music.

He made the mistake of casually criticizing Billy Ray Cyrus' monster novelty hit, "Achy Breaky Heart." When asked about the tune in an Associated Press interview, his disparaging comments were relatively bland. Yet the media (always starved for fresh celebrity high-jinx) fanned this tempest in a teapot into a full-blown feud that briefly pushed the war in Bosnia off the front pages of Nashville's daily papers.

In the country world, where the unwritten rule is to hear no evil and speak no evil (at least not in print, or to anybody's face), this little episode seemed to temporarily erode Tritt's popularity.

"I went from being the Number Two selling artist two years ago, beaten only by Garth Brooks...to not even being in the Top Ten sales bracket anymore, and not having as many Number One records on radio," Tritt told Michael McCall in a 1994 *Country Music Magazine* interview. "And it all started in June of 1991.

"I was asked a question, I answered it honestly," he added. "As a result, I got a tremendous cold shoulder. It's like Steve Earle once said, 'I like Nashville an awful lot. I just wonder sometimes if Nashville likes me.'"

As of the summer of 1994, Travis appeared to be on the rebound in a big way, as "Foolish Pride," the lead-off single from *Ten Feet Tall and Bullet Proof,* stormed to the Number One position in the country singles charts. —B.A.

Ernest Tubb

BORN: February 9, 1914
BIRTHPLACE: Crisp, Texas
DIED: September 6, 1984

E.T. might be a science fiction creature to kids. However, in Nashville, E.T. still means Ernest Dale Tubb, the "Texas Troubadour." A tangible link to the Jimmie Rodgers tradition, he was also far more: a founder of the honky tonk style of country music, humanitarian, businessman, talent scout, father figure and benefactor to many younger musicians who became stars.

Ask Hank Snow about Ernest Tubb. He'll tell you that without E.T.'s support in Nashville, his own career might have ended in the early 1950's. Ask Loretta Lynn about two decades of inspiration and friendship. Ask Jack Greene and Cal Smith, both ex-Texas Troubadours, how far their careers would have gone without his wise counsel. Johnny Cash and June Carter can also talk at length of the good advice he gave them. Carl Smith had one of his biggest hits literally handed to him by the man. Hank Williams got much fatherly advice from Ernest.

Ernest Tubb's birthplace was Crisp, Texas, south of Dallas; the year: 1914. The youngest of five children, he had little formal education. His folks separated in 1926 and he worked much of the time, staying with different relatives. By then he was marveling over Jimmie Rodgers' records, much as later generations would marvel over his own.

The year Tubb started singing—1933—was also the year Rodgers died of tuberculosis. Ernest bought his first guitar and started teaching himself many of Rodgers' songs after finishing his day job on a road-building crew. He moved to San Antonio where he met and married his first wife in 1934. He got a part time job playing mornings over KONO Radio.

The year 1935 was a turning point. Ernest's first child, Justin, was born in San Antonio. He also visited with Carrie Rodgers, Jimmie's widow, who lived in San Antonio. During their visit he asked her to listen to his radio show. Impressed with his knowledge of Rodgers' songs, Carrie got him two recording dates with RCA, Jimmie's label. In October 1936, he recorded six songs, two Rodgers tributes and four Tubb originals written in the Rodgers style. The following year he did two more songs, but none sold. Rodger Dale Tubb, his second child, was born in 1938 but died seven weeks later, inspiring Ernest's composition "Our Baby's Book." A daughter was born in 1939. Throughout this time Ernest alternated between singing on various Texas radio stations and working conventional day jobs.

He asked Carrie Rodgers, by then his informal adviser, if perhaps Decca Records (now MCA) might be interested in him. Both she and Ernest solicited them, and in April 1940, he went to Houston for his first session. That fall he moved to Fort Worth as KGKO Radio's "Gold Chain (Flour) Troubadour."

"Blue-Eyed Elaine" and "I'll Get Along Somehow," from the first Decca session, did well, and Ernest recorded 12 more numbers in Los Angeles in October 1940. These failed amid complaints from jukebox operators that nobody could hear Tubb's records in noisy bars. As a solution, Ernest brought electric guitarist "Smitty" Smith along for his April 1941 session in Dallas.

The first song they cut was Ernest's new composition, "Walking the Floor Over You." Smith, accustomed to playing from written music, simply played the song's melody for his solo, setting the style for every guitarist who worked for E.T. for the next 41 years. Ernest knew the commercial potential of "Walking the Floor." According to Tubb authority Ronnie Pugh, he urged Decca to release it first. They did, and it wound up a million-seller. Riding the crest of that wave, he appeared in two early 1940's Hollywood westerns, and RCA even went back and re-released two records he had done earlier for them. Legendary country music promoter Joe L. Frank brought Ernest to Nashville for his first Opry appearance in December of 1942. Three encores later he was an Opry regular, and his use of electric guitar helped make amplified instruments acceptable on the show.

Through the World War II years his stature rose with hits like "Try Me One More Time" and "I Ain't Goin' Honky Tonkin' Anymore." He'd formed his first Texas Troubadours band by 1943. His hits continued after the war with "There's a Little Bit of Everything in Texas" (1945), the sentimental ballad "Rainbow at

Midnight" (1946), "You Hit the Nail Right on the Head" and "Two Wrongs Don't Make a Right" (1947).

After fans griped that they couldn't find his records in local stores, he opened the Ernest Tubb Record Shop in Nashville. He was also among the first to see the potential of selling mail-order records over the airwaves. When he launched his *Midnight Jamboree* over 50,000-watt WSM from the record shop every Saturday night after the Opry, he used the show to hawk records. The store prospered. The same approach is still used by countless retailers on television 40 years later. Tubb also successfully pushed the music industry to replace the descriptive term "hillbilly" music, which he felt derogatory, with "country and western." In 1948 he cut "I'm Bitin' My Fingernails" and "Don't Rob Another Man's Castle" with The Andrews Sisters. In 1949 nearly every single he came out with—"Slippin' Around," "Warm Red Wine" and "Blue Christmas" among them—went Top Ten. By then he'd divorced Lois, his first wife, and married Olene Adams, who bore him five children.

He teamed with Red Foley for a series of duets, among them the single "Goodnight, Irene," which hit Number One. Decca later released *Red 'n' Ernie*, a duet album. In 1951 he gave "Don't Just Stand There," a song he co-wrote, to a hot new singer named Carl Smith. It became Carl's second Number One in a row.

In the throes of the Korean War, Ernest wrote the hit "Missing in Action," and toured Korea to entertain the troops. While there, he offered to call the families of soldiers he met once he got home. (He fulfilled that promise only to be staggered by families' indifference to their loved ones. His good intentions resulted in total frustration.)

Illness plagued him, and for a time he was forced to leave the Opry. A heavy drinker and smoker, he also had his wilder moments. In 1957, well in his cups, he shot up WSM's lobby with a .357 Magnum, fortunately injuring no one. From 1955 to 1958 he wasn't on the charts at all, then came back in 1958 with his own "Half a Mind" and "Hey, Mr. Bluebird," a duet with The Wilburn Brothers.

His final Top Five success came in 1963 with "Thanks a Lot." From then on his records generally stayed at the upper end of the Top 50. His excellent mid-1960's duets with Loretta Lynn resulted in four hits, the best of which was "Mr. and Mrs. Used-To-Be," in 1964. By then his own albums had a standard form, balancing his hits with covers of everyone else's.

He was inducted into the Country Music Hall of Fame in 1965.

Ernest was surprisingly candid about his vocal limitations. In a 1967 interview he admitted, "I've never been able to hold one note longer than one beat.". "All over the country...guys sit in bars trying to impress their girl... My voice comes on the jukebox and they say 'I can sing better than that.' And in about 90 percent of the cases, they're right."

By the 70's, emphysema was causing him constant respiratory problems—less serious, yet no less debilitating than those experienced by Jimmie Rodgers. He quit smoking. According to Justin Tubb that decision "probably added four, five or six years onto his life." He kept an oxygen tank on the bus and took more offstage breaks between singing, but otherwise was on the road as much as ever.

On June 18, 1975, Ernest completed his last session for MCA. His last MCA release in 1973 barely scratched the Top 100. Sagging sales led the company to drop a man whose success had made it a giant in the country field. Though deeply hurt, he wasn't alone. MCA also dropped Kitty Wells.

He moved to steel player and record producer Pete Drake's First Generation label, and recut many of his old hits in 1977 and 1978. Without telling Ernest, Drake overdubbed Willie Nelson, Charlie Rich, Waylon Jennings, Conway Twitty, Loretta Lynn, George Jones, Merle Haggard, Johnny Paycheck and other stars dueting with him. Justin Tubb recalled how his dad became misty-eyed when Drake finally played the tracks for him.

The album *The Legend and the Legacy* showed how artists, not record executives, felt about Ernest Tubb. On tour he packed them in. He was an elder statesman; the road was his life. He enjoyed it so much that friends speculated he'd probably die in the back of his bus.

That didn't happen. But emphysema was gaining ground. On November 13, 1982, he played his last show in Berlin, Ohio. He remained at home, following doctor's orders, struggling to recover. He saw few people before he was hospitalized for the last time in the fall of 1984. He died September 6. Tributes poured in from everywhere.

Ernest Tubb epitomized the spirit of country music old and new. His generosity, modesty and quiet dignity were of an earlier era. Yet his music and its popularity helped turn "the business" into "the industry." Perhaps his old drummer Jack Greene, a star himself, summed it up best. "Ernest Tubb gave more to the world than any politician or head of state or famous person in this world and asked for nothing in return. Remember, for God so loved the world, he gave us Ernest Tubb." —R.K.

Justin Tubb

BORN: August 20, 1935
BIRTHPLACE: San Antonio, Texas

Son of country music legend Ernest Tubb, Justin began performing with his guitar as a teenager. He signed with Decca in 1953 and had a Top Ten hit a year later, a duet with Goldie Hill called "Looking Back to See." He joined the Grand Ole Opry in 1955 and continued to record prolifically. His single releases during that period included "Sure Fire Kisses" and his own "I'm Just a Fool Enough." Beginning in 1959 Justin hopped from label to label, landing at RCA Victor in 1962. In the 60's his compositions were recorded by Patsy Cline, Jim Reeves and Skeeter Davis. Meanwhile, Justin toured extensively and scored hits of his own, including "Dern Ya" in 1964. Justin's recording career dwindled as his very traditional brand of country fell out of favor in the 1970's. He's still a member of the Opry and hosts the *Midnight Jamboree* over WSM. —M.B.

Tanya Tucker

BORN: October 10, 1958
BIRTHPLACE: Seminole, Texas

Few even imagined the longevity that lay ahead when Tanya Tucker began her recording career as a saucy, 13-year-old teen tease with semi-risqué 70's hits like "Delta Dawn" (a big pop-crossover hit, written by sometime recording artist Alex Harvey, which was about a small town woman's gradual descent into insanity), "What's Your Mama's Name" (about an illegitimate child's reunion with her long-lost father),

"Blood Red and Goin' Down," David Allan Coe's "Would You Lay With Me (In a Field of Stone)," "Lizzie and The Rainman," "The Jamestown Ferry," "The Man That Turned My Mama On" and "San Antonio Stroll."

Yet in the two decades since, Tucker has survived punishment for the worst sin a child star can commit (growing up), an ill-fated trampy-vampy foray into hard rock, drug and alcohol abuse, a series of tumultuous romances (including a highly publicized and tempestuous engagement to singer Glen Campbell), and a long dry stretch when she didn't record at all.

In the late 80's and early 90's, Tucker has, somewhat remarkably, emerged as a devoted and outspoken single mother, as well as one of country's hardest working and most stalwart entertainers and hit-makers.

Tucker was born in Seminole, Texas, in 1958, and grew up in Wilcox, Arizona, and Utah. Her father worked a series of menial jobs while struggling to launch Tanya and her talented older sister, La Costa (who had a couple of brief chart successes herself in the 70's) in show business. The elder Tucker eventu-

ally moved the family to Las Vegas in search of the big break. Though they didn't find it there, a demo tape of Tanya given to a Las Vegas songwriter eventually found its way to kingpin Nashville producer Billy Sherrill, who signed Tucker to Columbia Records at age 13, in the very early 70's.

Knowing a good gimmick when he saw one, Sherrill quickly began cranking out a string of very frank and explicit "adult" songs on the pixie-ish, fresh-faced Tucker. The public fascination quickly caught hold, and young Tanya even ended up on the cover of *Rolling Stone*.

Yet a few years passed and Tucker gradually lost the bloom of innocence (or, in her case, at least something like it). And the country world, which seemed to delight in the novelty of a cutey-pie young adolescent singing semi-prurient songs, just as quickly turned off when Tucker, as a tarty and none-too-cutesy 20-something began serving up similar material with a hard rock beat. She hit the bottom in 1979 with a full-blown, ill-conceived rock 'n' roll album called *TNT*, which featured her on the cover in skin-tight pink leotards and layers of make-up, looking like she'd stepped out of a second-rate cathouse.

In 1985, after a three-year absence, Tucker, having gotten her confused, hedonistic young life back together again, signed with Capitol Records and launched what would eventually unfold as one of the most dramatic comebacks of the decade. When her single, "Just Another Love," hit Number One in 1986, it was her first trip to the top of the charts in more than ten years.

The platinum records continued for Tucker, and Country Music Association awards. (She was the 1991 Female Vocalist of the Year.) "I Won't Take Less Than Your Love," "Strong Enough to Bend," "Highway Robbery," "What Do I Do With Me," "If Your Heart Ain't Busy Tonight," "Soon," "Two Sparrows in a Hurricane" and the Grammy-nominated "Down to My Last Teardrop" are just a few of the songs she's had resounding success with since her comeback. —B.A.

Nathan Turk

Though the man himself remains a mystery figure, Nathan Turk was a pioneer in the production of Western show clothing, in the business nearly a decade before Nudie Cohen began making Western outfits for Tex Williams in the late 40's. His Los Angeles shop was in business in the 1920's, and pro-

ducing Western outfits by the 1930's. Two of his earliest celebrity customers were Gene Autry and Tom Mix. In the days before sequins became popular, Turk costumes became known for their detail and their rich, dazzling color combinations and fancy appliqué. Turk made many outfits for the California country artists of the 1940's, outfitting the entire Spade Cooley band as well as The Maddox Brothers and Rose, who used their Turk outfits to proclaim themselves "The Most Colorful Hillbilly Band in the Land." Some of the finest examples of the Maddox outfits are now in the Country Music Hall of Fame. Though eclipsed by the more flamboyant Nudie, Turk continued to make Western outfits into the late 1970's. Today, Turk outfits are highly collectible, and artists like Marty Stuart actively seek specimens. —R.K.

Grant Turner

BORN: May 17, 1912
BIRTHPLACE: Abilene, Texas
DIED: October 19, 1991

Grant Turner, known as "The Dean of Grand Ole Opry Announcers," began his broadcasting career at age 16 at a station he helped build in his hometown of Abilene, Texas, using a windmill as a broadcast tower. He worked briefly as a newspaperman and as a DJ at various stations throughout the South before coming to Nashville's WSM Radio in 1944. In fact, his first day as an announcer at WSM was D-Day, June 6, 1944. A former protégé of Grand Ole Opry founder and original emcee George D. Hay, Turner became a central figure on the Opry, and on other WSM shows, as announcer and emcee. He was one of the first inductees into the Disc Jockey Hall of Fame and was elected to the Country Music Hall of Fame in 1981. He was active on the Opry up until his death. —B.A.

Zeb and Zeke Turner

BORN: Zeb, June 23, 1915, Lynchburg, Virginia
       Zeke, Unknown
DIED: Zeb, January 10, 1978

William Grishaw grew up around Columbia, South Carolina, and while playing with the South Carolina-based Hi Neighbor Boys in 1938, he made his first

records for the American Recording Company. Among them were "Zeb Turner's Stomp," which provided the origin of his stage name. In 1944 he relocated to Nashville, becoming a sideman with singer Wally Fowler. In 1945 Zeb had the first release on the Nashville-based Bullet label, and "Mountain Boogie," his brilliant instrumental, helped launch the country-boogie movement. James (William's brother), an equally talented guitarist, took the name Zeke Turner. Zeb and Zeke also recorded together for Bullet. Alone, Zeb wrote "It's a Sin," Eddy Arnold's 1947 hit, and the Western swing standard, "Texas in My Soul." Zeke became a popular studio guitarist, recording with many artists and working with Red Foley. He later worked out of Cincinnati with Foley's backup group, The Pleasant Valley Boys. This studio band included Jerry Byrd on steel guitar and fiddler Tommy Jackson. It was Zeke who created the classic guitar riff on The Delmore Brothers' "Blues Stay Away from Me." Zeb started recording for King in 1949 and had two hits, "Tennessee Boogie" in 1949 and the novelty "Chew Tobacco Rag" in 1950. He worked extensively around Baltimore and Washington in the early 1950's before moving to New Jersey. He later moved to Montreal, Canada, where he became a folksinger. Zeke worked for years on the WLW *Midwestern Hayride* before leaving the music business. —R.K.

Wesley Tuttle

BORN: December 30, 1917
BIRTHPLACE: Lamar, Colorado

Wesley Tuttle was one of a handful of West Coast-based country singers who worked in California before World War II. He worked with The Beverly Hillbillies and other such acts before briefly relocating to WLW in Cincinnati in the late 1930's. After returning to Los Angeles, he became part of Stuart Hamblen's *Covered Wagon Jubilee* radio show during World War II. One of the early performers signed to Capitol, he recorded with his friend, Merle Travis, in 1944 as The Coon Hunters. He and Travis also worked in a trio with Jimmy Dean, brother of Western singer Eddie Dean. Tuttle also appeared in western films, and found his biggest hits in 1945 and 1946: "With Tears in My Eyes," "Detour," "I Wish I Had Never Met Sunshine" and "Tho' I Tried (I Can't Forget You)." Tuttle worked extensively with Cliffie Stone through the 1940's and stuck mostly to the West Coast, working on the L.A.-based *Foreman Phillips Show* with his wife, Marilyn, in 1951, then spending several years as a regular on *Town Hall Party* and its nationally syndicated version, *Ranch Party*. He and Marilyn had a Top 20 hit in 1954 with "Never." He made other recordings, but by the late 50's decided to end his career to become a minister, though he did continue to sing, both religious and secular songs. Failing eyesight ended his ministry, though he ran a Christian bookstore with Marilyn and has remained in touch with fellow entertainers of his generation. —R.K.

Conway Twitty

BORN: September 1, 1933
BIRTHPLACE: Friars Point, Mississippi
DIED: June 5, 1993

Born Harold Jenkins on September 1, 1933, in Friars Point, Mississippi, Conway Twitty began playing guitar at the age of five. After his family moved to Helena, Arkansas, when he was a teenager, he formed his first band, a country-blues group called The Phillips County Ramblers. In between playing a weekly radio show on station KFFA, Jenkins contemplated a career in pro baseball, nearly signing with the Philadelphia Phillies before being drafted to serve in the Korean War during the early 1950's.

After his discharge in 1956 Jenkins auditioned unsuccessfully for Sun Records producer Sam Phillips. Undaunted, he hooked up with an agent who suggest he find himself a snappier stage name. Jenkins dug out a map and spotted Conway, Arkansas, and Twitty, Texas, and Conway Twitty was born.

Though he would go on to become one of the most popular country performers of all time, it was as a pop singer that Conway first made his mark as an entertainer. In 1958 he recorded the single "It's Only Make Believe," which went on to become the biggest hit of his career. He continued to record pop ballads through the mid-1960's before turning to country. During his teen heartthrob years Twitty also tried his hand at acting, appearing in three forgettable teen-age B-movies in the 1950's: *Sex Kittens Go to College, Platinum High School* and *College Confidential.*

Twitty's first country hit was "Next in Line," in 1968. He received a Gold record award for his album, *Hello Darlin'*, in 1970. In the 1970's Twitty dominated country charts thanks to a series of successful duets with Loretta Lynn. The duo made their Grand Ole Opry debut in February 1971. Their most successful singles included "After the Fire Is Gone," "Lead Me On," "Louisiana Woman, Mississippi Man," "As Soon As I Hang Up the Phone" and "Feelins'." Together the two recorded three Gold albums: *We Only Make Believe* in 1971, *Lead Me On* in 1972 and *The Very Best of Conway Twitty & Loretta Lynn* in 1979.

The pair was awarded a 1971 Grammy award for Best Performance by a Country Duo or Group and, that same year, the first of four consecutive Country Music Association awards for their duet work.

Twitty's work with Lynn did much to establish his credibility as a country artist and paved the way for a seemingly endless string of solo hits. Among his most popular 1970's singles were "I Can't Stop Loving You" (1972), "She Needs Someone to Hold Her (When She Cries)" (1973), "Linda on My Mind," "Touch the Hand" and "This Time I've Hurt Her More than She Loves Me" (all three 1975), "The Games That Daddies Play" (1976), "Play, Guitar, Play" (1977), "Don't Take It Away" and "Happy Birthday Darlin'" (both 1979). He also scored a Gold record award for the album *You've Never Been This Far Before* (1973) and for his two greatest hits collections, *Volume 1* (1972) and *Volume 2* (1976).

Between 1968 and 1977 Twitty cut 30 successive Number One singles, a feat unmatched by any coun-

try artist to date, and enough to fill the *Number Ones* album he cut in 1982 two times over. He was honored with 22 Country Music Association award nominations (but the only CMA awards he won were for his duets with Lynn), and was voted a "living legend" in the 1988 *Music City News* Awards. He spent his entire career recording for Decca/MCA, except for a brief period in the mid-80's when he moved to Warner Bros./Elektra. He was back with MCA by 1987, though, and continued recording right up until his death. His final album, *Final Touches*, was released posthumously in late 1993.

Conway Twitty, a lifelong workaholic, will also be remembered as a shrewd businessman. He owned a music promotion company, a minor league baseball team called the Nashville Sounds, and substantial real estate including Twitty City, his Nashville theme park. Ironically, at the time of his death in 1993, he was in the process of divesting himself of his various holdings in order to devote more time to songwriting and enjoying the fruits of his many years' labor. He suffered an abdominal aneurysm and died on his way home to Nashville from a concert in Branson.

Among the many honors Twitty received during

his lifetime was the honorary title of chief of the Choctaw nation. The Choctaws gave Twitty the Indian name "Hatako-Chtokchito-A-Yakni-Toloa," which means "Great Man of Country Music."   —M.B.

T. Texas Tyler

BORN: June 20, 1916
BIRTHPLACE: Mena, Arkansas
DIED: January 28, 1972

T. Texas Tyler (born David Luke Myrick) was raised in Texas and educated in Philadelphia. He appeared on the *Major Bowes Amateur Hour* in New York in the late 30's before rising to prominence as a member of Shreveport's *Louisiana Hayride*, which he joined in 1942. Moving to California in 1946, Tyler fronted a Western swing band and recorded a string of sentimental hits for which he is most often remembered: "Bummin' Around," "Remember Me" (1945), "It Makes No Difference Now" and the classic, "Deck of Cards" (1948), a recitation which he wrote and which has since been recorded by Tex Ritter, Tex Williams and other Texes of note. Later in life, he starred in a number of "singing cowboy" Hollywood westerns. *Horsemen of the Sierras* was one. He dabbling in TV acting, briefly having his own series, *Range Round-Up*, Tyler found renewed inspiration as a gospel writer and singer before his death in 1972.   —B.A.

Ian Tyson

BORN: September 25, 1933
BIRTHPLACE: British Columbia, Canada

Ian Tyson first attained stardom as the male half of Ian and Sylvia, a Canadian husband-and-wife folk duo. Ian and Sylvia moved to New York City in the early 1960's and played an influential role in ushering in the Greenwich Village folk scene. During this period, the couple wrote and recorded some memorable tunes, such as Ian's "Four Strong Winds" (a Number Three country hit for Bobby Bare in 1964 and also a minor pop single for rock singer Neil Young in 1979) and "Someday Soon" (a major hit for Suzy Bogguss nearly 30 years after Tyson first recorded it) and Sylvia's "You Were on My Mind," which in 1965 was a Top Five pop hit for the folk group, We Five. In 1975, the couple divorced and went their own ways—Ian devoting most of his time to ranching and cutting horses on his 160-acre ranch nestled in the foothills of southern Alberta's Canadian Rockies. Starting in the early 1980's, how-

ever, Ian began writing and recording songs that related his experiences as a cattle rancher and rodeo rider. His 1987 release, *Cowboyography*, went platinum in Canada—signifying sales of more than 100,000 copies. The recording also earned him a Juno award, which is the Canadian equivalent of a Grammy. In 1993, Ian signed with Vanguard Records and recorded the critically-acclaimed *Eighteen Inches of Rain*.   —R.P.

Urban Cowboy

This hit 1980 Hollywood feature film, starring John Travolta and Debra Winger, was the catalyst for a national music craze that made country music excessively trendy with urban audiences for a while. It also resulted in the making of some rather monumentally mediocre records as Nashville producers began watering country music down into a bubblegum-ish brand of pop- and rock-flavored pop crossover-oriented sound in order to try and pander to these city folks and the huge new market they represented.

Urban Cowboy, the film, had, in the words of one jaundiced reviewer, a "Lookin' for Mr. Goodbeer" plot that romanticized the singles scene, as it existed in urban neo-honky-tonks like Gilley's Club in

Texas—on which its story was based, and where the movie was filmed.

Just a year or so before *Urban Cowboy*, John Travolta had fanned the disco craze by donning white high-heeled dancing shoes and prancing across the silver screen in *Saturday Night Fever*. With *Urban Cowboy*, he slipped on his cowboy boots, hit the dance floor, and briefly helped launch a similar craze for all things Western as trendy America eagerly traded in its go-go boots for its cowboy boots. Largely as a result of *Urban Cowboy*'s popularity with youthful audiences, country music sales shot up to almost $250 million a year; and, by 1981, country became one of America's top-selling form of music.

For better or worse, most of the music directly associated with *Urban Cowboy* (the movie and the surrounding mania) had little to do with traditional and/or honky tonk music—what purists call "real country music." Instead, the major beneficiaries of this renewed popularity were country artists whose music had a soft rock or pop fuzziness to it. These artists—Kenny Rogers and Mickey Gilley, among them—flourished while more devoted traditional and hard-core country singers went begging.

Predictably, America's fascination with mechanical bucking bulls and high-collared Western shirts lasted little longer than had the national obsession with hula hoops and bob-a-loops. And most of the music spawned by this craze has, in retrospect, proven as superficial as the trend itself. By the mid-1980's, the *Urban Cowboy*-inspired country sales boom had turned into a bust.

The bright side of the *Urban Cowboy* era's rapid deflation was that it precipitated a major shakedown and reassessment about what country music was and where it was heading. This, in turn, precipitated the mid-1980's renaissance of New Traditionalism. Many of the brightest stars and most vital artists who would come to the fore in this new "back-to-the-basics" movement were motivated in part by their alienation from (and, in some cases, even disgust with) the general plasticity of the great *Urban Cowboy* sellout. (See also, Gilley's.)   —B.A.

Leroy Van Dyke

BORN: October 4, 1929
BIRTHPLACE: Spring Fork, Missouri

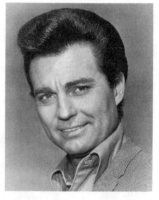

Leroy Van Dyke did not harbor the musical aspirations that most successful stars did. He grew up planning a career in agriculture, even majoring in animal husbandry at the University of Missouri. He didn't even learn to play guitar until his senior year in college. Though he loved Western music, he kept it to a hobby that stood him in good stead when he joined the Army in 1951. While working in military intelligence in Korea in 1953, he wrote "The Auctioneer," a song complete with auction-like chants about his cousin, livestock auctioneer Ray Sims. He first performed the song on a live show for the troops, preceding an appearance by Marilyn Monroe. After discharge, he started writing for livestock newspapers in Chicago and played music strictly as a sideline. On a 1956 amateur show appearance on WGN-TV in Chicago, his performance of "The Auctioneer" went over so well that a local DJ arranged for him to record it. Released on Dot in 1957, it became a pop and country hit. Though he did other recordings on Dot, they went nowhere. Then he signed with Mercury. His 1961 "Walk On By" remained Number One on the country charts for 19 weeks and became a Top Five pop hit. In 1962 "If a Woman Answers" also became a Number Three country hit. Van Dyke recorded for Warner Bros., Kapp, Decca and ABC through the 1970's. In the 1980's, he performed at fairs and even as a celebrity auctioneer. —R.K.

Porter Wagoner

BORN: August 12, 1927
BIRTHPLACE: Near West Plains, Missouri

At first inspection, Porter Wagoner seems to be the countriest of the country. Who can argue that the rhinestone suits, the folksy banter, the sad songs and the serious recitations all bespeak a performer determined to stay true to his rural roots? And yet, a closer look reveals that around this country core, Porter Wagoner has always experimented, always innovated.

But for all his unimpeachable credentials, ability and accomplishments, it's sometimes hard to take seriously the message of "Men with Broken Hearts" or "Skid Row Joe" when the next moment (no—the *same* moment) he's prancing, preening, showing off his gaudy $8,000 outfits for picture-takers. Anything for a laugh, whether it's changing lyrics to a song he's performing or the title of a song he's introducing. Many remember Carl Smith's disgusted "Always gotta be funny, don't you?" after Wagoner introduced his song on *That Good Ole Nashville Music* as "Faded Love and Winter Noses," instead of roses.

Like most of his generation, Porter Wayne Wagoner came up the hard way. Born near West Plains, Missouri, Wagoner showed a love for country music early on, and a desire to sing it. His boss at a West Plains grocery store, and some of the customers as well, took a liking to Porter's singing, and soon the young man was featured on local station KWPM, singing from the store three times a week. Later, KWTO in Springfield, Missouri, hired him away from West Plains to become a full-time entertainer on the bigger station. On the strength of some audition discs shopped to New York, Wagoner was signed to RCA Victor Records in 1952. His first few releases, much in the style of Hank Williams, went nowhere, but as Springfield became home base to country music's first real foray into network television, with radio's *Ozark Jubilee* becoming *Jubilee USA*, Wagoner's career caught fire. His 1955 hit, "A Satisfied Mind," topped *Billboard*'s disc jockey poll of America's fa-

vorite hillbilly records, besting versions of the same song by Jean Shepard and Porter's Springfield mentor, Red Foley. Not yet 30 years old, Wagoner had come far, and would go much further.

He left Springfield for Nashville in 1957 when he was invited to join the Grand Ole Opry, and there he has remained. With TV experience behind him, Wagoner was approached in 1959 by producer Willis "Bill" Graham, and asked to put together a cast for a TV show planned by the Chattanooga Medicine Company. Porter expanded his two-piece Wagonmasters band, found a girl singer—"Pretty Miss" Norma Jean, then on *Jubilee USA*—and hired comedian and bassist "Speck" Rhodes. This basic crew, plus top guest stars, made for a hit show. Airing first in 1960, *The Porter Wagoner Show* grew in syndication from a handful of initial markets to well over 100 at its peak, and remained in production for 21 years. "I was hoping I could last a year...get myself well enough known to get show dates," Wagoner told Graig Baguley of *Country Music People*. Wagoner's show dates did indeed pick up; so did his recording career. Between "Your Old Love Letters" (1961) and "Big Wind" (1969) came a string of Top Ten hits, great songs by some of the finest writers in the business, including the Curly Putman masterpiece, "Green, Green Grass of

Home," Bill Anderson's "The Cold Hard Facts of Life" and Bob Ferguson's "The Carroll County Accident."

By mutual agreement, Norma Jean left *The Porter Wagoner Show* in 1967, and Wagoner's choice for a new girl singer, about as different from Norma Jean as anyone could be, was petite, chesty, blonde Dolly Parton, then an up-and-coming 21-year-old with a few charted records behind her on the Monument label. For the next seven years, much of Wagoner's energy went into building both the Parton and Parton-Wagoner careers, an investment from which both parties profited handsomely. Porter worked to win Norma Jean's fans over to Dolly; he also worked to convince RCA Victor to give Parton a contract; to build them into a musical duet; and to help Parton hone her own considerable songwriting talents. On all points, his success was smashing. For several years, the Porter and Dolly duet career far outstripped what either was doing as a solo artist. They were named Country Music Association's Vocal Group of the Year in 1968 and Vocal Duo of the Year for both 1970 and 1971. Parton's growing renown as a singer-songwriter inspired Wagoner to undertake energetic songwriting on his own, and alongside a few disasters were some first-rate titles like "Be a Little Quieter," "What Ain't to Be Just Might Happen," "Katy Did," "Lightening the Load" and "Highway Headin' South."

After seven terrific years, Parton grew eager to spread her wings; she left Wagoner's TV and road show in 1974, not under the best of terms. Wagoner sued for breach of a contract which, he maintained, kept Dolly under his control for ten more years. Settlement was finally reached in 1980. Part of the settlement stipulated the release of some previously recorded duet material; and sure enough, their version of Johnny Russell's "Making Plans" zoomed to the Top Ten, the last such hit (to date) that Wagoner has had. Their breach seemed to be healed when Wagoner appeared on Dolly's late 1980's ABC-TV variety show, *Dolly*, and reminisced at length and in good spirits about their former days together.

The Porter Wagoner Show ceased production in 1981, about the same time that Wagoner's contract with RCA was terminated. Warner-Viva released a few Wagoner recordings over the next few years, including a couple from the soundtrack of the Clint Eastwood motion picture, *Honky Tonk Man*, in which Porter had a role.

Though Wagoner's days as a recording star seem to be behind him, he revived a dormant road career

in the 1980's with his famous "all-girl band," The Right Combination, proving that his penchant for restless experimentation had not deserted him. Wagoner obviously is still the same man who tested the rockabilly waters in the mid-1950's with "Let's Squiggle"; who welcomed Buck Trent's electrified banjo into his 1960's Wagonmasters band; who cut a bluegrass album and several gospel albums with The Blackwood Brothers (three of which won Grammy awards); who moved his TV show outdoors in the 1970's to Opryland USA; who created a firestorm of protest (and publicity) by bringing soul legend James Brown onto the Grand Ole Opry; and who produced at his Fireside Studios talents as diverse as his own and soul star Joe Simon.

In the early 90's, Porter remains active on the Opry, and serves as the official "meeter and greeter" for Opryland USA. The world of country music will not see his like again. —R.F.P.

Jimmy Wakely

BORN: February 16, 1914
BIRTHPLACE: Mineola, Arkansas
DIED: September 23, 1982

Jimmy grew up in Oklahoma and began playing music in the 1930's. After forming The Jimmy Wakely Trio with Johnny Bond and Dick Reinhart, the group performed on WKY in Oklahoma City beginning in 1937. Gene Autry heard the trio while touring Oklahoma and invited them west. They left Oklahoma in 1940 after Scotty Harrell replaced Dick Reinhart. Autry added them to his films and to the cast of his *Melody Ranch* radio show. After Wakely struck out on his own, he became a top western film star, ultimately starring in over 50 Hollywood movies and achieving popularity second only to Roy Rogers and Gene Autry. He had one hit on Decca with "I'm Sending You Red Roses" in 1944 before joining Capitol. There, he had even bigger hits including the crossover smash, "One Has My Name, The Other Has My Heart," in 1948. He had other Top Tens through 1949, his biggest being his duet with Capitol pop singer Margaret Whiting. Their cover version of Tillman's "Slippin' Around" topped both country and pop charts. Wakely had other hits with Whiting and on his own until 1951. In 1952 he began hosting a CBS radio program and in 1961, he and Tex Ritter co-hosted *Five Star Jubilee*, an extension of the old *Ozark Jubilee* TV series. Wakely formed Shasta Records in the mid-60's, recording others as well as himself. He recorded and performed with son Johnny and daughter Linda Lee. In the mid-70's he began reissuing material from his CBS radio shows on Shasta until his death in 1982 of lung disease.   —R.K.

Billy Walker

BORN: January 14, 1929
BIRTHPLACE: Ralls, Texas

Billy Walker got his start in the late 1940's backing various country stars including Hank Thompson. He performed on a number of country radio programs throughout the 1950's, including *Big D Jamboree* in Dallas (1951 to 1952), *Louisiana Hayride* in Shreveport (1952 to 1955) and *Ozark Jubilee* (1955 to 1959).

Billy's music, a lively hybrid of Tex-Mex, honky tonk and Western swing heavily influenced by the sound of Jimmie Rodgers, scored big enough with country audiences to get him invited to join the Grand Ole Opry in 1960. He went on to record a number of hits, including "Charlie's Shoes" (1962) and "Cross the Brazos at Waco" (1964).

By the late 60's Billy had become a big enough star to be featured in a number of promotional campaigns, including the Music City Pro-Celebrity Golf Tournament, where he appeared along with Kentucky Fried Chicken founder Colonel Sanders. Walker continues as an Opry member in the 90's.   —M.B.

Charlie Walker

BORN: November 2, 1926
BIRTHPLACE: Copeville, Texas

Charlie Walker wanted to be a country singer from the time he was in the fifth grade. He began his career at age 17, playing around Texas with The Cowboy Ramblers before joining the Army. There, he wound up as a DJ on the Armed Forces Radio Network, and continued in radio after his discharge. By the early 50's, based in San Antonio, he was becoming known as one of the top country DJ's in America. Still, he wanted to sing, and after landing a Decca recording contract, his "Only You, Only You" became a Top Ten record in 1956. In 1958, after joining Columbia, he had his biggest hit of all with "Pick Me Up on Your Way Down," a raw honky tonk number. Having established his singing talents, he had moderate hits over the next several years including "Close Up the Honky Tonks," a Number 11 record in 1961. His next big hit came with the Top Ten (now on CBS's Epic label) "Wild As a Wildcat" in 1965. In 1967 he joined the Grand Ole Opry and had another Top Ten with "Don't Squeeze My Sharmon." Walker never again had anything more than a moderate hit, though his 1969 album, *Live in Dallas, Texas*, is a minor country classic. Even when he moved to RCA in 1973, and on to Capitol in 1974, no more hits came his way. He did additional recording for Plantation Records in the late 70's. He became a member of the Grand Ole Opry in 1967 and remains a regular today.   —R.K.

Clay Walker

BORN: August 19, 1969
BIRTHPLACE: Beaumont, Texas

Giant Records newcomer Clay Walker found instant success when his 1993 debut single, "What's It to You," went straight to Number One. He followed it

up with another Number One, "Live Until I Die," and went Gold with his self-titled debut album. The young Texan hails from Beaumont (as do Mark Chesnutt and Tracy Byrd), and has been playing in the clubs since he was 16. Cast in the neo-honky tonk vein, his musical influences—like many of country music's new entrants—include James Taylor, Bob Seger and Lionel Richie right along with Haggard, Jones and Strait. —G.F.

Jerry Jeff Walker

BORN: March 16, 1942
BIRTHPLACE: Oneonta, New York

Though he's from upstate New York, the "progressive country" sound of Jerry Jeff Walker (born Ronald Clyde Crosby) is more identified with Texas, where he's resided since 1971. He made his first recordings with the band Circus Maximus in 1967, and his first solo recordings in 1968 for Atco Records, where he

had a pop hit with "Mr. Bojangles," a song inspired by a street singer he met in jail in New Orleans. Over the course of his career, he's released some 24 albums (on six different labels), including classics like *Viva Terlingua* (1973) and *Live at Gruene Hall* (1989). Though he hasn't had a large number of hits, he's amassed a loyal group of fans (President Clinton and First Lady Hillary showed up at one of his concerts in northern Virginia), much critical praise, and counts fellow artists like Willie Nelson and Guy Clark among his friends. Most recently he's been recording for his

own label, Tried and True Music, in conjunction with Ryko; in 1994, the label issued a live recording, *Viva Luckenbach*. —G.F.

Steve Wariner

BORN: December 25, 1954
BIRTHPLACE: Noblesville, Indiana

Since his recording debut a little over a decade ago, Steve Wariner has proven to be an artist who possesses all the right talents—he's a fabulous singer, an impressive songwriter and a consummate guitarist. Yet, until recently, he has never quite managed to parlay his assets into superstardom.

Within the Nashville record industry, Wariner's fine musicianship has long been recognized. As a guitarist he has frequently collaborated with his mentor and former producer, Chet Atkins, as well as with newgrass/country maestros Vince Gill, Ricky Skaggs and Mark O'Connor. "Restless," a collaboration by these four released as a single from O'Connor's 1991 album, *New Nashville Cats,* won both a Grammy and a Country Music Association award. His original tunes have been covered by the late Bob Luman and the late Conway Twitty, and he's also written or co-written a fair number of his own hits. His warm, expansive vocal style has often won comparisons with a young Glen Campbell and has earned him a string of Number One records, including "All Roads Lead to You," "Some Fools Never Learn," "You Can Dream of Me," "Life's Highway," "Lynda," "Where Did I Go Wrong," "I Got Dreams," "The Domino Theory" and "The Tips of My Fingers," among others.

Yet despite hits on three different labels (RCA, MCA, and most recently, Arista), and despite the strong backing of blue chip producers like Atkins and Tony Brown, Wariner has yet to forge a solid identity in country listeners' collective imagination. He's the classic example of the nice guy who never does quite manage to finish first. Born in Noblesville, Indiana, on Christmas Day 1954, Wariner began performing with his father, Roy, at age ten, on weekly radio and TV shows. Wariner was 17 and still in high school when he opened a show for Dottie West at the Nashville Country Club, in Indianapolis. West was so impressed with Wariner's vocal abilities, and his exceedingly friendly personal style, that she quickly signed him on as a bass player in her road band.

Three years later he moved on to similar duties in the late Bob Luman's band, where he remained for two-and-a-half years. He was with Luman when RCA Records producer Chet Atkins spotted him, inked him to RCA in 1977, and produced his first records.

In the years since, Wariner has seldom been out of the charts for long. Since his 1991 signing with Arista, his career has taken a significant leap forward. *I Am Ready* and *Drive*, his two most recent Arista albums, have done better chart-wise and sales-wise than any of the dozen or so previous albums he's recorded since 1982.

"This has been my biggest year ever, on the radio, in record sales, and even at live shows," Warner confirmed in a 1993 interview. "But regardless of sales or success, I'm going to be making music, one way or the other. That's the way I look at it. I love it too much. It's all I've ever done since childhood."

Another outstanding moment from his long career is *Christmas Memories*, a Christmas album he did with Nanci Griffith, Chet Atkins, Maura O'Connell, and The Chieftans.   —B.A.

Doc Watson

BORN: March 2, 1923
BIRTHPLACE: Deep Gap, North Carolina

Arthel "Doc" Watson, one of this era's most brilliant finger and flatpicking guitarists, is among the few remaining links to pre-war country stringband music. He is able to seamlessly synthesize that music into a repertoire that mixes the old with country music of later generations. Blind since birth, he drank in the music of Jimmie Rodgers, The Delmore Brothers and The Carter Family. He first played harmonica and then clawhammer banjo before graduating to guitar. He started playing around his home area in the early 40's, and got his name while being introduced on a local radio show. In the 50's he played electric guitar with a mainstream country band that also did rock 'n' roll. To compensate for their lack of a fiddler, he began flatpicking fiddle tunes, which became his specialty, though Joe Maphis had preceded him with this technique. He also kept playing traditional music, backing veteran old-timey artist Clarence Ashley, who lived nearby. When folklorist Ralph Rinzler traveled to North Carolina to record Ashley in 1960, he discovered Doc as well. In 1961 Doc and Ashley performed in New York together, and Doc soon began performing solo, as he did to great acclaim at the 1963 Newport Folk Festival.

In 1964 Doc signed with the Vanguard label. By then his guitar-playing teenage son, Eddy Merle (named for Eddy Arnold and Merle Travis), was regularly performing with him onstage. Then, as now, Doc's repertoire encompassed everything from Jimmie Rodgers and ancient folk tunes to blues, to Hank Snow hits of the 50's, to Delmore Brothers favorites and plenty of instrumentals. After Vanguard, he moved on to Poppy Records. Recording often with Merle, he hopped over to United Artists, then to Flying Fish and Sugar Hill. Doc participated in The Nitty Gritty Dirt Band's landmark *Will the Circle Be Unbroken* album in 1971 (where he first met Merle Travis). Doc and his son continued to ride a growing wave of popularity with various TV and stage appearances, and in 1980 Doc recorded *Reflections*, an album teaming him and Chet Atkins. Doc and Merle's popularity continued until Merle's tragic death in a October 23, 1985, tractor accident on his farm. Doc has persevered, though the intensity of his and Merle's special guitar interplay is much missed. Though he has "re-

held him in high esteem, due both to his spare but powerful, country-to-the-core vocal style and his fine selection of material. Some of his best known songs include "Paper Rosie," "Farewell Party," "Pick the Wildwood Flower," "Should I Come Home (Or Should I Go Crazy)," "Fourteen Carat Mind," "You're Out Doing What I'm Here Doing Without" and "Don't Waste It on the Blues." Sticking close to his traditional roots, Watson has been able to weather the many ups and downs and cycles of country music; he consistently scored hits through the Outlaw movement, the Urban Cowboy era and the crossover movement, until the industry finally caught back up to

him with the rise of New Traditionalism. Ironically, that's when his hits began to trickle off. He label-hopped through the 80's, moving to MCA in 1981, Epic in 1985 and Warner Bros. in 1988. His most recent chart appearance came in early 1993 on the independent label, Broadland. —G.F.

tired" from touring more than once, Doc nonetheless remains active. His annual Merle Watson Memorial Festival in North Carolina each year draws huge crowds and attests to his timeless appeal. —R.K.

Gene Watson

BORN: October 11, 1943
BIRTHPLACE: Palestine, Texas

A staunchly traditional honky tonker in the classic sense of Lefty Frizzell or Ernest Tubb, Gary Gene Watson's career in music goes back as far as age 13, when he first started singing professionally. He worked for years in the clubs of Houston, Texas, supplementing his income as an auto mechanic, before signing with Capitol Records in 1975. His first Capitol single, the sensual, racy (for its time) "Love in the Hot Afternoon" shot up to Number Three, thus beginning a long string of Top Ten singles throughout the 70's and 80's. Critics—and fans—have always

Kevin Welch

BORN: August 17, 1955
BIRTHPLACE: Long Beach, California

A well-respected Nashville singer-songwriter whose Jimmie Rodgers-meets-Jack Kerouac lyrics evoked images of the open, Western road, Kevin Welch was born in Long Beach, California, on August 17, 1955.

Raised in Oklahoma, Welch dropped out of school at 17 and headed to Nashville, where he spent the next few years playing in bluegrass bands and honing his songwriting and performance skills.

In the mid-1980's, he formed a band of crack Nashville musicians called The Overtones and began playing the Nashville club circuit. Critical acclaim and a cult-like following developed. On the heels of the rave reviews, record companies began to take notice, and in 1988, Welch signed a recording contract with Warner Bros. His self-titled debut for the Warner affiliate label, Reprise, yielded three minor country hits, "Stay November" (1989), "Till I See You Again" (1990) and "True Love Never Dies" (1991). His second Warner Bros. release, *Western Beat*, received critical acclaim in the rock as well as the country press and became a best seller de-

spite the absence of a hit single. Welch's reputation as an outstanding songwriter remained solid throughout the late 1980's and into the 1990's. His songs have been recorded by The Judds, Ricky Skaggs, Gary Morris, Don Williams and Sweethearts of the Rodeo.   —R.P.

Freddy Weller

BORN: September 9, 1947
BIRTHPLACE: Atlanta, Georgia

Atlanta-born guitarist Freddy Weller toured with Billy Joe Royal before joining the rock band, Paul Revere and The Raiders, in 1967.

Freddy signed a solo contract with Columbia in 1969 and was touring in Europe with The Raiders when he discovered his single, a Joe South tune called "Games People Play," was climbing the country charts.

Encouraged, Freddy left The Raiders in the early 1970's to concentrate on country. The result was a string of hits that made Freddy an immensely popular country performer.

Among his successful singles were "Sexy Lady" (1974), "Liquor, Love and Life" (1976), "Bar Wars" (1978) and "Lost in Austin" (1980), to name just a few of them. His final appearance on the chart came in 1980.   —M.B.

Kitty Wells

BORN: August 30, 1919
BIRTHPLACE: Nashville, Tennessee

Country music's first major female star, born Muriel Deason, spent her early years on a farm west of Nashville before her family moved to Nashville. Her father enjoyed singing and playing guitar, and she became a fan of the Grand Ole Opry at an early age. In the mid-1930's she began singing with her cousin, Bessie Choate, as The Deason Sisters. By 1936 they were working on Nashville radio station WSIX. After she married singer Johnny Wright in 1938, they formed a new act with Johnny's sister, Louise, before Wright teamed with Jack Anglin of The Anglin Brothers to form Johnnie and Jack. (See separate entry). When the duo began working radio stations around the country (Chet Atkins was one of their fiddlers), Muriel sang part-time with them. She was also raising a family, and they moved frequently. After they moved to WNOX in Knoxville, Johnny gave her the stage name

that stuck with her (from the traditional number "Sweet Kitty Wells"). Johnnie and Jack were recording for RCA in 1949, and Kitty made some solo gospel recordings, backed by Johnnie and Jack's band. Their records sold; Kitty's didn't.

In 1952, while they worked the *Louisiana Hayride*, Johnny Wright tried to interest Decca A&R man Paul Cohen in recording Kitty, as Johnnie and Jack prepared to move to the Opry. But Kitty was ready to retire for good and concentrate on raising her family. As fate would have it, Cohen found a song that he thought might work for her: an answer song to Hank Thompson's "Wild Side of Life." Not particularly impressed with the song, "It Wasn't God Who Made Honky Tonk Angels," Kitty nonetheless recorded it for Decca. To her surprise it blasted to the top of the charts that year, paving the way for every female country singer who later become a star.

Kitty's low-key dignity, which distinguished her from more upbeat, boisterous female singers like

Martha Carson, appealed to record buyers. She enjoyed 28 Top Ten hits through the 1950's and 60's including 1954's "One by One" (with Red Foley), "Makin' Believe" in 1955, "Searching (For Someone Like You)" in 1956, "Heartbreak U.S.A." (Number One in 1961) and "Password" (1964). By proving women could turn out hits consistently, Kitty made life a little easier for subsequent female singers, from Loretta Lynn and Dolly Parton to Dottie West and Reba McEntire. For 11 years *Billboard* named her the Number One female country singer.

By the late 1960's she had peaked, though her records still sold. Elected to the Country Music Hall of Fame in 1976, she briefly recorded for the Southern rock-oriented Capricorn label, and later for her own Ruboca label. Kitty and Johnny still tour with their son Bobby, work on the Opry and operate a museum in the Nashville suburb of Madison. —R.K.

West Coast Country

For years, differences have existed between country performers based in California and those based in Nashville. Nashville partisans have questioned whether certain types of California country have been too "uptown," a result of the influence of the film industry and the sophisticated California music scene, while West Coast supporters have considered Nashville too parochial and narrow. Those arguments are heard less often today, but the West Coast country scene has had a major impact on the music's development. The first major West Coast act was The Beverly Hillbillies, created by the manager of Los Angeles radio station KMPC in 1930. One member, Stuart Hamblen, was to become one of the major figures on the West Coast before World War II, and singers like Wesley Tuttle worked with Hamblen. By the late 30's Hamblen was a solo performer hosting his own radio show. Western singers like Gene Autry and The Sons of The Pioneers (with Roy Rogers) were also based in Hollywood.

But the Depression and World War II did more than anything to create the West Coast scene. The Dust Bowl forced many Southern families west in search of a better life. That's how the families of Merle Haggard, Rose Maddox and Buck Owens first arrived there. World War II brought millions to the West Coast to work in defense industry jobs, and they brought their music with them. Promoters like Foreman Phillips brought Bob Wills, Roy Acuff and Ernest Tubb to his Venice Pier and did turn-away business. Phillips ran some of his dancehalls 24 hours a day to accommodate different shifts in the defense factories. Additional Western singers like Tex Ritter and a number of Southern and Texas acts—including Bob Wills, Curly Williams, Ted Daffan and Al Dexter—relocated there, as did Hank Penny and Merle Travis from the Midwest. Capitol Records' founding in 1942, and the presence of recording studios, made it a natural recording center. West Coast music was more sophisticated, willing to use everything from trumpet on records (Gene Autry, Al Dexter and Merle Travis) to classical harp (Spade Cooley and Tex Willliams). Bob Wills settled for a time in Fresno and then Sacramento.

In the years at the end and just after World War II, the majority of the big West Coast country hits came from Ritter, Dexter, Wills, Tuttle and Travis. The presence of electric instrument makers like Rickenbacker, Bigsby and Fender also helped define the sound of country. Capitol became one of the major sources of top West Coast artists, with Cliffie Stone, Travis, Tennessee Ernie Ford and others. New local barn dance style TV shows like *Hometown Jamboree* and, in 1952, *Town Hall Party* showcased country talent in the region. Other performers like Joe and Rose Lee Maphis relocated to California and became permanent residents. The influence of West Coast performers, their use of drums and electric instruments, all had a major impact on mainstream country music.

By the late 40's into the early 50's, in central and northern California, around Bakersfield, an area heavily settled by Texans and Okies, The Maddox Brothers and Rose emerged as major talents. So did Ferlin Husky, local musician Bill Woods and Tommy Collins. Jean Shepard, another Okie, grew up there. These musicians would become cornerstones of the Bakersfield Sound, all recorded by Capitol and joined by Wynn Stewart, Buck Owens and later by Merle Haggard in the late 50's and early 60's. A small but healthy bluegrass scene also blossomed in California in the 60's, exemplified by The Dillards, The Kentucky Colonels (with Clarence White) and The Hillmen, led by future Byrds/Flying Burritos/Desert Rose Band founder Chris Hillman.

As Western swing faded, Buck Owens became America's top country singer in the 60's, his twanging recordings selling in the millions. Merle Haggard's deeply personal songs also swept the country in the mid- to late 60's, proving that California remained a major fountainhead. Owens and others barely concealed their disdain for Nashville politics, the excessive control of producers and their view of what an artist should record. The view that California artists were too sophisticated to be drawn into all that became widespread among the performers.

The Academy of Country Music, founded in 1964, began in part because of a view that Nashville ignored West Coast performers, and that the Nashville-based Country Music Association consistently gave short shrift to California-based artists. A healthy club scene in Southern California—built around clubs like L.A.'s legendary Palomino—continued for years. California spawned an innovative circle of country-rock acts that included The Byrds, Flying Burrito Brothers, Gram Parsons, The Eagles and Linda Ronstadt, all based around Los Angeles, and all of whom would have their own impact on mainstream country.

Today, California artists remain, though the industry has dropped some of its regional chauvinism. Nonetheless, in the mid-80's, when Kentucky native Dwight Yoakam emerged from the L.A. club scene with his hard-edged, Bakersfield-influenced sound, he talked contemptuously of the indifference he'd met in Nashville for being too country. Groups like Highway 101 and The Desert Rose Band emerged in the late 80's, as did the 90's "Western Beat" acts. California may appear to be less influential than it was, as Nashville has become the worldwide center of country music. Yet the West Coast is anything but dead musically, and without its influence country music as we know it might be very different. —R.K.

Dottie West

BORN: October 11, 1932
BIRTHPLACE: McMinnville, Tennessee
DIED: September 4, 1991

Dottie West was born in McMinnville, Tennessee, on October 11, 1932. As a student at Tennessee Technological University she met a boy named Bill West, an engineering student who played a mean steel guitar; the two Wests married, graduated and moved to Cleveland, where they performed on the local country music television program, *Landmark Jamboree.* In 1959 Dottie landed a recording contract with

Starday Records and the couple moved to Nashville, where their circle of friends included such struggling young performers as Willie Nelson and Hank Cochran.

Dottie's first composition, "Is This Me?," became a hit for Jim Reeves and earned Dottie a BMI Songwriter's Award. At the same time, Reeves brought her singing abilities to the attention of Chet Atkins, who was instrumental in helping her land a recording contract with RCA Records in 1962. The following year Dottie realized a lifelong dream when she became a regular cast member of the Grand Ole Opry. Still, it was another two years before Dottie scored her first hit, "Here Comes My Baby," co-written with Bill. The song was later covered by Perry Como, the first of more than a hundred different artists to record it, and soon became something of a pop and country standard. It won Dottie a Grammy nomination in 1964, the first of 16 such nominations and, to date, her only win.

On the heels of "Here Comes My Baby" Dottie headed into the studio to record her first duet, a format that would serve her well throughout her career. Her partner was Jim Reeves, and the song was Justin Tubb's "Love Is No Excuse." The duet became a Top Ten hit, and Dottie and Jim seemed to be a combination that couldn't miss, but the collaboration was cut short when Reeves was killed in a tragic plane crash on July 31, 1964. With an increasingly large following she recorded several hits of her own, including "Would You Hold It Against Me?" in 1966, "Paper Mansions" in 1967 and a duet with on Gibson titled "Rings of Gold," which was both a Number One single and title song of a top-selling album in 1967.

Throughout this time Dottie maintained a busy touring schedule throughout the U.S., Canada and Europe, and as many country performers have discovered, the constant traveling wreaks havoc on a marriage. In 1969, after four children and many years of successful collaboration, she and Bill West divorced.

In 1970 Dottie agreed to write a jingle for a Coca-Cola commercial based on her song "Country Sunshine." The popular commercial made Dottie's voice as familiar as a relative's to most of America and won her a Clio award for best commercial of the year, the first country performer to be so honored. The commercial was so successful, moreover, that the Coca-Cola Company offered Dottie a lifetime contract to write ad jingles. The agreement turned out to be incredibly lucrative for West, who had produced 15 such tunes by the late 70's.

In the mid-1970's Dottie married her drummer, Byron Metcalf. Around the same time she switched to the United Artists label and cut "When It's Just You and Me," her biggest selling single to that point. The switch also paved the way for a tremendously successful collaboration with another UA performer, Kenny Rogers. They recorded two duet albums, *Every Time Two Fools Collide* and *Classics*. Both albums went Gold, and the Country Music Association named Dottie and Kenny Vocal Duo of the Year in both 1978 and 1979. In November 1979 she had another solo album, *Special Delivery*. By this time Dottie was a regular fixture on TV talk shows and maintained an exhausting touring schedule.

In the midst of her 1980 divorce from Metcalf, Dottie had another string of successful singles, including "A Lesson in Leavin'," "You Pick Me Up (And Put Me Down)," "Leavin's for Unbelievers," the Number One "Are You Happy Baby?" and the Gold-selling "What Are We Doin' in Love?"

Plagued by financial troubles in the late 80's, West's life was cut tragically short in 1991 in a freak car accident while she was on her way to perform at the Opry. Daughter Shelly is also a country singer.—M.B.

Shelly West

BORN: May 23, 1958
BIRTHPLACE: Cleveland, Ohio

Shelly West, daughter of the late country music star and Grand Ole Opry favorite Dottie West, had a fleeting run of chart success in the early 1980's, during country music's Urban Cowboy crossover era. The high point of her recording career came with the 1981 Number One duet, "You're the Reason God Made Oklahoma," which she recorded with David Frizzell, her then-brother-in-law, also the younger brother of legendary singer Lefty Frizzell. (She was married to Allen Frizzell.) "You're the Reason God Made Oklahoma," which was also featured in the Clint Eastwood action comedy film, *Any Which Way But Loose*, was co-written by Larry Collins and Sandy Pinkard—the latter being half of the R-rated country comedy duo, Pinkard & Bowden.

After several more years and three more Top Ten singles—"A Texas State of Mind," "Another Honky-Tonk Night on Broadway" and "I Just Came Here to Dance"—the West/Frizzell string ran out.

On her own, West did manage to make one more trip to Number One—with 1983's "Jose Cuervo," a good-timey ode to the worm in the tequila bottle. She followed with a couple of other Top Ten singles— "Flight 309 to Tennessee" and "Another Motel Memory," along with other less successful singles, before fading from the charts.

West was born in Cleveland, Ohio, to Bill and Dottie West on May 23, 1958, and was raised in Nashville. She began her professional career singing backup on the road with her mother. Her first marriage, to Allen Frizzell, younger brother of Lefty and David, lasted until 1983. Shelly, Allen and David all began singing together in California night clubs in the late 1970's, and eventually fell into the clutches of veteran West Coast country producer Snuff Garrett, who first paired Shelly and David.

For a time, before her mother's death, she and Dottie toured together. As of the early 90's, Shelly was married to a TV production manager, and still singing on occasion. —B.A.

Speedy West

BORN: January 25, 1924
BIRTHPLACE: Springfield, Missouri

Wesley Webb "Speedy" West grew up on a family farm and began playing acoustic steel guitar as a child. Married at age 16, he farmed during World War II and played electric steel locally (he got his nickname at a local jam session). Moving with his family to Los Angeles in 1946, he worked days and played steel at night. In 1948 he acquired a custom-built Bigsby pedal steel guitar and turned pro. He worked briefly with Spade Cooley, and in 1949 with Hank Penny. Speedy's first record session was Eddie Kirk's 1949 hit recording of "Candy Kisses," which featured pedal steel four years before Webb Pierce's "Slowly." In 1949 Speedy joined Cliffie Stone's *Hometown Jamboree*. He and the show's new lead guitarist, Jimmy Bryant, created amazing guitar and steel ensembles and were in demand for recording sessions with all types of artists. Between 1950 and 1955 Speedy alone did 6,000 recordings with 177 artists, while he and Bryant recorded extraordinary guitar-steel instrumentals for Capitol. In 1960 Speedy produced Loretta Lynn's first hit: "Honky Tonk Girl" on the Zero label. Later that year he became manager of Fender Musical Instruments' regional distribution center in Tulsa, Oklahoma. He recorded two later albums for Capitol: *West of Hawaii* and *Guitar Spectacular*. After owning a Tulsa trailer business from 1968 to 1973, he drifted back into playing, and recorded a final album with Bryant in 1975. In April of 1981, a serious stroke paralyzed Speedy's right side, and though he regained movement, constant pain in his right arm ended his playing days. Nonetheless, he still appears at steel guitar conventions, combining comedy with entertaining stories of his past. —R.K.

Johnny Western

BORN: October 28, 1934
BIRTHPLACE: Two Harbors, Minnesota

Born in Two Harbors, Minnesota, in 1934, Johnny Western is a smooth cowboy singer best known as the writer of "The Ballad of Palladin," the theme song to *Have Gun Will Travel*, a popular western TV series that ran from 1957 until 1963, starring Richard Boone.

Western's career first got under way in earnest in 1956, when Gene Autry heard him singing at a party and put him to work on his road show. With this boost from Autry, Western eventually went on to enjoy modest success as a film and television actor., His credits include appearances on popular TV shows like *Gunsmoke, Wells Fargo* and *Pony Express.* Throughout the 60's, Western also enjoyed considerable popularity while touring with mainstream country artists like Kitty Wells and his friend Johnny Cash. Western has continued singing his inspired brand of cowboy music well into the 90's, and in recent years has also distinguished himself as a radio show host. —B.A.

Western Swing

Western swing was a form of music that could only have emerged from the eclectic musical atmosphere of Texas. During a night in a dancehall in the 30's and 40's, one could hear a Western swing band perform a traditional fiddle breakdown, a Benny Goodman big band favorite of the moment, a raunchy black blues and a Jimmie Rodgers number, with occasional overtones of mariachi music.

Bob Wills, the Texas fiddler credited with creating the music, grew up playing for dancers and always loved a good dance beat, be it in fiddling, pop, jazz or, particularly, the blues. When he formed the band that became The Light Crust Doughboys in the early 1930's with vocalist Milton Brown, they drew on all types of music that would please dancers. Being on the radio, sponsored by the Burrus Mill and Elevator Company of Dallas, gave their music exposure throughout Texas. Burrus general manager W. Lee O'Daniel, who hosted their radio show, discouraged their dancehall work, so Milton Brown left in 1932 to form The Musical Brownies.

The Brownies became the first swing band to take on the characteristics that would define most Western bands, boasting the first pianist (Fred "Papa" Calhoun) and electric steel guitar (Bob Dunn). After leaving The Doughboys, Wills' music went in much the same direction. He founded The Playboys in 1933, gradually adding full horn sections after he relocated to Tulsa in 1934. In Texas, the music remained the property of smaller bands. The Light Crust Doughboys continued performing and recording and, after W. Lee O'Daniel's dismissal from Burrus Mills, he continued with The Hillbilly Boys. These groups may have used a saxophone, but largely featured fiddles, piano, guitar, steel and bass. The Texas Playboys moved between a big band and smaller ensembles. Nashville was loath to embrace the music initially. Bob Wills defied the Grand Ole Opry by using his drums when he appeared there in 1944. Pee Wee King's Golden West Cowboys, Curley Williams and World War II brought swing to the West Coast, as Southerners moved to California seeking well-paying defense plant jobs and bands followed them to provide entertainment. But if anyone made California a hotbed of Western swing, Spade Cooley deserves the credit. His band, formed during World War II, featured more polish than even The Texas Playboys. He used a classical harp and tightly organized fiddle sections. In general, postwar West Coast swing had greater sophistication and made more creative use of electric instruments. Since innovative instrument makers like Leo Fender and

Paul Bigsby were perfecting their instruments, California players had state-of-the-art equipment. Cooley's hit-making streak ended when his vocalist, Tex Williams, quit in 1946 and most of his band followed him to become Williams' Western Caravan. Cooley then went to a large Lawrence Welk-style pop orchestra that also included fiddles and steel guitar. Nonetheless, most West Coast bands remained small, usually no more than eight pieces. Nationally, Cooley, Williams and Wills managed to have an impact on national record sales in the post-war 40's, which for the most part were their peak years in the charts.

In the Southwest and on the West Coast the music's popularity began fading in the early 50's, as television became the new form of diversion and the crowds tapered off in the dancehalls. Gradually, all but the larger ones either closed or changed their focus. Rock 'n' roll, a musical style that Western swing in some ways anticipated, hurt the entire country music industry. The music didn't disappear, but only a few of the bigger-name acts like the bands of Bob Wills, Leon McAuliffe and Tommy Duncan continued. Eventually, only Wills still worked. Many musicians left the business entirely. Aside from Wills' newer albums on Kapp, a Columbia reissue and a swing anthology on Arhoolie, little vintage material remained available on records.

The music was in danger of becoming an isolated, fading regional phenomenon when Merle Haggard's 1970 Bob Wills tribute album, *A Tribute to the Best Damn Fiddle Player in the World (Or My Salute to Bob Wills)* reintroduced Wills' music to a broader and younger audience. Young bands like Commander Cody and His Lost Planet Airmen and Asleep at the Wheel embraced Wills' music, and Western swing reissues began in the early 70's. Bob Wills, in failing health but sometimes well enough to travel, was honored throughout Texas and in Nashville. He had the chance to record part of a final album in 1973 with members of The Playboys, but a stroke left him comatose. Members of The Playboys including Leon McAuliffe and Al Stricklin reorganized for performing and recording. By the early 80's, George Strait helped revive Western swing by combining it with honky tonk music, as Hank Thompson had done in his time. Today, with reissues available and interest in Wills remaining high, Western swing is clearly in no further danger of extinction.
—R.K.

Billy Edd Wheeler

BORN: December 9, 1932
BIRTHPLACE: Whitesville, West Virginia

Billy Edd Wheeler has the rare distinction of being perhaps the only hit country songwriter and recording artist to also enjoy success as a playwright, Navy pilot, music executive, Yale Drama School attendee and college instructor (at his alma mater, Berea College, in Kentucky).

Raised in the mining town of Highcoal, West Virginia, Wheeler first turned to songwriting to put bread on the table in the early 1960's when he was an aspiring (and starving) playwright in New York City. He became a protégé of Jerry Leiber (of Leiber & Stoller songwriting fame), who also produced his earliest records. He had an early songwriting success when The Kingston Trio, the popular folk group, had a Top Ten hit with "The Reverend Mr. Black" in 1963. He wrote some of the most performed country hits of the 60's, 70's, and 80's: "Jackson," a Number Two country hit for Johnny Cash and June Carter and a minor pop hit for Nancy Sinatra and Lee Hazelwood in 1967. (Wheeler, ironically enough, was inspired to write "Jackson" after reading the Edward Albee play *Who's Afraid of Virginia Wolfe?*) Wheeler also penned the 1979 Kenny Rogers Number One, "Coward of the County," which was the inspiration for a Rogers-starring made-for-TV movie outing of the same name.

Wheeler, who is also a folklorist of some repute, enjoyed sporadic chart success of his own through the years. He hit his biggest lick in 1964 with the Top Five country novelty number, "Ode to the Little Brown Shack Out Back," which also made a minor ripple in the pop charts. Wheeler's later releases (on Kapp, United Artists and RCA, between 1968 and 1980), which also made brief entries in the country charts, include "I Ain't the Worryin' Kind," "West Virginia Woman," "Daddy" and "Fried Chicken and a Country Tune."   —B.A.

Cheryl Wheeler

BORN: July 10, 1951
BIRTHPLACE: Timonium, Maryland

In the 70's, Cheryl Wheeler left her native Maryland and settled in Newport, Rhode Island, a hotbed of the East Coast folk scene. She played bass in Jonathan

Edwards' band; he, in turn, produced some of her albums. Earning critical raves for both her singing and her songwriting—brilliant, sometimes humorous, sometimes haunting, slices of life—Wheeler released two albums and an EP on North Star Records during the 80's. In 1990, after her songs had been covered by Dan Seals and Juice Newton, among others, Wheeler was signed to Capitol Records. That affiliation produced another critically-acclaimed album, *Circles & Arrows*, which featured the compelling "Aces" (later covered by Suzy Bogguss) and the humorous "Estate Sale." In 1994, she released her fourth full-length album, *Driving Home*, on Philo/Rounder Records. As usual, it was highly praised.   —G.F.

The Whippoorwills

In 1940, country-jazz guitarist Roy Lanham founded a stringband inspired by Knoxville's Stringdusters, which included Homer Haynes and Jethro Burns. Lanham called the group—which included mandolinist Doug Dalton—The Fidgety Four. When they toured with pop singer Gene Austin, their name was changed to The Whippoorwills, and they added sophisticated four-part vocal harmonies. They disbanded during World War II, but Lanham and Doug Dalton reunited in Dayton, Ohio, in 1947 and added three new members: bassist Dusty Rhodes, rhythm guitarist Gene Mombeck and vocalist Juanita Vastine, who went by the name "Georgia Brown." They recorded for the Vita label, but their rich harmonies and country-jazz fusion was simply too far ahead of its time for most listeners. The group toured the Midwest in the late 40's, and briefly settled at KWTO in Springfield, Missouri. They also recorded transcribed radio shows with Smiley Burnette and George Morgan and toured extensively with Roy Rogers. They disbanded in 1955, when Lanham joined Cliffie Stone's *Hometown Jamboree* as guitarist.   —R.K.

Clarence White

BORN: July 7, 1944
BIRTHPLACE: Lewiston, Maine
DIED: July 14, 1973

Clarence White was a groundbreaking bluegrass flatpicker as well as a breathtakingly superb electric guitarist. He was born on June 7, 1944, in Lewiston, Maine, to a family who lived and breathed country and traditional Appalachian music.

In 1954, the family moved to Burbank, California, where ten-year-old Clarence and his brothers, Roland and Eric, formed The Country Boys. Throughout the mid- to late 1950's, the band performed on local stage, radio and television shows such as *The Squeakin' Deacon Show*, Cliffie Stone's *Hometown Jamboree* and *Town Hall Party*, and even *The Andy Griffith Show*.

After personnel changes, the group changed its name to The Kentucky Colonels in 1961 and cut its first album, *New Sounds of Bluegrass America*, released on the Briar label. During this period, White fell under the spell of bluegrass flatpicking legend Doc Watson, and subsequently began incorporating syncopated, unorthodox lead guitar runs and fills into his style of playing. That style would become a life-long trademark.

In 1964, The Colonels cut *Appalachian Swing*, a bluegrass masterpiece. The group disbanded in 1965, and White, who had begun to take an interest in electric guitar—thanks to some coaching and encouragement from James Burton—became a Hollywood session man, accompanying artists such as The Everly Brothers, Pat Boone, Rick Nelson, Randy Newman, Arlo Guthrie, Linda Ronstadt, Joe Cocker, Jackson Browne, The Monkees and The Byrds.

In 1968, White, banjoist-guitarist-drummer Gene Parsons, Cajun fiddler Gib Guilbeau and bassist Wayne Moore formed Nashville West—an early country-rock band. The group worked the Southern California club circuit for about a year. At this time, White was also making extensive use of the Parsons/White String Bender, a device that he invented with Gene Parsons. It enabled his Fender Telecaster to sound like a pedal steel by bending the B-string.

White's big break came in September 1968, when The Byrds hired him to play on their classic, country-rock album, *Sweetheart of the Rodeo*. When Gram Parsons (no relation to Gene) left the band shortly after the record's release, Chris Hillman and Roger McGuinn asked Clarence to become a full-fledged member. He obliged, and his association with the band lasted more than five years. In fact, some of Clarence's most dynamic electric—as well as acoustic—guitar playing can be heard on The Byrds' "The Ballad of Easy Rider" and other releases.

When The Byrds formally disbanded in 1973, Clarence joined Richard Greene, David Grisman, Peter Rowan and Bill Keith on the progressive bluegrass *Muleskinner* album, a favorite among modern bluegrass aficionados.

Around the same time, Clarence also began working on a solo album for Warner Bros. He'd only recorded a few tracks when, on July 14, 1973, while loading equipment into his car after a gig in Palmdale, California, he was struck and killed by a drunk driver.

Clarence's astonishing guitar playing inspired countless guitarists. Among the many musicians he influenced are Tony Rice, Bernie Leadon and Marty Stuart. In honor of the virtuoso guitarist, Fender Musical Instruments unveiled the Clarence White Signature Series Telecaster.　—R.P.

Lari White

BORN: May 13, 1965
BIRTHPLACE: Dunedin, Florida

Florida born and raised Lari White first took to performing as a child in her family's group, The White Family Singers. Attending the University of Miami, White sang in bands at night, did commercial jingle work and began writing songs. After a win on The Nashville Network's *You Can Be a Star*, White became a staff writer for Ronnie Milsap's publishing company. In 1991, she sang backing vocals for Rodney Crowell, who saw huge potential for the big-voiced, soulful White. When she signed with RCA, Crowell co-produced her 1993 debut, *Lead Me On*, along with guitarist and former Crowell sideman Steuart Smith and White herself. Critics raved about her voice and style—from bluesy torch numbers to roof-raising gospel, to contemporary country. While her early singles failed to connect at radio, White's talent is undeniable, and "That's My Baby," the lead single off of her 1994 sophomore album, provided the breakthrough she needed.

—G.F.

The Whites

A family band, and early practitioners of the New Traditional style of country music, The Whites (consisting of Buck White on piano and daughters Cheryl and Sharon on bass and guitar, respectively) have been playing together since 1971. They were then known as Buck White and The Down Home Folks, and Buck's wife, Pat, was part of the group. Buck grew up in Texas, where he met and married Pat and played in Western swing bands. The family moved to Arkansas in the early 1960's, and began playing bluegrass. After success on the bluegrass festival circuit, The Whites made the move to Nashville. They recorded several albums on independent labels, with Buck working construction to keep the family fed. Around this time, dobro ace Jerry Douglas joined the band, remaining with them until 1987.

In 1981, they signed with Capitol, putting "Send Me the Pillow You Dream On" onto the lower reaches of the singles chart. Moving over to Elektra in 1982, they scored Top Tens with "You Put the Blue in Me" and "Hangin' Around." Two more Top

Tens followed on the Warner label in 1983 before they settled in with MCA/Curb for the bulk of the 80's, where they hit the Top Ten once, with "Pins and Needles." Though country radio never warmed up to The Whites—the old saw about being "too country for country radio" applies here—fans and critics alike applauded their traditional mix of country, bluegrass and gospel. They were made members of the Grand Ole Opry in 1984, and still perform there regularly. In 1989, after leaving MCA, they released a gospel album on the Canaan label. Sharon is married to Ricky Skaggs, and she and her father and sister record and perform frequently with him.

—G.F.

Margaret Whiting

BORN: July 22, 1924
BIRTHPLACE: Detroit, Michigan

Margaret Whiting was not a country singer by anyone's definition. The daughter of pop composer Richard Whiting, she began singing as a guest vocalist on Capitol recordings in the 40's. Her brief period of country success came when Capitol teamed her with Cowboy singer Jimmy Wakely. From 1949 through 1951 they had nine Top Ten records, the first, Floyd Tillman's "Slippin' Around," being the biggest. They also did well with "Wedding Bells" that year, and Tillman's follow-up song, "I'll Never Slip Around Again." In 1950 the duo had one hit after another with "Broken Down Merry-Go-Round," "The Gods Were Angry With Me," "Let's Go to Church (Next Sunday Morning)" and "A Bushel and a Peck." In 1951 they had "When You and I Were Young Maggie Blues" and "I Don't Want to Be Free," an answer to the Tennessee Ernie-Kay Starr hit duet "I Want to Be Free."

Whiting's major success, however always remained in the pop field.

—R.K.

Keith Whitley

BORN: July 1, 1955
BIRTHPLACE: Sandy Hook, Kentucky
DIED: May 9, 1989

When Keith Whitley died suddenly and tragically in 1989, at age 33, it was the abrupt and somewhat sordid collapse of a musical promise left largely unfulfilled.

Though frequently overshadowed during his lifetime by more commercially successful peers like Randy Travis and George Strait, Whitley had, by the end of his life, matured into a hard country vocal stylist second to none and an accomplished and moving songwriter. The pity is he took his own life just at a point where the rest of the world was starting to recognize this. As Mark Coleman, writing for *The Journal Of Country Music*, noted in a brilliant essay on Whitley's slender but significant musical legacy: "All of Keith's Number One singles—'Don't Close Your Eyes,' 'When You Say Nothing at All,' 'No Stranger to the Rain,' 'I Wonder Do You Think of Me'—achieve a remarkable balance between pop accessibility and emotional purity. Keith Whitley discovered his musical niche—a place where traditional culture and popular concerns overlap—just around the same time he was dealing with some related personal problems."

Though he often seemed at a loss to fully channel it, Whitley's immense musical talent became apparent within a few years after he was born, in Sandy Hook, Kentucky, in 1955. By age 9, he'd made his radio debut on a station in Charleston, West Virginia, singing a Hank Williams song. By his early teens, he was singing tight bluegrass/gospel harmonies with long-time friend Ricky Skaggs in Ralph Stanley's legendary Clinch Mountain Boys. (Some of these early Whitely/Skaggs duets can be heard on the reissue CD, *Second Generation Bluegrass*.)

"Ricky and I met at a fiddlers' convention in Ezel, Kentucky," Whitley told *Country Music Magazine*. "We got to talking, and we ended up playing and singing together. Before long, he joined this little band that I had, The East Kentucky Mountain Boys. After that, we sang together constantly, night and day. Our voices just had a natural blend."

By the time Whitley was in his early 20's, he was already a star on the bluegrass circuit. Yet it is indicative of his long-time musical schizophrenia that all through his bluegrass years, it was Lefty Frizzell-style honky tonk music that he really longed to sing. Whitley got a rare opportunity to merge his bluegrass background and his closet honky tonk inclinations when he left Ralph Stanley's Clinch Mountain Boys and joined forces with newgrass master J.D. Crowe. As lead singer and front man with Crowe's respected ensemble, The New South, Whitley recorded several albums—most notably *My Home Ain't in the Hall of Fame* and 1981's masterful *Somewhere Between* which launched his steady, inexorable drift from bluegrass, where he was a prodigy and up-and-coming star, to the mainstream country field where he was, at that point, completely unknown.

It was on the strength of the rough tapes of *Somewhere Between*, Whitley's final album with Crowe and The New South—which were floating around Nashville even before the album's 1981 release—that Whitley landed his first major label solo contract, with RCA. But *A Hard Act to Follow*, his 1984 RCA debut, simply revealed too much of Whitley's Lefty Frizzell influence and not quite enough of Whitley himself. Whitley had his first real chart success with "Miami (My Amy)," a breezy love song off his 1986 *L.A. to Miami* album, which, ironically, went too far in the other direction—toward sultry balladry—to fully capture the quintessential Keith Whitley.

It was only when Whitley finally seized the reins of musical control, scrapped an album he'd completed with producer Blake Meavis and teamed up with producer Garth Fundis (of Trisha Yearwood and Don Williams fame) that he at long last hit his stride. His final two albums—*Don't Close Your Eyes* (1988) and *I Wonder Do You Think Of Me* (1989), both produced by Fundis—were, by far, his best ever, and resulted in his first Number One hits.

There is especially sad irony in the fact that in the couple of years just before his untimely death, Whitley's personal life at least also appeared to be on the mend. He married singer Lorrie Morgan (his second marriage) in 1986 and had his first child. After years of struggle, he claimed to have finally conquered his ferocious alcoholism.

But when he left this life, on an otherwise uneventful spring day, just a week or two before the release of *I Wonder Do You Think Of Me,* everything had, by accounts, come unraveled for him again. Cause of death was acute alcoholic poisoning: a .477 alcohol level—roughly the equivalent of 20 shots of 100-proof liquor drunk in two hours' time.

"Nobody really knew the depth of his problem," his widow Lorrie Morgan, who in 1994 was putting together a tribute album to her husband, explained in an interview with *Country Music Magazine* a year or so after her husband's death. "I don't even know a word to describe just how serious his problem was....He could only go so long without drinking, and nobody—not me, not any clinic, or any psychiatrist he went to—could help him."

"Knowing the incredible pressure Keith was under, I do not blame him for taking that first drink," she added. "Everyone needs an escape, but his schedule was so hectic it didn't permit him one, did not permit him to just be Keith. And somebody with an illness like that can only go so far before he reaches the end of his rope."

—B.A.

Ray Whitley

BORN: December 5, 1901
BIRTHPLACE: Atlanta, Georgia
DIED: February 21, 1979

Ray Whitley did not set out to be a singer. After Navy service, he worked on the East Coast at laboring jobs, playing music strictly as a diversion. In New York

City in the 1930's he auditioned for a radio show and along with another transplanted Southerner, Tex Ritter, began hosting the *WHN Barn Dance* there. As a singing cowboy, Whitley began recording for American Recording and for Decca, and by the mid-1930's was in Hollywood doing some of the earliest singing cowboy films. Signed to RKO Pictures, he did 18 musical shorts and appeared in films with Tim Holt and George O'Brien. In addition, he continued recording throughout this time. Whitley, with Fred Rose, also wrote such classics as Gene Autry's theme song, "Back in the Saddle Again," and "I Hang My Head and Cry." In 1937 he had Gibson build him a custom guitar that emphasized a deep bass sound and became their classic J-200 model. During World War II, Whitley briefly led a Western swing dance band in Los Angeles known as The Rhythm Wranglers, playing the many ballrooms that opened to serve defense plant workers. The band included much California Western swing talent: guitarist Merle Travis along with steel guitarists Noel Boggs, Joaquin Murphey and Herb Remington, and fiddler Tex Atchison. Whitley also worked in the business end of music, managing the Sons of The Pioneers and Jimmy Wakely. He remained active for some years before his death.

—R.K.

Slim Whitman

BORN: January 20, 1924
BIRTHPLACE: Tampa, Florida

Singer/guitarist Slim Whitman was born Otis Dewey Whitman Jr., in Tampa, Florida, on January 20, 1924. Both prolific and popular throughout his three-decade career, Whitman recorded over 30 Top 50 country singles and 19 Gold-selling albums. An outstanding athlete, Slim was a star pitcher in high school and dreamed of playing professionally. After learning to play the guitar during World War II, Slim began playing local clubs for extra money and sang on local radio station WDAE in Tampa in 1948. He signed a recording contract with RCA Victor the following year. Before long he moved to Shreveport and became a regular cast member of *Louisiana Hayride*.

In 1952 he switched to the West Coast independent label Imperial Records. Within a year he had a Top Ten hit with "Keep It a Secret," the first of a long string of hit singles that extended through the 1950's and 60's, including "North Wind," "Secret Love," "Rose Marie," "China Doll" and "Indian Love Call." From the 1950's through the 1970's Whitman recorded literally dozens of albums, on Imperial and, later, Liberty and United Artists. Among his 1960's releases were *Heart Songs and Love Songs, Yodeling, Love Song of the Waterfall* (1965), *Birmingham Jail* (Camden Records, 1966), *Travelin' Man* (1966) and *Memories* (1968).

Whitman continued to place singles in the country charts through the 1970's on United Artists, where he recorded after it bought Liberty. Meanwhile he had developed quite an international following: In

the late 1970's, his single of "Rose Marie" spent 11 consecutive weeks at Number One on British pop charts, an accomplishment that had eluded even The Beatles. At the same time, and for years afterward, "Rose Marie" held the record for the all-time best-selling 45 in Australia.

Known mostly for his very traditional country interpretations of old standards, Whitman was more of a revolutionary when it came to marketing his records. He enjoyed a phenomenal resurgence in the early 1980's when he became one of the first country performers to take advantage of television marketing. His outrageously successful *All My Best* collection, sold exclusively through TV spots, sold two million copies, making old Slim Whitman a hot new commodity in the record industry. He was courted by Cleveland International Records president Steve Popovich and ultimately signed a recording/distribution agreement with Cleveland and Epic Records. His debut single on Epic/Cleveland, "When,"

had an easy climb to the top of the charts and his first album was in record stores by early 1981. His second Epic album, *Mr. Songman*, was released later that year. With a career total of over 50 million records sold worldwide, Slim Whitman enjoys a comfortable retirement in Middleberg, Florida, with his wife Jerry.
—M.B.

The Wilburn Brothers

BORN: Doyle, July 7, 1930, Thayer, Missouri
      Teddy, November 30, 1931, Thayer, Missouri
DIED: Doyle, October 16, 1982

The Wilburn Brothers began as a family act, with four brothers, Lester, Leslie, Virgil Doyle Thurman, Theodore (or "Teddy") and a sister, Geraldine. They remained a family act during the 1930's, and in 1940 did a brief stint on the Opry. Child labor laws involving the youngest members, Doyle and Teddy, forced them to leave. In 1948 they joined the new KWKH *Louisiana Hayride* in Shreveport. Geraldine had left to marry, so the four Wilburn Brothers remained.

By the late 40's they were closely associated with *Hayride* star Webb Pierce. Teddy recorded for Pierce's Pacemaker label, and The Wilburn Family recorded for Four Star. After Army service during the Korean War, Doyle and Teddy worked with Pierce until 1954. In 1953 they were made members of the Grand Ole Opry. Their first hit was a duet with Pierce, "Sparkling Brown Eyes," followed by "I Wanna Wanna Wanna" and "You're Not Playing Love," in 1955. In 1956 "I'm So in Love With You" and "Go Away with Me" went Top Ten. Two hit duets with Ernest Tubb followed: "Mister Love" in 1957 and "Hey Mr. Bluebird" in 1958. Around that time they founded the Wil-Helm booking agency with steel guitarist Don Helms, and started Sure-Fire Music publishing. In 1959, "Which One Is to Blame" and "A Woman's Intuition" were also big hits. They not only signed Loretta Lynn to Sure-Fire, but got her her first Opry guest appearance and her Decca recording contract. Their

1962 hits were "Trouble's Back in Town." and "Roll Muddy River." In 1963 it was "Tell Her So." That year they began their syndicated TV program, *The Wilburn Brothers Show* which ran until 1974. Late in 1966, their biggest hit "Hurt Her Once for Me," remained on the charts for 20 weeks.

In the early 70's after Loretta left their show, the Wilburns added 15-year-old Kentucky singer Patty Ramey to their tours during her school vacations. She became a star in the 80's as Patty Loveless. After Doyle's death from cancer, Teddy concentrated on running Sure-Fire with his brother, Leslie. Teddy no longer tours but is still an Opry member, appearing there with Leslie playing guitar behind him.   —R.K.

Audrey Williams

BORN: February 28, 1923
BIRTHPLACE: Banks, Alabama
DIED: November 4, 1975

Audrey Williams in many ways was as tragic a figure as her husband Hank. Born Audrey Mae Sheppard, she grew up poor. She'd briefly married Erskine Guy with whom she had a daughter, Lycrecia, born in 1941. She already wanted to be a country singer when she met Hank Williams, who was still was playing rural Alabama honky tonks in the early 40's. She and Hank married December 15, 1944, and she "sang" with him and his band, The Drifting Cowboys, despite a near total inability to carry a tune. The marriage was volatile even after Hank gained his Acuff-Rose songwriting contract and his record deals with Sterling and MGM. Following the success of "Lovesick Blues," which brought Hank to the Opry, Hank got her a recording contract (with Decca in 1950) that resulted in several unlistenable records. Audrey divorced Hank in 1952; yet despite Hank's subsequent marriage to Billie Jean Eshlimar, she managed to make herself Hank's "legal" widow after his death. She later performed for MGM (with little success) and worked the road for several years. After that, she became a talent scout while pushing her son, Hank Jr.'s career. But mother and son grew estranged in the 1970's, and Audrey's problems (including alcoholism) worsened. Following a lengthy legal battle, Audrey ended up losing part of Hank's song royalties to Billie Jean (Hank's second wife and, later, Johnny Horton's widow). Audrey's tax problems also worsened as her health deteriorated. The IRS was to seize her Nashville home the day she died in 1975.   —R.K.

Curley Williams

BORN: June 3, 1913
BIRTHPLACE: Georgia
DIED: September 5, 1970

Doc Williams, a fiddler whose family named him "Doc" in the hope he'd pursue a medical career, made his initial mark around Albany, Georgia, and in late 1942 he and his band The Santa Fe Trail Riders, came to the Grand Ole Opry. Because WWVA singer Doc Williams called his band The Border Riders (as well as using the name "Doc"), George D. Hay of the Opry renamed the act. They became Curley Williams and The Georgia Peach Pickers. They worked on the Opry through the early 40's, before moving to California toward the end of World War II. Williams then relocated to Shreveport in 1948. The Peach Pickers, featuring pianist Joe Pope and former Hank Williams steel guitarist Boots Harris, made many excellent Western swing records for Columbia, including "Southern Gal (From Nashville, Tennessee)" and "Georgia Steel Guitar." Williams was also a gifted songwriter, and in 1951, wrote the ballad "Half as Much," which both he and Hank Williams recorded a year later. Williams' daughter, Georgia Anne, also sang with The Peach Pickers. They worked in Alabama in the mid-50's.   —R.K.

Doc Williams

BORN: June 26, 1914
BIRTHPLACE: Cleveland, Ohio

Though he and Curley Williams shared the same name, it came under very different circumstances. This Doc Williams was born Andrew John Smik Jr. in

Cleveland. Growing up in western Pennsylvania in the counties surrounding Pittsburgh, he heard the Slovak music of his heritage but also became attracted to country. At age 18, he returned to Cleveland and joined Doc McCaulley and His Kansas Clodhoppers. That band later became The Cherokee Hillbillies and  eventually relocated to KQV. In 1937, Smik took the name Doc Williams and changed The Cherokee Hillbillies into The Border Riders (he used the name Doc first, so Curley Williams changed his). They moved to Pittsburgh, then to Wheeling's *WWVA Jamboree*, mixing polka-style music with their country songs. They quickly became one of the show's top acts, remaining there ever since. His wife, Chickie, whom he married in 1946, became a vocalist who excelled in recitations. They toured and released records on their own Wheeling label. They never signed with a major label in part because they remained dedicated to hardcore country music, despite any trends. The Williamses remain associated with the *Jamboree* today, though they perform less frequently. They also own a souvenir shop across from the show's headquarters at the Capitol Music Hall in Wheeling.   —R.K.

Don Williams

BORN: May 27, 1939
BIRTHPLACE: Floydada, Texas

Don Williams, born in Floydada, Texas on May 27, 1939, was like a calming voice of reason and serenity during country music's tumultuous 1970's and droll early 80's. While artists like Waylon Jennings and Hank Williams Jr. were busy re-configuring the country landscape with rowdy, good-timey musical anthems, Williams, a founding member of the 60's folk trio, The Pozo Seco Singers (which scored a few pop hits in the late 60's and early 70's), held a steady course with his quiet, at times almost other-worldly brand of country, personified by soothing hits like "Amanda,"

"Till All the Rivers Run Dry," "You're My Best Friend" and "I'm Just a Country Boy."

Nicknamed "The Gentle Giant" for his imposing physical stature, quiet nature and introspective musical persona, Williams stormed the top of the charts again and again (17 Number Ones between 1974 and 1986) with his warm, laconic baritone, which was usually backed by low-key, minimalist arrangements furnished by producer Allen Reynolds and, later, Garth Fundis.

Williams worked briefly in the furniture business before moving to Nashville in 1967, where he became a staff songwriter for legendary producer Jack Clement, and first broke into the country charts (on Clement's label, JMI) in 1972, with the Top 20 hit, "The Shelter of Your Eyes." In the next decade, he would follow up with numerous hits, including high-spirited celebrations like "Tulsa Time" and "Rake and Ramblin' Man," and soulful ballads like "You're My Best Friend," "(Turn Out the Light and) Love Me Tonight," "Say It Again," "Some Broken Hearts Never Mend," "I Believe In You," "Lord, I Hope This Day Is Good" and "Love Is on a Roll." Along the way, he made some of the best music to come out of Nashville during the 70's and early 80's. Courtesy of his buddy Burt Reynolds, Williams also made a few light-hearted forays into acting, appearing in  forgettable comedy films like *Smokey and the Bandit 2* and *W.W. and the Dixie Dance Kings*.

Williams, who has continued recording— with less commercial success—during the late 1980's and early 1990's, has always scrupulously shied away from the more ostentatious aspects of the lifestyle and image associated with many artists of his generation. As his music suggests, he is a quiet, reclusive man, deeply anchored in the twin tenets of family and faith. In recent years, he's toured less frequently (he has a particularly huge following in Europe and The United Kingdom where he was proclaimed "Country Music Star of the Decade" in 1980), and has granted few interviews, preferring instead to let the power of positive suggestion embodied in the straightforward simplicity of his music speak for itself.   —B.A.

Hank Williams

BORN: September 17, 1923
BIRTHPLACE: Mount Olive, Alabama
DIED: January 1, 1953

Hank. You don't have to say the last name.

People know who you mean. His legacy outlasted the Nashville Sound, Sherrillization and every other short-lived trendy notion. Yet the lasting changes, from rockabilly to Outlaw to the music of Steve Earle and Randy Travis—and even Hank Jr.—have their roots, spiritually and musically, in Hank.

Everyone knows the tragedy: dominant mother, weak father, domineering wife, deep dependence on the bottle and later drugs, a crippling birth defect and terminal insecurity all stacked against him. His legend obsessed some of his followers. A few died trying to keep up with him. But Hank's genius was—and always will be—music. From the beginning, it overwhelmed everything else.

Hiram Hank (not Hiram King as some have written) Williams was born in Mt. Olive, Alabama, September 17, 1923, the son of Lilly and Lonnie Williams. Lonnie was a shell-shocked World War I veteran who drove an Alabama logging train. By the time Hank was 6, the marriage was over. Lonnie went into a VA hospital, and the family moved to various small Alabama towns before settling in Montgomery in 1937.

School bored him. He cared only about music, and learned his Jimmie Rodgers and Roy Acuff songs well. In mid-1937 he won a Montgomery talent contest singing "W.P.A. Blues," an original number that, according to Bob Pinson, the pre-eminent expert on Hank's music, he modeled on an old Riley Puckett number. He wound up with his own show on WSFA Radio and a hardcore group of fans—proof of his charisma even then.

In 1942 he tried to join the Army, but an old back injury disqualified him. He worked on and off in the shipyards of Mobile, Alabama, but never totally quit playing. By 1944 he was regrouping his band, as some of them left the service. Drifting Cowboys steel guitarist Don Helms, whose keening, high-pitched chords became a trademark of Hank's sound, had joined him in 1943.

Hank didn't like Audrey Sheppard Guy when he first met her. Her first marriage ending, she was obsessed with being a country singer, a desire complicated by a total lack of musical talent. Eventually they became attracted to each other. She started singing with the band and they married in December of 1944. Audrey would be the subject of some of his greatest songs—and the cause of his greatest pain.

By September of 1946 he and Audrey, confident of his songwriting, went to see Fred Rose at Acuff-Rose, the Nashville song publishing company Rose and Roy Acuff had founded. Rose, a master songsmith, saw Hank's genius immediately and took him on as a writer. On occasion he would touch up some of Hank's songs, rarely taking credit for it. Sterling Records asked Rose to suggest a country singer for their label; he suggested Hank. That December, with Rose producing and The Oklahoma Wranglers (the three Willis brothers, later known as The Drifting Cowboys) backing him, Hank cut four songs at the WSM studios in Nashville that sold well enough to justify another session in February of 1947.

Rose recommended Hank to Frank Walker, president of the new MGM Records, as the label was short on country talent except for Carson Robison and Bob Wills. That year he recorded "Move It on Over," which sold well enough to get him some notice—and also served as the musical model for the song "Rock Around the Clock." He and Audrey were divorced in 1948, shortly before Hank landed an audition on the new *Louisiana Hayride* show out of Shreveport. He quickly became one of the show's foremost artists and even cut down on the bottle.

That December he recorded "Lovesick Blues" for MGM in Cincinnati. It was an old pop song first recorded in the 1920's by yodeler Emmett Miller and later by Alabama singer Rex Griffin. Charles Wolfe's research reveals that Rose discouraged Hank from cutting the song; Hank insisted because his audiences liked it. After it topped the country charts in the spring of 1949, shortly after Hank's Jr. birth, the Opry—Hank's real goal—overlooked his reputation as a boozer and invited him as a guest on Red Foley's June 11th segment. Six explosive encores later, he was the Opry's newest star.

He reorganized The Drifting Cowboys and by

August, Audrey, seeing another chance at stardom, nullified the divorce. That year, "Wedding Bells," written by Claude Boone, Hank's own songs "Mind Your Own Business" and "You're Gonna Change," Leon Payne's "Lost Highway" and Hank's version of the old jazz tune "My Bucket's Got a Hole In It" were all huge hits for Hank.

Audrey took on a free-spending lifestyle, acquiring clothes, appliances, a new, ostentatious Nashville home and a rural retreat south of the city. By 1950, with more hits on the charts, Hank was selling millions of records and getting $1,000 a show. In 1951 he and Audrey opened a Western wear store in Nashville. Using the name "Luke the Drifter," he also recorded maudlin, moralistic recitations for MGM. Meanwhile Rose gave some of Hank's songs to Mitch Miller of Columbia Records, and in the hands of singers like Tony Bennett, who recorded "Cold, Cold Heart," they became huge pop hits.

But as he drank more, the good will he'd built started fading. He straightened up for the 1951 Hadacol Caravan tour, where he and the Cowboys outdid even Bob Hope. However, even as some of his most enduring numbers—songs like "I Can't Help It" and "Hey, Good Lookin'"—were topping the charts, he himself was deteriorating. Chet Flippo's controversial 1981 book, *Your Cheatin' Heart,* revealed that, regardless of his success, Hank was doomed anyway by spina bifida occulta—a birth defect fatal unless treated in childhood. His wasn't.

By early 1952 Hank and Audrey had re-separated; in May they divorced again. He moved into a house with his protégé Ray Price. He started missing shows, or worse yet, sometimes performed roaring drunk. In August, as "Jambalaya" headed for Number One, the Opry management, long uncomfortable with Hank's reputation, fired him. The *Louisiana Hayride* readily took him back.

A photo of him in custody for drunkenness that August shows a wasted, sickly figure clearly heading for oblivion. In October he privately married Billie Jean Jones Eshlimar, then married her a second time in Shreveport's Municipal Auditorium. As "Settin' the Woods on Fire" and the satirical "I'll Never Get Out of This World Alive" headed for the top, his body was failing fast. On a visit home to Alabama, he played a new song titled "The Log Train" for his relatives. A beautiful, folk-like number about his dad's days as an engineer, it showed glimpses of a new maturity never fulfilled.

Everyone knows the rest. He was booked to do a New Year's Day show in Canton, Ohio, for which he and his driver left Montgomery on December 30. Hank drank and took pills, and died along the way. His driver found him dead when he checked the back seat of the Caddie in Oak Hill, West Virginia. The funeral in Montgomery attracted at least 25,000. The tribute songs poured into the record bins and continue to this day.

When he died, the legend took over. His records never stopped selling. The horrible film, *Your Cheatin' Heart,* starring George Hamilton, appeared in 1964. Audrey got herself recognized as Hank's "official" widow and never quit using his legacy to try and promote herself. Hank Jr. nearly killed himself trying to follow the legend, which helped kill Audrey in 1975. Hank Jr.'s real success—a solid string of hits recalling his daddy's—came when he found his own voice and freed himself of his past. In 1961, Hank Sr. was one of the first members elected to the Country Music Hall of Fame. Few American performers manage to touch our consciousness long after they die, but Hank certainly did. His fame is assured for the rest of our lifetimes—and beyond.   —R.K.

Hank Williams Jr.

BORN: May 26, 1949
BIRTHPLACE: Shreveport, Louisiana

Hank Williams Jr. was a towering, and sometimes controversial figure on the country music landscape of the late 1970's and 1980's. With his fiery, brazenly outspoken brand of macho, redneck country-rock and his hell-raising persona, he became a favorite with the same rowdy, youthful grassroots masses that had revered early 70's southern rockers like The Marshall Tucker Band and Lynyrd Skynyrd—bands which also had a heavy influence on Williams himself in his early years.

The son of country legend Hank Williams Sr., Williams Jr. was born in Shreveport, Louisiana, on

May 26, 1949, just a few years before his father died. Williams, the Second, not only inherited a portion of the perennial financial windfalls from his father's lucrative catalogue of original songs; he also inherited a potent measure of the old man's musical talent and restless temperament.

"I'm not going to lie to you," Williams explained in his brutally candid 1979 autobiography, *Living Proof*, which was written with *Country Music Magazine*'s Michael Bane. "I was born with a safety net. Daddy's royalties, which come whether I'm a star or not....that's why I don't compromise my music. Success or failure, the responsibility is mine and mine alone."

By the time he was eight years old, Williams Jr. was already in the midst of what he later categorized as a "normal-abnormal childhood," having been pushed prematurely into the spotlight by his mother. He began his career as a gifted, but feckless imitator of his father's unforgettable style, and for quite a few years made a mint serving up hillbilly nostalgia to

the hard country masses hungry for a posthumous memories of their beloved anti-hero Hank Sr. (A headline from the time—"Hank Williams Had A Son; Son Sings"—seemed, for better or worse, to sum it all up.) Though in later years, Williams would step out from behind his father's dark, towering shadow, he has never entirely escaped it, or let his fans forget his family's dark tradition.

By the time Williams was in his late teens, the string had run out on the Father/Son schtick, and the big money and wild times of child stardom degenerated into quite a few late adolescent lost years, during which he was plagued by drug abuse, marital problems and at least one half-baked suicide attempt.

But there soon followed one of the most dramatic cases of musical—and personal—self-invention that country music has ever seen. Not only did Williams survive a near-fatal plunge off a Montana mountain top, he also transformed himself from a second-generation Hank Senior imitator that nobody wanted anymore, to one of the most immensely popular stars of his generation.

Not only did he gradually come into his own as a songwriter—adept at spinning out straight country weepers, as well as angry, hard-edged country protest songs ("A Country Boy Can Survive," "The Coalition to End Coalitions," "I've Got Rights," etc.); he also matured into a singer of even greater versatility than his father. Early albums on which he first found his own voice—*Family Tradition* (1979), *Habits Old & New* (1980), and *Whiskey Bent & Hellbound* (1981)—stand as classic examples of early Southern rock-country fusion. In the years since, he's also recorded some of the finest country-blues, Dixieland and Southern boogie heard in recent years.

Of course, the very qualities that made Williams an outsider and something of a pariah in Nashville's staid music industry—his outspoken, rowdy persona, redneck rock 'n' roll attitude and shoot-from-the-hip, politically-tinged anthems—made him a demigod with the wild-ass, youthful blue-collar masses. Hank Jr.'s music became the national theme song of redneck party animals everywhere. His hits weren't just full-tilt country-rockers to drink beer by; they were soundtracks to a lifestyle of rowdy excess: wild and woolly testimonials of grassroots defiance to get smashed to. Near riots would sometimes ensue when promoters at his sold-out coliseum concerts, out of fear for their lives and property, would shut down the beer concessions.

Ultimately, though, the righteous indignation and sincere fervor that inspired Williams' best music and earned him a formidable string of Number One hits, platinum-certified albums and two Country Music Association Entertainer of the Year awards (1987 and '88) began to degenerate into droll, arrogant, thematic redundancy by the late 80's; and even the most die-hard Hank fans began to weary of his interminable musical posturing and his endless musical references to his late father's legend.

The 1990's, thus far, have not been terribly kind to "Bocephus" (as his father long ago nicknamed him, and as he is sometimes known to his fans). Like a lot of 70's and 80's superstars, he's hung on long enough to see much of his thunder—and gate receipts—stolen by a younger, and determinedly more clean-cut and conventional generation of superstars.

Yet Williams always seems to have another trick up his sleeve. In 1993, he turned over yet another new musical leaf when he emerged with *Out of Left Field*. This tasteful and uncharacteristically low-key

collection of soulful, R&B-tinged tunes proved that even for an unregenerate hell-raiser of yesteryear like Hank Jr. there was indeed life—musical and otherwise—after 40.   —B.A.

Lucinda Williams

BORN: January 26, 1953
BIRTHPLACE: Lake Charles, Louisiana

Lucinda Williams, an influential fringe player on the 90's country scene, actually owes as much to Delta blues, rock, rhythm & blues and Cajun music for her singular style as she does to mainstream country music.

To date, Williams' biggest successes in the country field have been as a songwriter rather than as an artist. Patty Loveless had a Top 20 hit in 1990 with Williams' haunting "The Night's Too Long." And in 1992, Williams' "Passionate Kisses" became a Top Five single for Mary-Chapin Carpenter.

Born in Lake Charles, Louisiana, Williams, the daughter of a college professor and noted poet, Miller Williams, came of age in Atlanta, New Orleans, Mexico

City, and even Santiago, Chile, as her father moved from one academic post to the next. In her late teens, Williams began performing in clubs in Houston, Austin and New Orleans. Her earliest albums—*Ramblin'* (1979), an acoustic collection of Delta blues and traditional country; and *Happy Woman Blues* (1980)—were released on the Smithsonian/Folkways label.

It was not until 1988, after a move to Los Angeles, that Williams re-emerged with her third album, *Lucinda Williams*, on the Rough Trade label. This album ultimately earned her rave reviews and a healthy cult following. Next came an EP, *Passionate Kisses*, before Rough Trade folded. After an aborted deal with RCA Records, Williams landed on Chameleon Records, releasing the critically-acclaimed *Sweet Ole World* in 1992. "If someone asked me what kinds of songs I write," Williams says, "I'd say, 'Go read Flannery O'Connor or Eudora Welty.' It has that same feel to me, a sort of Southern Gothic thing."   —B.A.

Tex Williams

BORN: August 23, 1917
BIRTHPLACE: Ramsey, Illinois
DIED: October 11, 1985

Sollie Paul Williams grew up in rural Illinois, was playing over radio by age 13 and worked in a local band for a few years before moving to Washington State to pick apples. There, he played several more years in bands until moving to Los Angeles in 1942. He soon joined fiddler Spade Cooley as bass player and vocalist in Cooley's new band. Signed to Columbia, they recorded "Shame on You," a major country hit in 1945. By 1946, Tex's growing fame as a singer landed him a Capitol recording contract, but, when he and Cooley began clashing, Spade fired Tex. Most Cooley sidemen quit to join Tex's new band, The Western Caravan. With only one hit record, Tex was on the verge of being dropped by Capitol when Merle Travis wrote

for him the talking blues "Smoke! Smoke! Smoke! (That Cigarette)," a country and pop smash that became the label's first million-seller. Tex had other hits in the same vein, including "That's What I Like About the West," "Never Trust a Woman" (1947), "Suspicion," "Banjo Polka," "Who? Me?" "Talking Boogie" and Carson Robison's "Life Gits Tee-Jus, Don't It" (1948). For several years he ran the Riverside Rancho nightclub in Los Angeles. After 1949, he had no hits but toured extensively, recording for RCA, Decca, Capitol (again), Liberty and Boone Records with no success. He operated his Tex Williams Village club in Newhall, California, until 1965, then dissolved his band and worked as a solo artist. In 1972 he had a minor hit on Monument with "The Night Miss Nancy Ann's Hotel For Single Girls Burned Down" and briefly recorded for Granite. Tex's drawback was the limitations of the talking blues format that made him popular. Though he toured in the 70's and recorded a final album in 1981 with the band, Country Express, his health declined even before his death from lung cancer in 1985.   —R.K.

Foy Willing

BORN: 1915
BIRTHPLACE: Bosque County, Texas
DIED: July 24, 1978

Foy Willing, born Foy Willingham, began his musical career by singing on the radio in his teens. He even worked in New York City, sponsored by Crazy Water Crystals, the laxative company that sponsored many country acts on radio, from 1933 to 1935. He worked in Texas over the next several years before moving to California in 1940. There, he founded the Western vocal group The Riders of the Purple Sage with Al Sloey and Eddie Dean's older brother, Jimmy Dean (not the singer of "Big Bad John" fame). The group was comprised of former members of the *Hollywood Barn Dance* radio series and worked extensively on radio there. In 1944 they recorded for Capitol, having a hit with "Texas Blues." In 1946 their version of "Detour" became a hit, as did their recording of "Have I Told You Lately That I Love You" for Majestic Records. A number of excellent sidemen worked with the band including accordionists Billy Liebert and Paul Sells, fiddler Johnny Paul and steel gui-

tarist Freddie Tavares (who later helped Leo Fender design guitars). The Riders had other hits for Capitol; in 1952 Willing disbanded the group. Willing recorded several times after that and performed occasionally until his death.　　　　—R.K.

Kelly Willis

BORN: October 1, 1968
BIRTHPLACE: Annandale, Virginia

Of all the progressive country artists to storm into Nashville by way of Austin, Texas, on the heels of the late 1980's New Traditionalist movement, none seemed more an anomaly than Kelly Willis. This girlishly demure, almost wall-flowerish singer comes from a military family and grew up in the staid white-collar Northern Virginia suburbs of Washington, D.C. Yet, despite her relatively sheltered background and her quiet off-stage bearing, she possesses a voice of magnificent, at times almost guttural intensity—like

a latter-day Patsy Cline or Wanda Jackson at their earthiest. "Kelly Willis sings like an angel with hell-scorched wings," Nick Tosches wrote in *Texas Monthly* magazine. Added Rob Tannenbaum of *Rolling Stone*: "Willis has a rich, libidinal delivery.... Closer than most to Patsy Cline's true spirit."

"I get on stage, I'm a wild woman," Willis herself joked in a 1991 interview with *Country Music Magazine*. "But, really, I get off stage, I'm just this scared little person."

Willis began singing in her mid-teens in various D.C.-area rock bands—most notably in a "garage, thrashy, rockabilly" ensemble called The Fireballs, which also included her ex-husband and former drummer, Mas Palermo. "I discovered all kinds of music I wasn't aware of before," she recalled. "We would play Wanda Jackson songs, Gene Vincent, Patsy Cline—not the pretty Patsy Cline songs, but the rockin' Patsy Cline songs. We'd do rootsy rockabilly stuff, like Los Lobos, The Tailgaters, The Blasters. That sort of thing."

Willis, Palermo and the rest of The Fireballs moved to Austin, Texas, and scrambled around for gigs in Texas' music capitol. After they disbanded, Willis embarked on a solo career that soon won her a place as one of Austin's hottest club singers. She eventually came to the attention of then-Austinite Nanci Griffith, who in turn brought her to the attention of Tony Brown, executive producer and label head at MCA/Nashville.

As immensely talented as she is, Willis, even after recording three noteworthy albums for MCA—*Well Traveled Love* (1990), *Bang Bang* (1991) and *Kelly Willis* (1993)—has proven a little too gutsy and a little too real for country radio. Thus, without much airplay, she has yet to find a niche beyond the relatively slender market of the progressive post-punk country/college scene. And considering Willis' marvelous vocal talents and fiery innovative spirit, this is most surely country fans' great loss.　　　　—B.A.

The Willis Brothers

Guitarist James "Guy" Willis (born July 15, 1915, died April 13, 1981), his fiddling brother Charles "Skeeter" Willis (born December 20, 1907, died in 1976) and their third brother, accordionist Richard "Vic" Willis (born May 31, 1922), started out (along with bass player "Cherokee" Chuck Wright) as an eclectic western band called The Oklahoma Wranglers on KGEF in Shawnee in 1932. The group worked regularly with Eddy Arnold's touring shows. In 1946, they backed Hank Williams on his first sessions for Sterling Records and, that same year, joined the Grand Ole Opry, staying until 1949. During this time they recorded for RCA. They toured with Arnold until 1957 and rejoined the Grand Ole Opry in 1960. In the mid-60's, now known as The Willis Brothers, they scored big with truck driving songs, the most famous being "Give Me 40 Acres (To Turn This Rig Around)" (1964). After Guy's and Skeeter's deaths, Vic formed The Vic Willis Trio, which is still a popular Opry act in the 90's.   —B.A.

Billy Jack Wills

BORN: February 26, 1926
BIRTHPLACE: Memphis, Texas
DIED: March 2, 1991

Billy Jack Wills, Bob Wills' youngest brother, gravitated to the bass like his older brother Luke. He also played drums with brother Johnnie Lee Wills' band in Tulsa in the early 1940's.

During the mid-40's he joined Bob's Texas Playboys in California and became one of the band's principal vocalists after Bob fired Tommy Duncan in 1948. He sang such upbeat Wills favorites as "Rock-a-Bye Baby Blues" (which he wrote) and "Cadillac in Model 'A'," and also functioned as one of the Playboys' finest songwriters. Billy wrote the lyrics to the classic Wills ballad, "Faded Love," and co-wrote the ballad "Lily Dale" with Playboy fiddler-mandolinist Tiny Moore. When Bob moved to Oklahoma City in 1949, he built a band around Billy Jack, based at Bob's Wills Point Ballroom in Sacramento.

Billy and ex-Playboy mandolinist-fiddler Tiny Moore formed a memorable band that played dances throughout the region and did a daily show over KFBK radio.

Their sophisticated instrumental sound combined jazz with strong hints of rock 'n' roll, though their Four Star and MGM recordings didn't reflect this.

They disbanded when Bob Wills returned to Sacramento late in 1954 and incorporated Billy's musicians into The Texas Playboys. Billy Jack's career stalled and he left music by 1960.

Two early 1980's reissues of KFBK radio transcriptions showed Billy Jack's band at their progressive best.   —R.K.

Bob Wills

BORN: March 6, 1905
BIRTHPLACE: Kosse, Texas
DIED: May 13, 1975

Bob Wills was a musical revolutionary. Nobody thinks twice about horns, drums and electric instruments in country music today, but before he demonstrated their potential, they were taboo. He brought together the ethnic sounds of his native Texas—old-time fiddling, Western and Mexican music and blues—then mixed them with pop standards, big band and small-group jazz to create a hybrid music called Western swing.

Several numbers associated with him—"New San Antonio Rose," "Steel Guitar Rag," "Time Changes Everything" and "Faded Love"—have become country music standards. For these contributions he was inducted into the Country Music Hall of Fame in 1968, though he and most of his legendary Texas Playboys never considered themselves country musicians. Western swing became the musical basis of honky tonk music. The twin fiddles/steel honky tonk sound used by everyone from Ray Price to George Strait was popularized first by Wills.

Shortly after James Robert "Jim Rob" Wills was born near Kosse, Texas, in 1905, his dad and grandfather, both gifted local fiddlers, made up their minds to nurture another prodigy. However, fiddling didn't interest the boy until one day in 1915 when his dad was late for a dance. Ten-year-old Jim Rob played the six fiddle tunes he knew—over and over—until his dad arrived. He discovered he so enjoyed playing for dancing crowds that he became just what his elders hoped for.

His adolescence was a checkered one. He hoboed, worked odd jobs and preached before marrying and settling on a farm. Farm work battered his hands, so he became a barber in Turkey, Texas, which he adopted as his hometown until he angrily left after being jailed for rowdiness in 1929. In Fort Worth he joined a medicine show, where he learned much about showmanship. Late that year he and a guitarist played dances and parties in the area calling themselves The Wills Fiddle Band.

At one party they met vocalist Milton Brown, then a young cigar salesman. Jim Rob, by then known as "Bob," brought him into the group and they became close friends. By 1930 they were performing on Fort Worth radio. Burris Mill and Elevator Company, mak-

ers of Light Crust Flour, picked up their sponsorship in 1931 and Burris' General Manager W. Lee O'Daniel renamed them The Light Crust Doughboys. Soon they were so popular that several other Texas and Oklahoma stations picked up the show.

O'Daniel, who later became Governor of Texas, was a hard man to work for. After he barred the group from earning extra income by playing dances in 1932, Milton Brown quit and started The Musical Brownies, the first real Western swing band. Wills replaced Brown with vocalist Tommy Duncan.

Wills' drinking ended his relationship with O'Daniel in 1933, and intermittent binges caused him problems—some serious—throughout his career. He, Duncan and a fiddler moved to Waco and formed The Playboys, which at that point included his brother Johnnie Lee Wills. Though they did well there, Bob wanted a bigger audience and decided to move to Oklahoma in 1934.

He settled in Tulsa at radio station KVOO, boasting 50,000 watts, where he expanded the renamed Texas Playboys by adding horns, drums and three instrumental greats—steel guitarist Leon McAuliffe, pianist Al Stricklin and hot swing fiddler Jesse Ashlock. The band quickly became a success. Their daily broadcasts over KVOO and dances at Cain's in Tulsa and other towns made them stars, able to pack a dancehall even on weeknights.

In 1935 they began recording for the American Recording Company (later part of Columbia) with the legendary Uncle Art Satherley producing. Though Bob and Satherley initially disagreed over Bob's hollering and jive talking on the records (Bob won), they worked as a team in the studio for 12 years. Tommy Duncan's Bing Crosby-styled vocals gave the band a strong commercial edge, and their records sold well.

Bob's personal life was less successful. His first marriage ended in 1936. Over the next five years, three more marriages failed. Money was no problem; The Playboys didn't mind his high standards, for he paid them top dollar. His generosity even extended to fans. O.W. Mayo, his Tulsa manager, recalled in 1982 that "Bob came up the hard way. He just had a big heart."

By 1938, at the height of the big band era, Bob wanted The Playboys to sound as good as the best orchestras. When he hired Tulsa guitarist Eldon Shamblin, a gifted arranger, their sometimes ragged sound improved to the point where they attracted jazz musicians and expanded to 18 pieces. That year he recorded "San Antonio Rose," a fiddle instrumental. In 1940 he recorded it again with lyrics sung by Tommy Duncan. "New San Antonio Rose" did well, and when Bing Crosby recorded it, the song crossed over to pop success.

At that point The Playboys were popular enough to merit a call to Hollywood to begin filming Westerns. For a while, they commuted between Tulsa and California. As World War II intervened, Bob started losing musicians (including Tommy Duncan) to the military. In 1942 he married Betty Anderson, a marriage that lasted 33 years. He disbanded The Playboys in 1943 to join the Army himself; but Wills was 38 and used to being the boss: Private Wills and the Army didn't get along. He was discharged that July.

With Tommy Duncan also discharged, the two men moved to California that fall where Bob organized a smaller Playboy band, truly ahead of its time. Horns were minimized. Instead, electric steel and standard guitar (and later mandolins) played in harmony as horns normally would be—an idea copied by many country acts. Wills had huge hit records on Columbia with "Roly Poly," "Hang Your Head in Shame" and "New Spanish Two Step," and the many Texans and Okies who moved West to find defense jobs packed dancehalls to see The Playboys.

On December 30, 1944 Wills and his band caused a stir when they played the Grand Ole Opry. Opry officials demanded that Wills conceal drummer Monte Mountjoy behind a curtain. At the last minute he defiantly moved the drums out front, and though the audience (and many Opry stars) loved the music, the Opry's stuffed shirts denied an encore.

Wills bought a Sacramento ballroom in 1947, the same year he signed with MGM Records. Tensions between himself and Tommy Duncan, aggravated by Duncan's ego and Wills' drinking, led Bob to fire him in the fall of 1948. He had other fine singers but none comparable to Duncan.

Bob soon hit the road again. Fiddler Johnny Gimble, who joined The Playboys in 1949, recalled, "Bob had such a payroll (to meet) he couldn't stay in one place. He couldn't work the territory like he could in Tulsa before the war." He moved to Oklahoma City in 1949, then to Fort Worth in 1950 where he opened the Bob Wills Ranch House, a huge dancehall. He naively hired employees who stole him blind and left him deeply in debt.

He could still draw crowds at dances through the mid-1950's throughout the Southwest, but as TV an-

tennas sprouted, his dance audiences shrank. He made some mediocre recordings for Decca, and though he returned to work in Tulsa in 1958, it just wasn't the same. A year later he and Tommy Duncan reunited to do shows and record some respectable music for Liberty.

After Wills recovered from a 1962 coronary, he and The Playboys played to aging Southwestern audiences until a 1964 heart attack convinced him to disband the group and work as a solo act. The musical gulf that had existed between Wills and Nashville continued even into these last days of his career. Under contract with Kapp Records in 1964, he agreed to record with Nashville studio musicians. The resulting slick records sounded nothing like Bob Wills, and deeply embarrassed him. On May 30, 1969, he was honored by the Texas State Legislature in Austin. The next morning at his Dallas home, he suffered a massive stroke that paralyzed his entire right side. When he recovered enough to function, he was confined to a wheelchair.

In April of 1970 Merle Haggard, a Wills fan since childhood, assembled his band, The Strangers, and several ex-Texas Playboys in Hollywood to record *A Tribute to the Best Damn Fiddle Player in the World*, a Wills tribute album that sparked a worldwide revival of interest in his music even among people who'd never before heard Western swing.

By 1971 Bob was well enough to attend various events in his honor, many featuring performances by various former Playboys. In December 1973, producer Tommy Allsup and Merle Haggard reassembled many of the Tulsa-era Texas Playboys in Dallas for a recording session with Bob (released in 1974 as *For the Last Time*). Though his speech was impaired, he managed to talk a bit on one number. Before the second day's session, another massive stroke left him comatose. On May 13, 1975, Bob Wills died; on May 15 he was buried in Tulsa.

Today his music remains a touchstone. In 1975 Leon McAuliffe assembled various ex-Playboys and other swing musicians as The Original Texas Playboys and worked together until pianist Al Stricklin, a member of the Tulsa band, died in 1986. They had promised to disband when the first of the old Tulsa group died, and they did.

No matter. More Bob Wills records are available now than when he was living. Haggard and Asleep at the Wheel pay constant homage to the Wills sound. Fellow Texans Waylon and Willie both consider Bob Wills a major inspiration, as does George Strait. It was Waylon who sang, "Bob Wills Is Still the King." And so he is. —R.K.

Johnnie Lee Wills

BORN: September 2, 1912
BIRTHPLACE: Jewett, Texas
DIED: October 25, 1984

Like his brother, Bob Wills, Johnnie Lee Wills learned fiddle from their father, Uncle John Wills. After Bob left The Light Crust Doughboys in 1933, Johnnie Lee became tenor banjoist for Bob's band, The Playboys, and continued after they moved to Tulsa in 1934 and became The Texas Playboys. Except for a brief period in 1938 when he led his own band—The Rhythmaires—Johnnie Lee remained a Playboy until 1940. In 1940, Bob no longer needed a tenor banjo. He formed a band around Johnnie Lee to handle the overflow of dance jobs offered The Playboys. Johnnie Lee soon had a Decca recording contract and in 1940 recorded the superb "Milk Cow Blues." After Bob went to the Army in 1943 (and moved to California after his discharge), Johnnie Lee continued Bob's daily broadcasts over KVOO in Tulsa. In the late 40's, he began recording for Bullet Records and in 1950 had two hits: the novelty "Rag Mop" (The Ames Brothers' version became a pop hit), and the Easter song, "Peter Cottontail." In 1952 and 1953 he recorded unsuccessfully for RCA and later recorded for Oklahoma-based Sims Records. He also owned a Tulsa Western wear store and ran an annual rodeo, The Johnnie Lee Wills Stampede. For a time in the 1950's, when Bob returned to Tulsa, he and Johnnie Lee shared the KVOO broadcast. The daily show ended in 1958. The Western swing revival brought him back into prominence and he made occasional albums until his death. —R.K.

Luke Wills

BORN: September 10, 1920
BIRTHPLACE: Memphis, Texas

Luther J. Wills, brother of Bob Wills, was a part of the Texas Playboys for over 20 years as bass player and occasional vocalist. He started working with brother Johnnie Lee's band at age 18, playing dance dates that Bob, based in Tulsa and much in demand, couldn't play. He was included in several of Bob's early 40's Western film appearances, and after spending 1944-1946 in the Navy, he returned to Johnnie Lee's band in Tulsa. Bob Wills brought Luke to his home base in Fresno, California, and decided to form another band around Luke.

Originally dubbed "Luke Wills and The Texas Playboys No. 2," they recorded four songs for King Records in 1947. Luke got another contract with RCA under the name "Luke Wills and His Rhythm Busters." They made 20 RCA recordings during 1947 with a recording band including Eldon Shamblin, Junior Barnard and other Playboys combined with Luke's own band. The group disbanded in 1948, and, except for a brief revival in 1950, Luke remained with The Texas Playboys until they disbanded in 1964. He often fronted the band if Bob was unable to perform. After the Playboys disbanded, Luke moved to Las Vegas where he worked in non-musical jobs, except for occasional appearances at Bob Wills tributes and Playboy reunion shows. —R.K.

Mac Wiseman

BORN: May 23, 1925
BIRTHPLACE: Waynesboro, Virginia

Malcolm "Mac" Wiseman studied music for a time at Shenandoah Conservatory before finding work as a DJ. In the 1940's he played with Bill Monroe and The Blue Grass Boys, and cut several of the all-time great bluegrass duets with Monroe. Mac left The Blue Grass Boys in 1948, when he and fellow band member Lester Flatt started their own band, The Foggy Mountain Boys. Mac went solo in 1951, landing a regular spot on the *Louisiana Hayride* and signing a contract with Dot Records. He had a number of national hits, including "Shackles and Chains," "The Ballad of Davy Crockett" and "Love Letters in the Sand"; his "Jimmy Brown the Newsboy" remained on the national charts for 33 weeks.

In the coming years, Mac would spend less and less time performing country music and more time producing it. From 1957 to 1961 he served as an A&R (artists and repertoire) executive for Dot, running their entire country division. In 1961 Mac took his performing and production talents to Capitol and became a regular performer at national bluegrass festivals. He switched labels again in 1969; his RCA debut album, *Johnny's Cash and Charley's Pride*, appeared in June 1970. Throughout the decade Mac benefited from the mushrooming popularity of bluegrass, and remained one of the most popular performers in national bluegrass festivals.   —M.B.

WLS National Barn Dance

From the late 1920's through the mid-40's, the Chicago-based *National Barn Dance* was radio's most popular country music program. At one point, more than 20 million listeners regularly tuned to WLS every Saturday night to hear the show's family-oriented blend of ballads, cowboy songs, pop tunes, raucous novelties and occasional hymns.

The *National Barn Dance* was launched April 19, 1924, one week after WLS went on the air. Early performers included fiddler Tommy Dandurand, dance caller Tom Owens, vaudeville veterans Ford Rush and Glenn Rowell, and singer Grace Wilson. The initial announcer was "The Solemn Old Judge," George B. Hay, who soon left for WSM in Nashville, where he would help create the Grand Ole Opry in 1925. Balladeer Bradley Kincaid joined the *Barn Dance* in 1926; for the next five years he was the show's most popular artist. The *Barn Dance*'s heyday was the 1930's. Among the artists featured during that decade were Gene Autry, Lulu Belle and Scotty, The Hoosier Hot Shots, Luther "Arkie, The Arkansas Woodchopper" Ossenbrink, George Gobel, Red Foley, Patsy Montana, The Prairie Ramblers and The Cumberland Ridge Runners. Between 1933 and 1946, NBC carried the show's final half-hour to affiliates across the country.

After World War II, the *Barn Dance*'s popularity declined as the Grand Ole Opry's rose, primarily because WLS management refused to adjust to changing audience tastes and new trends in country music. The show left the air April 30, 1960. The *WGN Barn Dance*, a scaled-down version of the WLS program, debuted March 11, 1961; it ran through January 6, 1968. WGN syndicated a separate series for television between 1963 and 1971.   —D.S.

WLW Boone County Jamboree/ Midwestern Hayride

Cincinnati radio station WLW, founded in 1922 by inventor Powel Crosley, once boasted a signal of 500,000 watts before the government forced it to cut back to a still-potent 50,000. Their audience included early-rising farmers in numerous states, WLW began playing to them with their rural-oriented *Top O' The Morning* program in 1929. In 1937 John Lair began broadcasting his *Renfro Valley Barn Dance* from WLW. When that show decided to move to Kentucky, the station hired WLS *National Barn Dance* honcho George Biggar to create WLW's own program. Named the *Boone County Jamboree* (Boone County, Kentucky, was just across the river from Cincinnati), it debuted as a Friday night show in 1939. The talent roster would expand over the next few years, and

become an important stable for many important artists. Included were Ma and Pa McCormick, The Drifting Pioneers (with Merle Travis), Hugh Cross, Lazy Jim Day, Captain Stubby and The Buccaneers, and announcers Bill McCluskey (who became Biggar's right hand man) and Happy Hal O' Halloran. During World War II, The Delmore Brothers, Lulu Belle and Scotty, Smiley Burnette, Hank Penny, Grandpa Jones, Curly Fox and Texas Ruby, Sunshine Sue and her Rock Creek Rangers (with "Cousin" Joe Maphis) and Chet Atkins were also regulars. In addition to the broadcasts, many of the artists had their own shows on WLW and played stage shows in the area as well. World War II and the draft forced many changes in the lineup. New talent like Bonnie Lou and Homer and Jethro came to the station. In 1945 Crosley sold WLW to another company and the show was renamed the *Midwestern Hayride*. It continued on radio and, beginning in 1948, on TV with different cast members. NBC carried it as a network show from 1951-1957. Later hosts included Hugh Cherry, Kenny Price, Paul Dixon and Henson Cargill, who took over when the show was syndicated as *Country Hayride*. The show finally ended in 1974. —R.K

Del Wood

BORN: February 22, 1920
BIRTHPLACE: Nashville, Tennessee
DIED: October 3, 1989

Pianist Adelaide Hazelwood was a one-hit artist, but that one record gave her a lifetime career on the Grand Ole Opry and made her among the handful of pioneering women instrumentalists in country music (Maybelle Carter, guitarist Velma Williams and pianist Anita Kerr were others). Her ragtime piano recording of the 1934 Gid Tanner favorite, "Down Yonder," became a Top Five country and pop hit in 1951, released on the small Tennessee label. A large, jolly woman with considerable stage presence, Wood became a quintessential Grand Ole Opry favorite, performing "Down Yonder" on hundreds of shows. She never had another hit to follow it, but she recorded a number of Extended Play, four-song 45 r.p.m. discs for RCA in the mid-50's, as well as 19 ragtime piano instrumental albums for various labels, including RCA, Mercury (in the early 60's), Republic Records, and one for Columbia in 1966.

Wood's piano playing was influential, one of her admirers being Jerry Lee Lewis. During one of his rare Opry appearances, The Killer even called Wood out onstage so he could play "Down Yonder" with her. Wood continued on the Opry despite health problems, until a fatal stroke ended things in 1989. —R.K.

Sheb Wooley

BORN: April 10, 1921
BIRTHPLACE: Erick, Oklahoma

Hollywood Western character actor, singer of hit novelty songs, country comedian.... These are all hats that Sheb Wooley, a former rodeo rider, has worn since the 1940's, when he began his career performing on his own network radio show from Fort Worth, Texas.

Shelby Wooley (his real name) made his mark in Hollywood as well as Nashville. Since the late 1940's, he's appeared in more than 40 films, including *Giant*, with James Dean, *Rocky Mountain*, with Errol Flynn, *Little Big Horn, Distant Drums* and *Hoosiers*, with Gene Hackman. He played Ben Miller, the killer, in the Gary Cooper classic, *High Noon*. Years later, in the role of Pete Nolan he supported a young Clint Eastwood in the 60's TV series, *Rawhide*. He has since had small parts in several of Eastwood's popular western films.

In 1959, Wooley tried another hat on for size and cashed in on the U.F.O. craze with the wacky and wildly popular novelty hit, "Purple People Eater," which spent three weeks at the top of the pop charts. His similar spoofs, done in a country vein, include: "Peeping Through a Keyhole," "15 Beers Ago" (a parody of the Conway Twitty ballad "Fifteen Years Ago"), "That's My Pa" and "Harper Valley P.T.A. (Later the Same Day)."

Wooley was also, for several years, a cast member of the long-running country comedy TV show, *Hee Haw,* and wrote the show's theme song. His numerous comedy recordings (many of them done under the pseudonym of Ben Colder) made him Country Music Association Comedian of the Year in 1968.   —B.A.

Tom Wopat

BORN: September 9, 1951
BIRTHPLACE: Lodi, Wisconsin

Actor/singer Wopat is best-known for his portrayal of Luke Duke on the television series *The Dukes of Hazzard*. To a lesser degree than his *Dukes* co-star, John Schneider, Wopat made a few ripples in the country charts in the mid-80's. His Top 20's included "The Rock and Roll of Love," "Susannah" and "A Little Bit Closer," all on EMI. Later, he recorded—briefly—for Capitol and Epic. In the 90's, he refocused on acting.   —G.F.

Jimmy Work

BORN: March 29, 1924
BIRTHPLACE: Akron, Ohio

Ohio-born, Jimmy Work grew up on a farm in Dukedom, Tennessee. He loved music and played harmonica. He also learned to play guitar, as well as learning milling work. By 1945 he was living in Detroit, performing for the thousands of Southerners who'd migrated there to work in defense factories. Work did his first recordings for small local labels, including "Tennessee Border," an original he recorded in 1948. In 1949 Red Foley's version of "Tennessee Border" became a huge national hit (as did versions by Bob Atcher, Tennessee Ernie Ford and Jimmie Skinner). Work received a Decca recording contract that yielded no success. Recordings for Bullet, London and Capitol from 1950 to 1953 also failed to attract attention. Success finally came in 1955 with two recordings from his first Dot session: the classic ballads, "Making Believe" and "That's What Makes the Jukebox Play," both Work compositions. Both became Top Five singles in 1955. Kitty Wells' version of "Making Believe" reached Number Two. Other Dot recordings failed to take off, but Work still had several good years. Unfortunately the sort of raw honky tonk music he excelled in was losing favor as rockabilly and the Nashville Sound took over. He returned to Dukedom, where he still does milling work—and still writes songs.   —R.K.

Marion Worth

BORN: July 4, 1933
BIRTHPLACE: Birmingham, Alabama

A native of Birmingham, Alabama, Marion Worth, born Maryann Wilson was an impressive singer and songwriter who flourished in the 1960's. Her sophisticated singing and stylish stage presence got her on the Grand Ole Opry, as well as posh lounges in Las Vegas. Her career began in the Birmingham country music scene, where she scored her first hit Top Ten (in 1960) with "That's My Kind of Love." She signed with—and later married—regional promoter Happy Wilson, and soon had a second Top Ten hit, "I Think I Know," on Columbia Records. Coming to Nashville in the early 1960's, she had a hit duet with George Morgan (a revival of

"Slippin' Around") and did a number that has become a Christmas favorite: "Shake Me I Rattle (Squeeze Me I Cry)," in 1963. In 1966, she left Columbia Records and did some recording for Decca, putting two singles on the charts in the late 60's. She's currently residing in Birmingham once again.　　　　　　　—S.W.

Michelle Wright

BORN: July 1, 1961
BIRTHPLACE: Morpeth, Ontario, Canada

Michelle Wright, one of Canada's recent talents, possesses a sultry, intriguing low-register vocal style, reminiscent of fellow Canadian Anne Murray. She also has the rare ability to express both sensuality and wholesomeness— qualities that made her an electrifying performer. She is best known for early 90's hits like "Take It Like a Man," "New Kind of Love," "One Time Around" and "He Would Be Sixteen."

Wright parents (both talented country musicians around Ontario just north of Detroit) separated when she was just a year and a half old. Not surprisingly, she grew up listening to a steady radio diet of Motown greats like Diana Ross, Otis Redding and The Four Tops, as well as the country stars of the day.

When Wright was nine, her mother remarried and they relocated to Merlin, Ontario, a small farming community. There, Wright got her start by winning local talent contests and her first professional gig when a local group called in hopes of enlisting her mother as their lead vocalist. Wright replied that she also sang. She auditioned and landed the job.

Wright had been playing in top-flight club circuit bands and touring Canada extensively and the U.S. for quite a few years when, in 1985, Nashville songwriter/ producer Rick Giles caught her act at an Ottawa music festival. Giles and his songwriting partner, Steve Bogard (who have since co-produced and co-written most of Wright's hits), later flew Wright to Nashville and made some demo tapes on her. They were promptly turned down by every major label. Eventually, though, their persistence got Wright a contract with the new country division of Arista Records. And the hits, and awards, have been coming in a steady stream almost ever since.

In 1989, Wright won the prestigious Canadian Juno Award as Most Promising Female Vocalist. And in 1987, '89 and '90, she bested k.d. lang as the Canadian Country Music Association's Best Female Vocalist of the Year. She also won the Canadian CMA's '89 Entertainer of the Year citation.　　　　　　　—B.A.

WWVA Jamboree

During its heyday in the 1940's and 50's, Wheeling, West Virginia's *Wheeling Jamboree*, broadcast over the powerful 50,000-watt clear-channel AM signal of WWVA, was one of the most widely listened to "barn dance"-style live country radio shows in the eastern half of the nation. In popularity and influence it was rivaled only by the likes of Nashville's Grand Ole Opry and Shreveport's *Louisiana Hayride*.

The *Jamboree* began broadcasting in 1926, and, aside from a brief interruption during the war years, it has been on the air ever since. It has numbered among its cast members over the years notables like Hawkshaw Hawkins, Grandpa Jones, Floyd Tillman, Wilma Lee and Stoney Cooper, The Osborne Brothers, Red Allen, Mac Wiseman, Red Smiley and Dick Curless. There is not a country music artist of note from the 50's and 60's who did not make frequent guest appearances there.

Most important, the *Jamboree*, which since 1933 has been broadcast from Wheeling's atmospheric old Capitol Theater (which even has its own "Walkway of the Stars"), just a few blocks from the banks of the mighty Ohio River, was also a showcase for a wealth of indigenous country music talent that sprang from the surrounding mountains of northernmost West Virginia and the nearby Ohio Valley. (Veteran *Jamboree* member Doc Williams has actually been with the show longer than Roy Acuff was with the Opry.)

Though its impact (like that of all barn dance shows, save the Opry) has diminished in recent decades, the *Wheeling Jamboree*'s Saturday night shows still play host to a wealth of national country music talent—most of it by way of touring stars of the day like Tom T. Hall and West Virginian Kathy Mattea, who has always had a strong affinity for the show.　　—B.A.

Tammy Wynette

BORN: May 5, 1942

BIRTHPLACE: Itawamba County, Mississippi

For better or worse, Tammy Wynette was the unofficial spokesperson for the unliberated rural American women of the 70's—the women who might be more apt to pad their bra than burn it, and whose idea of "empowerment" might be wearing a mini-skirt to the office Christmas party. Admittedly, some of the more "enlightened" or "liberated" music critics have disparaged Wynette's late 60's and 70's anthems as "music to wash dishes by," or even condemned her songs as portrayals of women as victims. Even director Bob Rafelson's use of Wynette's music as the soundtrack for his classic film, *Five Easy Pieces,* suggested a stark ambivalence toward the lifestyle of big hair, bowling alleys, trailer parks and painted fingernails that the songs implied. So pervasive was this image that Hillary Clinton even took potshots at Wynette and "Stand By Your Man" when defending herself against media attacks during Bill Clinton's Presidential campaign.

Yet Wynette's hallmark hits—"Stand By Your Man" (which sold six million copies worldwide), "Your Good Girl's Gonna Go Bad," "D-I-V-O-R-C-E," "I Don't Wanna Play House" and others—were redeemed by a fervent honesty. And, in truth, they probably spoke directly to the hopes and dreams of the vast majority of 60's and 70's American women who were just beginning to chafe at the bit of traditional sexual roles and taking their first tentative steps toward forging a sense of identity outside the shadow of the man they stood by. And though her most memorable songs are the flip side of Loretta Lynn's earthy sass, their impact was nonetheless resounding enough to eventually earn Wynette the unequivocal title of "The First Lady of Country Music." Along the way, she had 39 Top Ten hits, 20 Number One singles, 11 Number One albums and sold more than 30 million records.

Above all, Tammy Wynette is a survivor—a stalwart artist who has prevailed over everything, including victimization at the hands of the 70's male-dominated music industry, stalkers (she was, at one point, the victim of a bizarre kidnapping), and husbands.

She was born Virginia Wynette Pugh in Itawamba County, Mississippi, on May 5, 1942. (Her stage name, along with many of her songs and her early musical persona, would be provided by iron-handed producer/starmaker Billy Sherrill, who also co-wrote many of her above-mentioned hits.) Wynette's father died of a brain tumor just nine months after her birth, and as a child, she endured her share of hard times. She picked cotton and labored as a hairdresser, barmaid and waitress. She married for the first of four times at age 17, and by age 24 was already divorced and raising her three young children on a beautician's salary.

In 1966, after being turned down by nearly every Nashville record label, Wynette stumbled unannounced into producer Billy Sherrill's office. Though Sherrill would became the most influential producer of the 70's, he was at this point still just another struggling staff producer in search of that one big hit. He didn't sign Wynette right away, but sent her home and told her to come back when she found better material. Wynette merely took this as just one more rejection.

Sherrill soon found the song that would be Wynette's first hit: "Apartment #9." (Ironically he only summoned her to record it when he could not obtain the licensing to re-release a small-label version of the song that had already been recorded by someone else.) "Apartment #9" was the first in a decade and a half's worth of hits that Wynette's and Sherrill's artist/producer relationship would produce.

For many, Wynette's name will never cease to be uttered in the same breath as that of singer George Jones, to whom she was married for six years (1968-1974). The string of hit duets she recorded with Jones—"Golden Ring," "We're Gonna Hold On," "Near You," "Southern California," "We're Not the Jet Set"—seemed to offer painful glimpses into their troubled lives. Their tumultuous marriage was chronicled so extensively in the tabloids that they came to be referred to as "The Sonny & Cher of Country Music."

Even after she and Jones split (though divorced, the duet hits would continued, including the classic "Two Story House"), Wynette's controversial lifestyle (a highly publicized fling with Burt Reynolds, a mysterious abduction from a Nashville parking lot, harassment and stalkings of all sorts, and myriad health

problems) often overshadowed her music.

Though Wynette has not been nearly the commercial force in the 80's and early 90's that she was in her heyday, she has managed to shuck the 70's image. In the process, she's become her own woman, and has recorded some of the best and most diverse music of her career (beginning with her 1987 album, *Higher Ground*). She also seems to have found happiness in her fourth marriage, to songwriter George Richey. And gradually the respect and universal recognition so long overdue has finally come her way. The surprise of all surprises was her international dance hit, "Justified and Ancient," a 1992 collaboration with the British synth-pop group, The KLF. The song was a Number One hit worldwide. She's still recording for Epic as the 90's progress, with 1993 bringing *Honky Tonk Angels*, a Gold-selling album recorded with Dolly Parton and Loretta Lynn, and '94 bringing *Without Walls*, an album of duets. Future plans include new duet recordings with George Jones. Indeed, Tammy Wynette has shown us all that older can be better.   —B.A.

Trisha Yearwood

BORN: September 19, 1964
BIRTHPLACE: Monticello, Georgia

Since her chart debut in 1991, Trisha Yearwood has quickly become one of the most commercially successful women of the 90's. Unlike a more roots-oriented country vocal genius like Patty Loveless, or an eclectic country-folkie like Kathy Mattea, Yearwood's ticket has always been her sheer middle-of-the-road appeal. There is a whole lot more Linda Ronstadt (her biggest childhood influence) in her voice than there is Loretta Lynn or Tammy Wynette.

Born in the small town of Monticello, Georgia, on September 19, 1964, Yearwood is the daughter of a banker and a school teacher. She arrived in Nashville in 1985 and earned a music business degree at

Belmont College. Like so many before her, she infiltrated the music business at the entry level, singing on demo records and answering phones at the now-defunct MTM Records. She also sang backup on Garth Brooks' first album.

Signed by MCA in 1991, her debut album (produced by Garth Fundis) resulted in the Number One single, "She's in Love with the Boy." Her subsequent albums—*Hearts in Armor* (1992) and *The Song Remembers When* (1993)—have all been best-sellers, enlarging on her popularity.   —B.A.

Dwight Yoakam

BORN: October 23, 1956
BIRTHPLACE: Pikeville, Kentucky

It's hard to recall any artist during the 1980's whose debut album caused as much stir in Nashville as did Dwight Yoakam's *Guitars, Cadillacs, Etc., Etc.* in 1986. This is particularly telling when you consider that Yoakam's first album was made in Hollywood rather than on Music Row.

This weird state of affairs spoke volumes about just how far Nashville had, musically speaking, gotten off the track and out of touch with grassroots tastes. It took Yoakam and his hard-boiled, hard-hitting West Coast brand of neo-honky tonk and hillbilly music to telegraph the message to Nashville that the Kenny Rogers leisure suit era of country music was over, and if Music City didn't wake up, it was about to miss out on something big. That something, about which Nashville did soon get the message, was the so-called New Traditionalist movement and it quickly brought the swaggering, instrumentally lean and mean, 50's style honky tonk/hard country back into vogue.

"The West Coast is the last bastion of pure honky tonk records, country records," Yoakam, who can rockabilly like a reborn Johnny Horton, but who can also be as ponderous and erudite as a self-styled professor of country music history, explained to John Morthland of *Country Music Magazine* back near the start of his recording career. "There were moments of 'tonk' music recurring in Nashville—Gary Stewart, early Moe Bandy, Gene Watson," added the Kentucky-born, Ohio-raised singer whose contempt for the musical blandness of the Urban Cowboy days has never been more than thinly veiled, and who

himself had to pay his dues in the Los Angeles area roots-rock/country punk scene after more or less getting the brush-off from Nashville in the 1970's. "But today we are tragically close to eliminating pure country music entirely. Hillbilly music, white American hillbilly music, is real close to extinction... I think that's not of the audience's choosing or doing; it's the marketing structure that's been established in the record business. But there's a segment of the country audience, I don't have to tell them what I do— they know."

Yoakam, the grandson of a coal miner, was born in Pikeville, Kentucky, October 23, 1956, and grew up and attended college in Ohio before heading for the West Coast. What's particularly unusual about Yoakam and his background is that he's absorbed his honky tonk/rockabilly/neo-hillbilly styles, attitudes, and posturing not only through his heart and gut, but through his intellect, as well. Not only is he vastly knowledgeable about country music's roots; he's been able to revitalize them with his own impeccably original songwriting and purist honky tonk/rockabilly musicianship.

Along the way, he's taken this music of old and made it fascinating to today's younger listeners by serving it up with a James-Dean-by-the-jukebox scowl, some latter-day Elvis hip-shaking, and a bit of early rock 'n' roll surliness. In short, he's made it his own and retrofitted it for the youthful masses of the 80's and 90's—taken it out of history books and put it back on the jukebox.

Besides Yoakam's immense contribution toward "opening up" country music in the 80's, and the credit he deserves for sustaining his hard-fought musical vision over nearly a half dozen albums, country fans also have Yoakam to thank for coaxing Bakersfield legend Buck Owens (an immense influence on both Yoakam and on his longtime guitarist/producer Pete Anderson) out of retirement. Owens and Yoakam dueted on a spirited version of the old Owens chestnut, "The Streets of Bakersfield," which resulted in both a hit single and a hit video.

This former college drama student has also dabbled in acting; in the Spring of 1993, he had the lead in a play, *Southern Rapture*, directed in Los Angeles by actor Peter Fonda. In 1993 he released *This Time*, his sixth album, and one of his best yet. Among the hits from the album were "Ain't That Lonely Yet," "A Thousand Miles from Nowhere," "Fast as You" and "Pocket of a Clown."   —B.A.

Faron Young

BORN: February 25, 1932
BIRTHPLACE: Shreveport, Louisiana

Hank Williams' success inspired a generation of honky tonkers. Brash, energetic and raw-edged, they began emerging from Hank's shadow even during his lifetime; and since some knew him, the influence was direct. One, Ray Price, was Hank's friend and roommate. Carl Smith, Webb Pierce and Lefty Frizzell were likewise of this generation.

So was a black-haired, spangle-shirted kid from Shreveport, Louisiana, named Faron Young, barely out of his teens when he became a star. Stonewall Jackson, George Jones and Willie Nelson all fell in his age group, but Faron got to the top first. His vocal style was raw, but not so rough that he couldn't handle music that went beyond hillbilly songs. His first big hit, the ballad "Goin' Steady," was the stylistic ancestor of Sonny James' "Young Love." However, most of the time Faron was short on subtlety, long on vigor. On his greatest recordings, he sang with all stops out, his voice soaring over steel guitars and fiddles. The now-classic shouted "Hey!" on "I've Got Five Dollars and It's Saturday Night" symbolized Faron's style.

His intuition when it came to unknown songwriters also made a difference. By recording songs by new writers like Don Gibson, Bill Anderson and, most notably, Willie Nelson, Young not only made a major difference in their careers (particularly Willie's); he helped others survive when they needed a paycheck. Roger Miller was his drummer for a time. In the late 1960's, Young hired an ex-Army chopper pilot as a laborer. The pilot was looking for rent money while he pitched songs around Nashville, and Kris Kristofferson never forgot the break.

Faron grew up on a farm and began singing in his teens. The advent of KWKH Radio's *Louisiana Hayride* in 1948, a show styled much like the Opry, aided his career. Around 1951 he met Webb Pierce, one of the *Hayride's* biggest stars. Pierce hired him as his warm-up singer, got him onto the *Hayride* and even recorded Faron, with little success, for his own Pacemaker label. For a time the pair did a KWKH disc jockey program.

The *Hayride's* success led WSM to hire away some of its bigger acts, including Webb and, in 1952, Faron. Capitol Records signed Faron that year, but he was soon drafted. In the Korean War, he was assigned to Army Special Services and performed for the troops. On leave, he recorded "Goin' Steady," which reached Number Two early in 1953. Discharged in 1954, he returned to the Opry. The Top Ten records came quickly—1955 brought his now-classic "If You Ain't Lovin'," followed by his first Number One hit, the lusty "Live Fast, Love Hard, Die Young." The follow-up, "All Right," a Faron original, was Number Two nationwide for four weeks that year.

Ted Daffan's honky tonk anthem, "I've Got Five Dollars," became a standard in Faron's hands, a virtual ode to the offstage "roaring" (hillbilly slang for hell-raising and wild partying) for which Faron himself was becoming notorious. That same year he covered a ballad by a promising new songwriter named Don Gibson. The song, "Sweet Dreams," made it to Number Two and remained on the country charts for 33 weeks. Gibson's original version became a Top Ten hit a couple of months later.

Faron's good looks made him a natural for the movies, and *Hidden Guns* gave him more than a film credit. He became known as the "Young Sheriff," later the "Singing Sheriff," and his band became the "Country Deputies." Other film appearances followed in *Daniel Boone* and *Raiders of Old California*. In 1958, the year "Alone With You" remained at Number One for 13 weeks, he co-starred with Ferlin Husky, June Carter, boxer Rocky Graziano and Zsa Zsa Gabor in *Country Music Holiday*, possibly the worst movie ever made on the subject. Faron didn't let that disaster deter him from working in other films, including appearances in westerns with his friend, Marty Robbins.

His third Number One hit came in 1959 with "Country Girl," a Roy Drusky number. He followed with "Riverboat," a Bill Anderson number that went to Number Four in 1960. Faron's recording of "Hello Walls," written by an unknown Willie Nelson, started Willie's career. Faron's recording of "Walls" was Number One for six weeks. And through 1962, he had a solid string of Top Tens, including "Backtrack," Willie's "Three Days," "The Comeback" and "Down by the River." In late 1962 Faron left Capitol for Mercury Records. Initially, this didn't seem the smartest move. After his first release, "The Yellow Bandana," he had plenty of chart records but only four solo Top Tens and one hit duet with Margie Singleton. He left the Opry in 1964 with a number of others in a dispute over the number of annual appearances required.

In 1969, "Wine Me Up," reached Number Two. Over the next five years all but one of his singles made the Top Ten. He even remade "Goin' Steady" as a Number Five record in 1970. Amid the crossover pop of the time, his basic honky tonk sound made him stand out. In 1972 the waltz-tempo ballad, "It's Four in the Mornin'," became his final Number One record, winning the Country Music Association's Single of the Year award. By the mid-70's, the hits trailed off. One of his best later efforts, made in the 80's, was a duet album with Willie.

Having seen Webb Pierce put his business sense to work in both Shreveport and Nashville, Faron followed suit. In 1963, he and Preston Temple co-founded the publication, *Music City News*. Other wise investments made him one of Nashville's wealthier entertainers. At the same time, his hard-drinking, outspoken lifestyle earned him some unwanted publicity and even an occasional scrape with the law.   —R.K.

Zydeco

Zydeco, a sub-style of Cajun, blends soul, boogie and honky tonk into the basic Cajun mix. Among the leaders in the field are Rockin' Sidney, who brought Zydeco to the country charts with his 1985 Top 20 hit, "My Toot Toot," and the band, Buckwheat Zydeco. That same year, New Orleans soul singer Jean Knight put the song on the pop charts. Later, Buckwheat Zydeco recorded a Zydeco version of Hank Williams' "Hey, Good Lookin'" with Dwight Yoakam. While Zydeco didn't turn out to be as big a chart presence as some anticipated after Rockin' Sidney's breakthrough, the style is still alive and well, especially in New Orleans. (See also, Cajun Music.)   —G.F.

Photo Credits

Listed below in page number order are sources of photographs used by permission in this book. All other photographs are from *Country Music Magazine*'s collection or are provided courtesy of the following recording companies: Arista, Atlantic Records, Capitol Records, Columbia Records, Decca, Elektra, Epic Records, MCA, Mercury Records, PolyGram Records, RCA Records and Warner Bros.

Acuff-Rose Publishing Company, p. 4, *Les Leverett Collection*; Rex Allen, p. 6, *Gene Bear Archives*; Eddy Arnold, p. 11, *Les Leverett*; Bob Atcher, p. 14, *Dave Samuelson Collection*; Chet Atkins, p. 15, *Les Leverett*; Gene Autry, p. 18, *Country Music Foundation*; Gene Autry, p. 19, *Country Music Foundation*; DeFord Bailey, p. 21, *David C. Morton Collection*; Bobby Bare, p. 24, *Marshall Falwell*; Blue Sky Boys, p.30, *Gary Reid Collection*; Hank Snow, p. 36, *Richard Wieze*; Milton Brown, p. 41, *Southern Folklife Collection*; Carl and Pearl Butler, p. 47, *Les Leverett*; The Byrds, p. 49, *Gram Parsons International*; The Carlisles, p. 53, *Lewis E. Witt Collection*; Johnny Cash, p. 60, *CBS Records*; Harry Choates, p. 66, *Crawford Vincent Collection*; Patsy Cline, p. 70, *Les Leverett*; Patsy Cline, p. 71, *Les Leverett*; Wilma Lee and Stoney Cooper, p. 80, *Frank Driggs Collection*; The Crook Brothers, p. 86, *Les Leverett Collection*; Darby and Tarlton, p. 94, *Robert A. Nobley Collection*; The Delmore Brothers, p. 99, *Southern Folklife Collection*; Little Jimmy Dickens, p. 103, *Charles Wolfe Collection*; Pete Drake, p. 106, *Marshall Falwell*; Jimmy Driftwood, p. 107, *Les Leverett*; Tommy Duncan, p. 109, *M. Geddings Collection*; Bob Dylan, p. 111, *Frank Driggs Collection*; Dale Evans, p. 116, *Gene Bear Archives*; The Everly Brothers, p. 117, *Frank Driggs Collection*; Flatt and Scruggs, p. 124, *Southern Folklife Collection*; Red Foley, p. 126, *Country Music Foundation*; Tennessee Ernie Ford, p. 127, *Charles Wolfe Collection*; Curly Fox, p. 130, *Les Leverett*; Kinky Friedman, p. 132, *Stephanie Chernikowski*; Lefty Frizzell, p. 133, *Country Music Foundation*; Hank Garland, p. 134, *Eddy Arnold Collection*; Johnny Gimble, p. 143, *Les Leverett*; Girls of the Golden West, p. 144, *Southern Folklife Collection*; Woody Guthrie, p. 156, *Frank Driggs Collection*; Tom T. Hall, p. 161, *Les Leverett*; Stuart Hamblen, p. 162, *Southern Folklife Collection*; Hometown Jamboree, p. 173, *Gene Bear Archives*; Hoosier Hot Shots, p. 175, *Gene Bear Archives*; Wanda Jackson, p. 182, *Lewis E. Witt Collection*; Jim and Jesse, p. 186, *Les Leverett*; Johnnie and Jack, p. 187, *Southern Folklife Collection*; George Jones, p. 189, *Lewis E. Witt Collection*; The Jordanaires, p. 192, *Frank Driggs Collection*; Jerry Lee Lewis, p. 210, *Les Leverett*; Lulu Belle and Scotty, p. 218, *John Morris Collection*; Mac and Bob, p. 222, *WLS Archives*; Rose Maddox, p. 224, *Rose Maddox Collection*; Wade Mainer, p. 225, *John Morris Collection*; Rose Lee and Joe Maphis, p. 228, *Gene Bear Archives*; Clayton McMichen, *Juanita McMichen Lynch Collection*; Patsy Montana, p. 248, *Gene Bear Archives*; Monroe Brothers, p. 248, *Southern Folklife Collection*; George Morgan, p. 251, *Marshall Falwell*; Moon Mullican, p. 253, *Gene Bear Archives*; Molly O'Day, p. 271, *John Morris Collection*; Roy Orbison, p. 274, *Stephanie Chernikowski*; Roy Orbison, p. 275, *Frank Driggs Collection*; Buck Owens, p. 282, *Buck Owens Collection*; Leon Payne, p. 291, *Lewis E. Witt Collection*; Ralph Peer, p. 295, *Country Music Foundation*; Sam Phillips, p. 297, *Marshall Falwell;* Charlie Poole, p. 302, *Kinney Rorer Collection*; Prairie Ramblers, p. 303, *Gene Bear Archives*; Elvis Presley, p. 306, *Frank Driggs Collection*; Riley Puckett, p. 313, *Georgia State University Archives*; Marvin Rainwater, p. 134, *Gene Bear Archives*; Wayne Raney, p. 315, *M. Geddings Collection*; Wade Ray, p. 316, *M. Geddings Collection*; Reno and Smiley, p. 324, *Gary Reid Collection*; Marty Robbins, p. 330, *CBS Records*; Kenny Roberts, p. 333, *Craig Sugerman Collection*; Jimmie Rodgers, p. 335, *Nolan Porterfield Collection*; Roy Rogers, p. 339, *Gene Bear Archives*; Jeannie Seely, p. 347, *Marshall Falwell*; Billy Joe Shaver, p. 348, *Marshall Falwell*; Asher and Little Jimmy Sizemore, p. 354, *Southern Folklife Collection*; Jimmie Skinner, p. 355, *M. Geddings Collection*; Carl Smith, p. 357, *Donna Jackson Collection*; Hank Snow, p. 361, *Richard Weize Collection*; Stanley Brothers, p.365, *Faye Elam Collection*; Wynn Stewart, p. 371, *Donna Jackson Collection*; Stringbean, p. 376, *Les Leverett*; Ernest Tubb, p. 396, *Gene Bear Archives*; Justin Tubb, p. 399, *Lillian Ferguson Collection*; Zeb and Zeke Turner, p. 400, *Harold Bradley Collection*; T. Texas Tyler, p. 403, *Gene Bear Archives*; Ray Whitley, p. 422, *Gene Bear Archives*; Foy Willing, p. 431, *Douglas B. Green Collection*; Bob Wills, p. 436, *Glenn White Collection*; WLW, p. 441, *Cincinnati Historical Society*; Marion Worth, p. 442, *Gene Bear Archives*.